FLORIDA STATUTES

CIVIL PRACTICE AND PROCEDURE

2018 EDITION

Updated as of April 30, 2018

THE LAW LIBRARY

TABLE OF CONTENTS

CHAPTER 45. CIVIL PROCEDURE: GENERAL PROVISIONS

45.011. Definitions.

In all statutes about practice and procedure "plaintiff" means any party seeking affirmative relief whether plaintiff, counterclaimant, cross-claimant; or third-party plaintiff, counterclaimant or cross-claimant; "defendant" means any party against whom such relief is sought; "bond with surety" means a bond with two good and sufficient sureties, each with unencumbered property not subject to any exemption afforded by law equal in value to the penal sum of the bond or a bond with a licensed surety company as surety or a cash deposit conditioned as for a bond.

45.021. Applicability.

Chapters 45-51, 55-57, 68 and 69 apply to all actions, whether heretofore at law or in chancery, unless specifically provided otherwise in such chapters or parts thereof.

45.031. Judicial sales procedure.

In any sale of real or personal property under an order or judgment, the procedures provided in this section and ss. 45.0315-45.035 may be followed as an alternative to any other sale procedure if so ordered by the court.

(1) FINAL JUDGMENT.—

(a) In the order or final judgment, the court shall direct the clerk to sell the property at public sale on a specified day that shall be not less than 20 days or more than 35 days after the date thereof, on terms and conditions specified in the order or judgment. A sale may be held more than 35 days after the date of final judgment or order if the plaintiff or plaintiff's attorney consents to such time. The final judgment shall contain the following statement in conspicuous type:

(b) If the property being foreclosed on has qualified for the homestead tax exemption in the most recent approved tax roll, the final judgment shall additionally contain the following statement in conspicuous type:

(c) A copy of the final judgment shall be furnished by the clerk by first class mail to the last known address of every party to the action or to the attorney of record for such party. Any irregularity in such mailing, including the failure to include this statement in any final judgment or order, shall not affect the validity or finality of the final judgment or order or any sale held pursuant to the final judgment or order. Any sale held more than 35 days after the final judgment or order shall not affect the validity or finality of the final judgment or order or any sale held pursuant to such judgment or order.

(2) PUBLICATION OF SALE.—Notice of sale shall be published once a week for 2 consecutive weeks in a newspaper of general circulation, as defined in chapter 50, published in the county where the sale is to be held. The second publication shall be at least 5 days before the sale. The notice shall contain:

(a) A description of the property to be sold.

(b) The time and place of sale.

(c) A statement that the sale will be made pursuant to the order or final judgment.

(d) The caption of the action.

(e) The name of the clerk making the sale.

(f) A statement that any person claiming an interest in the surplus from the sale, if any, other than the property owner as of the date of the lis pendens must file a claim within 60 days after the sale.

(3) CONDUCT OF SALE; DEPOSIT REQUIRED.—The sale shall be conducted at public auction at the time and place set forth in the final judgment. The clerk shall receive the service charge imposed in s. 45.035 for services in making, recording, and certifying the sale and title that shall be assessed as costs. At the time of the sale, the successful high bidder shall post with the clerk a deposit equal to 5 percent of the final bid. The deposit shall be applied to the sale price at the time of payment. If final payment is not made within the prescribed period, the clerk shall readvertise the sale as provided in this section and pay all costs of the sale from the deposit. Any remaining funds shall be applied toward the judgment.

(4) CERTIFICATION OF SALE.—After a sale of the property the clerk shall promptly file a certificate of sale and serve a copy of it on each party in substantially the following form:

(5) CERTIFICATE OF TITLE.—If no objections to the sale are filed within 10 days after filing the certificate of sale, the clerk shall file a certificate of title and serve a copy of it on each party in substantially the following form:

(6) CONFIRMATION; RECORDING.—When the certificate of title is filed the sale shall stand confirmed, and title to the property shall pass to the purchaser named in the certificate without the necessity of any further proceedings or instruments. The certificate of title shall be recorded by the clerk.

(7) DISBURSEMENTS OF PROCEEDS.—

(a) On filing a certificate of title, the clerk shall disburse the proceeds of the sale in accordance with the order or final judgment and shall file a report of such disbursements and serve a copy of it on each party, and on the Department of Revenue if the department was named as a defendant in the action or if the Department of Economic Opportunity or the former Agency for Workforce Innovation was named as a defendant while the Department of Revenue was providing reemployment assistance tax collection services under contract with the Department of Economic Opportunity or the former Agency for Workforce Innovation through an interagency agreement pursuant to s. 443.1316.

(b) The certificate of disbursements shall be in substantially the following form:

(c) If no objections to the report are served within 10 days after it is filed, the disbursements by the clerk shall stand approved as reported. If timely objections to the report are served, they shall be heard by the court. Service of objections to the report does not affect or cloud the title of the purchaser of the property in any manner.

(d) If there are funds remaining after payment of all disbursements required by the final judgment of foreclosure and shown on the certificate of disbursements, the surplus shall be distributed as provided in this section and ss. 45.0315-45.035.

(8) VALUE OF PROPERTY.—The amount of the bid for the property at the sale shall be conclusively presumed to be sufficient consideration for the sale. Any party may serve an objection to the amount of the bid within 10 days after the clerk files the certificate of sale. If timely objections to the bid are served, the objections shall be heard by the court. Service of objections to the amount of the bid does not affect or cloud the title of the purchaser in any manner. If the case is one in which a deficiency judgment may be sought and application is made for a deficiency, the amount bid at the sale may be considered by the court as one of the factors in determining a deficiency under the usual equitable principles.

(9) EXECUTION SALES.—This section shall not apply to property sold under executions.

(10) ELECTRONIC SALES.—The clerk may conduct the sale of real or personal property under an order or judgment pursuant to this section by electronic means. Such electronic sales shall comply with the procedures provided in this chapter, except that electronic proxy bidding shall be allowed and the clerk may require bidders to advance sufficient funds to pay the deposit required by subsection (3). The clerk shall provide access to the electronic sale by computer terminals open

to the public at a designated location and shall accept an advance credit proxy bid from the plaintiff of any amount up to the maximum allowable credit bid of the plaintiff. A clerk who conducts such electronic sales may receive electronic deposits and payments related to the sale.

45.0315. Right of redemption.

At any time before the later of the filing of a certificate of sale by the clerk of the court or the time specified in the judgment, order, or decree of foreclosure, the mortgagor or the holder of any subordinate interest may cure the mortgagor's indebtedness and prevent a foreclosure sale by paying the amount of moneys specified in the judgment, order, or decree of foreclosure, or if no judgment, order, or decree of foreclosure has been rendered, by tendering the performance due under the security agreement, including any amounts due because of the exercise of a right to accelerate, plus the reasonable expenses of proceeding to foreclosure incurred to the time of tender, including reasonable attorney's fees of the creditor. Otherwise, there is no right of redemption.

45.032. Disbursement of surplus funds after judicial sale.

(1) For purposes of ss. 45.031-45.035, the term:
(a) "Owner of record" means the person or persons who appear to be owners of the property that is the subject of the foreclosure proceeding on the date of the filing of the lis pendens. In determining an owner of record, a person need not perform a title search and examination but may rely on the plaintiff's allegation of ownership in the complaint when determining the owner of record.
(b) "Subordinate lienholder" means the holder of a subordinate lien shown on the face of the pleadings as an encumbrance on the property. The lien held by the party filing the foreclosure lawsuit is not a subordinate lien. A subordinate lienholder includes, but is not limited to, a subordinate mortgage, judgment, tax warrant, assessment lien, or construction lien. However, the holder of a subordinate lien shall not be deemed a subordinate lienholder if the holder was paid in full from the proceeds of the sale.
(c) "Surplus funds" or "surplus" means the funds remaining after payment of all disbursements required by the final judgment of foreclosure and shown on the certificate of disbursements.
(d) "Surplus trustee" means a person qualifying as a surplus trustee pursuant to s. 45.034.
(2) There is established a rebuttable legal presumption that the owner of record on the date of the filing of a lis pendens is the person entitled to surplus funds after payment of subordinate lienholders who have timely filed a claim. A person claiming a legal right to the surplus as an assignee of the rights of the owner of record must prove to the court that such person is entitled to the funds. At any hearing regarding such entitlement, the court shall consider the factors set forth in s. 45.033 in determining whether an assignment is sufficient to overcome the presumption. It is the intent of the Legislature to abrogate the common law rule that surplus proceeds in a foreclosure case are the property of the owner of the property on the date of the foreclosure sale.
(3) During the 60 days after the clerk issues a certificate of disbursements, the clerk shall hold the surplus pending a court order.
(a) If the owner of record claims the surplus during the 60-day period and there is no subordinate lienholder, the court shall order the clerk to deduct any applicable service charges from the surplus and pay the remainder to the owner of record. The clerk may establish a reasonable requirement that the owner of record prove his or her identity before receiving the disbursement. The clerk may assist an owner of record in making a claim. An owner of record may use the following form in making a claim:
(b) If any person other than the owner of record claims an interest in the proceeds during the 60-

day period or if the owner of record files a claim for the surplus but acknowledges that one or more other persons may be entitled to part or all of the surplus, the court shall set an evidentiary hearing to determine entitlement to the surplus. At the evidentiary hearing, an equity assignee has the burden of proving that he or she is entitled to some or all of the surplus funds. The court may grant summary judgment to a subordinate lienholder prior to or at the evidentiary hearing. The court shall consider the factors in s. 45.033 when hearing a claim that any person other than a subordinate lienholder or the owner of record is entitled to the surplus funds.

(c) If no claim is filed during the 60-day period, the clerk shall appoint a surplus trustee from a list of qualified surplus trustees as authorized in s. 45.034. Upon such appointment, the clerk shall prepare a notice of appointment of surplus trustee and shall furnish a copy to the surplus trustee. The form of the notice may be as follows:

(4) If the surplus trustee is unable to locate the owner of record entitled to the surplus within 1 year after appointment, the appointment shall terminate and the clerk shall notify the surplus trustee that his or her appointment was terminated. Thirty days after termination of the appointment of the surplus trustee, the clerk shall treat the remaining funds as unclaimed property to be deposited with the Chief Financial Officer pursuant to chapter 717.

(5) Proceedings regarding surplus funds in a foreclosure case do not in any manner affect or cloud the title of the purchaser at the foreclosure sale of the property.

45.033. Sale or assignment of rights to surplus funds in a property subject to foreclosure.

(1) There is established a rebuttable presumption that the owner of record of real property on the date of the filing of a lis pendens is the person entitled to surplus funds after payment of subordinate lienholders who have timely filed a claim. A person claiming a legal right to the surplus as an assignee of the rights of the owner of record must prove entitlement to the surplus funds pursuant to this section. It is the intent of the Legislature to abrogate the common law rule that surplus proceeds in a foreclosure case are the property of the owner of the property on the date of the foreclosure sale.

(2) The presumption may be rebutted only by:

(a) The grantee or assignee of a voluntary transfer or assignment establishing a right to collect the surplus funds or any portion or percentage of the surplus funds by proving that the transfer or assignment qualifies as a voluntary transfer or assignment as provided in subsection (3); or

(b) The grantee or assignee proving that the grantee or assignee is a grantee or assignee by virtue of an involuntary transfer or assignment of the right to collect the surplus. An involuntary transfer or assignment may be as a result of inheritance or as a result of the appointment of a guardian.

(3) A voluntary transfer or assignment shall be a transfer or assignment qualified under this subsection, thereby entitling the transferee or assignee to the surplus funds or a portion or percentage of the surplus funds, if:

(a) The transfer or assignment is in writing and the instrument:

1. If executed prior to the foreclosure sale, includes a financial disclosure that specifies the assessed value of the property, a statement that the assessed value may be lower than the actual value of the property, the approximate amount of any debt encumbering the property, and the approximate amount of any equity in the property. If the instrument was executed after the foreclosure sale, the instrument must also specify the foreclosure sale price and the amount of the surplus.

2. Includes a statement that the owner does not need an attorney or other representative to recover surplus funds in a foreclosure.

3. Specifies all forms of consideration paid for the rights to the property or the assignment of the rights to any surplus funds.

(b) The transfer or assignment is filed with the court on or before 60 days after the filing of the certificate of disbursements.

(c) There are funds available to pay the transfer or assignment after payment of timely filed claims of subordinate lienholders.

(d) The transferor or assignee is qualified as a surplus trustee, or could qualify as a surplus trustee, pursuant to s. 45.034.

(e) The total compensation paid or payable, or earned or expected to be earned, by the transferee or assignee does not exceed 12 percent of the surplus.

(4) The court shall honor a transfer or assignment that complies with the requirements of subsection (3), in which case the court shall order the clerk to pay the transferor or assignee from the surplus.

(5) If the court finds that a voluntary transfer or assignment does not qualify under subsection (3) but that the transfer or assignment was procured in good faith and with no intent to defraud the transferor or assignor, the court may order the clerk to pay the claim of the transferee or assignee after payment of timely filed claims of subordinate lienholders.

(6) If a voluntary transfer or assignment of the surplus is set aside, the owner of record shall be entitled to payment of the surplus after payment of timely filed claims of subordinate lienholders, but the transferee or assignee may seek in a separate proceeding repayment of any consideration paid for the transfer or assignment.

(7) This section does not apply to a deed, mortgage, or deed in lieu of foreclosure unless a person other than the owner of record is claiming that a deed or mortgage entitles the person to surplus funds. Nothing in this section affects the title or marketability of the real property that is the subject of the deed or other instrument. Nothing in this section affects the validity of a lien evidenced by a mortgage.

45.034. Qualifications and appointment of a surplus trustee in foreclosure actions.

(1) A surplus trustee is a third-party trustee approved pursuant to this section by the Department of Financial Services. A surplus trustee must be willing to accept cases on a statewide basis; however, a surplus trustee may employ subcontractors that are not qualified as a surplus trustee provided the surplus trustee remains primarily responsible for the duties set forth in this section.

(2) A surplus trustee is an entity that holds and administers surplus proceeds from a foreclosure pursuant to ss. 45.031-45.035.

(3) To be a surplus trustee, an entity must apply for certification with the Department of Financial Services. The application must contain:

(a) The name and address of the entity and of one or more principals of the entity.

(b) A certificate of good standing from the Secretary of State indicating that the entity is an entity registered in this state.

(c) A statement under oath by a principal of the entity certifying that the entity, or a principal of the entity, has a minimum of 12 months' experience in the recovery of surplus funds in foreclosure actions.

(d) Proof that the entity holds a valid Class "A" private investigator license pursuant to chapter 493.

(e) Proof that the entity carries a minimum of $500,000 in liability insurance, cash reserves, or bonding.

(f) A statement from an attorney licensed to practice in this state certifying that the attorney is a principal of the entity or is employed by the entity on a full-time basis and that the attorney will supervise the management of the entity during the entity's tenure as a surplus trustee.

(g) A statement under oath by a principal of the entity certifying that the principal understands his or her duty to immediately notify the department if the principal ever fails to qualify as an entity entitled to be a surplus trustee.

(h) A nonrefundable application fee of $25.

(4) The Department of Financial Services shall certify any surplus trustee that applies and qualifies. Applications must be filed by June 1, and all applications that qualify shall be certified by the department by June 30 and shall be effective for 1 year commencing July 1. The department shall renew a certification upon receipt of the $25 fee and a statement under oath from a principal of the surplus trustee certifying that the surplus trustee continues to qualify under this section.

(5) The Department of Financial Services shall develop a rotation system for assignment of cases to all qualified surplus trustees.

(6) The primary duty of a surplus trustee is to locate the owner of record within 1 year after appointment. Upon locating the owner of record, the surplus trustee shall file a petition with the court on behalf of the owner of record seeking disbursement of the surplus funds. If more than one person appears to be the owner of record, the surplus trustee shall obtain agreement between such persons as to the payment of the surplus or file an interpleader. The interpleader may be filed as part of the foreclosure case.

(7) A surplus trustee is entitled to the following service charges and fees which shall be disbursed by the clerk and payable from the surplus:

(a) Upon obtaining a court order, a cost advance of 2 percent of the surplus.

(b) Upon obtaining a court order disbursing the surplus to the owner of record, a service charge of 10 percent of the surplus.

45.035. Clerk's fees.

In addition to other fees or service charges authorized by law, the clerk shall receive service charges related to the judicial sales procedure set forth in ss. 45.031-45.034 and this section:

(1) The clerk shall receive a service charge of $70 for services in making, recording, and certifying the sale and title, which service charge shall be assessed as costs and shall be advanced by the plaintiff before the sale.

(2) If there is a surplus resulting from the sale, the clerk may receive the following service charges, which shall be deducted from the surplus:

(a) The clerk may withhold the sum of $28 from the surplus which may only be used for purposes of educating the public as to the rights of homeowners regarding foreclosure proceedings.

(b) The clerk is entitled to a service charge of $15 for notifying a surplus trustee of his or her appointment.

(c) The clerk is entitled to a service charge of $15 for each disbursement of surplus proceeds.

(d) The clerk is entitled to a service charge of $15 for appointing a surplus trustee, furnishing the surplus trustee with a copy of the final judgment and the certificate of disbursements, and disbursing to the surplus trustee the trustee's cost advance.

(3) If the sale is conducted by electronic means, as provided in s. 45.031(10), the clerk shall receive an additional service charge not to exceed $70 for services in conducting or contracting for the electronic sale, which service charge shall be assessed as costs and paid when filing for an electronic sale date. If the clerk requires advance electronic deposits to secure the right to bid, such deposits shall not be subject to the fee under s. 28.24(10). The portion of an advance deposit from a winning bidder required by s. 45.031(3) shall, upon acceptance of the winning bid, be subject to the fee under s. 28.24(10).

45.041. Amendment of bonds.

When any bond required or authorized in any action is defective in form or substance, the party giving the bond may give a new bond which is sufficient in form and substance and the new bond is as sufficient as though given in the first instance. The new bond may be given at any time before a motion attacking the sufficiency of the bond is served. Thereafter the new bond may be given by leave of court and on such terms as the court fixes. Leave to file an amended bond shall be freely given when justice so requires. If any amendment is made to a bond, the amended bond relates back to the commencement of the action and affords protection to the person in whose favor it is given from commencement although it was not theretofore binding on the surety.

45.045. Limitations on supersedeas bond; exception.

(1) Except for certified class actions subject to s. 768.733, in any civil action brought under any legal theory, the amount of a supersedeas bond necessary to obtain an automatic stay of execution of a judgment granting any type of relief during the entire course of all appeals or discretionary reviews, may not exceed $50 million for each appellant, regardless of the amount of the judgment appealed. The $50 million amount shall be adjusted annually to reflect changes in the Consumer Price Index compiled by the United States Department of Labor.

(2) In any civil action brought under any legal theory, a party seeking a stay of execution of a judgment pending review of any amount may move the court to reduce the amount of a supersedeas bond required to obtain such a stay. The court, in the interest of justice and for good cause shown, may reduce the supersedeas bond or may set other conditions for the stay with or without a bond. The court may not reduce the supersedeas bond if the appellant has an insurance or indemnification policy applicable to the case. This subsection does not apply to certified class actions subject to s. 768.733.

(3) If an appellant has posted a supersedeas bond for an amount less than that which would be required for an automatic stay pursuant to Rule 9.310(b)(1), Florida Rules of Appellate Procedure, the appellee may engage in discovery for the limited purpose of determining whether the appellant has dissipated or diverted assets outside the course of its ordinary business or is in the process of doing so.

(4) If the trial or appellate court determines that an appellant has dissipated or diverted assets outside the course of its ordinary business or is in the process of doing so, the court may enter orders necessary to protect the appellee, require the appellant to post a supersedeas bond in an amount up to, but not more than, the amount that would be required for an automatic stay pursuant to Rule 9.310(b)(1), Florida Rules of Appellate Procedure, and impose other remedies and sanctions as the court deems appropriate.

45.051. Execution of supersedeas bond when required of the state or its political subdivisions.

(1) When a supersedeas bond is required by the appellate court under Rule 9.310(b)(2), Florida Rules of Appellate Procedure or an appeal or other proceeding is taken in any court and there is no court rule or statute exempting the parties from giving supersedeas, cost, or other required bond, the parties are authorized to make and execute the required bond with a corporate surety thereon duly licensed to do business in this state. The premium or other cost for the bond may be paid from the general necessary and regular appropriation of the party taking the appeal, in the case of the state or any of its officers, boards, commissioners or other agencies, and from the county general fund, district school general fund, or otherwise as the case may be, in the case of a political subdivision of the state or any of its officers, boards, commissions or other agencies. The officers of the state and its political subdivisions and the executive officers of their boards,

commissions, and other agencies aforesaid, are authorized to make and execute the bonds on behalf of the parties.

(2) In connection with an appeal taken by a state employee or official of a judgment against that employee or official in an individual capacity, as part of the legal defense being provided by the state risk management program, the Division of Risk Management may enter into an indemnification agreement for the purpose of securing an appellate supersedeas bond, provided that, under any such agreement, the liability of the State of Florida is limited to the amount of the judgment being appealed and any costs imposed by law or the appropriate court.

45.061. Offers of settlement.

(1) At any time more than 60 days after the service of a summons and complaint on a party but not less than 60 days (or 45 days if it is a counteroffer) before trial, any party may serve upon an adverse party a written offer, which offer shall not be filed with the court and shall be denominated as an offer under this section, to settle a claim for the money, property, or relief specified in the offer and to enter into a stipulation dismissing the claim or to allow judgment to be entered accordingly. The offer shall remain open for 45 days unless withdrawn sooner by a writing served on the offeree prior to acceptance by the offeree. An offer that is neither withdrawn nor accepted within 45 days shall be deemed rejected. The fact that an offer is made but not accepted does not preclude the making of a subsequent offer. Evidence of an offer is not admissible except in proceedings to enforce a settlement or to determine sanctions under this section.

(2) If, upon a motion by the offeror within 30 days after the entry of judgment, the court determines that an offer was rejected unreasonably, resulting in unnecessary delay and needless increase in the cost of litigation, it may impose an appropriate sanction upon the offeree. In making this determination the court shall consider all of the relevant circumstances at the time of the rejection, including:

(a) Whether, upon specific request by the offeree, the offeror had unreasonably refused to furnish information which was necessary to evaluate the reasonableness of the offer.

(b) Whether the suit was in the nature of a "test case," presenting questions of far-reaching importance affecting nonparties.

(3) In determining the amount of any sanction to be imposed under this section, the court shall award:

(a) The amount of the parties' costs and expenses, including reasonable attorneys' fees, investigative expenses, expert witness fees, and other expenses which relate to the preparation for trial, incurred after the making of the offer of settlement; and

(b) The statutory rate of interest that could have been earned at the prevailing statutory rate on the amount that a claimant offered to accept to the extent that the interest is not otherwise included in the judgment.

(4) This section shall not apply to any class action or shareholder derivative suit or to matters relating to dissolution of marriage, alimony, nonsupport, eminent domain, or child custody.

(5) Sanctions authorized under this section may be imposed notwithstanding any limitation on recovery of costs or expenses which may be provided by contract or in other provisions of Florida law. This section shall not be construed to waive the limits of sovereign immunity set forth in s. 768.28.

(6) This section does not apply to causes of action that accrue after the effective date of this act.

45.062. Settlements, conditions, or orders when an agency of the executive branch is a party.

(1) In any civil action in which a state executive branch agency or officer is a party in state or federal court, the officer, agent, official, or attorney who represents or is acting on behalf of such agency or officer may not settle such action, consent to any condition, or agree to any order in connection therewith, if the settlement, condition, or order requires the expenditure of or the obligation to expend any state funds or other state resources exceeding $1 million, the refund or future loss of state revenues exceeding $10 million, or the establishment of any new program, unless:

(a) The expenditure is provided for by an existing appropriation or program established by law.

(b) At the time settlement negotiations have begun in earnest, written notification is given to the President of the Senate, the Speaker of the House of Representatives, the Senate and House of Representatives minority leaders, the chairs of the appropriations committees of the Legislature, and the Attorney General.

(c) Prior written notification is given at least 5 business days, or as soon thereafter as practicable, before the date the settlement or presettlement agreement or order is to be made final to the President of the Senate, the Speaker of the House of Representatives, the Senate and House of Representatives minority leaders, the chairs of the appropriations committees of the Legislature, and the Attorney General. Such notification shall specify how the agency involved will address the costs in future years within the limits of current appropriations.

1. The Division of Risk Management need not give the notification required by this paragraph when settling any claim covered by the state self-insurance program for an amount less than $250,000.

2. The notification specified in this paragraph is not required if:

a. The only settlement obligation of the state resulting from the claim is to pay court costs in an amount less than $10,000;

b. Notification would preclude the state's participation in multistate litigation;

c. Notification is precluded by federal law or regulation;

d. Notification is precluded by court rule or sanction;

e. The head of the primary state agency involved in the litigation certifies to the President of the Senate and the Speaker of the House of Representatives, in writing within 5 days after the settlement, the specific reasons prior notification could not be provided;

f. Settlement or presettlement negotiations are being conducted with fewer than all of the opposing parties; or

g. The President of the Senate and the Speaker of the House of Representatives or the chairs of the appropriations committees of the Legislature, acting in the best interest of the state, waive notification.

(2) The state executive branch agency or officer shall negotiate a closure date as soon as possible for the civil action.

(3) The state executive branch agency or officer may not pledge any current or future action of another branch of state government as a condition for settling the civil action.

(4) Any settlement that commits the state to spending in excess of current appropriations or to policy changes inconsistent with current state law shall be contingent upon and subject to legislative appropriation or statutory amendment. The state agency or officer may agree to use all efforts to procure legislative funding or statutory amendment.

(5) When a state agency or officer settles an action or legal claim in which the state asserted a right to recover money, all moneys paid to the state by a party in full or partial exchange for a release of the state's claim shall be placed into the General Revenue Fund or the appropriate trust fund.

(6) State executive branch agencies and officers shall report to each substantive and fiscal committee of the Legislature having jurisdiction over the reporting agency on all potential settlements that may commit the state to:

(a) Spend in excess of current appropriations; or

(b) Make policy changes inconsistent with current state law.

45.075. Expedited trials.

Upon the joint stipulation of the parties to any civil case, the court may conduct an expedited trial as provided in this section. Where two or more plaintiffs or defendants have a unity of interest, such as a husband and wife, they shall be considered one party for the purpose of this section. Unless otherwise ordered by the court or agreed to by the parties with approval of the court, an expedited trial shall be conducted as follows:

(1) All discovery shall be completed within 60 days after the court enters an order adopting the joint expedited trial stipulation.

(2) All interrogatories and requests for production must be served within 10 days after the court enters the order adopting the joint expedited trial stipulation, and all responses must be served within 20 days after receipt.

(3) The court shall determine the number of depositions required.

(4) The case may be tried to a jury.

(5) The case may be tried within 30 days after the 60-day discovery cutoff, if such schedule would not impose an undue burden on the court calendar.

(6) The trial must be limited to 1 day.

(7) The jury selection must be limited to 1 hour.

(8) The plaintiff will have no more than 3 hours to present its case, including the opening, all testimony and evidence, and the closing.

(9) The defendant will have no more than 3 hours to present its case, including the opening, all testimony and evidence, and the closing.

(10) The jury may be given "plain language" jury instructions at the beginning of the trial as well as a "plain language" jury verdict form. The parties must agree to the jury instructions and verdict form.

(11) The parties may introduce a verified written report of any expert and an affidavit of the expert's curriculum vitae instead of calling the expert to testify at trial.

(12) At trial the parties may use excerpts from depositions, including video depositions, regardless of where the deponent lives or whether the deponent is available to testify.

(13) Except as otherwise provided in this section, the Florida Evidence Code and the Florida Rules of Civil Procedure apply.

(14) The court may refuse to grant continuances of the trial absent extraordinary circumstances.

CHAPTER 46. PARTIES

46.011. Parties for contribution.

When a person executes any bond, note, draft, or bill of exchange and two or more persons execute it jointly with him or her, merely as his or her sureties, or endorse any note or draft or bill of exchange as sureties for the maker or drawer for his or her accommodation and without consideration, said persons are bound to each other for a proportional contribution of the amount of said bond, note, draft, or bill of exchange. If any person is compelled to pay any part of said bond, note, draft, or bill of exchange, he or she may sue his or her cosurety for contribution separately or jointly. Defendants, whether sureties, accommodation joint makers or accommodation endorsers may be sued separately or jointly.

46.015. Release of parties.

(1) A written covenant not to sue or release of a person who is or may be jointly and severally liable with other persons for a claim shall not release or discharge the liability of any other person who may be liable for the balance of such claim.

(2) At trial, if any person shows the court that the plaintiff, or his or her legal representative, has delivered a written release or covenant not to sue to any person in partial satisfaction of the damages sued for, the court shall set off this amount from the amount of any judgment to which the plaintiff would be otherwise entitled at the time of rendering judgment.

(3) The fact that a written release or covenant not to sue exists or the fact that any person has been dismissed because of such release or covenant not to sue shall not be made known to the jury.

46.021. Actions; surviving death of party.

No cause of action dies with the person. All causes of action survive and may be commenced, prosecuted, and defended in the name of the person prescribed by law.

46.031. Actions by husband and wife, parent or guardian and child.

In any action brought by a husband and his wife, parent or guardian and child for an injury done to the wife or child, in which the wife or child is necessarily joined as coplaintiff, the husband, parent or guardian may join claims of any nature in his or her own right.

46.041. Joinder of certain makers, endorsers, etc., of negotiable instruments.

(1) The makers of negotiable instruments and all other persons who, at or before the execution and delivery thereof, endorsed, guaranteed, or became surety for payment thereof, or are otherwise secondarily liable for payment, may be sued in the same action.

(2) In such action the final judgment shall specify the defendants who are liable for payment only as endorser, surety, guarantor or otherwise secondarily.

(3) When a final judgment authorized by this section is paid by one or more defendants who are liable only as endorser, surety, guarantor, or otherwise secondarily, the holder of such judgment shall, on request, assign such judgment to the defendants paying it. Such defendants are entitled to all the rights and remedies of the original plaintiff to enforce collection from the other defendants who are liable.

46.051. Joinder of products liability insurers.

(1) No products liability insurer shall be joined as a party defendant in an action to determine the insured's liability. However, each insurer which does or may provide products liability insurance coverage to pay all or a portion of any judgment which might be entered in the action shall file with the court, under oath, a statement by a corporate officer setting forth the following

information with regard to each known policy of insurance:

(a) The name of the insurer;

(b) The name of each insured;

(c) The limits of liability coverage; and

(d) A statement of any policy or coverage defense which said insurer reasonably believes is available to the insurer filing the statement at the time of filing.

(2) The statement required by subsection (1) shall be amended immediately upon discovery of facts calling for an amendment to such statement.

(3) If the statement or any amendment thereto indicates that a policy or coverage defense has been or will be asserted, then the insurer may be joined as a party.

(4) After the rendition of a verdict, or final judgment by the court if the case is tried without a jury, the insurer may be joined as a party and judgment may be entered by the court based upon the statement or statements herein required.

(5) The rules of discovery shall be available to discover the existence of liability insurance coverage and its provisions.

(6) This act is applicable to products liability actions based on either tort or contract causes of action.

CHAPTER 47. VENUE

47.011. Where actions may be begun.

Actions shall be brought only in the county where the defendant resides, where the cause of action accrued, or where the property in litigation is located. This section shall not apply to actions against nonresidents.

47.021. Actions against defendants residing in different counties.

Actions against two or more defendants residing in different counties may be brought in any county in which any defendant resides.

47.025. Actions against contractors.

Any venue provision in a contract for improvement to real property which requires legal action involving a resident contractor, subcontractor, sub-subcontractor, or materialman, as defined in 1part I of chapter 713, to be brought outside this state is void as a matter of public policy. To the extent that the venue provision in the contract is void under this section, any legal action arising out of that contract shall be brought only in this state in the county where the defendant resides, where the cause of action accrued, or where the property in litigation is located, unless, after the dispute arises, the parties stipulate to another venue.

47.031. Venue of receiverships when property in more than one circuit.

When an application is made for a receiver of property and it is located in more than one judicial circuit, the court appointing the receiver has jurisdiction over the entire property for the purposes of that action but the application for the receiver must be made to the circuit court in which the principal place of business, residence or office of defendant is located.

47.041. Actions on several causes of action.

Actions on several causes of action may be brought in any county where any of the causes of action arose. When two or more causes of action joined arose in different counties, venue may be laid in any of such counties, but the court may order separate trials if expedient.

47.051. Actions against corporations.

Actions against domestic corporations shall be brought only in the county where such corporation has, or usually keeps, an office for transaction of its customary business, where the cause of action accrued, or where the property in litigation is located. Actions against foreign corporations doing business in this state shall be brought in a county where such corporation has an agent or other representative, where the cause of action accrued, or where the property in litigation is located.

47.061. Action on promissory notes.

Actions on unsecured negotiable or nonnegotiable promissory notes shall be brought only in the county in which such notes were signed by the maker or one of the makers or in which the maker or one of the makers resides. When any such note was signed by the makers in more than one county, action may be brought thereon in any such county. This section shall be liberally construed in favor of the makers of such notes.

47.071. Jurisdiction over navigable waters.

When the territorial jurisdiction of a court extends to one bank of any navigable water, such court has jurisdiction across such navigable water from shore to shore. If the territorial jurisdiction of different courts, whether of the same county or not, extends to the opposite bank of any navigable water, such courts have concurrent jurisdiction across said navigable water from shore to shore.

47.081. Military, naval, or other service as residence.

Any person in any branch of the Armed Forces of the United States, and the husband or the wife of any such person, if he or she is living within the borders of the state, shall be prima facie a resident of the state for the purpose of maintaining any action.

47.091. Change of venue; power to grant.

All courts have power and it is their duty to grant changes of venue as hereinafter provided. The order of transfer shall require the movant or, if the action was initially filed in the improper venue, the initially filing party to pay the filing fee required to file a new action in the court to which the action is moved. The payment of such filing fee shall be considered a transfer fee.

47.101. Change of venue; application.

(1) If a party desires a change of venue he or she may move therefor stating the belief that he or she will not receive a fair trial in the court where the action is pending:
(a) Because the adverse party has an undue influence over the minds of the inhabitants of the county.
(b) Because movant is so odious to the inhabitants of the county that he or she could not receive a fair trial.
(2) Such motion shall be verified and filed not less than 10 days after the action is at issue unless good cause is shown for failure to so file. It shall set forth the facts on which the motion is based and be supported by affidavits of at least two reputable citizens of the county not of kin to the defendant or his or her attorney.

47.111. Change of venue; denial of motion.

The adverse party has the right to deny the allegations of the motion. The court shall hear the evidence on the motion.

47.121. Change of venue; when unable to obtain jury.

A change of venue shall be granted when it appears impracticable to obtain a qualified jury in the county where the action is pending.

47.122. Change of venue; convenience of parties or witnesses or in the interest of justice.

For the convenience of the parties or witnesses or in the interest of justice, any court of record may transfer any civil action to any other court of record in which it might have been brought.

47.131. Change of venue; second change, when permitted.

When it appears to the court to which an action has been transferred by a change of venue that any of the grounds for change of venue exist in the county to which the action has been transferred, the court may order a second change of venue, but it shall not be made to the county from which it was originally transferred.

47.141. Change of venue; same jurisdiction.

The order granting change of venue shall transfer the action to a court of the same jurisdiction in another county. If the judge of such court is disqualified, some other court shall be selected.

47.151. Change of venue; to another county of circuit.

If a change of venue is granted on grounds other than the disqualification or prejudice of a judge of the circuit court, the action may be removed to any other county in the same circuit.

47.172. Change of venue; transfer of papers, etc.

On a change of venue the clerk of the court in which such action was pending shall transmit all papers filed in said action, a certified copy of all entries of record in the progress docket and a copy of the order of transfer to the court to which the action is transferred, which court has full power to hear and determine the action.

47.181. Change of venue; testimony of witnesses.

After a change of venue, testimony of witnesses residing in the county from which the action is removed may be taken in the manner provided for taking testimony of witnesses residing out of the county in which any action is pending.

47.191. Change of venue; payment of costs.

No change of venue shall be granted except on condition that the movant, unless otherwise provided by the order of transfer, shall pay all costs that have accrued in the action including the required transfer fee. No change is effective until the costs are paid.

CHAPTER 48. PROCESS AND SERVICE OF PROCESS

48.011. Process; how directed.

Summons, subpoenas, and other process in civil actions run throughout the state. All process except subpoenas shall be directed to all and singular the sheriffs of the state.

48.021. Process; by whom served.

(1) All process shall be served by the sheriff of the county where the person to be served is found, except initial nonenforceable civil process, criminal witness subpoenas, and criminal summonses may be served by a special process server appointed by the sheriff as provided for in this section or by a certified process server as provided for in ss. 48.25-48.31. Civil witness subpoenas may be served by any person authorized by rules of civil procedure.

(2)(a) The sheriff of each county may, in his or her discretion, establish an approved list of natural persons designated as special process servers. The sheriff shall add to such list the names of those natural persons who have met the requirements provided for in this section. Each natural person whose name has been added to the approved list is subject to annual recertification and reappointment by the sheriff. The sheriff shall prescribe an appropriate form for application for appointment. A reasonable fee for the processing of the application shall be charged.

(b) A person applying to become a special process server shall:

1. Be at least 18 years of age.

2. Have no mental or legal disability.

3. Be a permanent resident of the state.

4. Submit to a background investigation that includes the right to obtain and review the criminal record of the applicant.

5. Obtain and file with the application a certificate of good conduct that specifies there is no pending criminal case against the applicant and that there is no record of any felony conviction, nor a record of a misdemeanor involving moral turpitude or dishonesty, with respect to the applicant within the past 5 years.

6. Submit to an examination testing the applicant's knowledge of the laws and rules regarding the service of process. The content of the examination and the passing grade thereon, and the frequency and the location at which the examination is offered must be prescribed by the sheriff. The examination must be offered at least once annually.

7. Take an oath that the applicant will honestly, diligently, and faithfully exercise the duties of a special process server.

(c) The sheriff may prescribe additional rules and requirements directly related to subparagraphs (b)1.-7. regarding the eligibility of a person to become a special process server or to have his or her name maintained on the list of special process servers.

(d) An applicant who completes the requirements of this section must be designated as a special process server provided that the sheriff of the county has determined that the appointment of special process servers is necessary or desirable. Each special process server must be issued an identification card bearing his or her identification number, printed name, signature and photograph, and an expiration date. Each identification card must be renewable annually upon proof of good standing.

(e) The sheriff shall have the discretion to revoke an appointment at any time that he or she determines a special process server is not fully and properly discharging the duties as a special process server. The sheriff shall institute a program to determine whether the special process servers appointed as provided for in this section are faithfully discharging their duties pursuant to such appointment, and a reasonable fee may be charged for the costs of administering such program.

(3) A special process server appointed in accordance with this section shall be authorized to serve process in only the county in which the sheriff who appointed him or her resides and may charge a reasonable fee for his or her services.

(4) Any special process server shall be disinterested in any process he or she serves; and if the special process server willfully and knowingly executes a false return of service or otherwise violates the oath of office, he or she shall be guilty of a felony of the third degree, punishable as provided for in s. 775.082, s. 775.083, or s. 775.084, and shall be permanently barred from serving process in Florida.

48.031. Service of process generally; service of witness subpoenas.

(1)(a) Service of original process is made by delivering a copy of it to the person to be served with a copy of the complaint, petition, or other initial pleading or paper or by leaving the copies at his or her usual place of abode with any person residing therein who is 15 years of age or older and informing the person of their contents. Minors who are or have been married shall be served as provided in this section.

(b) An employer, when contacted by an individual authorized to serve process, shall allow the authorized individual to serve an employee in a private area designated by the employer. An employer who fails to comply with this paragraph commits a noncriminal violation, punishable by a fine of up to $1,000.

(2)(a) Substitute service may be made on the spouse of the person to be served at any place in the county, if the cause of action is not an adversary proceeding between the spouse and the person to be served, if the spouse requests such service, and if the spouse and person to be served are residing together in the same dwelling.

(b) Substitute service may be made on an individual doing business as a sole proprietorship at his or her place of business, during regular business hours, by serving the person in charge of the business at the time of service if two attempts to serve the owner have been made at the place of business.

(3)(a) The service of process of witness subpoenas, whether in criminal cases or civil actions, shall be made as provided in subsection (1). However, service of a subpoena on a witness in a civil traffic case, a criminal traffic case, a misdemeanor case, or a second degree or third degree felony may be made by United States mail directed to the witness at the last known address, and the service must be mailed at least 7 days prior to the date of the witness's required appearance. Failure of a witness to appear in response to a subpoena served by United States mail that is not certified may not be grounds for finding the witness in contempt of court.

(b) A criminal witness subpoena commanding the witness to appear for a court appearance may be posted by a person authorized to serve process at the witness's residence if three attempts to serve the subpoena, made at different times of the day or night on different dates, have failed. A criminal witness subpoena commanding the witness to appear for a deposition may be posted by a person authorized to serve process at the witness's residence if one attempt to serve the subpoena has failed. The subpoena must be posted at least 5 days before the date of the witness's required appearance.

(4)(a) Service of a criminal witness subpoena upon a law enforcement officer or upon any federal, state, or municipal employee called to testify in an official capacity in a criminal case may be made as provided in subsection (1) or by delivery to a designated supervisory or administrative employee at the witness's place of employment if the agency head or highest ranking official at the witness's place of employment has designated such employee to accept such service. However, no such designated employee is required to accept service:

1. For a witness who is no longer employed by the agency at that place of employment;

2. If the witness is not scheduled to work prior to the date the witness is required to appear; or

3. If the appearance date is less than 5 days from the date of service.

(b) Service may also be made in accordance with subsection (3) provided that the person who requests the issuance of the criminal witness subpoena shall be responsible for mailing the subpoena in accordance with that subsection and for making the proper return of service to the court.

(5) A person serving process shall place, on the first page of at least one of the processes served, the date and time of service and his or her identification number and initials for all service of

process. The person serving process shall list on the return-of-service form all initial pleadings delivered and served along with the process. The person requesting service or the person authorized to serve the process shall file the return-of-service form with the court.

(6)(a) If the only address for a person to be served which is discoverable through public records is a private mailbox, a virtual office, or an executive office or mini suite, substitute service may be made by leaving a copy of the process with the person in charge of the private mailbox, virtual office, or executive office or mini suite, but only if the process server determines that the person to be served maintains a mailbox, a virtual office, or an executive office or mini suite at that location.

(b) For purposes of this subsection, the term "virtual office" means an office that provides communications services, such as telephone or facsimile services, and address services without providing dedicated office space, and where all communications are routed through a common receptionist. The term "executive office or mini suite" means an office that provides communications services, such as telephone and facsimile services, a dedicated office space, and other supportive services, and where all communications are routed through a common receptionist.

(7) A gated residential community, including a condominium association or a cooperative, shall grant unannounced entry into the community, including its common areas and common elements, to a person who is attempting to serve process on a defendant or witness who resides within or is known to be within the community.

48.041. Service on minor.

(1) Process against a minor who has never been married shall be served:

(a) By serving a parent or guardian of the minor as provided for in s. 48.031 or, when there is a legal guardian appointed for the minor, by serving the guardian as provided for in s. 48.031.

(b) By serving the guardian ad litem or other person, if one is appointed by the court to represent the minor. Service on the guardian ad litem is unnecessary when he or she appears voluntarily or when the court orders the appearance without service of process on him or her.

(2) In all cases heretofore adjudicated in which process was served on a minor as prescribed by any law heretofore existing, the service was lawfully made, and no proceeding shall be declared irregular or illegal if a guardian ad litem appeared for the minor.

48.042. Service on incompetent.

(1) Process against an incompetent shall be served:

(a) By serving two copies of the process to the person who has care or custody of the incompetent or, when there is a legal guardian appointed for the incompetent, by serving the guardian as provided in s. 48.031.

(b) By serving the guardian ad litem or other person, if one is appointed by the court to represent the incompetent. Service on the guardian ad litem is unnecessary when he or she appears voluntarily or when the court orders the appearance without service of process on him or her.

(2) In all cases heretofore adjudicated in which process was served on an incompetent as prescribed by any law heretofore existing, the service was lawfully made, and no proceeding shall be declared irregular or illegal if a guardian ad litem appeared for the incompetent.

48.051. Service on state prisoners.

Process against a state prisoner shall be served on the prisoner.

48.061. Service on partnerships and limited partnerships.

(1) Process against a partnership shall be served on any partner and is as valid as if served on each individual partner. If a partner is not available during regular business hours to accept service on behalf of the partnership, he or she may designate an employee to accept such service. After one attempt to serve a partner or designated employee has been made, process may be served on the person in charge of the partnership during regular business hours. After service on any partner, plaintiff may proceed to judgment and execution against that partner and the assets of the partnership. After service on a designated employee or other person in charge, plaintiff may proceed to judgment and execution against the partnership assets but not against the individual assets of any partner.

(2) Process against a domestic limited partnership may be served on any general partner or on the agent for service of process specified in its certificate of limited partnership or in its certificate as amended or restated and is as valid as if served on each individual member of the partnership. After service on a general partner or the agent, the plaintiff may proceed to judgment and execution against the limited partnership and all of the general partners individually. If a general partner cannot be found in this state and service cannot be made on an agent because of failure to maintain such an agent or because the agent cannot be found or served with the exercise of reasonable diligence, service of process may be effected by service upon the Secretary of State as agent of the limited partnership as provided for in s. 48.181. Service of process may be made under ss. 48.071 and 48.21 on limited partnerships.

(3) Process against a foreign limited partnership may be served on any general partner found in the state or on any agent for service of process specified in its application for registration and is as valid as if served on each individual member of the partnership. If a general partner cannot be found in this state and an agent for service of process has not been appointed or, if appointed, the agent's authority has been revoked or the agent cannot be found or served with the exercise of reasonable diligence, service of process may be effected by service upon the Secretary of State as agent of the limited partnership as provided for in s. 48.181, or process may be served as provided in ss. 48.071 and 48.21.

48.062. Service on a limited liability company.

(1) Process against a limited liability company, domestic or foreign, may be served on the registered agent designated by the limited liability company under chapter 605. A person attempting to serve process pursuant to this subsection may serve the process on any employee of the registered agent during the first attempt at service even if the registered agent is a natural person and is temporarily absent from his or her office.

(2) If service cannot be made on a registered agent of the limited liability company because of failure to comply with chapter 605 or because the limited liability company does not have a registered agent, or if its registered agent cannot with reasonable diligence be served, process against the limited liability company, domestic or foreign, may be served:

(a) On a member of a member-managed limited liability company;

(b) On a manager of a manager-managed limited liability company; or

(c) If a member or manager is not available during regular business hours to accept service on behalf of the limited liability company, he, she, or it may designate an employee of the limited liability company to accept such service. After one attempt to serve a member, manager, or designated employee has been made, process may be served on the person in charge of the limited liability company during regular business hours.

(3) If, after reasonable diligence, service of process cannot be completed under subsection (1) or subsection (2), service of process may be effected by service upon the Secretary of State as agent of the limited liability company as provided for in s. 48.181.

(4) If the address provided for the registered agent, member, or manager is a residence or private mailbox, service on the limited liability company, domestic or foreign, may be made by serving the registered agent, member, or manager in accordance with s. 48.031.

(5) This section does not apply to service of process on insurance companies.

48.071. Service on agents of nonresidents doing business in the state.

When any natural person or partnership not residing or having a principal place of business in this state engages in business in this state, process may be served on the person who is in charge of any business in which the defendant is engaged within this state at the time of service, including agents soliciting orders for goods, wares, merchandise or services. Any process so served is as valid as if served personally on the nonresident person or partnership engaging in business in this state in any action against the person or partnership arising out of such business. A copy of such process with a notice of service on the person in charge of such business shall be sent forthwith to the nonresident person or partnership by registered or certified mail, return receipt requested. An affidavit of compliance with this section shall be filed before the return day or within such further time as the court may allow.

48.081. Service on corporation.

(1) Process against any private corporation, domestic or foreign, may be served:

(a) On the president or vice president, or other head of the corporation;

(b) In the absence of any person described in paragraph (a), on the cashier, treasurer, secretary, or general manager;

(c) In the absence of any person described in paragraph (a) or paragraph (b), on any director; or

(d) In the absence of any person described in paragraph (a), paragraph (b), or paragraph (c), on any officer or business agent residing in the state.

(2) If a foreign corporation has none of the foregoing officers or agents in this state, service may be made on any agent transacting business for it in this state.

(3)(a) As an alternative to all of the foregoing, process may be served on the agent designated by the corporation under s. 48.091. However, if service cannot be made on a registered agent because of failure to comply with s. 48.091, service of process shall be permitted on any employee at the corporation's principal place of business or on any employee of the registered agent. A person attempting to serve process pursuant to this paragraph may serve the process on any employee of the registered agent during the first attempt at service even if the registered agent is temporarily absent from his or her office.

(b) If the address for the registered agent, officer, director, or principal place of business is a residence, a private mailbox, a virtual office, or an executive office or mini suite, service on the corporation may be made by serving the registered agent, officer, or director in accordance with s. 48.031.

(4) This section does not apply to service of process on insurance companies.

(5) When a corporation engages in substantial and not isolated activities within this state, or has a business office within the state and is actually engaged in the transaction of business therefrom, service upon any officer or business agent while on corporate business within this state may personally be made, pursuant to this section, and it is not necessary in such case that the action,

suit, or proceeding against the corporation shall have arisen out of any transaction or operation connected with or incidental to the business being transacted within the state.

48.091. Corporations; designation of registered agent and registered office.

(1) Every Florida corporation and every foreign corporation now qualified or hereafter qualifying to transact business in this state shall designate a registered agent and registered office in accordance with part I of chapter 607.

(2) Every corporation shall keep the registered office open from 10 a.m. to 12 noon each day except Saturdays, Sundays, and legal holidays, and shall keep one or more registered agents on whom process may be served at the office during these hours. The corporation shall keep a sign posted in the office in some conspicuous place designating the name of the corporation and the name of its registered agent on whom process may be served.

48.092. Service on financial institutions.

Service on financial institutions must be made in accordance with s. 655.0201.

48.101. Service on dissolved corporations.

Process against the directors of any corporation which was dissolved before July 1, 1990, as trustees of the dissolved corporation shall be served on one or more of the directors of the dissolved corporation as trustees thereof and binds all of the directors of the dissolved corporation as trustees thereof. Process against any other dissolved corporation shall be served in accordance with s. 48.081.

48.111. Service on public agencies and officers.

(1) Process against any municipal corporation, agency, board, or commission, department, or subdivision of the state or any county which has a governing board, council, or commission or which is a body corporate shall be served:

(a) On the president, mayor, chair, or other head thereof; and in his or her absence;

(b) On the vice president, vice mayor, or vice chair, or in the absence of all of the above;

(c) On any member of the governing board, council, or commission.

(2) Process against any public agency, board, commission, or department not a body corporate or having a governing board or commission shall be served on the public officer being sued or the chief executive officer of the agency, board, commission, or department.

(3) In any suit in which the Department of Revenue or its successor is a party, process against the department shall be served on the executive director of the department. This procedure is to be in lieu of any other provision of general law, and shall designate said department to be the only state agency or department to be so served.

48.121. Service on the state.

When the state has consented to be sued, process against the state shall be served on the state attorney or an assistant state attorney for the judicial circuit within which the action is brought and by sending two copies of the process by registered or certified mail to the Attorney General. The state may serve motions or pleadings within 40 days after service is made. This section is not intended to authorize the joinder of the Attorney General or a state attorney as a party in such suit or prosecution.

48.131. Service on alien property custodian.

In every action or proceeding in any court or before any administrative board involving real, personal, or mixed property, or any interest therein, when service of process or notice is required or directed to be made upon any person, firm or corporation located, or believed to be located, within any country or territory in the possession of or under the control of any country between which and the United States a state of war exists, in addition to the giving of the notice or service of process, a copy of the notice or process shall be sent by registered or certified mail to the alien property custodian, addressed to him or her at Washington, District of Columbia; but failure to mail a copy of the notice or process to the alien property custodian does not invalidate the action or proceeding.

48.141. Service on labor unions.

Process against labor organizations shall be served on the president or other officer, business agent, manager or person in charge of the business of such labor organization.

48.151. Service on statutory agents for certain persons.

(1) When any law designates a public officer, board, agency, or commission as the agent for service of process on any person, firm, or corporation, service of process thereunder shall be made by leaving one copy of the process with the public officer, board, agency, or commission or in the office thereof, or by mailing one copy to the public officer, board, agency, or commission. The public officer, board, agency, or commission so served shall retain a record copy and promptly send the copy served, by registered or certified mail, to the person to be served as shown by his or her or its records. Proof of service on the public officer, board, agency, or commission shall be by a notice accepting the process which shall be issued by the public officer, board, agency, or commission promptly after service and filed in the court issuing the process. The notice accepting service shall state the date upon which the copy of the process was mailed by the public officer, board, agency, or commission to the person being served and the time for pleading prescribed by the rules of procedure shall run from this date. The service is valid service for all purposes on the person for whom the public officer, board, agency, or commission is statutory agent for service of process.
(2) This section does not apply to substituted service of process on nonresidents.
(3) The Chief Financial Officer or his or her assistant or deputy or another person in charge of the office is the agent for service of process on all insurers applying for authority to transact insurance in this state, all licensed nonresident insurance agents, all nonresident disability insurance agents licensed pursuant to s. 626.835, any unauthorized insurer under s. 626.906 or s. 626.937, domestic

reciprocal insurers, fraternal benefit societies under chapter 632, warranty associations under chapter 634, prepaid limited health service organizations under chapter 636, and persons required to file statements under s. 628.461. As an alternative to service of process made by mail or personal service on the Chief Financial Officer, on his or her assistant or deputy, or on another person in charge of the office, the Department of Financial Services may create an Internet-based transmission system to accept service of process by electronic transmission of documents.

(4) The Director of the Office of Financial Regulation of the Financial Services Commission is the agent for service of process for any issuer as defined in s. 517.021, or any dealer, investment adviser, or associated person registered with that office, for any violation of any provision of chapter 517.

(5) The Secretary of State is the agent for service of process for any retailer, dealer or vendor who has failed to designate an agent for service of process as required under s. 212.151 for violations of chapter 212.

(6) For purposes of this section, records may be retained as paper or electronic copies.

48.161. Method of substituted service on nonresident.

(1) When authorized by law, substituted service of process on a nonresident or a person who conceals his or her whereabouts by serving a public officer designated by law shall be made by leaving a copy of the process with a fee of $8.75 with the public officer or in his or her office or by mailing the copies by certified mail to the public officer with the fee. The service is sufficient service on a defendant who has appointed a public officer as his or her agent for the service of process. Notice of service and a copy of the process shall be sent forthwith by registered or certified mail by the plaintiff or his or her attorney to the defendant, and the defendant's return receipt and the affidavit of the plaintiff or his or her attorney of compliance shall be filed on or before the return day of the process or within such time as the court allows, or the notice and copy shall be served on the defendant, if found within the state, by an officer authorized to serve legal process, or if found without the state, by a sheriff or a deputy sheriff of any county of this state or any duly constituted public officer qualified to serve like process in the state or jurisdiction where the defendant is found. The officer's return showing service shall be filed on or before the return day of the process or within such time as the court allows. The fee paid by the plaintiff to the public officer shall be taxed as cost if he or she prevails in the action. The public officer shall keep a record of all process served on him or her showing the day and hour of service.

(2) If any person on whom service of process is authorized under subsection (1) dies, service may be made on his or her administrator, executor, curator, or personal representative in the same manner.

(3) This section does not apply to persons on whom service is authorized under s. 48.151.

(4) The public officer may designate some other person in his or her office to accept service.

48.171. Service on nonresident motor vehicle owners, etc.

Any nonresident of this state, being the operator or owner of any motor vehicle, who accepts the privilege extended by the laws of this state to nonresident operators and owners, of operating a motor vehicle or of having it operated, or of permitting any motor vehicle owned, or leased, or controlled by him or her to be operated with his or her knowledge, permission, acquiescence, or consent, within the state, or any resident of this state, being the licensed operator or owner of or the lessee, or otherwise entitled to control any motor vehicle under the laws of this state, who becomes a nonresident or conceals his or her whereabouts, by the acceptance or licensure and by the operation of the motor vehicle, either in person, or by or through his or her servants, agents, or employees, or by persons with his or her knowledge, acquiescence, and consent within the state constitutes the Secretary of State his or her agent for the service of process in any civil action begun in the courts of the state against such operator or owner, lessee, or other person entitled to control of the motor vehicle, arising out of or by reason of any accident or collision occurring within the state in which the motor vehicle is involved.

48.181. Service on nonresident engaging in business in state.

(1) The acceptance by any person or persons, individually or associated together as a copartnership or any other form or type of association, who are residents of any other state or country, and all foreign corporations, and any person who is a resident of the state and who subsequently becomes a nonresident of the state or conceals his or her whereabouts, of the privilege extended by law to nonresidents and others to operate, conduct, engage in, or carry on a business or business venture in the state, or to have an office or agency in the state, constitutes an appointment by the persons and foreign corporations of the Secretary of State of the state as their agent on whom all process in any action or proceeding against them, or any of them, arising out of any transaction or operation connected with or incidental to the business or business venture may be served. The acceptance of the privilege is signification of the agreement of the persons and foreign corporations that the process against them which is so served is of the same validity as if served personally on the persons or foreign corporations.
(2) If a foreign corporation has a resident agent or officer in the state, process shall be served on the resident agent or officer.
(3) Any person, firm, or corporation which sells, consigns, or leases by any means whatsoever tangible or intangible personal property, through brokers, jobbers, wholesalers, or distributors to any person, firm, or corporation in this state is conclusively presumed to be both engaged in substantial and not isolated activities within this state and operating, conducting, engaging in, or carrying on a business or business venture in this state.

48.183. Service of process in action for possession of premises.

(1) In an action for possession of any residential premises, including those under chapters 83, 723, and 513, or nonresidential premises, if the tenant cannot be found in the county or there is no person 15 years of age or older residing at the tenant's usual place of abode in the county after at least two attempts to obtain service as provided above in this subsection, summons may be served by attaching a copy to a conspicuous place on the property described in the complaint or summons. The minimum time delay between the two attempts to obtain service shall be 6 hours. Nothing herein shall be construed as prohibiting service of process on a tenant as is otherwise provided on defendants in civil cases.
(2) If a landlord causes or anticipates causing a defendant to be served with a summons and complaint solely by attaching them to some conspicuous place on the property described in the complaint or summons, the landlord shall provide the clerk of the court with an additional copy of the complaint and a prestamped envelope addressed to the defendant at the premises involved in the proceeding. The clerk of the court shall immediately mail the copy of the summons and complaint by first-class mail, note the fact of mailing in the docket, and file a certificate in the court file of the fact and date of mailing. Service shall be effective on the date of posting or mailing, whichever occurs later, and at least 5 days must elapse from the date of service before a

judgment for final removal of the defendant may be entered.

48.19. Service on nonresidents operating aircraft or watercraft in the state.

The operation, navigation, or maintenance by a nonresident of an aircraft or a boat, ship, barge, or other watercraft in the state, either in person or through others, and the acceptance thereby by the nonresident of the protection of the laws of this state for the aircraft or watercraft, or the operation, navigation, or maintenance by a nonresident of an aircraft or a boat, ship, barge, or other watercraft in the state, either in person or through others, other than under the laws of the state, or any person who is a resident of the state and who subsequently becomes a nonresident or conceals his or her whereabouts, constitutes an appointment by the nonresident of the Secretary of State as the agent of the nonresident or concealed person on whom all process may be served in any action or proceeding against the nonresident or concealed person growing out of any accident or collision in which the nonresident or concealed person may be involved while, either in person or through others, operating, navigating, or maintaining an aircraft or a boat, ship, barge, or other watercraft in the state. The acceptance by operation, navigation, or maintenance in the state of the aircraft or watercraft is signification of the nonresident's or concealed person's agreement that process against him or her so served shall be of the same effect as if served on him or her personally.

48.193. Acts subjecting person to jurisdiction of courts of state.

(1)(a) A person, whether or not a citizen or resident of this state, who personally or through an agent does any of the acts enumerated in this subsection thereby submits himself or herself and, if he or she is a natural person, his or her personal representative to the jurisdiction of the courts of this state for any cause of action arising from any of the following acts:
1. Operating, conducting, engaging in, or carrying on a business or business venture in this state or having an office or agency in this state.
2. Committing a tortious act within this state.
3. Owning, using, possessing, or holding a mortgage or other lien on any real property within this state.
4. Contracting to insure a person, property, or risk located within this state at the time of contracting.
5. With respect to a proceeding for alimony, child support, or division of property in connection with an action to dissolve a marriage or with respect to an independent action for support of dependents, maintaining a matrimonial domicile in this state at the time of the commencement of this action or, if the defendant resided in this state preceding the commencement of the action, whether cohabiting during that time or not. This paragraph does not change the residency requirement for filing an action for dissolution of marriage.
6. Causing injury to persons or property within this state arising out of an act or omission by the defendant outside this state, if, at or about the time of the injury, either:
a. The defendant was engaged in solicitation or service activities within this state; or
b. Products, materials, or things processed, serviced, or manufactured by the defendant anywhere were used or consumed within this state in the ordinary course of commerce, trade, or use.
7. Breaching a contract in this state by failing to perform acts required by the contract to be performed in this state.
8. With respect to a proceeding for paternity, engaging in the act of sexual intercourse within this

state with respect to which a child may have been conceived.

9. Entering into a contract that complies with s. 685.102.

(b) Notwithstanding any other provision of this subsection, an order issued, or a penalty or fine imposed, by an agency of another state is not enforceable against any person or entity incorporated or having its principal place of business in this state if the other state does not provide a mandatory right of review of the agency decision in a state court of competent jurisdiction.

(2) A defendant who is engaged in substantial and not isolated activity within this state, whether such activity is wholly interstate, intrastate, or otherwise, is subject to the jurisdiction of the courts of this state, whether or not the claim arises from that activity.

(3) Service of process upon any person who is subject to the jurisdiction of the courts of this state as provided in this section may be made by personally serving the process upon the defendant outside this state, as provided in s. 48.194. The service shall have the same effect as if it had been personally served within this state.

(4) If a defendant in his or her pleadings demands affirmative relief on causes of action unrelated to the transaction forming the basis of the plaintiff's claim, the defendant shall thereafter in that action be subject to the jurisdiction of the court for any cause of action, regardless of its basis, which the plaintiff may by amendment assert against the defendant.

(5) Nothing contained in this section limits or affects the right to serve any process in any other manner now or hereinafter provided by law.

48.194. Personal service outside state.

(1) Except as otherwise provided herein, service of process on persons outside of this state shall be made in the same manner as service within this state by any officer authorized to serve process in the state where the person is served. No order of court is required. An affidavit of the officer shall be filed, stating the time, manner, and place of service. The court may consider the affidavit, or any other competent evidence, in determining whether service has been properly made. Service of process on persons outside the United States may be required to conform to the provisions of the Hague Convention on the Service Abroad of Judicial and Extrajudicial Documents in Civil or Commercial Matters.

(2) Where in rem or quasi in rem relief is sought in a foreclosure proceeding as defined by s. 702.09, service of process on a person outside of this state where the address of the person to be served is known may be made by registered mail as follows:

(a) The party's attorney or the party, if the party is not represented by an attorney, shall place a copy of the original process and the complaint, petition, or other initial pleading or paper and, if applicable, the order to show cause issued pursuant to s. 702.10 in a sealed envelope with adequate postage addressed to the person to be served.

(b) The envelope shall be placed in the mail as registered mail.

(c) Service under this subsection shall be considered obtained upon the signing of the return receipt by the person allowed to be served by law.

(3) If the registered mail which is sent as provided for in subsection (2) is returned with an endorsement or stamp showing "refused," the party's attorney or the party, if the party is not represented by an attorney, may serve original process by first-class mail. The failure to claim registered mail is not refusal of service within the meaning of this subsection. Service of process pursuant to this subsection shall be perfected as follows:

(a) The party's attorney or the party, if the party is not represented by an attorney, shall place a copy of the original process and the complaint, petition, or other initial pleading or paper and, if applicable, the order to show cause issued pursuant to s. 702.10 in a sealed envelope with adequate postage addressed to the person to be served.

(b) The envelope shall be mailed by first-class mail with the return address of the party's attorney or the party, if the party is not represented by an attorney, on the envelope.

(c) Service under this subsection shall be considered obtained upon the mailing of the envelope.

(4) If service of process is obtained under subsection (2), the party's attorney or the party, if the party is not represented by an attorney, shall file an affidavit setting forth the return of service. The affidavit shall state the nature of the process; the date on which the process was mailed by registered mail; the name and address on the envelope containing the process; the fact that the process was mailed registered mail return receipt requested; who signed the return receipt, if known, and the basis for that knowledge; and the relationship between the person who signed the receipt and the person to be served, if known, and the basis for that knowledge. The return receipt from the registered mail shall be attached to the affidavit. If service of process is perfected under subsection (3), the party's attorney or the party, if the party is not represented by an attorney, shall file an affidavit setting forth the return of service. The affidavit shall state the nature of the process; the date on which the process was mailed by registered mail; the name and address on the envelope containing the process that was mailed by registered mail; the fact that the process was mailed registered mail and was returned with the endorsement or stamp "refused"; the date, if known, the process was "refused"; the date on which the process was mailed by first-class mail; the name and address on the envelope containing the process that was mailed by first-class mail; and the fact that the process was mailed by first-class mail with a return address of the party or the party's attorney on the envelope. The return envelope from the attempt to mail process by registered mail and the return envelope, if any, from the attempt to mail the envelope by first-class mail shall be attached to the affidavit.

48.195. Service of foreign process.

(1) The service of process issued by a court of a state other than Florida may be made by the sheriffs of this state in the same manner as service of process issued by Florida courts. The provisions of this section shall not be interpreted to permit a sheriff to take any action against personal property, real property, or persons.

(2) An officer serving such foreign process shall be deemed as acting in the performance of his or her duties for the purposes of ss. 30.01, 30.02, 843.01, and 843.02, but shall not be held liable as provided in s. 839.19 for failure to execute any process delivered to him or her for service.

(3) The sheriffs shall be entitled to charge fees for the service of foreign process, and the fees shall be the same as fees for the service of comparable process for the Florida courts. When the service of foreign process requires duties to be performed in excess of those required by Florida courts, the sheriff may perform the additional duties and may collect reasonable additional compensation for the additional duties performed.

48.196. Service of process in connection with actions under the Florida International Commercial Arbitration Act.

(1) Any process in connection with the commencement of an action before the courts of this state under chapter 684, the Florida International Commercial Arbitration Act, shall be served:

(a) In the case of a natural person, by service upon:

1. That person;

2. Any agent for service of process appointed in, or pursuant to, any applicable agreement or by operation of any law of this state; or

3. Any person authorized by the law of the jurisdiction where process is being served to accept service for that person.

(b) In the case of any person other than a natural person, by service upon:

1. Any agent for service of process appointed in, or pursuant to, any applicable agreement or by operation of any law of this state;

2. Any person authorized by the law of the jurisdiction where process is being served to accept service for that person; or

3. Any person, whether natural or otherwise and wherever located, who by operation of law or internal action is an officer, business agent, director, general partner, or managing agent or director of the person being served; or

4. Any partner, joint venturer, member or controlling shareholder, wherever located, of the person being served, if the person being served does not by law or internal action have any officer, business agent, director, general partner, or managing agent or director.

(2) The process served under subsection (1) shall include a copy of the application to the court together with all attachments thereto and shall be served in the following manner:

(a) In any manner agreed upon, whether service occurs within or without this state;

(b) If service is within this state:

1. In the manner provided in ss. 48.021 and 48.031, or

2. If applicable under their terms, in the manner provided in ss. 48.161, 48.183, 48.23, or chapter 49; or

(c) If service is outside this state:

1. By personal service by any person authorized to serve process in the jurisdiction where service is being made or by any person appointed to do so by any competent court in that jurisdiction;

2. In any other manner prescribed by the laws of the jurisdiction where service is being made for service in an action before a local court of competent jurisdiction;

3. In the manner provided in any applicable treaty to which the United States is a party;

4. In the manner prescribed by order of the court;

5. By any form of mail requiring a signed receipt, to be addressed and dispatched by the clerk of the court to the person being served; or

6. If applicable, in the manner provided in chapter 49.

(3) No order of the court is required for service of process outside this state. The person serving process shall make proof of service to the court by affidavit or as prescribed by the law of the jurisdiction where process is being served or as prescribed in an order of the court. Such proof shall be made prior to expiration of the time within which the person served must respond. If service is by mail, the proof of service shall state the date and place of mailing and shall include a receipt signed by the addressee or other evidence of delivery satisfactory to the court.

48.20. Service of process on Sunday.

Service or execution on Sunday of any writ, process, warrant, order, or judgment is void and the person serving or executing, or causing it to be served or executed, is liable to the party aggrieved for damages for so doing as if he or she had done it without any process, writ, warrant, order, or judgment. If affidavit is made by the person requesting service or execution that he or she has good reason to believe that any person liable to have any such writ, process, warrant, order, or judgment served on him or her intends to escape from this state under protection of Sunday, any officer furnished with an order authorizing service or execution by the trial court judge may serve or execute such writ, process, warrant, order, or judgment on Sunday, and it is as valid as if it had been done on any other day.

48.21. Return of execution of process.

(1) Each person who effects service of process shall note on a return-of-service form attached thereto, the date and time when it comes to hand, the date and time when it is served, the manner of service, the name of the person on whom it was served and, if the person is served in a representative capacity, the position occupied by the person. The return-of-service form must be signed by the person who effects the service of process. However, a person employed by a sheriff who effects the service of process may sign the return-of-service form using an electronic signature certified by the sheriff.

(2) A failure to state the facts or to include the signature required by subsection (1) invalidates the service, but the return is amendable to state the facts or to include the signature at any time on application to the court from which the process issued. On amendment, service is as effective as if the return had originally stated the omitted facts or included the signature. A failure to state all the facts in or to include the signature on the return shall subject the person effecting service to a fine not exceeding $10, in the court's discretion.

48.22. Cumulative to other laws.

All provisions of this chapter are cumulative to other provisions of law or rules of court about service of process, and all other provisions about service of process are cumulative to this chapter.

48.23. Lis pendens.

(1)(a) An action in any of the state or federal courts in this state operates as a lis pendens on any real or personal property involved therein or to be affected thereby only if a notice of lis pendens is recorded in the official records of the county where the property is located and such notice has not expired pursuant to subsection (2) or been withdrawn or discharged.

(b)1. An action that is filed for specific performance or that is not based on a duly recorded instrument has no effect, except as between the parties to the proceeding, on the title to, or on any lien upon, the real or personal property unless a notice of lis pendens has been recorded and has not expired or been withdrawn or discharged.

2. Any person acquiring for value an interest in the real or personal property during the pendency of an action described in subparagraph 1., other than a party to the proceeding or the legal successor by operation of law, or personal representative, heir, or devisee of a deceased party to the proceeding, shall take such interest exempt from all claims against the property that were filed in such action by the party who failed to record a notice of lis pendens or whose notice expired or was withdrawn or discharged, and from any judgment entered in the proceeding, notwithstanding the provisions of s. 695.01, as if such person had no actual or constructive notice of the proceeding or of the claims made therein or the documents forming the causes of action against the property in the proceeding.

(c)1. A notice of lis pendens must contain the following:

a. The names of the parties.

b. The date of the institution of the action, the date of the clerk's electronic receipt, or the case number of the action.

c. The name of the court in which it is pending.

d. A description of the property involved or to be affected.

e. A statement of the relief sought as to the property.

2. In the case of any notice of lis pendens filed on the same date as the pleading upon which the notice is based, the clerk's notation of the date of receipt on the notice shall satisfy the requirement that the notice contain the date of the institution of the action.

(d) Except for the interest of persons in possession or easements of use, the recording of such notice of lis pendens, provided that during the pendency of the proceeding it has not expired pursuant to subsection (2) or been withdrawn or discharged, constitutes a bar to the enforcement against the property described in the notice of all interests and liens, including, but not limited to, federal tax liens and levies, unrecorded at the time of recording the notice unless the holder of any such unrecorded interest or lien intervenes in such proceedings within 30 days after the recording of the notice. If the holder of any such unrecorded interest or lien does not intervene in the proceedings and if such proceedings are prosecuted to a judicial sale of the property described in the notice, the property shall be forever discharged from all such unrecorded interests and liens. If the notice of lis pendens expires or is withdrawn or discharged, the expiration, withdrawal, or discharge of the notice does not affect the validity of any unrecorded interest or lien.

(2) A notice of lis pendens is not effectual for any purpose beyond 1 year from the commencement of the action and will expire at that time, unless the relief sought is disclosed by the pending pleading to be founded on a duly recorded instrument or on a lien claimed under part I of chapter 713 against the property involved, except when the court extends the time of expiration on reasonable notice and for good cause. The court may impose such terms for the extension of time as justice requires.

(3) When the pending pleading does not show that the action is founded on a duly recorded instrument or on a lien claimed under part I of chapter 713 or when the action no longer affects the subject property, the court shall control and discharge the recorded notice of lis pendens as the court would grant and dissolve injunctions.

(4) This section applies to all actions now or hereafter pending in any state or federal courts in this state, but the period of time specified in subsection (2) does not include the period of pendency of any action in an appellate court.

48.25. Short title.

Sections 48.25-48.31 may be cited as the "Florida Certified Process Server Act."

48.27. Certified process servers.

(1) The chief judge of each judicial circuit may establish an approved list of natural persons designated as certified process servers. The chief judge may periodically add to such list the names of those natural persons who have met the requirements for certification provided for in s. 48.29. Each person whose name has been added to the approved list is subject to annual recertification and reappointment by the chief judge of a judicial circuit. The chief judge shall prescribe appropriate forms for application for inclusion on the list of certified process servers. A reasonable fee for the processing of any such application must be charged.

(2)(a) The addition of a person's name to the list authorizes him or her to serve initial nonenforceable civil process on a person found within the circuit where the process server is certified when a civil action has been filed against such person in the circuit court or in a county court in the state. Upon filing an action in circuit or county court, a person may select from the list for the circuit where the process is to be served one or more certified process servers to serve initial nonenforceable civil process.

(b) The addition of a person's name to the list authorizes him or her to serve criminal witness subpoenas and criminal summonses on a person found within the circuit where the process server is certified. The state in any proceeding or investigation by a grand jury or any party in a criminal action, prosecution, or proceeding may select from the list for the circuit where the process is to be served one or more certified process servers to serve the subpoena or summons.

(3) Nothing herein shall be interpreted to exclude a sheriff or deputy or other person appointed by

the sheriff pursuant to s. 48.021 from serving process or to exclude a person from appointment by individual motion and order to serve process in any civil action in accordance with Rule 1.070(b) of the Florida Rules of Civil Procedure.

48.29. Certification of process servers.

(1) The circuit court administrator and the clerk of the court in each county in the circuit shall maintain the list of process servers approved by the chief judge of the circuit. Such list may, from time to time, be amended or modified to add or delete a person's name in accordance with the provisions of this section or s. 48.31.

(2) A person seeking the addition of his or her name to the approved list in any circuit shall submit an application to the chief judge of the circuit or to the chief judge's designee on a form prescribed by the court. A reasonable fee for processing the application may be charged.

(3) A person applying to become a certified process server shall:

(a) Be at least 18 years of age;

(b) Have no mental or legal disability;

(c) Be a permanent resident of the state;

(d) Submit to a background investigation, which shall include the right to obtain and review the criminal record of the applicant;

(e) Obtain and file with his or her application a certificate of good conduct, which specifies there is no pending criminal case against the applicant and that there is no record of any felony conviction, nor a record of a conviction of a misdemeanor involving moral turpitude or dishonesty, with respect to the applicant within the past 5 years;

(f) If prescribed by the chief judge of the circuit, submit to an examination testing his or her knowledge of the laws and rules regarding the service of process. The content of the examination and the passing grade thereon, and the frequency and location at which such examination shall be offered shall be prescribed by the chief judge of the circuit. The examination, if any, shall be offered at least once annually;

(g) Execute a bond in the amount of $5,000 with a surety company authorized to do business in this state for the benefit of any person wrongfully injured by any malfeasance, misfeasance, neglect of duty, or incompetence of the applicant, in connection with his or her duties as a process server. Such bond shall be renewable annually; and

(h) Take an oath of office that he or she will honestly, diligently, and faithfully exercise the duties of a certified process server.

(4) The chief judge of the circuit may, from time to time by administrative order, prescribe additional rules and requirements regarding the eligibility of a person to become a certified process server or to have his or her name maintained on the list of certified process servers.

(5)(a) An applicant who completes the requirements set forth in this section and whose name the chief judge by order enters on the list of certified process servers shall be designated as a certified process server.

(b) Each certified process server shall be issued an identification card bearing his or her identification number, printed name, signature and photograph, the seal of the circuit court, and an expiration date. Each identification card shall be renewable annually upon proof of good standing and current bond.

(6) A certified process server shall place the information required in s. 48.031(5) on the first page of at least one of the processes served. Return of service shall be made by a certified process server on a form which has been reviewed and approved by the court.

(7)(a) A person may qualify as a certified process server and have his or her name entered on the list in more than one circuit.

(b) A process server whose name is on a list of certified process servers in more than one circuit may serve process on a person found in any such circuits.

(c) A certified process server may serve foreign process in any circuit in which his or her name has been entered on the list of certified process servers for that circuit.

(8) A certified process server may charge a fee for his or her services.

48.31. Removal of certified process servers; false return of service.

(1) A certified process server may be removed from the list of certified process servers for any malfeasance, misfeasance, neglect of duty, or incompetence, as provided by court rule.

(2) A certified process server must be disinterested in any process he or she serves; if the certified process server willfully and knowingly executes a false return of service, he or she is guilty of a felony of the third degree, punishable as provided in s. 775.082, s. 775.083, or s. 775.084, and shall be permanently barred from serving process in this state.

CHAPTER 49. CONSTRUCTIVE SERVICE OF PROCESS

49.011. Service of process by publication; cases in which allowed.

Service of process by publication may be made in any court on any party identified in s. 49.021 in any action or proceeding:

(1) To enforce any legal or equitable lien or claim to any title or interest in real or personal property within the jurisdiction of the court or any fund held or debt owing by any party on whom process can be served within this state.

(2) To quiet title or remove any encumbrance, lien, or cloud on the title to any real or personal property within the jurisdiction of the court or any fund held or debt owing by any party on whom process can be served within this state.

(3) To partition real or personal property within the jurisdiction of the court.

(4) For dissolution or annulment of marriage.

(5) For the construction of any will, deed, contract, or other written instrument and for a judicial declaration or enforcement of any legal or equitable right, title, claim, lien, or interest thereunder.

(6) To reestablish a lost instrument or record which has or should have its situs within the jurisdiction of the court.

(7) In which a writ of replevin, garnishment, or attachment has been issued and executed.

(8) In which any other writ or process has been issued and executed which places any property, fund, or debt in the custody of a court.

(9) To revive a judgment by motion or scire facias.

(10) For adoption.

(11) In which personal service of process or notice is not required by the statutes or constitution of this state or by the Constitution of the United States.

(12) In probate or guardianship proceedings in which personal service of process or notice is not required by the statutes or constitution of this state or by the Constitution of the United States.

(13) For termination of parental rights pursuant to part VIII of chapter 39 or chapter 63.

(14) For temporary custody of a minor child, under chapter 751.

(15) To determine paternity, but only as to the legal father in a paternity action in which another

man is alleged to be the biological father, in which case it is necessary to serve process on the legal father in order to establish paternity with regard to the alleged biological father.

49.021. Service of process by publication, upon whom.

Where personal service of process or, if appropriate, service of process under s. 48.194 cannot be had, service of process by publication may be had upon any party, natural or corporate, known or unknown, including:
(1) Any known or unknown natural person, and, when described as such, the unknown spouse, heirs, devisees, grantees, creditors, or other parties claiming by, through, under, or against any known or unknown person who is known to be dead or is not known to be either dead or alive;
(2) Any corporation or other legal entity, whether its domicile be foreign, domestic, or unknown, and whether dissolved or existing, including corporations or other legal entities not known to be dissolved or existing, and, when described as such, the unknown assigns, successors in interest, trustees, or any other party claiming by, through, under, or against any named corporation or legal entity;
(3) Any group, firm, entity, or persons who operate or do business, or have operated or done business, in this state, under a name or title which includes the word "corporation," "company," "incorporated," "inc.," or any combination thereof, or under a name or title which indicates, tends to indicate or leads one to think that the same may be a corporation or other legal entity; and
(4) All claimants under any of such parties.

49.031. Sworn statement as condition precedent.

(1) As a condition precedent to service by publication, a statement shall be filed in the action executed by the plaintiff, the plaintiff's agent or attorney, setting forth substantially the matters hereafter required, which statement may be contained in a verified pleading, or in an affidavit or other sworn statement.
(2) As used in this chapter:
(a) The word "plaintiff" means any party in the action who is entitled to service of original process on any other party to the action or any person who may be brought in or allowed to come in as a party by any lawful means.
(b) The word "defendant" means any party on whom service by publication is authorized by this chapter, without regard to his or her designation in the pleadings or position in the action.
(c) The word "publication" includes the posting of the notice of action as provided for in ss. 49.10(1)(b) and 49.11.
(3) After the entry of a final judgment or decree in any action no sworn statement shall ever be held defective for failure to state a required fact if the fact otherwise appears from the record in the action.

49.041. Sworn statement, natural person as defendant.

The sworn statement of the plaintiff, his or her agent or attorney, for service of process by publication against a natural person, shall show:
(1) That diligent search and inquiry have been made to discover the name and residence of such person, and that the same is set forth in said sworn statement as particularly as is known to the affiant; and
(2) Whether such person is over or under the age of 18 years, if his or her age is known, or that the

person's age is unknown; and

(3) In addition to the above, that the residence of such person is, either:

(a) Unknown to the affiant; or

(b) In some state or country other than this state, stating said residence if known; or

(c) In the state, but that he or she has been absent from the state for more than 60 days next preceding the making of the sworn statement, or conceals himself or herself so that process cannot be personally served, and that affiant believes that there is no person in the state upon whom service of process would bind said absent or concealed defendant.

49.051. Sworn statement, corporation as defendant.

The sworn statement of the plaintiff, his or her agent or attorney, for service of process by publication against a corporation, shall show:

(1) That diligent search and inquiry have been made to discover the true name, domicile, principal place of business, and status (that is, whether foreign, domestic, or dissolved) of the corporate defendant, and that the same is set forth in said sworn statement as particularly as is known to the affiant, and that diligent search and inquiry have also been made, to discover the names and whereabouts of all persons upon whom the service of process would bind the said corporation and that the same is specified as particularly as is known to the affiant; and

(2) Whether or not the corporation has ever qualified to do business in this state, unless shown to be a Florida corporation; and

(3) That all officers, directors, general managers, cashiers, resident agents, and business agents of the corporation, either:

(a) Are absent from the state; or

(b) Cannot be found within the state; or

(c) Conceal themselves so that process cannot be served upon them so as to bind the said corporation; or

(d) That their whereabouts are unknown to the affiant; or

(e) That said officers, directors, general managers, cashiers, resident agents, and business agents of the corporation are unknown to affiant.

49.061. Sworn statement, parties doing business under a corporate name as defendants.

The sworn statement of the plaintiff, his or her agent or attorney, for service of process by publication against parties who have or may have done business under a corporate name, shall show:

(1) The name under which said parties have operated or done business; and

(2) That, after diligent search and inquiry, the affiant has been unable to ascertain whether or not the organization operating under said name was a corporation, either domestic or foreign; and

(3) The names, and places of residence if known, of all persons known to have been interested in such organization, and whether or not other or unknown persons may have been interested in such organization; or that, after diligent search and inquiry, all persons interested in such organization are unknown to the affiant, and, unless all such persons are unknown to the affiant,

(4) That the known persons interested in such organization, either:

(a) Are absent from this state; or

(b) Cannot be found within this state; or

(c) Conceal themselves so that process cannot be personally served upon them; or

(d) That their whereabouts are unknown to the affiant.

49.071. Sworn statement, unknown parties as defendants.

(1) If relief is demanded against unknown parties, the sworn statement for service of process by publication against them shall show:

(a) That affiant believes that there are persons who are or may be interested in the subject matter of the action or proceedings whose names, after diligent search and inquiry, are unknown to the affiant; and

(b) Whether said unknown parties claim as heirs, devisees, grantees, assignees, lienors, creditors, trustees, or other claimants:

1. By, through, under or against a known person who is dead or not known to be dead or alive; or

2. By, through, under or against some corporation, domestic or foreign, that has been dissolved or which is not known to be existing or dissolved; or

3. By, through, under or against some organization which operated or did business under a name indicating a corporation; or

4. Otherwise as the case may be.

(2) In any case alleged against a named defendant, natural or corporate, who is stated, either in the pleadings or in the sworn statement, to be either dead or dissolved, or not known to be dead or alive, or dissolved or existing, any judgment, decree or order rendered against such defendant shall be as good, valid and effectual as if it had not been so stated.

49.08. Notice of action, form.

On filing the sworn statement, and otherwise complying with the foregoing requirements, the plaintiff is entitled to have issued by the clerk or judge, not later than 60 days after filing the sworn statement, a notice of action which notice shall set forth:

(1) The names of the known natural defendants; the names, status and description of the corporate defendants; a description of the unknown defendants who claim by, through, under or against a known party which may be described as "all parties claiming interests by, through, under or against (name of known party)" and a description of all unknown defendants which may be described as "all parties having or claiming to have any right, title or interest in the property herein described";

(2) The nature of the action or proceeding in short and simple terms (but neglect to do so is not jurisdictional);

(3) The name of the court in which the action or proceeding was instituted and an abbreviated title of the case;

(4) The description of real property, if any, proceeded against.

49.09. Notice of action, return day.

The notice of action, except in foreclosure proceedings as defined in s. 702.09, shall require the defendant to file written defenses with the clerk of the court and to serve a copy not later than the date fixed in said notice, which date shall be not less than 28 nor more than 60 days after the first publication of the notice on plaintiff or his or her attorney whose name and address shall appear in, or be annexed to, said notice. In foreclosure proceedings, the notice of action shall require the defendant to file written defenses with the clerk of the court and to serve a copy within 30 days after the first publication of the notice on plaintiff or his or her attorney whose name and address shall appear in, or be annexed to, said notice.

49.10. Notice of action, publication, proof.

(1)(a) All notices of action, except those referred to in paragraphs (b) and (c), shall be published once during each week for 4 consecutive weeks (four publications being sufficient) in some newspaper published in the county where the court is located. The newspaper shall meet such requirements as are prescribed by law for such purpose.

(b) In proceedings described in s. 49.011(4), (10), and (11), the clerk of the court shall post notices of action in the manner prescribed by s. 49.11 when such notices are required of persons authorized to proceed as indigent under s. 57.081.

(c) Notices of action in foreclosure proceedings as defined in s. 702.09 shall be published once during each week for 2 consecutive weeks (two publications being sufficient) in some newspaper published in the county where the court is located. The newspaper shall meet such requirements as are prescribed by law for such purpose.

(2) Proof of publication shall be made by affidavit of the owner, publisher, proprietor, editor, business manager, foreman or other officer or employee of the newspaper having knowledge of such publication. The affidavit shall set forth or have attached a copy of the notice, shall set forth the dates of each publication and otherwise comply with the requirements of law.

49.11. Notice of action, posting, proof.

If there is no newspaper published in the county, three copies of the notice shall be posted at least 28 days before the return day thereof in three different and conspicuous places in such county, one of which shall be at the front door of the courthouse in said county. Proof of posting shall be by affidavit of the person posting the notices, which affidavit shall include a copy of the notice posted and the date and places of its posting.

49.12. Mailing of notice of action.

If the residence of any party to be served by publication is stated in the sworn statement with more particularity than the name of the state or country in which the defendant resides, the clerk or the judge shall mail a copy of the notice by United States mail, with postage prepaid, to each defendant within 10 days after making or posting the notice, the date of mailing to be noted on the docket with a copy of the pleading for which the notice was issued.

49.31. Appointment of ad litem.

(1) As used in this section, the term "ad litem" means an attorney, administrator, or guardian ad litem.

(2) The court may appoint an ad litem for any party, whether known or unknown, upon whom service of process by publication under this chapter has been properly made and who has failed to file or serve any paper in the action within the time required by law. A court may not appoint an ad litem to represent an interest for which a personal representative, guardian of property, or trustee is serving.

(a) If the court has appointed an ad litem and the ad litem discovers that a personal representative, guardian of property, or trustee is serving who represents the interest for which the ad litem was appointed, the ad litem must promptly report that finding to the court and must file a petition for discharge as to any interest for which the personal representative, guardian of property, or trustee is serving.

(b) If the court has appointed an ad litem to represent an interest and the ad litem discovers that the person whose interest he or she represents is deceased and there is no personal representative, guardian of property, or trustee to represent the decedent's interest, the ad litem must make a reasonable attempt to locate any spouse, heir, devisee, or beneficiary of the decedent, must report to the court the name and address of all such persons whom the ad litem locates, and must petition for discharge as to any interest of the person located.

(3) The court may not require an ad litem to post a bond or designate a resident agent in order to serve as an ad litem.

(4) The court shall discharge the ad litem when the final judgment is entered or as otherwise ordered by the court.

(5) The ad litem is entitled to an award of a reasonable fee for services rendered and costs, which shall be assessed against the party requesting the appointment of the ad litem, or as otherwise ordered by the court. State funds may not be used to pay fees for services rendered by the ad litem unless state funds would have been expended for such services in the same circumstance before July 1, 2015.

(6) In all cases adjudicated in which the court appointed an ad litem, a proceeding may not be declared ineffective solely due to lack of statutory authority to appoint an ad litem.

(7) This section does not abrogate a court's common law authority to appoint an ad litem.

CHAPTER 50. LEGAL AND OFFICIAL ADVERTISEMENTS

50.011. Where and in what language legal notices to be published.

Whenever by statute an official or legal advertisement or a publication, or notice in a newspaper has been or is directed or permitted in the nature of or in lieu of process, or for constructive service, or in initiating, assuming, reviewing, exercising or enforcing jurisdiction or power, or for any purpose, including all legal notices and advertisements of sheriffs and tax collectors, the contemporaneous and continuous intent and meaning of such legislation all and singular, existing or repealed, is and has been and is hereby declared to be and to have been, and the rule of interpretation is and has been, a publication in a newspaper printed and published periodically once a week or oftener, containing at least 25 percent of its words in the English language, entered or qualified to be admitted and entered as periodicals matter at a post office in the county where published, for sale to the public generally, available to the public generally for the publication of official or other notices and customarily containing information of a public character or of interest or of value to the residents or owners of property in the county where published, or of interest or of value to the general public.

50.021. Publication when no newspaper in county.

When any law, or order or decree of court, shall direct advertisements to be made in any county and there be no newspaper published in the said county, the advertisement may be made by posting three copies thereof in three different places in said county, one of which shall be at the front door of the courthouse, and by publication in the nearest county in which a newspaper is published.

50.0211. Internet website publication.

(1) This section applies to legal notices that must be published in accordance with this chapter unless otherwise specified.

(2) Each legal notice must be posted on the newspaper's website on the same day that the printed notice appears in the newspaper, at no additional charge, in a separate web page titled "Legal Notices," "Legal Advertising," or comparable identifying language. A link to the legal notices web page shall be provided on the front page of the newspaper's website that provides access to the legal notices. If there is a specified size and placement required for a printed legal notice, the size and placement of the notice on the newspaper's website must optimize its online visibility in keeping with the print requirements. The newspaper's web pages that contain legal notices must present the legal notices as the dominant and leading subject matter of those pages. The newspaper's website must contain a search function to facilitate searching the legal notices. A fee may not be charged, and registration may not be required, for viewing or searching legal notices on a newspaper's website if the legal notice is published in a newspaper.

(3)(a) If a legal notice is published in a newspaper, the newspaper publishing the notice shall place the notice on the statewide website established and maintained as an initiative of the Florida Press Association as a repository for such notices located at the following address: www.floridapublicnotices.com.

(b) A legal notice placed on the statewide website created under this subsection must be:

1. Accessible and searchable by party name and case number.

2. Posted for a period of at least 90 consecutive days after the first day of posting.

(c) The statewide website created under this subsection shall maintain a searchable archive of all legal notices posted on the publicly accessible website on or after October 1, 2014, for 18 months after the first day of posting. Such searchable archive shall be provided and accessible to the general public without charge.

(4) Newspapers that publish legal notices shall, upon request, provide e-mail notification of new legal notices when they are printed in the newspaper and added to the newspaper's website. Such e-mail notification shall be provided without charge, and notification for such an e-mail registry shall be available on the front page of the legal notices section of the newspaper's website.

50.031. Newspapers in which legal notices and process may be published.

No notice or publication required to be published in a newspaper in the nature of or in lieu of process of any kind, nature, character or description provided for under any law of the state, whether heretofore or hereafter enacted, and whether pertaining to constructive service, or the initiating, assuming, reviewing, exercising or enforcing jurisdiction or power, by any court in this state, or any notice of sale of property, real or personal, for taxes, state, county or municipal, or sheriff's, guardian's or administrator's or any sale made pursuant to any judicial order, decree or statute or any other publication or notice pertaining to any affairs of the state, or any county, municipality or other political subdivision thereof, shall be deemed to have been published in accordance with the statutes providing for such publication, unless the same shall have been published for the prescribed period of time required for such publication, in a newspaper which at the time of such publication shall have been in existence for 1 year and shall have been entered as periodicals matter at a post office in the county where published, or in a newspaper which is a direct successor of a newspaper which together have been so published; provided, however, that nothing herein contained shall apply where in any county there shall be no newspaper in existence which shall have been published for the length of time above prescribed. No legal publication of any kind, nature or description, as herein defined, shall be valid or binding or held to be in compliance with the statutes providing for such publication unless the same shall have been published in accordance with the provisions of this section. Proof of such publication shall be made by uniform affidavit.

50.041. Proof of publication; uniform affidavits required.

(1) All affidavits of publishers of newspapers (or their official representatives) made for the purpose of establishing proof of publication of public notices or legal advertisements shall be uniform throughout the state.

(2) Each such affidavit shall be printed upon white paper and shall be 81/2 inches in width and of convenient length, not less than 51/2 inches. A white margin of not less than 21/2 inches shall be left at the right side of each affidavit form and upon or in this space shall be substantially pasted a clipping which shall be a true copy of the public notice or legal advertisement for which proof is executed. Alternatively, the affidavit may be provided in electronic rather than paper form, provided the notarization of the affidavit complies with the requirements of s. 117.021.

(3) In all counties having a population in excess of 450,000 according to the latest official decennial census, in addition to the charges which are now or may hereafter be established by law for the publication of every official notice or legal advertisement, there may be a charge not to exceed $2 for the preparation and execution of each such proof of publication or publisher's affidavit.

50.051. Proof of publication; form of uniform affidavit.

The printed form upon which all such affidavits establishing proof of publication are to be executed shall be substantially as follows:

50.061. Amounts chargeable.

(1) The publisher of any newspaper publishing any and all official public notices or legal advertisements shall charge therefor the rates specified in this section without rebate, commission or refund.

(2) The charge for publishing each such official public notice or legal advertisement shall be 70 cents per square inch for the first insertion and 40 cents per square inch for each subsequent insertion, except that government notices required to be published more than once, the cost of which is paid for by the government and not paid in advance by or allowed to be recouped from private parties, may not be charged for the second and successive insertions at a rate greater than 85 percent of the original rate.

(3) Where the regular established minimum commercial rate per square inch of the newspaper publishing such official public notices or legal advertisements is in excess of the rate herein stipulated, said minimum commercial rate per square inch may be charged for all such legal advertisements or official public notices for each insertion, except that government notices required to be published more than once, the cost of which is paid for by the government and not paid in advance by or allowed to be recouped from private parties, may not be charged for the second and successive insertions at a rate greater than 85 percent of the original rate.

(4) A governmental agency publishing an official public notice or legal advertisement may procure publication by soliciting and accepting written bids from newspapers published in the county, in which case the specified charges in this section do not apply.

(5) If the public notice is published in a newspaper, the posting of the notice on the newspaper's website pursuant to s. 50.0211(2) must be done at no additional charge.

(6) All official public notices and legal advertisements shall be charged and paid for on the basis of 6-point type on 6-point body, unless otherwise specified by statute.

(7) Any person violating this section, either by allowing or accepting any rebate, commission, or refund, commits a misdemeanor of the second degree, punishable as provided in s. 775.082 or s. 775.083.

(8) Failure to charge the rates prescribed by this section shall in no way affect the validity of any official public notice or legal advertisement and shall not subject same to legal attack upon such grounds.

50.0711. Court docket fund; service charges; publications.

(1) The clerk of the court in each county may establish a court docket fund for the purpose of paying the cost of publication of the fact of the filing of any civil case in the circuit court of the county by the style and of the calendar relating to such cases. This court docket fund shall be funded by $1 mandatory court cost for all civil actions, suits, or proceedings filed in the circuit court of the county. The clerk shall maintain such funds separate and apart, and the proceeds from this court cost shall not be diverted to any other fund or for any purpose other than that established in this section. The clerk of the court shall dispense the fund to the designated record newspaper in the county on a quarterly basis.

(2) A newspaper qualified under the terms of s. 50.011 shall be designated as the record newspaper for such publication by an order of the majority of the judges in the judicial circuit in which such county is located, and such order shall be filed and recorded with the clerk of the circuit court for such county. The designated record newspaper may be changed at the end of any fiscal year of the county by a majority vote of the judges of the judicial circuit of the county ordering such change 30 days prior to the end of the fiscal year, notice of which order shall be given to the previously designated record newspaper.

(3) The publishers of any designated record newspapers receiving payment from this court docket fund shall publish, without additional charge, the fact of the filing of any civil case, suit, or action filed in such county in the circuit. Such publication shall be in accordance with a schedule agreed upon between the record newspaper and the clerk of the court in such county.

(4) The publishers of any designated record newspapers receiving revenues from the court docket fund established in subsection (1) shall, without charge, accept legal advertisements for the purpose of service of process by publication under s. 49.011(4), (10), and (11) when such publication is required of persons authorized to proceed as indigent persons under s. 57.081.

CHAPTER 51. SUMMARY PROCEDURE

51.011. Summary procedure.

The procedure in this section applies only to those actions specified by statute or rule. Rules of procedure apply to this section except when this section or the statute or rule prescribing this section provides a different procedure. If there is a difference between the time period prescribed in a rule and in this section, this section governs.

(1) PLEADINGS.—Plaintiff's initial pleading shall contain the matters required by the statute or rule prescribing this section or, if none is so required, shall state a cause of action. All defenses of law or fact shall be contained in defendant's answer which shall be filed within 5 days after service of process. If the answer incorporates a counterclaim, plaintiff shall include all defenses of law or fact in his or her answer to the counterclaim and shall serve it within 5 days after service of the counterclaim. No other pleadings are permitted. All defensive motions, including motions to quash, shall be heard by the court prior to trial.

(2) DISCOVERY.—Depositions on oral examination may be taken by any party at any time. Other discovery and admissions may be had only on order of court setting the time for compliance. No discovery postpones the time for trial except for good cause shown or by stipulation of the parties.

(3) JURY.—If a jury trial is authorized by law, any party may demand it in any pleading or by a separate paper served not later than 5 days after the action comes to issue. When a jury is in attendance at the close of pleading or the time of demand for jury trial, the action may be tried immediately; otherwise, the court shall order a special venire to be summoned immediately. If a special venire be summoned, the party demanding the jury shall deposit sufficient money with the clerk to pay the jury fees which shall be taxed as costs if he or she prevails.

(4) NEW TRIAL.—Motion for new trial shall be filed and served within 5 days after verdict, if a jury trial was had, or after entry of judgment, if trial was by the court. A reserved motion for directed verdict shall be renewed within the period for moving for a new trial.

(5) APPEAL.—Notice of appeal shall be filed and served within 30 days from the rendition of the judgment appealed from.

CHAPTER 55. JUDGMENTS

55.01. Judgments; general form.

(1) In all actions where either party recovers a sum of money, the amount to which he or she is entitled may be awarded by the judgment generally, without any distinction being therein made as to whether such sum is recovered by way of debt or damages.

(2) Each final judgment shall contain thereon the address and the social security number, if known to the prevailing party, of each person against whom judgment is rendered. Errors in names, addresses, or social security numbers or failure to include same shall in no way affect the validity or finality of a final judgment.

55.03. Judgments; rate of interest, generally.

(1) On December 1, March 1, June 1, and September 1 of each year, the Chief Financial Officer shall set the rate of interest that shall be payable on judgments or decrees for the calendar quarter beginning January 1 and adjust the rate quarterly on April 1, July 1, and October 1 by averaging the discount rate of the Federal Reserve Bank of New York for the preceding 12 months, then adding 400 basis points to the averaged federal discount rate. The Chief Financial Officer shall inform the clerk of the courts and chief judge for each judicial circuit of the rate that has been established for the upcoming quarter. The interest rate established by the Chief Financial Officer shall take effect on the first day of each following calendar quarter. Judgments obtained on or after January 1, 1995, shall use the previous statutory rate for time periods before January 1, 1995, for which interest is due and shall apply the rate set by the Chief Financial Officer for time periods after January 1, 1995, for which interest is due. Nothing contained herein shall affect a rate of

interest established by written contract or obligation.

(2) Any judgment for money damages or order for a judicial sale and any process or writ directed to a sheriff for execution shall bear, on its face, the rate of interest that is payable on the judgment. The rate of interest stated in the judgment, as adjusted in subsection (3), accrues on the judgment until it is paid.

(3) The interest rate is established at the time a judgment is obtained and such interest rate shall be adjusted annually on January 1 of each year in accordance with the interest rate in effect on that date as set by the Chief Financial Officer until the judgment is paid, except for judgments entered by the clerk of the court pursuant to ss. 55.141, 61.14, 938.29, and 938.30, which shall not be adjusted annually.

(4) A sheriff shall not be required to docket and index or collect on any process, writ, judgment, or decree, described in subsection (2), and entered after the effective date of this act, unless such process, writ, judgment, or decree indicates the rate of interest. For purposes of this subsection, if the process, writ, judgment, or decree refers to the statutory rate of interest described in subsection (1), such reference shall be deemed to indicate the rate of interest.

55.04. Judgments; rate of interest, bonds of county, etc.

All judgments and decrees rendered on any bonds or other written evidence of debt of any county, special road and bridge districts or any county for the use and benefit of any special road and bridge districts or incorporated city or town or taxing district bear interest at the rate of 5 percent a year. When a judgment or decree is rendered on a bond or other written evidence of debt providing for a lesser rate of interest, the judgment or decree bears interest at the rate specified in such bond or other written evidence of debt.

55.05. Judgments; power of attorney to confess invalid.

All powers of attorney for confessing or suffering judgment to pass by default or otherwise, and all general releases of error, heretofore made or to be made hereafter by any person whatsoever within or without this state, before such action brought, shall be absolutely null and void.

55.07. Judgments; effect of failure to record.

The failure to record any order, judgment or decree shall not affect the validity of any proceedings had thereon when collaterally attacked; provided, rendition of such order, judgment or decree is shown by the progress docket in the cause. This section shall apply to all proceedings heretofore had as well as to those hereafter had.

55.071. Judgments; effect of invalid affidavit or oath.

No order, judgment or decree heretofore or hereafter entered (including decrees pro confesso, defaults and judgments by default) which was or shall be predicated on a sworn statement, affidavit or oath shall be set aside or held void or voidable because the officer before whom such sworn statement or affidavit was or shall be made or such oath was or shall be administered was the attorney of record or otherwise the attorney for the person making such sworn statement, affidavit or oath.

55.081. Statute of limitations, lien of judgment.

Subject to the provisions of s. 55.10, no judgment, order, or decree of any court shall be a lien upon real or personal property within the state after the expiration of 20 years from the date of the entry of such judgment, order, or decree.

55.10. Judgments, orders, and decrees; lien of all, generally; extension of liens; transfer of liens to other security.

(1) A judgment, order, or decree becomes a lien on real property in any county when a certified copy of it is recorded in the official records or judgment lien record of the county, whichever is maintained at the time of recordation, provided that the judgment, order, or decree contains the address of the person who has a lien as a result of such judgment, order, or decree or a separate affidavit is recorded simultaneously with the judgment, order, or decree stating the address of the person who has a lien as a result of such judgment, order, or decree. A judgment, order, or decree does not become a lien on real property unless the address of the person who has a lien as a result of such judgment, order, or decree is contained in the judgment, order, or decree or an affidavit with such address is simultaneously recorded with the judgment, order, or decree. If the certified copy was first recorded in a county in accordance with this subsection between July 1, 1987, and June 30, 1994, then the judgment, order, or decree shall be a lien in that county for an initial period of 7 years from the date of the recording. If the certified copy is first recorded in accordance with this subsection on or after July 1, 1994, then the judgment, order, or decree shall be a lien in that county for an initial period of 10 years from the date of the recording.

(2) The lien provided for in subsection (1) or an extension of that lien as provided by this subsection may be extended for an additional period of 10 years, subject to the limitation in subsection (3), by rerecording a certified copy of the judgment, order, or decree prior to the expiration of the lien or the expiration of the extended lien and by simultaneously recording an affidavit with the current address of the person who has a lien as a result of the judgment, order, or decree. The extension shall be effective from the date the certified copy of the judgment, order, or decree is rerecorded. The lien or extended lien will not be extended unless the affidavit with the current address is simultaneously recorded.

(3) In no event shall the lien upon real property created by this section be extended beyond the period provided for in s. 55.081 or beyond the point at which the lien is satisfied, whichever occurs first.

(4) This act shall apply to all judgments, orders, and decrees of record which constitute a lien on real property; except that any judgment, order, or decree recorded prior to July 1, 1987, shall remain a lien on real property until the period provided for in s. 55.081 expires or until the lien is satisfied, whichever occurs first.

(5) Any lien claimed under this section may be transferred, by any person having an interest in the real property upon which the lien is imposed or the contract under which the lien is claimed, from such real property to other security by either depositing in the clerk's office a sum of money or filing in the clerk's office a bond executed as surety by a surety insurer licensed to do business in this state. Such deposit or bond shall be in an amount equal to the amount demanded in such claim of lien plus interest thereon at the legal rate for 3 years plus $500 to apply on any court costs which may be taxed in any proceeding to enforce said lien. Such deposit or bond shall be conditioned to pay any judgment, order, or decree which may be rendered for the satisfaction of

the lien for which such claim of lien was recorded and costs plus $500 for court costs. Upon such deposit being made or such bond being filed, the clerk shall make and record a certificate showing the transfer of the lien from the real property to the security and mail a copy thereof by registered or certified mail to the lienor named in the claim of lien so transferred, at the address stated therein. Upon the filing of the certificate of transfer, the real property shall thereupon be released from the lien claimed, and such lien shall be transferred to said security. The clerk shall be entitled to a service charge of up to $15 for making and serving the certificate. If the transaction involves the transfer of multiple liens, an additional service charge of up to $7.50 for each additional lien shall be charged. Any number of liens may be transferred to one such security.

(6) Any excess of the security over the aggregate amount of any judgments, orders, or decrees rendered, plus costs actually taxed, shall be repaid to the party filing the security or his or her successor in interest. Any deposit of money shall be considered as paid into court and shall be subject to the provisions of law relative to payments of money into court and the disposition of these payments.

(7) Any party having an interest in such security or the property from which the lien was transferred may at any time, and any number of times, file a complaint in chancery in the circuit court of the county where such security is deposited for an order:

(a) To require additional security;

(b) To require reduction of security;

(c) To require change or substitution of sureties;

(d) To require payment or discharge thereof; or

(e) Relating to any other matter affecting said security.

55.11. Judgments; no lien against municipalities.

No money judgment or decree against a municipal corporation is a lien on its property nor shall any execution or any writ in the nature of an execution based on the judgment or decree be issued or levied.

55.13. Judgments; rights of sureties, etc.

Any person paying money as surety for the principal in any bond or note, which he or she has signed as surety, upon which judgment has been obtained, shall have the same right to control the said judgment and collect the same, with principal, interest and costs, as the plaintiff creditor would have had if the debt had not been paid. Such judgment, and execution thereon, shall have the same lien on property of the principal as though the surety were the original plaintiff.

55.141. Satisfaction of judgments and decrees; duties of clerk.

(1) All judgments and decrees for the payment of money rendered in the courts of this state and which have become final, may be satisfied at any time prior to the actual levy of execution issued thereon by payment of the full amount of such judgment or decree, with interest thereon, plus the costs of the issuance, if any, of execution thereon into the registry of the court where rendered.

(2) Upon such payment, the clerk shall execute and record in the official records a satisfaction of judgment upon payment of the recording charge prescribed in s. 28.24(12). Upon payment of the amount required in subsection (1) and the recording charge required by this subsection and

execution and recordation of the satisfaction by the clerk, any lien created by the judgment is satisfied and discharged.

(3) The satisfaction of judgment executed by the clerk must be substantially in the following form:

(4) If an address for the judgment holder was provided under s. 55.10(1), the clerk shall formally send a copy of the satisfaction to the judgment holder at that address by certified mail with return receipt or by registered mail if the notice is to be sent outside the continental United States. If an address is not provided under s. 55.10(1) or if delivery cannot be effected to such address, the clerk may, but is not obligated to, make reasonable attempts to locate the judgment holder. The discharge of the lien by the issuance of the satisfaction is not dependent upon the delivery of notice by the clerk.

(5) Upon application of the judgment holder, the clerk shall pay over to the judgment holder the full amount of the payment received, less the clerk's fees for issuing execution on such judgment, if any has been issued; less the clerk's fees for receiving into and paying out of the registry of the court such payment; less the clerk's fees for recording the satisfaction of judgment; and, if the clerk incurred expenses in locating the judgment holder, less the reasonable expenses so incurred.

55.145. Discharge of judgments in bankruptcy.

At any time after 1 year has elapsed since a bankrupt or debtor was discharged from his or her debts, pursuant to the act of congress relating to bankruptcy, the bankrupt or debtor, his or her receiver or trustee, or any interested party may petition the court in which the judgment was rendered against such bankrupt or debtor for an order to cancel and discharge such judgment. The petition shall be accompanied by a certified copy of the discharge of said bankrupt or by a certified copy of the order of confirmation of the arrangement filed by said debtor. The petition, accompanied by copies of the papers upon which it is made, shall be served upon the judgment creditor in the manner prescribed for service of process in a civil action. If it appears upon the hearing that the bankrupt or debtor has been discharged from the payment of that judgment or of the debt upon which it was recovered, the court shall enter an order canceling and discharging said judgment. The order of cancellation and discharge shall have the same effect as a satisfaction of judgment, and a certified copy thereof may be recorded in the same manner as a satisfaction of judgment. This section shall apply only to liens under judgments or obligations duly scheduled in the bankruptcy proceedings.

55.146. Certain property exempt.

All property in this state of a judgment debtor where the judgment is in favor of any state for failure to pay that state's income tax on benefits received from a pension or other retirement plan is exempt from forced sale under process of any court, and no such judgment or execution based thereon shall be a lien on such property.

55.201. Central database of judgment liens on personal property.

The Department of State shall maintain a database of judgment lien files established in accordance with ss. 55.201-55.209.

55.202. Judgments, orders, and decrees; lien on personal property.

(1) A judgment lien securing the unpaid amount of any money judgment may be acquired by the holder of a judgment:

(a) Enforceable in this state under its laws or the laws of the United States;

(b) Entered by an issuing tribunal with respect to a support order being enforced in this state pursuant to chapter 88; or

(c) Enforceable by operation of law pursuant to s. 61.14(6).

(2) A judgment lien may be acquired on a judgment debtor's interest in all personal property in this state subject to execution under s. 56.061, other than fixtures, money, negotiable instruments, and mortgages.

(a) A judgment lien is acquired by filing a judgment lien certificate in accordance with s. 55.203 with the Department of State after the judgment has become final and if the time to move for rehearing has lapsed, no motion for rehearing is pending, and no stay of the judgment or its enforcement is then in effect. A court may authorize, for cause shown, the filing of a judgment lien certificate before a judgment has become final when the court has authorized the issuance of a writ of execution in the same matter. A judgment lien certificate not filed in compliance with this subsection is permanently void and of no effect.

(b) For any lien, warrant, assessment, or judgment collected by the Department of Revenue, a judgment lien may be acquired by filing the judgment lien certificate information or warrant with the Department of State in accordance with subsection (5).

(c) Except as provided in s. 55.208, the effective date of a judgment lien is the date, including the time of day, of filing. Although no lien attaches to property, and a creditor does not become a lien creditor as to liens under chapter 679, until the debtor acquires an interest in the property, priority among competing judgment liens is determined in order of filing date and time.

(d) Except as provided in s. 55.204(3), a judgment creditor may file only one effective judgment lien certificate based upon a particular judgment.

(3) Except as otherwise provided in s. 55.208, the priority of a judgment lien acquired in accordance with this section or s. 55.204(3) is established at the date and time the judgment lien certificate is filed.

(4) As used in ss. 55.201-55.209, the terms "holder of a judgment" and "judgment creditor" include the Department of Revenue with respect to a judgment being enforced by the Department of Revenue as the state IV-D agency.

(5) Liens, assessments, warrants, or judgments filed pursuant to paragraph (2)(b) may be filed directly into the central database by the Department of Revenue, or its designee as determined by its executive director, through electronic or information data exchange programs approved by the Department of State. Such filings must contain the information set forth in s. 55.203(1).

55.203. Judgment lien certificate; content, filing, and indexing.

(1) An original judgment lien certificate must include:

(a) The legal name of each judgment debtor and, if a recorded legal entity, the registered name and document filing number as shown in the records of the Department of State.

(b) The last known address and the social security number or federal employer identification number of each judgment debtor if shown on the judgment itself.

(c) The legal name of the judgment creditor and, if a recorded legal entity, the registered name and document filing number as shown in the records of the Department of State, and the name of the judgment creditor's attorney or duly authorized representative, if any.

(d) The address of the judgment creditor.

(e) The identity of the court which entered the judgment and the case number and the date the written judgment was entered.

(f) The amount due on the money judgment and the applicable interest rate.

(g) The signature of the judgment creditor or the judgment creditor's attorney or duly authorized representative.

(2) A second judgment lien certificate, as provided in s. 55.204(3), must include the information required in subsection (1) and must state the file number assigned to the file of the original judgment lien certificate, the money amount remaining unpaid, and the interest accrued thereon.

(3) An amendment, as provided in s. 55.206, or a correction statement, as provided in s. 55.207, must state the file number of the judgment lien file to which the amendment or correction statement relates and must state the action, change, or statement to be added.

(4) The Department of State shall examine, for compliance with ss. 55.201-55.209, each document submitted for filing and shall accept or reject the document accordingly. For each judgment lien certificate filed, the department shall:

(a) Create a file.

(b) Assign a unique file number to the record.

(c) Include the date and time of filing of the judgment lien certificate.

(d) Maintain the file in a database accessible to the public via the Internet.

(e) Index the judgment lien certificate according to the name of each judgment debtor.

(f) Index all subsequently filed documents relating to an original judgment lien certificate in a manner that associates them to the original judgment lien certificate.

(5) A judgment lien certificate substantially satisfying the requirements of this section is effective even if it has minor errors or omissions that make the filing seriously misleading.

(6) The Department of State shall prescribe mandatory forms of all documents to be filed under this section.

55.204. Duration and continuation of judgment lien; destruction of records.

(1) Except as provided in this section, a judgment lien acquired under s. 55.202 lapses and becomes invalid 5 years after the date of filing the judgment lien certificate.

(2) Liens securing the payment of child support or tax obligations under s. 95.091(1)(b) lapse 20 years after the date of the original filing of the warrant or other document required by law to establish a lien. Liens securing the payment of reemployment assistance tax obligations lapse 10 years after the date of the original filing of the notice of lien. A second lien based on the original filing may not be obtained.

(3) At any time within 6 months before or 6 months after the scheduled lapse of a judgment lien under subsection (1), the judgment creditor may acquire a second judgment lien by filing a new judgment lien certificate. The effective date of the second judgment lien is the date and time on which the judgment lien certificate is filed. The second judgment lien is a new judgment lien and not a continuation of the original judgment lien. The second judgment lien permanently lapses and becomes invalid 5 years after its filing date, and additional liens based on the original judgment or any judgment based on the original judgment may not be acquired.

(4) A judgment lien continues only as to itemized property for an additional 90 days after lapse of the lien. Such judgment lien continues only if:

(a) The property was itemized and its location described with sufficient particularity in the instructions for levy to permit the sheriff to act;

(b) The instructions for the levy had been delivered to the sheriff before the date of lapse of the lien; and

(c) The property was located in the county in which the sheriff has jurisdiction at the time of delivery of the instruction for levy. Subsequent removal of the property does not defeat the lien. A court may order continuation of the lien beyond the 90-day period on a showing that extraordinary circumstances have prevented levy.

(5) The date of lapse of a judgment lien whose enforceability has been temporarily stayed or enjoined as a result of any legal or equitable proceeding is tolled until 30 days after the stay or injunction is terminated.

(6) If a second judgment lien is not filed, the Department of State shall maintain each judgment lien file and all information contained therein for a minimum of 1 year after the judgment lien lapses in accordance with this section. If a second judgment lien is filed, the department shall maintain both files and all information contained in such files for a minimum of 1 year after the second judgment lien lapses.

(7) This section does not extend the life of a judgment lien beyond the time that the underlying judgment, order, decree, or warrant otherwise expires or becomes invalid pursuant to law.

55.205. Effect of judgment lien.

(1) A judgment creditor who has not acquired a judgment lien as provided in s. 55.202 or whose lien has lapsed may nevertheless proceed against the judgment debtor's property through any appropriate judicial process. Such judgment creditor proceeding by writ of execution acquires a lien as of the time of levy and only on the property levied upon. Except as provided in s. 55.208, such judgment creditor takes subject to the claims and interest of priority judgment creditors.

(2) A buyer in the ordinary course of business as defined in s. 671.201(9) takes free of a judgment lien acquired as provided in s. 55.202 or s. 55.204 even though the buyer knows of its existence. A valid security interest as defined in chapter 679 in after-acquired property of the judgment debtor which is perfected before the debtor acquires an interest in the property takes priority over the judgment lien on the after-acquired property.

(3) An individual buyer of goods for personal, family, or household use who buys the goods from a seller who held the goods for personal, family, or household use, and who pays value without knowledge that the goods are subject to a judgment lien, is entitled, to the extent of the value paid, to a lien on the goods superior to the judgment lien. If the buyer has made improvements to the goods, or other reasons justify doing so, a court may adjust the amount secured by the lien as the equities may require. This subsection shall not apply to:

(a) A transfer to a relative or an insider of the judgment debtor, as such are defined at s. 726.102;

(b) A fraudulent transfer, as defined by s. 726.105, s. 726.106, or 11 U.S.C. s. 548;

(c) A fraudulent asset conversion as defined by s. 222.30;

(d) Twenty-five percent of the transfer of goods by a judgment debtor the value of which, in the aggregate, exceeds $10,000;

(e) Fifty percent of the transfer of goods by a judgment debtor the value of which, in the aggregate, exceeds $20,000;

(f) Seventy-five percent of the transfer of goods by a judgment debtor the value of which, in the aggregate, exceeds $25,000; or

(g) Any transfer of goods by a judgment debtor the value of which, in the aggregate, exceeds $30,000.

(4) A buyer of stock in a corporation takes free of a judgment lien hereunder if the buyer pays value in good faith without notice as defined in s. 678.1051.

55.206. Amendment of judgment lien file; termination, partial release, assignment, continuation, tolling, correction.

(1) An amendment to a judgment lien acquired as provided under s. 55.202 may be filed by or on behalf of the judgment creditor of record, which may provide for:

(a) The termination, partial release, or assignment of the judgment creditor's interest in a judgment lien;

(b) The continuation and termination of the continuation of a judgment lien, as provided in s. 55.204(4);

(c) The tolling and termination of the tolling of a lapse of a judgment lien, as provided in s. 55.204(5); or

(d) The correction or change of any other information provided in the judgment lien file.

(2) Within 30 days following receipt of a written demand by a judgment debtor after the obligation underlying a judgment lien has been fully or partially released, the judgment lienholder must deliver to the judgment debtor a written statement indicating that there is no longer a claim for a lien on the personal property of the judgment debtor or that the judgment lien has been partially released and setting forth the value of the lien remaining unpaid as of the date of the statement. A statement signed by an assignee must include or be accompanied by a separate written acknowledgment of assignment signed by or for the benefit of the judgment creditor of record. If the judgment lienholder fails to deliver such a statement within 30 days after proper written demand therefor, the judgment lienholder is liable to the judgment debtor for $100, and for any actual or consequential damages, including reasonable attorney's fees, caused by such failure to the judgment debtor. The judgment debtor, the judgment creditor, or assignee may file such statement with the Department of State.

55.207. Correction of judgment lien file.

(1) A person may file with the Department of State a correction statement with respect to a judgment lien file, as provided in s. 55.203, indexed under any person's name, if the person believes that the file is inaccurate or that the judgment lien certificate was wrongfully filed.

(2) A correction statement must:

(a) State the judgment debtor named and the file number assigned to the judgment lien file to which the correction statement relates;

(b) Indicate that it is a correction statement;

(c) Provide the basis for the person's belief that the judgment lien certificate was wrongfully filed or the file is inaccurate; and

(d) Indicate the manner in which the person believes the file should be corrected to cure any inaccuracy.

(3) The department shall ensure that a correction statement is indexed and available in the same manner as any filed lien certificate in the central database of judgment lien files.

(4) The filing of a correction statement does not affect the effectiveness of the judgment lien or other filing.

55.208. Effect of filed judgment lien on writs of execution previously delivered to a sheriff.

(1) Any lien created by a writ of execution which has been delivered to the sheriff of any county before October 1, 2001, remains in effect for 2 years thereafter as to any property of the judgment debtor located in that county before October 1, 2001, and remaining within that county after that date. As to any property of the judgment debtor brought into the county on or after October 1, 2001, such writs create no lien, inchoate or otherwise.

(2) If a judgment creditor who has delivered a writ of execution to a sheriff in any county prior to October 1, 2001, properly files a judgment lien certificate with the Department of State by October 1, 2003, the resulting judgment lien is deemed filed on the date the writ was delivered to the sheriff as to all property of the judgment debtor subject to execution in this state under s. 56.061 which is located in that county on October 1, 2001, and that remains continuously in that county thereafter. Priority of such judgment liens is determined as of the effective date they are considered to have been filed. As to all other property of the judgment debtor, the effective date of the judgment lien is as provided in s. 55.202. The duration of all judgment liens is as provided in s. 55.204.

(3) If a judgment creditor who has delivered a writ of execution to a sheriff in any county before October 1, 2001, does not properly file a judgment lien certificate with the Department of State by October 1, 2003, such writ is considered to have been abandoned and to be of no effect after October 1, 2003.

55.209. Department of State; processing fees, responsibilities.

(1) Except for liens, assessments, warrants, or judgments filed electronically as provided in s. 55.202(2)(b), the Department of State shall collect the following nonrefundable processing fees for all documents filed in accordance with ss. 55.201-55.209:

(a) For any judgment lien certificate or other documents permitted to be filed, $20.

(b) For the certification of any filed document, $10.

(c) For copies of judgment lien documents which are produced by the Department of State, $1 per page or part thereof. However, no charge may be collected for copies provided in an online electronic format via the Internet.

(d) For indexing a judgment lien by multiple judgment debtor names, $5 per additional name.

(e) For each additional facing page attached to a judgment lien certificate or document permitted to be filed, $5.

(2) Unless otherwise provided by law, the Department of State may not conduct any search of the database established under s. 55.201 to determine the existence of any judgment lien file or to perform any service other than in connection with those services for which payment of services are required under this section. The information maintained in the database is for public notice purposes only and the department may make no certification or determination of the validity of any judgment lien acquired under ss. 55.202 and 55.204(3).

55.501. Florida Enforcement of Foreign Judgments Act; short title.

Sections 55.501-55.509 may be cited as the "Florida Enforcement of Foreign Judgments Act."

55.502. Construction of act.

(1) As used in ss. 55.501-55.509, the term "foreign judgment" means a judgment, decree, or order of a court of any other state, territory or commonwealth of the United States, or of the United States if such judgment, decree, or order is entitled to full faith and credit in this state.

(2) This act shall not be construed to impair the right of a judgment creditor to bring an action to enforce his or her judgment instead of proceeding under this act.

(3) This act shall be interpreted and construed to effectuate its general purpose to make uniform the law with respect to the subject of this act among states enacting it.

(4) Nothing contained in this act shall be construed to alter, modify, or extend the limitation period applicable for the enforcement of foreign judgments.

55.503. Recording and status of foreign judgments; fees.

(1) A copy of any foreign judgment certified in accordance with the laws of the United States or of this state may be recorded in the office of the clerk of the circuit court of any county. The clerk shall file, record, and index the foreign judgment in the same manner as a judgment of a circuit or county court of this state. A judgment so recorded shall have the same effect and shall be subject to the same rules of civil procedure, legal and equitable defenses, and proceedings for reopening, vacating, or staying judgments, and it may be enforced, released, or satisfied, as a judgment of a circuit or county court of this state.

(2) Any person recording a foreign judgment shall pay to the clerk of the circuit court a service charge as is required for the recording of an original action demanding the relief or judgment granted in the foreign judgment.

55.505. Notice of recording; prerequisite to enforcement.

(1) At the time of the recording of a foreign judgment, the judgment creditor shall make and record with the clerk of the circuit court an affidavit setting forth the name, social security number, if known, and last known post office address of the judgment debtor and of the judgment creditor.

(2) Promptly upon the recording of the foreign judgment and the affidavit, the clerk shall mail notice of the recording of the foreign judgment, by registered mail with return receipt requested, to the judgment debtor at the address given in the affidavit and shall make a note of the mailing in the docket. The notice shall include the name and post office address of the judgment creditor and of the judgment creditor's attorney, if any, in this state. In addition, the judgment creditor may mail a notice of the recording of the judgment to the judgment debtor and may record proof of mailing with the clerk. The failure of the clerk to mail notice of recording will not affect the enforcement proceedings if proof of mailing by the judgment creditor has been recorded.

(3) No execution or other process for enforcement of a foreign judgment recorded hereunder shall issue until 30 days after the mailing of notice by the clerk and payment of a service charge of up to $42 to the clerk. When an action authorized in s. 55.509(1) is filed, it acts as an automatic stay of the effect of this section.

55.507. Lien; when effective.

A foreign judgment does not operate as a lien until 30 days after the mailing of notice by the clerk. When an action authorized in s. 55.509(1) is filed, it acts as an automatic stay of the effect of this section.

55.509. Stay of enforcement of foreign judgment.

(1) If, within 30 days after the date the foreign judgment is recorded, the judgment debtor files an action contesting the jurisdiction of the court which entered the foreign judgment or the validity of the foreign judgment and records a lis pendens directed toward the foreign judgment, the court shall stay enforcement of the foreign judgment and the judgment lien upon the filing of the action by the judgment debtor.

(2) If the judgment debtor shows the circuit or county court any ground upon which enforcement of a judgment of any circuit or county court of this state would be stayed, the court shall stay enforcement of the foreign judgment for an appropriate period, upon requiring the same security for satisfaction of the judgment which is required in this state.

55.601. Uniform Out-of-country Foreign Money-Judgment Recognition Act; short title.

Sections 55.601-55.607 may be cited as the "Uniform Out-of-country Foreign Money-Judgment Recognition Act."

55.602. Definitions.

As used in this act, the term:

(1) "Foreign state" means any governmental unit other than the United States, or any state, district, commonwealth, territory, insular possession thereof, or the Panama Canal Zone, the Trust Territory of the Pacific Islands, or the Ryukyu Islands.

(2) "Out-of-country foreign judgment" means any judgment of a foreign state granting or denying recovery of a sum of money, other than a judgment for taxes, a fine, or other penalty.

55.603. Applicability.

This act applies to any out-of-country foreign judgment that is final and conclusive and enforceable where rendered, even though an appeal therefrom is pending or is subject to appeal.

55.604. Recognition and enforcement.

Except as provided in s. 55.605, an out-of-country foreign judgment meeting the requirements of s. 55.603 is conclusive between the parties to the extent that it grants or denies recovery of a sum of money. Procedures for recognition and enforceability of an out-of-country foreign judgment shall be as follows:

(1) The out-of-country foreign judgment shall be filed with the clerk of the court and recorded in the public records in the county or counties where enforcement is sought.

(a) At the time of the recording of an out-of-country foreign judgment, the judgment creditor shall make and record with the clerk of the circuit court an affidavit setting forth the name, social security number, if known, and last known post-office address of the judgment debtor and of the judgment creditor.

(b) Promptly upon the recording of the out-of-country foreign judgment and the affidavit, the clerk shall mail notice of the recording of the out-of-country foreign judgment, by registered mail with return receipt requested, to the judgment debtor at the address given in the affidavit and shall make a note of the mailing in the docket. The notice shall include the name and address of the judgment creditor and of the judgment creditor's attorney, if any, in this state. In addition, the judgment creditor may mail a notice of the recording of the judgment to the judgment debtor and may record proof of mailing with the clerk. The failure of the clerk to mail notice of recording will not affect the enforcement proceedings if proof of mailing by the judgment creditor has been recorded.

(2) The judgment debtor shall have 30 days after service of the notice to file a notice of objection with the clerk of the court specifying the grounds for nonrecognition or nonenforceability under this act.

(3) Upon the application of any party, and after proper notice, the circuit court shall have jurisdiction to conduct a hearing, determine the issues, and enter an appropriate order granting or denying recognition in accordance with the terms of this act.

(4) If the judgment debtor fails to file a notice of objection within the required time, the clerk of the court shall record a certificate stating that no objection has been filed.

(5) Upon entry of an order recognizing the out-of-country foreign judgment, or upon recording of the clerk's certificate set forth above, the out-of-country foreign judgment shall be enforced in the same manner as the judgment of a court of this state.

(6) Once an order recognizing the out-of-country foreign judgment has been entered by a court of this state, the order and a copy of the judgment may be recorded in any other county of this state without further notice or proceedings, and shall be enforceable in the same manner as the judgment of a court of this state.

(7) A lien on real estate in any county shall be created only when there has been recorded in the official records of the county (a) a certified copy of the judgment, and (b) a copy of the clerk's certificate or the order recognizing the out-of-country foreign judgment. The priority of such lien will be established as of the time the latter of the two recordings has occurred.

(8) A judgment lien on personal property is acquired only when a judgment lien certificate is filed in accordance with s. 55.203 with the Department of State.

55.605. Grounds for nonrecognition.

(1) An out-of-country foreign judgment is not conclusive if:
(a) The judgment was rendered under a system which does not provide impartial tribunals or procedures compatible with the requirements of due process of law.
(b) The foreign court did not have personal jurisdiction over the defendant.
(c) The foreign court did not have jurisdiction over the subject matter.
(2) An out-of-country foreign judgment need not be recognized if:
(a) The defendant in the proceedings in the foreign court did not receive notice of the proceedings in sufficient time to enable him or her to defend.
(b) The judgment was obtained by fraud.
(c) The cause of action or claim for relief on which the judgment is based is repugnant to the public policy of this state.
(d) The judgment conflicts with another final and conclusive order.
(e) The proceeding in the foreign court was contrary to an agreement between the parties under which the dispute in question was to be settled otherwise than by proceedings in that court.
(f) In the case of jurisdiction based only on personal service, the foreign court was a seriously inconvenient forum for the trial of the action.
(g) The foreign jurisdiction where judgment was rendered would not give recognition to a similar judgment rendered in this state.
(h) The cause of action resulted in a defamation judgment obtained in a jurisdiction outside the United States, unless the court sitting in this state before which the matter is brought first

determines that the defamation law applied in the foreign court's adjudication provided at least as much protection for freedom of speech and press in that case as would be provided by the United States Constitution and the State Constitution.

55.6055. Foreign defamation judgment.

(1) For the purposes of rendering declaratory relief with respect to a person's liability for a foreign defamation judgment and determining whether the foreign defamation judgment should be deemed nonrecognizable under s. 55.605, the courts of this state have personal jurisdiction over any person who obtains a judgment in a defamation proceeding outside the United States against any person who:
(a) Is a resident of this state;
(b) Is a person or entity amenable to the jurisdiction of this state;
(c) Has assets in this state; or
(d) May have to take action in this state to comply with the judgment.
(2) This section applies to judgments rendered in defamation proceedings outside the United States before, on, or after July 1, 2009.

55.606. Personal jurisdiction.

The out-of-country foreign judgment shall not be refused recognition for lack of personal jurisdiction if:
(1) The defendant was served personally in the foreign state;
(2) The defendant voluntarily appeared in the proceedings, other than for the purpose of protecting property seized or threatened with seizure in the proceedings or of contesting the jurisdiction of the court over him or her;
(3) The defendant, prior to the commencement of the proceedings, had agreed to submit to the jurisdiction of the foreign court with respect to the subject matter involved;
(4) The defendant was domiciled in the foreign state when the proceedings were instituted, or, being a body corporate, had its principal place of business, was incorporated, or had otherwise acquired corporate status, in the foreign state;
(5) The defendant had a business office in the foreign state and the proceedings in the foreign court involved a cause of action or a claim for relief arising out of business done by the defendant through that office in the foreign state; or
(6) The defendant operated a motor vehicle or airplane in the foreign state and the proceedings involved a cause of action or claim for relief arising out of such operation.

55.607. Stay in case of appeal.

If the defendant satisfies the court that an appeal is pending, or that he or she intends to appeal, and that he or she has obtained a stay of judgment from the foreign court, the court may stay the proceedings until the appeal has been determined or until the expiration of a period of time sufficient to enable the defendant to prosecute the appeal.

CHAPTER 56. FINAL PROCESS

56.0101. Definitions.

As used in this chapter, the term:

(1) "Claimant" means any person other than the judgment debtor who claims any property levied on.

(2) "Corporate judgment debtor" means a judgment debtor other than an individual, an estate, or a trust that is not a business trust.

(3) "Judgment creditor" means the holder of an unsatisfied judgment, order, or decree for the payment of money, including a transferee or a surety having the right to control and collect the judgment under s. 55.13.

(4) "Judgment debtor" means each person who is liable on a judgment, an order, or a decree subject to execution under this chapter.

(5) "Levying creditor" means the levying judgment creditor.

(6) "Person" means an individual, partnership, corporation, association, organization, government or governmental subdivision or agency, business trust, estate, trust, or any other legal or commercial entity.

(7) "Relative" means an individual related by consanguinity within the third degree as determined by the common law, a spouse, or an individual related to a spouse within the third degree as determined by the common law, and includes an individual in an adoptive relationship within the third degree.

56.011. Executions; capias ad satisfaciendum abolished.

A capias ad satisfaciendum may not be issued upon a judgment, nor may the body of any person be subject to arrest or confinement for the payment of money, except for fines imposed by lawful authority.

56.021. Executions; issuance and return, alias, etc.

When issued, an execution is valid and effective during the life of the judgment, order, or decree on which it is issued. When fully paid, the officer executing it shall make his or her return and file it in the court which issued the execution. If the execution is lost or destroyed, the party entitled thereto may have an alias, pluries or other copies on making proof of such loss or destruction by affidavit and filing it in the court issuing the execution.

56.031. Executions; form.

All executions shall be dated on the day on which they are issued, shall be directed to all and singular the sheriffs of the state and shall be in full force throughout the state.

56.041. Executions; collection and return.

(1) All executions shall be returnable when satisfied, and the officers to whom they are delivered shall collect the amounts thereof as soon as possible and shall furnish the judgment debtor with a satisfaction of judgment. All receipts shall be endorsed on the execution.

(2) All unsatisfied executions in the hands of the sheriff docketed before October 1, 2001, or 20 years after the date of issuance of final judgment upon which the execution was issued may be returned to the court issuing the execution. Upon such return, the clerk of the court of issuance shall provide a receipt to the sheriff submitting the return acknowledging the return of the unsatisfied execution.

56.051. Executions; collection when against principal and sureties.

Where there are executions against principals and sureties, or an execution against a principal and surety or sureties, it shall be the duty of the sheriff or other officer to make the money out of the property of the principal, unless the principal be insolvent or has no property, in which case the execution may proceed against the property of the sureties.

56.061. Property subject to execution.

Lands and tenements, goods and chattels, equities of redemption in real and personal property, and stock in corporations, shall be subject to levy and sale under execution. Likewise, the interest in personal property in possession of a vendee under a retained title contract or conditional sale contract shall be subject to levy and sale under execution to satisfy a judgment against the vendee. This shall be done by making the levy on such personal property.

56.071. Executions on equities of redemption; discovery of value.

On motion made by the person causing a levy to be made on an equity of redemption, the court from which the execution issued shall order the mortgagor, mortgagee, and all other persons interested in the mortgaged property levied on to appear and be examined about the amount remaining due on the mortgage, the amount that has been paid, the person to whom that amount has been paid, and the date when that amount was paid so that the value of the equity of redemption may be ascertained before the property is sold. The court may appoint a general or special magistrate to conduct the examination. This section shall also apply to the interest of and personal property in possession of a vendee under a retained title contract or conditional sales contract.

56.09. Executions against corporate judgment debtors; generally.

On any judgment against a corporate judgment debtor, the judgment creditor may have an execution levied on the current money as well as on the goods and chattels, lands and tenements of the corporate judgment debtor.

56.10. Executions against corporate judgment debtors; receivership.

If an execution cannot be satisfied in whole or in part for lack of property of the corporate judgment debtor subject to levy and sale, on motion of the judgment creditor the circuit court in chancery within whose circuit such corporate judgment debtor is or has been doing business, or in which any of its effects are found, may sequestrate the property, things in action, goods and chattels of the corporate judgment debtor for the purpose of enforcing the judgment, and may appoint a receiver for the corporate judgment debtor. A receiver so appointed is subject to the rules prescribed by law for receivers of the property of other judgment debtors. His or her power shall extend throughout the state.

56.12. Executions; levy, forthcoming bond.

If a judgment debtor wants to retake possession of any property levied on, the judgment debtor may do so by executing a bond with surety to be approved by the officer in favor of the judgment creditor in a sum double the value of the property retaken as fixed by the officer holding the execution and conditioned that the property will be forthcoming on the day of sale stated in the bond.

56.13. Executions; forfeiture of forthcoming bond.

Should the execution remain unpaid, and the parties to the bond fail to produce such property by the day specified, said bond shall be returned to the court from which the execution issued, as forfeited; and the clerk, or the court if it has no clerk, shall enter up judgment forthwith against the sureties for the value fixed as aforesaid of the property so bonded, or if the value of the property exceed the amount of the execution, then for the amount of the execution, and execution shall issue therefor. Such proceedings shall not affect the liability of the principal upon the original judgment.

56.14. Executions upon forthcoming bond; levy.

No bonds, as hereinbefore provided, shall be allowed to be given for property seized upon the execution on the judgment upon the forfeited bond.

56.15. Executions; stay of illegal writs.

If any execution issues illegally, the judgment debtor may obtain a stay by making and delivering an affidavit to the officer having the execution, stating the illegality and whether any part of the execution is due, with a bond with surety payable to the judgment creditor in double the amount of the execution or the part of which a stay is sought conditioned to pay the execution or part claimed to be illegal and any damages for delay if the affidavit is not well founded. On receipt of such affidavit and bond the officer shall stay proceedings on the execution and return the bond and affidavit to the court from which the execution issued. The court shall pass on the question of illegality as soon as possible. If the execution is adjudged illegal in any part, the court shall stay it as to the part but if it is adjudged legal in whole or in part, the court shall enter judgment against the principal and surety on such bond for the amount of so much of the execution as is adjudged to be legal and execution shall issue thereon.

56.16. Executions; claims of third parties to property levied on.

If any person, including a person to whom a Notice to Appear has been issued pursuant to s. 56.29(2), other than the judgment debtor claims any property levied on, he or she may obtain possession of the property by filing with the officer having the execution an affidavit by the claimant, or the claimant's agent or attorney, that the property claimed belongs to the claimant and by furnishing the officer a bond with surety to be approved by the officer in favor of the judgment creditor in double the value of the goods claimed as the value is fixed by the officer and conditioned to deliver said property on demand of said officer if it is adjudged to be the property of the judgment debtor and to pay the judgment creditor all damages found against the claimant if it appears that the claim was interposed for the purpose of delay.

56.17. Executions; duty of officer on claim of third person being filed.

On receipt of the bond and affidavit the officer shall deliver the property to the claimant and desist from any further proceedings under the execution until the right of property is tried. The officer shall return the execution to the court from which it issued with the affidavit and bond.

56.18. Executions; trial of claims of third persons.

As soon as possible after the return, or after service of a Notice to Appear pursuant to s. 56.29(2), a jury, if not waived, shall be impaneled to try the right of property. If the verdict is in favor of the judgment creditor and it appears that the claim brought pursuant to s. 56.16 was interposed for delay, the judgment creditor may be awarded reasonable damages, not exceeding 20 percent of the value of the property claimed. If the claimant denies in writing under oath filed at least 3 days before the trial, the correctness of the appraisement of the value of the property by the officer levying the execution, and the verdict is in favor of the judgment creditor, the jury if not waived, shall fix the value of each item thereof, or of the items covered by such denial.

56.19. Judgments upon claims of third persons.

Upon the verdict of the jury, the court shall enter judgment deciding the right of property, and if the verdict is for the judgment creditor, awarding a recovery by the judgment creditor from the claimant and the claimant's sureties, of the value (as fixed by the officer, or as fixed by the jury if fixed by it) of such parts of the property as the jury may have found subject to execution that were delivered to the claimant, and awarding separately such damages as may be awarded under s. 56.18, and of all costs attending the presentation and trial of the claim.

56.20. Executions on judgments against third person claimants.

If the execution issued on the judgment is not paid, it shall be satisfied in the usual manner unless on demand of the officer holding it, the principal and surety in the claim bond deliver the property released under the claim bond to the officer and pay him or her the damages and costs awarded to the judgment creditor. If the property is returned to the officer but damages and costs are not paid, execution shall be enforced for the damages and costs. If part of the property is returned to the officer, the execution shall be enforced for the value, fixed as aforesaid, of that not returned. All property returned shall be sold under the original execution against the judgment debtor.

56.21. Execution sales; notice.

Notice of all sales under execution shall be given by advertisement once each week for 4 successive weeks in a newspaper published in the county in which the sale is to take place. The time of such notice may be shortened in the discretion of the court from which the execution issued, upon affidavit that the property to be sold is subject to decay and will not sell for its full value if held until date of sale. On or before the date of the first publication or posting of the notice of sale, a copy of the notice of sale shall be furnished by the sheriff by certified mail to the attorney of record of the judgment debtor, or to the judgment debtor at the judgment debtor's last known address if the judgment debtor does not have an attorney of record. Such copy of the notice of sale shall be mailed even though a default judgment was entered. When levying upon real or personal property, a notice of such levy and execution sale and a copy of the affidavit required by s. 56.27(4) shall be sent by the sheriff to the attorneys of record of all judgment creditors and other lienholders, or to all judgment creditors and other lienholders who do not have an attorney of record, who have acquired a lien as provided in s. 55.10(1) and (2), s. 55.202, s. 55.204(3), or s. 695.01, and whose liens have not lapsed at the time of levy, at the address listed in the judgment lien certificate or other recorded liens, or, if amended, in any amendment thereto, and to all secured creditors who have filed financing statements as provided in part V of chapter 679 in the name of the judgment debtor reflecting a security interest in property of the kind to be sold at the execution sale at the address listed in the financing statement, or, if amended, in any amendment to the financing statement. Such notice shall be made in the same manner as notice is made to any judgment debtor under this section. When levying upon real property, notice of such levy and execution sale and affidavit required by s. 56.27(4) shall be made to the property owner of record in the same manner as notice is made to any judgment debtor pursuant to this section, and shall be made to each other person holding a mortgage or other lien against the real property as disclosed by the affidavit. When selling real or personal property, the sale date shall not be earlier than 30 days after the date of the first advertisement.

56.22. Execution sales.

(1) All sales of property under legal process shall take place at the time, date, and place advertised in the notice of the sheriff's sale on any day of the week except Saturday and Sunday and shall continue from day to day until such property is disposed of.
(2) Property not effectively disposed of at the initial sheriff's sale may be readvertised, as provided in s. 56.21, upon receipt of an additional deposit to cover costs incurred in connection with the maintenance of the property under legal process. If no additional deposit is received by the sheriff, the property may be returned to the judgment debtor; if the judgment debtor refuses to accept such

property, the property may be returned to a third party, such as a lienholder, upon presentation of a proper court order directing such return. If the property cannot be returned as described in this subsection, such property shall be disposed of as unclaimed or abandoned.

56.25. Execution sale; bill of sale or deed.

When a sale is made under an execution, the officer making the sale shall execute and deliver to the purchaser a deed or bill of sale to the property on payment of the purchase money and the cost of the deed or bill of sale.

56.26. Executions; mandamus to force levy and sale.

When an officer holds an unsatisfied execution and refuses to levy on property liable thereunder and on which it is his or her duty to levy or having levied, refuses to advertise and sell the property levied on, the judgment creditor is entitled to an alternative writ of mandamus requiring the officer to levy such execution or advertise and sell the property levied on, or both, as the case may be.

56.27. Executions; payment of money collected.

(1) All money received under executions shall be paid, in the order prescribed, to the following: the sheriff, for costs; the levying creditor in the amount of $500 as liquidated expenses; and the priority lienholder under s. 55.10(1) and (2), s. 55.202, s. 55.204(3), or s. 55.208(2), as set forth in an affidavit required by subsection (4), or the levying creditor's attorney, in satisfaction of the judgment lien, if the judgment lien has not lapsed at the time of the levy. The receipt of the attorney shall be a release of the officer paying the money to him or her. If the name of more than one attorney appears in the court file, the money shall be paid to the attorney who originally commenced the action or who made the original defense unless the file shows that another attorney has been substituted.
(2)(a) If property sold under execution brings more than the amount needed to satisfy the provisions of subsection (1), the surplus shall be paid in the order of priority to any judgment lienholders whose judgment liens have not lapsed, unless the affidavit required by subsection (4) discloses that the property is also subject to any recorded mortgage, financing statement, tax warrant, or other lien, other than a judgment lien, which is junior in priority to the levying creditor's judgment lien. For the purpose of the sheriff's distribution of the surplus to judgment lienholders under this paragraph, priority of judgment liens on personal property shall be based on the effective date of the judgment lien acquired under s. 55.202, s. 55.204(3), or s. 55.208(2), and priority of judgment liens on real property shall be based on the effective date of the judgment lien acquired under s. 55.10(1) and (2), as set forth in an affidavit required under subsection (4). If there is a surplus after all valid judgment liens and execution liens have been satisfied under this paragraph, the surplus must be paid to the owner of the property sold.
(b) If the affidavit required by subsection (4) discloses that the property is also subject to any recorded mortgage, financing statement, tax warrant, or other lien, other than a judgment lien, which is junior in priority to the levying creditor's judgment lien, any surplus from the sale of the property shall be paid over to the registry of the court from which the execution issued for further proceedings to determine the priority in which such surplus shall be distributed among judgment lienholders, other lienholders, and the owner of the property sold.
(3) The value of the property levied upon shall not be considered excessive unless the value unreasonably exceeds the total debt reflected in all unsatisfied judgment liens that have not lapsed

and any unsatisfied lien of the levying creditor.

(4) Before the date of the first publication or posting of the notice of sale provided for under s. 56.21, at the time of the levy request to the sheriff, the levying creditor shall deliver to the sheriff an affidavit setting forth all of the following as to the judgment debtor:

(a) For a personal property levy, an attestation by the levying creditor or the levying creditor's attorney of record that he or she has reviewed the database or judgment lien records established in accordance with ss. 55.201-55.209 and that the information contained in the affidavit based on that review is true and correct. For a real property levy in accordance with s. 55.10(1) and (2), an attestation by the levying creditor or the levying creditor's attorney of record that he or she has reviewed the records of the clerk of the court of the county where the property is situated, or that he or she has performed or reviewed a title search, and that the information contained in the affidavit, including a disclosure of all judgment liens, mortgages, financing statements, tax warrants, and other liens against the real property, based on that review or title search is true and correct.

(b) The information required under s. 55.203(1) and (2) for each judgment lien certificate indexed under the name of the judgment debtor as to each judgment creditor; the file number assigned to the record of the original and, if any, the second judgment lien; and the date of filing for each judgment lien certificate under s. 55.202 or s. 55.204(3). For each judgment lien recorded on real property, the information contained in the certified copy of recordation of lien under s. 55.10(1) and (2), and for each other lien recorded on real property, the name and address of the lienholder as shown in the copy of the recorded lien disclosed by the title search.

(c) A statement that the levying creditor either does not have any other levy in process or, if another levy is in process, the levying creditor believes in good faith that the total value of the property under execution does not exceed the amount of outstanding judgments.

(5) A sheriff may rely on the affidavit submitted as required under this section, and a sheriff paying money received under an execution in accordance with the information contained in the affidavit required under subsection (4) is not liable to anyone for damages arising from a wrongful levy or wrongful distribution of funds.

(6) A sheriff who is uncertain as to whom to disburse the proceeds from the sale of the levied property may apply for instructions from:

(a) The court that entered the judgment that is the basis of the judgment lien; or

(b) The appropriate court where the levied property was located at the time of the levy,

56.275. Disposition of unclaimed money collected.

All unclaimed proceeds from sheriff's sales or money collected under execution shall be disposed of as provided in s. 116.21.

56.28. Executions; failure of officer to pay over moneys collected.

If any officer collecting money under execution fails or refuses to pay it over within 30 days after it has been received by him or her, or within 10 days after demand by the levying creditor or the levying creditor's attorney of record made in writing and delivered during regular business hours to the civil process bureau, the officer is liable to pay the same and 20 percent damages, to be recovered by motion in court.

56.29. Proceedings supplementary.

(1) When any judgment creditor holds an unsatisfied judgment or judgment lien obtained under chapter 55, the judgment creditor may file a motion and an affidavit so stating, identifying, if applicable, the issuing court, the case number, and the unsatisfied amount of the judgment or judgment lien, including accrued costs and interest, and stating that the execution is valid and outstanding, and thereupon the judgment creditor is entitled to these proceedings supplementary to execution.

(2) The judgment creditor shall, in the motion described in subsection (1) or in a supplemental affidavit, describe any property of the judgment debtor not exempt from execution in the hands of any person or any property, debt, or other obligation due to the judgment debtor which may be applied toward the satisfaction of the judgment. Upon filing of the motion and affidavits that property of the judgment debtor, or any debt, or other obligation due to the judgment debtor in the custody or control of any other person may be applied to satisfy the judgment, then the court shall issue a Notice to Appear. The Notice to Appear shall direct such person to file an affidavit, as provided in s. 56.16, with the court by a date certain, which date shall not be less than 7 business days from the date of service of the Notice to Appear, stating why the property, debt, or other obligation should not be applied to satisfy the judgment. For good cause shown, the court may shorten the time for serving an affidavit. The Notice to Appear must describe with reasonable particularity the property, debt, or other obligation that may be available to satisfy the judgment, must provide such person with the opportunity to present defenses, and must indicate that discovery as provided under the rules of civil procedure is available and that there is a right to a jury trial as provided in s. 56.18. The Notice to Appear must be served as provided for in chapter 48. A responding affidavit must raise any fact or defense opposing application of the property described in the Notice to Appear to satisfy the judgment, including legal defenses, such as lack of personal jurisdiction. Legal defenses need not be filed under oath but must be served contemporaneously with the affidavit.

(3)(a) When, within 1 year before the service of process on the judgment debtor in the original proceeding or action, the judgment debtor has had title to, or paid the purchase price of, any personal property to which the judgment debtor's spouse, any relative, or any person on confidential terms with the judgment debtor claims title and right of possession, the judgment debtor has the burden of proof to establish that such transfer or gift was not made to delay, hinder, or defraud creditors.

(b) When any gift, transfer, assignment or other conveyance of personal property has been made or contrived by the judgment debtor to delay, hinder, or defraud creditors, the court shall order the gift, transfer, assignment or other conveyance to be void and direct the sheriff to take the property to satisfy the execution. This does not authorize seizure of property exempted from levy and sale under execution or property which has passed to a bona fide purchaser for value and without notice. Any person aggrieved by the levy or Notice to Appear may proceed under ss. 56.16-56.20.

(4) At any time the court may refer the proceeding to a general or special magistrate who may be directed to report findings of law or fact, or both. The general or special magistrate has all the powers thereof, including the power to issue subpoena, and shall be paid the fees provided by the court.

(5) A party or a witness examined under these provisions is not excused from answering a question on the ground that the answer will tend to show him or her guilty of the commission of a fraud, or prove that he or she has been a party or privy to, or knowing of a conveyance, assignment, transfer, or other disposition of property for any purpose, or that the party or witness or another person claims to have title as against the judgment debtor or to hold property derived from or through the judgment debtor, or to be discharged from the payment of a debt which was due to the judgment debtor or to a person on behalf of the judgment debtor. An answer cannot be used as evidence against the person so answering in any criminal proceeding.

(6) The court may order any property of the judgment debtor, not exempt from execution, or any

property, debt, or other obligation due to the judgment debtor, in the hands of or under the control of any person subject to the Notice to Appear, to be levied upon and applied toward the satisfaction of the judgment debt. The court may enter any orders, judgments, or writs required to carry out the purpose of this section, including those orders necessary or proper to subject property or property rights of any judgment debtor to execution, and including entry of money judgments as provided in ss. 56.16-56.19 against any person to whom a Notice to Appear has been directed and over whom the court obtained personal jurisdiction irrespective of whether such person has retained the property, subject to applicable principles of equity, and in accordance with chapters 76 and 77 and all applicable rules of civil procedure. Sections 56.16-56.20 apply to any order issued under this subsection.

(7) Any person failing to obey any order issued under this section by a judge or general or special magistrate or failing to attend in response to a subpoena served on him or her may be held in contempt.

(8) Costs for proceedings supplementary shall be taxed against the judgment debtor as well as all other incidental costs determined to be reasonable and just by the court including, but not limited to, docketing the execution, sheriff's service fees, and court reporter's fees. Reasonable attorney fees may be taxed against the judgment debtor.

(9) The court may entertain claims concerning the judgment debtor's assets brought under chapter 726 and enter any order or judgment, including a money judgment against any initial or subsequent transferee, in connection therewith, irrespective of whether the transferee has retained the property. Claims under chapter 726 brought under this section shall be initiated by a supplemental complaint and served as provided by the rules of civil procedure, and the claims under the supplemental complaint are subject to chapter 726 and the rules of civil procedure. The clerk of the court shall docket a supplemental proceeding under the same case number assigned to the original complaint filed by the judgment creditor or the case number assigned to a judgment domesticated pursuant to 1s. 55.01, shall assign a separate supplemental proceeding number, and shall assign such supplemental proceeding to the same division and judge assigned to the main case or domesticated judgment.

56.30. Discovery in proceedings supplementary.

(1) In addition to any other discovery permitted under the rules of civil procedure, on the judgment creditor's motion the court shall require the judgment debtor to appear before it or a general or special magistrate at a time and place specified by the order in the county of the judgment debtor's residence or principal place of business to be examined concerning property subject to execution. This examination may occur before issuance of a Notice to Appear.

(2) The order shall be served in a reasonable time before the date of the examination in the manner provided for service of summons or may be served on the judgment debtor or the judgment debtor's attorney of record as provided for service of papers in the rules of civil procedure.

(3) Testimony shall be under oath, shall be comprehensive, and cover all matters and things pertaining to the business and financial interests of the judgment debtor which may tend to show what property the judgment debtor has and its location. Any testimony tending directly or indirectly to aid in satisfying the execution is admissible. A corporate judgment debtor must attend and answer by a designee with knowledge or an identified officer or manager who may be specified in the order. Examination of witnesses shall be as at trial, and any party may call other witnesses to be examined concerning property that may be subject to execution.

CHAPTER 57. COURT COSTS

57.021. Costs; taxing.

The clerk or the judge shall tax the costs accruing in each action when it is determined and shall keep a duplicate of the costs bill on file among the original papers in the action. Each item of costs shall be enumerated in the bill.

57.031. Costs; record.

All officers who are allowed to charge fees and costs shall keep a book in which they shall record an itemized account of all the costs and fees which they charge against parties having business with them. The book shall be open at all times for inspection of parties wishing to examine the costs charged for any service rendered by the officers.

57.041. Costs; recovery from losing party.

(1) The party recovering judgment shall recover all his or her legal costs and charges which shall be included in the judgment; but this section does not apply to executors or administrators in actions when they are not liable for costs.
(2) Costs may be collected by execution on the judgment or order assessing costs.

57.051. Costs; prohibition against unlawful exaction.

(1) PROHIBITION.—No officer shall make two charges for the same official act or service, nor charge for any constructive service. No fee shall be charged for any official service performed or claimed to be performed by any officer unless the fee is specifically authorized and its amount is specified by law.
(2) PENALTY.—When any officer willfully charges or levies more than he or she is entitled to, the officer shall forfeit and pay to the party injured 4 times the amount unjustly claimed which may be recovered on motion in the court where the services were rendered.

57.061. Costs; recovery of illegally exacted; procedure.

(1) SUMMARY PROCEEDINGS.—Any person aggrieved by any charge for costs by any officer may have its correctness determined by a court and jury by giving 5 days' notice to the officer making the charge, stating in the notice the time and place of trial. The judge shall enter the action for trial on the day specified in the notice unless he or she extends the time.
(2) VERDICT AND JUDGMENT.—If the jury finds for plaintiff, it shall find the amount which has been improperly collected and the court shall enter judgment for 4 times the amount on which execution shall issue.

57.071. Costs; what taxable.

(1) If costs are awarded to any party, the following shall also be allowed:

(a) The reasonable premiums or expenses paid on all bonds or other security furnished by such party.
(b) The expense of the court reporter for per diem, transcribing proceedings and depositions, including opening statements and arguments by counsel.
(c) Any sales or use tax due on legal services provided to such party, notwithstanding any other provision of law to the contrary.
(2) Expert witness fees may not be awarded as taxable costs unless the party retaining the expert witness furnishes each opposing party with a written report signed by the expert witness which summarizes the expert witness's opinions and the factual basis of the opinions, including documentary evidence and the authorities relied upon in reaching the opinions. Such report shall be filed at least 5 days prior to the deposition of the expert or at least 20 days prior to discovery cutoff, whichever is sooner, or as otherwise determined by the court. This subsection does not apply to any action proceeding under the Florida Family Law Rules of Procedure.

57.081. Costs; right to proceed where prepayment of costs and payment of filing fees waived.

(1) Any indigent person, except a prisoner as defined in s. 57.085, who is a party or intervenor in any judicial or administrative agency proceeding or who initiates such proceeding shall receive the services of the courts, sheriffs, and clerks, with respect to such proceedings, despite his or her present inability to pay for these services. Such services are limited to filing fees; service of process; certified copies of orders or final judgments; a single photocopy of any court pleading, record, or instrument filed with the clerk; examining fees; mediation services and fees; private court-appointed counsel fees; subpoena fees and services; service charges for collecting and disbursing funds; and any other cost or service arising out of pending litigation. In any appeal from an administrative agency decision, for which the clerk is responsible for preparing the transcript, the clerk shall record the cost of preparing the transcripts and the cost for copies of any exhibits in the record. A party who has obtained a certification of indigence pursuant to s. 27.52 or s. 57.082 with respect to a proceeding is not required to prepay costs to a court, clerk, or sheriff and is not required to pay filing fees or charges for issuance of a summons.
(2) Any sheriff who, in complying with the terms of this section, expends personal funds for automotive fuel or ordinary carfare in serving the process of those qualifying under this section may requisition the board of county commissioners of the county for the actual expense, and on the submission to the board of county commissioners of appropriate proof of any such expenditure, the board of county commissioners shall pay the amount of the actual expense from the general fund of the county to the requisitioning officer.
(3) If an applicant prevails in an action, costs shall be taxed in his or her favor as provided by law and, when collected, shall be applied to pay filing fees or costs that have not been paid.

57.082. Determination of civil indigent status.

(1) APPLICATION TO THE CLERK.—A person seeking appointment of an attorney in a civil case eligible for court-appointed counsel, or seeking relief from payment of filing fees and prepayment of costs under s. 57.081, based upon an inability to pay must apply to the clerk of the court for a determination of civil indigent status using an application form developed by the Florida Clerks of Court Operations Corporation with final approval by the Supreme Court.
(a) The application must include, at a minimum, the following financial information:
1. Net income, consisting of total salary and wages, minus deductions required by law, including court-ordered support payments.

2. Other income, including, but not limited to, social security benefits, union funds, veterans' benefits, workers' compensation, other regular support from absent family members, public or private employee pensions, reemployment assistance or unemployment compensation, dividends, interest, rent, trusts, and gifts.

3. Assets, including, but not limited to, cash, savings accounts, bank accounts, stocks, bonds, certificates of deposit, equity in real estate, and equity in a boat or a motor vehicle or in other tangible property.

4. All liabilities and debts.

(b) The clerk shall assist a person who appears before the clerk and requests assistance in completing the application, and the clerk shall notify the court if a person is unable to complete the application after the clerk has provided assistance.

(c) The clerk shall accept an application that is signed by the applicant and submitted on his or her behalf by a private attorney who is representing the applicant in the applicable matter.

(d) A person who seeks appointment of an attorney in a proceeding under chapter 39, at shelter hearings or during the adjudicatory process, during the judicial review process, upon the filing of a petition to terminate parental rights, or upon the filing of any appeal, or if the person seeks appointment of an attorney in a reopened proceeding, for which an indigent person is eligible for court-appointed representation must pay a $50 application fee to the clerk for each application filed. A person is not required to pay more than one application fee per case. However, an appeal or the reopening of a proceeding shall be deemed to be a distinct case. The applicant must pay the fee within 7 days after submitting the application. If the applicant has not paid the fee within 7 days, the court shall enter an order requiring payment, and the clerk shall pursue collection under s. 28.246. The clerk shall transfer monthly all application fees collected under this paragraph to the Department of Revenue for deposit into the Indigent Civil Defense Trust Fund, to be used as appropriated by the Legislature. The clerk may retain 10 percent of application fees collected monthly for administrative costs prior to remitting the remainder to the Department of Revenue. If the person cannot pay the application fee, the clerk shall enroll the person in a payment plan pursuant to s. 28.246.

(2) DETERMINATION BY THE CLERK.—The clerk of the court shall determine whether an applicant seeking such designation is indigent based upon the information provided in the application and the criteria prescribed in this subsection.

(a)1. An applicant, including an applicant who is a minor or an adult tax-dependent person, is indigent if the applicant's income is equal to or below 200 percent of the then-current federal poverty guidelines prescribed for the size of the household of the applicant by the United States Department of Health and Human Services.

2. There is a presumption that the applicant is not indigent if the applicant owns, or has equity in, any intangible or tangible personal property or real property or the expectancy of an interest in any such property having a net equity value of $2,500 or more, excluding the value of the person's homestead and one vehicle having a net value not exceeding $5,000.

(b) Based upon its review, the clerk shall make one of the following determinations:

1. The applicant is not indigent.

2. The applicant is indigent.

(c) If the clerk determines that the applicant is indigent, the clerk shall immediately file the determination in the case record.

(d) The duty of the clerk in determining whether an applicant is indigent is limited to receiving the application and comparing the information provided in the application to the criteria prescribed in this subsection. The determination of indigent status is a ministerial act of the clerk and may not be based on further investigation or the exercise of independent judgment by the clerk. The clerk may contract with third parties to perform functions assigned to the clerk under this section.

(e) The applicant may seek review of the clerk's determination that the applicant is not indigent in the court having jurisdiction over the matter by filing a petition to review the clerk's determination of nonindigent status, for which a filing fee may not be charged. If the applicant seeks review of the clerk's determination of indigent status, the court shall make a final determination as provided in subsection (4).

(3) APPOINTMENT OF COUNSEL ON AN INTERIM BASIS.—If the clerk of the court has not made a determination of indigent status at the time a person requests appointment of an attorney in a civil case eligible for court-appointed counsel, the court shall make a preliminary determination of indigent status, pending further review by the clerk, and may, by court order, appoint counsel on an interim basis.

(4) REVIEW OF THE CLERK'S DETERMINATION.—

(a) If the clerk of the court determines that the applicant is not indigent and the applicant seeks review of the clerk's determination, the court shall make a final determination of indigent status by reviewing the information provided in the application against the criteria prescribed in subsection (2) and by considering the following additional factors:

1. Whether paying for private counsel or other fees and costs creates a substantial hardship for the applicant or the applicant's family.

2. Whether the applicant is proceeding pro se or is represented by a private attorney for a fee or on a pro bono basis.

3. When the applicant retained private counsel.

4. The amount of any attorney's fees and who is paying the fees.

5. Any other relevant financial circumstances of the applicant or the applicant's family.

(b) Based upon its review, the court shall make one of the following determinations and shall, if appropriate, appoint counsel:

1. The applicant is not indigent.

2. The applicant is indigent.

(5) APPOINTMENT OF COUNSEL.—In appointing counsel after a determination that a person is indigent under this section, the court shall first appoint the office of criminal conflict and civil regional counsel, as provided in s. 27.511, unless specific provision is made in law for the appointment of the public defender in the particular civil proceeding. The court shall also order the person to pay the application fee under subsection (1), or enroll in a payment plan if he or she is unable to pay the fee, if the fee remains unpaid or if the person has not enrolled in a payment plan at the time the court appoints counsel. However, a person who is found to be indigent may not be refused counsel.

(6) PROCESSING CHARGE; PAYMENT PLANS.—A person who the clerk or the court determines is indigent for civil proceedings under this section shall be enrolled in a payment plan under s. 28.246 and shall be charged a one-time administrative processing charge under s. 28.24(26)(c). A monthly payment amount, calculated based upon all fees and all anticipated costs, is presumed to correspond to the person's ability to pay if it does not exceed 2 percent of the person's annual net income, as defined in subsection (1), divided by 12. The person may seek review of the clerk's decisions regarding a payment plan established under s. 28.246 in the court having jurisdiction over the matter. A case may not be impeded in any way, delayed in filing, or delayed in its progress, including the final hearing and order, due to nonpayment of any fees or costs by an indigent person. Filing fees waived from payment under s. 57.081 may not be included in the calculation related to a payment plan established under this section.

(7) FINANCIAL DISCREPANCIES; FRAUD; FALSE INFORMATION.—

(a) If the court learns of discrepancies between the application and the actual financial status of the person found to be indigent, the court shall determine whether the status and any relief provided as a result of that status shall be revoked. The person may be heard regarding the information learned by the court. If the court, based on the information, determines that the person is not indigent, the court shall revoke the provision of any relief under this section.

(b) If the court has reason to believe that any applicant, through fraud or misrepresentation, was improperly determined to be indigent, the matter shall be referred to the state attorney. Twenty-five percent of any amount recovered by the state attorney as reasonable value of the services rendered, including fees, charges, and costs paid by the state on the person's behalf, shall be remitted to the Department of Revenue for deposit into the Grants and Donations Trust Fund within the Justice Administrative Commission. Seventy-five percent of any amount recovered shall be remitted to the Department of Revenue for deposit into the General Revenue Fund.

(c) A person who knowingly provides false information to the clerk or the court in seeking a determination of indigent status under this section commits a misdemeanor of the first degree, punishable as provided in s. 775.082 or s. 775.083.

57.085. Deferral of prepayment of court costs and fees for indigent prisoners.

(1) For the purposes of this section, the term "prisoner" means a person who has been convicted of a crime and is incarcerated for that crime or who is being held in custody pending extradition or sentencing.

(2) When a prisoner who is intervening in or initiating a judicial proceeding seeks to defer the prepayment of court costs and fees because of indigence, the prisoner must file an affidavit of indigence with the appropriate clerk of the court. The affidavit must contain complete information about the prisoner's identity; the nature and amount of the prisoner's income; all real property owned by the prisoner; all tangible and intangible property worth more than $100 which is owned by the prisoner; the amount of cash held by the prisoner; the balance of any checking, savings, or money market account held by the prisoner; the prisoner's dependents, including their names and ages; the prisoner's debts, including the name of each creditor and the amount owed to each creditor; and the prisoner's monthly expenses. The prisoner must certify in the affidavit whether the prisoner has been adjudicated indigent under this section, certified indigent under s. 57.081, or authorized to proceed as an indigent under 28 U.S.C. s. 1915 by a federal court. The prisoner must attach to the affidavit a photocopy of the prisoner's trust account records for the preceding 6 months or for the length of the prisoner's incarceration, whichever period is shorter. The affidavit must contain the following statements: "I am presently unable to pay court costs and fees. Under penalty of perjury, I swear or affirm that all statements in this affidavit are true and complete."

(3) Before a prisoner may receive a deferral of prepayment of any court costs and fees for an action brought under this section, the clerk of court must review the affidavit and determine the prisoner to be indigent.

(4) When the clerk has found the prisoner to be indigent but concludes the prisoner is able to pay part of the court costs and fees required by law, the court shall order the prisoner to make, prior to service of process, an initial partial payment of those court costs and fees. The initial partial payment must total at least 20 percent of the average monthly balance of the prisoner's trust account for the preceding 6 months or for the length of the prisoner's incarceration, whichever period is shorter.

(5) When the clerk has found the prisoner to be indigent, the court shall order the prisoner to make monthly payments of no less than 20 percent of the balance of the prisoner's trust account as payment of court costs and fees. When a court orders such payment, the Department of Corrections or the local detention facility shall place a lien on the inmate's trust account for the full amount of the court costs and fees, and shall withdraw money maintained in that trust account and forward the money, when the balance exceeds $10, to the appropriate clerk of the court until the prisoner's court costs and fees are paid in full.

(6) Before an indigent prisoner may intervene in or initiate any judicial proceeding, the court must review the prisoner's claim to determine whether it is legally sufficient to state a cause of action for which the court has jurisdiction and may grant relief. The court shall dismiss all or part of an indigent prisoner's claim which:

(a) Fails to state a claim for which relief may be granted;

(b) Seeks monetary relief from a defendant who is immune from such relief;

(c) Seeks relief for mental or emotional injury where there has been no related allegation of a physical injury; or

(d) Is frivolous, malicious, or reasonably appears to be intended to harass one or more named defendants.

(7) A prisoner who has twice in the preceding 3 years been adjudicated indigent under this section, certified indigent under s. 57.081, or authorized to proceed as an indigent under 28 U.S.C. s. 1915 by a federal court may not be adjudicated indigent to pursue a new suit, action, claim, proceeding, or appeal without first obtaining leave of court. In a request for leave of court, the prisoner must provide a complete listing of each suit, action, claim, proceeding, or appeal brought by the prisoner or intervened in by the prisoner in any court or other adjudicatory forum in the preceding 5 years. The prisoner must attach to a request for leave of court a copy of each complaint, petition, or other document purporting to commence a lawsuit and a record of disposition of the proceeding.

(8) In any judicial proceeding in which a certificate of indigence has been issued to a prisoner, the court may at any time dismiss the prisoner's action, in whole or in part, upon a finding that:

(a) The prisoner's claim of indigence is false or misleading;

(b) The prisoner provided false or misleading information regarding another judicial or administrative proceeding in which the prisoner was a party;

(c) The prisoner failed to pay court costs and fees under this section despite having the ability to pay; or

(d) The prisoner's action or a portion of the action is frivolous or malicious.

(9) In determining whether an action is frivolous or malicious, the court may consider whether:

(a) The prisoner's claim has no arguable basis in law or fact;

(b) The prisoner's claim reasonably appears intended solely to harass a party filed against;

(c) The prisoner's claim is substantially similar to a previous claim in that it involves the same parties or arises from the same operative facts as a previous claim;

(d) The prisoner's claim has little likelihood of success on its merits; or

(e) The allegations of fact in the prisoner's claim are fanciful or not credible.

(10) This section does not apply to a criminal proceeding or a collateral criminal proceeding.

57.104. Computation of attorneys' fees.

In any action in which attorneys' fees are to be determined or awarded by the court, the court shall consider, among other things, time and labor of any legal assistants who contributed nonclerical, meaningful legal support to the matter involved and who are working under the supervision of an attorney. For purposes of this section "legal assistant" means a person, who under the supervision and direction of a licensed attorney engages in legal research, and case development or planning in relation to modifications or initial proceedings, services, processes, or applications; or who prepares or interprets legal documents or selects, compiles, and uses technical information from references such as digests, encyclopedias, or practice manuals and analyzes and follows procedural problems that involve independent decisions.

57.105. Attorney's fee; sanctions for raising unsupported claims or defenses; exceptions; service of motions; damages for delay of litigation.

(1) Upon the court's initiative or motion of any party, the court shall award a reasonable attorney's fee, including prejudgment interest, to be paid to the prevailing party in equal amounts by the losing party and the losing party's attorney on any claim or defense at any time during a civil proceeding or action in which the court finds that the losing party or the losing party's attorney

knew or should have known that a claim or defense when initially presented to the court or at any time before trial:

(a) Was not supported by the material facts necessary to establish the claim or defense; or

(b) Would not be supported by the application of then-existing law to those material facts.

(2) At any time in any civil proceeding or action in which the moving party proves by a preponderance of the evidence that any action taken by the opposing party, including, but not limited to, the filing of any pleading or part thereof, the assertion of or response to any discovery demand, the assertion of any claim or defense, or the response to any request by any other party, was taken primarily for the purpose of unreasonable delay, the court shall award damages to the moving party for its reasonable expenses incurred in obtaining the order, which may include attorney's fees, and other loss resulting from the improper delay.

(3) Notwithstanding subsections (1) and (2), monetary sanctions may not be awarded:

(a) Under paragraph (1)(b) if the court determines that the claim or defense was initially presented to the court as a good faith argument for the extension, modification, or reversal of existing law or the establishment of new law, as it applied to the material facts, with a reasonable expectation of success.

(b) Under paragraph (1)(a) or paragraph (1)(b) against the losing party's attorney if he or she has acted in good faith, based on the representations of his or her client as to the existence of those material facts.

(c) Under paragraph (1)(b) against a represented party.

(d) On the court's initiative under subsections (1) and (2) unless sanctions are awarded before a voluntary dismissal or settlement of the claims made by or against the party that is, or whose attorneys are, to be sanctioned.

(4) A motion by a party seeking sanctions under this section must be served but may not be filed with or presented to the court unless, within 21 days after service of the motion, the challenged paper, claim, defense, contention, allegation, or denial is not withdrawn or appropriately corrected.

(5) In administrative proceedings under chapter 120, an administrative law judge shall award a reasonable attorney's fee and damages to be paid to the prevailing party in equal amounts by the losing party and a losing party's attorney or qualified representative in the same manner and upon the same basis as provided in subsections (1)-(4). Such award shall be a final order subject to judicial review pursuant to s. 120.68. If the losing party is an agency as defined in s. 120.52(1), the award to the prevailing party shall be against and paid by the agency. A voluntary dismissal by a nonprevailing party does not divest the administrative law judge of jurisdiction to make the award described in this subsection.

(6) The provisions of this section are supplemental to other sanctions or remedies available under law or under court rules.

(7) If a contract contains a provision allowing attorney's fees to a party when he or she is required to take any action to enforce the contract, the court may also allow reasonable attorney's fees to the other party when that party prevails in any action, whether as plaintiff or defendant, with respect to the contract. This subsection applies to any contract entered into on or after October 1, 1988.

57.111. Civil actions and administrative proceedings initiated by state agencies; attorneys' fees and costs.

(1) This section may be cited as the "Florida Equal Access to Justice Act."

(2) The Legislature finds that certain persons may be deterred from seeking review of, or defending against, unreasonable governmental action because of the expense of civil actions and administrative proceedings. Because of the greater resources of the state, the standard for an award of attorney's fees and costs against the state should be different from the standard for an award

against a private litigant. The purpose of this section is to diminish the deterrent effect of seeking review of, or defending against, governmental action by providing in certain situations an award of attorney's fees and costs against the state.

(3) As used in this section:

(a) The term "attorney's fees and costs" means the reasonable and necessary attorney's fees and costs incurred for all preparations, motions, hearings, trials, and appeals in a proceeding.

(b) The term "initiated by a state agency" means that the state agency:

1. Filed the first pleading in any state or federal court in this state;

2. Filed a request for an administrative hearing pursuant to chapter 120; or

3. Was required by law or rule to advise a small business party of a clear point of entry after some recognizable event in the investigatory or other free-form proceeding of the agency.

(c) A small business party is a "prevailing small business party" when:

1. A final judgment or order has been entered in favor of the small business party and such judgment or order has not been reversed on appeal or the time for seeking judicial review of the judgment or order has expired;

2. A settlement has been obtained by the small business party which is favorable to the small business party on the majority of issues which such party raised during the course of the proceeding; or

3. The state agency has sought a voluntary dismissal of its complaint.

(d) The term "small business party" means:

1.a. A sole proprietor of an unincorporated business, including a professional practice, whose principal office is in this state, who is domiciled in this state, and whose business or professional practice has, at the time the action is initiated by a state agency, not more than 25 full-time employees or a net worth of not more than $2 million, including both personal and business investments;

b. A partnership or corporation, including a professional practice, which has its principal office in this state and has at the time the action is initiated by a state agency not more than 25 full-time employees or a net worth of not more than $2 million; or

c. An individual whose net worth did not exceed $2 million at the time the action is initiated by a state agency when the action is brought against that individual's license to engage in the practice or operation of a business, profession, or trade; or

2. Any small business party as defined in subparagraph 1., without regard to the number of its employees or its net worth, in any action under s. 72.011 or in any administrative proceeding under that section to contest the legality of any assessment of tax imposed for the sale or use of services as provided in chapter 212, or interest thereon, or penalty therefor.

(e) A proceeding is "substantially justified" if it had a reasonable basis in law and fact at the time it was initiated by a state agency.

(f) The term "state agency" has the meaning described in s. 120.52(1).

(4)(a) Unless otherwise provided by law, an award of attorney's fees and costs shall be made to a prevailing small business party in any adjudicatory proceeding or administrative proceeding pursuant to chapter 120 initiated by a state agency, unless the actions of the agency were substantially justified or special circumstances exist which would make the award unjust.

(b)1. To apply for an award under this section, the attorney for the prevailing small business party must submit an itemized affidavit to the court which first conducted the adversarial proceeding in the underlying action, or by electronic means through the division's website to the Division of Administrative Hearings which shall assign an administrative law judge, in the case of a proceeding pursuant to chapter 120, which affidavit shall reveal the nature and extent of the services rendered by the attorney as well as the costs incurred in preparations, motions, hearings, and appeals in the proceeding.

2. The application for an award of attorney's fees must be made within 60 days after the date that the small business party becomes a prevailing small business party.

(c) The state agency may oppose the application for the award of attorney's fees and costs by affidavit.

(d) The court, or the administrative law judge in the case of a proceeding under chapter 120, shall promptly conduct an evidentiary hearing on the application for an award of attorney's fees and shall issue a judgment, or a final order in the case of an administrative law judge. The final order of an administrative law judge is reviewable in accordance with the provisions of s. 120.68. If the court affirms the award of attorney's fees and costs in whole or in part, it may, in its discretion, award additional attorney's fees and costs for the appeal.

1. No award of attorney's fees and costs shall be made in any case in which the state agency was a nominal party.

2. No award of attorney's fees and costs for an action initiated by a state agency shall exceed $50,000.

(5) If the state agency fails to tender payment of the award of attorney's fees and costs within 30 days after the date that the order or judgment becomes final, the prevailing small business party may petition the circuit court where the subject matter of the underlying action arose for enforcement of the award by writ of mandamus, including additional attorney's fees and costs incurred for issuance of the writ.

(6) This section does not apply to any proceeding involving the establishment of a rate or rule or to any action sounding in tort.

57.115. Execution on judgments; attorney's fees and costs.

(1) The court may award against a judgment debtor reasonable costs and attorney's fees incurred thereafter by a judgment creditor in connection with execution on a judgment.

(2) In determining the amount of costs, including attorney's fees, if any, to be awarded under this section, the court shall consider:

(a) Whether the judgment debtor had attempted to avoid or evade the payment of the judgment; and

(b) Other factors as may be appropriate in determining the value of the services provided or the necessity for incurring costs in connection with the execution.

CHAPTER 59. APPELLATE PROCEEDINGS

59.04. Appeal from order granting new trial.

Upon the entry of an order granting a new trial, the party aggrieved may prosecute an appeal to the proper appellate court without waiting for final judgment. If the judgment is reversed, the appellate court may direct that final judgment be entered in the trial court for the party obtaining the verdict unless a motion in arrest of judgment or for a judgment notwithstanding the verdict be made and prevail.

59.041. Harmless error; effect.

No judgment shall be set aside or reversed, or new trial granted by any court of the state in any cause, civil or criminal, on the ground of misdirection of the jury or the improper admission or rejection of evidence or for error as to any matter of pleading or procedure, unless in the opinion of the court to which application is made, after an examination of the entire case it shall appear that the error complained of has resulted in a miscarriage of justice. This section shall be liberally construed.

59.06. Matters reviewable on appeal.

(1) WHAT MAY BE ASSIGNED AS ERROR.—All judgments and orders made in any action wherein the trial court:
(a) May allow or refuse to allow any motion:
1. For a new trial or rehearing,
2. For leave to amend pleadings,
3. For leave to file new or additional pleadings,
4. To amend the record, or
5. For continuance of the action; or
(b) Shall sustain or overrule any motion to dismiss the action
(2) EFFECT OF PLEADING OVER OR AMENDING.—Pleading over or amending pleadings after order upon motion to dismiss shall not waive the right to have the judgment or order reviewed.

59.081. Time for invoking appellate jurisdiction of any court.

(1) The time within which and the method by which the jurisdiction of any court in this state possessed of power to review the action of any other court, commission, officer or bureau may be invoked by appeal, certiorari, petition for review or other process by whatever name designated, and the manner of computing such time shall be prescribed by rule of the Supreme Court.
(2) Failure to invoke the jurisdiction of any such court within the time prescribed by such rules shall divest such court of jurisdiction to review such cause.

59.13. Supersedeas on petition for certiorari.

When it appears to the trial court that a petition for certiorari has been or is about to be applied for in an appellate court, the trial court may grant a supersedeas upon petitioner giving a good and sufficient bond, conditioned that the petition shall be duly presented to the appellate court within the time prescribed by the Florida Rules of Appellate Procedure and to pay all costs, damages, and expenses occasioned by reason of the stay of proceedings with such other and further conditions as may be fixed by the trial court in the event the order or judgment for which a review is sought is not quashed, modified or reversed.

59.15. Proceedings in pais; authentication.

Proceedings in pais, not stenographically reported, may be authenticated by recitals in orders, judgments, or decrees, of the trial court, or of the judge thereof, or by a stipulation by the interested parties.

59.29. Amendment of appellate proceedings.

The appellate court may, at any time, in the furtherance of justice, upon such terms as may be just, permit appellate proceedings to be amended.

59.33. Quashing appeals; power of appellate court.

Appellate courts shall have power to quash appeals in all cases in which appeals do not lie, or where they are taken against good faith or merely for delay, and may decree in such case damages against the appellant not exceeding 10 percent.

59.35. Judgment; power of appellate court to direct a new trial upon one or more issues.

An appellate court may, in reversing a judgment of a lower court brought before it for review by appeal, by the order of reversal, if the error for which reversal is sought is such as to require a new trial, direct that a new trial be had on all the issues shown by the record or upon a part of such issues only. When a reversal is had, with direction for new trial on a part of the issues, all other issues shall be deemed settled conclusively in favor of the appellee.

59.45. Misconception of remedy; Supreme Court.

If an appeal be improvidently taken where the remedy might have been more properly sought by certiorari, this alone shall not be a ground for dismissal; but the notice of appeal and the record thereon shall be regarded and acted on as a petition for certiorari duly presented to the Supreme Court.

59.46. Attorney's fees.

In the absence of an expressed contrary intent, any provision of a statute or of a contract entered into after October 1, 1977, providing for the payment of attorney's fees to the prevailing party shall be construed to include the payment of attorney's fees to the prevailing party on appeal.

CHAPTER 60. INJUNCTIONS

60.01. Injunction; against levy of execution issued against another than the plaintiff.

When real estate is levied on, or an attempt to sell it under any execution or other process issued is made, or an attempt to sell it as the property of another person is made, chancery courts have jurisdiction to enjoin the sale on the application of the owner in possession of the real estate.

60.03. Injunction against removal of mortgaged personal property.

The removal from the state of any personal property mortgaged to secure a debt which has not matured at the time of the removal may be enjoined by any chancery court within whose territorial jurisdiction the property is located.

60.04. Injunction; sureties on bond of fiduciaries may restrain disposition of principal's property.

When actions are commenced on the bond of any executor, administrator, guardian or trustee, or for an accounting, the surety on the bond may apply to the court in which the action is pending, if in chancery, or if the action is at law, then to any chancery court having jurisdiction, for an injunction restraining any principal in the bond from disposing of his or her property and from encumbering or removing it from the county in which it is located until the final disposition of the action. If it appears on the application that there is danger that the principal may dispose of his or her property before final judgment so that there will not be sufficient property of the principal to satisfy any judgment that is rendered against the administrator, executor, guardian or trustee, the court shall issue an injunction on such terms as are proper, enjoining such principal from disposing of his or her property, or so much thereof as is necessary for the protection of the surety until the final disposition of the action. It is not necessary for the surety to show that any amounts are due by said administrator, executor, guardian or trustee but the judge granting the injunction may vacate it on the executor, administrator, guardian or trustee giving adequate security, to be approved by the court, to the surety conditioned to save him or her harmless for all loss or damage he or she sustains as surety.

60.05. Abatement of nuisances.

(1) When any nuisance as defined in s. 823.05 exists, the Attorney General, state attorney, city attorney, county attorney, or any citizen of the county may sue in the name of the state on his or her relation to enjoin the nuisance, the person or persons maintaining it, and the owner or agent of the building or ground on which the nuisance exists.
(2) The court may allow a temporary injunction without bond on proper proof being made. If it appears by evidence or affidavit that a temporary injunction should issue, the court, pending the determination on final hearing, may enjoin:
(a) The maintaining of a nuisance;
(b) The operating and maintaining of the place or premises where the nuisance is maintained;
(c) The owner or agent of the building or ground upon which the nuisance exists;
(d) The conduct, operation, or maintenance of any business or activity operated or maintained in the building or on the premises in connection with or incident to the maintenance of the nuisance.
(3) Evidence of the general reputation of the alleged nuisance and place is admissible to prove the existence of the nuisance. No action filed by a citizen shall be dismissed unless the court is satisfied that it should be dismissed. Otherwise the action shall continue and the state attorney notified to proceed with it. If the action is brought by a citizen and the court finds that there was no reasonable ground for the action, the costs shall be taxed against the citizen.
(4) On trial if the existence of a nuisance is shown, the court shall issue a permanent injunction

and order the costs to be paid by the persons establishing or maintaining the nuisance and shall adjudge that the costs are a lien on all personal property found in the place of the nuisance and on the failure of the property to bring enough to pay the costs, then on the real estate occupied by the nuisance. No lien shall attach to the real estate of any other than said persons unless 5 days' written notice has been given to the owner or his or her agent who fails to begin to abate the nuisance within said 5 days. In a proceeding abating a nuisance pursuant to s. 823.10 or s. 823.05, if a tenant has been convicted of an offense under chapter 893 or s. 796.07, the court may order the tenant to vacate the property within 72 hours if the tenant and owner of the premises are parties to the nuisance abatement action and the order will lead to the abatement of the nuisance.

(5) If the action was brought by the Attorney General, a state attorney, or any other officer or agency of state government; if the court finds either before or after trial that there was no reasonable ground for the action; and if judgment is rendered for the defendant, the costs and reasonable attorney's fees shall be taxed against the state.

60.06. Abatement of nuisances; enforcement.

The court shall make such orders on proper proof as will abate all nuisances mentioned in s. 823.05, and has authority to enforce injunctions by contempt but the jurisdiction hereby granted does not repeal or alter s. 823.01.

60.07. Assessment of damages after dissolution.

In injunction actions, on dissolution, the court may hear evidence and assess damages to which a defendant may be entitled under any injunction bond, eliminating the necessity for an action on the injunction bond if no party has requested a jury trial on damages.

60.08. Injunctions sought by the state pursuant to statute shall issue without bond.

In any action for injunctive relief sought by the state or one of its agencies as provided in ss. 501.207(1)(b), 542.23, and 895.05(5), any injunction sought shall issue without bond or surety and no bond or surety shall be required during the term of the injunction.

CHAPTER 61. DISSOLUTION OF MARRIAGE; SUPPORT; TIME-SHARING

PART I. GENERAL PROVISIONS (SS. 61.001-61.45)

61.001. Purpose of chapter.

(1) This chapter shall be liberally construed and applied.
(2) Its purposes are:

(a) To preserve the integrity of marriage and to safeguard meaningful family relationships;

(b) To promote the amicable settlement of disputes that arise between parties to a marriage; and

(c) To mitigate the potential harm to the spouses and their children caused by the process of legal dissolution of marriage.

61.011. Dissolution in chancery.

Proceedings under this chapter are in chancery.

61.021. Residence requirements.

To obtain a dissolution of marriage, one of the parties to the marriage must reside 6 months in the state before the filing of the petition.

61.031. Dissolution of marriage to be a vinculo.

No dissolution of marriage is from bed and board, but is from bonds of matrimony.

61.0401. Application of the law of a foreign country in courts relating to matters arising out of or relating to this chapter and chapter 88.

(1) As used in this section, the term "strong public policy" means public policy of sufficient importance to outweigh the policy of protecting freedom of contract.

(2) A court may not enforce:

(a) A choice of law provision in a contract selecting the law of a foreign country which contravenes the strong public policy of this state or that is unjust or unreasonable.

(b) A forum selection clause in a contract that selects a forum in a foreign country if the clause is shown to be unreasonable or unjust or if strong public policy would prohibit the enforceability of the clause under the specific facts of the case.

(3) Before enforcing a judgment or order of a court of a foreign country, a court must review the judgment or order to ensure that it complies with the rule of comity. A judgment or order of a court of a foreign country is not entitled to comity if the parties were not given adequate notice and the opportunity to be heard, the foreign court did not have jurisdiction, or the judgment or order of the foreign court offends the public policy of this state. As used in this subsection, a "foreign court" or "court of a foreign country" includes any court or tribunal that has jurisdiction under the laws of that nation over the subject of matters governed by this chapter or chapter 88.

(4) Any attempt to apply the law of a foreign country is void if it contravenes the strong public policy of this state or if the law is unjust or unreasonable.

(5) A trial court may not dismiss an action on the grounds that a satisfactory remedy may be more conveniently sought in a foreign country unless the trial court finds in accordance with all the applicable rules of civil procedure and this section that an adequate alternate forum exists.

(6) This section applies only to matters governed by or relating to this chapter or chapter 88.

61.043. Commencement of a proceeding for dissolution of marriage or for alimony and child support; dissolution questionnaire.

(1) A proceeding for dissolution of marriage or a proceeding under s. 61.09 shall be commenced by filing in the circuit court a petition entitled "In re the marriage of , husband, and , wife." A copy of the petition together with a copy of a summons shall be served upon the other party to the marriage in the same manner as service of papers in civil actions generally.

(2) Upon filing for dissolution of marriage, the petitioner must complete and file with the clerk of the circuit court an unsigned anonymous informational questionnaire. For purposes of anonymity, completed questionnaires must be kept in a separate file for later distribution by the clerk to researchers from the Florida State University Center for Marriage and Family. These questionnaires must be made available to researchers from the Florida State University Center for Marriage and Family at their request. The actual questionnaire shall be formulated by researchers from Florida State University who shall distribute them to the clerk of the circuit court in each county.

61.044. Certain existing defenses abolished.

The defenses to divorce and legal separation of condonation, collusion, recrimination, and laches are abolished.

61.046. Definitions.

As used in this chapter, the term:

(1) "Business day" means any day other than a Saturday, Sunday, or legal holiday.

(2) "Clerk of Court Child Support Collection System" or "CLERC System" means the automated system established pursuant to s. 61.181(2)(b)1., integrating all clerks of court and depositories and through which payment data and State Case Registry data is transmitted to the department's automated child support enforcement system.

(3) "Department" means the Department of Revenue.

(4) "Depository" means the central governmental depository established pursuant to s. 61.181, created by special act of the Legislature or other entity established before June 1, 1985, to perform depository functions and to receive, record, report, disburse, monitor, and otherwise handle alimony and child support payments not otherwise required to be processed by the State Disbursement Unit.

(5) "Electronic communication" means contact, other than face-to-face contact, facilitated by tools such as telephones, electronic mail or e-mail, webcams, video-conferencing equipment and software or other wired or wireless technologies, or other means of communication to supplement face-to-face contact between a parent and that parent's minor child.

(6) "Federal Case Registry of Child Support Orders" means the automated registry of support order abstracts and other information established and maintained by the United States Department of Health and Human Services as provided by 42 U.S.C. s. 653(h).

(7) "Health insurance" means coverage under a fee-for-service arrangement, health maintenance organization, or preferred provider organization, and other types of coverage available to either parent, under which medical services could be provided to a dependent child.

(8) "Income" means any form of payment to an individual, regardless of source, including, but not limited to: wages, salary, commissions and bonuses, compensation as an independent contractor,

worker's compensation, disability benefits, annuity and retirement benefits, pensions, dividends, interest, royalties, trusts, and any other payments, made by any person, private entity, federal or state government, or any unit of local government. United States Department of Veterans Affairs disability benefits and reemployment assistance or unemployment compensation, as defined in chapter 443, are excluded from this definition of income except for purposes of establishing an amount of support.

(9) "IV-D" means services provided pursuant to Title IV-D of the Social Security Act, 42 U.S.C. ss. 651 et seq.

(10) "Local officer" means an elected or appointed constitutional or charter government official including, but not limited to, the state attorney and clerk of the circuit court.

(11) "National medical support notice" means the notice required under 42 U.S.C. s. 666(a)(19).

(12) "Obligee" means the person to whom payments are made pursuant to an order establishing, enforcing, or modifying an obligation for alimony, for child support, or for alimony and child support.

(13) "Obligor" means a person responsible for making payments pursuant to an order establishing, enforcing, or modifying an obligation for alimony, for child support, or for alimony and child support.

(14) "Parenting plan" means a document created to govern the relationship between the parents relating to decisions that must be made regarding the minor child and must contain a time-sharing schedule for the parents and child. The issues concerning the minor child may include, but are not limited to, the child's education, health care, and physical, social, and emotional well-being. In creating the plan, all circumstances between the parents, including their historic relationship, domestic violence, and other factors must be taken into consideration.

(a) The parenting plan must be:

1. Developed and agreed to by the parents and approved by a court; or

2. Established by the court, with or without the use of a court-ordered parenting plan recommendation, if the parents cannot agree to a plan or the parents agreed to a plan that is not approved by the court.

(b) Any parenting plan formulated under this chapter must address all jurisdictional issues, including the Uniform Child Custody Jurisdiction and Enforcement Act, part II of this chapter, the International Child Abduction Remedies Act, 42 U.S.C. ss. 11601 et seq., the Parental Kidnapping Prevention Act, and the Convention on the Civil Aspects of International Child Abduction enacted at the Hague on October 25, 1980.

(c) For purposes of the Uniform Child Custody Jurisdiction and Enforcement Act, part II of this chapter, a judgment or order incorporating a parenting plan under this part is a child custody determination under part II of this chapter.

(d) For purposes of the International Child Abduction Remedies Act, 42 U.S.C. ss. 11601 et seq., and the Convention on the Civil Aspects of International Child Abduction, enacted at the Hague on October 25, 1980, rights of custody and rights of access are determined pursuant to the parenting plan under this part.

(15) "Parenting plan recommendation" means a nonbinding recommendation concerning one or more elements of a parenting plan made by a court-appointed mental health practitioner or other professional designated pursuant to s. 61.20, s. 61.401, or Florida Family Law Rules of Procedure 12.363.

(16) "Payor" means an employer or former employer or any other person or agency providing or administering income to the obligor.

(17) "Shared parental responsibility" means a court-ordered relationship in which both parents retain full parental rights and responsibilities with respect to their child and in which both parents confer with each other so that major decisions affecting the welfare of the child will be determined jointly.

(18) "Sole parental responsibility" means a court-ordered relationship in which one parent makes decisions regarding the minor child.

(19) "State Case Registry" means the automated registry maintained by the Title IV-D agency,

containing records of each Title IV-D case and of each support order established or modified in the state on or after October 1, 1998. Such records shall consist of data elements as required by the United States Secretary of Health and Human Services.

(20) "State Disbursement Unit" means the unit established and operated by the Title IV-D agency to provide one central address for collection and disbursement of child support payments made in cases enforced by the department pursuant to Title IV-D of the Social Security Act and in cases not being enforced by the department in which the support order was initially issued in this state on or after January 1, 1994, and in which the obligor's child support obligation is being paid through income deduction order.

(21) "Support order" means a judgment, decree, or order, whether temporary or final, issued by a court of competent jurisdiction or administrative agency for the support and maintenance of a child which provides for monetary support, health care, arrearages, or past support. When the child support obligation is being enforced by the Department of Revenue, the term "support order" also means a judgment, decree, or order, whether temporary or final, issued by a court of competent jurisdiction for the support and maintenance of a child and the spouse or former spouse of the obligor with whom the child is living which provides for monetary support, health care, arrearages, or past support.

(22) "Support," unless otherwise specified, means:

(a) Child support and, when the child support obligation is being enforced by the Department of Revenue, spousal support or alimony for the spouse or former spouse of the obligor with whom the child is living.

(b) Child support only in cases not being enforced by the Department of Revenue.

(23) "Time-sharing schedule" means a timetable that must be included in the parenting plan that specifies the time, including overnights and holidays, that a minor child will spend with each parent. The time-sharing schedule shall be:

(a) Developed and agreed to by the parents of a minor child and approved by the court; or

(b) Established by the court if the parents cannot agree or if their agreed-upon schedule is not approved by the court.

61.052. Dissolution of marriage.

(1) No judgment of dissolution of marriage shall be granted unless one of the following facts appears, which shall be pleaded generally:

(a) The marriage is irretrievably broken.

(b) Mental incapacity of one of the parties. However, no dissolution shall be allowed unless the party alleged to be incapacitated shall have been adjudged incapacitated according to the provisions of s. 744.331 for a preceding period of at least 3 years. Notice of the proceeding for dissolution shall be served upon one of the nearest blood relatives or guardian of the incapacitated person, and the relative or guardian shall be entitled to appear and to be heard upon the issues. If the incapacitated party has a general guardian other than the party bringing the proceeding, the petition and summons shall be served upon the incapacitated party and the guardian; and the guardian shall defend and protect the interests of the incapacitated party. If the incapacitated party has no guardian other than the party bringing the proceeding, the court shall appoint a guardian ad litem to defend and protect the interests of the incapacitated party. However, in all dissolutions of marriage granted on the basis of incapacity, the court may require the petitioner to pay alimony pursuant to the provisions of s. 61.08.

(2) Based on the evidence at the hearing, which evidence need not be corroborated except to establish that the residence requirements of s. 61.021 are met which may be corroborated by a valid Florida driver license, a Florida voter's registration card, a valid Florida identification card issued under s. 322.051, or the testimony or affidavit of a third party, the court shall dispose of the petition for dissolution of marriage when the petition is based on the allegation that the marriage is

irretrievably broken as follows:

(a) If there is no minor child of the marriage and if the responding party does not, by answer to the petition for dissolution, deny that the marriage is irretrievably broken, the court shall enter a judgment of dissolution of the marriage if the court finds that the marriage is irretrievably broken.

(b) When there is a minor child of the marriage, or when the responding party denies by answer to the petition for dissolution that the marriage is irretrievably broken, the court may:

1. Order either or both parties to consult with a marriage counselor, psychologist, psychiatrist, minister, priest, rabbi, or any other person deemed qualified by the court and acceptable to the party or parties ordered to seek consultation; or

2. Continue the proceedings for a reasonable length of time not to exceed 3 months, to enable the parties themselves to effect a reconciliation; or

3. Take such other action as may be in the best interest of the parties and the minor child of the marriage.

(3) During any period of continuance, the court may make appropriate orders for the support and alimony of the parties; the parenting plan, support, maintenance, and education of the minor child of the marriage; attorney's fees; and the preservation of the property of the parties.

(4) A judgment of dissolution of marriage shall result in each spouse having the status of being single and unmarried. No judgment of dissolution of marriage renders the child of the marriage a child born out of wedlock.

(5) The court may enforce an antenuptial agreement to arbitrate a dispute in accordance with the law and tradition chosen by the parties.

(6) Any injunction for protection against domestic violence arising out of the dissolution of marriage proceeding shall be issued as a separate order in compliance with chapter 741 and shall not be included in the judgment of dissolution of marriage.

(7) In the initial pleading for a dissolution of marriage as a separate attachment to the pleading, each party is required to provide his or her social security number and the full names and social security numbers of each of the minor children of the marriage.

(8) Pursuant to the federal Personal Responsibility and Work Opportunity Reconciliation Act of 1996, each party is required to provide his or her social security number in accordance with this section. Each party is also required to provide the full name, date of birth, and social security number for each minor child of the marriage. Disclosure of social security numbers obtained through this requirement shall be limited to the purpose of administration of the Title IV-D program for child support enforcement.

61.061. Proceedings against nonresidents.

Proceedings may be brought against persons residing out of the state.

61.071. Alimony pendente lite; suit money.

In every proceeding for dissolution of the marriage, a party may claim alimony and suit money in the petition or by motion, and if the petition is well founded, the court shall allow a reasonable sum therefor. If a party in any proceeding for dissolution of marriage claims alimony or suit money in his or her answer or by motion, and the answer or motion is well founded, the court shall allow a reasonable sum therefor.

61.075. Equitable distribution of marital assets and liabilities.

(1) In a proceeding for dissolution of marriage, in addition to all other remedies available to a court to do equity between the parties, or in a proceeding for disposition of assets following a dissolution of marriage by a court which lacked jurisdiction over the absent spouse or lacked jurisdiction to dispose of the assets, the court shall set apart to each spouse that spouse's nonmarital assets and liabilities, and in distributing the marital assets and liabilities between the parties, the court must begin with the premise that the distribution should be equal, unless there is a justification for an unequal distribution based on all relevant factors, including:

(a) The contribution to the marriage by each spouse, including contributions to the care and education of the children and services as homemaker.

(b) The economic circumstances of the parties.

(c) The duration of the marriage.

(d) Any interruption of personal careers or educational opportunities of either party.

(e) The contribution of one spouse to the personal career or educational opportunity of the other spouse.

(f) The desirability of retaining any asset, including an interest in a business, corporation, or professional practice, intact and free from any claim or interference by the other party.

(g) The contribution of each spouse to the acquisition, enhancement, and production of income or the improvement of, or the incurring of liabilities to, both the marital assets and the nonmarital assets of the parties.

(h) The desirability of retaining the marital home as a residence for any dependent child of the marriage, or any other party, when it would be equitable to do so, it is in the best interest of the child or that party, and it is financially feasible for the parties to maintain the residence until the child is emancipated or until exclusive possession is otherwise terminated by a court of competent jurisdiction. In making this determination, the court shall first determine if it would be in the best interest of the dependent child to remain in the marital home; and, if not, whether other equities would be served by giving any other party exclusive use and possession of the marital home.

(i) The intentional dissipation, waste, depletion, or destruction of marital assets after the filing of the petition or within 2 years prior to the filing of the petition.

(j) Any other factors necessary to do equity and justice between the parties.

(2) If the court awards a cash payment for the purpose of equitable distribution of marital assets, to be paid in full or in installments, the full amount ordered shall vest when the judgment is awarded and the award shall not terminate upon remarriage or death of either party, unless otherwise agreed to by the parties, but shall be treated as a debt owed from the obligor or the obligor's estate to the obligee or the obligee's estate, unless otherwise agreed to by the parties.

(3) In any contested dissolution action wherein a stipulation and agreement has not been entered and filed, any distribution of marital assets or marital liabilities shall be supported by factual findings in the judgment or order based on competent substantial evidence with reference to the factors enumerated in subsection (1). The distribution of all marital assets and marital liabilities, whether equal or unequal, shall include specific written findings of fact as to the following:

(a) Clear identification of nonmarital assets and ownership interests;

(b) Identification of marital assets, including the individual valuation of significant assets, and designation of which spouse shall be entitled to each asset;

(c) Identification of the marital liabilities and designation of which spouse shall be responsible for each liability;

(d) Any other findings necessary to advise the parties or the reviewing court of the trial court's rationale for the distribution of marital assets and allocation of liabilities.

(4) The judgment distributing assets shall have the effect of a duly executed instrument of conveyance, transfer, release, or acquisition which is recorded in the county where the property is

located when the judgment, or a certified copy of the judgment, is recorded in the official records of the county in which the property is located.

(5) If the court finds good cause that there should be an interim partial distribution during the pendency of a dissolution action, the court may enter an interim order that shall identify and value the marital and nonmarital assets and liabilities made the subject of the sworn motion, set apart those nonmarital assets and liabilities, and provide for a partial distribution of those marital assets and liabilities. An interim order may be entered at any time after the date the dissolution of marriage is filed and served and before the final distribution of marital and nonmarital assets and marital and nonmarital liabilities.

(a) Such an interim order shall be entered only upon good cause shown and upon sworn motion establishing specific factual basis for the motion. The motion may be filed by either party and shall demonstrate good cause why the matter should not be deferred until the final hearing.

(b) The court shall specifically take into account and give appropriate credit for any partial distribution of marital assets or liabilities in its final allocation of marital assets or liabilities. Further, the court shall make specific findings in any interim order under this section that any partial distribution will not cause inequity or prejudice to either party as to either party's claims for support or attorney's fees.

(c) Any interim order partially distributing marital assets or liabilities as provided in this subsection shall be pursuant to and comport with the factors in subsections (1) and (3) as such factors pertain to the assets or liabilities made the subject of the sworn motion.

(d) As used in this subsection, the term "good cause" means extraordinary circumstances that require an interim partial distribution.

(6) As used in this section:

(a)1. "Marital assets and liabilities" include:

a. Assets acquired and liabilities incurred during the marriage, individually by either spouse or jointly by them.

b. The enhancement in value and appreciation of nonmarital assets resulting either from the efforts of either party during the marriage or from the contribution to or expenditure thereon of marital funds or other forms of marital assets, or both.

c. Interspousal gifts during the marriage.

d. All vested and nonvested benefits, rights, and funds accrued during the marriage in retirement, pension, profit-sharing, annuity, deferred compensation, and insurance plans and programs.

2. All real property held by the parties as tenants by the entireties, whether acquired prior to or during the marriage, shall be presumed to be a marital asset. If, in any case, a party makes a claim to the contrary, the burden of proof shall be on the party asserting the claim that the subject property, or some portion thereof, is nonmarital.

3. All personal property titled jointly by the parties as tenants by the entireties, whether acquired prior to or during the marriage, shall be presumed to be a marital asset. In the event a party makes a claim to the contrary, the burden of proof shall be on the party asserting the claim that the subject property, or some portion thereof, is nonmarital.

4. The burden of proof to overcome the gift presumption shall be by clear and convincing evidence.

(b) "Nonmarital assets and liabilities" include:

1. Assets acquired and liabilities incurred by either party prior to the marriage, and assets acquired and liabilities incurred in exchange for such assets and liabilities;

2. Assets acquired separately by either party by noninterspousal gift, bequest, devise, or descent, and assets acquired in exchange for such assets;

3. All income derived from nonmarital assets during the marriage unless the income was treated, used, or relied upon by the parties as a marital asset;

4. Assets and liabilities excluded from marital assets and liabilities by valid written agreement of the parties, and assets acquired and liabilities incurred in exchange for such assets and liabilities; and

5. Any liability incurred by forgery or unauthorized signature of one spouse signing the name of

the other spouse. Any such liability shall be a nonmarital liability only of the party having committed the forgery or having affixed the unauthorized signature. In determining an award of attorney's fees and costs pursuant to s. 61.16, the court may consider forgery or an unauthorized signature by a party and may make a separate award for attorney's fees and costs occasioned by the forgery or unauthorized signature. This subparagraph does not apply to any forged or unauthorized signature that was subsequently ratified by the other spouse.

(7) The cut-off date for determining assets and liabilities to be identified or classified as marital assets and liabilities is the earliest of the date the parties enter into a valid separation agreement, such other date as may be expressly established by such agreement, or the date of the filing of a petition for dissolution of marriage. The date for determining value of assets and the amount of liabilities identified or classified as marital is the date or dates as the judge determines is just and equitable under the circumstances. Different assets may be valued as of different dates, as, in the judge's discretion, the circumstances require.

(8) All assets acquired and liabilities incurred by either spouse subsequent to the date of the marriage and not specifically established as nonmarital assets or liabilities are presumed to be marital assets and liabilities. Such presumption is overcome by a showing that the assets and liabilities are nonmarital assets and liabilities. The presumption is only for evidentiary purposes in the dissolution proceeding and does not vest title. Title to disputed assets shall vest only by the judgment of a court. This section does not require the joinder of spouses in the conveyance, transfer, or hypothecation of a spouse's individual property; affect the laws of descent and distribution; or establish community property in this state.

(9) The court may provide for equitable distribution of the marital assets and liabilities without regard to alimony for either party. After the determination of an equitable distribution of the marital assets and liabilities, the court shall consider whether a judgment for alimony shall be made.

(10) To do equity between the parties, the court may, in lieu of or to supplement, facilitate, or effectuate the equitable division of marital assets and liabilities, order a monetary payment in a lump sum or in installments paid over a fixed period of time.

(11) Special equity is abolished. All claims formerly identified as special equity, and all special equity calculations, are abolished and shall be asserted either as a claim for unequal distribution of marital property and resolved by the factors set forth in subsection (1) or as a claim of enhancement in value or appreciation of nonmarital property.

61.076. Distribution of retirement plans upon dissolution of marriage.

(1) All vested and nonvested benefits, rights, and funds accrued during the marriage in retirement, pension, profit-sharing, annuity, deferred compensation, and insurance plans and programs are marital assets subject to equitable distribution.

(2) If the parties were married for at least 10 years, during which at least one of the parties who was a member of the federal uniformed services performed at least 10 years of creditable service, and if the division of marital property includes a division of uniformed services retired or retainer pay, the final judgment shall include the following:

(a) Sufficient information to identify the member of the uniformed services;

(b) Certification that the Servicemembers Civil Relief Act was observed if the decree was issued while the member was on active duty and was not represented in court;

(c) A specification of the amount of retired or retainer pay to be distributed pursuant to the order, expressed in dollars or as a percentage of the disposable retired or retainer pay.

(3) An order which provides for distribution of retired or retainer pay from the federal uniformed services shall not provide for payment from this source more frequently than monthly and shall

not require the payor to vary normal pay and disbursement cycles for retired or retainer pay in order to comply with the order.

61.077. Determination of entitlement to setoffs or credits upon sale of marital home.

A party is not entitled to any credits or setoffs upon the sale of the marital home unless the parties' settlement agreement, final judgment of dissolution of marriage, or final judgment equitably distributing assets or debts specifically provides that certain credits or setoffs are allowed or given at the time of the sale. In the absence of a settlement agreement involving the marital home, the court shall consider the following factors before determining the issue of credits or setoffs in its final judgment:

(1) Whether exclusive use and possession of the marital home is being awarded, and the basis for the award;

(2) Whether alimony is being awarded to the party in possession and whether the alimony is being awarded to cover, in part or otherwise, the mortgage and taxes and other expenses of and in connection with the marital home;

(3) Whether child support is being awarded to the party in possession and whether the child support is being awarded to cover, in part or otherwise, the mortgage and taxes and other expenses of and in connection with the marital home;

(4) The value to the party in possession of the use and occupancy of the marital home;

(5) The value of the loss of use and occupancy of the marital home to the party out of possession;

(6) Which party will be entitled to claim the mortgage interest payments, real property tax payments, and related payments in connection with the marital home as tax deductions for federal income tax purposes;

(7) Whether one or both parties will experience a capital gains taxable event as a result of the sale of the marital home; and

(8) Any other factor necessary to bring about equity and justice between the parties.

61.079. Premarital agreements.

(1) SHORT TITLE.—This section may be cited as the "Uniform Premarital Agreement Act" and this section applies only to proceedings under the Florida Family Law Rules of Procedure.

(2) DEFINITIONS.—As used in this section, the term:

(a) "Premarital agreement" means an agreement between prospective spouses made in contemplation of marriage and to be effective upon marriage.

(b) "Property" includes, but is not limited to, an interest, present or future, legal or equitable, vested or contingent, in real or personal property, tangible or intangible, including income and earnings, both active and passive.

(3) FORMALITIES.—A premarital agreement must be in writing and signed by both parties. It is enforceable without consideration other than the marriage itself.

(4) CONTENT.—

(a) Parties to a premarital agreement may contract with respect to:

1. The rights and obligations of each of the parties in any of the property of either or both of them whenever and wherever acquired or located;

2. The right to buy, sell, use, transfer, exchange, abandon, lease, consume, expend, assign, create a security interest in, mortgage, encumber, dispose of, or otherwise manage and control property;

3. The disposition of property upon separation, marital dissolution, death, or the occurrence or nonoccurrence of any other event;

4. The establishment, modification, waiver, or elimination of spousal support;

5. The making of a will, trust, or other arrangement to carry out the provisions of the agreement;

6. The ownership rights in and disposition of the death benefit from a life insurance policy;

7. The choice of law governing the construction of the agreement; and

8. Any other matter, including their personal rights and obligations, not in violation of either the public policy of this state or a law imposing a criminal penalty.

(b) The right of a child to support may not be adversely affected by a premarital agreement.

(5) EFFECT OF MARRIAGE.—A premarital agreement becomes effective upon marriage of the parties.

(6) AMENDMENT; REVOCATION OR ABANDONMENT.—After marriage, a premarital agreement may be amended, revoked, or abandoned only by a written agreement signed by the parties. The amended agreement, revocation, or abandonment is enforceable without consideration.

(7) ENFORCEMENT.—

(a) A premarital agreement is not enforceable in an action proceeding under the Florida Family Law Rules of Procedure if the party against whom enforcement is sought proves that:

1. The party did not execute the agreement voluntarily;

2. The agreement was the product of fraud, duress, coercion, or overreaching; or

3. The agreement was unconscionable when it was executed and, before execution of the agreement, that party:

a. Was not provided a fair and reasonable disclosure of the property or financial obligations of the other party;

b. Did not voluntarily and expressly waive, in writing, any right to disclosure of the property or financial obligations of the other party beyond the disclosure provided; and

c. Did not have, or reasonably could not have had, an adequate knowledge of the property or financial obligations of the other party.

(b) If a provision of a premarital agreement modifies or eliminates spousal support and that modification or elimination causes one party to the agreement to be eligible for support under a program of public assistance at the time of separation or marital dissolution, a court, notwithstanding the terms of the agreement, may require the other party to provide support to the extent necessary to avoid that eligibility.

(c) An issue of unconscionability of a premarital agreement shall be decided by the court as a matter of law.

(8) ENFORCEMENT; VOID MARRIAGE.—If a marriage is determined to be void, an agreement that would otherwise have been a premarital agreement is enforceable only to the extent necessary to avoid an inequitable result.

(9) LIMITATION OF ACTIONS.—Any statute of limitations applicable to an action asserting a claim for relief under a premarital agreement is tolled during the marriage of the parties to the agreement. However, equitable defenses limiting the time for enforcement, including laches and estoppel, are available to either party.

(10) APPLICATION TO PROBATE CODE.—This section does not alter the construction, interpretation, or required formalities of, or the rights or obligations under, agreements between spouses under s. 732.701 or s. 732.702.

61.08. Alimony.

(1) In a proceeding for dissolution of marriage, the court may grant alimony to either party, which alimony may be bridge-the-gap, rehabilitative, durational, or permanent in nature or any combination of these forms of alimony. In any award of alimony, the court may order periodic payments or payments in lump sum or both. The court may consider the adultery of either spouse and the circumstances thereof in determining the amount of alimony, if any, to be awarded. In all

dissolution actions, the court shall include findings of fact relative to the factors enumerated in subsection (2) supporting an award or denial of alimony.

(2) In determining whether to award alimony or maintenance, the court shall first make a specific factual determination as to whether either party has an actual need for alimony or maintenance and whether either party has the ability to pay alimony or maintenance. If the court finds that a party has a need for alimony or maintenance and that the other party has the ability to pay alimony or maintenance, then in determining the proper type and amount of alimony or maintenance under subsections (5)-(8), the court shall consider all relevant factors, including, but not limited to:

(a) The standard of living established during the marriage.

(b) The duration of the marriage.

(c) The age and the physical and emotional condition of each party.

(d) The financial resources of each party, including the nonmarital and the marital assets and liabilities distributed to each.

(e) The earning capacities, educational levels, vocational skills, and employability of the parties and, when applicable, the time necessary for either party to acquire sufficient education or training to enable such party to find appropriate employment.

(f) The contribution of each party to the marriage, including, but not limited to, services rendered in homemaking, child care, education, and career building of the other party.

(g) The responsibilities each party will have with regard to any minor children they have in common.

(h) The tax treatment and consequences to both parties of any alimony award, including the designation of all or a portion of the payment as a nontaxable, nondeductible payment.

(i) All sources of income available to either party, including income available to either party through investments of any asset held by that party.

(j) Any other factor necessary to do equity and justice between the parties.

(3) To the extent necessary to protect an award of alimony, the court may order any party who is ordered to pay alimony to purchase or maintain a life insurance policy or a bond, or to otherwise secure such alimony award with any other assets which may be suitable for that purpose.

(4) For purposes of determining alimony, there is a rebuttable presumption that a short-term marriage is a marriage having a duration of less than 7 years, a moderate-term marriage is a marriage having a duration of greater than 7 years but less than 17 years, and long-term marriage is a marriage having a duration of 17 years or greater. The length of a marriage is the period of time from the date of marriage until the date of filing of an action for dissolution of marriage.

(5) Bridge-the-gap alimony may be awarded to assist a party by providing support to allow the party to make a transition from being married to being single. Bridge-the-gap alimony is designed to assist a party with legitimate identifiable short-term needs, and the length of an award may not exceed 2 years. An award of bridge-the-gap alimony terminates upon the death of either party or upon the remarriage of the party receiving alimony. An award of bridge-the-gap alimony shall not be modifiable in amount or duration.

(6)(a) Rehabilitative alimony may be awarded to assist a party in establishing the capacity for self-support through either:

1. The redevelopment of previous skills or credentials; or

2. The acquisition of education, training, or work experience necessary to develop appropriate employment skills or credentials.

(b) In order to award rehabilitative alimony, there must be a specific and defined rehabilitative plan which shall be included as a part of any order awarding rehabilitative alimony.

(c) An award of rehabilitative alimony may be modified or terminated in accordance with s. 61.14 based upon a substantial change in circumstances, upon noncompliance with the rehabilitative plan, or upon completion of the rehabilitative plan.

(7) Durational alimony may be awarded when permanent periodic alimony is inappropriate. The purpose of durational alimony is to provide a party with economic assistance for a set period of time following a marriage of short or moderate duration or following a marriage of long duration if there is no ongoing need for support on a permanent basis. An award of durational alimony

terminates upon the death of either party or upon the remarriage of the party receiving alimony. The amount of an award of durational alimony may be modified or terminated based upon a substantial change in circumstances in accordance with s. 61.14. However, the length of an award of durational alimony may not be modified except under exceptional circumstances and may not exceed the length of the marriage.

(8) Permanent alimony may be awarded to provide for the needs and necessities of life as they were established during the marriage of the parties for a party who lacks the financial ability to meet his or her needs and necessities of life following a dissolution of marriage. Permanent alimony may be awarded following a marriage of long duration if such an award is appropriate upon consideration of the factors set forth in subsection (2), following a marriage of moderate duration if such an award is appropriate based upon clear and convincing evidence after consideration of the factors set forth in subsection (2), or following a marriage of short duration if there are written findings of exceptional circumstances. In awarding permanent alimony, the court shall include a finding that no other form of alimony is fair and reasonable under the circumstances of the parties. An award of permanent alimony terminates upon the death of either party or upon the remarriage of the party receiving alimony. An award may be modified or terminated based upon a substantial change in circumstances or upon the existence of a supportive relationship in accordance with s. 61.14.

(9) The award of alimony may not leave the payor with significantly less net income than the net income of the recipient unless there are written findings of exceptional circumstances.

(10)(a) With respect to any order requiring the payment of alimony entered on or after January 1, 1985, unless the provisions of paragraph (c) or paragraph (d) apply, the court shall direct in the order that the payments of alimony be made through the appropriate depository as provided in s. 61.181.

(b) With respect to any order requiring the payment of alimony entered before January 1, 1985, upon the subsequent appearance, on or after that date, of one or both parties before the court having jurisdiction for the purpose of modifying or enforcing the order or in any other proceeding related to the order, or upon the application of either party, unless the provisions of paragraph (c) or paragraph (d) apply, the court shall modify the terms of the order as necessary to direct that payments of alimony be made through the appropriate depository as provided in s. 61.181.

(c) If there is no minor child, alimony payments need not be directed through the depository.

(d)1. If there is a minor child of the parties and both parties so request, the court may order that alimony payments need not be directed through the depository. In this case, the order of support shall provide, or be deemed to provide, that either party may subsequently apply to the depository to require that payments be made through the depository. The court shall provide a copy of the order to the depository.

2. If the provisions of subparagraph 1. apply, either party may subsequently file with the depository an affidavit alleging default or arrearages in payment and stating that the party wishes to initiate participation in the depository program. The party shall provide copies of the affidavit to the court and the other party or parties. Fifteen days after receipt of the affidavit, the depository shall notify all parties that future payments shall be directed to the depository.

3. In IV-D cases, the IV-D agency shall have the same rights as the obligee in requesting that payments be made through the depository.

61.09. Alimony and child support unconnected with dissolution.

If a person having the ability to contribute to the maintenance of his or her spouse and support of his or her minor child fails to do so, the spouse who is not receiving support may apply to the court for alimony and for support for the child without seeking dissolution of marriage, and the court shall enter an order as it deems just and proper.

61.10. Adjudication of obligation to support spouse or minor child unconnected with dissolution; parenting plan.

Except when relief is afforded by some other pending civil action or proceeding, a spouse residing in this state apart from his or her spouse and minor child, whether or not such separation is through his or her fault, may obtain an adjudication of obligation to maintain the spouse and minor child, if any. The court shall adjudicate his or her financial obligations to the spouse and child and shall establish the parenting plan for the parties. Such an action does not preclude either party from maintaining any other proceeding under this chapter for other or additional relief at any time.

61.11. Writs.

(1) When either party is about to remove himself or herself or his or her property out of the state, or fraudulently convey or conceal it, the court may award a ne exeat or injunction against the party or the property and make such orders as will secure alimony or support to the party who should receive it.

(2)(a) When the court issues a writ of bodily attachment in connection with a court-ordered support obligation, the writ or attachment to the writ must include, at a minimum, such information on the respondent's physical description and location as is required for entry of the writ into the Florida Crime Information Center telecommunications system and authorization for the assessment and collection of the actual costs associated with the service of the writ and transportation of the respondent in compliance thereof. The writ shall direct that service and execution of the writ may be made on any day of the week and any time of the day or night.

(b) The clerk of the court shall forward a copy of the writ for service to the sheriff of the county in which the writ is issued.

(c) Upon receipt of a writ from the clerk of the court, the sheriff shall enter the information on any unserved writ into the Florida Crime Information Center telecommunications system to make the information available to other law enforcement agencies within the state. The writ shall be enforceable in all counties of the state.

(d) Upon receipt of the purge payment, the receiving agency shall provide the subject with a written receipt acknowledging such payment, which must be carried on the person of the respondent for a period of at least 30 days from the date of payment as proof of such payment. A sheriff receiving such payment shall forward the funds to the sheriff who entered the information about the writ into the Florida Crime Information Center telecommunications system and who shall forward the funds to the appropriate clerk of court.

(e) After a writ is modified, purged, recalled, terminated, or otherwise rendered ineffective by ruling of the court, the clerk of the court shall notify the sheriff receiving the original writ. That agency shall modify or cancel the entry in the Florida Crime Information Center telecommunications system in accordance with such notification.

61.12. Attachment or garnishment of amounts due for alimony or child support.

(1) So much as the court orders of the money or other things due to any person or public officer, state or county, whether the head of a family residing in this state or not, when the money or other thing is due for the personal labor or service of the person or otherwise, is subject to attachment or garnishment to enforce and satisfy the orders and judgments of the court of this state for alimony, suit money, or child support, or other orders in proceedings for dissolution, alimony, or child support; when the money or other thing sought to be attached or garnisheed is the salary of a public officer, state or county, the writ of attachment or garnishment shall be served on the public officer whose duty it is to pay the salary, who shall obey the writ as provided by law in other cases. It is the duty of the officer to notify the public officer whose duty it is to audit or issue a warrant for the salary sought to be attached immediately upon service of the writ. A warrant for as much of the salary as is ordered held under the writ shall not issue except pursuant to court order unless the writ is dissolved. No more of the salary shall be retained by virtue of the writ than is provided for in the order.

(2) The provisions of chapter 77 or any other provision of law to the contrary notwithstanding, the court may issue a continuing writ of garnishment to an employer to enforce the order of the court for periodic payment of alimony or child support or both. The writ may provide that the salary of any person having a duty of support pursuant to such order be garnisheed on a periodic and continuing basis for so long as the court may determine or until otherwise ordered by the court or a court of competent jurisdiction in a further proceeding. Any disciplinary action against the employee by an employer to whom a writ is issued pursuant to this section solely because such writ is in effect constitutes a contempt of court, and the court may enter such order as it deems just and proper.

61.122. Parenting plan recommendation; presumption of psychologist's good faith; prerequisite to parent's filing suit; award of fees, costs, reimbursement.

(1) A psychologist who has been appointed by the court to develop a parenting plan recommendation in a dissolution of marriage, a case of domestic violence, or a paternity matter involving the relationship of a child and a parent, including time-sharing of children, is presumed to be acting in good faith if the psychologist's recommendation has been reached under standards that a reasonable psychologist would use to develop a parenting plan recommendation.

(2) An administrative complaint against a court-appointed psychologist which relates to a parenting plan recommendation conducted by the psychologist may not be filed anonymously. The individual who files an administrative complaint must include in the complaint his or her name, address, and telephone number.

(3) A parent who desires to file a legal action against a court-appointed psychologist who has acted in good faith in developing a parenting plan recommendation must petition the judge who presided over the dissolution of marriage, case of domestic violence, or paternity matter involving the relationship of a child and a parent, including time-sharing of children, to appoint another psychologist. Upon the parent's showing of good cause, the court shall appoint another psychologist. The court shall determine who is responsible for all court costs and attorney's fees associated with making such an appointment.

(4) If a legal action, whether it be a civil action, a criminal action, or an administrative proceeding, is filed against a court-appointed psychologist in a dissolution of marriage, case of domestic violence, or paternity matter involving the relationship of a child and a parent, including time-sharing of children, the claimant is responsible for all reasonable costs and reasonable attorney's fees associated with the action for both parties if the psychologist is held not liable. If the psychologist is held liable in civil court, the psychologist must pay all reasonable costs and reasonable attorney's fees for the claimant.

61.125. Parenting coordination.

(1) PURPOSE.—The purpose of parenting coordination is to provide a child-focused alternative dispute resolution process whereby a parenting coordinator assists the parents in creating or implementing a parenting plan by facilitating the resolution of disputes between the parents by providing education, making recommendations, and, with the prior approval of the parents and the court, making limited decisions within the scope of the court's order of referral.

(2) REFERRAL.—In any action in which a judgment or order has been sought or entered adopting, establishing, or modifying a parenting plan, except for a domestic violence proceeding under chapter 741, and upon agreement of the parties, the court's own motion, or the motion of a party, the court may appoint a parenting coordinator and refer the parties to parenting coordination to assist in the resolution of disputes concerning their parenting plan.

(3) DOMESTIC VIOLENCE ISSUES.—

(a) If there has been a history of domestic violence, the court may not refer the parties to parenting coordination unless both parents consent. The court shall offer each party an opportunity to consult with an attorney or domestic violence advocate before accepting the party's consent. The court must determine whether each party's consent has been given freely and voluntarily.

(b) In determining whether there has been a history of domestic violence, the court shall consider whether a party has committed an act of domestic violence as defined s. 741.28, or child abuse as defined in s. 39.01, against the other party or any member of the other party's family; engaged in a pattern of behaviors that exert power and control over the other party and that may compromise the other party's ability to negotiate a fair result; or engaged in behavior that leads the other party to have reasonable cause to believe he or she is in imminent danger of becoming a victim of domestic violence. The court shall consider and evaluate all relevant factors, including, but not limited to, the factors listed in s. 741.30(6)(b).

(c) If there is a history of domestic violence, the court shall order safeguards to protect the safety of the participants, including, but not limited to, adherence to all provisions of an injunction for protection or conditions of bail, probation, or a sentence arising from criminal proceedings.

(4) QUALIFICATIONS OF A PARENTING COORDINATOR.—A parenting coordinator is an impartial third person whose role is to assist the parents in successfully creating or implementing a parenting plan. Unless there is a written agreement between the parties, the court may appoint only a qualified parenting coordinator.

(a) To be qualified, a parenting coordinator must:

1. Meet one of the following professional requirements:

a. Be licensed as a mental health professional under chapter 490 or chapter 491.

b. Be licensed as a physician under chapter 458, with certification by the American Board of Psychiatry and Neurology.

c. Be certified by the Florida Supreme Court as a family law mediator, with at least a master's degree in a mental health field.

d. Be a member in good standing of The Florida Bar.

2. Complete all of the following:

a. Three years of postlicensure or postcertification practice.

b. A family mediation training program certified by the Florida Supreme Court.

c. A minimum of 24 hours of parenting coordination training in parenting coordination concepts and ethics, family systems theory and application, family dynamics in separation and divorce, child and adolescent development, the parenting coordination process, parenting coordination techniques, and Florida family law and procedure, and a minimum of 4 hours of training in domestic violence and child abuse which is related to parenting coordination.

(b) The court may require additional qualifications to address issues specific to the parties.

(c) A qualified parenting coordinator must be in good standing, or in clear and active status, with his or her respective licensing authority, certification board, or both, as applicable.

(5) DISQUALIFICATIONS OF PARENTING COORDINATOR.—

(a) The court may not appoint a person to serve as parenting coordinator who, in any jurisdiction:

1. Has been convicted or had adjudication withheld on a charge of child abuse, child neglect, domestic violence, parental kidnapping, or interference with custody;

2. Has been found by a court in a child protection hearing to have abused, neglected, or abandoned a child;

3. Has consented to an adjudication or a withholding of adjudication on a petition for dependency; or

4. Is or has been a respondent in a final order or injunction of protection against domestic violence.

(b) A parenting coordinator must discontinue service as a parenting coordinator and immediately report to the court and the parties if any of the disqualifying circumstances described in paragraph (a) occur, or if he or she no longer meets the minimum qualifications in subsection (4), and the court may appoint another parenting coordinator.

(6) FEES FOR PARENTING COORDINATION.—The court shall determine the allocation of fees and costs for parenting coordination between the parties. The court may not order the parties to parenting coordination without their consent unless it determines that the parties have the financial ability to pay the parenting coordination fees and costs.

(a) In determining if a nonindigent party has the financial ability to pay the parenting coordination fees and costs, the court shall consider the party's financial circumstances, including income, assets, liabilities, financial obligations, resources, and whether paying the fees and costs would create a substantial hardship.

(b) If a party is found to be indigent based upon the factors in s. 57.082, the court may not order the party to parenting coordination unless public funds are available to pay the indigent party's allocated portion of the fees and costs or the nonindigent party consents to paying all of the fees and costs.

(7) CONFIDENTIALITY.—Except as otherwise provided in this section, all communications made by, between, or among the parties and the parenting coordinator during parenting coordination sessions are confidential. The parenting coordinator and each party designated in the order appointing the coordinator may not testify or offer evidence about communications made by, between, or among the parties and the parenting coordinator during parenting coordination sessions, except if:

(a) Necessary to identify, authenticate, confirm, or deny a written agreement entered into by the parties during parenting coordination;

(b) The testimony or evidence is necessary to identify an issue for resolution by the court without otherwise disclosing communications made by any party or the parenting coordinator;

(c) The testimony or evidence is limited to the subject of a party's compliance with the order of referral to parenting coordination, orders for psychological evaluation, counseling ordered by the court or recommended by a health care provider, or for substance abuse testing or treatment;

(d) The parenting coordinator reports that the case is no longer appropriate for parenting coordination;

(e) The parenting coordinator is reporting that he or she is unable or unwilling to continue to serve and that a successor parenting coordinator should be appointed;

(f) The testimony or evidence is necessary pursuant to paragraph (5)(b) or subsection (8);

(g) The parenting coordinator is not qualified to address or resolve certain issues in the case and a more qualified coordinator should be appointed;

(h) The parties agree that the testimony or evidence be permitted; or

(i) The testimony or evidence is necessary to protect any person from future acts that would constitute domestic violence under chapter 741; child abuse, neglect, or abandonment under chapter 39; or abuse, neglect, or exploitation of an elderly or disabled adult under chapter 825.

(8) REPORT OF EMERGENCY TO COURT.—

(a) A parenting coordinator must immediately inform the court by affidavit or verified report without notice to the parties of an emergency situation if:

1. There is a reasonable cause to suspect that a child will suffer or is suffering abuse, neglect, or abandonment as provided under chapter 39;

2. There is a reasonable cause to suspect a vulnerable adult has been or is being abused, neglected, or exploited as provided under chapter 415;

3. A party, or someone acting on a party's behalf, is expected to wrongfully remove or is wrongfully removing the child from the jurisdiction of the court without prior court approval or compliance with the requirements of s. 61.13001. If the parenting coordinator suspects that the parent has relocated within the state to avoid domestic violence, the coordinator may not disclose the location of the parent and child unless required by court order.

(b) Upon such information and belief, a parenting coordinator shall immediately inform the court by affidavit or verified report and serve a copy on each party of an emergency in which a party obtains a final order or injunction of protection against domestic violence or is arrested for an act of domestic violence as provided under chapter 741.

(9) LIMITATION ON LIABILITY.—A parenting coordinator appointed by the court is not liable for civil damages for any act or omission in the scope of his or her duties pursuant to an order of referral unless such person acted in bad faith or with malicious purpose or in a manner exhibiting wanton and willful disregard for the rights, safety, or property of the parties.

61.13. Support of children; parenting and time-sharing; powers of court.

(1)(a) In a proceeding under this chapter, the court may at any time order either or both parents who owe a duty of support to a child to pay support to the other parent or, in the case of both parents, to a third party who has custody in accordance with the child support guidelines schedule in s. 61.30.

1. All child support orders and income deduction orders entered on or after October 1, 2010, must provide:

a. For child support to terminate on a child's 18th birthday unless the court finds or previously found that s. 743.07(2) applies, or is otherwise agreed to by the parties;

b. A schedule, based on the record existing at the time of the order, stating the amount of the monthly child support obligation for all the minor children at the time of the order and the amount of child support that will be owed for any remaining children after one or more of the children are no longer entitled to receive child support; and

c. The month, day, and year that the reduction or termination of child support becomes effective.

2. The court initially entering an order requiring one or both parents to make child support payments has continuing jurisdiction after the entry of the initial order to modify the amount and terms and conditions of the child support payments if the modification is found by the court to be in the best interests of the child; when the child reaches majority; if there is a substantial change in the circumstances of the parties; if s. 743.07(2) applies; or when a child is emancipated, marries, joins the armed services, or dies. The court initially entering a child support order has continuing jurisdiction to require the obligee to report to the court on terms prescribed by the court regarding the disposition of the child support payments.

(b) Each order for support shall contain a provision for health insurance for the minor child when health insurance is reasonable in cost and accessible to the child. Health insurance is presumed to be reasonable in cost if the incremental cost of adding health insurance for the child or children does not exceed 5 percent of the gross income, as defined in s. 61.30, of the parent responsible for providing health insurance. Health insurance is accessible to the child if the health insurance is available to be used in the county of the child's primary residence or in another county if the parent who has the most time under the time-sharing plan agrees. If the time-sharing plan provides for equal time-sharing, health insurance is accessible to the child if the health insurance is available to be used in either county where the child resides or in another county if both parents agree. The court may require the obligor to provide health insurance or to reimburse the obligee for the cost of health insurance for the minor child when insurance is provided by the obligee. The presumption of reasonable cost may be rebutted by evidence of any of the factors in s. 61.30(11)(a). The court may deviate from what is presumed reasonable in cost only upon a written finding explaining its determination why ordering or not ordering the provision of health insurance or the reimbursement of the obligee's cost for providing health insurance for the minor child would be unjust or inappropriate. In any event, the court shall apportion the cost of health insurance, and any noncovered medical, dental, and prescription medication expenses of the child, to both parties by adding the cost to the basic obligation determined pursuant to s. 61.30(6). The court may order that payment of noncovered medical, dental, and prescription medication expenses of the minor child be made directly to the obligee on a percentage basis. In a proceeding for medical support only, each parent's share of the child's noncovered medical expenses shall equal the parent's percentage share of the combined net income of the parents. The percentage share shall be calculated by dividing each parent's net monthly income by the combined monthly net income of both parents. Net income is calculated as specified by s. 61.30(3) and (4).

1. In a non-Title IV-D case, a copy of the court order for health insurance shall be served on the obligor's union or employer by the obligee when the following conditions are met:

a. The obligor fails to provide written proof to the obligee within 30 days after receiving effective notice of the court order that the health insurance has been obtained or that application for health insurance has been made;

b. The obligee serves written notice of intent to enforce an order for health insurance on the obligor by mail at the obligor's last known address; and

c. The obligor fails within 15 days after the mailing of the notice to provide written proof to the obligee that the health insurance existed as of the date of mailing.

2.a. A support order enforced under Title IV-D of the Social Security Act which requires that the obligor provide health insurance is enforceable by the department through the use of the national medical support notice, and an amendment to the support order is not required. The department shall transfer the national medical support notice to the obligor's union or employer. The department shall notify the obligor in writing that the notice has been sent to the obligor's union or employer, and the written notification must include the obligor's rights and duties under the national medical support notice. The obligor may contest the withholding required by the national medical support notice based on a mistake of fact. To contest the withholding, the obligor must file a written notice of contest with the department within 15 business days after the date the obligor receives written notification of the national medical support notice from the department. Filing with the department is complete when the notice is received by the person designated by the department in the written notification. The notice of contest must be in the form prescribed by the department. Upon the timely filing of a notice of contest, the department shall, within 5 business days, schedule an informal conference with the obligor to discuss the obligor's factual dispute. If the informal conference resolves the dispute to the obligor's satisfaction or if the obligor fails to attend the informal conference, the notice of contest is deemed withdrawn. If the informal conference does not resolve the dispute, the obligor may request an administrative hearing under chapter 120 within 5 business days after the termination of the informal conference, in a form and manner prescribed by the department. However, the filing of a notice of contest by the obligor does not delay the withholding of premium payments by the union, employer, or health plan administrator. The union, employer, or health plan administrator must implement the withholding as directed by the national medical support notice unless notified by the department that the national medical support notice is terminated.

b. In a Title IV-D case, the department shall notify an obligor's union or employer if the obligation to provide health insurance through that union or employer is terminated.

3. In a non-Title IV-D case, upon receipt of the order pursuant to subparagraph 1., or upon application of the obligor pursuant to the order, the union or employer shall enroll the minor child

as a beneficiary in the group health plan regardless of any restrictions on the enrollment period and withhold any required premium from the obligor's income. If more than one plan is offered by the union or employer, the child shall be enrolled in the group health plan in which the obligor is enrolled.

4.a. Upon receipt of the national medical support notice under subparagraph 2. in a Title IV-D case, the union or employer shall transfer the notice to the appropriate group health plan administrator within 20 business days after the date on the notice. The plan administrator must enroll the child as a beneficiary in the group health plan regardless of any restrictions on the enrollment period, and the union or employer must withhold any required premium from the obligor's income upon notification by the plan administrator that the child is enrolled. The child shall be enrolled in the group health plan in which the obligor is enrolled. If the group health plan in which the obligor is enrolled is not available where the child resides or if the obligor is not enrolled in group coverage, the child shall be enrolled in the lowest cost group health plan that is accessible to the child.

b. If health insurance or the obligor's employment is terminated in a Title IV-D case, the union or employer that is withholding premiums for health insurance under a national medical support notice must notify the department within 20 days after the termination and provide the obligor's last known address and the name and address of the obligor's new employer, if known.

5.a. The amount withheld by a union or employer in compliance with a support order may not exceed the amount allowed under s. 303(b) of the Consumer Credit Protection Act, 15 U.S.C. s. 1673(b), as amended. The union or employer shall withhold the maximum allowed by the Consumer Credit Protection Act in the following order:

(I) Current support, as ordered.

(II) Premium payments for health insurance, as ordered.

(III) Past due support, as ordered.

(IV) Other medical support or insurance, as ordered.

b. If the combined amount to be withheld for current support plus the premium payment for health insurance exceed the amount allowed under the Consumer Credit Protection Act, and the health insurance cannot be obtained unless the full amount of the premium is paid, the union or employer may not withhold the premium payment. However, the union or employer shall withhold the maximum allowed in the following order:

(I) Current support, as ordered.

(II) Past due support, as ordered.

(III) Other medical support or insurance, as ordered.

6. An employer, union, or plan administrator who does not comply with the requirements in sub-subparagraph 4.a. is subject to a civil penalty not to exceed $250 for the first violation and $500 for subsequent violations, plus attorney's fees and costs. The department may file a petition in circuit court to enforce the requirements of this subparagraph.

7. The department may adopt rules to administer the child support enforcement provisions of this section that affect Title IV-D cases.

(c) To the extent necessary to protect an award of child support, the court may order the obligor to purchase or maintain a life insurance policy or a bond, or to otherwise secure the child support award with any other assets which may be suitable for that purpose.

(d)1. All child support orders shall provide the full name and date of birth of each minor child who is the subject of the child support order.

2. If both parties request and the court finds that it is in the best interest of the child, support payments need not be subject to immediate income deduction. Support orders that are not subject to immediate income deduction may be directed through the depository under s. 61.181 or made payable directly to the obligee. Payments made by immediate income deduction shall be made to the State Disbursement Unit. The court shall provide a copy of the order to the depository.

3. For support orders payable directly to the obligee, any party, or the department in a IV-D case, may subsequently file an affidavit with the depository alleging a default in payment of child support and stating that the party wishes to require that payments be made through the depository.

The party shall provide copies of the affidavit to the court and to each other party. Fifteen days after receipt of the affidavit, the depository shall notify all parties that future payments shall be paid through the depository, except that income deduction payments shall be made to the State Disbursement Unit.

(2)(a) The court may approve, grant, or modify a parenting plan, notwithstanding that the child is not physically present in this state at the time of filing any proceeding under this chapter, if it appears to the court that the child was removed from this state for the primary purpose of removing the child from the court's jurisdiction in an attempt to avoid the court's approval, creation, or modification of a parenting plan.

(b) A parenting plan approved by the court must, at a minimum:

1. Describe in adequate detail how the parents will share and be responsible for the daily tasks associated with the upbringing of the child;

2. Include the time-sharing schedule arrangements that specify the time that the minor child will spend with each parent;

3. Designate who will be responsible for:

a. Any and all forms of health care. If the court orders shared parental responsibility over health care decisions, the parenting plan must provide that either parent may consent to mental health treatment for the child.

b. School-related matters, including the address to be used for school-boundary determination and registration.

c. Other activities; and

4. Describe in adequate detail the methods and technologies that the parents will use to communicate with the child.

(c) The court shall determine all matters relating to parenting and time-sharing of each minor child of the parties in accordance with the best interests of the child and in accordance with the Uniform Child Custody Jurisdiction and Enforcement Act, except that modification of a parenting plan and time-sharing schedule requires a showing of a substantial, material, and unanticipated change of circumstances.

1. It is the public policy of this state that each minor child has frequent and continuing contact with both parents after the parents separate or the marriage of the parties is dissolved and to encourage parents to share the rights and responsibilities, and joys, of childrearing. There is no presumption for or against the father or mother of the child or for or against any specific time-sharing schedule when creating or modifying the parenting plan of the child.

2. The court shall order that the parental responsibility for a minor child be shared by both parents unless the court finds that shared parental responsibility would be detrimental to the child. Evidence that a parent has been convicted of a misdemeanor of the first degree or higher involving domestic violence, as defined in s. 741.28 and chapter 775, or meets the criteria of s. 39.806(1)(d), creates a rebuttable presumption of detriment to the child. If the presumption is not rebutted after the convicted parent is advised by the court that the presumption exists, shared parental responsibility, including time-sharing with the child, and decisions made regarding the child, may not be granted to the convicted parent. However, the convicted parent is not relieved of any obligation to provide financial support. If the court determines that shared parental responsibility would be detrimental to the child, it may order sole parental responsibility and make such arrangements for time-sharing as specified in the parenting plan as will best protect the child or abused spouse from further harm. Whether or not there is a conviction of any offense of domestic violence or child abuse or the existence of an injunction for protection against domestic violence, the court shall consider evidence of domestic violence or child abuse as evidence of detriment to the child.

a. In ordering shared parental responsibility, the court may consider the expressed desires of the parents and may grant to one party the ultimate responsibility over specific aspects of the child's welfare or may divide those responsibilities between the parties based on the best interests of the child. Areas of responsibility may include education, health care, and any other responsibilities that the court finds unique to a particular family.

b. The court shall order sole parental responsibility for a minor child to one parent, with or without time-sharing with the other parent if it is in the best interests of the minor child.

3. Access to records and information pertaining to a minor child, including, but not limited to, medical, dental, and school records, may not be denied to either parent. Full rights under this subparagraph apply to either parent unless a court order specifically revokes these rights, including any restrictions on these rights as provided in a domestic violence injunction. A parent having rights under this subparagraph has the same rights upon request as to form, substance, and manner of access as are available to the other parent of a child, including, without limitation, the right to in-person communication with medical, dental, and education providers.

(d) The circuit court in the county in which either parent and the child reside or the circuit court in which the original order approving or creating the parenting plan was entered may modify the parenting plan. The court may change the venue in accordance with s. 47.122.

(3) For purposes of establishing or modifying parental responsibility and creating, developing, approving, or modifying a parenting plan, including a time-sharing schedule, which governs each parent's relationship with his or her minor child and the relationship between each parent with regard to his or her minor child, the best interest of the child shall be the primary consideration. A determination of parental responsibility, a parenting plan, or a time-sharing schedule may not be modified without a showing of a substantial, material, and unanticipated change in circumstances and a determination that the modification is in the best interests of the child. Determination of the best interests of the child shall be made by evaluating all of the factors affecting the welfare and interests of the particular minor child and the circumstances of that family, including, but not limited to:

(a) The demonstrated capacity and disposition of each parent to facilitate and encourage a close and continuing parent-child relationship, to honor the time-sharing schedule, and to be reasonable when changes are required.

(b) The anticipated division of parental responsibilities after the litigation, including the extent to which parental responsibilities will be delegated to third parties.

(c) The demonstrated capacity and disposition of each parent to determine, consider, and act upon the needs of the child as opposed to the needs or desires of the parent.

(d) The length of time the child has lived in a stable, satisfactory environment and the desirability of maintaining continuity.

(e) The geographic viability of the parenting plan, with special attention paid to the needs of school-age children and the amount of time to be spent traveling to effectuate the parenting plan. This factor does not create a presumption for or against relocation of either parent with a child.

(f) The moral fitness of the parents.

(g) The mental and physical health of the parents.

(h) The home, school, and community record of the child.

(i) The reasonable preference of the child, if the court deems the child to be of sufficient intelligence, understanding, and experience to express a preference.

(j) The demonstrated knowledge, capacity, and disposition of each parent to be informed of the circumstances of the minor child, including, but not limited to, the child's friends, teachers, medical care providers, daily activities, and favorite things.

(k) The demonstrated capacity and disposition of each parent to provide a consistent routine for the child, such as discipline, and daily schedules for homework, meals, and bedtime.

(l) The demonstrated capacity of each parent to communicate with and keep the other parent informed of issues and activities regarding the minor child, and the willingness of each parent to adopt a unified front on all major issues when dealing with the child.

(m) Evidence of domestic violence, sexual violence, child abuse, child abandonment, or child neglect, regardless of whether a prior or pending action relating to those issues has been brought. If the court accepts evidence of prior or pending actions regarding domestic violence, sexual violence, child abuse, child abandonment, or child neglect, the court must specifically acknowledge in writing that such evidence was considered when evaluating the best interests of the child.

(n) Evidence that either parent has knowingly provided false information to the court regarding any prior or pending action regarding domestic violence, sexual violence, child abuse, child abandonment, or child neglect.

(o) The particular parenting tasks customarily performed by each parent and the division of parental responsibilities before the institution of litigation and during the pending litigation, including the extent to which parenting responsibilities were undertaken by third parties.

(p) The demonstrated capacity and disposition of each parent to participate and be involved in the child's school and extracurricular activities.

(q) The demonstrated capacity and disposition of each parent to maintain an environment for the child which is free from substance abuse.

(r) The capacity and disposition of each parent to protect the child from the ongoing litigation as demonstrated by not discussing the litigation with the child, not sharing documents or electronic media related to the litigation with the child, and refraining from disparaging comments about the other parent to the child.

(s) The developmental stages and needs of the child and the demonstrated capacity and disposition of each parent to meet the child's developmental needs.

(t) Any other factor that is relevant to the determination of a specific parenting plan, including the time-sharing schedule.

(4)(a) When a parent who is ordered to pay child support or alimony fails to pay child support or alimony, the parent who should have received the child support or alimony may not refuse to honor the time-sharing schedule presently in effect between the parents.

(b) When a parent refuses to honor the other parent's rights under the time-sharing schedule, the parent whose time-sharing rights were violated shall continue to pay any ordered child support or alimony.

(c) When a parent refuses to honor the time-sharing schedule in the parenting plan without proper cause, the court:

1. Shall, after calculating the amount of time-sharing improperly denied, award the parent denied time a sufficient amount of extra time-sharing to compensate for the time-sharing missed, and such time-sharing shall be ordered as expeditiously as possible in a manner consistent with the best interests of the child and scheduled in a manner that is convenient for the parent deprived of time-sharing. In ordering any makeup time-sharing, the court shall schedule such time-sharing in a manner that is consistent with the best interests of the child or children and that is convenient for the nonoffending parent and at the expense of the noncompliant parent.

2. May order the parent who did not provide time-sharing or did not properly exercise time-sharing under the time-sharing schedule to pay reasonable court costs and attorney's fees incurred by the nonoffending parent to enforce the time-sharing schedule.

3. May order the parent who did not provide time-sharing or did not properly exercise time-sharing under the time-sharing schedule to attend a parenting course approved by the judicial circuit.

4. May order the parent who did not provide time-sharing or did not properly exercise time-sharing under the time-sharing schedule to do community service if the order will not interfere with the welfare of the child.

5. May order the parent who did not provide time-sharing or did not properly exercise time-sharing under the time-sharing schedule to have the financial burden of promoting frequent and continuing contact when that parent and child reside further than 60 miles from the other parent.

6. May, upon the request of the parent who did not violate the time-sharing schedule, modify the parenting plan if modification is in the best interests of the child.

7. May impose any other reasonable sanction as a result of noncompliance.

(d) A person who violates this subsection may be punished by contempt of court or other remedies as the court deems appropriate.

(5) The court may make specific orders regarding the parenting plan and time-sharing schedule as such orders relate to the circumstances of the parties and the nature of the case and are equitable and provide for child support in accordance with the guidelines schedule in s. 61.30. An order for

equal time-sharing for a minor child does not preclude the court from entering an order for child support of the child.

(6) In any proceeding under this section, the court may not deny shared parental responsibility and time-sharing rights to a parent solely because that parent is or is believed to be infected with human immunodeficiency virus, but the court may, in an order approving the parenting plan, require that parent to observe measures approved by the Centers for Disease Control and Prevention of the United States Public Health Service or by the Department of Health for preventing the spread of human immunodeficiency virus to the child.

(7)(a) Each party to any paternity or support proceeding is required to file with the tribunal as defined in s. 88.1011 and State Case Registry upon entry of an order, and to update as appropriate, information on location and identity of the party, including social security number, residential and mailing addresses, telephone number, driver license number, and name, address, and telephone number of employer. Each party to any paternity or child support proceeding in a non-Title IV-D case shall meet the above requirements for updating the tribunal and State Case Registry.

(b) Pursuant to the federal Personal Responsibility and Work Opportunity Reconciliation Act of 1996, each party is required to provide his or her social security number in accordance with this section. Disclosure of social security numbers obtained through this requirement shall be limited to the purpose of administration of the Title IV-D program for child support enforcement.

(c) In any subsequent Title IV-D child support enforcement action between the parties, upon sufficient showing that diligent effort has been made to ascertain the location of such a party, the court of competent jurisdiction shall deem state due process requirements for notice and service of process to be met with respect to the party, upon delivery of written notice to the most recent residential or employer address filed with the tribunal and State Case Registry pursuant to paragraph (a). In any subsequent non-Title IV-D child support enforcement action between the parties, the same requirements for service shall apply.

(8) At the time an order for child support is entered, each party is required to provide his or her social security number and date of birth to the court, as well as the name, date of birth, and social security number of each minor child that is the subject of such child support order. Pursuant to the federal Personal Responsibility and Work Opportunity Reconciliation Act of 1996, each party is required to provide his or her social security number in accordance with this section. All social security numbers required by this section shall be provided by the parties and maintained by the depository as a separate attachment in the file. Disclosure of social security numbers obtained through this requirement shall be limited to the purpose of administration of the Title IV-D program for child support enforcement.

(9)(a) A time-sharing plan may not require that a minor child visit a parent who is a resident of a recovery residence, as defined by s. 397.311, between the hours of 9 p.m. and 7 a.m., unless the court makes a specific finding that such visitation is in the best interest of the child. In determining the best interest of the minor child in such cases, the court shall take into account factors including, but not limited to, whether the parent resides in a specialized residence for pregnant women or parents whose children reside with them, the number of adults living in the recovery residence, and the parent's level of recovery.

(b) A time-sharing plan that does not mention a recovery residence may not be interpreted to require that a minor child visit a parent who is a resident of a recovery residence, as defined by s. 397.311, between the hours of 9 p.m. and 7 a.m.

(c) A court may not order visitation at a recovery residence if any resident of the recovery residence is currently required to register as a sexual predator under s. 775.21 or as a sexual offender under s. 943.0435.

61.13001. Parental relocation with a child.

(1) DEFINITIONS.—As used in this section, the term:

(a) "Child" means any person who is under the jurisdiction of a state court pursuant to the Uniform Child Custody Jurisdiction and Enforcement Act or is the subject of any order granting to a parent or other person any right to time-sharing, residential care, kinship, or custody, as provided under state law.

(b) "Court" means the circuit court in an original proceeding which has proper venue and jurisdiction in accordance with the Uniform Child Custody Jurisdiction and Enforcement Act, the circuit court in the county in which either parent and the child reside, or the circuit court in which the original action was adjudicated.

(c) "Other person" means an individual who is not the parent, but with whom the child resides pursuant to court order, or who has the right of access to, time-sharing with, or visitation with the child.

(d) "Parent" means any person so named by court order or express written agreement who is subject to court enforcement or a person reflected as a parent on a birth certificate and who is entitled to access to or time-sharing with the child.

(e) "Relocation" means a change in the location of the principal residence of a parent or other person from his or her principal place of residence at the time of the last order establishing or modifying time-sharing, or at the time of filing the pending action to establish or modify time-sharing. The change of location must be at least 50 miles from that residence, and for at least 60 consecutive days not including a temporary absence from the principal residence for purposes of vacation, education, or the provision of health care for the child.

(2) RELOCATION BY AGREEMENT.—

(a) If the parents and every other person entitled to access to or time-sharing with the child agree to the relocation of the child, they may satisfy the requirements of this section by signing a written agreement that:

1. Reflects consent to the relocation;

2. Defines an access or time-sharing schedule for the nonrelocating parent and any other persons who are entitled to access or time-sharing; and

3. Describes, if necessary, any transportation arrangements related to access or time-sharing.

(b) If there is an existing cause of action, judgment, or decree of record pertaining to the child's residence or a time-sharing schedule, the parties shall seek ratification of the agreement by court order without the necessity of an evidentiary hearing unless a hearing is requested, in writing, by one or more of the parties to the agreement within 10 days after the date the agreement is filed with the court. If a hearing is not timely requested, it shall be presumed that the relocation is in the best interest of the child and the court may ratify the agreement without an evidentiary hearing.

(3) PETITION TO RELOCATE.—Unless an agreement has been entered as described in subsection (2), a parent or other person seeking relocation must file a petition to relocate and serve it upon the other parent, and every other person entitled to access to or time-sharing with the child. The pleadings must be in accordance with this section:

(a) The petition to relocate must be signed under oath or affirmation under penalty of perjury and include:

1. A description of the location of the intended new residence, including the state, city, and specific physical address, if known.

2. The mailing address of the intended new residence, if not the same as the physical address, if known.

3. The home telephone number of the intended new residence, if known.

4. The date of the intended move or proposed relocation.

5. A detailed statement of the specific reasons for the proposed relocation. If one of the reasons is based upon a job offer that has been reduced to writing, the written job offer must be attached to the petition.

6. A proposal for the revised postrelocation schedule for access and time-sharing together with a proposal for the postrelocation transportation arrangements necessary to effectuate time-sharing with the child. Absent the existence of a current, valid order abating, terminating, or restricting access or time-sharing or other good cause predating the petition, failure to comply with this

provision renders the petition to relocate legally insufficient.

7. Substantially the following statement, in all capital letters and in the same size type, or larger, as the type in the remainder of the petition:

(b) The petition to relocate must be served on the other parent and on every other person entitled to access to and time-sharing with the child. If there is a pending court action regarding the child, service of process may be according to court rule. Otherwise, service of process shall be according to chapters 48 and 49 or via certified mail, restricted delivery, return receipt requested.

(c) A parent or other person seeking to relocate has a continuing duty to provide current and updated information required by this section when that information becomes known.

(d) If the other parent and any other person entitled to access to or time-sharing with the child fails to timely file a response objecting to the petition to relocate, it is presumed that the relocation is in the best interest of the child and that the relocation should be allowed, and the court shall, absent good cause, enter an order specifying that the order is entered as a result of the failure to respond to the petition and adopting the access and time-sharing schedule and transportation arrangements contained in the petition. The order may be issued in an expedited manner without the necessity of an evidentiary hearing. If a response is timely filed, the parent or other person may not relocate, and must proceed to a temporary hearing or trial and obtain court permission to relocate.

(e) Relocating the child without complying with the requirements of this subsection subjects the party in violation to contempt and other proceedings to compel the return of the child and may be taken into account by the court in any initial or postjudgment action seeking a determination or modification of the parenting plan or the access or time-sharing schedule as:

1. A factor in making a determination regarding the relocation of a child.

2. A factor in determining whether the parenting plan or the access or time-sharing schedule should be modified.

3. A basis for ordering the temporary or permanent return of the child.

4. Sufficient cause to order the parent or other person seeking to relocate the child to pay reasonable expenses and attorney's fees incurred by the party objecting to the relocation.

5. Sufficient cause for the award of reasonable attorney's fees and costs, including interim travel expenses incident to access or time-sharing or securing the return of the child.

(4) APPLICABILITY OF PUBLIC RECORDS LAW.—If the parent or other person seeking to relocate a child, or the child, is entitled to prevent disclosure of location information under a public records exemption, the court may enter any order necessary to modify the disclosure requirements of this section in compliance with the public records exemption.

(5) OBJECTION TO RELOCATION.—An answer objecting to a proposed relocation must be verified and include the specific factual basis supporting the reasons for seeking a prohibition of the relocation, including a statement of the amount of participation or involvement the objecting party currently has or has had in the life of the child.

(6) TEMPORARY ORDER.—

(a) The court may grant a temporary order restraining the relocation of a child, order the return of the child, if a relocation has previously taken place, or order other appropriate remedial relief, if the court finds:

1. That the petition to relocate does not comply with subsection (3);

2. That the child has been relocated without a written agreement of the parties or without court approval; or

3. From an examination of the evidence presented at the preliminary hearing that there is a likelihood that upon final hearing the court will not approve the relocation of the child.

(b) The court may grant a temporary order permitting the relocation of the child pending final hearing, if the court finds:

1. That the petition to relocate was properly filed and is otherwise in compliance with subsection (3); and

2. From an examination of the evidence presented at the preliminary hearing, that there is a likelihood that on final hearing the court will approve the relocation of the child, which findings must be supported by the same factual basis as would be necessary to support approving the

relocation in a final judgment.

(c) If the court has issued a temporary order authorizing a party seeking to relocate or move a child before a final judgment is rendered, the court may not give any weight to the temporary relocation as a factor in reaching its final decision.

(d) If temporary relocation of a child is approved, the court may require the person relocating the child to provide reasonable security, financial or otherwise, and guarantee that the court-ordered contact with the child will not be interrupted or interfered with by the relocating party.

(7) NO PRESUMPTION; FACTORS TO DETERMINE CONTESTED RELOCATION.—A presumption in favor of or against a request to relocate with the child does not arise if a parent or other person seeks to relocate and the move will materially affect the current schedule of contact, access, and time-sharing with the nonrelocating parent or other person. In reaching its decision regarding a proposed temporary or permanent relocation, the court shall evaluate all of the following:

(a) The nature, quality, extent of involvement, and duration of the child's relationship with the parent or other person proposing to relocate with the child and with the nonrelocating parent, other persons, siblings, half-siblings, and other significant persons in the child's life.

(b) The age and developmental stage of the child, the needs of the child, and the likely impact the relocation will have on the child's physical, educational, and emotional development, taking into consideration any special needs of the child.

(c) The feasibility of preserving the relationship between the nonrelocating parent or other person and the child through substitute arrangements that take into consideration the logistics of contact, access, and time-sharing, as well as the financial circumstances of the parties; whether those factors are sufficient to foster a continuing meaningful relationship between the child and the nonrelocating parent or other person; and the likelihood of compliance with the substitute arrangements by the relocating parent or other person once he or she is out of the jurisdiction of the court.

(d) The child's preference, taking into consideration the age and maturity of the child.

(e) Whether the relocation will enhance the general quality of life for both the parent or other person seeking the relocation and the child, including, but not limited to, financial or emotional benefits or educational opportunities.

(f) The reasons each parent or other person is seeking or opposing the relocation.

(g) The current employment and economic circumstances of each parent or other person and whether the proposed relocation is necessary to improve the economic circumstances of the parent or other person seeking relocation of the child.

(h) That the relocation is sought in good faith and the extent to which the objecting parent has fulfilled his or her financial obligations to the parent or other person seeking relocation, including child support, spousal support, and marital property and marital debt obligations.

(i) The career and other opportunities available to the objecting parent or other person if the relocation occurs.

(j) A history of substance abuse or domestic violence as defined in s. 741.28 or which meets the criteria of s. 39.806(1)(d) by either parent, including a consideration of the severity of such conduct and the failure or success of any attempts at rehabilitation.

(k) Any other factor affecting the best interest of the child or as set forth in s. 61.13.

(8) BURDEN OF PROOF.—The parent or other person wishing to relocate has the burden of proving by a preponderance of the evidence that relocation is in the best interest of the child. If that burden of proof is met, the burden shifts to the nonrelocating parent or other person to show by a preponderance of the evidence that the proposed relocation is not in the best interest of the child.

(9) ORDER REGARDING RELOCATION.—If relocation is approved:

(a) The court may, in its discretion, order contact with the nonrelocating parent or other person, including access, time-sharing, telephone, Internet, webcam, and other arrangements sufficient to ensure that the child has frequent, continuing, and meaningful contact with the nonrelocating parent or other person, if contact is financially affordable and in the best interest of the child.

(b) If applicable, the court shall specify how the transportation costs are to be allocated between the parents and other persons entitled to contact, access, and time-sharing and may adjust the child support award, as appropriate, considering the costs of transportation and the respective net incomes of the parents in accordance with the state child support guidelines schedule.

(10) PRIORITY FOR HEARING OR TRIAL.—An evidentiary hearing or nonjury trial on a pleading seeking temporary or permanent relief filed under this section shall be accorded priority on the court's calendar. If a motion seeking a temporary relocation is filed, absent good cause, the hearing must occur no later than 30 days after the motion for a temporary relocation is filed. If a notice to set the matter for a nonjury trial is filed, absent good cause, the nonjury trial must occur no later than 90 days after the notice is filed.

(11) APPLICABILITY.—

(a) This section applies:

1. To orders entered before October 1, 2009, if the existing order defining custody, primary residence, the parenting plan, time-sharing, or access to or with the child does not expressly govern the relocation of the child.

2. To an order, whether temporary or permanent, regarding the parenting plan, custody, primary residence, time-sharing, or access to the child entered on or after October 1, 2009.

3. To any relocation or proposed relocation, whether permanent or temporary, of a child during any proceeding pending on October 1, 2009, wherein the parenting plan, custody, primary residence, time-sharing, or access to the child is an issue.

(b) To the extent that a provision of this section conflicts with an order existing on October 1, 2009, this section does not apply to the terms of that order which expressly govern relocation of the child or a change in the principal residence address of a parent or other person.

61.13002. Temporary time-sharing modification and child support modification due to military service.

(1) If a supplemental petition or a motion for modification of time-sharing and parental responsibility is filed because a parent is activated, deployed, or temporarily assigned to military service and the parent's ability to comply with time-sharing is materially affected as a result, the court may not issue an order or modify or amend a previous judgment or order that changes time-sharing as it existed on the date the parent was activated, deployed, or temporarily assigned to military service, except that a court may enter a temporary order to modify or amend time-sharing if there is clear and convincing evidence that the temporary modification or amendment is in the best interests of the child. However, a parent's activation, deployment, or temporary assignment to military service and the resultant temporary disruption to the child may not be the sole factor in a court's decision to grant a petition for or modification of permanent time-sharing and parental responsibility. When entering a temporary order under this section, the court shall consider and provide for, if feasible, contact between the military servicemember and his or her child, including, but not limited to, electronic communication by webcam, telephone, or other available means. The court shall also permit liberal time-sharing during periods of leave from military service, as it is in the child's best interests to maintain the parent-child bond during the parent's military service.

(2) If a parent is activated, deployed, or temporarily assigned to military service on orders in excess of 90 days and the parent's ability to comply with time-sharing is materially affected as a result, the parent may designate a person or persons to exercise time-sharing with the child on the parent's behalf. The designation shall be limited to a family member, a stepparent, or a relative of the child by marriage. The designation shall be made in writing and provided to the other parent at least 10 working days before the court-ordered period of time-sharing commences. The other parent may only object to the appointment of the designee on the basis that the designee's time-

sharing visitation is not in the best interests of the child. When unable to reach agreement on the delegation, either parent may request an expedited court hearing for a determination on the designation.

(3) The servicemember and the nonmilitary parent shall cooperate with each other in an effort to reach a mutually agreeable resolution of custody, visitation, delegation of visitation, and child support. Each party shall provide information to the other party in an effort to facilitate agreement on custody, visitation, delegation of visitation, and child support. Agreements on designation of persons to exercise time-sharing with the child on the parent's behalf may also be made at the time of dissolution of marriage or other child custody proceedings.

(4) If a temporary order is issued under this section, the court shall reinstate the time-sharing order previously in effect upon the servicemember parent's return from active military service, deployment, or temporary assignment.

(5) Upon motion of either parent for enforcement of rights under this section, the court shall, for good cause shown, hold an expedited hearing in custody and visitation matters instituted under this section, and shall permit the servicemember to testify by telephone, video teleconference, webcam, affidavit, or other means where the military duties of the servicemember parent have a material effect on the parent's ability, or anticipated ability, to appear in person at a regularly scheduled hearing.

(6) If a temporary order is entered under this section, the court may address the issue of support for the child by:

(a) Entering an order of temporary support from the servicemember to the other parent under s. 61.30;

(b) Requiring the servicemember to enroll the child as a military dependent with DEERs, TriCare, or other similar benefits available to military dependents as provided by the service member's branch of service and federal regulations; or

(c) Suspending, abating, or reducing the child support obligation of the nonservice member until the custody judgment or time-share order previously in effect is reinstated.

(7) This section does not apply to permanent change of station moves by military personnel, which shall be governed by s. 61.13001.

61.13003. Court-ordered electronic communication between a parent and a child.

(1)(a) In connection with proceedings under this chapter, a court may order electronic communication between a parent and a child. Before ordering electronic communication, a court must consider:

1. Whether electronic communication is in a child's best interests;

2. Whether communication equipment and technology to provide electronic communication is reasonably available, accessible, and affordable;

3. Each parent's history of substance abuse or domestic violence; and

4. Any other factor that the court considers material.

(b) Notwithstanding paragraph (a), a rebuttable presumption is created providing that it is in the best interests of a child for a parent and child to have reasonable telephone communication. Unless this presumption is rebutted, the court shall order telephone communication.

(c) The court may set safeguards or guidelines for electronic communication.

(2) If the court finds that one or both parents will incur additional costs in order to implement electronic communication with the child, the court shall allocate such expenses arising solely from the electronic communication between the parents after considering the respective parent's financial circumstances.

(3) If the court enters an order granting electronic communication, each parent shall furnish the

other parent with the access information necessary to facilitate electronic communication. Each parent shall notify the other parent of any change in the access information within 7 days after the change.

(4) Electronic communication may be used only to supplement a parent's face-to-face contact with his or her minor child. Electronic communication may not be used to replace or as a substitute for face-to-face contact.

(5) A party to a child custody order that does not prohibit electronic communication may move a court to order electronic communication. Such a party need not prove a substantial change in circumstances.

(6) The court may not consider the availability of electronic communication as the sole determinative factor when considering relocation.

(7) The extent or amount of time that electronic communication with the child is ordered under s. 61.13 may not be used as a factor when the court calculates child support.

(8) This section does not apply to any judgment or order issued before October 1, 2007.

61.1301. Income deduction orders.

(1) ISSUANCE IN CONJUNCTION WITH AN ORDER ESTABLISHING, ENFORCING, OR MODIFYING AN OBLIGATION FOR ALIMONY OR CHILD SUPPORT.—

(a) Upon the entry of an order establishing, enforcing, or modifying an obligation for alimony, for child support, or for alimony and child support, other than a temporary order, the court shall enter a separate order for income deduction if one has not been entered. Upon the entry of a temporary order establishing support or the entry of a temporary order enforcing or modifying a temporary order of support, the court may enter a separate order of income deduction. Copies of the orders shall be served on the obligee and obligor. If the order establishing, enforcing, or modifying the obligation directs that payments be made through the depository, the court shall provide to the depository a copy of the order establishing, enforcing, or modifying the obligation. If the obligee is a recipient of Title IV-D services, the court shall furnish to the Title IV-D agency a copy of the income deduction order and the order establishing, enforcing, or modifying the obligation.

1. In Title IV-D cases, the Title IV-D agency may implement income deduction after receiving a copy of an order from the court under this paragraph or a forwarding agency under UIFSA, URESA, or RURESA by issuing an income deduction notice to the payor.

2. The income deduction notice must state that it is based upon a valid support order and that it contains an income deduction requirement or upon a separate income deduction order. The income deduction notice must contain the notice to payor provisions specified by paragraph (2)(e). The income deduction notice must contain the following information from the income deduction order upon which the notice is based: the case number, the court that entered the order, and the date entered.

3. Payors shall deduct support payments from income, as specified in the income deduction notice, in the manner provided under paragraph (2)(e).

4. In non-Title IV-D cases, the income deduction notice must be accompanied by a copy of the support order upon which the notice is based. In Title IV-D cases, upon request of a payor, the Title IV-D agency shall furnish the payor a copy of the income deduction order.

5. If a support order entered before January 1, 1994, in a non-Title IV-D case does not specify income deduction, income deduction may be initiated upon a delinquency without the need for any amendment to the support order or any further action by the court. In such case the obligee may implement income deduction by serving a notice of delinquency on the obligor as provided for under paragraph (f).

(b) The income deduction order shall:

1. Direct a payor to deduct from all income due and payable to an obligor the amount required by the court to meet the obligor's support obligation including any attorney's fees or costs owed and

forward the deducted amount pursuant to the order.

2. State the amount of arrearage owed, if any, and direct a payor to withhold an additional 20 percent or more of the periodic amount specified in the order establishing, enforcing, or modifying the obligation, until full payment is made of any arrearage, attorney's fees and costs owed, provided no deduction shall be applied to attorney's fees and costs until the full amount of any arrearage is paid.

3. Provide that if a delinquency accrues after the order establishing, modifying, or enforcing the obligation has been entered and there is no order for repayment of the delinquency or a preexisting arrearage, a payor shall deduct an additional 20 percent of the current support obligation or other amount agreed to by the parties until the delinquency and any attorney's fees and costs are paid in full. No deduction may be applied to attorney's fees and costs until the delinquency is paid in full.

4. Direct a payor not to deduct in excess of the amounts allowed under s. 303(b) of the Consumer Credit Protection Act, 15 U.S.C. s. 1673(b), as amended.

5. Direct whether a payor shall deduct all, a specified portion, or no income which is paid in the form of a bonus or other similar one-time payment, up to the amount of arrearage reported in the income deduction notice or the remaining balance thereof, and forward the payment to the governmental depository. For purposes of this subparagraph, "bonus" means a payment in addition to an obligor's usual compensation and which is in addition to any amounts contracted for or otherwise legally due and shall not include any commission payments due an obligor.

6. In Title IV-D cases, direct a payor to provide to the court depository the date on which each deduction is made.

7. In Title IV-D cases, if an obligation to pay current support is reduced or terminated due to emancipation of a child and the obligor owes an arrearage, retroactive support, delinquency, or costs, direct the payor to continue the income deduction at the rate in effect immediately prior to emancipation until all arrearages, retroactive support, delinquencies, and costs are paid in full or until the amount of withholding is modified.

8. Direct that, at such time as the State Disbursement Unit becomes operational, all payments in those cases in which the obligee is receiving Title IV-D services and in those cases in which the obligee is not receiving Title IV-D services in which the initial support order was issued in this state on or after January 1, 1994, and in which the obligor's child support obligation is being paid through income deduction, be made payable to and delivered to the State Disbursement Unit. Notwithstanding any other statutory provision to the contrary, funds received by the State Disbursement Unit shall be held, administered, and disbursed by the State Disbursement Unit pursuant to the provisions of this chapter.

(c) The income deduction order is effective immediately unless the court upon good cause shown finds that the income deduction order shall be effective upon a delinquency in an amount specified by the court but not to exceed 1 month's payment, pursuant to the order establishing, enforcing, or modifying the obligation. In order to find good cause, the court must at a minimum make written findings that:

1. Explain why implementing immediate income deduction would not be in the child's best interest;

2. There is proof of timely payment of the previously ordered obligation without an income deduction order in cases of modification; and

3.a. There is an agreement by the obligor to advise the IV-D agency and court depository of any change in payor and health insurance; or

b. There is a signed written agreement providing an alternative arrangement between the obligor and the obligee and, at the option of the IV-D agency, by the IV-D agency in IV-D cases in which there is an assignment of support rights to the state, reviewed and entered in the record by the court.

(d) The income deduction order shall be effective as long as the order upon which it is based is effective or until further order of the court. Notwithstanding the foregoing, however, at such time as the State Disbursement Unit becomes operational, in those cases in which the obligee is receiving Title IV-D services and in those cases in which the obligee is not receiving Title IV-D services in which the initial support order was issued in this state on or after January 1, 1994, and in which the obligor's child support obligation is being paid through income deduction, such payments shall be made payable to and delivered to the State Disbursement Unit.

(e) When the court orders the income deduction to be effective immediately, the court shall furnish to the obligor a statement of his or her rights, remedies, and duties in regard to the income deduction order. The statement shall state:

1. All fees or interest which shall be imposed.

2. The total amount of income to be deducted for each pay period until the arrearage, if any, is paid in full and shall state the total amount of income to be deducted for each pay period thereafter. The amounts deducted may not be in excess of that allowed under s. 303(b) of the Consumer Credit Protection Act, 15 U.S.C. s. 1673(b), as amended.

3. That the income deduction order applies to current and subsequent payors and periods of employment.

4. That a copy of the income deduction order or, in Title IV-D cases, the income deduction notice will be served on the obligor's payor or payors.

5. That enforcement of the income deduction order may only be contested on the ground of mistake of fact regarding the amount owed pursuant to the order establishing, enforcing, or modifying the obligation, the arrearages, or the identity of the obligor, the payor, or the obligee.

6. That the obligor is required to notify the obligee and, when the obligee is receiving IV-D services, the IV-D agency within 7 days of changes in the obligor's address, payors, and the addresses of his or her payors.

7. That in a Title IV-D case, if an obligation to pay current support is reduced or terminated due to emancipation of a child and the obligor owes an arrearage, retroactive support, delinquency, or costs, income deduction continues at the rate in effect immediately prior to emancipation until all arrearages, retroactive support, delinquencies, and costs are paid in full or until the amount of withholding is modified.

(f) If a support order was entered before January 1, 1994, the court orders the income deduction to be effective upon a delinquency as provided in paragraph (c), or a delinquency has accrued under an order entered before July 1, 2006, that established, modified, or enforced the obligation and there is no order for repayment of the delinquency or a preexisting arrearage, the obligee or, in Title IV-D cases, the Title IV-D agency may enforce the income deduction by serving a notice of delinquency on the obligor under this paragraph.

1. The notice of delinquency shall state:

a. The terms of the order establishing, enforcing, or modifying the obligation.

b. The period of delinquency and the total amount of the delinquency as of the date the notice is mailed.

c. All fees or interest which may be imposed.

d. The total amount of income to be deducted for each pay period until the arrearage, and all applicable fees and interest, is paid in full and shall state the total amount of income to be deducted for each pay period thereafter. The amounts deducted may not be in excess of that allowed under s. 303(b) of the Consumer Credit Protection Act, 15 U.S.C. s. 1673(b), as amended.

e. That the income deduction order applies to current and subsequent payors and periods of employment.

f. That a copy of the notice of delinquency will be served on the obligor's payor or payors, together with a copy of the income deduction order or, in Title IV-D cases, the income deduction notice, unless the obligor applies to the court to contest enforcement of the income deduction. If the income deduction order being enforced was rendered by the Title IV-D agency pursuant to s. 409.2563 and the obligor contests the deduction, the obligor shall file a petition for an administrative hearing with the Title IV-D agency. The application or petition shall be filed within 15 days after the date the notice of delinquency was served.

g. That enforcement of the income deduction order may only be contested on the ground of mistake of fact regarding the amount owed pursuant to the order establishing, enforcing, or modifying the obligation, the amount of arrearages, or the identity of the obligor, the payor, or the obligee.

h. That the obligor is required to notify the obligee of the obligor's current address and current payors and of the address of current payors. All changes shall be reported by the obligor within 7 days. If the IV-D agency is enforcing the order, the obligor shall make these notifications to the agency instead of to the obligee.

2. The failure of the obligor to receive the notice of delinquency does not preclude subsequent service of the income deduction order or, in Title IV-D cases, the income deduction notice on the obligor's payor. A notice of delinquency which fails to state an arrearage does not mean that an arrearage is not owed.

(g) At any time, any party, including the IV-D agency, may apply to the court to:

1. Modify, suspend, or terminate the income deduction order in accordance with a modification, suspension, or termination of the support provisions in the underlying order; or

2. Modify the amount of income deducted when the arrearage has been paid.

(2) ENFORCEMENT OF INCOME DEDUCTION ORDERS.—

(a) The obligee or his or her agent shall serve an income deduction order and notice to payor, or, in Title IV-D cases, the Title IV-D agency shall issue an income deduction notice, and in the case of a delinquency a notice of delinquency, on the obligor's payor unless the obligor has applied for a hearing to contest the enforcement of the income deduction pursuant to paragraph (c).

(b)1. Service by or upon any person who is a party to a proceeding under this section shall be made in the manner prescribed in the Florida Rules of Civil Procedure for service upon parties.

2. Service upon an obligor's payor or successor payor under this section shall be made by prepaid certified mail, return receipt requested, or in the manner prescribed in chapter 48.

(c)1. The obligor, within 15 days after service of a notice of delinquency, may apply for a hearing to contest the enforcement of the income deduction on the ground of mistake of fact regarding the amount owed pursuant to an order establishing, enforcing, or modifying an obligation for alimony, for child support, or for alimony and child support, the amount of the arrearage, or the identity of the obligor, the payor, or the obligee. The obligor shall send a copy of the pleading to the obligee and, if the obligee is receiving IV-D services, to the IV-D agency. The timely filing of the pleading shall stay service of an income deduction order or, in Title IV-D cases, income deduction notice on all payors of the obligor until a hearing is held and a determination is made as to whether enforcement of the income deduction order is proper. The payment of a delinquent obligation by an obligor upon entry of an income deduction order shall not preclude service of the income deduction order or, in Title IV-D cases, an income deduction notice on the obligor's payor.

2. When an obligor timely requests a hearing to contest enforcement of an income deduction order, the court, after due notice to all parties and the IV-D agency if the obligee is receiving IV-D services, shall hear the matter within 20 days after the application is filed. The court shall enter an order resolving the matter within 10 days after the hearing. A copy of this order shall be served on the parties and the IV-D agency if the obligee is receiving IV-D services. If the court determines that income deduction is proper, it shall specify the date the income deduction order must be served on the obligor's payor.

(d) When a court determines that an income deduction order is proper pursuant to paragraph (c), the obligee or his or her agent shall cause a copy of the notice of delinquency to be served on the obligor's payors. A copy of the income deduction order or, in Title IV-D cases, income deduction notice, and in the case of a delinquency a notice of delinquency, shall also be furnished to the obligor.

(e) Notice to payor and income deduction notice. The notice to payor or, in Title IV-D cases, income deduction notice shall contain only information necessary for the payor to comply with the order providing for income deduction. The notice shall:

1. Provide the obligor's social security number.

2. Require the payor to deduct from the obligor's income the amount specified in the income deduction order, and in the case of a delinquency the amount specified in the notice of delinquency, and to pay that amount to the obligee or to the depository, as appropriate. The amount actually deducted plus all administrative charges shall not be in excess of the amount

allowed under s. 303(b) of the Consumer Credit Protection Act, 15 U.S.C. s. 1673(b);

3. Instruct the payor to implement income deduction no later than the first payment date which occurs more than 14 days after the date the income deduction notice was served on the payor, and the payor shall conform the amount specified in the income deduction order or, in Title IV-D cases, income deduction notice to the obligor's pay cycle. The court should request at the time of the order that the payment cycle reflect that of the payor;

4. Instruct the payor to forward, within 2 days after each date the obligor is entitled to payment from the payor, to the obligee or to the depository the amount deducted from the obligor's income, a statement as to whether the amount totally or partially satisfies the periodic amount specified in the income deduction order or, in Title IV-D cases, income deduction notice, and the specific date each deduction is made. If the IV-D agency is enforcing the order, the payor shall make these notifications to the agency instead of the obligee;

5. Specify that if a payor fails to deduct the proper amount from the obligor's income, the payor is liable for the amount the payor should have deducted, plus costs, interest, and reasonable attorney's fees;

6. Provide that the payor may collect up to $5 against the obligor's income to reimburse the payor for administrative costs for the first income deduction and up to $2 for each deduction thereafter;

7. State that the notice to payor or, in Title IV-D cases, income deduction notice, and in the case of a delinquency the notice of delinquency, are binding on the payor until further notice by the obligee, IV-D agency, or the court or until the payor no longer provides income to the obligor;

8. Instruct the payor that, when he or she no longer provides income to the obligor, he or she shall notify the obligee and shall also provide the obligor's last known address and the name and address of the obligor's new payor, if known; and that, if the payor violates this provision, the payor is subject to a civil penalty not to exceed $250 for the first violation or $500 for any subsequent violation. If the IV-D agency is enforcing the order, the payor shall make these notifications to the agency instead of to the obligee. Penalties shall be paid to the obligee or the IV-D agency, whichever is enforcing the income deduction order;

9. State that the payor shall not discharge, refuse to employ, or take disciplinary action against an obligor because of the requirement for income deduction and shall state that a violation of this provision subjects the payor to a civil penalty not to exceed $250 for the first violation or $500 for any subsequent violation. Penalties shall be paid to the obligee or the IV-D agency, whichever is enforcing the income deduction, if any alimony or child support obligation is owing. If no alimony or child support obligation is owing, the penalty shall be paid to the obligor;

10. State that an obligor may bring a civil action in the courts of this state against a payor who refuses to employ, discharges, or otherwise disciplines an obligor because of income deduction. The obligor is entitled to reinstatement and all wages and benefits lost, plus reasonable attorney's fees and costs incurred;

11. Inform the payor that the requirement for income deduction has priority over all other legal processes under state law pertaining to the same income and that payment, as required by the notice to payor or income deduction notice, is a complete defense by the payor against any claims of the obligor or his or her creditors as to the sum paid;

12. Inform the payor that, when the payor receives notices to payor or income deduction notices requiring that the income of two or more obligors be deducted and sent to the same depository, the payor may combine the amounts that are to be paid to the depository in a single payment as long as the payments attributable to each obligor are clearly identified;

13. Inform the payor that if the payor receives more than one notice to payor or income deduction notice against the same obligor, the payor shall contact the court or, in Title IV-D cases, the Title IV-D agency for further instructions. Upon being so contacted, the court or, in Title IV-D cases when all the cases upon which the notices are based are Title IV-D cases, the Title IV-D agency shall allocate amounts available for income deduction as provided in subsection (4); and

14. State that in a Title IV-D case, if an obligation to pay current support is reduced or terminated due to the emancipation of a child and the obligor owes an arrearage, retroactive support, delinquency, or costs, income deduction continues at the rate in effect immediately prior to

emancipation until all arrearages, retroactive support, delinquencies, and costs are paid in full or until the amount of withholding is modified.

(f) At any time an income deduction order is being enforced, the obligor may apply to the court for a hearing to contest the continued enforcement of the income deduction on the same grounds set out in paragraph (c), with a copy to the obligee and, in IV-D cases, to the IV-D agency. If the income deduction order being enforced was rendered by the IV-D agency pursuant to s. 409.2563 and the obligor contests the withholding, the obligor shall file a petition for an administrative hearing with the IV-D agency. The application or petition does not affect the continued enforcement of the income deduction until the court or IV-D agency, if applicable, enters an order granting relief to the obligor. The obligee or the IV-D agency is released from liability for improper receipt of moneys pursuant to an income deduction order upon return to the appropriate party of any moneys received.

(g) An obligee or his or her agent shall enforce an income deduction order against an obligor's successor payor who is located in this state in the same manner prescribed in this section for the enforcement of an income deduction order against a payor.

(h)1. When an income deduction order is to be enforced against a payor located outside the state, the obligee who is receiving IV-D services or his or her agent shall promptly request the agency responsible for income deduction in the other state to enforce the income deduction order. The request shall contain all information necessary to enforce the income deduction order, including the amount to be periodically deducted, a copy of the order establishing, enforcing, or modifying the obligation, and a statement of arrearages, if applicable.

2. When the IV-D agency is requested by the agency responsible for income deduction in another state to enforce an income deduction order against a payor located in this state for the benefit of an obligee who is being provided IV-D services by the agency in the other state, the IV-D agency shall act promptly pursuant to the applicable provisions of this section.

3. When an obligor who is subject to an income deduction order enforced against a payor located in this state for the benefit of an obligee who is being provided IV-D services by the agency responsible for income deduction in another state terminates his or her relationship with his or her payor, the IV-D agency shall notify the agency in the other state and provide it with the name and address of the obligor and the address of any new payor of the obligor, if known.

4.a. The procedural rules and laws of this state govern the procedural aspects of income deduction whenever the agency responsible for income deduction in another state requests the enforcement of an income deduction order in this state.

b. Except with respect to when withholding must be implemented, which is controlled by the state where the order establishing, enforcing, or modifying the obligation was entered, the substantive law of this state shall apply whenever the agency responsible for income deduction in another state requests the enforcement of an income deduction in this state.

c. When the IV-D agency is requested by an agency responsible for income deduction in another state to implement income deduction against a payor located in this state for the benefit of an obligee who is being provided IV-D services by the agency in the other state or when the IV-D agency in this state initiates an income deduction request on behalf of an obligee receiving IV-D services in this state against a payor in another state, pursuant to this section or the Uniform Interstate Family Support Act, the IV-D agency shall file the interstate income deduction documents, or an affidavit of such request when the income deduction documents are not available, with the depository and if the IV-D agency in this state is responding to a request from another state, provide copies to the payor and obligor in accordance with subsection (1). The depository created pursuant to s. 61.181 shall accept the interstate income deduction documents or affidavit and shall establish an account for the receipt and disbursement of child support or child support and alimony payments and advise the IV-D agency of the account number in writing within 2 days after receipt of the documents or affidavit.

(i) Certified copies of payment records maintained by a depository shall, without further proof, be admitted into evidence in any legal proceeding in this state.

(j)1. A person may not discharge, refuse to employ, or take disciplinary action against an employee because of the enforcement of an income deduction order. An employer who violates this subsection is subject to a civil penalty not to exceed $250 for the first violation or $500 for any subsequent violation. Penalties shall be paid to the obligee or the IV-D agency, whichever is enforcing the income deduction, if any alimony or child support is owing. If no alimony or child support is owing, the penalty shall be paid to the obligor.

2. An employee may bring a civil action in the courts of this state against an employer who refuses to employ, discharges, or otherwise disciplines an employee because of an income deduction order. The employee is entitled to reinstatement and all wages and benefits lost plus reasonable attorney's fees and costs incurred.

(k) When a payor no longer provides income to an obligor, he or she shall notify the obligee and, if the obligee is a IV-D applicant, the IV-D agency and shall also provide the obligor's last known address and the name and address of the obligor's new payor, if known. A payor who violates this subsection is subject to a civil penalty not to exceed $250 for the first violation or $500 for a subsequent violation. Penalties shall be paid to the obligee or the IV-D agency, whichever is enforcing the income deduction order.

(3)(a) It is the intent of the Legislature that this section may be used to collect arrearages in child support or in alimony payments.

(b) In a Title IV-D case, if an obligation to pay current support is reduced or terminated due to the emancipation of a child and the obligor owes an arrearage, retroactive support, delinquency, or costs, income deduction continues at the rate in effect immediately prior to emancipation until all arrearages, retroactive support, delinquencies, and costs are paid in full or until the amount of withholding is modified. Any income-deducted amount that is in excess of the obligation to pay current support shall be credited against the arrearages, retroactive support, delinquency, and costs owed by the obligor. The department shall send notice of this requirement by regular mail to the payor and the depository operated pursuant to s. 61.181, and the notice shall state the amount of the obligation to pay current support, if any, and the amount owed for arrearages, retroactive support, delinquency, and costs. For income deduction orders entered before July 1, 2004, which do not include this requirement, the department shall send by certified mail, restricted delivery, return receipt requested, to the obligor at the most recent address provided by the obligor to the tribunal that issued the order or a more recent address if known, notice of this requirement, that the obligor may contest the withholding as provided by paragraph (2)(f), and that the obligor may request the tribunal that issued the income deduction to modify the amount of the withholding. This paragraph provides an additional remedy for collection of unpaid support and applies to cases in which a support order or income deduction order was entered before, on, or after July 1, 2004.

(c) If a delinquency accrues after an order establishing, modifying, or enforcing a support obligation has been entered, an income deduction order entered after July 1, 2006, is in effect, and there is no order for repayment of the delinquency or a preexisting arrearage, a payor who is served with an income deduction order or, in a Title IV-D case, an income deduction notice shall deduct an additional 20 percent of the current support obligation or other amount agreed to by the parties until the delinquency and any attorney's fees and costs are paid in full. No deduction may be applied to attorney's fees and costs until the delinquency is paid in full.

(4) When there is more than one income deduction notice against the same obligor, the amounts available for income deduction must be allocated among all obligee families as follows:

(a) For computation purposes, all obligations must be converted to a common payroll frequency, and the percentage of deduction allowed under s. 303(b) of the Consumer Credit Protection Act, 15 U.S.C. s. 1673(b), as amended, must be determined. The amount of income available for deduction is determined by multiplying that percentage by the obligor's net income.

(b) If the total monthly support obligation to all families is less than the amount of income available for deduction, the full amount of each obligation must be deducted.

(c) If the total monthly support obligation to all families is greater than the amount of income available for deduction, the amount of the deduction must be prorated, giving priority to current support, so that each family is allocated a percentage of the amount deducted. The percentage to be allocated to each family is determined by dividing each current support obligation by the total of all current support obligations. If the total of all current support obligations is less than the income available for deduction, and past due support is owed to more than one family, then the remainder of the available income must be prorated so that each family is allocated a percentage of the remaining income available for deduction. The percentage to be allocated to each family is determined by dividing each past due support obligation by the total of all past due support obligations.

(5) By July 1, 2006, the department shall provide a payor with Internet access to income deduction and national medical support notices issued by the department on or after July 1, 2006, concerning an obligor to whom the payor pays income. The department shall provide a payor who requests Internet access with a user code and password to allow the payor to receive notices electronically and to download the information necessary to begin income deduction and health insurance enrollment. If a participating payor does not respond to electronic notice by accessing the data posted by the department within 48 hours, the department shall mail the income deduction or medical support notice to the payor.

61.13015. Petition for suspension or denial of professional licenses and certificates.

(1) An obligee may petition the court which entered the support order or the court which is enforcing the support order for an order to suspend or deny the license or certificate issued pursuant to chapters 409, 455, 456, 559, and 1012 of any obligor with a delinquent support obligation. However, no petition may be filed until the obligee has exhausted all other available remedies. The purpose of this section is to promote the public policy of s. 409.2551.

(2) The obligee shall give notice to any obligor when a delinquency exists in the support obligation. The notice shall specify that the obligor has 30 days from the date on which service of the notice is complete to pay the delinquency or to reach an agreement with the obligee to pay the delinquency. The notice shall specify that, if payment is not made or an agreement cannot be reached, the license or certificate may be denied or suspended pursuant to a court order.

(3) If a delinquency exists and the obligor fails to pay the delinquency or to reach an agreement to pay the delinquency within 30 days following completion of service of the notice of the delinquency, the obligee shall send a second notice to the obligor stating that the obligor has 30 days to pay the delinquency or reach an agreement with the obligee to pay the delinquency. If the obligor fails to respond to either notice from the obligee or if the obligor fails to pay the delinquency or to reach an agreement to pay the delinquency after the second notice, the obligee may petition the court to deny the application for the license or certificate or to suspend the license or certificate of the obligor. The court may find that it would be inappropriate to deny or suspend a license or certificate if:

(a) Denial or suspension would result in irreparable harm to the obligor or employees of the obligor or would not accomplish the objective of collecting the delinquency; or

(b) The obligor demonstrates that he or she has made a good faith effort to reach an agreement with the obligee.

(4) If the court denies or suspends a license or certificate and the obligor subsequently pays the delinquency or reaches an agreement with the obligee to settle the delinquency and makes the first payment required by the agreement, the license or certificate shall be issued or reinstated upon written proof to the court that the obligor has complied with the court order. Proof of payment shall consist of a certified copy of the payment record issued by the depository. The court shall order the appropriate department or licensing board to issue or reinstate the license or certificate without additional charge to the obligor.

(5) Notice shall be served under this section by mailing it by certified mail, return receipt requested, to the obligor at his or her last address of record with the local depository. If the obligor

has no address of record with the local depository, or if the last address of record with the local depository is incorrect, service shall be by publication as provided in chapter 49. When service of the notice is made by mail, service is complete upon the receipt of the notice by the obligor.

61.13016. Suspension of driver licenses and motor vehicle registrations.

(1) The driver license and motor vehicle registration of a support obligor who is delinquent in payment or who has failed to comply with subpoenas or a similar order to appear or show cause relating to paternity or support proceedings may be suspended. When an obligor is 15 days delinquent making a payment in support or failure to comply with a subpoena, order to appear, order to show cause, or similar order in IV-D cases, the Title IV-D agency may provide notice to the obligor of the delinquency or failure to comply with a subpoena, order to appear, order to show cause, or similar order and the intent to suspend by regular United States mail that is posted to the obligor's last address of record with the Department of Highway Safety and Motor Vehicles. When an obligor is 15 days delinquent in making a payment in support in non-IV-D cases, and upon the request of the obligee, the depository or the clerk of the court must provide notice to the obligor of the delinquency and the intent to suspend by regular United States mail that is posted to the obligor's last address of record with the Department of Highway Safety and Motor Vehicles. In either case, the notice must state:
(a) The terms of the order creating the support obligation;
(b) The period of the delinquency and the total amount of the delinquency as of the date of the notice or describe the subpoena, order to appear, order to show cause, or other similar order that has not been complied with;
(c) That notification will be given to the Department of Highway Safety and Motor Vehicles to suspend the obligor's driver license and motor vehicle registration unless, within 20 days after the date that the notice is mailed, the obligor:
1.a. Pays the delinquency in full and any other costs and fees accrued between the date of the notice and the date the delinquency is paid;
b. Enters into a written agreement for payment with the obligee in non-IV-D cases or with the Title IV-D agency in IV-D cases; or in IV-D cases, complies with a subpoena or order to appear, order to show cause, or a similar order;
c. Files a petition with the circuit court to contest the delinquency action;
d. Demonstrates that he or she receives reemployment assistance or unemployment compensation pursuant to chapter 443;
e. Demonstrates that he or she is disabled and incapable of self-support or that he or she receives benefits under the federal Supplemental Security Income program or Social Security Disability Insurance program;
f. Demonstrates that he or she receives temporary cash assistance pursuant to chapter 414; or
g. Demonstrates that he or she is making payments in accordance with a confirmed bankruptcy plan under chapter 11, chapter 12, or chapter 13 of the United States Bankruptcy Code, 11 U.S.C. ss. 101 et seq.; and
2. Pays any applicable delinquency fees.
(2)(a) Upon petition filed by the obligor in the circuit court within 20 days after the mailing date of the notice, the court may, in its discretion, direct the department to issue a license for driving privilege restricted to business purposes only, as defined by s. 322.271, if the person is otherwise qualified for such a license. As a condition for the court to exercise its discretion under this subsection, the obligor must agree to a schedule of payment on any child support arrearages and to maintain current child support obligations. If the obligor fails to comply with the schedule of payment, the court shall direct the Department of Highway Safety and Motor Vehicles to suspend

the obligor's driver license.

(b) The obligor must serve a copy of the petition on the Title IV-D agency in IV-D cases or on the depository or the clerk of the court in non-IV-D cases. When an obligor timely files a petition to set aside a suspension, the court must hear the matter within 15 days after the petition is filed. The court must enter an order resolving the matter within 10 days after the hearing, and a copy of the order must be served on the parties. The timely filing of a petition under this subsection stays the intent to suspend until the entry of a court order resolving the matter.

(3) If the obligor does not, within 20 days after the mailing date on the notice, pay the delinquency; enter into a written agreement; comply with the subpoena, order to appear, order to show cause, or other similar order; file a motion to contest; or satisfy sub-subparagraph (1)(c)1.d., sub-subparagraph (1)(c)1.e., sub-subparagraph (1)(c)1.f., or sub-subparagraph (1)(c)1.g., the Title IV-D agency in IV-D cases, or the depository or clerk of the court in non-IV-D cases, may file the notice with the Department of Highway Safety and Motor Vehicles and request the suspension of the obligor's driver license and motor vehicle registration in accordance with s. 322.058.

(4) The obligor may, within 20 days after the mailing date on the notice of delinquency or noncompliance and intent to suspend, file in the circuit court a petition to contest the notice of delinquency or noncompliance and intent to suspend on the ground of mistake of fact regarding the existence of a delinquency or the identity of the obligor. The obligor must serve a copy of the petition on the Title IV-D agency in IV-D cases or depository or clerk of the court in non-IV-D cases. When an obligor timely files a petition to contest, the court must hear the matter within 15 days after the petition is filed. The court must enter an order resolving the matter within 10 days after the hearing, and a copy of the order must be served on the parties. The timely filing of a petition to contest stays the notice of delinquency and intent to suspend until the entry of a court order resolving the matter.

(5) The procedures prescribed in this section and s. 322.058 may be used to enforce compliance with an order to appear for genetic testing.

61.1354. Sharing of information between consumer reporting agencies and the IV-D agency.

(1) Upon receipt of a request from a consumer reporting agency as defined in s. 603(f) of the Fair Credit Reporting Act, the IV-D agency or the depository in non-Title IV-D cases shall make available information relating to the amount of current and overdue support owed by an obligor. The IV-D agency or the depository in non-Title IV-D cases shall give the obligor written notice, at least 15 days prior to the release of information, of the IV-D agency's or depository's authority to release information to consumer reporting agencies relating to the amount of current and overdue support owed by the obligor. The obligor shall be informed of his or her right to request a hearing with the IV-D agency or the court in non-Title IV-D cases to contest the accuracy of the information.

(2) The IV-D agency shall report periodically to appropriate consumer reporting agencies, as identified by the IV-D agency, the name and social security number of any delinquent obligor, the amount of overdue support owed by the obligor, and the amount of the obligor's current support obligation when the overdue support is paid. The IV-D agency, or its designee, shall provide the obligor with written notice, at least 15 days prior to the initial release of information, of the IV-D agency's authority to release the information periodically to the consumer reporting agencies. The notice shall state the amount of overdue support owed and the amount of current support owed when the overdue support is paid and shall inform the obligor of the right to request a hearing with the IV-D agency within 15 days after receipt of the notice to contest the accuracy of the information. After the initial notice is given, no further notice or opportunity for a hearing need be given when updated information concerning the same obligor is periodically released to the

consumer reporting agencies.

(3) For purposes of determining an individual's income and establishing an individual's capacity to make support payments or for determining the appropriate amount of child support payment to be made by the individual, consumer reporting agencies shall provide, upon request, consumer reports to the head of the IV-D agency pursuant to s. 604 of the Fair Credit Reporting Act, provided that the head of the IV-D agency, or its designee, certifies that:

(a) The consumer report is needed for the purpose of determining an individual's income and establishing an individual's capacity to make support payments or determining the appropriate amount of child support payment to be made by the individual;

(b) Paternity of the child of the individual whose report is sought, if that individual is the father of the child, has been established or acknowledged pursuant to the laws of Florida;

(c) The individual whose report is sought was provided with at least 15 days' prior notice, by certified or registered mail to the individual's last known address, that the report was requested; and

(d) The consumer report will be used solely for the purpose described in paragraph (a).

(4) For purposes of setting an initial or modified child support order, consumer reporting agencies shall provide, upon request, consumer reports to the IV-D agency.

(5) The Department of Revenue is authorized to adopt rules necessary to implement this section.

61.14. Enforcement and modification of support, maintenance, or alimony agreements or orders.

(1)(a) When the parties enter into an agreement for payments for, or instead of, support, maintenance, or alimony, whether in connection with a proceeding for dissolution or separate maintenance or with any voluntary property settlement, or when a party is required by court order to make any payments, and the circumstances or the financial ability of either party changes or the child who is a beneficiary of an agreement or court order as described herein reaches majority after the execution of the agreement or the rendition of the order, either party may apply to the circuit court of the circuit in which the parties, or either of them, resided at the date of the execution of the agreement or reside at the date of the application, or in which the agreement was executed or in which the order was rendered, for an order decreasing or increasing the amount of support, maintenance, or alimony, and the court has jurisdiction to make orders as equity requires, with due regard to the changed circumstances or the financial ability of the parties or the child, decreasing, increasing, or confirming the amount of separate support, maintenance, or alimony provided for in the agreement or order. A finding that medical insurance is reasonably available or the child support guidelines schedule in s. 61.30 may constitute changed circumstances. Except as otherwise provided in s. 61.30(11)(c), the court may modify an order of support, maintenance, or alimony by increasing or decreasing the support, maintenance, or alimony retroactively to the date of the filing of the action or supplemental action for modification as equity requires, giving due regard to the changed circumstances or the financial ability of the parties or the child.

(b)1. The court may reduce or terminate an award of alimony upon specific written findings by the court that since the granting of a divorce and the award of alimony a supportive relationship has existed between the obligee and a person with whom the obligee resides. On the issue of whether alimony should be reduced or terminated under this paragraph, the burden is on the obligor to prove by a preponderance of the evidence that a supportive relationship exists.

2. In determining whether an existing award of alimony should be reduced or terminated because of an alleged supportive relationship between an obligee and a person who is not related by consanguinity or affinity and with whom the obligee resides, the court shall elicit the nature and extent of the relationship in question. The court shall give consideration, without limitation, to circumstances, including, but not limited to, the following, in determining the relationship of an

obligee to another person:

a. The extent to which the obligee and the other person have held themselves out as a married couple by engaging in conduct such as using the same last name, using a common mailing address, referring to each other in terms such as "my husband" or "my wife," or otherwise conducting themselves in a manner that evidences a permanent supportive relationship.

b. The period of time that the obligee has resided with the other person in a permanent place of abode.

c. The extent to which the obligee and the other person have pooled their assets or income or otherwise exhibited financial interdependence.

d. The extent to which the obligee or the other person has supported the other, in whole or in part.

e. The extent to which the obligee or the other person has performed valuable services for the other.

f. The extent to which the obligee or the other person has performed valuable services for the other's company or employer.

g. Whether the obligee and the other person have worked together to create or enhance anything of value.

h. Whether the obligee and the other person have jointly contributed to the purchase of any real or personal property.

i. Evidence in support of a claim that the obligee and the other person have an express agreement regarding property sharing or support.

j. Evidence in support of a claim that the obligee and the other person have an implied agreement regarding property sharing or support.

k. Whether the obligee and the other person have provided support to the children of one another, regardless of any legal duty to do so.

3. This paragraph does not abrogate the requirement that every marriage in this state be solemnized under a license, does not recognize a common law marriage as valid, and does not recognize a de facto marriage. This paragraph recognizes only that relationships do exist that provide economic support equivalent to a marriage and that alimony terminable on remarriage may be reduced or terminated upon the establishment of equivalent equitable circumstances as described in this paragraph. The existence of a conjugal relationship, though it may be relevant to the nature and extent of the relationship, is not necessary for the application of the provisions of this paragraph.

(c) For each support order reviewed by the department as required by s. 409.2564(11), if the amount of the child support award under the order differs by at least 10 percent but not less than $25 from the amount that would be awarded under s. 61.30, the department shall seek to have the order modified and any modification shall be made without a requirement for proof or showing of a change in circumstances.

(d) The department shall have authority to adopt rules to implement this section.

(2) When an order or agreement is modified pursuant to subsection (1), the party having an obligation to pay shall pay only the amount of support, maintenance, or alimony directed in the new order, and the agreement or earlier order is modified accordingly. No person may commence an action for modification of a support, maintenance, or alimony agreement or order except as herein provided. No court has jurisdiction to entertain any action to enforce the recovery of separate support, maintenance, or alimony other than as herein provided.

(3) This section is declaratory of existing public policy and of the laws of this state.

(4) If a party applies for a reduction of alimony or child support and the circumstances justify the reduction, the court may make the reduction of alimony or child support regardless of whether or not the party applying for it has fully paid the accrued obligations to the other party at the time of the application or at the time of the order of modification.

(5)(a) When a court of competent jurisdiction enters an order for the payment of alimony or child support or both, the court shall make a finding of the obligor's imputed or actual present ability to comply with the order. If the obligor subsequently fails to pay alimony or support and a contempt hearing is held, the original order of the court creates a presumption that the obligor has the present ability to pay the alimony or support and to purge himself or herself from the contempt. At the contempt hearing, the obligor shall have the burden of proof to show that he or she lacks the ability to purge himself or herself from the contempt. This presumption is adopted as a presumption under s. 90.302(2) to implement the public policy of this state that children shall be maintained from the resources of their parents and as provided for in s. 409.2551, and that spouses be maintained as provided for in s. 61.08. The court shall state in its order the reasons for granting or denying the contempt.

(b) In a proceeding in circuit court to enforce a support order under this chapter, chapter 88, chapter 409, or chapter 742, or any other provision of law, if the court finds that payments due under the support order are delinquent or overdue and that the obligor is unemployed, underemployed, or has no income but is able to work or participate in job training, the court may order the obligor to:

1. Seek employment.

2. File periodic reports with the court, or with the department if the department is providing Title IV-D services, detailing the obligor's efforts to seek and obtain employment during the reporting period.

3. Notify the court or the department, as appropriate, upon obtaining employment, income, or property.

4. Participate in job training, job placement, work experience, or other work programs that may be available pursuant to chapter 445, chapter 446, or any other source.

(6)(a)1. When support payments are made through the local depository or through the State Disbursement Unit, any payment or installment of support which becomes due and is unpaid under any support order is delinquent; and this unpaid payment or installment, and all other costs and fees herein provided for, become, after notice to the obligor and the time for response as set forth in this subsection, a final judgment by operation of law, which has the full force, effect, and attributes of a judgment entered by a court in this state for which execution may issue. No deduction shall be made by the local depository from any payment made for costs and fees accrued in the judgment by operation of law process under paragraph (b) until the total amount of support payments due the obligee under the judgment has been paid.

2. A certified statement by the local depository evidencing a delinquency in support payments constitute evidence of the final judgment under this paragraph.

3. The judgment under this paragraph is a final judgment as to any unpaid payment or installment of support which has accrued up to the time either party files a motion with the court to alter or modify the support order, and such judgment may not be modified by the court. The court may modify such judgment as to any unpaid payment or installment of support which accrues after the date of the filing of the motion to alter or modify the support order. This subparagraph does not prohibit the court from providing relief from the judgment pursuant to Rule 1.540, Florida Rules of Civil Procedure.

(b)1. When an obligor is 15 days delinquent in making a payment or installment of support and the amount of the delinquency is greater than the periodic payment amount ordered by the court, the local depository shall serve notice on the obligor informing him or her of:

a. The delinquency and its amount.

b. An impending judgment by operation of law against him or her in the amount of the delinquency and all other amounts which thereafter become due and are unpaid, together with costs and a service charge of up to $25, for failure to pay the amount of the delinquency.

c. The obligor's right to contest the impending judgment and the ground upon which such contest can be made.

d. The local depository's authority to release information regarding the delinquency to one or more credit reporting agencies.

2. The local depository shall serve the notice by mailing it by first class mail to the obligor at his or her last address of record with the local depository. If the obligor has no address of record with the local depository, service shall be by publication as provided in chapter 49.

3. When service of the notice is made by mail, service is complete on the date of mailing.

(c) Within 15 days after service of the notice is complete, the obligor may file with the court that issued the support order, or with the court in the circuit where the local depository which served the notice is located, a motion to contest the impending judgment. An obligor may contest the impending judgment only on the ground of a mistake of fact regarding an error in whether a delinquency exists, in the amount of the delinquency, or in the identity of the obligor.

(d) The court shall hear the obligor's motion to contest the impending judgment within 15 days after the date of filing of the motion. Upon the court's denial of the obligor's motion, the amount of the delinquency and all other amounts that become due, together with costs and a service charge of up to $25, become a final judgment by operation of law against the obligor. The depository shall charge interest at the rate established in s. 55.03 on all judgments for support. Payments on judgments shall be applied first to the current child support due, then to any delinquent principal, and then to interest on the support judgment.

(e) If the obligor fails to file a motion to contest the impending judgment within the time limit prescribed in paragraph (c) and fails to pay the amount of the delinquency and all other amounts which thereafter become due, together with costs and a service charge of up to $25, such amounts become a final judgment by operation of law against the obligor at the expiration of the time for filing a motion to contest the impending judgment.

(f)1. Upon request of any person, the local depository shall issue, upon payment of a service charge of up to $25, a payoff statement of the total amount due under the judgment at the time of the request. The statement may be relied upon by the person for up to 30 days from the time it is issued unless proof of satisfaction of the judgment is provided.

2. When the depository records show that the obligor's account is current, the depository shall record a satisfaction of the judgment upon request of any interested person and upon receipt of the appropriate recording fee. Any person shall be entitled to rely upon the recording of the satisfaction.

3. The local depository, at the direction of the department, or the obligee in a non-IV-D case, may partially release the judgment as to specific real property, and the depository shall record a partial release upon receipt of the appropriate recording fee.

4. The local depository is not liable for errors in its recordkeeping, except when an error is a result of unlawful activity or gross negligence by the clerk or his or her employees.

(g) The local depository shall send the department monthly by electronic means a list of all Title IV-D and non-Title IV-D cases in which a judgment by operation of law has been recorded during the month for which the data is provided. At a minimum, the depository shall provide the names of the obligor and obligee, social security numbers of the obligor and obligee, if available, and depository number.

(7) When modification of an existing order of support is sought, the proof required to modify a settlement agreement and the proof required to modify an award established by court order shall be the same.

(8)(a) When an employee and an employer reach an agreement for a lump-sum settlement under s. 440.20(11), no proceeds of the settlement shall be disbursed to the employee, nor shall any attorney's fees be disbursed, until after a judge of compensation claims reviews the proposed disbursement and enters an order finding the settlement provides for appropriate recovery of any support arrearage. The employee, or the employee's attorney if the employee is represented, shall submit a written statement from the department that indicates whether the employee owes unpaid support and, if so, the amount owed. In addition, the judge of compensation claims may require the employee to submit a similar statement from a local depository established under s. 61.181. A sworn statement by the employee that all existing support obligations have been disclosed is also required. If the judge finds the proposed allocation of support recovery insufficient, the parties may amend the allocation of support recovery within the settlement agreement to make the allocation of proceeds sufficient. The Office of the Judges of Compensation Claims shall adopt procedural rules to implement this paragraph.

(b) In accordance with the provisions of s. 440.22, any compensation due or that may become due an employee under chapter 440 is exempt from garnishment, attachment, execution, and assignment of income, except for the purposes of enforcing child or spousal support obligations.

(9) Unless otherwise ordered by the court or agreed to by the parties, the obligation to pay the current child support for that child is terminated when the child reaches 18 years of age or the disability of nonage is removed. The termination of the current child support obligation does not otherwise terminate the obligation to pay any arrearage, retroactive support, delinquency, or costs owed by the obligor.

(10)(a) In a Title IV-D case, if an obligation to pay current child support is terminated due to the emancipation of the child and the obligor owes an arrearage, retroactive support, delinquency, or costs, the obligor shall continue to pay at the same rate in effect immediately prior to emancipation until all arrearages, retroactive support, delinquencies, and costs are paid in full or until the amount of the order is modified. Any income-deducted amount or amount paid by the obligor which is in excess of the obligation to pay current support shall be credited against the arrearages, retroactive support, delinquency, and costs owed by the obligor.

(b) In a Title IV-D case, if an obligation to pay current child support for multiple children is reduced due to the emancipation of one child and the obligor owes an arrearage, retroactive support, delinquency, or costs, the obligor shall continue to pay at the same rate in effect immediately prior to emancipation until all arrearages, retroactive support, delinquencies, and costs are paid in full or until the amount of the order is modified. Any income-deducted amount or amount paid by the obligor which is in excess of the obligation to pay current support shall be credited against the arrearages, retroactive support, delinquency, and costs owed by the obligor. If an obligation to pay current support for more than one child is not reduced when a child is emancipated because the order does not allocate support per child, this paragraph does not apply.

(c) Paragraphs (a) and (b) provide an additional remedy for collection of unpaid support and apply to cases in which a support order was entered before, on, or after July 1, 2004.

(11)(a) A court may, upon good cause shown, and without a showing of a substantial change of circumstances, modify, vacate, or set aside a temporary support order before or upon entering a final order in a proceeding.

(b) The modification of the temporary support order may be retroactive to the date of the initial entry of the temporary support order; to the date of filing of the initial petition for dissolution of marriage, initial petition for support, initial petition determining paternity, or supplemental petition for modification; or to a date prescribed in paragraph (1)(a) or s. 61.30(11)(c) or (17), as applicable.

61.16. Attorney's fees, suit money, and costs.

(1) The court may from time to time, after considering the financial resources of both parties, order a party to pay a reasonable amount for attorney's fees, suit money, and the cost to the other party of maintaining or defending any proceeding under this chapter, including enforcement and modification proceedings and appeals. In those cases in which an action is brought for enforcement and the court finds that the noncompliant party is without justification in the refusal to follow a court order, the court may not award attorney's fees, suit money, and costs to the noncompliant party. An application for attorney's fees, suit money, or costs, whether temporary or otherwise, shall not require corroborating expert testimony in order to support an award under this chapter. The trial court shall have continuing jurisdiction to make temporary attorney's fees and costs awards reasonably necessary to prosecute or defend an appeal on the same basis and criteria as though the matter were pending before it at the trial level. In all cases, the court may order that the amount be paid directly to the attorney, who may enforce the order in that attorney's name. In determining whether to make attorney's fees and costs awards at the appellate level, the court shall primarily consider the relative financial resources of the parties, unless an appellate party's cause is deemed to be frivolous. In Title IV-D cases, attorney's fees, suit money, and costs, including filing fees, recording fees, mediation costs, service of process fees, and other expenses incurred by

the clerk of the circuit court, shall be assessed only against the nonprevailing obligor after the court makes a determination of the nonprevailing obligor's ability to pay such costs and fees. The Department of Revenue shall not be considered a party for purposes of this section; however, fees may be assessed against the department pursuant to s. 57.105(1).

(2) In an action brought pursuant to Rule 3.840, Florida Rules of Criminal Procedure, whether denominated direct or indirect criminal contempt, the court shall have authority to:

(a) Appoint an attorney to prosecute said contempt.

(b) Assess attorney's fees and costs against the contemptor after the court makes a determination of the contemptor's ability to pay such costs and fees.

(c) Order that the amount be paid directly to the attorney, who may enforce the order in his or her name.

61.17. Alimony and child support; additional method for enforcing orders and judgments; costs, expenses.

(1) An order or judgment for the payment of alimony or child support or either entered by any court of this state may be enforced by another chancery court in this state in the following manner:

(a) The person to whom such alimony or child support is payable or for whose benefit it is payable may procure a certified copy of the order or judgment and file it with a complaint for enforcement in the circuit court for the county in which the person resides or in the county where the person charged with the payment of the alimony or child support resides or is found.

(b) If the pleadings seek a change in the amount of the alimony or child support money, the court has jurisdiction to adjudicate the application and change the order or judgment. In such event the clerk of the circuit court in which the order is entered changing the original order or judgment shall transmit a certified copy thereof to the court of original jurisdiction, and the new order shall be recorded and filed in the original action and become a part thereof. If the pleadings ask for a modification of the order or judgment, the court may determine that the action should be tried by the court entering the original order or judgment and shall then transfer the action to that court for determination as a part of the original action.

(c) Enforcement of a case certified under Title IV-D of the Social Security Act under this section shall grant to the registering court jurisdiction to address only those issues allowed and reimbursable under Title IV-D of the Social Security Act.

(2) The court in which such an action is brought has jurisdiction to award costs and expenses as are equitable, including the cost of certifying and recording the judgment entered in the action in the court of original jurisdiction and reasonable attorney's fees.

(3) The entry of a judgment for arrearages for child support, alimony, or attorney's fees and costs does not preclude a subsequent contempt proceeding or certification of a IV-D case for intercept, by the United States Internal Revenue Service, for failure of an obligor to pay the child support, alimony, attorney's fees, or costs for which the judgment was entered.

61.18. Alimony and child support; default in undertaking of bond posted to ensure payment.

(1) When there is a breach of the condition of any bond posted to ensure the payment of alimony or child support, either temporary or permanent, for a party or minor children of the parties, the court in which the order was issued may order payment to the party entitled thereto of the principal of the bond or the part thereof necessary to cure the existing default without further notice from time to time where the amount is liquidated.

(2) The sureties on the bond, or the sheriff or clerk holding a cash bond, shall be ordered to pay into the registry of court, or to any party the court may direct, the sum necessary to cure the default.

(3) If the principal or sureties or sheriff or clerk fails to pay within the time and as required by the order, the court may enforce the payment by contempt against the principal or sureties on the bond or sheriff or clerk without further notice, or may issue an execution against the principal, sureties, sheriff, or clerk for the amount unpaid under any prior order or orders, but no sureties on the bond are liable for more than the penalty of the bond.

61.181. Depository for alimony transactions, support, maintenance, and support payments; fees.

(1)(a) The office of the clerk of the court shall operate a depository unless the depository is otherwise created by special act of the Legislature or unless, prior to June 1, 1985, a different entity was established to perform such functions. The department shall, no later than July 1, 1998, extend participation in the federal child support cost reimbursement program to the central depository in each county, to the maximum extent possible under existing federal law. The depository shall receive reimbursement for services provided under a cooperative agreement with the department pursuant to s. 61.1826. Each depository shall participate in the State Disbursement Unit and shall implement all statutory and contractual duties imposed on the State Disbursement Unit. Each depository shall receive from and transmit to the State Disbursement Unit required data through the Clerk of Court Child Support Enforcement Collection System. Payments on non-Title IV-D cases without income deduction orders shall not be sent to the State Disbursement Unit.

(b) Upon request by the department, the depository created pursuant to paragraph (a) shall establish an account for the receipt and disbursement of support payments for Title IV-D interstate cases. The department shall provide a copy of the other state's order with the request, and the depository shall advise the department of the account number in writing within 4 business days after receipt of the request.

(2)(a) For payments not required to be processed through the State Disbursement Unit, the depository shall impose and collect a fee on each payment made for receiving, recording, reporting, disbursing, monitoring, or handling alimony or child support payments as required under this section. For non-Title IV-D cases required to be processed by the State Disbursement Unit pursuant to this chapter, the State Disbursement Unit shall, on each payment received, collect a fee, and shall transmit to the depository in which the case is located 40 percent of such service charge for the depository's administration, management, and maintenance of such case. If a payment is made to the State Disbursement Unit which is not accompanied by the required fee, the State Disbursement Unit shall not deduct any moneys from the support payment for payment of the fee. The fee shall be a flat fee based, to the extent practicable, upon estimated reasonable costs of operation. The fee shall be reduced in any case in which the fixed fee results in a charge to any party of an amount greater than 3 percent of the amount of any support payment made in satisfaction of the amount which the party is obligated to pay, except that no fee shall be less than $1 nor more than $5 per payment made. The fee shall be considered by the court in determining the amount of support that the obligor is, or may be, required to pay.

(b)1. The fee imposed in paragraph (a) shall be increased to 4 percent of the support payments which the party is obligated to pay, except that no fee shall be more than $5.25. The fee shall be considered by the court in determining the amount of support that the obligor is, or may be, required to pay. Notwithstanding the provisions of s. 145.022, 75 percent of the additional revenues generated by this paragraph shall be remitted monthly to the Clerk of the Court Child Support Enforcement Collection System Trust Fund administered by the department as provided in subparagraph 2. These funds shall be used exclusively for the development, implementation, and operation of the Clerk of the Court Child Support Enforcement Collection System to be operated by the depositories, including the automation of civil case information necessary for the State Case Registry. The department shall contract with the Florida Association of Court Clerks and the depositories to design, establish, operate, upgrade, and maintain the automation of the depositories to include, but not be limited to, the provision of online electronic transfer of information to the IV-D agency as otherwise required by this chapter. The department's obligation to fund the automation of the depositories is limited to the state share of funds available in the Clerk of the Court Child Support Enforcement Collection System Trust Fund. Each depository created under this section shall fully participate in the Clerk of the Court Child Support Enforcement Collection System and transmit data in a readable format as required by the contract between the Florida Association of Court Clerks and the department.

2. Moneys to be remitted to the department by the depository shall be done daily by electronic funds transfer and calculated as follows:

a. For each support payment of less than $33, 18.75 cents.

b. For each support payment between $33 and $140, an amount equal to 18.75 percent of the fee charged.

c. For each support payment in excess of $140, 18.75 cents.

3. The fees established by this section shall be set forth and included in every order of support entered by a court of this state which requires payment to be made into the depository.

(3)(a) For payments not required to be processed through the State Disbursement Unit, the depository shall collect and distribute all support payments paid into the depository to the appropriate party. On or after July 1, 1998, if a payment is made on a Title IV-D case which is not accompanied by the required transaction fee, the depository shall not deduct any moneys from the support payment for payment of the fee. Nonpayment of the required fee shall be considered a delinquency, and when the total of fees and costs which are due but not paid exceeds $50, the judgment by operation of law process set forth in s. 61.14(6)(a) shall become applicable and operational. As part of its collection and distribution functions, the depository shall maintain records listing:

1. The obligor's name, address, social security number, place of employment, and any other sources of income.

2. The obligee's name, address, and social security number.

3. The amount of support due as provided in the court order.

4. The schedule of payment as provided in the court order.

5. The actual amount of each support payment received, the date of receipt, the amount disbursed, and the recipient of the disbursement.

6. The unpaid balance of any arrearage due as provided in the court order.

7. Other records as necessary to comply with federal reporting requirements.

(b) The depository may require a payor or obligor to complete an information form, which shall request the following about the payor or obligor who provides payment by check:

1. Full name, address, and home phone number.

2. Driver license number.

3. Social security number.

4. Name, address, and business phone number of obligor's employer.

5. Date of birth.

6. Weight and height.

7. Such other information as may be required by the State Attorney if prosecution for an insufficient check becomes necessary.

(c) Parties using the depository for support payments shall inform the depository of changes in their names or addresses. An obligor shall, additionally, notify the depository of all changes in employment or sources of income, including the payor's name and address, and changes in the amounts of income received. Notification of all changes shall be made in writing to the depository within 7 days of a change.

(d) When time-sharing of a child is relinquished by a parent who is entitled to receive child support moneys from the depository to the custody of a licensed or registered long-term care child agency, that agency may request from the court an order directing child support payments that would otherwise be distributed to the parent be distributed to the agency for the period of time that the child is with the agency. Thereafter, payments shall be distributed to the agency as if the agency were the parent until further order of the court.

(4) The depository shall provide to the IV-D agency, at least once a month, a listing of IV-D accounts which identifies all delinquent accounts, the period of delinquency, and total amount of delinquency. The list shall be in alphabetical order by name of obligor, shall include the obligee's name and case number, and shall be provided at no cost to the IV-D agency.

(5) The depository shall accept a support payment tendered in the form of a check drawn on the account of a payor or obligor, unless the payor or obligor has previously remitted a check which was returned to the depository due to lack of sufficient funds in the account. If the payor or obligor has had a check returned for this reason, the depository shall accept payment by cash, cashier's check, or money order, or may accept a check upon deposit by the payor or obligor of an amount equal to 1 month's payment. Upon payment by cash, cashier's check, or money order, the depository shall disburse the proceeds to the obligee within 2 working days. Payments drawn by check on the account of a payor or obligor shall be disbursed within 4 working days. Notwithstanding the provisions of s. 28.243, the administrator of the depository shall not be personally liable if the check tendered by the payor or obligor is not paid by the bank.

(6) Certified copies of payment records maintained by a depository shall without further proof be admitted into evidence in any legal proceeding in this state.

(7) The depository shall provide to the Title IV-D agency the date provided by a payor, as required in s. 61.1301, for each payment received and forwarded to the agency. If no date is provided by the payor, the depository shall provide the date of receipt by the depository and shall report to the Title IV-D agency those payors who fail to provide the date the deduction was made.

(8) On or before July 1, 1994, the depository shall provide information required by this chapter to be transmitted to the Title IV-D agency by online electronic transmission pursuant to rules promulgated by the Title IV-D agency.

(9) If the increase in fees as provided by paragraph (2)(b) expires or is otherwise terminated, the depository shall not be required to provide the Title IV-D agency the date provided by a payor as required by s. 61.1301.

(10) Compliance with the requirements of this section shall be included as part of the annual county audit required pursuant to s. 218.39.

61.1811. Clerk of the Court Child Support Enforcement Collection System Trust Fund.

There is hereby created the Clerk of the Court Child Support Enforcement Collection System Trust Fund to be used to deposit the department's share of the fees generated in s. 61.181(2)(b).

61.1812. Child Support Incentive Trust Fund.

(1) The Child Support Incentive Trust Fund is hereby created, to be administered by the Department of Revenue. All child support enforcement incentive earnings and that portion of the state share of Title IV-A public assistance collections recovered in fiscal year 1996-1997 by the Title IV-D program of the department which is in excess of the amount estimated by the February 1997 Social Services Estimating Conference to be recovered in fiscal year 1996-1997 shall be credited to the trust fund, and no other receipts, except interest earnings, shall be credited thereto. For fiscal years beginning with 1997-1998, in addition to incentive earnings and interest earnings,

that portion of the state share of Title IV-A public assistance collections recovered in each fiscal year by the Title IV-D program of the department which is in excess of the amount estimated by the February 1997 Social Services Estimating Conference to be recovered in fiscal year 1997-1998 shall be credited to the trust fund. The purpose of the trust fund is to account for federal incentive payments to the state for child support enforcement and to support the activities of the child support enforcement program under Title IV-D of the Social Security Act. The department shall invest the money in the trust fund pursuant to s. 17.61 and retain all interest earnings in the trust fund. The department shall separately account for receipts credited to the trust fund. When all general revenue appropriations for the child support enforcement program have been shifted to the trust fund, then annually thereafter, on June 30, if revenues deposited into the trust fund, including federal child support incentive earnings, have exceeded state expenditures for the child support enforcement program administered by the department for the prior 12-month period, the revenues in excess of cash flow needs are transferred to the General Revenue Fund.

(2) Notwithstanding the provisions of s. 216.301, and pursuant to s. 216.351, any balance in the trust fund at the end of any fiscal year shall remain in the trust fund and shall be available for carrying out the purposes of the trust fund.

61.1814. Child Support Enforcement Application and Program Revenue Trust Fund.

(1) The Child Support Enforcement Application and Program Revenue Trust Fund is hereby created, to be administered by the Department of Revenue. The purpose of the trust fund is to account for Title IV-D program income and to support the activities of the child support enforcement program under Title IV-D of the Social Security Act. The department shall invest the money in the trust fund pursuant to s. 17.61 and retain all interest earnings in the trust fund. Notwithstanding the provisions of s. 216.301, and pursuant to s. 216.351, any balance in the trust fund at the end of any fiscal year shall remain in the trust fund and shall be available for carrying out the purposes of the trust fund. In accordance with federal requirements, the federal share of program income shall be credited to the Federal Government.

(2) With the exception of fees required to be deposited in the Clerk of the Court Child Support Enforcement Collection System Trust Fund under s. 61.181(2)(b) and collections determined to be undistributable or unidentifiable under s. 409.2558, the fund shall be used for the deposit of Title IV-D program income received by the department. Each type of program income received shall be accounted for separately. Program income received by the department includes, but is not limited to:

(a) Application fees of nonpublic assistance applicants for child support enforcement services;

(b) Court-ordered costs recovered from child support obligors;

(c) Interest on child support collections;

(d) The balance of fees received under s. 61.181(2)(a) on non-Title IV-D cases required to be processed through the State Disbursement Unit after the clerk's share is paid;

(e) Fines imposed under ss. 409.256(7)(b), 409.2564(7), and 409.2578; and

(f) The annual fee required under s. 409.2567.

61.1816. Child Support Clearing Trust Fund.

(1) The Child Support Clearing Trust Fund is hereby created, to be administered by the Department of Revenue. Funds shall be credited to the trust fund from child support payments. The purpose of the trust fund is to account for child support collections pending distribution to custodial parents and other state trust funds.

(2) Notwithstanding the provisions of s. 216.301 and pursuant to s. 216.351, any balance in the trust fund at the end of any fiscal year shall remain in the trust fund and shall be available for carrying out the purposes of the trust fund.

61.1824. State Disbursement Unit.

(1) The State Disbursement Unit is hereby created and shall be operated by the Department of Revenue or by a contractor responsible directly to the department. The State Disbursement Unit shall be responsible for the collection and disbursement of payments for:

(a) All support cases enforced by the department pursuant to Title IV-D of the Social Security Act; and

(b) All child support cases not being enforced by the department pursuant to Title IV-D of the Social Security Act in which the initial support order was issued in this state on or after January 1, 1994, and in which the obligor's child support obligation is being paid through income deduction.

(2) The State Disbursement Unit must be operated in coordination with the department's child support enforcement automated system in Title IV-D cases.

(3) The State Disbursement Unit shall perform the following functions:

(a) Disburse all receipts from intercepts, including, but not limited to, United States Internal Revenue Service, reemployment assistance or unemployment compensation, lottery, and administrative offset intercepts.

(b) Provide employers and payors with one address to which all income deduction collections are sent.

(c) When there is more than one income deduction order being enforced against the same obligor by the payor, allocate the amounts available for income deduction in the manner set forth in s. 61.1301.

(d) To the extent feasible, use automated procedures for the collection and disbursement of support payments, including, but not limited to, having procedures for:

1. Receipt of payments from obligors, employers, other states and jurisdictions, and other entities.

2. Timely disbursement of payments to obligees, the department, and other state Title IV-D agencies.

3. Accurate identification of payment source and amount.

4. Furnishing any parent, upon request, timely information on the current status of support payments under an order requiring payments to be made by or to the parent, except that in cases described in paragraph (1)(b), prior to the date the State Disbursement Unit becomes fully operational, the State Disbursement Unit shall not be required to convert and maintain in automated form records of payments kept pursuant to s. 61.181.

5. Electronic disbursement of support payments to obligees. The State Disbursement Unit shall notify obligees of electronic disbursement options. Any payments made to the State Disbursement Unit that are owed to the obligee shall be disbursed electronically. The obligee may designate a personal account for deposit of payments. If the obligee does not designate a personal account, the State Disbursement Unit shall deposit any payments into a stored value account that can be accessed by the obligee.

(e) Information regarding disbursement must be transmitted in the following manner:

1. In Title IV-D cases, the State Disbursement Unit shall transmit, in an electronic format as prescribed by the department, all required information to the department on the same business day the information is received from the employer or other source of periodic income, if sufficient information identifying the payee is provided. The department shall determine distribution allocation of a collection and shall electronically transmit that information to the State Disbursement Unit, whereupon the State Disbursement Unit shall disburse the collection. The State Disbursement Unit may delay the disbursement of payments toward arrearages until the resolution of any timely appeal with respect to such arrearages. The State Disbursement Unit may

delay the disbursement of Title IV-D collections until authorization by the Title IV-D agency has been received.

2. In non-Title IV-D cases, payment information is not transmitted to the department. The State Disbursement Unit may delay the disbursement of payments toward arrearages until the resolution of any timely appeal with respect to such arrearages.

(f) Reconcile all cash receipts and all disbursements daily and provide the department with a daily reconciliation report in a format as prescribed by the department.

(g) Disburse support payments to foreign countries as may be required.

(h) Receive and convert support payments made in foreign currency.

(i) Remit to the department payments for costs due the department.

(j) Handle insufficient funds payments, claims of lost or stolen checks, and stop payment orders.

(k) Issue billing notices and statements of account, in accordance with federal requirements, in a format and frequency prescribed by the department to persons who pay and receive child support in Title IV-D cases.

(l) Provide the department with a weekly report that summarizes and totals all financial transaction activity.

(m) Provide toll-free access to customer assistance representatives and an automated voice response system that will enable the parties to a support case to obtain payment information.

(4) For cases in which the obligor or payor fails to submit payment directly to the central address provided by the State Disbursement Unit, the depositories shall have procedures for accepting a support payment tendered in the form of cash or a check drawn on the account of a payor or obligor, unless the payor or obligor has previously remitted a check which was returned to the depository due to lack of sufficient funds in the account. If the payor or obligor has had a check returned for this reason, the depository shall accept payment by cash, cashier's check, or money order, or may accept a check upon deposit by the payor or obligor of an amount equal to 1 month's payment. Upon payment by cash, cashier's check, or money order, the depository shall remit the payment to the State Disbursement Unit within 1 business day after receipt.

(5) Obligees receiving payments through the State Disbursement Unit shall inform the State Disbursement Unit of changes in their names and addresses. Notification of all changes must be made directly to the State Disbursement Unit within 7 business days after a change. In Title IV-D cases, the State Disbursement Unit shall transmit the information to the department, in an electronic format prescribed by the department, within 1 business day after receipt.

(6) All support payments for cases to which the requirements of this section apply shall be made payable to and delivered to the State Disbursement Unit.

(a) An employer that is required to remit tax payments electronically to the department under s. 213.755 or s. 443.163 shall remit support payments deducted pursuant to an income deduction order or income deduction notice and provide associated case data to the State Disbursement Unit by electronic means approved by the department. The department may waive the requirement to remit payments electronically for an employer that is unable to comply despite good faith efforts or due to circumstances beyond the employer's reasonable control. Grounds for approving a waiver include, but are not limited to, circumstances in which:

1. The employer does not have a computer that meets the minimum standards necessary for electronic remittance.

2. Additional time is needed to program the employer's computer.

3. The employer does not currently file data electronically with any business or government agency.

4. Compliance conflicts with the employer's business procedures.

5. Compliance would cause a financial hardship.

(b) The department shall adopt by rule standards for electronic remittance, data transfer, and waivers that, to the extent feasible, are consistent with the department's rules for electronic filing and remittance of taxes under ss. 213.755 and 443.163. A waiver granted by the department from the requirement to file and remit electronically under s. 213.755 or s. 443.163 constitutes a waiver from the requirement under this subsection.

(7) Notwithstanding any other statutory provision to the contrary, funds received by the State Disbursement Unit shall be held, administered, and disbursed by the State Disbursement Unit pursuant to the provisions of this chapter.

61.1825. State Case Registry.

(1) The Department of Revenue or its agent shall operate and maintain a State Case Registry as provided by 42 U.S.C. s. 654A. The State Case Registry must contain records for:
(a) Each case in which services are being provided by the department as the state's Title IV-D agency; and
(b) By October 1, 1998, each support order established or modified in the state on or after October 1, 1998, in which services are not being provided by the Title IV-D agency.
(2) By October 1, 1998, for each support order established or modified by a court of this state on or after October 1, 1998, the depository for the court that enters the support order in a non-Title IV-D case shall provide, in an electronic format prescribed by the department, the following information to that component of the State Case Registry that receives, maintains, and transmits support order information for non-Title IV-D cases:
(a) The names of the obligor, obligee, and child or children;
(b) The social security numbers of the obligor, obligee, and child or children;
(c) The dates of birth of the obligor, obligee, and child or children;
(d) Whether a family violence indicator is present;
(e) The date the support order was established or modified;
(f) The case identification number, which is the two-digit numeric county code followed by the civil circuit case number;
(g) The federal information processing system numeric designation for the county and state where the support order was established or modified; and
(h) Any other data as may be required by the United States Secretary of Health and Human Services.
(3)(a) For the purpose of this section, a family violence indicator must be placed on a record when:
1. A party executes a sworn statement requesting that a family violence indicator be placed on that party's record which states that the party has reason to believe that release of information to the Federal Case Registry may result in physical or emotional harm to the party or the child; or
2. A temporary or final injunction for protection against domestic violence has been granted pursuant to s. 741.30(6), an injunction for protection against domestic violence has been issued by a court of a foreign state pursuant to s. 741.315, or a temporary or final injunction for protection against repeat violence has been granted pursuant to s. 784.046; or
3. The department has received information on a Title IV-D case from the Domestic, Dating, Sexual, and Repeat Violence Injunction Statewide Verification System, established pursuant to s. 784.046(8)(b), that a court has granted a party a domestic violence or repeat violence injunction.
(b) Before the family violence indicator can be removed from a record, the protected person must be afforded notice and an opportunity to appear before the court on the issue of whether the disclosure will result in harm.
(4) The depository, using standardized data elements, shall provide the support order information required by subsection (2) to the entity that maintains the non-Title IV-D support order information for the State Case Registry at a frequency and in a format prescribed by the department.
(5) The entity that maintains State Case Registry information for non-Title IV-D cases shall make the information available to the department in a readable and searchable electronic format that is compatible with the department's automated child support enforcement system.
(6) State Case Registry information must be transmitted electronically to the Federal Case Registry of Child Support Orders by the department in a manner and frequency prescribed by the

United States Secretary of Health and Human Services.

61.1826. Procurement of services for State Disbursement Unit and the non-Title IV-D component of the State Case Registry; contracts and cooperative agreements; penalties; withholding payment.

(1) LEGISLATIVE FINDINGS.—The Legislature finds that the clerks of court play a vital role, as essential participants in the establishment, modification, collection, and enforcement of child support, in securing the health, safety, and welfare of the children of this state. The Legislature further finds and declares that:

(a) It is in the state's best interest to preserve the essential role of the clerks of court in disbursing child support payments and maintaining official records of child support orders entered by the courts of this state.

(b) As official recordkeeper for matters relating to court-ordered child support, the clerks of court are necessary parties to obtaining, safeguarding, and providing child support payment and support order information.

(c) As provided by the federal Personal Responsibility and Work Opportunity Reconciliation Act of 1996, the state must establish and operate a State Case Registry in full compliance with federal law by October 1, 1998, and a State Disbursement Unit by October 1, 1999.

(d) Noncompliance with federal law could result in a substantial loss of federal funds for the state's child support enforcement program and the temporary assistance for needy families welfare block grant.

(e) The potential loss of substantial federal funds poses a direct and immediate threat to the health, safety, and welfare of the children and citizens of the state and constitutes an emergency for purposes of s. 287.057(3)(a).

(f) The clerks of court maintain the official payment record of the court for amounts received, payments credited, arrearages owed, liens attached, and current mailing addresses of all parties, payor, obligor, and payee.

(g) The clerks of court have established a statewide Clerk of Court Child Support Enforcement Collection System for the automation of all payment processing using state and local government funds as provided under s. 61.181(2)(b)1.

(h) The Legislature acknowledges the improvements made by and the crucial role of the Clerk of the Court Child Support Enforcement Collection System in speeding payments to the children of Florida.

(i) There is no viable alternative to continuing the role of the clerks of court in collecting, safeguarding, and providing essential child support payment information.

(2) COOPERATIVE AGREEMENTS.—Each depository shall enter into a standard cooperative agreement with the department for participation in the State Disbursement Unit and the non-Title IV-D component of the State Case Registry through the Clerk of Court Child Support Enforcement Collection System within 60 days after the effective date of this section. The cooperative agreement shall be a uniform document, mutually developed by the department and the Florida Association of Court Clerks, that applies to all depositories and complies with all state and federal requirements. Each depository shall also enter into a written agreement with the Florida Association of Court Clerks and the department within 60 days after the effective date of this section that requires each depository to participate fully in the State Disbursement Unit and the non-Title IV-D component of the State Case Registry.

(3) CONTRACT.—The Florida Association of Court Clerks shall enter into a written contract with the department that fully complies with all federal and state laws within 60 days after the

effective date of this section. The contract shall be mutually developed by the department and the Florida Association of Court Clerks. As required by s. 287.057 and 45 C.F.R. s. 74.43, any subcontracts entered into by the Florida Association of Court Clerks, except for a contract between the Florida Association of Court Clerks and its totally owned subsidiary corporation, must be procured through competitive bidding.

(4) COOPERATIVE AGREEMENT AND CONTRACT TERMS.—The contract between the Florida Association of Court Clerks and the department, and cooperative agreements entered into by the depositories and the department, must contain, but are not limited to, the following terms:

(a) The initial term of the contract and cooperative agreements is for 5 years. The subsequent term of the contract and cooperative agreements is for 3 years, with the option of two 1-year renewal periods, at the sole discretion of the department.

(b) The duties and responsibilities of the Florida Association of Court Clerks, the depositories, and the department.

(c) Under s. 287.058(1)(a), all providers and subcontractors shall submit to the department directly, or through the Florida Association of Court Clerks, a report of monthly expenditures in a format prescribed by the department and in sufficient detail for a proper preaudit and postaudit thereof.

(d) All providers and subcontractors shall submit to the department directly, or through the Florida Association of Court Clerks, management reports in a format prescribed by the department.

(e) All subcontractors shall comply with chapter 280, as may be required.

(f) Federal financial participation for eligible Title IV-D expenditures incurred by the Florida Association of Court Clerks and the depositories shall be at the maximum level permitted by federal law for expenditures incurred for the provision of services in support of child support enforcement in accordance with 45 C.F.R. part 74 and Federal Office of Management and Budget Circulars A-87 and A-122 and based on an annual cost allocation study of each depository. The depositories shall submit directly, or through the Florida Association of Court Clerks, claims for Title IV-D expenditures monthly to the department in a standardized format as prescribed by the department. The Florida Association of Court Clerks shall contract with a certified public accounting firm, selected by the Florida Association of Court Clerks and the department, to audit and certify quarterly to the department all claims for expenditures submitted by the depositories for Title IV-D reimbursement.

(g) Upon termination of the contracts between the department and the Florida Association of Court Clerks or the depositories, the Florida Association of Court Clerks, its agents, and the depositories shall assist the department in making an orderly transition to a private vendor.

(h) Interest on late payment by the department shall be in accordance with s. 215.422.

(5) CONTRACT TERMINATION.—If any of the following events occur, the department may discontinue its plans to contract, or terminate its contract, with the Florida Association of Court Clerks and the depositories upon 30 days' written notice by the department and may, through competitive bidding, procure services from a private vendor to perform functions necessary for the department to operate the State Disbursement Unit and the non-Title IV-D component of the State Case Registry with a minimum amount of disruption in service to the children and citizens of the state:

(a) Receipt by the department of final notice by the United States Secretary of Health and Human Services or the secretary's designee that the contractual arrangement between the department, the Florida Association of Court Clerks, and the depositories does not satisfy federal requirements for a State Disbursement Unit or a State Case Registry and that the state's Title IV-D State Plan will not be approved, or that federal Title IV-D funding is not made available to fund the non-Title IV-D component of the State Case Registry or the State Disbursement Unit;

(b) The Florida Association of Court Clerks, a depository, or any subcontractor fails to comply with any material contractual term or state or federal requirement;

(c) The non-Title IV-D component of the State Case Registry is not established and operational, consistent with the terms of the contract, by October 1, 1998; or

(d) The State Disbursement Unit is not established and operational, consistent with the terms of the contract, by October 1, 1999.

(6) PARTICIPATION BY DEPOSITORIES.—

(a) Each depository shall participate in the non-Title IV-D component of the State Case Registry by using an automated system compatible with the department's automated child support enforcement system.

(b) For participation in the State Disbursement Unit, each depository shall:

1. Use the CLERC System;

2. Receive electronically and record payment information from the State Disbursement Unit for each support order entered by the court.

(7) TITLE IV-D PROGRAM INCOME.—Pursuant to 45 C.F.R. s. 304.50, all transaction fees and interest income realized by the State Disbursement Unit constitute and must be reported as program income under federal law and must be transmitted to the Title IV-D agency for deposit in the Child Support Enforcement Application and Program Revenue Trust Fund.

(8) PENALTIES.—All depositories must participate in the State Disbursement Unit and the non-Title IV-D component of the State Case Registry as provided in this chapter. If, after notice and an opportunity to cure an otherwise curable default, a depository fails to comply with the material terms of the cooperative agreement, the failure to comply subjects the county officer or officers responsible for the depository to the sanctions provided in Art. IV of the State Constitution. However, no county officer or officers shall be subject to sanctions under Art. IV of the State Constitution for any noncurable default resulting from circumstances or conditions outside the control of the depository.

(9) WITHHOLDING PAYMENT UNDER CONTRACTS.—If the Florida Association of Court Clerks, its agent, a subcontractor, or a depository does not comply with any material contractual term or state or federal requirement, the department may withhold funds otherwise due under the individual contract with the Florida Association of Court Clerks or the individual cooperative agreement with the depository, or both, at the department's election, to enforce compliance. The department shall provide written notice of noncompliance before withholding funds. Within 10 business days after receipt of written notification of noncompliance, the department must be provided with a written proposed corrective action plan. Within 10 business days after receipt of a corrective action plan, the department shall accept the plan or allow 5 business days within which a revised plan may be submitted. Upon the department's acceptance of a corrective action plan, the agreed-upon plan must be fully completed within 30 business days unless a longer period is permitted by the department. If a proposed corrective action plan is not submitted, is not accepted, or is not fully completed, any funds withheld by the department for noncompliance are forfeited to the department. Withholding or forfeiture of funds may be contested by filing a petition or request for a hearing under the applicable provisions of chapter 120. For the purposes of this section, no party to a dispute involving less than $5,000 in withheld or forfeited funds is deemed to be substantially affected by the dispute or to have a substantial interest in the decision resolving the dispute.

61.1827. Identifying information concerning applicants for and recipients of child support services.

(1) Any information that reveals the identity of applicants for or recipients of child support services, including the name, address, and telephone number of such persons, held by a non-Title IV-D county child support enforcement agency is confidential and exempt from s. 119.07(1) and s. 24(a) of Art. I of the State Constitution. The use or disclosure of such information by the non-Title IV-D county child support enforcement agency is limited to the purposes directly connected with:

(a) Any investigation, prosecution, or criminal or civil proceeding connected with the administration of any non-Title IV-D county child support enforcement program;

(b) Mandatory disclosure of identifying and location information as provided in s. 61.13(7) by the non-Title IV-D county child support enforcement agency when providing non-Title IV-D services;

(c) Mandatory disclosure of information as required by ss. 409.2577, 61.181, 61.1825, and 61.1826 and Title IV-D of the Social Security Act; or

(d) Disclosure to an authorized person, as defined in 45 C.F.R. s. 303.15, for purposes of enforcing any state or federal law with respect to the unlawful taking or restraint of a child or making or enforcing a parenting plan. As used in this paragraph, the term "authorized person" includes a parent with whom the child does not currently reside, unless a court has entered an order under s. 741.30, s. 741.31, or s. 784.046.

(2) The non-Title IV-D county child support enforcement agency shall not disclose information that identifies by name and address an applicant for or recipient of child support services or the whereabouts of such party or child to another person against whom a protective order with respect to the former party or the child has been entered if the county agency has reason to believe that the release of information to such person could result in physical or emotional harm to the party or the child.

(3) As used in this section, "non-Title IV-D county child support enforcement agency" means a department, division, or other agency of a county government which is operated by the county, excluding local depositories pursuant to s. 61.181 operated by the clerk of the court, to provide child support enforcement and depository services to county residents.

61.183. Mediation of certain contested issues.

(1) In any proceeding in which the issues of parental responsibility, primary residence, access to, visitation with, or support of a child are contested, the court may refer the parties to mediation in accordance with rules promulgated by the Supreme Court. In Title IV-D cases, any costs, including filing fees, recording fees, mediation costs, service of process fees, and other expenses incurred by the clerk of the circuit court, shall be assessed only against the nonprevailing obligor after the court makes a determination of the nonprevailing obligor's ability to pay such costs and fees.

(2) If an agreement is reached by the parties on the contested issues, a consent order incorporating the agreement shall be prepared by the mediator and submitted to the parties and their attorneys for review. Upon approval by the parties, the consent order shall be reviewed by the court and, if approved, entered. Thereafter, the consent order may be enforced in the same manner as any other court order.

(3) Any information from the files, reports, case summaries, mediator's notes, or other communications or materials relating to a mediation proceeding pursuant to this section obtained by any person performing mediation duties is exempt from the provisions of s. 119.07(1).

61.19. Entry of judgment of dissolution of marriage, delay period.

No final judgment of dissolution of marriage may be entered until at least 20 days have elapsed from the date of filing the original petition for dissolution of marriage; but the court, on a showing that injustice would result from this delay, may enter a final judgment of dissolution of marriage at an earlier date.

61.191. Application.

(1) This act applies to all proceedings commenced on or after July 1, 1971. However, pending actions for divorce are deemed to have been commenced on the bases provided in s. 61.052, and evidence as to such bases for dissolution of marriage after July 1, 1971, shall be in compliance with this act.

(2) This act applies to all proceedings commenced after July 1, 1971, for the modification of a judgment or order entered prior to July 1, 1971.

(3) In any action or proceeding in which an appeal was pending or a new trial was ordered prior to July 1, 1971, the law in effect at the time of the order sustaining the appeal or the new trial governs the appeal, the new trial, and any subsequent trial or appeal.

61.20. Social investigation and recommendations regarding a parenting plan.

(1) In any action where the parenting plan is at issue because the parents are unable to agree, the court may order a social investigation and study concerning all pertinent details relating to the child and each parent when such an investigation has not been done and the study therefrom provided to the court by the parties or when the court determines that the investigation and study that have been done are insufficient. The agency, staff, or person conducting the investigation and study ordered by the court pursuant to this section shall furnish the court and all parties of record in the proceeding a written study containing recommendations, including a written statement of facts found in the social investigation on which the recommendations are based. The court may consider the information contained in the study in making a decision on the parenting plan, and the technical rules of evidence do not exclude the study from consideration.

(2) A social investigation and study, when ordered by the court, shall be conducted by qualified staff of the court; a child-placing agency licensed pursuant to s. 409.175; a psychologist licensed pursuant to chapter 490; or a clinical social worker, marriage and family therapist, or mental health counselor licensed pursuant to chapter 491. If a certification of indigence based on an affidavit filed with the court pursuant to s. 57.081 is provided by an adult party to the proceeding and the court does not have qualified staff to perform the investigation and study, the court may request that the Department of Children and Families conduct the investigation and study.

(3) Except as to persons who obtain certification of indigence as specified in subsection (2), for whom no costs are incurred, the parents involved in a proceeding to determine a parenting plan where the court has ordered the performance of a social investigation and study are responsible for paying the costs of the investigation and study. Upon submitting the study to the court, the agency, staff, or person performing the study shall include a bill for services, which shall be taxed and ordered paid as costs in the proceeding.

61.21. Parenting course authorized; fees; required attendance authorized; contempt.

(1) LEGISLATIVE FINDINGS; PURPOSE.—It is the finding of the Legislature that:

(a) A large number of children experience the separation or divorce of their parents each year. Parental conflict related to divorce is a societal concern because children suffer potential short-term and long-term detrimental economic, emotional, and educational effects during this difficult period of family transition. This is particularly true when parents engage in lengthy legal conflict.

(b) Parents are more likely to consider the best interests of their children when determining parental arrangements if courts provide families with information regarding the process by which courts make decisions on issues affecting their children and suggestions as to how parents may ease the coming adjustments in family structure for their children.

(c) It has been found to be beneficial to parents who are separating or divorcing to have available an educational program that will provide general information regarding:

1. The issues and legal procedures for resolving time-sharing and child support disputes.

2. The emotional experiences and problems of divorcing adults.

3. The family problems and the emotional concerns and needs of the children.

4. The availability of community services and resources.

(d) Parents who are separating or divorcing are more likely to receive maximum benefit from a program if they attend such program at the earliest stages of their dispute, before extensive litigation occurs and adversarial positions are assumed or intensified.

(2) The Department of Children and Families shall approve a parenting course which shall be a course of a minimum of 4 hours designed to educate, train, and assist divorcing parents in regard to the consequences of divorce on parents and children.

(a) The parenting course referred to in this section shall be named the Parent Education and Family Stabilization Course and may include, but need not be limited to, the following topics as they relate to court actions between parents involving custody, care, time-sharing, and support of a child or children:

1. Legal aspects of deciding child-related issues between parents.

2. Emotional aspects of separation and divorce on adults.

3. Emotional aspects of separation and divorce on children.

4. Family relationships and family dynamics.

5. Financial responsibilities to a child or children.

6. Issues regarding spousal or child abuse and neglect.

7. Skill-based relationship education that may be generalized to parenting, workplace, school, neighborhood, and civic relationships.

(b) Information regarding spousal and child abuse and neglect shall be included in every parent education and family stabilization course. A list of local agencies that provide assistance with such issues shall also be provided.

(c) The parent education and family stabilization course shall be educational in nature and shall not be designed to provide individual mental health therapy for parents or children, or individual legal advice to parents or children.

(d) Course providers shall not solicit participants from the sessions they conduct to become private clients or patients.

(e) Course providers shall not give individual legal advice or mental health therapy.

(3) Each course provider offering a parenting course pursuant to this section must be approved by the Department of Children and Families.

(a) The Department of Children and Families shall provide each judicial circuit with a list of approved course providers and sites at which the parent education and family stabilization course may be completed. Each judicial circuit must make information regarding all course providers approved for their circuit available to all parents.

(b) The Department of Children and Families shall include on the list of approved course providers and sites for each circuit at least one site in that circuit where the parent education and family stabilization course may be completed on a sliding fee scale, if available.

(c) The Department of Children and Families shall include on the list of approved course providers, without limitation as to the area of the state for which the course is approved, a minimum of one statewide approved course to be provided through the Internet and one statewide approved course to be provided through correspondence. The purpose of the Internet and correspondence courses is to ensure that the parent education and stabilization course is available in the home county of each state resident and to those out-of-state persons subject to this section.

(d) The Department of Children and Families may remove a provider who violates this section, or its implementing rules, from the list of approved court providers.

(e) The Department of Children and Families shall adopt rules to administer subsection (2) and this subsection.

(4) All parties to a dissolution of marriage proceeding with minor children or a paternity action that involves issues of parental responsibility shall be required to complete the Parent Education and Family Stabilization Course prior to the entry by the court of a final judgment. The court may excuse a party from attending the parenting course, or from completing the course within the required time, for good cause.

(5) All parties required to complete a parenting course under this section shall begin the course as expeditiously as possible. For dissolution of marriage actions, unless excused by the court pursuant to subsection (4), the petitioner must complete the course within 45 days after the filing of the petition, and all other parties must complete the course within 45 days after service of the petition. For paternity actions, unless excused by the court pursuant to subsection (4), the petitioner must complete the course within 45 days after filing the petition, and any other party must complete the course within 45 days after an acknowledgment of paternity by that party, an adjudication of paternity of that party, or an order granting time-sharing to or support from that party. Each party to a dissolution or paternity action shall file proof of compliance with this subsection with the court prior to the entry of the final judgment.

(6) All parties to a modification of a final judgment involving a parenting plan or a time-sharing schedule may be required to complete a court-approved parenting course prior to the entry of an order modifying the final judgment.

(7) A reasonable fee may be charged to each parent attending the course.

(8) Information obtained or statements made by the parties at any educational session required under this statute shall not be considered in the adjudication of a pending or subsequent action, nor shall any report resulting from such educational session become part of the record of the case unless the parties have stipulated in writing to the contrary.

(9) The court may hold any parent who fails to attend a required parenting course in contempt, or that parent may be denied shared parental responsibility or time-sharing or otherwise sanctioned as the court deems appropriate.

(10) Nothing in this section shall be construed to require the parties to a dissolution of marriage to attend a court-approved parenting course together.

(11) The court may, without motion of either party, prohibit the parenting course from being taken together, if there is a history of domestic violence between the parties.

61.29. Child support guidelines; principles.

The following principles establish the public policy of the State of Florida in the creation of the child support guidelines:

(1) Each parent has a fundamental obligation to support his or her minor or legally dependent child.

(2) The guidelines schedule is based on the parent's combined net income estimated to have been allocated to the child as if the parents and children were living in an intact household.

(3) The guidelines encourage fair and efficient settlement of support issues between parents and minimizes the need for litigation.

61.30. Child support guidelines; retroactive child support.

(1)(a) The child support guideline amount as determined by this section presumptively establishes the amount the trier of fact shall order as child support in an initial proceeding for such support or in a proceeding for modification of an existing order for such support, whether the proceeding arises under this or another chapter. The trier of fact may order payment of child support which varies, plus or minus 5 percent, from the guideline amount, after considering all relevant factors, including the needs of the child or children, age, station in life, standard of living, and the financial status and ability of each parent. The trier of fact may order payment of child support in an amount which varies more than 5 percent from such guideline amount only upon a written finding explaining why ordering payment of such guideline amount would be unjust or inappropriate. Notwithstanding the variance limitations of this section, the trier of fact shall order payment of child support which varies from the guideline amount as provided in paragraph (11)(b) whenever any of the children are required by court order or mediation agreement to spend a substantial amount of time with either parent. This requirement applies to any living arrangement, whether temporary or permanent.

(b) The guidelines may provide the basis for proving a substantial change in circumstances upon which a modification of an existing order may be granted. However, the difference between the existing monthly obligation and the amount provided for under the guidelines shall be at least 15 percent or $50, whichever amount is greater, before the court may find that the guidelines provide a substantial change in circumstances.

(c) For each support order reviewed by the department as required by s. 409.2564(11), if the amount of the child support award under the order differs by at least 10 percent but not less than $25 from the amount that would be awarded under this section, the department shall seek to have the order modified and any modification shall be made without a requirement for proof or showing of a change in circumstances.

(2) Income shall be determined on a monthly basis for each parent as follows:

(a) Gross income shall include, but is not limited to, the following:

1. Salary or wages.

2. Bonuses, commissions, allowances, overtime, tips, and other similar payments.

3. Business income from sources such as self-employment, partnership, close corporations, and independent contracts. "Business income" means gross receipts minus ordinary and necessary expenses required to produce income.

4. Disability benefits.

5. All workers' compensation benefits and settlements.

6. Reemployment assistance or unemployment compensation.

7. Pension, retirement, or annuity payments.

8. Social security benefits.

9. Spousal support received from a previous marriage or court ordered in the marriage before the court.

10. Interest and dividends.

11. Rental income, which is gross receipts minus ordinary and necessary expenses required to produce the income.

12. Income from royalties, trusts, or estates.

13. Reimbursed expenses or in kind payments to the extent that they reduce living expenses.

14. Gains derived from dealings in property, unless the gain is nonrecurring.

(b) Monthly income shall be imputed to an unemployed or underemployed parent if such unemployment or underemployment is found by the court to be voluntary on that parent's part, absent a finding of fact by the court of physical or mental incapacity or other circumstances over which the parent has no control. In the event of such voluntary unemployment or underemployment, the employment potential and probable earnings level of the parent shall be determined based upon his or her recent work history, occupational qualifications, and prevailing earnings level in the community if such information is available. If the information concerning a parent's income is unavailable, a parent fails to participate in a child support proceeding, or a parent fails to supply adequate financial information in a child support proceeding, income shall be automatically imputed to the parent and there is a rebuttable presumption that the parent has income equivalent to the median income of year-round full-time workers as derived from current population reports or replacement reports published by the United States Bureau of the Census.

However, the court may refuse to impute income to a parent if the court finds it necessary for that parent to stay home with the child who is the subject of a child support calculation or as set forth below:

1. In order for the court to impute income at an amount other than the median income of year-round full-time workers as derived from current population reports or replacement reports published by the United States Bureau of the Census, the court must make specific findings of fact consistent with the requirements of this paragraph. The party seeking to impute income has the burden to present competent, substantial evidence that:

a. The unemployment or underemployment is voluntary; and

b. Identifies the amount and source of the imputed income, through evidence of income from available employment for which the party is suitably qualified by education, experience, current licensure, or geographic location, with due consideration being given to the parties' time-sharing schedule and their historical exercise of the time-sharing provided in the parenting plan or relevant order.

2. Except as set forth in subparagraph 1., income may not be imputed based upon:

a. Income records that are more than 5 years old at the time of the hearing or trial at which imputation is sought; or

b. Income at a level that a party has never earned in the past, unless recently degreed, licensed, certified, relicensed, or recertified and thus qualified for, subject to geographic location, with due consideration of the parties' existing time-sharing schedule and their historical exercise of the time-sharing provided in the parenting plan or relevant order.

(c) Public assistance as defined in s. 409.2554 shall be excluded from gross income.

(3) Net income is obtained by subtracting allowable deductions from gross income. Allowable deductions shall include:

(a) Federal, state, and local income tax deductions, adjusted for actual filing status and allowable dependents and income tax liabilities.

(b) Federal insurance contributions or self-employment tax.

(c) Mandatory union dues.

(d) Mandatory retirement payments.

(e) Health insurance payments, excluding payments for coverage of the minor child.

(f) Court-ordered support for other children which is actually paid.

(g) Spousal support paid pursuant to a court order from a previous marriage or the marriage before the court.

(4) Net income for each parent shall be computed by subtracting allowable deductions from gross income.

(5) Net income for each parent shall be added together for a combined net income.

(6) The following guidelines schedule shall be applied to the combined net income to determine the minimum child support need:

Combined
Monthly Net
Child or Children
Income
One
Two
Three
Four
Five
Six
800.00
190
211
213
216

218
220
850.00
202
257
259
262
265
268
900.00
213
302
305
309
312
315
950.00
224
347
351
355
359
363
1000.00
235
365
397
402
406
410
1050.00
246
382
443
448
453
458
1100.00
258
400
489
495
500
505
1150.00
269
417
522
541
547
553
1200.00
280

435
544
588
594
600
1250.00
290
451
565
634
641
648
1300.00
300
467
584
659
688
695
1350.00
310
482
603
681
735
743
1400.00
320
498
623
702
765
790
1450.00
330
513
642
724
789
838
1500.00
340
529
662
746
813
869
1550.00
350
544
681
768
836

895
1600.00
360
560
701
790
860
920
1650.00
370
575
720
812
884
945
1700.00
380
591
740
833
907
971
1750.00
390
606
759
855
931
996
1800.00
400
622
779
877
955
1022
1850.00
410
638
798
900
979
1048
1900.00
421
654
818
923
1004
1074
1950.00
431
670

839
946
1029
1101
2000.00
442
686
859
968
1054
1128
2050.00
452
702
879
991
1079
1154
2100.00
463
718
899
1014
1104
1181
2150.00
473
734
919
1037
1129
1207
2200.00
484
751
940
1060
1154
1234
2250.00
494
767
960
1082
1179
1261
2300.00
505
783
980
1105
1204
1287

2350.00
515
799
1000
1128
1229
1314
2400.00
526
815
1020
1151
1254
1340
2450.00
536
831
1041
1174
1279
1367
2500.00
547
847
1061
1196
1304
1394
2550.00
557
864
1081
1219
1329
1420
2600.00
568
880
1101
1242
1354
1447
2650.00
578
896
1121
1265
1379
1473
2700.00
588
912
1141

1287
1403
1500
2750.00
597
927
1160
1308
1426
1524
2800.00
607
941
1178
1328
1448
1549
2850.00
616
956
1197
1349
1471
1573
2900.00
626
971
1215
1370
1494
1598
2950.00
635
986
1234
1391
1517
1622
3000.00
644
1001
1252
1412
1540
1647
3050.00
654
1016
1271
1433
1563
1671
3100.00

663
1031
1289
1453
1586
1695
3150.00
673
1045
1308
1474
1608
1720
3200.00
682
1060
1327
1495
1631
1744
3250.00
691
1075
1345
1516
1654
1769
3300.00
701
1090
1364
1537
1677
1793
3350.00
710
1105
1382
1558
1700
1818
3400.00
720
1120
1401
1579
1723
1842
3450.00
729
1135
1419
1599

1745
1867
3500.00
738
1149
1438
1620
1768
1891
3550.00
748
1164
1456
1641
1791
1915
3600.00
757
1179
1475
1662
1814
1940
3650.00
767
1194
1493
1683
1837
1964
3700.00
776
1208
1503
1702
1857
1987
3750.00
784
1221
1520
1721
1878
2009
3800.00
793
1234
1536
1740
1899
2031
3850.00
802

1248
1553
1759
1920
2053
3900.00
811
1261
1570
1778
1940
2075
3950.00
819
1275
1587
1797
1961
2097
4000.00
828
1288
1603
1816
1982
2119
4050.00
837
1302
1620
1835
2002
2141
4100.00
846
1315
1637
1854
2023
2163
4150.00
854
1329
1654
1873
2044
2185
4200.00
863
1342
1670
1892
2064

2207
4250.00
872
1355
1687
1911
2085
2229
4300.00
881
1369
1704
1930
2106
2251
4350.00
889
1382
1721
1949
2127
2273
4400.00
898
1396
1737
1968
2147
2295
4450.00
907
1409
1754
1987
2168
2317
4500.00
916
1423
1771
2006
2189
2339
4550.00
924
1436
1788
2024
2209
2361
4600.00
933
1450

1804
2043
2230
2384
4650.00
942
1463
1821
2062
2251
2406
4700.00
951
1477
1838
2081
2271
2428
4750.00
959
1490
1855
2100
2292
2450
4800.00
968
1503
1871
2119
2313
2472
4850.00
977
1517
1888
2138
2334
2494
4900.00
986
1530
1905
2157
2354
2516
4950.00
993
1542
1927
2174
2372
2535

5000.00
1000
1551
1939
2188
2387
2551
5050.00
1006
1561
1952
2202
2402
2567
5100.00
1013
1571
1964
2215
2417
2583
5150.00
1019
1580
1976
2229
2432
2599
5200.00
1025
1590
1988
2243
2447
2615
5250.00
1032
1599
2000
2256
2462
2631
5300.00
1038
1609
2012
2270
2477
2647
5350.00
1045
1619
2024

2283
2492
2663
5400.00
1051
1628
2037
2297
2507
2679
5450.00
1057
1638
2049
2311
2522
2695
5500.00
1064
1647
2061
2324
2537
2711
5550.00
1070
1657
2073
2338
2552
2727
5600.00
1077
1667
2085
2352
2567
2743
5650.00
1083
1676
2097
2365
2582
2759
5700.00
1089
1686
2109
2379
2597
2775
5750.00

1096
1695
2122
2393
2612
2791
5800.00
1102
1705
2134
2406
2627
2807
5850.00
1107
1713
2144
2418
2639
2820
5900.00
1111
1721
2155
2429
2651
2833
5950.00
1116
1729
2165
2440
2663
2847
6000.00
1121
1737
2175
2451
2676
2860
6050.00
1126
1746
2185
2462
2688
2874
6100.00
1131
1754
2196
2473

2700
2887
6150.00
1136
1762
2206
2484
2712
2900
6200.00
1141
1770
2216
2495
2724
2914
6250.00
1145
1778
2227
2506
2737
2927
6300.00
1150
1786
2237
2517
2749
2941
6350.00
1155
1795
2247
2529
2761
2954
6400.00
1160
1803
2258
2540
2773
2967
6450.00
1165
1811
2268
2551
2785
2981
6500.00
1170

1819
2278
2562
2798
2994
6550.00
1175
1827
2288
2573
2810
3008
6600.00
1179
1835
2299
2584
2822
3021
6650.00
1184
1843
2309
2595
2834
3034
6700.00
1189
1850
2317
2604
2845
3045
6750.00
1193
1856
2325
2613
2854
3055
6800.00
1196
1862
2332
2621
2863
3064
6850.00
1200
1868
2340
2630
2872

3074
6900.00
1204
1873
2347
2639
2882
3084
6950.00
1208
1879
2355
2647
2891
3094
7000.00
1212
1885
2362
2656
2900
3103
7050.00
1216
1891
2370
2664
2909
3113
7100.00
1220
1897
2378
2673
2919
3123
7150.00
1224
1903
2385
2681
2928
3133
7200.00
1228
1909
2393
2690
2937
3142
7250.00
1232
1915

2400
2698
2946
3152
7300.00
1235
1921
2408
2707
2956
3162
7350.00
1239
1927
2415
2716
2965
3172
7400.00
1243
1933
2423
2724
2974
3181
7450.00
1247
1939
2430
2733
2983
3191
7500.00
1251
1945
2438
2741
2993
3201
7550.00
1255
1951
2446
2750
3002
3211
7600.00
1259
1957
2453
2758
3011
3220

7650.00
1263
1963
2461
2767
3020
3230
7700.00
1267
1969
2468
2775
3030
3240
7750.00
1271
1975
2476
2784
3039
3250
7800.00
1274
1981
2483
2792
3048
3259
7850.00
1278
1987
2491
2801
3057
3269
7900.00
1282
1992
2498
2810
3067
3279
7950.00
1286
1998
2506
2818
3076
3289
8000.00
1290
2004
2513

2827
3085
3298
8050.00
1294
2010
2521
2835
3094
3308
8100.00
1298
2016
2529
2844
3104
3318
8150.00
1302
2022
2536
2852
3113
3328
8200.00
1306
2028
2544
2861
3122
3337
8250.00
1310
2034
2551
2869
3131
3347
8300.00
1313
2040
2559
2878
3141
3357
8350.00
1317
2046
2566
2887
3150
3367
8400.00

1321
2052
2574
2895
3159
3376
8450.00
1325
2058
2581
2904
3168
3386
8500.00
1329
2064
2589
2912
3178
3396
8550.00
1333
2070
2597
2921
3187
3406
8600.00
1337
2076
2604
2929
3196
3415
8650.00
1341
2082
2612
2938
3205
3425
8700.00
1345
2088
2619
2946
3215
3435
8750.00
1349
2094
2627
2955

3224
3445
8800.00
1352
2100
2634
2963
3233
3454
8850.00
1356
2106
2642
2972
3242
3464
8900.00
1360
2111
2649
2981
3252
3474
8950.00
1364
2117
2657
2989
3261
3484
9000.00
1368
2123
2664
2998
3270
3493
9050.00
1372
2129
2672
3006
3279
3503
9100.00
1376
2135
2680
3015
3289
3513
9150.00
1380

2141
2687
3023
3298
3523
9200.00
1384
2147
2695
3032
3307
3532
9250.00
1388
2153
2702
3040
3316
3542
9300.00
1391
2159
2710
3049
3326
3552
9350.00
1395
2165
2717
3058
3335
3562
9400.00
1399
2171
2725
3066
3344
3571
9450.00
1403
2177
2732
3075
3353
3581
9500.00
1407
2183
2740
3083
3363

3591
9550.00
1411
2189
2748
3092
3372
3601
9600.00
1415
2195
2755
3100
3381
3610
9650.00
1419
2201
2763
3109
3390
3620
9700.00
1422
2206
2767
3115
3396
3628
9750.00
1425
2210
2772
3121
3402
3634
9800.00
1427
2213
2776
3126
3408
3641
9850.00
1430
2217
2781
3132
3414
3647
9900.00
1432
2221

2786
3137
3420
3653
9950.00
1435
2225
2791
3143
3426
3659
10000.00
1437
2228
2795
3148
3432
3666

(a) If the obligor parent's net income is less than the amount in the guidelines schedule:

1. The parent should be ordered to pay a child support amount, determined on a case-by-case basis, to establish the principle of payment and lay the basis for increased support orders should the parent's income increase.

2. The obligor parent's child support payment shall be the lesser of the obligor parent's actual dollar share of the total minimum child support amount, as determined in subparagraph 1., and 90 percent of the difference between the obligor parent's monthly net income and the current poverty guidelines as periodically updated in the Federal Register by the United States Department of Health and Human Services pursuant to 42 U.S.C. s. 9902(2) for a single individual living alone.

(b) For combined monthly net income greater than the amount in the guidelines schedule, the obligation is the minimum amount of support provided by the guidelines schedule plus the following percentages multiplied by the amount of income over $10,000:

Child or Children
One
Two
Three
Four
Five
Six
5.0%
7.5%
9.5%
11.0%
12.0%
12.5%

(7) Child care costs incurred due to employment, job search, or education calculated to result in employment or to enhance income of current employment of either parent shall be added to the basic obligation. After the child care costs are added, any moneys prepaid by a parent for child care costs for the child or children of this action shall be deducted from that parent's child support obligation for that child or those children. Child care costs may not exceed the level required to provide quality care from a licensed source.

(8) Health insurance costs resulting from coverage ordered pursuant to s. 61.13(1)(b), and any noncovered medical, dental, and prescription medication expenses of the child, shall be added to the basic obligation unless these expenses have been ordered to be separately paid on a percentage basis. After the health insurance costs are added to the basic obligation, any moneys prepaid by a

parent for health-related costs for the child or children of this action shall be deducted from that parent's child support obligation for that child or those children.

(9) Each parent's percentage share of the child support need shall be determined by dividing each parent's net monthly income by the combined net monthly income.

(10) Each parent's actual dollar share of the total minimum child support need shall be determined by multiplying the minimum child support need by each parent's percentage share of the combined monthly net income.

(11)(a) The court may adjust the total minimum child support award, or either or both parents' share of the total minimum child support award, based upon the following deviation factors:

1. Extraordinary medical, psychological, educational, or dental expenses.

2. Independent income of the child, not to include moneys received by a child from supplemental security income.

3. The payment of support for a parent which has been regularly paid and for which there is a demonstrated need.

4. Seasonal variations in one or both parents' incomes or expenses.

5. The age of the child, taking into account the greater needs of older children.

6. Special needs, such as costs that may be associated with the disability of a child, that have traditionally been met within the family budget even though fulfilling those needs will cause the support to exceed the presumptive amount established by the guidelines.

7. Total available assets of the obligee, obligor, and the child.

8. The impact of the Internal Revenue Service Child & Dependent Care Tax Credit, Earned Income Tax Credit, and dependency exemption and waiver of that exemption. The court may order a parent to execute a waiver of the Internal Revenue Service dependency exemption if the paying parent is current in support payments.

9. An application of the child support guidelines schedule that requires a person to pay another person more than 55 percent of his or her gross income for a child support obligation for current support resulting from a single support order.

10. The particular parenting plan, a court-ordered time-sharing schedule, or a time-sharing arrangement exercised by agreement of the parties, such as where the child spends a significant amount of time, but less than 20 percent of the overnights, with one parent, thereby reducing the financial expenditures incurred by the other parent; or the refusal of a parent to become involved in the activities of the child.

11. Any other adjustment that is needed to achieve an equitable result which may include, but not be limited to, a reasonable and necessary existing expense or debt. Such expense or debt may include, but is not limited to, a reasonable and necessary expense or debt that the parties jointly incurred during the marriage.

(b) Whenever a particular parenting plan, a court-ordered time-sharing schedule, or a time-sharing arrangement exercised by agreement of the parties provides that each child spend a substantial amount of time with each parent, the court shall adjust any award of child support, as follows:

1. In accordance with subsections (9) and (10), calculate the amount of support obligation apportioned to each parent without including day care and health insurance costs in the calculation and multiply the amount by 1.5.

2. Calculate the percentage of overnight stays the child spends with each parent.

3. Multiply each parent's support obligation as calculated in subparagraph 1. by the percentage of the other parent's overnight stays with the child as calculated in subparagraph 2.

4. The difference between the amounts calculated in subparagraph 3. shall be the monetary transfer necessary between the parents for the care of the child, subject to an adjustment for day care and health insurance expenses.

5. Pursuant to subsections (7) and (8), calculate the net amounts owed by each parent for the expenses incurred for day care and health insurance coverage for the child.

6. Adjust the support obligation owed by each parent pursuant to subparagraph 4. by crediting or debiting the amount calculated in subparagraph 5. This amount represents the child support which must be exchanged between the parents.

7. The court may deviate from the child support amount calculated pursuant to subparagraph 6. based upon the deviation factors in paragraph (a), as well as the obligee parent's low income and ability to maintain the basic necessities of the home for the child, the likelihood that either parent will actually exercise the time-sharing schedule set forth in the parenting plan, a court-ordered time-sharing schedule, or a time-sharing arrangement exercised by agreement of the parties, and whether all of the children are exercising the same time-sharing schedule.

8. For purposes of adjusting any award of child support under this paragraph, "substantial amount of time" means that a parent exercises time-sharing at least 20 percent of the overnights of the year.

(c) A parent's failure to regularly exercise the time-sharing schedule set forth in the parenting plan, a court-ordered time-sharing schedule, or a time-sharing arrangement exercised by agreement of the parties not caused by the other parent which resulted in the adjustment of the amount of child support pursuant to subparagraph (a)10. or paragraph (b) shall be deemed a substantial change of circumstances for purposes of modifying the child support award. A modification pursuant to this paragraph is retroactive to the date the noncustodial parent first failed to regularly exercise the court-ordered or agreed time-sharing schedule.

(12)(a) A parent with a support obligation may have other children living with him or her who were born or adopted after the support obligation arose. If such subsequent children exist, the court, when considering an upward modification of an existing award, may disregard the income from secondary employment obtained in addition to the parent's primary employment if the court determines that the employment was obtained primarily to support the subsequent children.

(b) Except as provided in paragraph (a), the existence of such subsequent children should not as a general rule be considered by the court as a basis for disregarding the amount provided in the guidelines schedule. The parent with a support obligation for subsequent children may raise the existence of such subsequent children as a justification for deviation from the guidelines schedule. However, if the existence of such subsequent children is raised, the income of the other parent of the subsequent children shall be considered by the court in determining whether or not there is a basis for deviation from the guideline amount.

(c) The issue of subsequent children under paragraph (a) or paragraph (b) may only be raised in a proceeding for an upward modification of an existing award and may not be applied to justify a decrease in an existing award.

(13) If the recurring income is not sufficient to meet the needs of the child, the court may order child support to be paid from nonrecurring income or assets.

(14) Every petition for child support or for modification of child support shall be accompanied by an affidavit which shows the party's income, allowable deductions, and net income computed in accordance with this section. The affidavit shall be served at the same time that the petition is served. The respondent, whether or not a stipulation is entered, shall make an affidavit which shows the party's income, allowable deductions, and net income computed in accordance with this section. The respondent shall include his or her affidavit with the answer to the petition or as soon thereafter as is practicable, but in any case at least 72 hours prior to any hearing on the finances of either party.

(15) For purposes of establishing an obligation for support in accordance with this section, if a person who is receiving public assistance is found to be noncooperative as defined in s. 409.2572, the department may submit to the court an affidavit or written declaration signed under penalty of perjury as specified in s. 92.525(2) attesting to the income of that parent based upon information available to the department.

(16) The Legislature shall review the guidelines schedule established in this section at least every 4 years beginning in 1997.

(17) In an initial determination of child support, whether in a paternity action, dissolution of marriage action, or petition for support during the marriage, the court has discretion to award child support retroactive to the date when the parents did not reside together in the same household with the child, not to exceed a period of 24 months preceding the filing of the petition, regardless of whether that date precedes the filing of the petition. In determining the retroactive award in such

cases, the court shall consider the following:

(a) The court shall apply the guidelines schedule in effect at the time of the hearing subject to the obligor's demonstration of his or her actual income, as defined by subsection (2), during the retroactive period. Failure of the obligor to so demonstrate shall result in the court using the obligor's income at the time of the hearing in computing child support for the retroactive period.

(b) All actual payments made by a parent to the other parent or the child or third parties for the benefit of the child throughout the proposed retroactive period.

(c) The court should consider an installment payment plan for the payment of retroactive child support.

61.401. Appointment of guardian ad litem.

In an action for dissolution of marriage or for the creation, approval, or modification of a parenting plan, if the court finds it is in the best interest of the child, the court may appoint a guardian ad litem to act as next friend of the child, investigator or evaluator, not as attorney or advocate. The court in its discretion may also appoint legal counsel for a child to act as attorney or advocate; however, the guardian and the legal counsel shall not be the same person. In such actions which involve an allegation of child abuse, abandonment, or neglect as defined in s. 39.01, which allegation is verified and determined by the court to be well-founded, the court shall appoint a guardian ad litem for the child. The guardian ad litem shall be a party to any judicial proceeding from the date of the appointment until the date of discharge.

61.402. Qualifications of guardians ad litem.

(1) A person appointed as a guardian ad litem pursuant to s. 61.401 must be:

(a) Certified by the Guardian Ad Litem Program pursuant to s. 39.821;

(b) Certified by a not-for-profit legal aid organization as defined in s. 68.096; or

(c) An attorney who is a member in good standing of The Florida Bar.

(2)(a) Prior to certifying a guardian ad litem pursuant to paragraph (1)(b), the not-for-profit legal aid organization must:

1. Conduct a security background investigation as described in s. 39.821 for which the not-for-profit legal aid organization has the sole discretion in determining whether to certify a person based on his or her security background investigation; and

2. Provide training using the uniform objective statewide training program for guardians ad litem developed by The Florida Bar.

(b) The security background investigation and the training program requirements as provided in this subsection must be paid for by the not-for-profit legal aid organization or the person seeking certification as a guardian ad litem through the not-for-profit legal aid organization.

(3) Only a guardian ad litem who qualifies under paragraph (1)(a) or paragraph (1)(c) may be appointed to a case in which the court has determined that there are well-founded allegations of child abuse, abandonment, or neglect as defined in s. 39.01.

(4) Nothing in this section requires the Guardian Ad Litem Program or a not-for-profit legal aid organization to train or certify guardians ad litem appointed under this chapter.

(5) It is a misdemeanor of the first degree, punishable as provided in s. 775.082 or s. 775.083, for any person to willfully, knowingly, or intentionally fail, by false statement, misrepresentation, impersonation, or other fraudulent means, to disclose in an application for a guardian ad litem any material fact used in making a determination as to the applicant's qualifications for such position.

61.403. Guardians ad litem; powers and authority.

A guardian ad litem when appointed shall act as next friend of the child, investigator or evaluator, not as attorney or advocate but shall act in the child's best interest. A guardian ad litem shall have the powers, privileges, and responsibilities to the extent necessary to advance the best interest of the child, including, but not limited to, the following:

(1) The guardian ad litem may investigate the allegations of the pleadings affecting the child, and, after proper notice to interested parties to the litigation and subject to conditions set by the court, may interview the child, witnesses, or any other person having information concerning the welfare of the child.

(2) The guardian ad litem, through counsel, may petition the court for an order directed to a specified person, agency, or organization, including, but not limited to, hospitals, medical doctors, dentists, psychologists, and psychiatrists, which order directs that the guardian ad litem be allowed to inspect and copy any records and documents which relate to the minor child or to the child's parents or other custodial persons or household members with whom the child resides. Such order shall be obtained only after notice to all parties and hearing thereon.

(3) The guardian ad litem, through counsel, may request the court to order expert examinations of the child, the child's parents, or other interested parties in the action, by medical doctors, dentists, and other providers of health care including psychiatrists, psychologists, or other mental health professionals.

(4) The guardian ad litem may assist the court in obtaining impartial expert examinations.

(5) The guardian ad litem may address the court and make written or oral recommendations to the court. The guardian ad litem shall file a written report which may include recommendations and a statement of the wishes of the child. The report must be filed and served on all parties at least 20 days prior to the hearing at which it will be presented unless the court waives such time limit. The guardian ad litem must be provided with copies of all pleadings, notices, and other documents filed in the action and is entitled to reasonable notice before any action affecting the child is taken by either of the parties, their counsel, or the court.

(6) A guardian ad litem, acting through counsel, may file such pleadings, motions, or petitions for relief as the guardian ad litem deems appropriate or necessary in furtherance of the guardian's function. The guardian ad litem, through counsel, is entitled to be present and to participate in all depositions, hearings, and other proceedings in the action, and, through counsel, may compel the attendance of witnesses.

(7) The duties and rights of nonattorney guardians do not include the right to practice law.

(8) The guardian ad litem shall submit his or her recommendations to the court regarding any stipulation or agreement, whether incidental, temporary, or permanent, which affects the interest or welfare of the minor child, within 10 days after the date such stipulation or agreement is served upon the guardian ad litem.

61.404. Guardians ad litem; confidentiality.

The guardian ad litem shall maintain as confidential all information and documents received from any source described in s. 61.403(2) and may not disclose such information or documents except, in the guardian ad litem's discretion, in a report to the court, served upon both parties to the action and their counsel or as directed by the court.

61.405. Guardians ad litem; immunity.

Any person participating in a judicial proceeding as a guardian ad litem shall be presumed prima facie to be acting in good faith and in so doing shall be immune from any liability, civil or criminal, that otherwise might be incurred or imposed.

61.45. Court-ordered parenting plan; risk of violation; bond.

(1) In any proceeding in which the court enters a parenting plan, including a time-sharing schedule, including in a modification proceeding, upon the presentation of competent substantial evidence that there is a risk that one party may violate the court's parenting plan by removing a child from this state or country or by concealing the whereabouts of a child, upon stipulation of the parties, upon the motion of another individual or entity having a right under the law of this state, or if the court finds evidence that establishes credible risk of removal of the child, the court may:

(a) Order that a parent may not remove the child from this state without the notarized written permission of both parents or further court order;

(b) Order that a parent may not remove the child from this country without the notarized written permission of both parents or further court order;

(c) Order that a parent may not take the child to a country that has not ratified or acceded to the Hague Convention on the Civil Aspects of International Child Abduction unless the other parent agrees in writing that the child may be taken to the country;

(d) Require a parent to surrender the passport of the child or require that:

1. The petitioner place the child's name in the Children's Passport Issuance Alert Program of the United States Department of State;

2. The respondent surrender to the court or the petitioner's attorney any United States or foreign passport issued in the child's name, including a passport issued in the name of both the parent and the child; and

3. The respondent not apply on behalf of the child for a new or replacement passport or visa; or

(e) Require that a party post bond or other security in an amount sufficient to serve as a financial deterrent to abduction, the proceeds of which may be used to pay the reasonable expenses of recovery of the child, including reasonable attorney's fees and costs, if the child is abducted.

(2) If the court enters a parenting plan, including a time-sharing schedule, including in a modification proceeding, that includes a provision entered under paragraph (1)(b) or paragraph (1)(c), a certified copy of the order should be sent by the parent who requested the restriction to the Passport Services Office of the United States Department of State requesting that they not issue a passport to the child without their signature or further court order.

(3) If the court enters an order under paragraph (1)(a) or paragraph (1)(b) to prevent the removal of the child from this state or country, the order may include one or more of the following:

(a) An imposition of travel restrictions that require that a party traveling with the child outside a designated geographic area provide the other party with the following:

1. The travel itinerary of the child.

2. A list of physical addresses and telephone numbers at which the child can be reached at specified times.

3. Copies of all travel documents.

(b) A prohibition of the respondent directly or indirectly:

1. Removing the child from this state or country or another specified geographic area without permission of the court or the petitioner's written consent;

2. Removing or retaining the child in violation of a child custody determination;

3. Removing the child from school or a child care or similar facility; or

4. Approaching the child at any location other than a site designated for supervised visitation.

(c) A requirement that a party register the order in another state as a prerequisite to allowing the child to travel to that state.

(d) As a prerequisite to exercising custody or visitation, a requirement that the respondent provide the following:

1. An authenticated copy of the order detailing passport and travel restrictions for the child to the Office of Children's Issues within the Bureau of Consular Affairs of the United States Department of State and the relevant foreign consulate or embassy.

2. Proof to the court that the respondent has provided the information in subparagraph 1.

3. An acknowledgment to the court in a record from the relevant foreign consulate or embassy that no passport application has been made, or passport issued, on behalf of the child.

4. Proof to the petitioner and court of registration with the United States embassy or other United States diplomatic presence in the destination country and with the destination country's central authority for the Hague Convention on the Civil Aspects of International Child Abduction, if that convention is in effect between this country and the destination country, unless one of the parties objects.

5. A written waiver under the Privacy Act, 5 U.S.C. s. 552a, as amended, with respect to any document, application, or other information pertaining to the child or the respondent authorizing its disclosure to the court.

6. A written waiver with respect to any document, application, or other information pertaining to the child or the respondent in records held by the United States Bureau of Citizenship and Immigration Services authorizing its disclosure to the court.

7. Upon the court's request, a requirement that the respondent obtain an order from the relevant foreign country containing terms identical to the child custody determination issued in this country.

8. Upon the court's request, a requirement that the respondent be entered in the Prevent Departure Program of the United States Department of State or a similar federal program designed to prevent unauthorized departures to foreign countries.

(e) The court may impose conditions on the exercise of custody or visitation that limit visitation or require that visitation with the child by the respondent be supervised until the court finds that supervision is no longer necessary and orders the respondent to pay the costs of supervision.

(4) In assessing the need for a bond or other security, the court may consider any reasonable factor bearing upon the risk that a party may violate a parenting plan by removing a child from this state or country or by concealing the whereabouts of a child, including but not limited to whether:

(a) A court has previously found that a party previously removed a child from Florida or another state in violation of a parenting plan, or whether a court had found that a party has threatened to take a child out of Florida or another state in violation of a parenting plan;

(b) The party has strong family and community ties to Florida or to other states or countries, including whether the party or child is a citizen of another country;

(c) The party has strong financial reasons to remain in Florida or to relocate to another state or country;

(d) The party has engaged in activities that suggest plans to leave Florida, such as quitting employment; sale of a residence or termination of a lease on a residence, without efforts to acquire an alternative residence in the state; closing bank accounts or otherwise liquidating assets; applying for a passport or visa; or obtaining travel documents for the respondent or the child;

(e) Either party has had a history of domestic violence as either a victim or perpetrator, child abuse or child neglect evidenced by criminal history, including but not limited to, arrest, an injunction for protection against domestic violence issued after notice and hearing under s. 741.30, medical records, affidavits, or any other relevant information;

(f) The party has a criminal record;

(g) The party is likely to take the child to a country that:

1. Is not a party to the Hague Convention on the Civil Aspects of International Child Abduction and does not provide for the extradition of an abducting parent or for the return of an abducted child;

2. Is a party to the Hague Convention on the Civil Aspects of International Child Abduction, but:

a. The Hague Convention on the Civil Aspects of International Child Abduction is not in force between this country and that country;

b. Is noncompliant or demonstrating patterns of noncompliance according to the most recent compliance report issued by the United States Department of State; or

c. Lacks legal mechanisms for immediately and effectively enforcing a return order under the Hague Convention on the Civil Aspects of International Child Abduction;

3. Poses a risk that the child's physical or emotional health or safety would be endangered in the country because of specific circumstances relating to the child or because of human rights violations committed against children;

4. Has laws or practices that would:

a. Enable the respondent, without due cause, to prevent the petitioner from contacting the child;

b. Restrict the petitioner from freely traveling to or exiting from the country because of the petitioner's gender, nationality, marital status, or religion; or

c. Restrict the child's ability to legally leave the country after the child reaches the age of majority because of a child's gender, nationality, or religion;

5. Is included by the United States Department of State on a current list of state sponsors of terrorism;

6. Does not have an official United States diplomatic presence in the country; or

7. Is engaged in active military action or war, including a civil war, to which the child may be exposed;

(h) The party is undergoing a change in immigration or citizenship status that would adversely affect the respondent's ability to remain in this country legally;

(i) The party has had an application for United States citizenship denied;

(j) The party has forged or presented misleading or false evidence on government forms or supporting documents to obtain or attempt to obtain a passport, a visa, travel documents, a social security card, a driver license, or other government-issued identification card or has made a misrepresentation to the United States government;

(k) The party has used multiple names to attempt to mislead or defraud;

(l) The party has been diagnosed with a mental health disorder that the court considers relevant to the risk of abduction; or

(m) The party has engaged in any other conduct that the court considers relevant to the risk of abduction.

(5) The court must consider the party's financial resources prior to setting the bond amount under this section. Under no circumstances may the court set a bond that is unreasonable.

(6) Any deficiency of bond or security does not absolve the violating party of responsibility to pay the full amount of damages determined by the court.

(7)(a) Upon a material violation of any parenting plan by removing a child from this state or country or by concealing the whereabouts of a child, the court may order the bond or other security forfeited in whole or in part.

(b) This section, including the requirement to post a bond or other security, does not apply to a parent who, in a proceeding to order or modify a parenting plan or time-sharing schedule, is determined by the court to be a victim of an act of domestic violence or provides the court with reasonable cause to believe that he or she is about to become the victim of an act of domestic violence, as defined in s. 741.28. An injunction for protection against domestic violence issued pursuant to s. 741.30 for a parent as the petitioner which is in effect at the time of the court proceeding shall be one means of demonstrating sufficient evidence that the parent is a victim of domestic violence or is about to become the victim of an act of domestic violence, as defined in s. 741.28, and shall exempt the parent from this section, including the requirement to post a bond or other security. A parent who is determined by the court to be exempt from the requirements of this section must meet the requirements of s. 787.03(6) if an offense of interference with the parenting plan or time-sharing schedule is committed.

(8)(a) Upon an order of forfeiture, the proceeds of any bond or other security posted pursuant to this subsection may only be used to:

1. Reimburse the nonviolating party for actual costs or damages incurred in upholding the court's parenting plan.

2. Locate and return the child to the residence as set forth in the parenting plan.

3. Reimburse reasonable fees and costs as determined by the court.

(b) Any remaining proceeds shall be held as further security if deemed necessary by the court, and if further security is not found to be necessary; applied to any child support arrears owed by the parent against whom the bond was required, and if no arrears exists; all remaining proceeds will be allocated by the court in the best interest of the child.

(9) At any time after the forfeiture of the bond or other security, the party who posted the bond or other security, or the court on its own motion may request that the party provide documentation substantiating that the proceeds received as a result of the forfeiture have been used solely in accordance with this subsection. Any party using such proceeds for purposes not in accordance with this section may be found in contempt of court.

(10) A violation of this section may subject the party committing the violation to civil or criminal penalties or a federal or state warrant under federal or state laws, including the International Parental Kidnapping Crime Act, and may subject the violating parent to apprehension by a law enforcement officer.

PART II. UNIFORM CHILD CUSTODY JURISDICTION AND ENFORCEMENT ACT (SS. 61.501-61.542)

61.501. Short title.

This part may be cited as the "Uniform Child Custody Jurisdiction and Enforcement Act."

61.502. Purposes of part; construction of provisions.

The general purposes of this part are to:

(1) Avoid jurisdictional competition and conflict with courts of other states in matters of child custody which have in the past resulted in the shifting of children from state to state with harmful effects on their well-being.

(2) Promote cooperation with the courts of other states to the end that a custody decree is rendered in the state that can best decide the case in the interest of the child.

(3) Discourage the use of the interstate system for continuing controversies over child custody.

(4) Deter abductions.

(5) Avoid relitigating the custody decisions of other states in this state.

(6) Facilitate the enforcement of custody decrees of other states.

(7) Promote and expand the exchange of information and other forms of mutual assistance between the courts of this state and those of other states concerned with the same child.

(8) Make uniform the law with respect to the subject of this part among the states enacting it.

61.503. Definitions.

As used in this part, the term:

(1) "Abandoned" means left without provision for reasonable and necessary care or supervision.

(2) "Child" means an individual who has not attained 18 years of age.

(3) "Child custody determination" means a judgment, decree, or other order of a court providing for the legal custody, physical custody, residential care, or visitation with respect to a child. The term includes a permanent, temporary, initial, and modification order. The term does not include an order relating to child support or other monetary obligation of an individual.

(4) "Child custody proceeding" means a proceeding in which legal custody, physical custody, residential care, or visitation with respect to a child is an issue. The term includes a proceeding for divorce, separation, neglect, abuse, dependency, guardianship, paternity, termination of parental rights, and protection from domestic violence, in which the issue may appear. The term does not include a proceeding involving juvenile delinquency, contractual emancipation, or enforcement under ss. 61.524-61.540.

(5) "Commencement" means the filing of the first pleading in a proceeding.

(6) "Court" means an entity authorized under the laws of a state to establish, enforce, or modify a child custody determination.

(7) "Home state" means the state in which a child lived with a parent or a person acting as a parent for at least 6 consecutive months immediately before the commencement of a child custody proceeding. In the case of a child younger than 6 months of age, the term means the state in which the child lived from birth with any of the persons mentioned. A period of temporary absence of any of the mentioned persons is part of the period.

(8) "Initial determination" means the first child custody determination concerning a particular child.

(9) "Issuing court" means the court that makes a child custody determination for which enforcement is sought under this part.

(10) "Issuing state" means the state in which a child custody determination is made.

(11) "Modification" means a child custody determination that changes, replaces, supersedes, or is otherwise made after a previous determination concerning the same child, regardless of whether it is made by the court that made the previous determination.

(12) "Person" means an individual, corporation, business trust, estate, trust, partnership, limited liability company, association, joint venture, or government; governmental subdivision, agency, instrumentality, or public corporation; or any other legal or commercial entity.

(13) "Person acting as a parent" means a person, other than a parent, who:

(a) Has physical custody of the child or has had physical custody for a period of 6 consecutive months, including any temporary absence, within 1 year immediately before the commencement of a child custody proceeding; and

(b) Has been awarded a child-custody determination by a court or claims a right to a child-custody determination under the laws of this state.

(14) "Physical custody" means the physical care and supervision of a child.

(15) "State" means a state of the United States, the District of Columbia, Puerto Rico, the United States Virgin Islands, or any territory or insular possession subject to the jurisdiction of the United States.

(16) "Tribe" means an Indian tribe, or band, or Alaskan Native village that is recognized by federal law or formally acknowledged by a state.

(17) "Warrant" means an order issued by a court authorizing law enforcement officers to take physical custody of a child.

61.504. Proceedings governed by other law.

This part does not govern a proceeding pertaining to the authorization of emergency medical care for a child.

61.505. Application to Indian tribes.

(1) A child custody proceeding that pertains to an Indian child, as defined in the Indian Child Welfare Act, 25 U.S.C. ss. 1901 et seq., is not subject to this part to the extent that it is governed by the Indian Child Welfare Act.

(2) A court of this state shall treat a tribe as if it were a state of the United States for purposes of applying ss. 61.501-61.523.

(3) A child custody determination made by a tribe under factual circumstances in substantial conformity with the jurisdictional standards of this part must be recognized and enforced under ss. 61.524-61.540.

61.506. International application of part.

(1) A court of this state shall treat a foreign country as if it were a state of the United States for purposes of applying ss. 61.501-61.523.

(2) Except as otherwise provided in subsection (3), a child custody determination made in a foreign country under factual circumstances in substantial conformity with the jurisdictional standards of this part must be recognized and enforced under ss. 61.524-61.540.

(3) A court of this state need not apply this part if the child custody law of a foreign country violates fundamental principles of human rights.

61.507. Effect of child custody determination.

A child custody determination made by a court of this state which had jurisdiction under this part binds all persons who have been served in accordance with the laws of this state or notified in accordance with s. 61.509 or who have submitted to the jurisdiction of the court, and who have been given an opportunity to be heard. As to those persons, the determination is conclusive as to all decided issues of law and fact except to the extent the determination is modified.

61.508. Priority.

If a question of existence or exercise of jurisdiction under this part is raised in a child custody proceeding, the question, upon request of a party, must be given priority on the calendar and handled expeditiously.

61.509. Notice to persons outside the state.

(1) Notice required for the exercise of jurisdiction when a person is outside this state may be given in a manner prescribed by the laws of the state in which the service is made. Notice must be given in a manner reasonably calculated to give actual notice, but may be made by publication if other means are not effective.

(2) Proof of service may be made in the manner prescribed by the laws of the state in which the service is made.

(3) Notice is not required for the exercise of jurisdiction with respect to a person who submits to the jurisdiction of the court.

61.510. Appearance and limited immunity.

(1) A party to a child custody proceeding, including a modification proceeding, or a petitioner or respondent in a proceeding to enforce or register a child custody determination, is not subject to personal jurisdiction in this state for another proceeding or purpose solely by reason of having participated, or of having been physically present for the purpose of participating, in the proceeding.

(2) A person who is subject to personal jurisdiction in this state on a basis other than physical presence is not immune from service of process in this state. A party present in this state who is subject to the jurisdiction of another state is not immune from service of process allowable under the laws of that state.

(3) The immunity granted by subsection (1) does not extend to civil litigation based on an act unrelated to the participation in a proceeding under this part which was committed by an individual while present in this state.

61.511. Communication between courts.

(1) A court of this state may communicate with a court in another state concerning a proceeding arising under this part.

(2) The court shall allow the parties to participate in the communication. If the parties elect to participate in the communication, they must be given the opportunity to present facts and legal arguments before a decision on jurisdiction is made.

(3) Communication between courts on schedules, calendars, court records, and similar matters may occur without informing the parties. A record need not be made of the communication.

(4) Except as otherwise provided in subsection (3), a record must be made of a communication under this section. The parties must be informed promptly of the communication and granted access to the record.

(5) For purposes of this section, the term "record" means a form of information, including, but not limited to, an electronic recording or transcription by a court reporter which creates a verbatim memorialization of any communication between two or more individuals or entities.

61.512. Taking testimony in another state.

(1) In addition to other procedures available to a party, a party to a child custody proceeding may offer testimony of witnesses who are located in another state, including testimony of the parties and the child, by deposition or other means available in this state for testimony taken in another state. The court on its own motion may order that the testimony of a person be taken in another state and may prescribe the manner in which and the terms upon which the testimony is taken.

(2) Upon agreement of the parties, a court of this state may permit an individual residing in another state to be deposed or to testify by telephone, audiovisual means, or other electronic means before a designated court or at another location in that state. A court of this state shall cooperate with courts of other states in designating an appropriate location for the deposition or testimony.

(3) Documentary evidence transmitted from another state to a court of this state by technological means that do not produce an original writing may not be excluded from evidence on an objection based on the means of transmission.

61.513. Cooperation between courts; preservation of records.

(1) A court of this state may request the appropriate court of another state to:

(a) Hold an evidentiary hearing;

(b) Order a person to produce or give evidence pursuant to the laws of that state;

(c) Order that an evaluation be made with respect to the custody of a child involved in a pending proceeding pursuant to the laws of the state where the proceeding is pending;

(d) Forward to the court of this state a certified copy of the transcript of the record of the hearing, the evidence otherwise presented, and any evaluation prepared in compliance with the request; or

(e) Order a party to a child custody proceeding or any person having physical custody of the child to appear in the proceeding with or without the child.

(2) Upon request of a court of another state, a court of this state may hold a hearing or enter an order described in subsection (1).

(3) Travel and other necessary and reasonable expenses incurred under subsections (1) and (2) may be assessed against the parties according to the laws of this state if the court has personal jurisdiction over the party against whom these expenses are being assessed.

(4) A court of this state shall preserve the pleadings, orders, decrees, records of hearings, evaluations, and other pertinent records with respect to a child custody proceeding until the child attains 18 years of age. Upon appropriate request by a court or law enforcement official of another state, the court shall forward a certified copy of these records.

61.514. Initial child custody jurisdiction.

(1) Except as otherwise provided in s. 61.517, a court of this state has jurisdiction to make an initial child custody determination only if:

(a) This state is the home state of the child on the date of the commencement of the proceeding, or was the home state of the child within 6 months before the commencement of the proceeding and the child is absent from this state but a parent or person acting as a parent continues to live in this state;

(b) A court of another state does not have jurisdiction under paragraph (a), or a court of the home state of the child has declined to exercise jurisdiction on the grounds that this state is the more appropriate forum under s. 61.520 or s. 61.521, and:

1. The child and the child's parents, or the child and at least one parent or a person acting as a parent, have a significant connection with this state other than mere physical presence; and

2. Substantial evidence is available in this state concerning the child's care, protection, training, and personal relationships;

(c) All courts having jurisdiction under paragraph (a) or paragraph (b) have declined to exercise jurisdiction on the grounds that a court of this state is the more appropriate forum to determine the custody of the child under s. 61.520 or s. 61.521; or

(d) No court of any other state would have jurisdiction under the criteria specified in paragraph (a), paragraph (b), or paragraph (c).

(2) Subsection (1) is the exclusive jurisdictional basis for making a child custody determination by a court of this state.

(3) Physical presence of, or personal jurisdiction over, a party or a child is not necessary or sufficient to make a child custody determination.

61.515. Exclusive, continuing jurisdiction.

(1) Except as otherwise provided in s. 61.517, a court of this state which has made a child custody determination consistent with s. 61.514 or s. 61.516 has exclusive, continuing jurisdiction over the determination until:
(a) A court of this state determines that the child, the child's parents, and any person acting as a parent do not have a significant connection with this state and that substantial evidence is no longer available in this state concerning the child's care, protection, training, and personal relationships; or
(b) A court of this state or a court of another state determines that the child, the child's parent, and any person acting as a parent do not presently reside in this state.
(2) A court of this state which has made a child custody determination and does not have exclusive, continuing jurisdiction under this section may modify that determination only if it has jurisdiction to make an initial determination under s. 61.514.

61.516. Jurisdiction to modify a determination.

Except as otherwise provided in s. 61.517, a court of this state may not modify a child custody determination made by a court of another state unless a court of this state has jurisdiction to make an initial determination under s. 61.514(1)(a) or (b) and:
(1) The court of the other state determines it no longer has exclusive, continuing jurisdiction under s. 61.515 or that a court of this state would be a more convenient forum under s. 61.520; or
(2) A court of this state or a court of the other state determines that the child, the child's parents, and any person acting as a parent do not presently reside in the other state.

61.517. Temporary emergency jurisdiction.

(1) A court of this state has temporary emergency jurisdiction if the child is present in this state and the child has been abandoned or it is necessary in an emergency to protect the child because the child, or a sibling or parent of the child, is subjected to or threatened with mistreatment or abuse.
(2) If there is no previous child custody determination that is entitled to be enforced under this part, and a child custody proceeding has not been commenced in a court of a state having jurisdiction under ss. 61.514-61.516, a child custody determination made under this section remains in effect until an order is obtained from a court of a state having jurisdiction under ss. 61.514-61.516. If a child custody proceeding has not been or is not commenced in a court of a state having jurisdiction under ss. 61.514-61.516, a child custody determination made under this section becomes a final determination if it so provides and this state becomes the home state of the child.
(3) If there is a previous child custody determination that is entitled to be enforced under this part, or a child custody proceeding has been commenced in a court of a state having jurisdiction under ss. 61.514-61.516, any order issued by a court of this state under this section must specify in the order a period that the court considers adequate to allow the person seeking an order to obtain an order from the state having jurisdiction under ss. 61.514-61.516. The order issued in this state remains in effect until an order is obtained from the other state within the period specified or the period expires.
(4) A court of this state which has been asked to make a child custody determination under this section, upon being informed that a child custody proceeding has been commenced in, or a child custody determination has been made by, a court of a state having jurisdiction under ss. 61.514-

61.516, shall immediately communicate with the other court. A court of this state which is exercising jurisdiction under ss. 61.514-61.516, upon being informed that a child custody proceeding has been commenced in, or a child custody determination has been made by, a court of another state under a statute similar to this section shall immediately communicate with the court of that state to resolve the emergency, protect the safety of the parties and the child, and determine a period for the duration of the temporary order.

61.518. Notice; opportunity to be heard; joinder.

(1) Before a child custody determination is made under this part, notice and an opportunity to be heard in accordance with the standards of s. 61.509 must be given to all persons entitled to notice under the laws of this state as in child custody proceedings between residents of this state, any parent whose parental rights have not been previously terminated, and any person acting as a parent.

(2) This part does not govern the enforceability of a child custody determination made without notice or an opportunity to be heard.

(3) The obligation to join a party and the right to intervene as a party in a child custody proceeding under this part are governed by the laws of this state as in child custody proceedings between residents of this state.

61.519. Simultaneous proceedings.

(1) Except as otherwise provided in s. 61.517, a court of this state may not exercise its jurisdiction under ss. 61.514-61.524 if, at the time of the commencement of the proceeding, a proceeding concerning the custody of the child had been commenced in a court of another state having jurisdiction substantially in conformity with this part, unless the proceeding has been terminated or is stayed by the court of the other state because a court of this state is a more convenient forum under s. 61.520.

(2) Except as otherwise provided in s. 61.517, a court of this state, before hearing a child custody proceeding, shall examine the court documents and other information supplied by the parties pursuant to s. 61.522. If the court determines that a child custody proceeding was previously commenced in a court in another state having jurisdiction substantially in accordance with this part, the court of this state shall stay its proceeding and communicate with the court of the other state. If the court of the state having jurisdiction substantially in accordance with this part does not determine that the court of this state is a more appropriate forum, the court of this state shall dismiss the proceeding.

(3) In a proceeding to modify a child custody determination, a court of this state shall determine whether a proceeding to enforce the determination has been commenced in another state. If a proceeding to enforce a child custody determination has been commenced in another state, the court may:

(a) Stay the proceeding for modification pending the entry of an order of a court of the other state enforcing, staying, denying, or dismissing the proceeding for enforcement;

(b) Enjoin the parties from continuing with the proceeding for enforcement; or

(c) Proceed with the modification under conditions it considers appropriate.

61.520. Inconvenient forum.

(1) A court of this state which has jurisdiction under this part to make a child custody

determination may decline to exercise its jurisdiction at any time if it determines that it is an inconvenient forum under the circumstances and that a court of another state is a more appropriate forum. The issue of inconvenient forum may be raised upon motion of a party, the court's own motion, or request of another court.

(2) Before determining whether it is an inconvenient forum, a court of this state shall consider whether it is appropriate for a court of another state to exercise jurisdiction. For this purpose, the court shall allow the parties to submit information and shall consider all relevant factors, including:

(a) Whether domestic violence has occurred and is likely to continue in the future and which state could best protect the parties and the child;

(b) The length of time the child has resided outside this state;

(c) The distance between the court in this state and the court in the state that would assume jurisdiction;

(d) The relative financial circumstances of the parties;

(e) Any agreement of the parties as to which state should assume jurisdiction;

(f) The nature and location of the evidence required to resolve the pending litigation, including testimony of the child;

(g) The ability of the court of each state to decide the issue expeditiously and the procedures necessary to present the evidence; and

(h) The familiarity of the court of each state with the facts and issues in the pending litigation.

(3) If a court of this state determines that it is an inconvenient forum and that a court of another state is a more appropriate forum, it shall stay the proceedings upon condition that a child custody proceeding be promptly commenced in another designated state and may impose any other condition the court considers just and proper.

(4) A court of this state may decline to exercise its jurisdiction under this part if a child custody determination is incidental to an action for divorce or another proceeding while still retaining jurisdiction over the divorce or other proceeding.

61.521. Jurisdiction declined by reason of conduct.

(1) Except as otherwise provided in s. 61.517 or by other law of this state, if a court of this state has jurisdiction under this part because a person seeking to invoke its jurisdiction has engaged in unjustifiable conduct, the court shall decline to exercise its jurisdiction unless:

(a) The parents and all persons acting as parents have acquiesced in the exercise of jurisdiction;

(b) A court of the state otherwise having jurisdiction under ss. 61.514-61.516 determines that this state is a more appropriate forum under s. 61.520; or

(c) No court of any other state would have jurisdiction under the criteria specified in ss. 61.514-61.516.

(2) If a court of this state declines to exercise its jurisdiction under subsection (1), it may fashion an appropriate remedy to ensure the safety of the child and prevent a repetition of the unjustifiable conduct, including staying the proceeding until a child custody proceeding is commenced in a court having jurisdiction under ss. 61.514-61.516.

(3) If a court dismisses a petition or stays a proceeding because it declines to exercise its jurisdiction under subsection (1), it shall assess against the party seeking to invoke its jurisdiction necessary and reasonable expenses, including costs, communication expenses, attorney's fees, investigative fees, expenses for witnesses, travel expenses, and expenses for child care during the course of the proceedings, unless the party from whom fees are sought establishes that the assessment would be clearly inappropriate. The court may not assess fees, costs, or expenses against this state unless authorized by law other than this part.

61.522. Information to be submitted to the court.

(1) Subject to Florida law providing for the confidentiality of procedures, addresses, and other identifying information in a child custody proceeding, each party, in its first pleading or in an attached affidavit, shall give information, if reasonably ascertainable, under oath as to the child's present address or whereabouts, the places where the child has lived during the last 5 years, and the names and present addresses of the persons with whom the child has lived during that period. The pleading or affidavit must state whether the party:

(a) Has participated, as a party or witness or in any other capacity, in any other proceeding concerning the custody of or visitation with the child and, if so, identify the court, the case number, and the date of the child custody determination, if any;

(b) Knows of any proceeding that could affect the current proceeding, including proceedings for enforcement and proceedings relating to domestic violence, protective orders, termination of parental rights, and adoptions and, if so, identify the court, the case number, and the nature of the proceeding; and

(c) Knows the names and addresses of any person not a party to the proceeding who has physical custody of the child or claims rights of legal custody or physical custody of, or visitation with, the child and, if so, the names and addresses of those persons.

(2) If the information required by subsection (1) is not furnished, the court, upon motion of a party or its own motion, may stay the proceeding until the information is furnished.

(3) If the declaration as to any of the items described in paragraphs (1)(a)-(c) is in the affirmative, the declarant shall give additional information under oath as required by the court. The court may examine the parties under oath as to details of the information furnished and other matters pertinent to the court's jurisdiction and the disposition of the case.

(4) Each party has a continuing duty to inform the court of any proceeding in this or any other state which could affect the current proceeding.

61.523. Appearance of parties and child.

(1) In a child custody proceeding in this state, the court may order a party to the proceeding who is in this state to appear before the court in person with or without the child. The court may order any person who is in this state and who has physical custody or control of the child to appear in person with the child.

(2) If a party to a child custody proceeding whose presence is desired by the court is outside this state, the court may order that a notice given pursuant to s. 61.509 include a statement directing the party to appear in person with or without the child and informing the party that failure to appear may result in a decision adverse to the party.

(3) The court may enter any orders necessary to ensure the safety of the child and of any person ordered to appear under this section.

(4) If a party to a child custody proceeding who is outside this state is directed to appear under subsection (2) or desires to appear in person before the court with or without the child, the court may require another party to pay reasonable and necessary travel and other expenses of the party so appearing and of the child.

61.524. Definitions.

As used in ss. 61.524-61.540, the term:

(1) "Petitioner" means a person who seeks enforcement of an order for return of a child under the Hague Convention on the Civil Aspects of International Child Abduction or enforcement of a

child custody determination.

(2) "Respondent" means a person against whom a proceeding has been commenced for enforcement of an order for return of a child under the Hague Convention on the Civil Aspects of International Child Abduction or enforcement of a child custody determination.

61.525. Enforcement under the Hague Convention.

Under this part, a court of this state may enforce an order for the return of a child made under the Hague Convention on the Civil Aspects of International Child Abduction as if it were a child custody determination.

61.526. Duty to enforce.

(1) A court of this state shall recognize and enforce a child custody determination of a court of another state if the latter court exercised jurisdiction in substantial conformity with this part or the determination was made under factual circumstances meeting the jurisdictional standards of this part and the determination has not been modified in accordance with this part.

(2) A court of this state may use any remedy available under other laws of this state to enforce a child custody determination made by a court of another state. The remedies provided by ss. 61.524-61.540 are cumulative and do not affect the availability of other remedies to enforce a child custody determination.

61.527. Temporary visitation.

(1) A court of this state which does not have jurisdiction to modify a child custody determination may issue a temporary order enforcing:

(a) A visitation schedule made by a court of another state; or

(b) The visitation provisions of a child custody determination of another state which does not provide for a specific visitation schedule.

(2) If a court of this state makes an order under paragraph (1)(b), it shall specify in the order a period that it considers adequate to allow the petitioner to obtain an order from a court having jurisdiction under the criteria specified in ss. 61.514-61.523. The order remains in effect until an order is obtained from the other court or the period expires.

61.528. Registration of child custody determination.

(1) A child custody determination issued by a court of another state may be registered in this state, with or without a simultaneous request for enforcement, by sending to the circuit court of the county where the petitioner or respondent resides or where a simultaneous request for enforcement is sought:

(a) A letter or other document requesting registration;

(b) Two copies, including one certified copy, of the determination sought to be registered and a statement under penalty of perjury that, to the best of the knowledge and belief of the person seeking registration, the order has not been modified; and

(c) Except as otherwise provided in s. 61.522, the name and address of the person seeking registration and any parent or person acting as a parent who has been awarded custody or visitation in the child custody determination sought to be registered.

(2) On receipt of the documents required by subsection (1), the registering court shall:

(a) Cause the determination to be filed as a foreign judgment, together with one copy of any accompanying documents and information, regardless of their form; and

(b) Serve notice upon the persons named pursuant to paragraph (1)(c) and provide them with an opportunity to contest the registration in accordance with this section.

(3) The notice required by paragraph (2)(b) must state that:

(a) A registered determination is enforceable as of the date of the registration in the same manner as a determination issued by a court of this state;

(b) A hearing to contest the validity of the registered determination must be requested within 20 days after service of notice; and

(c) Failure to contest the registration will result in confirmation of the child custody determination and preclude further contest of that determination with respect to any matter that could have been asserted.

(4) A person seeking to contest the validity of a registered order must request a hearing within 20 days after service of the notice. At that hearing, the court shall confirm the registered order unless the person contesting registration establishes that:

(a) The issuing court did not have jurisdiction under ss. 61.514-61.523;

(b) The child custody determination sought to be registered has been vacated, stayed, or modified by a court having jurisdiction to do so under ss. 61.514-61.523; or

(c) The person contesting registration was entitled to notice, but notice was not given in accordance with the standards of s. 61.509 in the proceedings before the court that issued the order for which registration is sought.

(5) If a timely request for a hearing to contest the validity of the registration is not made, the registration is confirmed as a matter of law and the person requesting registration and all persons served must be notified of the confirmation.

(6) Confirmation of a registered order, whether by operation of law or after notice and hearing, precludes further contest of the order with respect to any matter that could have been asserted at the time of registration.

61.529. Enforcement of registered determination.

(1) A court of this state may grant any relief normally available under the laws of this state to enforce a registered child custody determination made by a court of another state.

(2) A court of this state shall recognize and enforce but may not modify, except in accordance with ss. 61.514-61.523, a registered child custody determination of another state.

61.530. Simultaneous proceedings.

If a proceeding for enforcement under ss. 61.524-61.540 is commenced in a court of this state and the court determines that a proceeding to modify the determination is pending in a court of another state having jurisdiction to modify the determination under ss. 61.514-61.523, the enforcing court shall immediately communicate with the modifying court. The proceeding for enforcement continues unless the enforcing court, after consultation with the modifying court, stays or dismisses the proceeding.

61.531. Expedited enforcement of child custody determination.

(1) A petition under ss. 61.524-61.540 must be verified. Certified copies of all orders sought to be enforced and of any order confirming registration must be attached to the petition. A copy of a certified copy of an order may be attached instead of the original.

(2) A petition for enforcement of a child custody determination must state:

(a) Whether the court that issued the determination identified the jurisdictional basis it relied upon in exercising jurisdiction and, if so, specify the basis;

(b) Whether the determination for which enforcement is sought has been vacated, stayed, or modified by a court whose decision must be enforced under this part and, if so, identify the court, the case number, and the nature of the proceeding;

(c) Whether any proceeding has been commenced that could affect the current proceeding, including proceedings relating to domestic violence, protective orders, termination of parental rights, and adoptions and, if so, identify the court, the case number, and the nature of the proceeding;

(d) The present physical address of the child and the respondent, if known;

(e) Whether relief in addition to the immediate physical custody of the child and attorney's fees is sought, including a request for assistance from law enforcement officers and, if so, the relief sought; and

(f) If the child custody determination has been registered and confirmed under s. 61.528, the date and place of registration.

(3) Upon the filing of a petition, the court shall issue an order directing the respondent to appear in person with or without the child at a hearing and may enter any order necessary to ensure the safety of the parties and the child. The hearing must be held on the next judicial day after service of the order unless that date is impossible. In that event, the court shall hold the hearing on the first judicial day possible. The court may extend the date of the hearing at the request of the petitioner.

(4) An order issued under subsection (3) must state the time and place of the hearing and advise the respondent that at the hearing the court will order that the petitioner may take immediate physical custody of the child and the payment of fees, costs, and expenses under s. 61.535 and may schedule a hearing to determine whether further relief is appropriate, unless the respondent appears and establishes that:

(a) The child custody determination has not been registered and confirmed under s. 61.528 and that:

1. The issuing court did not have jurisdiction under ss. 61.514-61.523;

2. The child custody determination for which enforcement is sought has been vacated, stayed, or modified by a court of a state having jurisdiction to do so under ss. 61.514-61.523; or

3. The respondent was entitled to notice, but notice was not given in accordance with the standards of s. 61.509 in the proceedings before the court that issued the order for which enforcement is sought; or

(b) The child custody determination for which enforcement is sought was registered and confirmed under s. 61.528, but has been vacated, stayed, or modified by a court of a state having jurisdiction to do so under ss. 61.514-61.523.

61.532. Service of petition and order.

Except as otherwise provided in s. 61.534, the petition and order must be served by any method authorized by the laws of this state upon the respondent and any person who has physical custody of the child.

61.533. Hearing and order.

(1) Unless the court enters a temporary emergency order under s. 61.517, upon a finding that a petitioner is entitled to immediate physical custody of the child, the court shall order that the petitioner may take immediate physical custody of the child unless the respondent establishes that:
(a) The child custody determination has not been registered and confirmed under s. 61.528 and that:
1. The issuing court did not have jurisdiction under ss. 61.514-61.523;
2. The child custody determination for which enforcement is sought has been vacated, stayed, or modified by a court of a state having jurisdiction to do so under ss. 61.514-61.523; or
3. The respondent was entitled to notice, but notice was not given in accordance with the standards of s. 61.509 in the proceedings before the court that issued the order for which enforcement is sought; or
(b) The child custody determination for which enforcement is sought was registered and confirmed under s. 61.528, but has been vacated, stayed, or modified by a court of a state having jurisdiction to do so under ss. 61.514-61.523.
(2) The court shall award the fees, costs, and expenses authorized under s. 61.535 and may grant additional relief, including a request for the assistance of law enforcement officers, and set a further hearing to determine whether additional relief is appropriate.
(3) If a party called to testify refuses to answer on the ground that the testimony may be self-incriminating, the court may draw an adverse inference from the refusal.
(4) A privilege against disclosure of communications between spouses and a defense of immunity based on the relationship of husband and wife or parent and child may not be invoked in a proceeding under ss. 61.524-61.540.

61.534. Warrant to take physical custody of child.

(1) Upon the filing of a petition seeking enforcement of a child custody determination, the petitioner may file a verified application for the issuance of a warrant to take physical custody of the child if the child is likely to imminently suffer serious physical harm or removal from this state.
(2) If the court, upon the testimony of the petitioner or other witness, finds that the child is likely to imminently suffer serious physical harm or removal from this state, it may issue a warrant to take physical custody of the child. The petition must be heard on the next judicial day after the warrant is executed unless that date is impossible. In that event, the court shall hold the hearing on the first judicial day possible. The application for the warrant must include the statements required by s. 61.531(2).
(3) A warrant to take physical custody of a child must:
(a) Recite the facts upon which a conclusion of imminent serious physical harm or removal from the jurisdiction is based;
(b) Direct law enforcement officers to take physical custody of the child immediately; and
(c) Provide for the placement of the child pending final relief.
(4) The respondent must be served with the petition, warrant, and order immediately after the child is taken into physical custody.
(5) A warrant to take physical custody of a child is enforceable throughout this state. If the court finds on the basis of the testimony of the petitioner or other witness that a less intrusive remedy is not effective, it may authorize law enforcement officers to enter private property to take physical custody of the child. If required by exigent circumstances of the case, the court may authorize law enforcement officers to make a forcible entry at any hour.

(6) The court may impose conditions upon placement of a child to ensure the appearance of the child and the child's custodian.

61.535. Costs, fees, and expenses.

(1) So long as the court has personal jurisdiction over the party against whom the expenses are being assessed, the court shall award the prevailing party, including a state, necessary and reasonable expenses incurred by or on behalf of the party, including costs, communication expenses, attorney's fees, investigative fees, expenses for witnesses, travel expenses, and expenses for child care during the course of the proceedings, unless the party from whom fees or expenses are sought establishes that the award would be clearly inappropriate.
(2) The court may not assess fees, costs, or expenses against a state unless authorized by law other than this part.

61.536. Recognition and enforcement.

A court of this state shall accord full faith and credit to an order issued by another state and consistent with this part which enforces a child custody determination by a court of another state unless the order has been vacated, stayed, or modified by a court having jurisdiction to do so under ss. 61.514-61.523.

61.537. Appeals.

An appeal may be taken from a final order in a proceeding under ss. 61.524-61.540 in accordance with expedited appellate procedures in other civil cases. Unless the court enters a temporary emergency order under s. 61.517, the enforcing court may not stay an order enforcing a child custody determination pending appeal.

61.538. Role of state attorney.

(1) In a case arising under this part or involving the Hague Convention on the Civil Aspects of International Child Abduction, the state attorney may take any lawful action, including resort to a proceeding under ss. 61.524-61.540 or any other available civil proceeding, to locate a child, obtain the return of a child, or enforce a child custody determination, if there is:
(a) An existing child custody determination;
(b) A request to do so from a court in a pending child custody proceeding;
(c) A reasonable belief that a criminal statute has been violated; or
(d) A reasonable belief that the child has been wrongfully removed or retained in violation of the Hague Convention on the Civil Aspects of International Child Abduction.
(2) A state attorney acting under this section acts on behalf of the court and may not represent any party.

61.539. Role of law enforcement officers.

At the request of a state attorney acting under s. 61.538, a law enforcement officer may take any lawful action reasonably necessary to locate a child or a party and assist a state attorney with responsibilities under s. 61.538.

61.540. Costs and expenses.

The court may assess against the nonprevailing party all direct expenses and costs incurred by the state attorney and law enforcement officers under s. 61.538 or s. 61.539 so long as the court has personal jurisdiction over the nonprevailing party.

61.541. Application and construction.

In applying and construing this part, consideration must be given to the need to promote uniformity of the law with respect to its subject matter among states that enact it.

61.542. Transitional provision.

A motion or other request for relief made in a child custody proceeding or to enforce a child custody determination that was commenced before the effective date of this part is governed by the law in effect at the time the motion or other request was made.

PART III. COLLABORATIVE LAW PROCESS ACT (SS. 61.55-61.58)

61.55. Purpose.

The purpose of this part is to create a uniform system of practice for the collaborative law process in this state. It is the policy of this state to encourage the peaceful resolution of disputes and the early resolution of pending litigation through a voluntary settlement process. The collaborative law process is a unique nonadversarial process that preserves a working relationship between the parties and reduces the emotional and financial toll of litigation.

61.56. Definitions.

As used in this part, the term:
(1) "Collaborative attorney" means an attorney who represents a party in a collaborative law process.
(2) "Collaborative law communication" means an oral or written statement, including a statement made in a record, or nonverbal conduct that:
(a) Is made in the conduct of or in the course of participating in, continuing, or reconvening for a collaborative law process; and
(b) Occurs after the parties sign a collaborative law participation agreement and before the collaborative law process is concluded or terminated.

(3) "Collaborative law participation agreement" means an agreement between persons to participate in a collaborative law process.

(4) "Collaborative law process" means a process intended to resolve a collaborative matter without intervention by a tribunal and in which persons sign a collaborative law participation agreement and are represented by collaborative attorneys.

(5) "Collaborative matter" means a dispute, a transaction, a claim, a problem, or an issue for resolution, including a dispute, a claim, or an issue in a proceeding which is described in a collaborative law participation agreement and arises under chapter 61 or chapter 742, including, but not limited to:

(a) Marriage, divorce, dissolution, annulment, and marital property distribution.

(b) Child custody, visitation, parenting plan, and parenting time.

(c) Alimony, maintenance, and child support.

(d) Parental relocation with a child.

(e) Parentage and paternity.

(f) Premarital, marital, and postmarital agreements.

(6) "Law firm" means:

(a) One or more attorneys who practice law in a partnership, professional corporation, sole proprietorship, limited liability company, or association; or

(b) One or more attorneys employed in a legal services organization, the legal department of a corporation or other organization, or the legal department of a governmental entity, subdivision, agency, or instrumentality.

(7) "Nonparty participant" means a person, other than a party and the party's collaborative attorney, who participates in a collaborative law process.

(8) "Party" means a person who signs a collaborative law participation agreement and whose consent is necessary to resolve a collaborative matter.

(9) "Person" means an individual; a corporation; a business trust; an estate; a trust; a partnership; a limited liability company; an association; a joint venture; a public corporation; a government or governmental subdivision, agency, or instrumentality; or any other legal or commercial entity.

(10) "Proceeding" means a judicial, an administrative, an arbitral, or any other adjudicative process before a tribunal, including related prehearing and posthearing motions, conferences, and discovery.

(11) "Prospective party" means a person who discusses with a prospective collaborative attorney the possibility of signing a collaborative law participation agreement.

(12) "Record" means information that is inscribed on a tangible medium or that is stored in an electronic or other medium and is retrievable in perceivable form.

(13) "Related to a collaborative matter" means involving the same parties, transaction or occurrence, nucleus of operative fact, dispute, claim, or issue as the collaborative matter.

(14) "Sign" means, with present intent to authenticate or adopt a record, to:

(a) Execute or adopt a tangible symbol; or

(b) Attach to or logically associate with the record an electronic symbol, sound, or process.

(15) "Tribunal" means a court, an arbitrator, an administrative agency, or other body acting in an adjudicative capacity which, after presentation of evidence or legal argument, has jurisdiction to render a decision affecting a party's interests in a matter.

61.57. Beginning, concluding, and terminating a collaborative law process.

(1) The collaborative law process begins, regardless of whether a legal proceeding is pending, when the parties enter into a collaborative law participation agreement.

(2) A tribunal may not order a party to participate in a collaborative law process over that party's

objection.

(3) A collaborative law process is concluded by any of the following:

(a) Resolution of a collaborative matter as evidenced by a signed record;

(b) Resolution of a part of the collaborative matter, evidenced by a signed record, in which the parties agree that the remaining parts of the collaborative matter will not be resolved in the collaborative law process; or

(c) Termination of the collaborative law process.

(4) A collaborative law process terminates when a party:

(a) Gives notice to the other parties in a record that the collaborative law process is concluded;

(b) Begins a proceeding related to a collaborative matter without the consent of all parties;

(c) Initiates a pleading, a motion, an order to show cause, or a request for a conference with a tribunal in a pending proceeding related to a collaborative matter;

(d) Requests that the proceeding be put on the tribunal's active calendar in a pending proceeding related to a collaborative matter;

(e) Takes similar action requiring notice to be sent to the parties in a pending proceeding related to a collaborative matter; or

(f) Discharges a collaborative attorney or a collaborative attorney withdraws from further representation of a party, except as otherwise provided in subsection (7).

(5) A party's collaborative attorney shall give prompt notice to all other parties in a record of a discharge or withdrawal.

(6) A party may terminate a collaborative law process with or without cause.

(7) Notwithstanding the discharge or withdrawal of a collaborative attorney, the collaborative law process continues if, not later than 30 days after the date that the notice of the discharge or withdrawal of a collaborative attorney required by subsection (5) is sent to the parties:

(a) The unrepresented party engages a successor collaborative attorney;

(b) The parties consent to continue the collaborative law process by reaffirming the collaborative law participation agreement in a signed record;

(c) The collaborative law participation agreement is amended to identify the successor collaborative attorney in a signed record; and

(d) The successor collaborative attorney confirms his or her representation of a party in the collaborative law participation agreement in a signed record.

(8) A collaborative law process does not conclude if, with the consent of the parties, a party requests a tribunal to approve a resolution of a collaborative matter or any part thereof as evidenced by a signed record.

(9) A collaborative law participation agreement may provide additional methods for concluding a collaborative law process.

61.58. Confidentiality of a collaborative law communication.

Except as provided in this section, a collaborative law communication is confidential to the extent agreed by the parties in a signed record or as otherwise provided by law.

(1) PRIVILEGE AGAINST DISCLOSURE FOR COLLABORATIVE LAW COMMUNICATION; ADMISSIBILITY; DISCOVERY.—

(a) Subject to subsections (2) and (3), a collaborative law communication is privileged as provided under paragraph (b), is not subject to discovery, and is not admissible into evidence.

(b) In a proceeding, the following privileges apply:

1. A party may refuse to disclose, and may prevent another person from disclosing, a collaborative law communication.

2. A nonparty participant may refuse to disclose, and may prevent another person from disclosing,

a collaborative law communication of a nonparty participant.

(c) Evidence or information that is otherwise admissible or subject to discovery does not become inadmissible or protected from discovery solely because of its disclosure or use in a collaborative law process.

(2) WAIVER AND PRECLUSION OF PRIVILEGE.—

(a) A privilege under subsection (1) may be waived orally or in a record during a proceeding if it is expressly waived by all parties and, in the case of the privilege of a nonparty participant, if it is expressly waived by the nonparty participant.

(b) A person who makes a disclosure or representation about a collaborative law communication that prejudices another person in a proceeding may not assert a privilege under subsection (1). This preclusion applies only to the extent necessary for the person prejudiced to respond to the disclosure or representation.

(3) LIMITS OF PRIVILEGE.—

(a) A privilege under subsection (1) does not apply to a collaborative law communication that is:

1. Available to the public under chapter 119 or made during a session of a collaborative law process that is open, or is required by law to be open, to the public;

2. A threat, or statement of a plan, to inflict bodily injury or commit a crime of violence;

3. Intentionally used to plan a crime, commit or attempt to commit a crime, or conceal an ongoing crime or ongoing criminal activity; or

4. In an agreement resulting from the collaborative law process, as evidenced by a record signed by all parties to the agreement.

(b) The privilege under subsection (1) for a collaborative law communication does not apply to the extent that such collaborative law communication is:

1. Sought or offered to prove or disprove a claim or complaint of professional misconduct or malpractice arising from or relating to a collaborative law process; or

2. Sought or offered to prove or disprove abuse, neglect, abandonment, or exploitation of a child or an adult unless the Department of Children and Families is a party to or otherwise participates in the process.

(c) A privilege under subsection (1) does not apply if a tribunal finds, after a hearing in camera, that the party seeking discovery or the proponent of the evidence has shown that the evidence is not otherwise available, the need for the evidence substantially outweighs the interest in protecting confidentiality, and the collaborative law communication is sought or offered in:

1. A proceeding involving a felony; or

2. A proceeding seeking rescission or reformation of a contract arising out of the collaborative law process or in which a defense is asserted to avoid liability on the contract.

(d) If a collaborative law communication is subject to an exception under paragraph (b) or paragraph (c), only the part of the collaborative law communication necessary for the application of the exception may be disclosed or admitted.

(e) Disclosure or admission of evidence excepted from the privilege under paragraph (b) or paragraph (c) does not make the evidence or any other collaborative law communication discoverable or admissible for any other purpose.

(f) The privilege under subsection (1) does not apply if the parties agree in advance in a signed record, or if a record of a proceeding reflects agreement by the parties, that all or part of a collaborative law process is not privileged. This paragraph does not apply to a collaborative law communication made by a person who did not receive actual notice of the collaborative law participation agreement before the communication was made.

CHAPTER 63. ADOPTION

63.012. Short title.

This chapter shall be known as the "Florida Adoption Act."

63.022. Legislative intent.

(1) The Legislature finds that:

(a) The state has a compelling interest in providing stable and permanent homes for adoptive children in a prompt manner, in preventing the disruption of adoptive placements, and in holding parents accountable for meeting the needs of children.

(b) An unmarried mother faced with the responsibility of making crucial decisions about the future of a newborn child is entitled to privacy, has the right to make timely and appropriate decisions regarding her future and the future of the child, and is entitled to assurance regarding an adoptive placement.

(c) Adoptive children have the right to permanence and stability in adoptive placements.

(d) Adoptive parents have a constitutional privacy interest in retaining custody of a legally adopted child.

(e) An unmarried biological father has an inchoate interest that acquires constitutional protection only when he demonstrates a timely and full commitment to the responsibilities of parenthood, both during the pregnancy and after the child's birth. The state has a compelling interest in requiring an unmarried biological father to demonstrate that commitment by providing appropriate medical care and financial support and by establishing legal paternity rights in accordance with the requirements of this chapter.

(2) It is the intent of the Legislature that in every adoption, the best interest of the child should govern and be of foremost concern in the court's determination. The court shall make a specific finding as to the best interests of the child in accordance with the provisions of this chapter.

(3) It is the intent of the Legislature to protect and promote the well-being of persons being adopted and their birth and adoptive parents and to provide to all children who can benefit by it a permanent family life, and, whenever appropriate, to maintain sibling groups.

(4) The basic safeguards intended to be provided by this chapter are that:

(a) The minor is legally free for adoption and that all adoptions are handled in accordance with the requirements of law.

(b) The required persons consent to the adoption or the parent-child relationship is terminated by judgment of the court.

(c) The required social studies are completed and the court considers the reports of these studies prior to judgment on adoption petitions.

(d) A sufficient period of time elapses during which the minor has lived within the proposed adoptive home under the guidance of an adoption entity, except stepparent adoptions or adoptions of a relative.

(e) All expenditures by adoption entities or adoptive parents relative to the adoption of a minor are reported to the court and become a permanent record in the file of the adoption proceedings, including, but not limited to, all legal fees and costs, all payments to or on behalf of a birth parent, and all payments to or on behalf of the minor.

(f) Social and medical information concerning the minor and the parents is furnished by the parent when available and filed with the court before a final hearing on a petition to terminate parental rights pending adoption, unless the petitioner is a stepparent or a relative.

(g) A new birth certificate is issued after entry of the adoption judgment.

(h) At the time of the hearing, the court may order temporary substitute care when it determines that the minor is in an unsuitable home.

(i) The records of all proceedings concerning custody and adoption of a minor are confidential and exempt from s. 119.07(1), except as provided in s. 63.162.

(j) The birth parent, the prospective adoptive parent, and the minor receive, at a minimum, the safeguards, guidance, counseling, and supervision required in this chapter.

(k) In all matters coming before the court under this chapter, the court shall enter such orders as it deems necessary and suitable to promote and protect the best interests of the person to be adopted.

(l) In dependency cases initiated by the department, where termination of parental rights occurs, and siblings are separated despite diligent efforts of the department, continuing postadoption communication or contact among the siblings may be ordered by the court if found to be in the best interests of the children.

(5) It is the intent of the Legislature to provide for cooperation between private adoption entities and the Department of Children and Families in matters relating to permanent placement options for children in the care of the department whose birth parents wish to participate in a private adoption plan with a qualified family.

63.032. Definitions.

As used in this chapter, the term:

(1) "Abandoned" means a situation in which the parent or person having legal custody of a child, while being able, makes little or no provision for the child's support or makes little or no effort to communicate with the child, which situation is sufficient to evince an intent to reject parental responsibilities. If, in the opinion of the court, the efforts of such parent or person having legal custody of the child to support and communicate with the child are only marginal efforts that do not evince a settled purpose to assume all parental duties, the court may declare the child to be abandoned. In making this decision, the court may consider the conduct of a father towards the child's mother during her pregnancy.

(2) "Adoption" means the act of creating the legal relationship between parent and child where it did not exist, thereby declaring the child to be legally the child of the adoptive parents and their heir at law and entitled to all the rights and privileges and subject to all the obligations of a child born to such adoptive parents in lawful wedlock.

(3) "Adoption entity" means the department, a child-caring agency registered under s. 409.176, an intermediary, a Florida child-placing agency licensed under s. 63.202, or a child-placing agency licensed in another state which is licensed by the department to place children in the State of Florida.

(4) "Adoption plan" means an arrangement made by a birth parent or other individual having a legal right to custody of a minor, born or to be born, with an adoption entity in furtherance of placing the minor for adoption.

(5) "Adult" means a person who is not a minor.

(6) "Agency" means any child-placing agency licensed by the department pursuant to s. 63.202 to place minors for adoption.

(7) "Child" means any unmarried person under the age of 18 years who has not been emancipated by court order.

(8) "Court" means a circuit court of this state and, if the context requires, the court of any state that is empowered to grant petitions for adoption.

(9) "Department" means the Department of Children and Families.

(10) "Intermediary" means an attorney who is licensed or authorized to practice in this state and who is placing or intends to place a child for adoption, including placing children born in another state with citizens of this state or country or placing children born in this state with citizens of another state or country.

(11) "Legal custody" has the meaning ascribed in s. 39.01.

(12) "Parent" means a woman who gives birth to a child and who is not a gestational surrogate as defined in s. 742.13 or a man whose consent to the adoption of the child would be required under

s. 63.062(1). If a child has been legally adopted, the term "parent" means the adoptive mother or father of the child. The term does not include an individual whose parental relationship to the child has been legally terminated or an alleged or prospective parent.

(13) "Person" includes a natural person, corporation, government or governmental subdivision or agency, business trust, estate, trust, partnership, or association, and any other legal entity.

(14) "Placement" means the process of a parent or legal guardian surrendering a child for adoption and the prospective adoptive parents receiving and adopting the child and all actions by any adoption entity participating in placing the child.

(15) "Primarily lives and works outside Florida" means that a person lives and works outside this state at least 6 months and 1 day per year, is a member of the military who designates a state other than Florida as his or her place of residence in accordance with the Servicemembers Civil Relief Act, Pub. L. No. 108-189, or is a citizen of the United States living in a foreign country who designates a state other than Florida as his or her place of residence.

(16) "Relative" means a person related by blood to the person being adopted within the third degree of consanguinity.

(17) "Suitability of the intended placement" means the fitness of the intended placement, with primary consideration being given to the best interests of the child.

(18) "To place" means the process whereby a parent or legal guardian surrenders a child for adoption and the prospective adoptive parents receive and adopt the child, and includes all actions by any person or adoption entity participating in the process.

(19) "Unmarried biological father" means the child's biological father who is not married to the child's mother at the time of conception or on the date of the birth of the child and who, before the filing of a petition to terminate parental rights, has not been adjudicated by a court of competent jurisdiction to be the legal father of the child or has not filed an affidavit pursuant to s. 382.013(2)(c).

63.037. Proceedings applicable to cases resulting from a termination of parental rights under chapter 39.

A case in which a minor becomes available for adoption after the parental rights of each parent have been terminated by a judgment entered pursuant to chapter 39 shall be governed by s. 39.812 and this chapter. Adoption proceedings initiated under chapter 39 are exempt from the following provisions of this chapter: requirement for search of the Florida Putative Father Registry provided in s. 63.054(7), if a search was previously completed and documentation of the search is contained in the case file; disclosure requirements for the adoption entity provided in s. 63.085(1); general provisions governing termination of parental rights pending adoption provided in s. 63.087; notice and service provisions governing termination of parental rights pending adoption provided in s. 63.088; and procedures for terminating parental rights pending adoption provided in s. 63.089.

63.039. Duty of adoption entity to prospective adoptive parents; sanctions.

(1) An adoption entity placing a minor for adoption has an affirmative duty to follow the requirements of this chapter and specifically the following provisions, which protect and promote the well-being of persons being adopted and their parents and prospective adoptive parents by promoting certainty, finality, and permanency for such persons. The adoption entity must:
(a) Provide written initial disclosure to the prospective adoptive parent at the time and in the manner required under s. 63.085.

(b) Provide written disclosure to the parent at the time and in the manner required under s. 63.085.

(c) When a written consent for adoption is obtained, obtain the consent at the time and in the manner required under s. 63.082.

(d) When a written consent or affidavit of nonpaternity for adoption is obtained, obtain a consent to adoption or affidavit of nonpaternity that contains the language required under s. 63.062 or s. 63.082.

(e) Include in the petition to terminate parental rights pending adoption all information required under s. 63.087.

(f) Obtain and file the affidavit of inquiry pursuant to s. 63.088(4), if the required inquiry is not conducted orally in the presence of the court.

(g) When the identity of a person whose consent to adoption is necessary under this chapter is known but the location of such a person is unknown, conduct the diligent search and file the affidavit required under s. 63.088(5).

(h) Serve a petition and notice of hearing to terminate parental rights pending adoption at the time and in the manner prescribed by law.

(i) Obtain the written waiver of venue required under s. 63.062, if applicable.

(j) Provide an adoption disclosure statement, as required under s. 63.085(1), to all persons whose consent is required under s. 63.062(1).

(2) With the exception of an adoption by a relative or stepparent, all adoptions of minor children require the use of an adoption entity that will assume the responsibilities provided in this section.

(3) If a court finds that a consent to adoption or an affidavit of nonpaternity taken under this chapter was obtained by fraud or duress attributable to the adoption entity, the court may award all sums paid by the prospective adoptive parents or on their behalf in anticipation of or in connection with the adoption. The court may also award reasonable attorney's fees and costs incurred by the prospective adoptive parents in connection with the adoption and any litigation related to placement or adoption of a minor. The court may award reasonable attorney's fees and costs, if any, incurred by the person whose consent or affidavit was obtained by fraud or duress. Any award under this subsection to the prospective adoptive parents or to the person whose consent or affidavit was obtained by fraud or duress must be paid directly to them by the adoption entity or by any applicable insurance carrier on behalf of the adoption entity if the court determines, after an evidentiary hearing held subsequent to the entry of a final order in the underlying termination of parental rights or adoption action, that the actions or failures of the adoption entity directly contributed to the finding of fraud or duress.

(4) The prevailing party in an action to set aside a judgment terminating parental rights pending adoption or a judgment of adoption may be awarded reasonable attorney's fees and costs pursuant to Rule 1.540(b)(3), Florida Rules of Civil Procedure. An award under this subsection must be paid by the adoption entity or by the applicable insurance carrier on behalf of the adoption entity if the court finds that the acts or omissions of the entity were the basis for the court's order granting relief to the prevailing party.

(5) Within 30 days after the entry of an order of the court finding sanctionable conduct on the part of an adoption entity, the clerk of the court must forward to:

(a) The Florida Bar any order that imposes sanctions under this section against an attorney acting as an adoption entity.

(b) The Department of Children and Families any order that imposes sanctions under this section against a licensed child-placing agency or a child-placing agency licensed in another state that is qualified by the department.

(c) The entity under s. 409.176 that certifies child-caring agencies any order that imposes sanctions under this section against a child-caring agency registered under s. 409.176.

(d) The Office of Attorney General any order that imposes sanctions under this section against the department.

63.042. Who may be adopted; who may adopt.

(1) Any person, a minor or an adult, may be adopted.
(2) The following persons may adopt:
(a) A husband and wife jointly;
(b) An unmarried adult; or
(c) A married person without the other spouse joining as a petitioner, if the person to be adopted is not his or her spouse, and if:
1. The other spouse is a parent of the person to be adopted and consents to the adoption; or
2. The failure of the other spouse to join in the petition or to consent to the adoption is excused by the court for good cause shown or in the best interest of the child.
(3) No person eligible under this section shall be prohibited from adopting solely because such person possesses a physical disability or handicap, unless it is determined by the court or adoption entity that such disability or handicap renders such person incapable of serving as an effective parent.
(4) No person eligible under this section shall be prohibited from adopting solely because he or she desires to educate the adopted child at home.

63.0422. Prohibited conditions on adoptions; firearms and ammunition.

An adoption agency or entity, whether public or private, may not:
(1) Make a determination that a person is unsuitable to adopt based on the lawful possession, storage, or use of a firearm or ammunition by any member of the adoptive home.
(2) Require an adoptive parent or prospective adoptive parent to disclose information relating to a person's lawful possession, storage, or use of a firearm or ammunition as a condition to adopt.
(3) Restrict the lawful possession, storage, or use of a firearm or ammunition as a condition for a person to adopt.

63.0423. Procedures with respect to surrendered infants.

(1) Upon entry of final judgment terminating parental rights, a licensed child-placing agency that takes physical custody of an infant surrendered at a hospital, emergency medical services station, or fire station pursuant to s. 383.50 assumes responsibility for the medical and other costs associated with the emergency services and care of the surrendered infant from the time the licensed child-placing agency takes physical custody of the surrendered infant.
(2) The licensed child-placing agency shall immediately seek an order from the circuit court for emergency custody of the surrendered infant. The emergency custody order shall remain in effect until the court orders preliminary approval of placement of the surrendered infant in the prospective home, at which time the prospective adoptive parents become guardians pending termination of parental rights and finalization of adoption or until the court orders otherwise. The guardianship of the prospective adoptive parents shall remain subject to the right of the licensed child-placing agency to remove the surrendered infant from the placement during the pendency of the proceedings if such removal is deemed by the licensed child-placing agency to be in the best interests of the child. The licensed child-placing agency may immediately seek to place the surrendered infant in a prospective adoptive home.
(3) The licensed child-placing agency that takes physical custody of the surrendered infant shall, within 24 hours thereafter, request assistance from law enforcement officials to investigate and

determine, through the Missing Children Information Clearinghouse, the National Center for Missing and Exploited Children, and any other national and state resources, whether the surrendered infant is a missing child.

(4) The parent who surrenders the infant in accordance with s. 383.50 is presumed to have consented to termination of parental rights, and express consent is not required. Except when there is actual or suspected child abuse or neglect, the licensed child-placing agency shall not attempt to pursue, search for, or notify that parent as provided in s. 63.088 and chapter 49. For purposes of s. 383.50 and this section, an infant who tests positive for illegal drugs, narcotic prescription drugs, alcohol, or other substances, but shows no other signs of child abuse or neglect, shall be placed in the custody of a licensed child-placing agency. Such a placement does not eliminate the reporting requirement under s. 383.50(7). When the department is contacted regarding an infant properly surrendered under this section and s. 383.50, the department shall provide instruction to contact a licensed child-placing agency and may not take custody of the infant unless reasonable efforts to contact a licensed child-placing agency to accept the infant have not been successful.

(5) A petition for termination of parental rights under this section may not be filed until 30 days after the date the infant was surrendered in accordance with s. 383.50. A petition for termination of parental rights may not be granted until a parent has failed to reclaim or claim the surrendered infant within the time period specified in s. 383.50.

(6) A claim of parental rights of the surrendered infant must be made to the entity having legal custody of the surrendered infant or to the circuit court before which proceedings involving the surrendered infant are pending. A claim of parental rights of the surrendered infant may not be made after the judgment to terminate parental rights is entered, except as otherwise provided by subsection (9).

(7) If a claim of parental rights of a surrendered infant is made before the judgment to terminate parental rights is entered, the circuit court may hold the action for termination of parental rights in abeyance for a period of time not to exceed 60 days.

(a) The court may order scientific testing to determine maternity or paternity at the expense of the parent claiming parental rights.

(b) The court shall appoint a guardian ad litem for the surrendered infant and order whatever investigation, home evaluation, and psychological evaluation are necessary to determine what is in the best interests of the surrendered infant.

(c) The court may not terminate parental rights solely on the basis that the parent left the infant at a hospital, emergency medical services station, or fire station in accordance with s. 383.50.

(d) The court shall enter a judgment with written findings of fact and conclusions of law.

(8) Within 7 business days after recording the judgment, the clerk of the court shall mail a copy of the judgment to the department, the petitioner, and any person whose consent was required, if known. The clerk shall execute a certificate of each mailing.

(9)(a) A judgment terminating parental rights pending adoption is voidable, and any later judgment of adoption of that minor is voidable, if, upon the motion of a parent, the court finds that a person knowingly gave false information that prevented the parent from timely making known his or her desire to assume parental responsibilities toward the minor or from exercising his or her parental rights. A motion under this subsection must be filed with the court originally entering the judgment. The motion must be filed within a reasonable time but not later than 1 year after the entry of the judgment terminating parental rights.

(b) No later than 30 days after the filing of a motion under this subsection, the court shall conduct a preliminary hearing to determine what contact, if any, will be permitted between a parent and the child pending resolution of the motion. Such contact may be allowed only if it is requested by a parent who has appeared at the hearing and the court determines that it is in the best interests of the child. If the court orders contact between a parent and the child, the order must be issued in writing as expeditiously as possible and must state with specificity any provisions regarding contact with persons other than those with whom the child resides.

(c) The court may not order scientific testing to determine the paternity or maternity of the minor until such time as the court determines that a previously entered judgment terminating the parental rights of that parent is voidable pursuant to paragraph (a), unless all parties agree that such testing is in the best interests of the child. Upon the filing of test results establishing that person's maternity or paternity of the surrendered infant, the court may order visitation only if it appears to be in the best interests of the child.

(d) Within 45 days after the preliminary hearing, the court shall conduct a final hearing on the motion to set aside the judgment and shall enter its written order as expeditiously as possible thereafter.

(10) Except to the extent expressly provided in this section, proceedings initiated by a licensed child-placing agency for the termination of parental rights and subsequent adoption of a newborn left at a hospital, emergency medical services station, or fire station in accordance with s. 383.50 shall be conducted pursuant to this chapter.

63.0425. Grandparent's right to notice.

(1) If a child has lived with a grandparent for at least 6 months within the 24-month period immediately preceding the filing of a petition for termination of parental rights pending adoption, the adoption entity shall provide notice to that grandparent of the hearing on the petition.

(2) This section does not apply if the placement for adoption is the result of the death of the child's parent and a different preference is stated in the parent's will.

(3) This section does not apply in stepparent adoptions.

(4) This section does not contravene the provisions of s. 63.142(4).

63.0427. Agreements for continued communication or contact between adopted child and siblings, parents, and other relatives.

(1) A child whose parents have had their parental rights terminated and whose custody has been awarded to the department pursuant to s. 39.811, and who is the subject of a petition for adoption under this chapter, shall have the right to have the court consider the appropriateness of postadoption communication or contact, including, but not limited to, visits, written correspondence, or telephone calls, with his or her siblings or, upon agreement of the adoptive parents, with the parents who have had their parental rights terminated or other specified biological relatives. The court shall consider the following in making such determination:

(a) Any orders of the court pursuant to s. 39.811(7).

(b) Recommendations of the department, the foster parents if other than the adoptive parents, and the guardian ad litem.

(c) Statements of the prospective adoptive parents.

(d) Any other information deemed relevant and material by the court.

(2) Notwithstanding s. 63.162, the adoptive parent may, at any time, petition for review of a communication or contact order entered pursuant to subsection (1), if the adoptive parent believes that the best interests of the adopted child are being compromised, and the court may order the communication or contact to be terminated or modified, as the court deems to be in the best interests of the adopted child; however, the court may not increase contact between the adopted child and siblings, birth parents, or other relatives without the consent of the adoptive parent or parents. As part of the review process, the court may order the parties to engage in mediation. The department shall not be required to be a party to such review.

63.043. Mandatory screening or testing for sickle-cell trait prohibited.

No person, firm, corporation, unincorporated association, state agency, unit of local government, or any public or private entity shall require screening or testing for the sickle-cell trait as a condition for becoming eligible for adoption if otherwise eligible for adoption under the laws of this state.

63.052. Guardians designated; proof of commitment.

(1) For minors who have been placed for adoption with an adoption entity, other than an intermediary, such adoption entity shall be the guardian of the person of the minor and has the responsibility and authority to provide for the needs and welfare of the minor.

(2) For minors who have been voluntarily surrendered to an intermediary through an execution of a consent to adoption, the intermediary shall be responsible for the minor until the time a court orders preliminary approval of placement of the minor in the prospective adoptive home, after which time the prospective adoptive parents shall become guardians pending finalization of adoption, subject to the intermediary's right and responsibility to remove the child from the prospective adoptive home if the removal is deemed by the intermediary to be in the best interests of the child. The intermediary may not remove the child without a court order unless the child is in danger of imminent harm. The intermediary does not become responsible for the minor child's medical bills that were incurred before taking physical custody of the child after the execution of adoption consents. Prior to the court's entry of an order granting preliminary approval of the placement, the intermediary shall have the responsibility and authority to provide for the needs and welfare of the minor. A minor may not be placed in a prospective adoptive home until that home has received a favorable preliminary home study, as provided in s. 63.092, completed and approved within 1 year before such placement in the prospective home. The provisions of s. 627.6578 shall remain in effect notwithstanding the guardianship provisions in this section.

(3) If a minor is surrendered to an adoption entity for subsequent adoption and a suitable prospective adoptive home is not available pursuant to s. 63.092 at the time the minor is surrendered to the adoption entity, the minor must be placed in a licensed foster care home, with a person or family that has received a favorable preliminary home study pursuant to subsection (2), or with a relative until a suitable prospective adoptive home is available.

(4) If a minor is voluntarily surrendered to an adoption entity for subsequent adoption and the adoption does not become final within 180 days after termination of parental rights, the adoption entity must report to the court on the status of the minor and the court may at that time proceed under s. 39.701 or take action reasonably necessary to protect the best interest of the minor.

(5) The recital in a written consent, answer, or recommendation filed by an adoption entity that the minor has been permanently committed to the adoption entity or that the adoption entity is duly licensed shall be prima facie proof of such commitment. A consent for adoption signed by an adoption entity need not comply with s. 63.082.

(6) Unless otherwise authorized by law or ordered by the court, the department is not responsible for expenses incurred by other adoption entities participating in a placement of a minor.

(7) The court retains jurisdiction of a minor who has been placed for adoption until the adoption is final. After a minor is placed with an adoption entity or prospective adoptive parent, the court may review the status of the minor and the progress toward permanent adoptive placement.

63.053. Rights and responsibilities of an unmarried biological father; legislative findings.

(1) In enacting the provisions contained in this chapter, the Legislature prescribes the conditions for determining whether an unmarried biological father's actions are sufficiently prompt and substantial so as to require protection of a constitutional right. If an unmarried biological father fails to take the actions that are available to him to establish a relationship with his child, his parental interest may be lost entirely, or greatly diminished, by his failure to timely comply with the available legal steps to substantiate a parental interest.

(2) The Legislature finds that the interests of the state, the mother, the child, and the adoptive parents described in this chapter outweigh the interest of an unmarried biological father who does not take action in a timely manner to establish and demonstrate a relationship with his child in accordance with the requirements of this chapter. An unmarried biological father has the primary responsibility to protect his rights and is presumed to know that his child may be adopted without his consent unless he strictly complies with this chapter and demonstrates a prompt and full commitment to his parental responsibilities.

(3) The Legislature finds that a birth mother and a birth father have a right of privacy.

63.054. Actions required by an unmarried biological father to establish parental rights; Florida Putative Father Registry.

(1) In order to preserve the right to notice and consent to an adoption under this chapter, an unmarried biological father must, as the "registrant," file a notarized claim of paternity form with the Florida Putative Father Registry maintained by the Office of Vital Statistics of the Department of Health which includes confirmation of his willingness and intent to support the child for whom paternity is claimed in accordance with state law. The claim of paternity may be filed at any time before the child's birth, but may not be filed after the date a petition is filed for termination of parental rights. In each proceeding for termination of parental rights, the petitioner must submit to the Office of Vital Statistics a copy of the petition for termination of parental rights or a document executed by the clerk of the court showing the style of the case, the names of the persons whose rights are sought to be terminated, and the date and time of the filing of the petition. The Office of Vital Statistics may not record a claim of paternity after the date a petition for termination of parental rights is filed. The failure of an unmarried biological father to file a claim of paternity with the registry before the date a petition for termination of parental rights is filed also bars him from filing a paternity claim under chapter 742.

(a) An unmarried biological father is excepted from the time limitations for filing a claim of paternity with the registry or for filing a paternity claim under chapter 742, if:

1. The mother identifies him to the adoption entity as a potential biological father by the date she executes a consent for adoption; and

2. He is served with a notice of intended adoption plan pursuant to s. 63.062(3) and the 30-day mandatory response date is later than the date the petition for termination of parental rights is filed with the court.

(b) If an unmarried biological father falls within the exception provided by paragraph (a), the petitioner shall also submit to the Office of Vital Statistics a copy of the notice of intended adoption plan and proof of service of the notice on the potential biological father.

(c) An unmarried biological father who falls within the exception provided by paragraph (a) may not file a claim of paternity with the registry or a paternity claim under chapter 742 after the 30-day mandatory response date to the notice of intended adoption plan has expired. The Office of

Vital Statistics may not record a claim of paternity 30 days after service of the notice of intended adoption plan.

(2) By filing a claim of paternity form with the Office of Vital Statistics, the registrant expressly consents to submit to and pay for DNA testing upon the request of any party, the registrant, or the adoption entity with respect to the child referenced in the claim of paternity.

(3) The Office of Vital Statistics of the Department of Health shall adopt by rule the appropriate claim of paternity form in English, Spanish, and Creole in order to facilitate the registration of an unmarried biological father with the Florida Putative Father Registry and shall, within existing resources, make these forms available through local offices of the Department of Health and the Department of Children and Families, the Internet websites of those agencies, and the offices of the clerks of the circuit court. The claim of paternity form shall be signed by the unmarried biological father and must include his name, address, date of birth, and physical description. In addition, the registrant shall provide, if known, the name, address, date of birth, and physical description of the mother; the date, place, and location of conception of the child; and the name, date, and place of birth of the child or estimated date of birth of the expected minor child, if known. The claim of paternity form shall be signed under oath by the registrant.

(4) Upon initial registration, or at any time thereafter, the registrant may designate a physical address other than his residential address for sending any communication regarding his registration. Similarly, upon initial registration, or at any time thereafter, the registrant may designate, in writing, an agent or representative to receive any communication on his behalf and receive service of process. The agent or representative must file an acceptance of the designation, in writing, in order to receive notice or service of process. The failure of the designated representative or agent of the registrant to deliver or otherwise notify the registrant of receipt of correspondence from the Florida Putative Father Registry is at the registrant's own risk and may not serve as a valid defense based upon lack of notice.

(5) The registrant may, at any time prior to the birth of the child for whom paternity is claimed, execute a notarized written revocation of the claim of paternity previously filed with the Florida Putative Father Registry, and upon receipt of such revocation, the claim of paternity shall be deemed null and void. If a court determines that a registrant is not the father of the minor or has no parental rights, the court shall order the Department of Health to remove the registrant's name from the registry.

(6) It is the obligation of the registrant or, if designated under subsection (4), his designated agent or representative to notify and update the Office of Vital Statistics of any change of address or change in the designation of an agent or representative. The failure of a registrant, or designated agent or representative, to report any such change is at the registrant's own risk and may not serve as a defense based upon lack of notice, and the adoption entity or petitioner has no further obligation to search for the registrant unless the person petitioning for termination of parental rights or adoption has actual notice of the registrant's address and whereabouts from another source.

(7) In each proceeding for termination of parental rights or each adoption proceeding in which parental rights are being terminated simultaneously with entry of the final judgment of adoption, as in a stepparent and relative adoption filed under this chapter, the petitioner must contact the Office of Vital Statistics by submitting an application for a search of the Florida Putative Father Registry. The petitioner must provide the same information, if known, on the search application form that the registrant furnished under subsection (3). Thereafter, the Office of Vital Statistics shall issue a certificate signed by the State Registrar certifying:

(a) The identity and contact information, if any, for each registered unmarried biological father whose information matches the search request sufficiently so that such person may be considered a possible father of the subject child; or

(b) That a diligent search has been made of the registrants who may be the unmarried biological father of the subject child and that no matching registration has been located in the registry.

(8) If an unmarried biological father does not know the county in which the birth mother resides, gave birth, or intends to give birth, he may initiate an action in any county in the state, subject to

the birth mother's right to change venue to the county where she resides.

(9) The Department of Health shall establish and maintain a Florida Putative Father Registry through its Office of Vital Statistics, in accordance with the requirements of this section. The Department of Health may charge a nominal fee to cover the costs of filing and indexing the Florida Putative Father Registry and the costs of searching the registry.

(10) The Department of Health shall, within existing resources, prepare and adopt by rule application forms for initiating a search of the Florida Putative Father Registry and shall make those forms available through the local offices of the Department of Health and the Department of Children and Families and the offices of the clerks of the circuit court.

(11) The Department of Health shall produce and distribute, within existing resources, a pamphlet or publication informing the public about the Florida Putative Father Registry and which is printed in English, Spanish, and Creole. The pamphlet shall indicate the procedures for voluntary acknowledgment of paternity, the consequences of acknowledgment of paternity, the consequences of failure to acknowledge paternity, and the address of the Florida Putative Father Registry. Such pamphlets or publications shall be made available for distribution at all offices of the Department of Health and the Department of Children and Families and shall be included in health class curricula taught in public and charter schools in this state. The Department of Health shall also provide such pamphlets or publications to hospitals, adoption entities, libraries, medical clinics, schools, universities, and providers of child-related services, upon request. In cooperation with the Department of Highway Safety and Motor Vehicles, each person applying for a Florida driver license, or renewal thereof, and each person applying for a Florida identification card shall be offered the pamphlet or publication informing the public about the Florida Putative Father Registry.

(12) The Department of Health shall, within existing resources, provide additional information about the Florida Putative Father Registry and its services to the public in English, Spanish, and Creole using public service announcements, Internet websites, and such other means as it deems appropriate.

(13) The filing of a claim of paternity with the Florida Putative Father Registry does not excuse or waive the obligation of a petitioner to comply with the requirements of s. 63.088(4) for conducting a diligent search and required inquiry with respect to the identity of an unmarried biological father or legal father which are set forth in this chapter.

(14) The Office of Vital Statistics of the Department of Health is authorized to adopt rules to implement this section.

63.0541. Public records exemption for the Florida Putative Father Registry.

(1) All information contained in the Florida Putative Father Registry is confidential and exempt from s. 119.07(1) and s. 24(a), Art. I of the State Constitution.

(2) Information made confidential and exempt by this section shall be disclosed to:

(a) An adoption entity, upon the filing of a request for a diligent search of the Florida Putative Father Registry in connection with the planned adoption of a child.

(b) The registrant unmarried biological father, upon receipt of a notarized request for a copy of his registry entry only.

(c) The birth mother, upon receipt of a notarized request for a copy of any registry entry in which she is identified as the birth mother.

(d) The court, upon issuance of a court order concerning a petitioner acting pro se in an action under this chapter.

(3) The database comprising the Florida Putative Father Registry shall remain separate from all other databases.

63.062. Persons required to consent to adoption; affidavit of nonpaternity; waiver of venue.

(1) Unless supported by one or more of the grounds enumerated under s. 63.089(3), a petition to terminate parental rights pending adoption may be granted only if written consent has been executed as provided in s. 63.082 after the birth of the minor or notice has been served under s. 63.088 to:

(a) The mother of the minor.

(b) The father of the minor, if:

1. The minor was conceived or born while the father was married to the mother;

2. The minor is his child by adoption;

3. The minor has been adjudicated by the court to be his child before the date a petition for termination of parental rights is filed;

4. He has filed an affidavit of paternity pursuant to s. 382.013(2)(c) or he is listed on the child's birth certificate before the date a petition for termination of parental rights is filed; or

5. In the case of an unmarried biological father, he has acknowledged in writing, signed in the presence of a competent witness, that he is the father of the minor, has filed such acknowledgment with the Office of Vital Statistics of the Department of Health within the required timeframes, and has complied with the requirements of subsection (2).

(c) The minor, if 12 years of age or older, unless the court in the best interest of the minor dispenses with the minor's consent.

(d) Any person lawfully entitled to custody of the minor if required by the court.

(e) The court having jurisdiction to determine custody of the minor, if the person having physical custody of the minor does not have authority to consent to the adoption.

(2) In accordance with subsection (1), the consent of an unmarried biological father shall be necessary only if the unmarried biological father has complied with the requirements of this subsection.

(a)1. With regard to a child who is placed with adoptive parents more than 6 months after the child's birth, an unmarried biological father must have developed a substantial relationship with the child, taken some measure of responsibility for the child and the child's future, and demonstrated a full commitment to the responsibilities of parenthood by providing reasonable and regular financial support to the child in accordance with the unmarried biological father's ability, if not prevented from doing so by the person or authorized agency having lawful custody of the child, and either:

a. Regularly visited the child at least monthly, when physically and financially able to do so and when not prevented from doing so by the birth mother or the person or authorized agency having lawful custody of the child; or

b. Maintained regular communication with the child or with the person or agency having the care or custody of the child, when physically or financially unable to visit the child or when not prevented from doing so by the birth mother or person or authorized agency having lawful custody of the child.

2. An unmarried biological father who openly lived with the child for at least 6 months within the 1-year period following the birth of the child and immediately preceding placement of the child with adoptive parents and who openly held himself out to be the father of the child during that period shall be deemed to have developed a substantial relationship with the child and to have otherwise met the requirements of this paragraph.

(b) With regard to a child who is 6 months of age or younger at the time the child is placed with the adoptive parents, an unmarried biological father must have demonstrated a full commitment to his parental responsibility by having performed all of the following acts prior to the time the mother executes her consent for adoption:

1. Filed a notarized claim of paternity form with the Florida Putative Father Registry within the Office of Vital Statistics of the Department of Health, which form shall be maintained in the confidential registry established for that purpose and shall be considered filed when the notice is entered in the registry of notices from unmarried biological fathers.

2. Upon service of a notice of an intended adoption plan or a petition for termination of parental rights pending adoption, executed and filed an affidavit in that proceeding stating that he is personally fully able and willing to take responsibility for the child, setting forth his plans for care of the child, and agreeing to a court order of child support and a contribution to the payment of living and medical expenses incurred for the mother's pregnancy and the child's birth in accordance with his ability to pay.

3. If he had knowledge of the pregnancy, paid a fair and reasonable amount of the living and medical expenses incurred in connection with the mother's pregnancy and the child's birth, in accordance with his financial ability and when not prevented from doing so by the birth mother or person or authorized agency having lawful custody of the child. The responsibility of the unmarried biological father to provide financial assistance to the birth mother during her pregnancy and to the child after birth is not abated because support is being provided to the birth mother or child by the adoption entity, a prospective adoptive parent, or a third party, nor does it serve as a basis to excuse the birth father's failure to provide support.

(c) The mere fact that a father expresses a desire to fulfill his responsibilities towards his child which is unsupported by acts evidencing this intent does not meet the requirements of this section.

(d) The petitioner shall file with the court a certificate from the Office of Vital Statistics stating that a diligent search has been made of the Florida Putative Father Registry of notices from unmarried biological fathers described in subparagraph (b)1. and that no filing has been found pertaining to the father of the child in question or, if a filing is found, stating the name of the putative father and the time and date of filing. That certificate shall be filed with the court prior to the entry of a final judgment of termination of parental rights.

(e) An unmarried biological father who does not comply with each of the conditions provided in this subsection is deemed to have waived and surrendered any rights in relation to the child, including the right to notice of any judicial proceeding in connection with the adoption of the child, and his consent to the adoption of the child is not required.

(3) Pursuant to chapter 48, an adoption entity shall serve a notice of intended adoption plan upon any known and locatable unmarried biological father who is identified to the adoption entity by the mother by the date she signs her consent for adoption if the child is 6 months of age or less at the time the consent is executed. Service of the notice of intended adoption plan is not required when the unmarried biological father signs a consent for adoption or an affidavit of nonpaternity or when the child is more than 6 months of age at the time of the execution of the consent by the mother. The notice may be served at any time before the child's birth or before placing the child in the adoptive home. The recipient of the notice may waive service of process by executing a waiver and acknowledging receipt of the plan. The notice of intended adoption plan must specifically state that if the unmarried biological father desires to contest the adoption plan he must, within 30 days after service, file with the court a verified response that contains a pledge of commitment to the child in substantial compliance with subparagraph (2)(b)2. and a claim of paternity form with the Office of Vital Statistics, and must provide the adoption entity with a copy of the verified response filed with the court and the claim of paternity form filed with the Office of Vital Statistics. The notice must also include instructions for submitting a claim of paternity form to the Office of Vital Statistics and the address to which the claim must be sent. If the party served with the notice of intended adoption plan is an entity whose consent is required, the notice must specifically state that the entity must file, within 30 days after service, a verified response setting forth a legal basis for contesting the intended adoption plan, specifically addressing the best interests of the child.

(a) If the unmarried biological father or entity whose consent is required fails to timely and properly file a verified response with the court and, in the case of an unmarried biological father, a claim of paternity form with the Office of Vital Statistics, the court shall enter a default judgment against the unmarried biological father or entity and the consent of that unmarried biological father or entity shall no longer be required under this chapter and shall be deemed to have waived any claim of rights to the child. To avoid an entry of a default judgment, within 30 days after receipt of service of the notice of intended adoption plan:

1. The unmarried biological father must:

a. File a claim of paternity with the Florida Putative Father Registry maintained by the Office of Vital Statistics;

b. File a verified response with the court which contains a pledge of commitment to the child in substantial compliance with subparagraph (2)(b)2.; and

c. Provide support for the birth mother and the child.

2. The entity whose consent is required must file a verified response setting forth a legal basis for contesting the intended adoption plan, specifically addressing the best interests of the child.

(b) If the mother identifies a potential unmarried biological father within the timeframes required by the statute, whose location is unknown, the adoption entity shall conduct a diligent search pursuant to s. 63.088. If, upon completion of a diligent search, the potential unmarried biological father's location remains unknown and a search of the Florida Putative Father Registry fails to reveal a match, the adoption entity shall request in the petition for termination of parental rights pending adoption that the court declare the diligent search to be in compliance with s. 63.088, that the adoption entity has no further obligation to provide notice to the potential unmarried biological father, and that the potential unmarried biological father's consent to the adoption is not required.

(4) Any person whose consent is required under paragraph (1)(b), or any other man, may execute an irrevocable affidavit of nonpaternity in lieu of a consent under this section and by doing so waives notice to all court proceedings after the date of execution. An affidavit of nonpaternity must be executed as provided in s. 63.082. The affidavit of nonpaternity may be executed prior to the birth of the child. The person executing the affidavit must receive disclosure under s. 63.085 prior to signing the affidavit. For purposes of this chapter, an affidavit of nonpaternity is sufficient if it contains a specific denial of parental obligations and does not need to deny the existence of a biological relationship.

(5) A person who signs a consent to adoption or an affidavit of nonpaternity must be given reasonable notice of his or her right to select a person who does not have an employment, professional, or personal relationship with the adoption entity or the prospective adoptive parents to be present when the consent to adoption or affidavit of nonpaternity is executed and to sign the consent or affidavit as a witness.

(6) The petitioner must make good faith and diligent efforts as provided under s. 63.088 to notify, and obtain written consent from, the persons required to consent to adoption under this section.

(7) If parental rights to the minor have previously been terminated, the adoption entity with which the minor has been placed for subsequent adoption may provide consent to the adoption. In such case, no other consent is required. The consent of the department shall be waived upon a determination by the court that such consent is being unreasonably withheld and if the petitioner has filed with the court a favorable preliminary adoptive home study as required under s. 63.092.

(8) A petition to adopt an adult may be granted if:

(a) Written consent to adoption has been executed by the adult and the adult's spouse, if any, unless the spouse's consent is waived by the court for good cause.

(b) Written notice of the final hearing on the adoption has been provided to the parents, if any, or proof of service of process has been filed, showing notice has been served on the parents as provided in this chapter.

(9) A petition for termination of parental rights must be filed in the appropriate county as determined under s. 63.087(2). If a parent whose consent is required objects to venue in the county where the action was filed, the court may transfer venue to a proper venue consistent with this chapter and chapter 47 unless the objecting parent has previously executed a waiver of venue.

(10) The waiver of venue must be a separate document containing no consents, disclosures, or other information unrelated to venue.

63.063. Responsibility of parents for actions; fraud or misrepresentation; contesting termination of parental rights and adoption.

(1) Each parent of a child conceived or born outside of marriage is responsible for his or her actions and is not excused from strict compliance with this chapter based upon any action, statement, or omission of the other parent or a third party, except as provided in s. 63.062(2)(a).

(2) Any person injured by a fraudulent representation or action in connection with an adoption may pursue civil or criminal penalties as provided by law. A fraudulent representation is not a defense to compliance with the requirements of this chapter and is not a basis for dismissing a petition for termination of parental rights or a petition for adoption, for vacating an adoption decree, or for granting custody to the offended party. Custody and adoption determinations must be based on the best interests of the child in accordance with s. 61.13.

(3) The Legislature finds no way to remove all risk of fraud or misrepresentation in adoption proceedings and has provided a method for absolute protection of an unmarried biological father's rights through compliance with this chapter. In balancing the rights and interests of the state and of all parties affected by fraud, including the child, the adoptive parents, and the unmarried biological father, the Legislature has determined that the unmarried biological father is in the best position to prevent or ameliorate the effects of fraud and, therefore, has the burden of preventing fraud.

(4) The Legislature finds that an unmarried biological father who resides in another state may not, in every circumstance, be reasonably presumed to know and comply with the requirements of this chapter. Therefore, if all of the following requirements have been met, an unmarried biological father may contest a termination of parental rights or subsequent adoption and, before entry of the final judgment of adoption, assert his interest in the child. Following such assertion, the court may proceed with an evidentiary hearing if:

(a) The unmarried biological father resides and has resided in another state where the unmarried mother was also located or resided.

(b) The unmarried mother left that state without notifying or informing the unmarried biological father that she could be located in this state.

(c) The unmarried biological father has, through every reasonable means, attempted to locate the mother but does not know or have reason to know that the mother is residing in this state.

(d) The unmarried biological father has substantially complied with the requirements of the state where the mother previously resided or was located in order to protect and preserve his parental interest and rights with regard to the child.

63.064. Persons whose consent to an adoption may be waived.

The court may waive the consent of the following individuals to an adoption:

(1) A parent who has deserted a child without means of identification or who has abandoned a child.

(2) A parent whose parental rights have been terminated by order of a court of competent jurisdiction.

(3) A parent who has been judicially declared incompetent and for whom restoration of competency is medically improbable.

(4) A legal guardian or lawful custodian of the person to be adopted, other than a parent, who has failed to respond in writing to a request for consent for a period of 60 days or who, after

examination of his or her written reasons for withholding consent, is found by the court to be withholding his or her consent unreasonably.

(5) The spouse of the person to be adopted, if the failure of the spouse to consent to the adoption is excused by reason of prolonged and unexplained absence, unavailability, incapacity, or circumstances that are found by the court to constitute unreasonable withholding of consent.

63.082. Execution of consent to adoption or affidavit of nonpaternity; family social and medical history; revocation of consent.

(1)(a) Consent to an adoption or an affidavit of nonpaternity shall be executed as follows:
1. If by the person to be adopted, by oral or written statement in the presence of the court or by being acknowledged before a notary public and in the presence of two witnesses.
2. If by an agency, by affidavit from its authorized representative.
3. If by any other person, in the presence of the court or by affidavit acknowledged before a notary public and in the presence of two witnesses.
4. If by a court, by an appropriate order or certificate of the court.
(b) A minor parent has the power to consent to the adoption of his or her child and has the power to relinquish his or her control or custody of the child to an adoption entity. Such consent or relinquishment is valid and has the same force and effect as a consent or relinquishment executed by an adult parent. A minor parent, having executed a consent or relinquishment, may not revoke that consent upon reaching the age of majority or otherwise becoming emancipated.
(c) A consent or an affidavit of nonpaternity executed by a minor parent who is 14 years of age or younger must be witnessed by a parent, legal guardian, or court-appointed guardian ad litem.
(d) The notice and consent provisions of this chapter as they relate to the father of a child do not apply in cases in which the child is conceived as a result of a violation of the criminal laws of this or another state or country, including, but not limited to, sexual battery, unlawful sexual activity with certain minors under s. 794.05, lewd acts perpetrated upon a minor, or incest.
(2) A consent that does not name or otherwise identify the adopting parent is valid if the consent contains a statement by the person consenting that the consent was voluntarily executed and that identification of the adopting parent is not required for granting the consent.
(3)(a) The department must provide a family social and medical history form to an adoption entity that intends to place a child for adoption. Forms containing, at a minimum, the same information as the forms promulgated by the department must be attached to the petition to terminate parental rights pending adoption and must contain biological and sociological information or information as to the family medical history regarding the minor and the parents. This form is not required for adoptions of relatives, adult adoptions, or adoptions of stepchildren, unless parental rights are being or were terminated pursuant to chapter 39. The information must be filed with the court in the termination of parental rights proceeding.
(b) A good faith and diligent effort must be made to have each parent whose identity is known and whose consent is required interviewed by a representative of the adoption entity before the consent is executed. A summary of each interview, or a statement that the parent is unidentified, unlocated, or unwilling or unavailable to be interviewed, must be filed with the petition to terminate parental rights pending adoption. The interview may be excused by the court for good cause. This interview is not required for adoptions of relatives, adult adoptions, or adoptions of stepchildren, unless parental rights are being or were terminated pursuant to chapter 39.
(c) If any person who is required to consent is unavailable because the person cannot be located, an affidavit of diligent search required under s. 63.088 shall be filed.
(d) If any person who is required to consent is unavailable because the person is deceased, the petition to terminate parental rights pending adoption must be accompanied by a certified copy of

the death certificate. In an adoption of a stepchild or a relative, the certified copy of the death certificate of the person whose consent is required may be attached to the petition for adoption if a separate petition for termination of parental rights is not being filed.

(4)(a) An affidavit of nonpaternity may be executed before the birth of the minor; however, the consent to an adoption may not be executed before the birth of the minor except in a preplanned adoption pursuant to s. 63.213.

(b) A consent to the adoption of a minor who is to be placed for adoption may be executed by the birth mother 48 hours after the minor's birth or the day the birth mother is notified in writing, either on her patient chart or in release paperwork, that she is fit to be released from the licensed hospital or birth center, whichever is earlier. A consent by any man may be executed at any time after the birth of the child. The consent is valid upon execution and may be withdrawn only if the court finds that it was obtained by fraud or duress.

(c) If the minor to be adopted is older than 6 months of age at the time of the execution of the consent, the consent to adoption is valid upon execution; however, it is subject to a revocation period of 3 business days.

(d) The consent to adoption or the affidavit of nonpaternity must be signed in the presence of two witnesses and be acknowledged before a notary public who is not signing as one of the witnesses. The notary public must legibly note on the consent or the affidavit the date and time of execution. The witnesses' names must be typed or printed underneath their signatures. The witnesses' home or business addresses must be included. The person who signs the consent or the affidavit has the right to have at least one of the witnesses be an individual who does not have an employment, professional, or personal relationship with the adoption entity or the prospective adoptive parents. The adoption entity must give reasonable advance notice to the person signing the consent or affidavit of the right to select a witness of his or her own choosing. The person who signs the consent or affidavit must acknowledge in writing on the consent or affidavit that such notice was given and indicate the witness, if any, who was selected by the person signing the consent or affidavit. The adoption entity must include its name, address, and telephone number on the consent to adoption or affidavit of nonpaternity.

(e) A consent to adoption being executed by the birth parent must be in at least 12-point boldfaced type and shall contain the following recitation of rights:

(5) A copy or duplicate original of each consent signed in an action for termination of parental rights pending adoption must be provided to the person who executed the consent to adoption. The copy must be hand delivered, with a written acknowledgment of receipt signed by the person whose consent is required at the time of execution. If a copy of a consent cannot be provided as required in this subsection, the adoption entity must execute an affidavit stating why the copy of the consent was not delivered. The original consent and acknowledgment of receipt, or an affidavit stating why the copy of the consent was not delivered, must be filed with the petition for termination of parental rights pending adoption.

(6)(a) If a parent executes a consent for adoption of a minor with an adoption entity or qualified prospective adoptive parents and the minor child is under the supervision of the department, or otherwise subject to the jurisdiction of the dependency court as a result of the entry of a shelter order, a dependency petition, or a petition for termination of parental rights pursuant to chapter 39, but parental rights have not yet been terminated, the adoption consent is valid, binding, and enforceable by the court.

(b) Upon execution of the consent of the parent, the adoption entity shall be permitted to intervene in the dependency case as a party in interest and must provide the court that acquired jurisdiction over the minor, pursuant to the shelter order or dependency petition filed by the department, a copy of the preliminary home study of the prospective adoptive parents and any other evidence of the suitability of the placement. The preliminary home study must be maintained with strictest confidentiality within the dependency court file and the department's file. A preliminary home study must be provided to the court in all cases in which an adoption entity has intervened pursuant to this section. Unless the court has concerns regarding the qualifications of the home study provider, or concerns that the home study may not be adequate to determine the best interests of the child, the home study provided by the adoption entity shall be deemed to be sufficient and no additional home study needs to be performed by the department.

(c) If an adoption entity files a motion to intervene in the dependency case in accordance with this chapter, the dependency court shall promptly grant a hearing to determine whether the adoption entity has filed the required documents to be permitted to intervene and whether a change of placement of the child is in the best interests of the child. Absent good cause or mutual agreement of the parties, the final hearing on the motion to intervene and the change of placement of the child must be held within 30 days after the filing of the motion, and a written final order shall be filed within 15 days after the hearing.

(d) If after consideration of all relevant factors, including those set forth in paragraph (e), the court determines that the prospective adoptive parents are properly qualified to adopt the minor child and that the adoption is in the best interests of the minor child, the court shall promptly order the transfer of custody of the minor child to the prospective adoptive parents, under the supervision of the adoption entity. The court may establish reasonable requirements for the transfer of custody in the transfer order, including a reasonable period of time to transition final custody to the prospective adoptive parents. The adoption entity shall thereafter provide monthly supervision reports to the department until finalization of the adoption. If the child has been determined to be dependent by the court, the department shall provide information to the prospective adoptive parents at the time they receive placement of the dependent child regarding approved parent training classes available within the community. The department shall file with the court an acknowledgment of the parent's receipt of the information regarding approved parent training classes available within the community.

(e) In determining whether the best interests of the child are served by transferring the custody of the minor child to the prospective adoptive parent selected by the parent or adoption entity, the court shall consider and weigh all relevant factors, including, but not limited to:

1. The permanency offered;
2. The established bonded relationship between the child and the current caregiver in any potential adoptive home in which the child has been residing;
3. The stability of the potential adoptive home in which the child has been residing as well as the desirability of maintaining continuity of placement;
4. The importance of maintaining sibling relationships, if possible;
5. The reasonable preferences and wishes of the child, if the court deems the child to be of sufficient maturity, understanding, and experience to express a preference;
6. Whether a petition for termination of parental rights has been filed pursuant to s. 39.806(1)(f), (g), or (h);
7. What is best for the child; and
8. The right of the parent to determine an appropriate placement for the child.

(f) The adoption entity shall be responsible for keeping the dependency court informed of the status of the adoption proceedings at least every 90 days from the date of the order changing placement of the child until the date of finalization of the adoption.

(g) At the arraignment hearing held pursuant to s. 39.506, in the order that approves the case plan pursuant to s. 39.603, and in the order that changes the permanency goal to adoption pursuant to s. 39.621, the court shall provide written notice to the biological parent who is a party to the case of his or her right to participate in a private adoption plan including written notice of the factors provided in paragraph (e).

(7) If a person is seeking to revoke consent for a child older than 6 months of age:

(a) The person seeking to revoke consent must, in accordance with paragraph (4)(c), notify the adoption entity in writing by certified mail, return receipt requested, within 3 business days after execution of the consent. As used in this subsection, the term "business day" means any day on which the United States Postal Service accepts certified mail for delivery.

(b) Upon receiving timely written notice from a person whose consent to adoption is required of that person's desire to revoke consent, the adoption entity must contact the prospective adoptive parent to arrange a time certain for the adoption entity to regain physical custody of the minor, unless, upon a motion for emergency hearing by the adoption entity, the court determines in written findings that placement of the minor with the person who had legal or physical custody of the child immediately before the child was placed for adoption may endanger the minor or that the person who desires to revoke consent is not required to consent to the adoption, has been determined to have abandoned the child, or is otherwise subject to a determination that the person's consent is waived under this chapter.

(c) If the court finds that the placement may endanger the minor, the court shall enter an order continuing the placement of the minor with the prospective adoptive parents pending further proceedings if they desire continued placement. If the prospective adoptive parents do not desire continued placement, the order must include, but need not be limited to, a determination of whether temporary placement in foster care, with the person who had legal or physical custody of the child immediately before placing the child for adoption, or with a relative is in the best interests of the child and whether an investigation by the department is recommended.

(d) If the person revoking consent claims to be the father of the minor but has not been established to be the father by marriage, court order, or scientific testing, the court may order scientific paternity testing and reserve ruling on removal of the minor until the results of such testing have been filed with the court.

(e) The adoption entity must return the minor within 3 business days after timely and proper notification of the revocation of consent or after the court determines that revocation is timely and in accordance with the requirements of this chapter upon consideration of an emergency motion, as filed pursuant to paragraph (b), to the physical custody of the person revoking consent or the person directed by the court. If the person seeking to revoke consent claims to be the father of the minor but has not been established to be the father by marriage, court order, or scientific testing, the adoption entity may return the minor to the care and custody of the mother, if she desires such placement and she is not otherwise prohibited by law from having custody of the child.

(f) Following the revocation period described in paragraph (a), consent may be set aside only when the court finds that the consent was obtained by fraud or duress.

(g) An affidavit of nonpaternity may be set aside only if the court finds that the affidavit was obtained by fraud or duress.

(h) If the consent of one parent is set aside or revoked in accordance with this chapter, any other consents executed by the other parent or a third party whose consent is required for the adoption of the child may not be used by the parent whose consent was revoked or set aside to terminate or diminish the rights of the other parent or third party whose consent was required for the adoption of the child.

63.085. Disclosure by adoption entity.

(1) DISCLOSURE REQUIRED TO PARENTS AND PROSPECTIVE ADOPTIVE PARENTS.—Within 14 days after a person seeking to adopt a minor or a person seeking to place a minor for adoption contacts an adoption entity in person or provides the adoption entity with a mailing address, the entity must provide a written disclosure statement to that person if the entity agrees or continues to work with the person. The adoption entity shall also provide the written disclosure to the parent who did not initiate contact with the adoption entity within 14 days after that parent is identified and located. For purposes of providing the written disclosure, a person is considered to be seeking to place a minor for adoption if that person has sought information or advice from the adoption entity regarding the option of adoptive placement. The written disclosure statement must be in substantially the following form:

(2) DISCLOSURE TO ADOPTIVE PARENTS.—

(a) At the time that an adoption entity is responsible for selecting prospective adoptive parents for a born or unborn child whose parents are seeking to place the child for adoption or whose rights were terminated pursuant to chapter 39, the adoption entity must provide the prospective adoptive parents with information concerning the background of the child to the extent such information is disclosed to the adoption entity by the parents, legal custodian, or the department. This subsection applies only if the adoption entity identifies the prospective adoptive parents and supervises the placement of the child in the prospective adoptive parents' home. If any information cannot be disclosed because the records custodian failed or refused to produce the background information, the adoption entity has a duty to provide the information if it becomes available. An individual or entity contacted by an adoption entity to obtain the background information must release the requested information to the adoption entity without the necessity of a subpoena or a court order. In all cases, the prospective adoptive parents must receive all available information by the date of the final hearing on the petition for adoption. The information to be disclosed includes:

1. A family social and medical history form completed pursuant to s. 63.162(6).

2. The biological mother's medical records documenting her prenatal care and the birth and delivery of the child.

3. A complete set of the child's medical records documenting all medical treatment and care since the child's birth and before placement.

4. All mental health, psychological, and psychiatric records, reports, and evaluations concerning the child before placement.

5. The child's educational records, including all records concerning any special education needs of the child before placement.

6. Records documenting all incidents that required the department to provide services to the child, including all orders of adjudication of dependency or termination of parental rights issued pursuant to chapter 39, any case plans drafted to address the child's needs, all protective services investigations identifying the child as a victim, and all guardian ad litem reports filed with the court concerning the child.

7. Written information concerning the availability of adoption subsidies for the child, if applicable.

(b) When disclosing information pursuant to this subsection, the adoption entity must redact any confidential identifying information concerning the child's parents, foster parents and their families, siblings, relatives, and perpetrators of crimes against the child or involving the child.

(c) If the prospective adoptive parents waive the receipt of any of the records described in paragraph (a), a copy of the written notification of the waiver to the adoption entity shall be filed with the court.

(3) ACKNOWLEDGMENT OF DISCLOSURE.—The adoption entity must obtain a written statement acknowledging receipt of the disclosures required under this section and signed by the persons receiving the disclosure or, if it is not possible to obtain such an acknowledgment, the adoption entity must execute an affidavit stating why an acknowledgment could not be obtained. If the disclosure was delivered by certified mail, return receipt requested, a return receipt signed by the person from whom acknowledgment is required is sufficient to meet the requirements of this subsection. A copy of the acknowledgment of receipt of the disclosure must be provided to the person signing it. A copy of the acknowledgment or affidavit executed by the adoption entity in lieu of the acknowledgment must be maintained in the file of the adoption entity. The original acknowledgment or affidavit must be filed with the court.

(4) REVOCATION OF CONSENT.—Failure to meet the requirements of this section does not constitute grounds for revocation of a consent to adoption or withdrawal of an affidavit of nonpaternity unless the extent and circumstances of such a failure result in a material failure of fundamental fairness in the administration of due process, or the failure constitutes or contributes materially to fraud or duress in obtaining a consent to adoption or affidavit of nonpaternity.

63.087. Proceeding to terminate parental rights pending adoption; general provisions.

(1) JURISDICTION.—A court of this state which is competent to decide child welfare or custody matters has jurisdiction to hear all matters arising from a proceeding to terminate parental rights pending adoption.

(2) VENUE.—

(a) A petition to terminate parental rights pending adoption must be filed:

1. In the county where the child resides; or

2. In the county where the adoption entity is located.

(b) If a petition for termination of parental rights has been filed and a parent whose consent is required objects to venue, there must be a hearing in which the court shall determine whether that parent intends to assert legally recognized grounds to contest a termination of parental rights and, if so, the court may transfer venue to a proper venue under this subsection. For purposes of selecting venue, the court shall consider the ease of access to the court for the parent and the factors set forth in s. 47.122.

(c) If there is a transfer of venue, the court may determine which party shall bear the cost of venue transfer.

(3) PREREQUISITE FOR ADOPTION.—A petition for adoption may not be filed until after the date the court enters the judgment terminating parental rights pending adoption. Adoptions of relatives, adult adoptions, or adoptions of stepchildren are not required to file a separate termination of parental rights proceeding pending adoption. In such cases, the petitioner may file a joint petition for termination of parental rights and adoption, attaching all required consents, affidavits, notices, and acknowledgments. Unless otherwise provided by law, this chapter applies to joint petitions.

(4) PETITION.—

(a) A proceeding seeking to terminate parental rights pending adoption pursuant to this chapter must be initiated by the filing of an original petition after the birth of the minor.

(b) The petition may be filed by a parent or person having physical custody of the minor. The petition may be filed by an adoption entity only if a parent or person having physical or legal custody who has executed a consent to adoption pursuant to s. 63.082 also consents in writing to the adoption entity filing the petition. The original of such consent must be filed with the petition.

(c) The petition must be entitled: "In the Matter of the Termination of Parental Rights for the Proposed Adoption of a Minor Child."

(d) The petition to terminate parental rights pending adoption must be in writing and signed by the petitioner under oath stating the petitioner's good faith in filing the petition. A written consent to adoption, affidavit of nonpaternity, or affidavit of diligent search under s. 63.088, for each person whose consent to adoption is required under s. 63.062, must be executed and attached.

(e) The petition must include:

1. The minor's name, gender, date of birth, and place of birth. The petition must contain all names by which the minor is or has been known, excluding the minor's prospective adoptive name but including the minor's legal name at the time of the filing of the petition. In the case of an infant child whose adoptive name appears on the original birth certificate, the adoptive name shall not be included in the petition, nor shall it be included elsewhere in the termination of parental rights proceeding.

2. All information required by the Uniform Child Custody Jurisdiction and Enforcement Act and the Indian Child Welfare Act.

3. A statement of the grounds under s. 63.089 upon which the petition is based.

4. The name, address, and telephone number of any adoption entity seeking to place the minor for adoption.

5. The name, address, and telephone number of the division of the circuit court in which the petition is to be filed.

6. A certification of compliance with the requirements of s. 63.0425 regarding notice to grandparents of an impending adoption.

(5) SUMMONS TO BE ISSUED.—The petitioner shall cause a summons to be issued substantially in the form provided in Form 1.902, Florida Rules of Civil Procedure. Petition and

summons shall be served upon any person whose consent has been provided but who has not waived service of the pleadings and notice of the hearing thereon and also upon any person whose consent is required but who has not provided that consent.

(6) ANSWER AND APPEARANCE REQUIRED.—An answer to the petition or any pleading requiring an answer must be filed in accordance with the Florida Family Law Rules of Procedure. Failure to file a written response to the petition constitutes grounds upon which the court may terminate parental rights. Failure to personally appear at the hearing constitutes grounds upon which the court may terminate parental rights. Any person present at the hearing to terminate parental rights pending adoption whose consent to adoption is required under s. 63.062 must:

(a) Be advised by the court that he or she has a right to ask that the hearing be reset for a later date so that the person may consult with an attorney; and

(b) Be given an opportunity to admit or deny the allegations in the petition.

63.088. Proceeding to terminate parental rights pending adoption; notice and service; diligent search.

(1) NOTICE REQUIRED.—An unmarried biological father, by virtue of the fact that he has engaged in a sexual relationship with a woman, is deemed to be on notice that a pregnancy and an adoption proceeding regarding that child may occur and that he has a duty to protect his own rights and interest. He is, therefore, entitled to notice of a birth or adoption proceeding with regard to that child only as provided in this chapter. If a mother fails to identify an unmarried biological father to the adoption entity by the date she signs her consent for adoption, the unmarried biological father's claim that he did not receive actual notice of the adoption proceeding is not a defense to the termination of his parental rights.

(2) INITIATE LOCATION PROCEDURES.—When the location of a person whose consent to an adoption is required but is not known, the adoption entity must begin the inquiry and diligent search process required by this section within a reasonable time period after the date on which the person seeking to place a minor for adoption has evidenced in writing to the adoption entity a desire to place the minor for adoption with that entity, or not later than 30 days after the date any money is provided as permitted under this chapter by the adoption entity for the benefit of the person seeking to place a minor for adoption.

(3) LOCATION AND IDENTITY KNOWN.—Before the court may determine that a minor is available for adoption, each person whose consent is required under s. 63.062, who has not executed a consent for adoption or an affidavit of nonpaternity, and whose location and identity have been determined by compliance with the procedures in this section must be personally served, pursuant to chapter 48, at least 20 days before the hearing with a copy of the petition to terminate parental rights pending adoption and with notice in substantially the following form:

(4) REQUIRED INQUIRY.—In proceedings initiated under s. 63.087, the court shall conduct an inquiry of the person who is placing the minor for adoption and of any relative or person having legal custody of the minor who is present at the hearing and likely to have the following information regarding the identity of:

(a) Any man to whom the mother of the minor was married at any time when conception of the minor may have occurred or at the time of the birth of the minor;

(b) Any man who has filed an affidavit of paternity pursuant to s. 382.013(2)(c) before the date that a petition for termination of parental rights is filed with the court;

(c) Any man who has adopted the minor;

(d) Any man who has been adjudicated by a court as the father of the minor child before the date a petition for termination of parental rights is filed with the court; and

(e) Any man whom the mother identified to the adoption entity as a potential biological father before the date she signed the consent for adoption.

(5) LOCATION UNKNOWN; IDENTITY KNOWN.—If the inquiry by the court under subsection (4) identifies any person who has not executed a consent to adoption or an affidavit of nonpaternity, and the location of the person is unknown, the adoption entity must conduct a diligent search for that person which must include inquiries concerning:

(a) The person's current address, or any previous address, through an inquiry of the United States Postal Service through the Freedom of Information Act;

(b) The last known employment of the person, including the name and address of the person's employer;

(c) Names and addresses of relatives to the extent they can be reasonably obtained from the petitioner or other sources, contacts with those relatives, and inquiry as to the person's last known address. The petitioner must pursue any leads to any addresses where the person may have moved;

(d) Information as to whether or not the person may have died and, if so, the date and location;

(e) Telephone listings in the area where the person last resided;

(f) Inquiries of law enforcement agencies in the area where the person last resided;

(g) Highway patrol records in the state where the person last resided;

(h) Department of Corrections records in the state where the person last resided;

(i) Hospitals in the area where the person last resided;

(j) Records of utility companies, including water, sewer, cable television, and electric companies, in the area where the person last resided;

(k) Records of the Armed Forces of the United States as to whether there is any information as to the person;

(l) Records of the tax assessor and tax collector in the area where the person last resided; and

(m) Search of one Internet databank locator service.

(6) CONSTRUCTIVE SERVICE.—This subsection only applies if, as to any person whose consent is required under s. 63.062 and who has not executed a consent to adoption or an affidavit of nonpaternity, the location of the person is unknown and the inquiry under subsection (4) fails to locate the person. The unlocated person must be served notice under subsection (3) by constructive service in the manner provided in chapter 49. The notice shall be published in the county where the person was last known to have resided. The notice, in addition to all information required under chapter 49, must include a physical description, including, but not limited to, age, race, hair and eye color, and approximate height and weight of the person, the minor's date of birth, and the place of birth of the minor. Constructive service by publication shall not be required to provide notice to an identified birth father whose consent is not required pursuant to ss. 63.062 and 63.064.

63.089. Proceeding to terminate parental rights pending adoption; hearing; grounds; dismissal of petition; judgment.

(1) HEARING.—The court may terminate parental rights pending adoption only after a hearing.

(2) HEARING PREREQUISITES.—The court may hold the hearing only when:

(a) For each person whose consent to adoption is required under s. 63.062:

1. A consent under s. 63.082 has been executed and filed with the court;

2. An affidavit of nonpaternity under s. 63.082 has been executed and filed with the court;

3. Notice has been provided under ss. 63.087 and 63.088; or

4. The certificate from the Office of Vital Statistics has been provided to the court stating that a diligent search has been made of the Florida Putative Father Registry created in s. 63.054 and that no filing has been found pertaining to the father of the child in question or, if a filing is found, stating the name of the putative father and the time and date of the filing.

(b) For each notice and petition that must be served under ss. 63.087 and 63.088:

1. At least 20 days have elapsed since the date of personal service and an affidavit of service has been filed with the court;

2. At least 30 days have elapsed since the first date of publication of constructive service and an affidavit of service has been filed with the court; or

3. An affidavit of nonpaternity, consent for adoption, or other document that affirmatively waives service has been executed and filed with the court.

(c) The minor named in the petition has been born.

(d) The petition contains all information required under s. 63.087 and all affidavits of inquiry, diligent search, and service required under s. 63.088 have been obtained and filed with the court.

(3) GROUNDS FOR TERMINATING PARENTAL RIGHTS PENDING ADOPTION.—The court may enter a judgment terminating parental rights pending adoption if the court determines by clear and convincing evidence, supported by written findings of fact, that each person whose consent to adoption is required under s. 63.062:

(a) Has executed a valid consent under s. 63.082 and the consent was obtained according to the requirements of this chapter;

(b) Has executed an affidavit of nonpaternity and the affidavit was obtained according to the requirements of this chapter;

(c) Has been served with a notice of the intended adoption plan in accordance with the provisions of s. 63.062(3) and has failed to respond within the designated time period;

(d) Has been properly served notice of the proceeding in accordance with the requirements of this chapter and has failed to file a written answer or personally appear at the evidentiary hearing resulting in the judgment terminating parental rights pending adoption;

(e) Has been properly served notice of the proceeding in accordance with the requirements of this chapter and has been determined under subsection (4) to have abandoned the minor;

(f) Is a parent of the person to be adopted, which parent has been judicially declared incapacitated with restoration of competency found to be medically improbable;

(g) Is a person who has legal custody of the person to be adopted, other than a parent, who has failed to respond in writing to a request for consent for a period of 60 days or, after examination of his or her written reasons for withholding consent, is found by the court to be withholding his or her consent unreasonably;

(h) Has been properly served notice of the proceeding in accordance with the requirements of this chapter, but has been found by the court, after examining written reasons for the withholding of consent, to be unreasonably withholding his or her consent; or

(i) Is the spouse of the person to be adopted who has failed to consent, and the failure of the spouse to consent to the adoption is excused by reason of prolonged and unexplained absence, unavailability, incapacity, or circumstances that are found by the court to constitute unreasonable withholding of consent.

(4) FINDING OF ABANDONMENT.—A finding of abandonment resulting in a termination of parental rights must be based upon clear and convincing evidence that a parent or person having legal custody has abandoned the child in accordance with the definition contained in s. 63.032. A finding of abandonment may also be based upon emotional abuse or a refusal to provide reasonable financial support, when able, to a birth mother during her pregnancy or on whether the person alleged to have abandoned the child, while being able, failed to establish contact with the child or accept responsibility for the child's welfare.

(a) In making a determination of abandonment at a hearing for termination of parental rights under this chapter, the court shall consider, among other relevant factors not inconsistent with this section:

1. Whether the actions alleged to constitute abandonment demonstrate a willful disregard for the safety or welfare of the child or the unborn child;

2. Whether the person alleged to have abandoned the child, while being able, failed to provide financial support;

3. Whether the person alleged to have abandoned the child, while being able, failed to pay for medical treatment; and

4. Whether the amount of support provided or medical expenses paid was appropriate, taking into consideration the needs of the child and relative means and resources available to the person alleged to have abandoned the child.

(b) The child has been abandoned when the parent of a child is incarcerated on or after October 1, 2001, in a federal, state, or county correctional institution and:

1. The period of time for which the parent has been or is expected to be incarcerated will constitute a significant portion of the child's minority. In determining whether the period of time is significant, the court shall consider the child's age and the child's need for a permanent and stable home. The period of time begins on the date that the parent enters into incarceration;

2. The incarcerated parent has been determined by a court of competent jurisdiction to be a violent career criminal as defined in s. 775.084, a habitual violent felony offender as defined in s. 775.084, convicted of child abuse as defined in s. 827.03, or a sexual predator as defined in s. 775.21; has been convicted of first degree or second degree murder in violation of s. 782.04 or a sexual battery that constitutes a capital, life, or first degree felony violation of s. 794.011; or has been convicted of a substantially similar offense in another jurisdiction. As used in this section, the term "substantially similar offense" means any offense that is substantially similar in elements and penalties to one of those listed in this subparagraph, and that is in violation of a law of any other jurisdiction, whether that of another state, the District of Columbia, the United States or any possession or territory thereof, or any foreign jurisdiction; or

3. The court determines by clear and convincing evidence that continuing the parental relationship with the incarcerated parent would be harmful to the child and, for this reason, termination of the parental rights of the incarcerated parent is in the best interests of the child.

(5) DISMISSAL OF PETITION.—If the court does not find by clear and convincing evidence that parental rights of a parent should be terminated pending adoption, the court must dismiss the petition and that parent's parental rights that were the subject of such petition shall remain in full force under the law. The order must include written findings in support of the dismissal, including findings as to the criteria in subsection (4) if rejecting a claim of abandonment.

(a) Parental rights may not be terminated based upon a consent that the court finds has been timely revoked under s. 63.082 or a consent to adoption or affidavit of nonpaternity that the court finds was obtained by fraud or duress.

(b) The court must enter an order based upon written findings providing for the placement of the minor, but the court may not proceed to determine custody between competing eligible parties. The placement of the child should revert to the parent or guardian who had physical custody of the child at the time of the placement for adoption unless the court determines upon clear and convincing evidence that this placement is not in the best interests of the child or is not an available option for the child. The court may not change the placement of a child who has established a bonded relationship with the current caregiver without providing for a reasonable transition plan consistent with the best interests of the child. The court may direct the parties to participate in a reunification or unification plan with a qualified professional to assist the child in the transition. The court may order scientific testing to determine the paternity of the minor only if the court has determined that the consent of the alleged father would be required, unless all parties agree that such testing is in the best interests of the child. The court may not order scientific testing to determine paternity of an unmarried biological father if the child has a father as described in s. 63.088(4)(a)-(d) whose rights have not been previously terminated. Further proceedings, if any, regarding the minor must be brought in a separate custody action under chapter 61, a dependency action under chapter 39, or a paternity action under chapter 742.

(6) JUDGMENT TERMINATING PARENTAL RIGHTS PENDING ADOPTION.—

(a) The judgment terminating parental rights pending adoption must be in writing and contain findings of fact as to the grounds for terminating parental rights.

(b) Within 7 days after filing, the court shall mail a copy of the judgment to the department. The clerk shall execute a certificate of the mailing.

(c) The judgment terminating parental rights pending adoption legally frees the child for subsequent adoption, adjudicates the child's status, and may not be challenged by a person claiming parental status who did not establish parental rights before the filing of the petition for termination, except as specifically provided in this chapter.

(7) RELIEF FROM JUDGMENT TERMINATING PARENTAL RIGHTS.—

(a) A motion for relief from a judgment terminating parental rights must be filed with the court originally entering the judgment. The motion must be filed within a reasonable time, but not later than 1 year after the entry of the judgment. An unmarried biological father does not have standing to seek relief from a judgment terminating parental rights if the mother did not identify him to the adoption entity before the date she signed a consent for adoption or if he was not located because the mother failed or refused to provide sufficient information to locate him.

(b) No later than 30 days after the filing of a motion under this subsection, the court must conduct a preliminary hearing to determine what contact, if any, shall be permitted between a parent and the child pending resolution of the motion. Such contact shall be considered only if it is requested by a parent who has appeared at the hearing and may not be awarded unless the parent previously established a bonded relationship with the child and the parent has pled a legitimate legal basis and established a prima facie case for setting aside the judgment terminating parental rights. If the court orders contact between a parent and child, the order must be issued in writing as expeditiously as possible and must state with specificity any provisions regarding contact with persons other than those with whom the child resides.

(c) At the preliminary hearing, the court, upon the motion of any party or upon its own motion, may order scientific testing to determine the paternity of the minor if the person seeking to set aside the judgment is alleging to be the child's father and that fact has not previously been determined by legitimacy or scientific testing. The court may order visitation with a person for whom scientific testing for paternity has been ordered and who has previously established a bonded relationship with the child.

(d) Unless otherwise agreed between the parties or for good cause shown, the court shall conduct a final hearing on the motion for relief from judgment within 45 days after the filing and enter its written order as expeditiously as possible thereafter.

(e) If the court grants relief from the judgment terminating parental rights and no new pleading is filed to terminate parental rights, the placement of the child should revert to the parent or guardian who had physical custody of the child at the time of the original placement for adoption unless the court determines upon clear and convincing evidence that this placement is not in the best interests of the child or is not an available option for the child. The court may not change the placement of a child who has established a bonded relationship with the current caregiver without providing for a reasonable transition plan consistent with the best interests of the child. The court may direct the parties to participate in a reunification or unification plan with a qualified professional to assist the child in the transition. The court may not direct the placement of a child with a person other than the adoptive parents without first obtaining a favorable home study of that person and any other persons residing in the proposed home and shall take whatever additional steps are necessary and appropriate for the physical and emotional protection of the child.

(8) RECORDS; CONFIDENTIAL INFORMATION.—All papers and records pertaining to a petition to terminate parental rights pending adoption are related to the subsequent adoption of the minor and are subject to s. 63.162. An unmarried biological father does not have standing to seek the court case number or access the court file if the mother did not identify him to the adoption entity before the date she signed the consent for adoption. The confidentiality provisions of this chapter do not apply to the extent information regarding persons or proceedings is made available as specified under s. 63.088.

63.092. Report to the court of intended placement by an adoption entity; at-risk placement; preliminary study.

(1) REPORT TO THE COURT.—The adoption entity must report any intended placement of a minor for adoption with any person who is not a relative or a stepparent if the adoption entity participates in the intended placement. The report must be made to the court before the minor is placed in the home or within 2 business days thereafter.

(2) AT-RISK PLACEMENT.—If the minor is placed in the prospective adoptive home before the parental rights of the minor's parents are terminated under s. 63.089, the placement is an at-risk placement. If the placement is an at-risk placement, the prospective adoptive parents must acknowledge in writing before the minor may be placed in the prospective adoptive home that the placement is at risk. The prospective adoptive parents shall be advised by the adoption entity, in writing, that the minor is subject to removal from the prospective adoptive home by the adoption entity or by court order at any time prior to the finalization of the adoption.

(3) PRELIMINARY HOME STUDY.—Before placing the minor in the intended adoptive home, a preliminary home study must be performed by a licensed child-placing agency, a child-caring agency registered under s. 409.176, a licensed professional, or an agency described in s. 61.20(2), unless the adoptee is an adult or the petitioner is a stepparent or a relative. If the adoptee is an adult or the petitioner is a stepparent or a relative, a preliminary home study may be required by the court for good cause shown. The department is required to perform the preliminary home study only if there is no licensed child-placing agency, child-caring agency registered under s. 409.176, licensed professional, or agency described in s. 61.20(2), in the county where the prospective adoptive parents reside. The preliminary home study must be made to determine the suitability of the intended adoptive parents and may be completed prior to identification of a prospective adoptive minor. A favorable preliminary home study is valid for 1 year after the date of its completion. Upon its completion, a signed copy of the home study must be provided to the intended adoptive parents who were the subject of the home study. A minor may not be placed in an intended adoptive home before a favorable preliminary home study is completed unless the adoptive home is also a licensed foster home under s. 409.175. The preliminary home study must include, at a minimum:

(a) An interview with the intended adoptive parents;

(b) Records checks of the department's central abuse registry and criminal records correspondence checks under s. 39.0138 through the Department of Law Enforcement on the intended adoptive parents;

(c) An assessment of the physical environment of the home;

(d) A determination of the financial security of the intended adoptive parents;

(e) Documentation of counseling and education of the intended adoptive parents on adoptive parenting;

(f) Documentation that information on adoption and the adoption process has been provided to the intended adoptive parents;

(g) Documentation that information on support services available in the community has been provided to the intended adoptive parents; and

(h) A copy of each signed acknowledgment of receipt of disclosure required by s. 63.085.

63.097. Fees.

(1) When the adoption entity is an agency, fees may be assessed if they are approved by the department within the process of licensing the agency and if they are for:

(a) Foster care expenses;

(b) Preplacement and postplacement social services; and

(c) Agency facility and administrative costs.

(2) The following fees, costs, and expenses may be assessed by the adoption entity or paid by the adoption entity on behalf of the prospective adoptive parents:

(a) Reasonable living expenses of the birth mother which the birth mother is unable to pay due to unemployment, underemployment, or disability. Reasonable living expenses are rent, utilities, basic telephone service, food, toiletries, necessary clothing, transportation, insurance, and expenses found by the court to be necessary for the health and well-being of the birth mother and the unborn child. Such expenses may be paid during the pregnancy and for a period of up to 6 weeks postpartum.

(b) Reasonable and necessary medical expenses. Such expenses may be paid during the pregnancy and for a period of up to 6 weeks postpartum.

(c) Expenses necessary to comply with the requirements of this chapter, including, but not limited to, service of process under s. 63.088, investigator fees, a diligent search under s. 63.088, a preliminary home study under s. 63.092, and a final home investigation under s. 63.125.

(d) Court filing expenses, court costs, and other litigation expenses and birth certificate and medical record expenses.

(e) Costs associated with advertising under s. 63.212(1)(g).

(f) The following professional fees:

1. A reasonable hourly fee or flat fee necessary to provide legal representation to the adoptive parents or adoption entity in a proceeding filed under this chapter.

2. A reasonable hourly fee or flat fee for contact with the parent related to the adoption. In determining a reasonable hourly fee under this subparagraph, the court must consider if the tasks done were clerical or of such a nature that the matter could have been handled by support staff at a lesser rate than the rate for legal representation charged under subparagraph 1. Such tasks include, but need not be limited to, transportation, transmitting funds, arranging appointments, and securing accommodations.

3. A reasonable hourly fee for counseling services provided to a parent or a prospective adoptive parent by a psychologist licensed under chapter 490 or a clinical social worker, marriage and family therapist, or mental health counselor licensed under chapter 491, or a counselor who is employed by an adoption entity accredited by the Council on Accreditation of Services for Children and Families to provide pregnancy counseling and supportive services.

(3) Approval of the court is not required until the total of amounts permitted under subsection (2) exceeds:

(a) $5,000 in legal or other fees;

(b) $800 in court costs; or

(c) $5,000 in reasonable and necessary living and medical expenses.

(4) Any fees, costs, or expenses not included in subsection (2) or prohibited under subsection (5) require court approval prior to payment and must be based on a finding of extraordinary circumstances.

(5) The following fees, costs, and expenses are prohibited:

(a) Any fee or expense that constitutes payment for locating a minor for adoption.

(b) Any payment which is not itemized and documented on the affidavit filed under s. 63.132.

(c) Any fee on the affidavit which does not specify the service that was provided and for which the fee is being charged, such as a fee for facilitation, acquisition, or other similar service, or which does not identify the date the service was provided, the time required to provide the service, the person or entity providing the service, and the hourly fee charged.

(6) Unless otherwise indicated in this section, when an adoption entity uses the services of a licensed child-placing agency, a professional, any other person or agency pursuant to s. 63.092, or, if necessary, the department, the person seeking to adopt the child must pay the licensed child-placing agency, professional, other person or agency, or the department an amount equal to the cost of all services performed, including, but not limited to, the cost of conducting the preliminary home study, counseling, and the final home investigation.

63.102. Filing of petition for adoption or declaratory statement; venue; proceeding for approval of fees and costs.

(1) PETITION FOR ADOPTION.—A petition for adoption may not be filed until after the entry of the judgment or decree terminating parental rights unless the adoptee is an adult or the petitioner is a stepparent or a relative. After a judgment terminating parental rights has been entered, a proceeding for adoption may be commenced by filing a petition entitled, "In the Matter of the Adoption of " in the circuit court. The person to be adopted shall be designated in the caption in the name by which he or she is to be known if the petition is granted. Except for a joint petition for the adoption of a stepchild, a relative, or an adult, any name by which the minor was previously known may not be disclosed in the petition, the notice of hearing, the judgment of adoption, or the court docket as provided in s. 63.162(3).

(2) VENUE.—A petition for adoption or for a declaratory statement as to the adoption contract must be filed in the county where the petition for termination of parental rights was filed or granted or where the adoption entity is located. The circuit court in this state shall retain jurisdiction over the matter until a final judgment is entered on the adoption, either within or outside the state. The Uniform Child Custody Jurisdiction and Enforcement Act does not apply until a final judgment is entered on the adoption.

(3) FILING OF ADOPTION PETITION REQUIRED.—Unless leave of court is granted for good cause shown, a petition for adoption shall be filed not later than 60 days after entry of the final judgment terminating parental rights.

(4) CONFIDENTIALITY.—If the filing of the petition for adoption or for a declaratory statement as to the adoption contract in the county where the petitioner or minor resides would tend to endanger the privacy of the petitioner or minor, the petition for adoption may be filed in a different county, provided the substantive rights of any person will not thereby be affected.

(5) PRIOR APPROVAL OF FEES AND COSTS.—A proceeding for prior approval of fees and costs may be commenced any time after an agreement is reached between the birth mother and the adoptive parents by filing a petition for declaratory statement on the agreement entitled "In the Matter of the Proposed Adoption of a Minor Child" in the circuit court.

(a) The petition must be filed by the adoption entity with the consent of the parties to the agreement.

(b) A contract for the payment of fees, costs, and expenses permitted under this chapter must be in writing, and any person who enters into the contract has 3 business days in which to cancel the contract unless placement of the child has occurred. To cancel the contract, the person must notify the adoption entity in writing by certified United States mail, return receipt requested, no later than 3 business days after signing the contract. For the purposes of this subsection, the term "business day" means a day on which the United States Postal Service accepts certified mail for delivery. If the contract is canceled within the first 3 business days, the person who cancels the contract does not owe any legal, intermediary, or other fees, but may be responsible for the adoption entity's actual costs during that time.

(c) The court may grant approval only of fees and expenses permitted under s. 63.097. A prior approval of prospective fees and costs shall create a presumption that these items will subsequently be approved by the court under s. 63.132. The court, under s. 63.132, may order an adoption entity to refund any amounts paid under this subsection that are subsequently found by the court to be greater than fees, costs, and expenses actually incurred.

(d) The contract may not require, and the court may not approve, any amount that constitutes payment for locating a minor for adoption.

(e) A declaratory statement as to the adoption contract, regardless of when filed, shall be consolidated with any related petition for adoption. The clerk of the court shall only assess one filing fee that includes the adoption action, the declaratory statement petition, and the petition for termination of parental rights.

(f) Prior approval of fees and costs by the court does not obligate the parent to ultimately relinquish the minor for adoption.

(6) STEPCHILD, RELATIVE, AND ADULT ADOPTIONS.—Petitions for the adoption of a stepchild, a relative, or an adult shall not require the filing of a separate judgment or separate proceeding terminating parental rights pending adoption. The final judgment of adoption shall have the effect of terminating parental rights simultaneously with the granting of the decree of adoption.

63.112. Petition for adoption; description; report or recommendation, exceptions; mailing.

(1) The petition for adoption shall be signed and verified by the petitioner and filed with the clerk of the court and shall state:

(a) The date and place of birth of the person to be adopted, if known;

(b) The name to be given to the person to be adopted;

(c) The date petitioner acquired custody of the minor and the name of the adoption entity placing the minor, if any;

(d) The full name, age, and place and duration of residence of the petitioner;

(e) The marital status of the petitioner, including the date and place of marriage, if married, and divorces, if applicable to the adoption by a stepparent;

(f) A statement that the petitioner is able to provide for the material needs of the child;

(g) A description and estimate of the value of any property of the person to be adopted;

(h) The case style and date of entry of the judgment terminating parental rights or, if the adoptee is an adult or a minor relative or a stepchild of the petitioner, the address, if known, of any person whose consent to the adoption is required and, if such person has not consented, the facts or circumstances that excuse the lack of consent to justify a termination of parental rights; and

(i) The reasons why the petitioner desires to adopt the person.

(2) The following documents are required to be filed with the clerk of the court at the time the petition is filed:

(a) A certified copy of the court judgment terminating parental rights under chapter 39 or under this chapter or, if the adoptee is an adult or a minor relative or stepchild of the petitioner, the required consent, unless such consent is excused by the court.

(b) The favorable preliminary home study of the department, licensed child-placing agency, or professional pursuant to s. 63.092, as to the suitability of the home in which the minor has been placed, unless the petitioner is a stepparent or a relative.

(c) A copy of any declaratory statement previously entered by the court pursuant to s. 63.102.

(d) Documentation that an interview was held with the minor, if older than 12 years of age, unless the court, in the best interest of the minor, dispenses with the minor's consent under s. 63.062(1)(c).

(3) Unless ordered by the court, no report or recommendation is required when the placement is a stepparent adoption or an adult adoption or when the minor is a relative of one of the adoptive parents.

63.122. Notice of hearing on petition.

(1) The hearing on the petition to adopt a minor may not be held sooner than 30 days after the date the judgment terminating parental rights was entered or sooner than 90 days after the date the minor was placed in the physical custody of the petitioner, unless good cause is shown for a

shortening of these time periods. The minor must remain under the supervision of the adoption entity until the adoption becomes final. When the adoptee is an adult, the hearing may be held immediately after the filing of the petition. If the petitioner is a stepparent or a relative of the adoptee, the hearing may be held immediately after the filing of the petition if all persons whose consent is required have executed a valid consent and the consent has been filed with the court.

(2) Notice of hearing must be given as prescribed by the Florida Rules of Civil Procedure, and service of process must be made as specified by law for civil actions.

(3) Upon a showing by the petitioner or parent that the privacy, safety, or welfare of the petitioner, parent, or minor may be endangered, the court may order that the names of the petitioner, parent, minor, or all be deleted from the notice of hearing and from the copy of the petition attached thereto if the substantive rights of any person are not affected.

(4) Notice of the hearing must be given by the petitioner to the adoption entity that places the minor.

(5) After filing the petition to adopt an adult, the court may order an appropriate investigation to assist in determining whether the adoption is in the best interest of the persons involved and is in accordance with state law.

63.125. Final home investigation.

(1) The final home investigation must be conducted before the adoption becomes final. The investigation may be conducted by a licensed child-placing agency or a professional in the same manner as provided in s. 63.092 to ascertain whether the adoptive home is a suitable home for the minor and whether the proposed adoption is in the best interest of the minor. Unless directed by the court, an investigation and recommendation are not required if the petitioner is a stepparent or if the minor is related to one of the adoptive parents within the third degree of consanguinity. The department is required to perform the home investigation only if there is no licensed child-placing agency or professional pursuant to s. 63.092 in the county in which the prospective adoptive parent resides.

(2) The department, the licensed child-placing agency, or the professional that performs the investigation must file a written report of the investigation with the court and the petitioner within 90 days after placement.

(3) The report of the investigation must contain an evaluation of the placement with a recommendation on the granting of the petition for adoption and any other information the court requires regarding the petitioner or the minor.

(4) The department, the licensed child-placing agency, or the professional making the required investigation may request other state agencies or child-placing agencies within or outside this state to make investigations of designated parts of the inquiry and to make a written report to the department, the professional, or other person or agency.

(5) The final home investigation must include:

(a) The information from the preliminary home study.

(b) After the minor is placed in the intended adoptive home, two scheduled visits with the minor and the minor's adoptive parent or parents, one of which visits must be in the home, to determine the suitability of the placement.

(c) The family social and medical history as provided in s. 63.082.

(d) Any other information relevant to the suitability of the intended adoptive home.

(e) Any other relevant information, as provided in rules that the department may adopt.

63.132. Affidavit of expenses and receipts.

(1) Before the hearing on the petition for adoption, the prospective adoptive parent and any adoption entity must file two copies of an affidavit under this section.

(a) The affidavit must be signed by the adoption entity and the prospective adoptive parents. A copy of the affidavit must be provided to the adoptive parents at the time the affidavit is executed.

(b) The affidavit must itemize all disbursements and receipts of anything of value, including professional and legal fees, made or agreed to be made by or on behalf of the prospective adoptive parent and any adoption entity in connection with the adoption or in connection with any prior proceeding to terminate parental rights which involved the minor who is the subject of the petition for adoption. The affidavit must also include, for each legal or counseling fee itemized, the service provided for which the fee is being charged, the date the service was provided, the time required to provide the service if the service was charged by the hour, the person or entity that provided the service, and the hourly fee charged.

(c) The affidavit must show any expenses or receipts incurred in connection with:

1. The birth of the minor.

2. The placement of the minor with the petitioner.

3. The medical or hospital care received by the mother or by the minor during the mother's prenatal care and confinement.

4. The living expenses of the birth mother. The living expenses must be itemized in detail to apprise the court of the exact expenses incurred.

5. The services relating to the adoption or to the placement of the minor for adoption that were received by or on behalf of the petitioner, the adoption entity, either parent, the minor, or any other person.

(2) The court may require such additional information as is deemed necessary.

(3) The court must issue a separate order approving or disapproving the fees, costs, and expenses itemized in the affidavit. The court may approve only fees, costs, and expenditures allowed under s. 63.097. The court may reject in whole or in part any fee, cost, or expenditure listed if the court finds that the expense is:

(a) Contrary to this chapter;

(b) Not supported by a receipt in the record, if the expense is not a fee of the adoption entity; or

(c) Not a reasonable fee or expense, considering the requirements of this chapter and the totality of the circumstances.

(4) This section does not apply to an adoption by a stepparent or an adoption of a relative or adult, the finalization of an adoption of a minor if the parental rights were terminated under chapter 39, or the domestication of an adoption decree of a minor child adopted in a foreign country.

63.135. Information to be submitted to the court.

(1) The adoption entity or petitioner must file an affidavit under the Uniform Child Custody Jurisdiction and Enforcement Act in the termination of parental rights proceeding in the first pleading or in an affidavit attached to that pleading.

(2) Each party has a continuing duty to inform the court of any custody proceeding concerning the child in this or any other state about which he or she obtained information during this proceeding.

63.142. Hearing; judgment of adoption.

(1) APPEARANCE.—The petitioner and the person to be adopted shall appear either in person or, with the permission of the court, telephonically before a person authorized to administer an oath at the hearing on the petition for adoption, unless:

(a) The person is a minor under 12 years of age; or

(b) The appearance of either is excused by the court for good cause.

(2) CONTINUANCE.—The court may continue the hearing from time to time to permit further observation, investigation, or consideration of any facts or circumstances affecting the granting of the petition.

(3) DISMISSAL.—

(a) If the petition is dismissed, further proceedings, if any, regarding the minor must be brought in a separate custody action under chapter 61, a dependency action under chapter 39, or a paternity action under chapter 742.

(b) If the petition is dismissed, the court shall state with specificity the reasons for the dismissal.

(4) JUDGMENT.—At the conclusion of the hearing, after the court determines that the date for a parent to file an appeal of a valid judgment terminating that parent's parental rights has passed and no appeal, pursuant to the Florida Rules of Appellate Procedure, is pending and that the adoption is in the best interest of the person to be adopted, a judgment of adoption shall be entered. A judgment terminating parental rights pending adoption is voidable and any later judgment of adoption of that minor is voidable if, upon a parent's motion for relief from judgment, the court finds that the adoption substantially fails to meet the requirements of this chapter. The motion must be filed within a reasonable time, but not later than 1 year after the date the judgment terminating parental rights was entered.

63.152. Application for new birth record.

Within 30 days after entry of a judgment of adoption, the clerk of the court or the adoption entity shall transmit a certified statement of the entry to the state registrar of vital statistics on a form provided by the registrar. A new birth record containing the necessary information supplied by the certificate shall be issued by the registrar on application of the adopting parents or the adopted person.

63.162. Hearings and records in adoption proceedings; confidential nature.

(1) All hearings held in proceedings under this act shall be held in closed court without admittance of any person other than essential officers of the court, the parties, witnesses, counsel, persons who have not consented to the adoption and are required to consent, and representatives of the agencies who are present to perform their official duties.

(2) All papers and records pertaining to the adoption, including the original birth certificate, whether part of the permanent record of the court or a file in the office of an adoption entity are confidential and subject to inspection only upon order of the court; however, the petitioner in any proceeding for adoption under this chapter may, at the option of the petitioner, make public the reasons for a denial of the petition for adoption. The order must specify which portion of the records are subject to inspection, and it may exclude the name and identifying information concerning the parent or adoptee. Papers and records of the department, a court, or any other governmental agency, which papers and records relate to adoptions, are exempt from s. 119.07(1). In the case of an adoption not handled by the department or a child-placing agency licensed by the department, the department must be given notice of hearing and be permitted to present to the court a report on the advisability of disclosing or not disclosing information pertaining to the adoption. In the case of an agency adoption, the licensed child-placing agency must be given notice of hearing and be permitted to present to the court a report on the advisability of disclosing or not disclosing information pertaining to the adoption. This subsection does not prohibit the department from inspecting and copying any official record pertaining to the adoption that is

maintained by the department or from inspecting and copying any of the official records maintained by an agency licensed by the department and does not prohibit an agency from inspecting and copying any official record pertaining to the adoption that is maintained by that agency.

(3) The court files, records, and papers in the adoption of a minor shall be indexed only in the name of the petitioner, and the name of the minor shall not be noted on any docket, index, or other record outside the court file, except that closed agency files may be cross-referenced in the original and adoptive names of the minor.

(4) A person may not disclose from the records the name and identity of a birth parent, an adoptive parent, or an adoptee unless:

(a) The birth parent authorizes in writing the release of his or her name;

(b) The adoptee, if 18 or more years of age, authorizes in writing the release of his or her name; or, if the adoptee is less than 18 years of age, written consent to disclose the adoptee's name is obtained from an adoptive parent;

(c) The adoptive parent authorizes in writing the release of his or her name; or

(d) Upon order of the court for good cause shown. In determining whether good cause exists, the court shall give primary consideration to the best interests of the adoptee, but must also give due consideration to the interests of the adoptive and birth parents. Factors to be considered in determining whether good cause exists include, but are not limited to:

1. The reason the information is sought;

2. The existence of means available to obtain the desired information without disclosing the identity of the birth parents, such as by having the court, a person appointed by the court, the department, or the licensed child-placing agency contact the birth parents and request specific information;

3. The desires, to the extent known, of the adoptee, the adoptive parents, and the birth parents;

4. The age, maturity, judgment, and expressed needs of the adoptee; and

5. The recommendation of the department, licensed child-placing agency, or professional which prepared the preliminary study and home investigation, or the department if no such study was prepared, concerning the advisability of disclosure.

(5) The adoptee or other person seeking information under this subsection shall pay the department or agency making reports or recommendations as required hereunder a reasonable fee for its services and expenses.

(6) Subject to the provisions of subsection (4), identifying information regarding the birth parents, adoptive parents, and adoptee may not be disclosed unless a birth parent, adoptive parent, or adoptee has authorized in writing the release of such information concerning himself or herself. Specific names or identifying information must not be given in a family medical history. All nonidentifying information, including the family medical history and social history of the adoptee and the birth parents, when available, must be furnished to the adoptive parents before the adoption becomes final and to the adoptee, upon the adoptee's request, after he or she reaches majority. Upon the request of the adoptive parents, all nonidentifying information obtained before or after the adoption has become final must be furnished to the adoptive parents.

(7) The court may, upon petition of an adult adoptee or birth parent, for good cause shown, appoint an intermediary or a licensed child-placing agency to contact a birth parent or adult adoptee, as applicable, who has not registered with the adoption registry pursuant to s. 63.165 and advise both of the availability of the intermediary or agency and that the birth parent or adult adoptee, as applicable, wishes to establish contact.

63.165. State registry of adoption information; duty to inform and explain.

Notwithstanding any other law to the contrary, the department shall maintain a registry with the last known names and addresses of an adoptee and his or her parents whose consent was required under s. 63.062, and adoptive parents and any other identifying information that the adoptee, parents whose consent was required under s. 63.062, or adoptive parents desire to include in the registry. The department shall maintain the registry records for the time required by rules adopted by the department in accordance with this chapter or for 99 years, whichever period is greater. The registry shall be open with respect to all adoptions in the state, regardless of when they took place. The registry shall be available for those persons choosing to enter information therein, but no one shall be required to do so.

(1) Anyone seeking to enter, change, or use information in the registry, or any agent of such person, shall present verification of his or her identity and, if applicable, his or her authority. A person who enters information in the registry shall be required to indicate clearly the persons to whom he or she is consenting to release this information, which persons shall be limited to the adoptee and the birth mother, father whose consent was required under s. 63.062, adoptive mother, adoptive father, birth siblings, and maternal and paternal birth grandparents of the adoptee. Except as provided in this section, information in the registry is confidential and exempt from s. 119.07(1). Consent to the release of this information may be made in the case of a minor adoptee by his or her adoptive parents or by the court after a showing of good cause. At any time, any person may withdraw, limit, or otherwise restrict consent to release information by notifying the department in writing.

(2) The department may charge a reasonable fee to any person seeking to enter, change, or use information in the registry. The department shall deposit such fees in a trust fund to be used by the department only for the efficient administration of this section. The department and agencies shall make counseling available for a fee to all persons seeking to use the registry, and the department shall inform all affected persons of the availability of such counseling.

(3) The adoption entity must inform the parents before parental rights are terminated, and the adoptive parents before placement, in writing, of the existence and purpose of the registry established under this section, but failure to do so does not affect the validity of any proceeding under this chapter.

63.167. State adoption information center.

(1) The department shall establish a state adoption information center for the purpose of increasing public knowledge about adoption and promoting to adolescents and pregnant women the availability of adoption services. The department shall contract with one or more licensed child-placing agencies to operate the state adoption information center.

(2) The functions of the state adoption information center shall include:

(a) Providing a training program for persons who counsel adolescents, including, but not limited to, school counselors, county child welfare services employees, and family planning clinic employees.

(b) Recruiting adoption services specialist trainees, and providing a training program for such specialists.

(c) Operating a toll-free telephone number to provide information and referral services. The state adoption information center shall provide contact information for all adoption entities in the caller's county or, if no adoption entities are located in the caller's county, the number of the nearest adoption entity when contacted for a referral to make an adoption plan and shall rotate the order in which the names of adoption entities are provided to callers.

(d) Distributing pamphlets which provide information on the availability of adoption services.

(e) Promoting adoption through the communications media.

(f) Maintaining a list of licensed child-placing agencies eligible and willing to take custody of and place newborn infants left at a hospital, pursuant to s. 383.50. The names and contact information for the licensed child-placing agencies on the list shall be provided on a rotating basis to the statewide central abuse hotline.

(3) The department shall ensure equitable distribution of referrals to licensed child-placing agencies.

63.172. Effect of judgment of adoption.

(1) A judgment of adoption, whether entered by a court of this state, another state, or of any other place, has the following effect:

(a) It relieves the birth parents of the adopted person, except a birth parent who is a petitioner or who is married to a petitioner, of all parental rights and responsibilities.

(b) It terminates all legal relationships between the adopted person and the adopted person's relatives, including the birth parents, except a birth parent who is a petitioner or who is married to a petitioner, so that the adopted person thereafter is a stranger to his or her former relatives for all purposes, including the interpretation or construction of documents, statutes, and instruments, whether executed before or after entry of the adoption judgment, that do not expressly include the adopted person by name or by some designation not based on a parent and child or blood relationship, except that rights of inheritance shall be as provided in the Florida Probate Code.

(c) Except for rights of inheritance, it creates the relationship between the adopted person and the petitioner and all relatives of the petitioner that would have existed if the adopted person were a blood descendant of the petitioner born within wedlock. This relationship shall be created for all purposes, including applicability of statutes, documents, and instruments, whether executed before or after entry of the adoption judgment, that do not expressly exclude an adopted person from their operation or effect.

(2) If one or both parents of a child die without the relationship of parent and child having been previously terminated and a spouse of the living parent or a close relative of the child thereafter adopts the child, the child's right of inheritance from or through the deceased parent is unaffected by the adoption and, unless the court orders otherwise, the adoption will not terminate any grandparental rights delineated under chapter 752. For purposes of this subsection, a close relative of a child is the child's brother, sister, grandparent, aunt, or uncle.

63.182. Statute of repose.

(1) Notwithstanding s. 95.031 or s. 95.11 or any other statute, an action or proceeding of any kind to vacate, set aside, or otherwise nullify a judgment of adoption or an underlying judgment terminating parental rights on any ground may not be filed more than 1 year after entry of the judgment terminating parental rights.

(2)(a) Except for the specific persons expressly entitled to be given notice of an adoption in accordance with this chapter, the interest that entitles a person to notice of an adoption must be direct, financial, and immediate, and the person must show that he or she will gain or lose by the direct legal operation and effect of the judgment. A showing of an indirect, inconsequential, or contingent interest is wholly inadequate, and a person with this indirect interest lacks standing to set aside a judgment of adoption.

(b) This subsection is remedial and shall apply to all adoptions, including those in which a judgment of adoption has already been entered.

63.192. Recognition of foreign judgment or decree affecting adoption.

A judgment terminating the relationship of parent and child or establishing the relationship by adoption, or a decree granting legal guardianship for purposes of adoption, issued pursuant to due process of law by a court or authorized body of any other jurisdiction within or without the United States shall be recognized in this state, and the rights and obligations of the parties shall be determined as though the judgment or decree were issued by a court of this state. A judgment or decree of a court or authorized body terminating the relationship of a parent and child, whether independent, incorporated in an adoption decree, or incorporated in a legal guardianship order issued pursuant to due process of law of any other jurisdiction within or without the United States, shall be deemed to effectively terminate parental rights for purposes of a proceeding on a petition for adoption in this state. If a minor child has been made available for adoption in a foreign state or foreign country and the parental rights of the minor child's parent have been terminated or the child has been declared to be abandoned or orphaned, no additional termination of parental rights proceeding need occur, and the adoption may be finalized according to the procedures set forth in this chapter.

63.202. Authority to license; adoption of rules.

(1) The Department of Children and Families is authorized and empowered to license child placement agencies that it determines to be qualified to place minors for adoption.
(2) No agency shall place a minor for adoption unless such agency is licensed by the department, except a child-caring agency registered under s. 409.176.
(3) The department may adopt rules necessary to ensure that all child-placing agencies comply with this chapter to receive or renew a license.

63.207. Out-of-state placement.

(1) Unless the parent placing a minor for adoption files an affidavit that the parent chooses to place the minor outside the state, giving the reason for that placement, or the minor is to be placed with a relative or with a stepparent, or the minor is a special needs child, as defined in s. 409.166, or for other good cause shown, an adoption entity may not:
(a) Take or send a minor out of the state for the purpose of placement for adoption; or
(b) Place or attempt to place a minor for the purpose of adoption with a family who primarily lives and works outside Florida in another state. If an adoption entity is acting under this subsection, the adoption entity must file a petition for declaratory statement pursuant to s. 63.102 for prior approval of fees and costs. The court shall review the costs pursuant to s. 63.097. The petition for declaratory statement must be converted to a petition for an adoption upon placement of the minor in the home. When a minor is placed for adoption with prospective adoptive parents who primarily live and work outside this state, the circuit court in this state may retain jurisdiction over the matter until the adoption becomes final. The prospective adoptive parents may finalize the adoption in this state.
(2) An adoption entity may not counsel a birth mother to leave the state for the purpose of giving birth to a child outside the state in order to secure a fee in excess of that permitted under s. 63.097 when it is the intention that the child is to be placed for adoption outside the state.
(3) When applicable, the Interstate Compact on the Placement of Children authorized in s. 409.401 shall be used in placing children outside the state for adoption.

63.212. Prohibited acts; penalties for violation.

(1) It is unlawful for any person:

(a) To place or attempt to place a minor for adoption with a person who primarily lives and works outside this state unless all of the requirements of the Interstate Compact for the Placement of Children, when applicable, have been met.

(b) Except an adoption entity, to place or attempt to place within the state a minor for adoption unless the minor is placed with a relative or with a stepparent. This prohibition, however, does not apply to a person who is placing or attempting to place a minor for the purpose of adoption with the adoption entity.

(c) To sell or surrender, or to arrange for the sale or surrender of, a minor to another person for money or anything of value or to receive such minor child for such payment or thing of value. If a minor is being adopted by a relative or by a stepparent, or is being adopted through an adoption entity, this paragraph does not prohibit the person who is contemplating adopting the child from paying, under ss. 63.097 and 63.132, the actual prenatal care and living expenses of the mother of the child to be adopted, or from paying, under ss. 63.097 and 63.132, the actual living and medical expenses of such mother for a reasonable time, not to exceed 6 weeks, if medical needs require such support, after the birth of the minor.

(d) Having the rights and duties of a parent with respect to the care and custody of a minor to assign or transfer such parental rights for the purpose of, incidental to, or otherwise connected with, selling or offering to sell such rights and duties.

(e) To assist in the commission of any act prohibited in paragraphs (a)-(d). In the case of a stepparent adoption, this paragraph does not preclude the forgiveness of vested child support arrearages owed by a parent.

(f) Except an adoption entity, to charge or accept any fee or compensation of any nature from anyone for making a referral in connection with an adoption.

(g) Except an adoption entity, to place an advertisement or offer to the public, in any way, by any medium whatever that a minor is available for adoption or that a minor is sought for adoption; and, further, it is unlawful for any person purchasing advertising space or purchasing broadcast time to advertise adoption services to fail to include in any publication or fail to include in the broadcast for such advertisement the Florida license number of the adoption entity or The Florida Bar number of the attorney placing the advertisement.

1. Only a person who is an attorney licensed to practice law in this state or an adoption entity licensed under the laws of this state may place a paid advertisement or paid listing of the person's telephone number, on the person's own behalf, in a telephone directory that:

a. A child is offered or wanted for adoption; or

b. The person is able to place, locate, or receive a child for adoption.

2. A person who publishes a telephone directory that is distributed in this state shall include, at the beginning of any classified heading for adoption and adoption services, a statement that informs directory users that only attorneys licensed to practice law in this state and licensed adoption entities may legally provide adoption services under state law.

3. A person who places an advertisement described in subparagraph 1. in a telephone directory must include the following information:

a. For an attorney licensed to practice law in this state, the person's Florida Bar number.

b. For a child-placing agency licensed under the laws of this state, the number on the person's adoption entity license.

(h) To contract for the purchase, sale, or transfer of custody or parental rights in connection with any child, in connection with any fetus yet unborn, or in connection with any fetus identified in any way but not yet conceived, in return for any valuable consideration. Any such contract is void and unenforceable as against the public policy of this state. However, fees, costs, and other incidental payments made in accordance with statutory provisions for adoption, foster care, and child welfare are permitted, and a person may agree to pay expenses in connection with a preplanned adoption agreement as specified below, but the payment of such expenses may not be conditioned upon the transfer of parental rights. Each petition for adoption which is filed in connection with a preplanned adoption agreement must clearly identify the adoption as a preplanned adoption arrangement and must include a copy of the preplanned adoption agreement for review by the court.

(2) Any person who is a birth mother, or a woman who holds herself out to be a birth mother, who is interested in making an adoption plan and who knowingly or intentionally benefits from the payment of adoption-related expenses in connection with that adoption plan commits adoption deception if:

(a) The person knows or should have known that the person is not pregnant at the time the sums were requested or received;

(b) The person accepts living expenses assistance from a prospective adoptive parent or adoption entity without disclosing that she is receiving living expenses assistance from another prospective adoptive parent or adoption entity at the same time in an effort to adopt the same child; or

(c) The person knowingly makes false representations to induce the payment of living expenses and does not intend to make an adoptive placement.

(3) This section does not prohibit an adoption entity from charging fees permitted under this chapter and reasonably commensurate to the services provided.

(4) It is unlawful for any adoption entity to fail to report to the court, within a reasonable time period, the intended placement of a minor for purposes of adoption with any person not a stepparent or a relative, if the adoption entity participates in such intended placement.

(5) It is unlawful for any adoption entity to charge any fee except those fees permitted under s. 63.097 and approved under s. 63.102.

(6) It is unlawful for any adoption entity to counsel a birth mother to leave the state for the purpose of giving birth to a child outside the state in order to secure a fee in excess of that permitted under s. 63.097 when it is the intention that the child be placed for adoption outside the state.

(7) It is unlawful for any adoption entity to obtain a preliminary home study or final home investigation and fail to disclose the existence of the study or investigation to the court when required by law to do so.

(8) Unless otherwise indicated, a person who willfully and with criminal intent violates any provision of this section, excluding paragraph (1)(g), commits a felony of the third degree, punishable as provided in s. 775.082, s. 775.083, or s. 775.084. A person who willfully and with criminal intent violates paragraph (1)(g) commits a misdemeanor of the second degree, punishable as provided in s. 775.083; and each day of continuing violation shall be considered a separate offense.

63.213. Preplanned adoption agreement.

(1) Individuals may enter into a preplanned adoption arrangement as specified in this section, but such arrangement may not in any way:

(a) Effect final transfer of custody of a child or final adoption of a child without review and approval of the court and without compliance with other applicable provisions of law.

(b) Constitute consent of a mother to place her biological child for adoption until 48 hours after the birth of the child and unless the court making the custody determination or approving the adoption determines that the mother was aware of her right to rescind within the 48-hour period after the birth of the child but chose not to rescind such consent. The volunteer mother's right to rescind her consent in a preplanned adoption applies only when the child is genetically related to her.

(2) A preplanned adoption agreement must include, but need not be limited to, the following terms:

(a) That the volunteer mother agrees to become pregnant by the fertility technique specified in the agreement, to bear the child, and to terminate any parental rights and responsibilities to the child she might have through a written consent executed at the same time as the preplanned adoption agreement, subject to a right of rescission by the volunteer mother any time within 48 hours after the birth of the child, if the volunteer mother is genetically related to the child.

(b) That the volunteer mother agrees to submit to reasonable medical evaluation and treatment and to adhere to reasonable medical instructions about her prenatal health.

(c) That the volunteer mother acknowledges that she is aware that she will assume parental rights and responsibilities for the child born to her as otherwise provided by law for a mother if the intended father and intended mother terminate the agreement before final transfer of custody is completed, if a court determines that a parent clearly specified by the preplanned adoption agreement to be the biological parent is not the biological parent, or if the preplanned adoption is not approved by the court pursuant to the Florida Adoption Act.

(d) That an intended father who is also the biological father acknowledges that he is aware that he will assume parental rights and responsibilities for the child as otherwise provided by law for a father if the agreement is terminated for any reason by any party before final transfer of custody is completed or if the planned adoption is not approved by the court pursuant to the Florida Adoption Act.

(e) That the intended father and intended mother acknowledge that they may not receive custody or the parental rights under the agreement if the volunteer mother terminates the agreement or if the volunteer mother rescinds her consent to place her child for adoption within 48 hours after the birth of the child, if the volunteer mother is genetically related to the child.

(f) That the intended father and intended mother may agree to pay all reasonable legal, medical, psychological, or psychiatric expenses of the volunteer mother related to the preplanned adoption arrangement and may agree to pay the reasonable living expenses and wages lost due to the pregnancy and birth of the volunteer mother and reasonable compensation for inconvenience, discomfort, and medical risk. No other compensation, whether in cash or in kind, shall be made pursuant to a preplanned adoption arrangement.

(g) That the intended father and intended mother agree to accept custody of and to assert full parental rights and responsibilities for the child immediately upon the child's birth, regardless of any impairment to the child.

(h) That the intended father and intended mother shall have the right to specify the blood and tissue typing tests to be performed if the agreement specifies that at least one of them is intended to be the biological parent of the child.

(i) That the agreement may be terminated at any time by any of the parties.

(3) A preplanned adoption agreement shall not contain any provision:

(a) To reduce any amount paid to the volunteer mother if the child is stillborn or is born alive but impaired, or to provide for the payment of a supplement or bonus for any reason.

(b) Requiring the termination of the volunteer mother's pregnancy.

(4) An attorney who represents an intended father and intended mother or any other attorney with whom that attorney is associated shall not represent simultaneously a female who is or proposes to be a volunteer mother in any matter relating to a preplanned adoption agreement or preplanned adoption arrangement.

(5) Payment to agents, finders, and intermediaries, including attorneys and physicians, as a finder's fee for finding volunteer mothers or matching a volunteer mother and intended father and intended mother is prohibited. Doctors, psychologists, attorneys, and other professionals may receive reasonable compensation for their professional services, such as providing medical services and procedures, legal advice in structuring and negotiating a preplanned adoption agreement, or counseling.

(6) As used in this section, the term:

(a) "Blood and tissue typing tests" include, but are not limited to, tests of red cell antigens, red cell isoenzymes, human leukocyte antigens, and serum proteins.

(b) "Child" means the child or children conceived by means of a fertility technique that is part of a preplanned adoption arrangement.

(c) "Fertility technique" means artificial embryonation, artificial insemination, whether in vivo or in vitro, egg donation, or embryo adoption.

(d) "Intended father" means a male who, as evidenced by a preplanned adoption agreement, intends to assert the parental rights and responsibilities for a child conceived through a fertility technique, regardless of whether the child is biologically related to the male.

(e) "Intended mother" means a female who, as evidenced by a preplanned adoption agreement, intends to assert the parental rights and responsibilities for a child conceived through a fertility technique, regardless of whether the child is biologically related to the female.

(f) "Party" means the intended father, the intended mother, the volunteer mother, or the volunteer mother's husband, if she has a husband.

(g) "Preplanned adoption agreement" means a written agreement among the parties that specifies the intent of the parties as to their rights and responsibilities in the preplanned adoption arrangement, consistent with the provisions of this section.

(h) "Preplanned adoption arrangement" means the arrangement through which the parties enter into an agreement for the volunteer mother to bear the child, for payment by the intended father and intended mother of the expenses allowed by this section, for the intended father and intended mother to assert full parental rights and responsibilities to the child if consent to adoption is not rescinded after birth by a volunteer mother who is genetically related to the child, and for the volunteer mother to terminate, subject to any right of rescission, all her parental rights and responsibilities to the child in favor of the intended father and intended mother.

(i) "Volunteer mother" means a female at least 18 years of age who voluntarily agrees, subject to a right of rescission if it is her biological child, that if she should become pregnant pursuant to a preplanned adoption arrangement, she will terminate her parental rights and responsibilities to the child in favor of the intended father and intended mother.

63.219. Sanctions.

Upon a finding by the court that an adoption entity has willfully violated any substantive provision of this chapter relative to the rights of the parties to the adoption and legality of the adoption process, the court is authorized to prohibit the adoption entity from placing a minor for adoption in the future in this state.

63.222. Effect on prior adoption proceedings.

Any adoption made before July 1, 2012, is valid, and any proceedings pending on that date and any subsequent amendments thereto are not affected thereby unless the amendment is designated as a remedial provision.

63.232. Duty of person adopting.

In order to protect the rights of all the parties involved in an adoption, any person adopting or attempting to adopt another person shall comply with the procedures established by this act.

63.2325. Conditions for invalidation of a consent to adoption or affidavit of nonpaternity.

Notwithstanding the requirements of this chapter, a failure to meet any of those requirements does not constitute grounds for invalidation of a consent to adoption or revocation of an affidavit of nonpaternity unless the extent and circumstances of such a failure result in a material failure of fundamental fairness in the administration of due process, or the failure constitutes or contributes to fraud or duress in obtaining a consent to adoption or affidavit of nonpaternity.

63.233. Rulemaking authority.

The department shall adopt rules pursuant to ss. 120.536(1) and 120.54 to implement the provisions of this chapter.

63.235. Petitions filed before effective date; governing law.

Any petition for adoption filed before the effective date of this act shall be governed by the law in effect at the time the petition was filed.

63.236. Petitions filed before July 1, 2008; governing law.

A petition for termination of parental rights filed before July 1, 2008, is governed by the law in effect at the time the petition was filed.

CHAPTER 64. PARTITION OF PROPERTY

64.011. Jurisdiction.

All actions for partition are in chancery.

64.022. Venue.

Partition shall be brought in any county where the lands or any part thereof lie which are the subject matter of the action.

64.031. Parties.

The action may be filed by any one or more of several joint tenants, tenants in common, or coparceners, against their cotenants, coparceners, or others interested in the lands to be divided.

64.041. Complaint.

The complaint shall allege a description of the lands of which partition is demanded, the names and places of residence of the owners, joint tenants, tenants in common, coparceners, or other persons interested in the lands according to the best knowledge and belief of plaintiff, the quantity held by each, and such other matters, if any, as are necessary to enable the court to adjudicate the rights and interests of the party. If the names, residence or quantity of interest of any owner or claimant is unknown to plaintiff, this shall be stated. If the name is unknown, the action may proceed as though such unknown persons were named in the complaint.

64.051. Judgment.

The court shall adjudge the rights and interests of the parties, and that partition be made if it appears that the parties are entitled to it. When the rights and interests of plaintiffs are established or are undisputed, the court may order partition to be made, and the interest of plaintiffs and such of the defendants as have established their interest to be allotted to them, leaving for future adjustment in the same action the interest of any other defendants.

64.061. Commissioners; special magistrate.

(1) APPOINTMENT AND REMOVAL.—When a judgment of partition is made, the court shall appoint three suitable persons as commissioners to make the partition. They shall be selected by the court unless agreed on by the parties. They may be removed by the court for good cause and others appointed in their places.
(2) POWERS, DUTIES, COMPENSATION AND REPORT OF COMMISSIONERS.—The commissioners shall be sworn to execute the trust imposed in them faithfully and impartially before entering on their duties; have power to employ a surveyor, if necessary, for the purpose of making partition; be allowed such sum as is reasonable for their services; to make partition of the lands in question according to the court's order and report it in writing to the court without delay.
(3) EXCEPTIONS TO REPORT AND FINAL JUDGMENT.—Any party may file objections to the report of the commissioners within 10 days after it is served. If no objections are filed or if the court is satisfied on hearing any such objections that they are not well-founded, the report shall be confirmed, and a final judgment entered vesting in the parties the title to the parcels of the lands allotted to them respectively, and giving each of them the possession of and quieting title to their respective shares as against the other parties to the action or those claiming through or under them.
(4) APPOINTMENT OF SPECIAL MAGISTRATE WHERE PROPERTY NOT SUBJECT TO PARTITION.—On an uncontested allegation in a pleading that the property sought to be partitioned is indivisible and is not subject to partition without prejudice to the owners of it or if a judgment of partition is entered and the court is satisfied that the allegation is correct, on motion of any party and notice to the others the court may appoint a special magistrate or the clerk to make sale of the property either at private sale or as provided by s. 64.071.

64.071. Sale where nondivisible.

(1) ORDER OF SALE.—If the commissioners report that the lands of which partition is directed

are so situated that partition cannot be made without prejudice to the owners and if the court is satisfied that such report is correct, the court may order the land to be sold at public auction to the highest bidder by the commissioners or the clerk and the money arising from such sale paid into the court to be divided among the parties in proportion to their interest.

(2) CONDITIONS OF SALE.—For good cause the court may order the sale made on reasonable credit for part or all of the purchase money, but at least one-third of the purchase money shall be paid down unless all parties consent to credit otherwise. The purchase money not paid down shall be secured by a mortgage on the land and such other security as the court directs.

(3) CONFIRMATION OF SALE AND CONVEYANCE.—The sale shall be reported to the court, unless sold by the clerk under s. 45.031, and the money arising therefrom paid into court and the sale approved by the court and a conveyance ordered before any conveyance pursuant to the sale is made.

64.081. Costs; taxes; attorneys' fees.

Every party shall be bound by the judgment to pay a share of the costs, including attorneys' fees to plaintiff's or defendant's attorneys or to each of them commensurate with their services rendered and of benefit to the partition, to be determined on equitable principles in proportion to the party's interest. Such judgment is binding on all his or her goods and chattels, lands, or tenements. In case of sale the court may order the costs and fees to be paid or retained out of the moneys arising from the sale and due to the parties who ought to pay the same. All taxes, state, county, and municipal, due thereon at the time of the sale, shall be paid out of the purchase money.

64.091. Personalty.

The laws applicable to partition and sale for partition of real estate are applicable to the partition and sale for partition of personal property and the proceedings therefor, as far as the nature of the property permits.

CHAPTER 65. QUIETING TITLE

65.011. Real estate; certain jurisdiction over.

Chancery courts have jurisdiction of actions by any person or corporation claiming to own any land or part thereof, or by two or more claiming to own the same land or part thereof under a common title against more than one person or corporation occupying or claiming title to the land or part thereof adversely to plaintiff, whether defendants claim or hold under a common title or not; and shall determine the title of plaintiff as against defendants and enter judgment quieting the title of, and awarding possession to, the plaintiff entitled thereto and may enter injunctions, temporary or perpetual, appoint receivers, and enter such orders about costs as are necessary to protect the rights of the parties.

65.021. Real estate; removing clouds.

Chancery courts have jurisdiction of actions brought by any person or corporation, whether in actual possession or not, claiming legal or equitable title to land against any person or corporation not in actual possession, who has, appears to have or claims an adverse legal or equitable estate, interest, or claim therein to determine such estate, interest, or claim and quiet or remove clouds from the title to the land. It is no bar to relief that the title has not been litigated at law or that there is only one litigant to each side of the controversy or that the adverse claim, estate, or interest is void upon its face, or though not void on its face, requires extrinsic evidence to establish its validity.

65.031. Real estate; removing clouds; plaintiffs.

An action in chancery for quieting title to, or clearing a cloud from, land may be maintained in the name of the owner or of any prior owner who warranted the title. All lands, the title to which is subject to a common defect, may be embraced in one action irrespective of the number of existing legal or equitable owners.

65.041. Real estate; removing clouds; defendants.

No person not a party to the action is bound by any judgment rendered adverse to his or her interest, but any judgment favorable to the person inures to that person's benefit to the extent of his or her legal or equitable title.

65.051. Real estate; removing clouds; joinder.

Two or more persons who are interested in removing a cloud from or quieting title to land as against the same clouds or adverse claims may join as plaintiffs in a single action to remove such clouds or quiet the title, although their interests relate to separate lands or parts thereof.

65.061. Quieting title; additional remedy.

(1) JURISDICTION.—Chancery courts have jurisdiction of actions by any person or corporation claiming legal or equitable title to any land, or part thereof, or when any two or more persons claim to own the same land, or any part thereof under a common title against all persons or corporations claiming title to or occupying the land adversely to plaintiff, whether defendants claim or hold under a common title or not, and shall determine the title of plaintiff and may enter judgment quieting the title and awarding possession to the party entitled thereto, but if any defendant is in actual possession of any part of the land, a trial by jury may be demanded by any party, whereupon the court shall order an issue in ejectment as to such lands to be made and tried by a jury. Provision for trial by jury does not affect the action on any lands that are not claimed to be in the actual possession of any defendant. The court may enter final judgment without awaiting the determination of the ejectment action.
(2) GROUNDS.—When a person or corporation not the rightful owner of land has any conveyance or other evidence of title thereto, or asserts any claim, or pretends to have any right or title thereto, which may cast a cloud on the title of the real owner, or when any person or corporation is the true and equitable owner of land the record title to which is not in the person or corporation because of the defective execution of any deed or mortgage because of the omission of a seal thereon, the lack of witnesses, or any defect or omission in the wording of the

acknowledgment of a party or parties thereto, when the person or corporation claims title thereto by the defective instrument and the defective instrument was apparently made and delivered by the grantor to convey or mortgage the real estate and was recorded in the county where the land lies, or when possession of the land has been held by any person or corporation adverse to the record owner thereof or his or her heirs and assigns until such adverse possession has ripened into a good title under the statutes of this state, such person or corporation may file complaint in any county in which any part of the land is situated to have the conveyance or other evidence of claim or title canceled and the cloud removed from the title and to have his or her title quieted, whether such real owner is in possession or not or is threatened to be disturbed in his or her possession or not, and whether defendant is a resident of this state or not, and whether the title has been litigated at law or not, and whether the adverse claim or title or interest is void on its face or not, or if not void on its face that it may require extrinsic evidence to establish its validity. A guardian ad litem shall not be appointed unless it shall affirmatively appear that the interest of minors, persons of unsound mind, or convicts are involved.

(3) DERAIGNMENT OF TITLE.—The plaintiff shall deraign his or her title from the original source or for a period of at least 7 years before filing the complaint unless the court otherwise directs, setting forth the book and page of the records where any instrument affecting the title is recorded, if it is recorded, unless plaintiff claims from a common source with defendant.

(4) JUDGMENT.—If it appears that plaintiff has legal title to the land or is the equitable owner thereof based on one or more of the grounds mentioned in subsection (2), or if a default is entered against defendant (in which case no evidence need be taken), the court shall enter judgment removing the alleged cloud from the title to the land and forever quieting the title in plaintiff and those claiming under him or her since the commencement of the action and adjudging plaintiff to have a good fee simple title to said land or the interest thereby cleared of cloud.

(5) RECORDING FINAL JUDGMENTS.—All final judgments may be recorded in the county or counties in which the land is situated and operate to vest title in like manner as though a conveyance were executed by a special magistrate or commissioner.

(6) OPERATION.—This section is cumulative to other existing remedies.

65.071. Quieting title; deeds without joinder of wife when separated for 30 years.

An action in chancery may be brought to quiet title to land to preclude any wife from claiming dower or any heirs from claiming any interest to land when the following facts exist:

(1) When any husband and wife have not cohabited as husband and wife for 30 years or more and during this time the husband has conveyed land as a single man and the land has come into the hands of purchasers for a valuable consideration without notice that the husband was married at the time he conveyed the land, and the purchasers have relied on the acknowledgment to deeds by the husband that he was a single man, and it afterwards became known that he was a married man at the time he deeded the land and his marriage has never been dissolved and he refuses to voluntarily get a dissolution of marriage to clear the title to preclude his wife from claiming any inchoate dower therein and his heirs from claiming any interest therein and when the wife has never lived in the county where the land is located with the husband as his wife and has never asserted any inchoate right to dower in the land, the inchoate right to dower is divested and is a cloud on the title to the land and the purchaser of the land has the right to remove the cloud and to prevent the wife or heirs from claiming any dower or other interest from such purchasers and their successors in title.

(2) When these facts are proven, the court shall adjudge that the wife and heirs of the husband are forever barred and perpetually enjoined from claiming any interest in the land arising out of dower or otherwise, and that the wife did not join in the execution of the deeds by which the husband

deeded the land as a single man under the facts above-stated is not effective to reserve an inchoate right of dower in the land held by such purchasers.

65.081. Tax titles; quieting title.

(1) PARTIES.—Any grantee under any tax deed issued by the state, or any municipality or other political subdivision thereof, or any purchaser from the state, or any municipality or other political subdivision thereof, of any land the title to which has been acquired by this state or such municipality or political subdivision through any proceeding or foreclosure for the nonpayment of taxes or special assessments, or the successor in title to the grantee or purchaser, may maintain an action in chancery to quiet title to the land included in the tax deed, or so purchased against the holder of the record title to the land, and against any other person or corporation claiming any interest in the land or any lien or encumbrance thereon, before issuance of the tax deed or before the loss of title to the land in the tax proceeding or foreclosure.

(2) DERAIGNING TITLE.—Actions may be maintained hereunder whether or not plaintiff is in possession of the land involved but when defendant is in actual possession of the land a jury trial may be had as provided in other actions to quiet title. When the action is based on a tax deed, the complaint need not deraign title beyond the issuance of the tax deed. When the action is based on a conveyance by this state, or any municipality or other political subdivision thereof, of land the title to which it has acquired through a foreclosure or other proceeding for the nonpayment of taxes, the complaint need not deraign title beyond the deed or other instrument or act vesting title in the state or municipality or other political subdivision of the state.

(3) WHEN TAXES HAVE BEEN PAID.—No defense to the action or attack upon the tax deed shall be made except the defense that the taxes assessed against the property had been paid by the former owner before issuance of the tax deed.

(4) WHEN TAX DEED HAS BEEN ISSUED BEFORE CONVEYANCE BY SOVEREIGN.— No defense shall be made to the action because of assessment of the property or issuance of the tax deed before the United States or the state has parted with title to the property, and no other attack shall be made on it, except the defense that the taxes assessed against the property had been paid by the person, or a claimant under him or her, to whom the United States patent or conveyance from the state was issued before the issuance of the tax deed.

CHAPTER 66. EJECTMENT

66.011. Common-law ejectment abolished.

In ejectment it is not necessary to have any fictitious parties. Plaintiff may bring action directly against the party in possession or claiming adversely.

66.021. Procedure.

(1) LANDLORD NOT A DEFENDANT.—When it appears before trial that a defendant in ejectment is in possession as a tenant and that his or her landlord is not a party, the landlord shall be made a party before further proceeding unless otherwise ordered by the court.

(2) DEFENSE MAY BE LIMITED.—A defendant in an action of ejectment may limit his or her defense to a part of the property mentioned in the complaint, describing such part with reasonable

certainty.

(3) WRIT OF POSSESSION; EXECUTION TO BE JOINT OR SEVERAL.—When plaintiff recovers in ejectment, he or she may have one writ for possession, damages and costs or, if the plaintiff elects, have separate writs for possession and damages.

(4) CHAIN OF TITLE.—Plaintiff with his or her complaint and defendant with his or her answer shall serve a statement setting forth chronologically the chain of title on which he or she will rely at trial. If any part of the chain of title is recorded, the statement shall set forth the names of the grantors and the grantees and the book and page of the record thereof; if an unrecorded instrument is relied on, a copy shall be attached. The court may require the original to be submitted to the opposite party for inspection. If the party relies on a claim or right without color of title, the statement shall specify how and when the claim originated and the facts on which the claim is based. If defendant and plaintiff claim under a common source, the statement need not deraign title before the common source.

(5) TESTING SUFFICIENCY.—If either party wants to test the legal sufficiency of any instrument or court proceeding in the chain of title of the opposite party, the party shall do so before trial by motion setting up his or her objections with a copy of the instrument or court proceedings attached. The motion shall be disposed of before trial. If either party determines that he or she will be unable to maintain his or her claim by reason of the order, that party may so state in the record and final judgment shall be entered for the opposite party.

66.031. Verdict and judgment.

(1) VERDICT.—A verdict for plaintiff shall state the quantity of the estate of plaintiff, and describe the land by metes and bounds, lot number or other certain description.

(2) JUDGMENT.—The judgment awarding possession shall state the quantity of the estate and give a description of the land recovered in like manner.

66.041. Betterment, petition.

If a judgment of eviction is rendered against defendant, within 60 days thereafter, or if he or she has appealed, within 20 days after filing the mandate affirming the judgment, defendant may file in the court in which the judgment was rendered a petition setting forth that:

(1) Defendant had been in possession and that he or she or those under whom defendant validly derived had permanently improved the value of the property in controversy before commencement of the action in which judgment was rendered;

(2) Defendant or those under whom defendant validly derives held the property at the time of such improvement under an apparently good legal or equitable title derived from the English, Spanish, or United States Governments or this state; or under a legal or equitable title plain and connected on the records of a public office or public offices; or under purchase at a regular sale made by an executor, administrator, guardian or other person by order of court; and

(3) When defendant made the improvements or purchased the property improved, he or she believed the title which he or she held or purchased to the land thus improved to be a good and valid title. The petition shall demand that the value of the improvements be assessed and compensation awarded to defendant therefor.

66.051. Betterment, answer.

The plaintiff in the judgment of eviction may file written defenses to the petition within 20 days after service of the petition.

66.061. Betterment, trial and verdict.

If an answer is filed, trial shall be on the issues made. If no answer is filed, trial shall be ex parte, but defendant is required to prove every allegation of the petition. If the jury (or if a jury is waived, the court) finds in favor of defendant, it shall assess:
(1) The value of the land at the time of the assessment, irrespective of the improvements put upon the land by defendant or those under whom he or she derives, and if any, the injury done to the land by defendant or those under whom he or she derives.
(2) The value of the permanent improvements at the time of the assessment.
(3) The injury, if any, done to the land by defendant or those under whom he or she derives.
(4) The value of the use of the land by defendant between the time of the judgment in ejectment and the time of the assessment or if defendant has been evicted from or has surrendered the premises, from the time of the judgment to the time of the surrender or eviction. The findings shall be specified separately on each of these matters.

66.071. Betterment, judgment for plaintiff.

On rendition of the verdict the clerk shall ascertain whether the balance of the last three assessments (that is, of the value of the improvements, the extent of the injury and the value of the use of land), is in favor of plaintiff or defendant and ascertain the amount of the balance; if the verdict is in favor of plaintiff, judgment shall be rendered against defendant for costs, whether the balance of the assessments is in favor of plaintiff or defendant; but if the balance of the assessments is in favor of plaintiff, he or she shall have a judgment for costs in addition to the judgment for the balance.

66.081. Betterment, judgment for defendant.

If the verdict is in favor of defendant and the balance of assessments is also in defendant's favor, a judgment for costs shall be entered against plaintiff, and a further judgment that unless plaintiff pays or secures as hereinafter provided the amount of the balance of assessments against him or her within 20 days, defendant may pay or secure to plaintiff the value of the land as assessed.

66.091. Betterment, payment by plaintiff.

The plaintiff may pay the balance in cash or may give defendant a bond with surety to be approved by the clerk, conditioned to pay said balance in two equal annual installments, with interest at 6 percent per annum to defendant. If plaintiff shall pay the sum within 20 days, or if the payment of the bond is received, satisfaction of the judgment shall be entered and all rights conferred on defendant by the judgment terminate.

66.101. Betterment, payment by defendant.

If plaintiff does not pay or secure the sum within 20 days, within 20 days thereafter defendant may pay to plaintiff the value of the land as assessed or give plaintiff a bond with surety, to be approved by the clerk, conditioned to pay plaintiff the value in two equal annual installments, with 6 percent interest; or if plaintiff fails to pay the bond given by him or her when it becomes due, for 20 days after the expiration of the time fixed in the bond for payment, defendant shall again have the privilege of paying to plaintiff in cash the value of the land assessed. On the payment of the sum to plaintiff at any of the times hereinbefore mentioned, title to the land shall vest in defendant and plaintiff or those holding under him or her shall give defendant a deed to the land, tenements, hereditaments, and appurtenances, and if defendant has been evicted from or has surrendered the property, it shall be restored to him or her by order of court on motion.

CHAPTER 68. MISCELLANEOUS PROCEEDINGS

68.01. Declaring tax assessment invalid.

When an assessment is made against any person, body politic or corporate and payment is refused on an allegation of illegality of the assessment, the person, body corporate or politic may file an action in chancery setting forth the alleged illegality. The court has jurisdiction to decide the matter and if the assessment is illegal, shall declare the assessment not lawfully made.

68.02. Ne exeat.

(1) WHEN TO ISSUE.—No writ of ne exeat shall be granted until a verified complaint is filed demanding the writ. It may issue in any case in equity, including support as defined in s. 409.2554, when the issuance is just.
(2) JUDGE TO FIX PENALTY OF BOND.—In granting the writ the court shall fix the penalty and conditions of the bond with surety to be approved by the clerk to be required of plaintiff in favor of defendant. The writ shall not issue until the bond is given.
(3) ABSENCE FROM STATE UNDER CERTAIN CONDITIONS PERMITTED.—An absence of the defendant from the state from which he or she returns before a personal appearance is necessary or before it is necessary to perform any order of the court is not a breach of the condition of the bond.
(4) SURRENDER OF DEFENDANT BY SURETIES.—The surety of defendant has the right personally or by attorney at any time before the bond is forfeited to take the body of the principal and surrender him or her in open court or deliver him or her to the executive officer of the court, who shall detain the principal as in cases of the surrender of the principal by special bail. At the time of delivery to the officer, the surety shall take a receipt for the body and file it with the clerk. If done before the bond is forfeited, the surrender or delivery discharges the surety from his or her undertaking.

68.03. Sequestration; proceedings prescribed.

(1) If any action is commenced in chancery against any defendant residing out of this state and any other defendant within the state has in his or her hands effects of, or is otherwise indebted to, the absent defendant and the absentee does not appear in the action and give security to the satisfaction of the court for performing the judgment and on affidavit that the absentee is out of the state, or that on inquiry at the absentee's usual place of abode he or she cannot be found to be

served with process, the court may restrain the defendant in this state from paying or conveying or secreting the debts owing by him or her to, or the effects in his or her hands of, the absentee or restrain the absentee from conveying or secreting or removing the property in litigation, or may sequestrate the property which may be necessary to secure plaintiff if he or she prevails, and may order such debts to be paid and effects to be delivered to plaintiff on his or her giving bond with surety for the return thereof.

(2) The court shall require the plaintiff to give bond with surety to be approved by the clerk, to abide the future orders made for restoring the estate or effects to the absent defendant on his or her appearance in the action. If the plaintiff does not furnish the bond, the effects shall remain under the direction of the court or in the hands of a receiver or otherwise for so long a time and shall be disposed of in such manner as the court deems fit.

68.04. Chancery jurisdiction over liens.

All liens of any kind, whether created by statute or the common law, and whether heretofore regarded as merely possessory or not, may be enforced in chancery.

68.05. Creditors' bills.

Creditors' bills may be filed in chancery before the claims of indebtedness of the persons filing them have been reduced to judgment, but no such action shall be entertained unless plaintiff has first commenced a separate action at law for the collection of the claims. No final judgment shall be entered on a creditor's bill until such claims have been reduced to judgment at law.

68.06. Actions upon negotiable and other instruments; consideration, etc.

All bonds, notes, covenants, deeds, bills of exchange, and other written instruments not under seal have the same force and effect (so far as the rules of pleading and evidence are concerned) as bonds and instruments under seal. The assignment or endorsement of any instrument vests the assignee or endorsee with the same rights, powers, and capacities as were possessed by the assignor or endorser. The assignee or endorsee may bring action thereon. It is not necessary for the plaintiff in any action on an instrument assignable by law to allege the consideration on which the instrument was given or on which the assignment or endorsement was made nor to prove the consideration or the execution of the instrument, unless it is denied by the defendant under oath. An executor or administrator may deny the execution or consideration by answer not under oath.

68.065. Actions to collect worthless payment instruments; attorney fees and collection costs.

(1) As used in this section, the term "payment instrument" or "instrument" means a check, draft, order of payment, debit card order, or electronic funds transfer.

(2) In lieu of a service charge authorized under subsection (3), s. 832.062(4)(a), or s. 832.07, the payee of a payment instrument, the payment of which is refused by the drawee because of lack of funds, lack of credit, or lack of an account, or where the maker or drawer stops payment on the

instrument with intent to defraud, may lawfully collect bank fees actually incurred by the payee in the course of tendering the payment, plus a service charge of $25 if the face value does not exceed $50; $30 if the face value exceeds $50 but does not exceed $300; $40 if the face value exceeds $300; or 5 percent of the face value of the payment instrument, whichever is greater. The right to damages under this subsection may be claimed without the filing of a civil action.

(3)(a) In any civil action brought for the purpose of collecting a payment instrument, the payment of which is refused by the drawee because of lack of funds, lack of credit, or lack of an account, or where the maker or drawer stops payment on the instrument with intent to defraud, and where the maker or drawer fails to pay the amount owing, in cash, to the payee within 30 days after a written demand therefor, as provided in subsection (4), the maker or drawer is liable to the payee, in addition to the amount owing upon such payment instrument, for damages of triple the amount so owing. However, in no case shall the liability for damages be less than $50. The maker or drawer is also liable for any court costs and reasonable attorney fees incurred by the payee in taking the action. Criminal sanctions, as provided in s. 832.07, may be applicable.

(b) The payee may also charge the maker or drawer of the payment instrument a service charge not to exceed the service fees authorized under s. 832.08(5) or 5 percent of the face amount of the instrument, whichever is greater, when making written demand for payment. In the event that a judgment or decree is rendered, interest at the rate and in the manner described in s. 55.03 may be added toward the total amount due. Any bank fees incurred by the payee may be charged to the maker or drawer of the payment instrument.

(4) Before recovery under subsection (3) may be claimed, a written demand must be delivered by certified or registered mail, evidenced by return receipt, or by first-class mail, evidenced by an affidavit of service of mail, to the maker or drawer of the payment instrument to the address on the instrument, to the address given by the drawer at the time the instrument was issued, or to the drawer's last known address. The form of such notice shall be substantially as follows:

(5) A subsequent person receiving a payment instrument from the original payee or a successor endorsee has the same rights that the original payee has against the maker of the instrument, if such subsequent person gives notice in a substantially similar form to that provided in subsection (4). A subsequent person providing such notice is immune from civil liability for the giving of such notice and for proceeding under the forms of such notice, so long as the maker of the instrument has the same defenses against the subsequent person as against the original payee. However, the remedies available under this section may be exercised only by one party in interest.

(6) After commencement of the action but before the hearing, the maker or drawer may tender to the payee, as satisfaction of the claim, an amount of money equal to the sum of the payment instrument, the service charge, court costs, and incurred bank fees. Other provisions notwithstanding, the maker or drawer is liable to the payee for all attorney fees and collection costs incurred by payee as a result of the payee's claim.

(7) If the court or jury determines that the failure of the maker or drawer to satisfy the dishonored payment instrument was due to economic hardship, the court or jury has the discretion to waive all or part of the statutory damages.

68.07. Change of name.

(1) Chancery courts have jurisdiction to change the name of any person residing in this state on petition of the person filed in the county in which he or she resides.

(2)(a) Before the court hearing on a petition for a name change, the petitioner must have fingerprints submitted for a state and national criminal history records check, except if a former name is being restored. Fingerprints for the petitioner shall be taken in a manner approved by the Department of Law Enforcement and shall be submitted electronically to the department for state processing for a criminal history records check. The department shall submit the fingerprints to the Federal Bureau of Investigation for national processing. The department shall submit the results of the state and national records check, which must indicate whether the petitioner has registered as a sexual predator or a sexual offender, to the clerk of the court. The court shall consider the results in reviewing the information contained in the petition and evaluating whether to grant the petition.

(b) When a petition is filed which requires a criminal history records check, the clerk of the court shall instruct the petitioner on the process for having fingerprints taken and submitted, including providing information on law enforcement agencies or service providers authorized to submit fingerprints electronically to the Department of Law Enforcement.

(c) The cost of processing fingerprints and conducting the state and national criminal history records check required under this subsection shall be borne by the petitioner for the name change or by the parent or guardian of a minor for whom a name change is being sought.

(3) Each petition shall be verified and show:

(a) That the petitioner is a bona fide resident of and domiciled in the county where the change of name is sought.

(b) If known, the date and place of birth of the petitioner, the petitioner's father's name, the petitioner's mother's maiden name, and where the petitioner has resided since birth.

(c) If the petitioner is married, the name of the petitioner's spouse and if the petitioner has children, the names and ages of each and where they reside.

(d) If the petitioner's name has previously been changed and when and where and by what court.

(e) The petitioner's occupation and where the petitioner is employed and has been employed for 5 years next preceding the filing of the petition. If the petitioner owns and operates a business, the name and place of it shall be stated and the petitioner's connection therewith and how long the petitioner has been identified with that business. If the petitioner is in a profession, the profession shall be stated, where the petitioner has practiced the profession, and if a graduate of a school or schools, the name or names thereof, date of graduation, and degrees received.

(f) Whether the petitioner has been generally known or called by any other names and if so, by what names and where.

(g) Whether the petitioner has ever been adjudicated a bankrupt and if so, where and when.

(h) Whether the petitioner has ever been arrested for or charged with, pled guilty or nolo contendere to, or been found to have committed a criminal offense, regardless of adjudication, and if so, when and where.

(i) Whether the petitioner has ever been required to register as a sexual predator under s. 775.21 or as a sexual offender under s. 943.0435.

(j) Whether any money judgment has ever been entered against the petitioner and if so, the name of the judgment creditor, the amount and date thereof, the court by which entered, and whether the judgment has been satisfied.

(k) That the petition is filed for no ulterior or illegal purpose and granting it will not in any manner invade the property rights of others, whether partnership, patent, good will, privacy, trademark, or otherwise.

(l) That the petitioner's civil rights have never been suspended or, if the petitioner's civil rights have been suspended, that full restoration of civil rights has occurred.

(4) The hearing on a petition for restoring a former name may be held immediately after it is filed. The hearing on any other petition for a name change may be held immediately after the clerk receives the results of the criminal history records check.

(5) On filing the final judgment, the clerk of the court shall, if the birth occurred in this state, send a report of the judgment to the Office of Vital Statistics of the Department of Health on a form to be furnished by the department. The form must contain sufficient information to identify the original birth certificate of the person, the new name, and the file number of the judgment. This report shall be filed by the department with respect to a person born in this state and shall become a part of the vital statistics of this state. With respect to a person born in another state, the clerk of the court shall provide the petitioner with a certified copy of the final judgment.

(6) The clerk of the court must, within 5 business days after the filing of the final judgment, send a report of the judgment to the Department of Law Enforcement on a form to be furnished by that department. If the petitioner is required to register as a sexual predator or a sexual offender

pursuant to s. 775.21 or s. 943.0435, the clerk of court shall electronically notify the Department of Law Enforcement of the name change, in a manner prescribed by that department, within 2 business days after the filing of the final judgment. The Department of Law Enforcement must send a copy of the report to the Department of Highway Safety and Motor Vehicles, which may be delivered by electronic transmission. The report must contain sufficient information to identify the petitioner, including the results of the criminal history records check if applicable, the new name of the petitioner, and the file number of the judgment. The Department of Highway Safety and Motor Vehicles shall monitor the records of any sexual predator or sexual offender whose name has been provided to it by the Department of Law Enforcement. If the sexual predator or sexual offender does not obtain a replacement driver license or identification card within the required time as specified in s. 775.21 or s. 943.0435, the Department of Highway Safety and Motor Vehicles shall notify the Department of Law Enforcement. The Department of Law Enforcement shall notify applicable law enforcement agencies of the predator's or offender's failure to comply with registration requirements. Any information retained by the Department of Law Enforcement and the Department of Highway Safety and Motor Vehicles may be revised or supplemented by said departments to reflect changes made by the final judgment. With respect to a person convicted of a felony in another state or of a federal offense, the Department of Law Enforcement must send the report to the respective state's office of law enforcement records or to the office of the Federal Bureau of Investigation. The Department of Law Enforcement may forward the report to any other law enforcement agency it believes may retain information related to the petitioner.

(7) A husband and wife and minor children may join in one petition for change of name and the petition must show the facts required of a petitioner as to the husband and wife and the names of the minor children may be changed at the discretion of the court.

(8) When only one parent petitions for a change of name of a minor child, process shall be served on the other parent and proof of such service shall be filed in the cause; however, if the other parent is a nonresident, constructive notice of the petition may be given pursuant to chapter 49, and proof of publication shall be filed in the cause without the necessity of recordation.

(9) This section does not apply to any change of name in proceedings for dissolution of marriage or for adoption of children.

68.081. Florida False Claims Act; short title.

Sections 68.081-68.092 may be cited as the "Florida False Claims Act."

68.082. False claims against the state; definitions; liability.

(1) As used in this section, the term:

(a) "Claim" means any request or demand, whether under a contract or otherwise, for money or property, regardless of whether the state has title to the money or property, that:

1. Is presented to any employee, officer, or agent of the state; or

2. Is made to a contractor, grantee, or other recipient if the state provides or has provided any portion of the money or property requested or demanded, or if the state will reimburse the contractor, grantee, or other recipient for any portion of the money or property that is requested or demanded.

(b) "Department" means the Department of Legal Affairs, except as specifically provided in ss. 68.083 and 68.084.

(c) "Knowing" or "knowingly" means, with respect to information, that a person:

1. Has actual knowledge of the information;

2. Acts in deliberate ignorance of the truth or falsity of the information; or

3. Acts in reckless disregard of the truth or falsity of the information.

(d) "Material" means having a natural tendency to influence, or be capable of influencing, the payment or receipt of money or property.

(e) "Obligation" means an established duty, fixed or otherwise, arising from an express or implied contractual, grantor-grantee, or licensor-licensee relationship, from a fee-based or similar relationship, from statute or regulation, or from the retention of any overpayment.

(f) "State" means the government of the state or any department, division, bureau, commission, regional planning agency, board, district, authority, agency, or other instrumentality of the state.

(2) Any person who:

(a) Knowingly presents or causes to be presented a false or fraudulent claim for payment or approval;

(b) Knowingly makes, uses, or causes to be made or used a false record or statement material to a false or fraudulent claim;

(c) Conspires to commit a violation of this subsection;

(d) Has possession, custody, or control of property or money used or to be used by the state and knowingly delivers or causes to be delivered less than all of that money or property;

(e) Is authorized to make or deliver a document certifying receipt of property used or to be used by the state and, intending to defraud the state, makes or delivers the receipt without knowing that the information on the receipt is true;

(f) Knowingly buys or receives, as a pledge of an obligation or a debt, public property from an officer or employee of the state who may not sell or pledge the property; or

(g) Knowingly makes, uses, or causes to be made or used a false record or statement material to an obligation to pay or transmit money or property to the state, or knowingly conceals or knowingly and improperly avoids or decreases an obligation to pay or transmit money or property to the state

(3) The court may reduce the treble damages authorized under subsection (2) if the court finds one or more of the following specific extenuating circumstances:

(a) The person committing the violation furnished the department with all information known to the person about the violation within 30 days after the date on which the person first obtained the information;

(b) The person fully cooperated with any official investigation of the violation; or

(c) At the time the person furnished the department with the information about the violation, no criminal prosecution, civil action, or administrative action had commenced under this section with respect to the violation, and the person did not have actual knowledge of the existence of an investigation into the violation;

68.083. Civil actions for false claims.

(1) The department may diligently investigate a violation under s. 68.082. If the department finds that a person has violated or is violating s. 68.082, the department may bring a civil action under the Florida False Claims Act against the person. The Department of Financial Services may bring a civil action under this section if the action arises from an investigation by that department and the Department of Legal Affairs has not filed an action under this act.

(2) A person may bring a civil action for a violation of s. 68.082 for the person and for the affected agency. Civil actions instituted under this act shall be governed by the Florida Rules of Civil Procedure and shall be brought in the name of the State of Florida. Prior to the court unsealing the complaint under subsection (3), the action may be voluntarily dismissed by the person bringing the action only if the department gives written consent to the dismissal and its reasons for such consent.

(3) The complaint shall be identified on its face as a qui tam action and shall be filed in the circuit court of the Second Judicial Circuit, in and for Leon County. Immediately upon the filing of the

complaint, a copy of the complaint and written disclosure of substantially all material evidence and information the person possesses shall be served on the Attorney General, as head of the department, and on the Chief Financial Officer, as head of the Department of Financial Services, by registered mail, return receipt requested. The department, or the Department of Financial Services under the circumstances specified in subsection (4), may elect to intervene and proceed with the action, on behalf of the state, within 60 days after it receives both the complaint and the material evidence and information.

(4) If a person brings an action under subsection (2) and the action is based upon the facts underlying a pending investigation by the Department of Financial Services, the Department of Financial Services, instead of the department, may take over the action on behalf of the state. In order to take over the action, the Department of Financial Services must give the department written notification within 20 days after the action is filed that the Department of Financial Services is conducting an investigation of the facts of the action and that the Department of Financial Services, instead of the department, will take over the action filed under subsection (2). If the Department of Financial Services takes over the action under this subsection, the word "department" as used in this act means the Department of Financial Services, and that department, for purposes of that action, shall have all rights and standing granted the department under this act.

(5) The department may, for good cause shown, request the court to extend the time during which the complaint remains under seal under subsection (2). Any such motion may be supported by affidavits or other submissions in camera. The defendant is not required to respond to any complaint filed under this section until 20 days after the complaint is unsealed and served upon the defendant in accordance with law.

(6) Before the expiration of the 60-day period or any extensions obtained under subsection (5), the department shall:

(a) Proceed with the action, in which case the action is conducted by the department on behalf of the state; or

(b) Notify the court that it declines to take over the action, in which case the person bringing the action has the right to conduct the action.

(7) When a person files an action under this section, no person other than the department may intervene or bring a related action based on the facts underlying the pending action.

(8)(a) Except as otherwise provided in this subsection, the complaint and information held by the department pursuant to an investigation of a violation of s. 68.082 is confidential and exempt from s. 119.07(1) and s. 24(a), Art. I of the State Constitution. This paragraph is subject to the Open Government Sunset Review Act in accordance with s. 119.15 and shall stand repealed on October 2, 2018, unless reviewed and saved from repeal through reenactment by the Legislature.

(b) Information made confidential and exempt under paragraph (a) may be disclosed by the department to a law enforcement agency or another administrative agency in the performance of its official duties and responsibilities.

(c) Information made confidential and exempt under paragraph (a) is no longer confidential and exempt once the investigation is completed, unless the information is otherwise protected by law.

(d) For purposes of this subsection, an investigation is considered complete:

1. Under subsection (1) once the department either files its own action or closes its investigation without filing an action.

2. Under subsection (2) upon the unsealing of the qui tam action or its voluntary dismissal prior to any unsealing.

68.0831. Subpoena.

(1) As used in this section, the term "department" means the Department of Legal Affairs.

(2) Whenever the department has reason to believe that any person may be in possession, custody, or control of any documentary material or may have any information, which documentary material

or information is relevant to a civil investigation authorized by s. 68.083, the department may, before the institution of a civil proceeding thereon, issue in writing and cause to be served upon the person a subpoena requiring the person to:

(a) Produce such documentary material for inspection and copying or reproduction;

(b) Answer, under oath and in writing, written interrogatories;

(c) Give sworn oral testimony concerning the documentary material or information; or

(d) Furnish any combination of such material, answers, or testimony.

(3) The subpoena shall:

(a) Be served upon the person in the manner required for service of process in this state or by certified mail showing receipt by the addressee or by the authorized agent of the addressee.

(b) State the nature of the conduct that constitutes the violation of this act and that is alleged to have occurred or to be imminent.

(c) Describe the class or classes of documentary material to be produced thereunder with such definiteness and certainty as to permit such materials to be reasonably identified.

(d) Prescribe a date and time at which the person must appear to testify, under oath or affirmation, or by which the person must answer written interrogatories or produce the documentary material for inspection or copying; however, such date shall not be earlier than 30 days after the date of service of the subpoena.

(e) Specify a place for the taking of testimony or for the submission of answers to interrogatories and identify the person who is to take custody of any documentary material. Inspection and copying of documentary material shall be carried out at the place where the documentary material is located or at such other place as may be thereafter agreed to by the person and such designated custodian. Upon written agreement between the person and the designated custodian, copies may be substituted for original documents.

(4) Such subpoena may not require the production of any documentary material, the submission of any answers to written interrogatories, or the giving of any oral testimony if such material, answers, or testimony would be protected from disclosure under:

(a) The standards applicable to subpoenas or subpoenas duces tecum issued by a court of this state in aid of a grand jury investigation; or

(b) The standards applicable to a discovery request under the Florida Rules of Civil Procedure, to the extent that the application of such standards to any such subpoena is appropriate and consistent with the provisions and purposes of this act.

(5) This section does not limit the power of the department to require the appearance of witnesses or production of documents or other tangible evidence located outside the state.

(6) Within 30 days after the service of a subpoena upon any person or at any time before the return date specified therein, whichever period is longer, the person served may file, and serve on the department, a petition for an order of the court modifying or setting aside the subpoena. Any such petition shall be filed in the circuit court of the Second Judicial Circuit in and for Leon County. The time allowed for compliance in whole or in part with the subpoena as deemed proper and ordered by the court shall not run while the petition is pending before the court. The petition shall specify each ground upon which the petitioner relies in seeking relief and may be based upon the failure of the subpoena to comply with this section or upon any constitutional or other legal right or privilege of such person.

(7) In case of the failure of any person to comply in whole or in part with a subpoena and when such person has not filed a petition under subsection (6), the circuit court of the Second Judicial Circuit in and for Leon County, upon application of the department, may issue an order requiring compliance. The failure to obey the order of the court shall be punishable as a contempt of court.

(8) The examination of all witnesses under this section shall be conducted by the department before an officer authorized to administer oaths in this state. The testimony shall be taken stenographically or by a sound-recording device. Any person compelled to appear under a subpoena for oral testimony pursuant to this section may be accompanied, represented, and advised by counsel. Counsel may advise such person, in confidence, either upon the request of such person or upon counsel's own initiative, with respect to any question asked of such person.

Such person or counsel may object on the record to any question, in whole or in part, and shall briefly state for the record the reason for any such objection. If such person refuses to answer any question, the person conducting the examination may petition the circuit court as provided by subsection (11).

(9) When the testimony is fully transcribed, the person conducting the deposition shall afford the witness, and counsel, if any, a reasonable opportunity to examine the transcript, and the transcript shall be read to or by the witness, unless such examination and reading is waived by the witness. Any changes in form or substance that the witness desires to make shall be entered and identified upon the transcript by the officer or the department, with a statement of the reasons given by the witness for making such changes. The transcript shall then be signed by the witness unless the witness waives the signing in writing, is ill, cannot be found, or refuses to sign. If the transcript is not signed by the witness within 30 days after his or her being afforded a reasonable opportunity to examine it, the person conducting the examination shall sign it and state on the record the fact of the waiver, illness, absence, or refusal to sign, together with the reason, if any, given therefor. Any person required to testify or to submit documentary evidence is entitled, on payment of reasonable costs, to procure a copy of any document produced by such person and of his or her own testimony as stenographically reported or, in the case of a deposition, as reduced to writing by or under the direction of the person taking the deposition.

(10) The department shall have the authority to stipulate to protective orders with respect to documents and information submitted in response to a subpoena under this section.

(11) The department may request that any natural person who refuses to comply with this section on the ground that the testimony or documents may incriminate him or her be ordered by the circuit court to provide the testimony or the documents. Except in a prosecution for perjury, a natural person who complies with a court order to provide testimony or documents after asserting a privilege against self-incrimination to which he or she is entitled by law may not be subject to a criminal proceeding with respect to the transaction to which he or she is required to testify or produce documents. Any natural person who fails to comply with such a court order to testify or produce documents may be adjudged in contempt and imprisoned until the time the person purges himself or herself of the contempt.

(12) While in the possession of the custodian, documentary material, answers to interrogatories, and transcripts of oral testimony shall be available, under such reasonable terms and conditions as the department shall prescribe, for examination by the person who produced such materials or answers or that person's duly authorized representative.

(13) This section does not impair the authority of the department to:

(a) Institute a civil proceeding under s. 68.083;

(b) Invoke the power of a court to compel the production of evidence before a grand jury; or

(c) Maintain the confidential and exempt status of the complaint and any other information as provided in s. 68.083(8).

(14)(a) A person who knows or has reason to believe that a subpoena pursuant to this section is pending shall not:

1. Alter, destroy, conceal, or remove any record, document, or thing with the purpose of impairing its verity or availability in such proceeding or investigation; or

2. Make, present, or use any record, document, or thing knowing it to be false.

(b) Any natural person who violates this subsection is subject to a civil penalty of not more than $100,000, reasonable attorney fees, and costs. Any other person who violates this subsection is subject to a civil penalty of not more than $1 million, reasonable attorney fees, and costs.

68.084. Rights of the parties in civil actions.

(1) If the department, on behalf of the state, proceeds with the action, it has the primary responsibility for prosecuting the action, and is not bound by any act of the person bringing the

action. The person bringing the action has the right to continue as a party to the action, subject to the limitations specified in subsection (2).

(2)(a) The department may at any point voluntarily dismiss the action notwithstanding the objections of the person initiating the action.

(b) Subject to s. 17.04, nothing in this act shall be construed to limit the authority of the department or the qui tam plaintiff to compromise a claim brought in a complaint filed under this act if the court determines, after a hearing, that the proposed settlement is fair, adequate, and reasonable under all the circumstances.

(c) Upon a showing by the department that unrestricted participation during the course of the litigation by the person initiating the action would interfere with or unduly delay the department's prosecution of the case, or would be repetitious, irrelevant, or for purposes of harassment, the court may, in its discretion, impose limitations on the person's participation, including, but not limited to:

1. Limiting the number of witnesses the person may call;
2. Limiting the length of the testimony of the person's witnesses;
3. Limiting the person's cross-examination of witnesses; or
4. Otherwise limiting the participation by the person in the litigation.

(d) Upon a showing by the defendant that unrestricted participation during the course of the litigation by the person initiating the action would be for purposes of harassment or would cause the defendant undue burden or unnecessary expense, the court may limit the participation by the person in the litigation.

(3) If the department elects not to proceed with the action, the person who initiated the action has the right to conduct the action. If the Attorney General, as head of the department, or the Chief Financial Officer, as head of the Department of Financial Services, so requests, it shall be served with copies of all pleadings and motions filed in the action along with copies of all deposition transcripts at the requesting department's expense. When a person proceeds with the action, the court, without limiting the rights of the person initiating the action, may nevertheless permit the department to intervene and take over the action on behalf of the state at a later date upon showing of good cause.

(4) Regardless of whether the department proceeds with the action, upon a showing by the department that certain actions of discovery by the person initiating the action would interfere with an investigation by the state or the prosecution of a criminal or civil matter arising out of the same facts, the court may stay such discovery for a period of not more than 60 days. Such a showing shall be conducted in camera. The court may extend the 60-day period upon a further showing in camera by the department that the criminal or civil investigation or proceeding has been pursued with reasonable diligence and any proposed discovery in the civil action will interfere with an ongoing criminal or civil investigation or proceeding.

(5) Notwithstanding paragraph (2)(b), the state may elect to pursue its claim through any available alternate remedy, including any administrative proceeding to determine a civil money penalty. If any such alternate remedy is pursued in another proceeding, the person initiating the action shall have the same rights in such proceeding as the person would have had if the action had continued under this section. Any finding of fact or conclusion of law made in such other proceeding that has become final shall be conclusive on all parties to an action under this section. For purposes of this subsection, a finding or conclusion is final if it has been finally determined on appeal to the appropriate court, if all time for filing such an appeal with respect to the finding or conclusion has expired, or if the finding or conclusion is not subject to judicial review.

(6) The Department of Financial Services, or the department, may intervene on its own behalf as a matter of right.

68.085. Awards to plaintiffs bringing action.

(1)(a) If the department proceeds with an action brought by a person under this act, subject to the requirements of paragraph (b), the person shall receive at least 15 percent but not more than 25 percent of the proceeds of the action or settlement of the claim, depending upon the extent to which the person substantially contributed to the prosecution of the action.

(b) If the court finds the action to be based primarily on disclosures of specific information, other than information provided by the person bringing the action, relating to allegations or transactions in a criminal, civil, or administrative hearing; a legislative, administrative, inspector general, or auditor general report, hearing, audit, or investigation; or from the news media, the court may award such sums as it considers appropriate, but in no case more than 10 percent of the proceeds, taking into account the significance of the information and the role of the person bringing the action in advancing the case to litigation.

(c) Any payment to a person under paragraph (a) or paragraph (b) shall be made from the proceeds. The person shall also receive an amount for reasonable expenses that the court finds to have been necessarily incurred, plus reasonable attorney fees and costs. All such expenses, fees, and costs shall be awarded against the defendant.

(2) If the department does not proceed with an action under this section, the person bringing the action or settling the claim shall receive an amount that the court decides is reasonable for collecting the civil penalty and damages. The amount shall be not less than 25 percent and not more than 30 percent of the proceeds of the action or settlement and shall be paid out of such proceeds. The person shall also receive an amount for reasonable expenses that the court finds to have been necessarily incurred, plus reasonable attorney fees and costs. All such expenses, fees, and costs shall be awarded against the defendant.

(3) Following any distributions under subsection (1) or subsection (2), the state entity injured by the submission of a false or fraudulent claim shall be awarded an amount not to exceed its compensatory damages. If the action was based on a claim of funds from the state Medicaid program, 10 percent of any remaining proceeds shall be deposited into the Operating Trust Fund to fund rewards for persons who report and provide information relating to Medicaid fraud pursuant to s. 409.9203. Any remaining proceeds, including civil penalties awarded under s. 68.082, shall be deposited in the General Revenue Fund.

(4) Regardless of whether the department proceeds with the action, if the court finds that the action was brought by a person who planned and initiated the violation of s. 68.082 upon which the action was brought, the court may, to the extent the court considers appropriate, reduce the share of the proceeds of the action that the person would otherwise receive under this section, taking into account the role of the person in advancing the case to litigation and any relevant circumstances pertaining to the violation. If the person bringing the action is convicted of criminal conduct arising from his or her role in the violation of s. 68.082, the person shall be dismissed from the civil action and shall not receive any share of the proceeds of the action. Such dismissal shall not prejudice the right of the department to continue the action.

68.086. Expenses; attorney fees and costs.

(1) If the department initiates an action under this act or assumes control of an action brought by a person under this act, the department shall be awarded its reasonable attorney fees, expenses, and costs.

(2) If the department does not proceed with an action under this act and the person bringing the action conducts the action, the court may award to the defendant its reasonable attorney fees and expenses if the defendant prevails in the action and the court finds that the claim of the person bringing the action was clearly frivolous, clearly vexatious, or brought primarily for purposes of harassment.

(3) No liability shall be incurred by the state or the department for any expenses, attorney fees, or other costs incurred by any person in bringing or defending an action under this act.

68.087. Exemptions to civil actions.

(1) No court shall have jurisdiction over an action brought under this act against a member of the Legislature, a member of the judiciary, or a senior executive branch official if the action is based on evidence or information known to the state government when the action was brought. For purposes of this subsection, the term "senior executive branch official" means any person employed in the executive branch of government holding a position in the Senior Management Service as defined in s. 110.402.

(2) In no event may a person bring an action under s. 68.083(2) based upon allegations or transactions that are the subject of a civil action or an administrative proceeding in which the state is already a party.

(3) The court shall dismiss an action brought under this act unless opposed by the department, if substantially the same allegations or transactions as alleged in the action were publicly disclosed:

(a) In a criminal, civil, or administrative hearing in which the state is a party;

(b) In a legislative, administrative, inspector general, or other state report, hearing, audit, or investigation; or

(c) From the news media,

(4) No court shall have jurisdiction over an action where the person bringing the action under s. 68.083(2) is:

(a) Acting as an attorney for state government; or

(b) An employee or former employee of state government,

(5) No court shall have jurisdiction over an action where the person bringing the action under s. 68.083(2) obtained the information from an employee or former employee of state government who was not acting in the course or scope of government employment.

(6) No court shall have jurisdiction over an action brought under this act against any county or municipality.

68.088. Protection for participating employees.

Any employee who is discharged, demoted, suspended, threatened, harassed, or in any other manner discriminated against in the terms and conditions of employment by his or her employer because of lawful acts done by the employee on behalf of the employee or others in furtherance of an action under this act, including investigation for initiation of, testimony for, or assistance in an action filed or to be filed under this act, shall have a cause of action under s. 112.3187.

68.089. Limitation of actions; effect of interventions by department.

(1) A civil action under this act may not be brought:

(a) More than 6 years after the date on which the violation of s. 68.082 is committed; or

(b) More than 3 years after the date when facts material to the right of action are known or reasonably should have been known by the department, but in no event more than 10 years after the date on which the violation is committed, whichever occurs last.

(2) If the department elects to intervene and proceed with an action brought under s. 68.083(2), the department may file its own complaint or amend the complaint of a person who has brought an action under s. 68.083(2) to clarify or add detail to the claims in which the department is

intervening and to add any additional claims with respect to which the department contends it is entitled to relief. For statute of limitations purposes, any such pleading shall relate back to the filing date of the complaint of the person who originally brought the action, to the extent that the claim of the state arises out of the conduct, transactions, or occurrences set forth, or attempted to be set forth, in the prior complaint of that person. This subsection applies to any actions under s. 68.083(2) pending on or filed after July 1, 2013.

68.09. Burden of proof.

(1) In any action brought under this act, the department or the qui tam plaintiff shall be required to prove all essential elements of the cause of action, including damages, by a preponderance of the evidence.

(2) Notwithstanding any other provision of law, a final judgment or decree rendered in favor of the state or the Federal Government in any criminal proceeding concerning the conduct of the defendant that forms the basis for a civil cause of action under this act, whether upon a verdict after trial or upon a plea of guilty or nolo contendere, shall estop the defendant in any action by the department pursuant to this act as to all matters as to which such judgment or decree would be an estoppel as if the department had been a party in the criminal proceeding.

68.091. Construction and severability of provisions.

(1) This act shall be liberally construed to effectuate its remedial and deterrent purposes.

(2) If any provision of this act or its application to any particular person or circumstance is held invalid, that provision or its application is severable and does not affect the validity of other provisions or applications of this act.

68.092. Deposit of recovered moneys.

All moneys recovered by the Chief Financial Officer as head of the Department of Financial Services under s. 68.086(1) in any civil action for violation of the Florida False Claims Act shall be deposited in the Administrative Trust Fund of the Department of Financial Services.

68.093. Florida Vexatious Litigant Law.

(1) This section may be cited as the "Florida Vexatious Litigant Law."

(2) As used in section, the term:

(a) "Action" means a civil action governed by the Florida Rules of Civil Procedure and proceedings governed by the Florida Probate Rules, but does not include actions concerning family law matters governed by the Florida Family Law Rules of Procedure or any action in which the Florida Small Claims Rules apply.

(b) "Defendant" means any person or entity, including a corporation, association, partnership, firm, or governmental entity, against whom an action is or was commenced or is sought to be commenced.

(c) "Security" means an undertaking by a vexatious litigant to ensure payment to a defendant in an amount reasonably sufficient to cover the defendant's anticipated, reasonable expenses of litigation, including attorney's fees and taxable costs.

(d) "Vexatious litigant" means:

1. A person as defined in s. 1.01(3) who, in the immediately preceding 5-year period, has commenced, prosecuted, or maintained, pro se, five or more civil actions in any court in this state, except an action governed by the Florida Small Claims Rules, which actions have been finally and adversely determined against such person or entity; or

2. Any person or entity previously found to be a vexatious litigant pursuant to this section.

(3)(a) In any action pending in any court of this state, including actions governed by the Florida Small Claims Rules, any defendant may move the court, upon notice and hearing, for an order requiring the plaintiff to furnish security. The motion shall be based on the grounds, and supported by a showing, that the plaintiff is a vexatious litigant and is not reasonably likely to prevail on the merits of the action against the moving defendant.

(b) At the hearing upon any defendant's motion for an order to post security, the court shall consider any evidence, written or oral, by witness or affidavit, which may be relevant to the consideration of the motion. No determination made by the court in such a hearing shall be admissible on the merits of the action or deemed to be a determination of any issue in the action. If, after hearing the evidence, the court determines that the plaintiff is a vexatious litigant and is not reasonably likely to prevail on the merits of the action against the moving defendant, the court shall order the plaintiff to furnish security to the moving defendant in an amount and within such time as the court deems appropriate.

(c) If the plaintiff fails to post security required by an order of the court under this section, the court shall immediately issue an order dismissing the action with prejudice as to the defendant for whose benefit the security was ordered.

(d) If a motion for an order to post security is filed prior to the trial in an action, the action shall be automatically stayed and the moving defendant need not plead or otherwise respond to the complaint until 10 days after the motion is denied. If the motion is granted, the moving defendant shall respond or plead no later than 10 days after the required security has been furnished.

(4) In addition to any other relief provided in this section, the court in any judicial circuit may, on its own motion or on the motion of any party, enter a prefiling order prohibiting a vexatious litigant from commencing, pro se, any new action in the courts of that circuit without first obtaining leave of the administrative judge of that circuit. Disobedience of such an order may be punished as contempt of court by the administrative judge of that circuit. Leave of court shall be granted by the administrative judge only upon a showing that the proposed action is meritorious and is not being filed for the purpose of delay or harassment. The administrative judge may condition the filing of the proposed action upon the furnishing of security as provided in this section.

(5) The clerk of the court shall not file any new action by a vexatious litigant pro se unless the vexatious litigant has obtained an order from the administrative judge permitting such filing. If the clerk of the court mistakenly permits a vexatious litigant to file an action pro se in contravention of a prefiling order, any party to that action may file with the clerk and serve on the plaintiff and all other defendants a notice stating that the plaintiff is a pro se vexatious litigant subject to a prefiling order. The filing of such a notice shall automatically stay the litigation against all defendants to the action. The administrative judge shall automatically dismiss the action with prejudice within 10 days after the filing of such notice unless the plaintiff files a motion for leave to file the action. If the administrative judge issues an order permitting the action to be filed, the defendants need not plead or otherwise respond to the complaint until 10 days after the date of service by the plaintiff, by United States mail, of a copy of the order granting leave to file the action.

(6) The clerk of a court shall provide copies of all prefiling orders to the Clerk of the Florida Supreme Court, who shall maintain a registry of all vexatious litigants.

(7) The relief provided under this section shall be cumulative to any other relief or remedy available to a defendant under the laws of this state and the Florida Rules of Civil Procedure, including, but not limited to, the relief provided under s. 57.105.

68.094. Short title.

This act may be cited as the "Florida Access to Civil Legal Assistance Act."

68.095. Legislative intent.

It is the intent of the Legislature to establish an administrative framework whereby public funds may be used in an effective and efficient manner to enhance the availability of civil legal assistance to the poor in this state. The Legislature finds that the lack of adequate and equitable legal services available to the indigent population, particularly the children and elderly of this state, unnecessarily burdens existing social and human services programs. It is the purpose of this act to promote the availability of civil legal assistance to the poor and improve access to justice by establishing a streamlined method to utilize available state funds in furtherance of this goal.

68.096. Definitions.

For purposes of this act:
(1) "Department" means the Department of Legal Affairs.
(2) "Eligible client" means a person whose income is equal to or below 150 percent of the then-current federal poverty guidelines prescribed for the size of the household of the person seeking assistance by the United States Department of Health and Human Services or disabled veterans who are in receipt of, or eligible to receive, Veterans Administration pension benefits or supplemental security income.
(3) "Legal assistance" means the provision of civil legal services consistent with the rules regulating The Florida Bar, subject to the limitations in s. 68.098.
(4) "Not-for-profit legal aid organization" means a not-for-profit organization operated in this state that provides as its primary purpose civil legal services without charge to eligible clients.

68.097. Authority and duties of the department.

The department shall have the powers necessary or appropriate to carry out the purposes and provisions of this act, including, but not limited to, the power to contract with a statewide not-for-profit organization that provides funding for civil legal assistance to the poor in this state to allocate funds to not-for-profit legal aid organizations consistent with the provisions of this act.

68.098. Limitations.

No funds received or allocated pursuant to this act shall be used to:
(1) Lobby or influence the passage or defeat of any legislation before any municipal, county, or state legislative or administrative body.
(2) Provide legal assistance or advice with respect to any criminal proceeding or any federal or state postconviction proceeding. For purposes of this subsection, "criminal proceeding" means an adversary judicial process prosecuted by a public officer and initiated by formal complaint, information, or indictment charging a person with an offense classified or denominated as criminal by applicable law and punishable by death, imprisonment, jail sentence, or criminal fine.

(3) Sue the state or any of its agencies or political subdivisions.

(4) Sue any college or university.

(5) Initiate or participate in a class action suit.

(6) Provide legal assistance or advice with respect to any noncriminal infraction or any enforcement proceeding instituted by the state or its agencies or political subdivisions pursuant to chapter 316, chapter 318, chapter 320, or chapter 322.

(7) Contest any regulatory decision by any municipal, county, or state administrative or legislative body.

(8) File or assist in the filing of private causes of action under federal or state statutes enforced by federal or state agencies relating to or arising out of employment or the terms or conditions of employment.

68.099. Funding.

In connection with funds received pursuant to this act, the department shall contract with a not-for-profit, charitable organization that meets the qualifications of s. 501(c)(3) of the United States Internal Revenue Code, as amended, that provides funding statewide for civil legal assistance to the poor for the administration, allocation, and distribution of any or all such funds in a manner consistent with the provisions of this act. Such contract shall provide that distribution of at least 80 percent of such funds shall be based annually by county on a per capita basis upon the number of persons in the county whose income is 125 percent or less of the then-current federal poverty guidelines of the United States Department of Health and Human Services. For purposes of this section, the source of data identifying the number of persons per county shall be the latest available figures of persons per county from the Bureau of the Census of the United States Department of Commerce. Such contract shall provide that up to 15 percent of such funds shall be distributed annually to statewide and regional not-for-profit legal aid organizations and that up to 5 percent of such funds shall be provided for administrative costs.

68.10. Eligible activities.

Funds received or allocated pursuant to this act may be used to secure the legal rights of eligible clients relating to family law, juvenile law, entitlements to federal government benefits, protection from domestic violence, elder and child abuse, and immigration by providing legal assistance and education regarding legal rights and duties under the law.

68.101. Accountability.

In any contract allocating funds pursuant to this act, the department shall ensure that funds received or allocated pursuant to this act are expended in a manner consistent with the terms and intent of this act and shall provide for an annual audit of such expenditures.

68.102. State support.

Programs funded pursuant to this act shall be eligible for state support, including, but not limited to, access to the SUNCOM Network services. Accounts for SUNCOM services furnished to program eligible entities shall be billed directly to the department, as program administrator, and paid with the funding provided.

68.103. Unconstitutionality or unenforceability of fund limitations.

If any of the limitations on the use of funds received or allocated under this act is found to violate the Constitution of the United States or the State Constitution or otherwise found to be unenforceable:
(1) The entire act shall be null and void.
(2) All appropriations made for the purposes of this act and not expended are repealed.
(3) All unspent funds received by any entity pursuant to this act or the act appropriating funds for the purpose of this act shall be returned to the department for transfer to the treasury to the credit of the fund from which they were appropriated.
(4) No further funds appropriated for the purposes of this act shall be distributed or expended.

68.104. Construction.

This act shall not be construed to create a statutory right to counsel in any proceeding. This act shall not be construed to create any statutory right accruing to any attorney.

68.105. Use of funds; reports.

All appropriations made for the purposes of the Florida Access to Civil Legal Assistance Act shall be used only for legal education or assistance in family law, juvenile law, entitlement to federal benefits, protection from domestic violence, elder abuse, child abuse, or immigration law. These funds may not be used in criminal or postconviction relief matters; for lobbying activities; to sue the state, its agencies or political subdivisions, or colleges or universities; for class action lawsuits; to provide legal assistance with respect to noncriminal infractions pursuant to chapter 316, chapter 318, chapter 320, or chapter 322; to contest regulatory decisions of any municipal, county, or state administrative or legislative body; or to file or assist in the filing of private causes of action under federal or state statutes relating to or arising out of employment or terms or conditions of employment. The contracting organization shall require pilot projects to provide data on the number of clients served, the types of cases, the reasons the cases were closed, and the state dollars saved and federal dollars brought into the state because of the legal services provided. The contracting organization shall provide to the department, within 60 days after completing the contract, a report on the legal services provided, the state dollars saved, and the federal dollars brought into the state.

CHAPTER 69. MISCELLANEOUS PROCEDURAL MATTERS

69.011. Supreme Court; bond not to be required of certain officers in certain original proceedings.

Constitutional officers of the state, boards of county commissioners, and school boards of the several counties of this state shall not be required to furnish any bond or other security for the procurement of or to render effective any restraining order, injunction, or other order, writ or judgment in cases of original jurisdiction in the Supreme Court of Florida.

69.021. Bondholders' committee.

(1) SELECTION.—In any action to foreclose the lien of any mortgage or deed of trust given to secure any issue of bonds or other obligations and encumbering real or personal property or both when the owners of the bonds or beneficiaries of the trust exceed ten in number, on motion of a party or on its own initiative, the court may appoint three persons, two of whom shall constitute a quorum for all purposes, as a committee for the protection of the holders of bonds or units or certificates of beneficial interest. The committee is vested with such powers and authority and shall discharge such duties in connection with the litigation and its subject matter as is necessary and proper in the court's discretion to protect the interest of the holders of the bonds and beneficiaries of the trust involved in, or affected by, the litigation. During the pendency of such litigation, the court may prescribe, modify, abrogate or nullify the powers and authority of the committee.

(2) QUALIFICATIONS.—No person is eligible for appointment to, nor qualified to act as a member of, the committee who is interested in the outcome of the action or in the subject matter thereof, or who is an officer, director or stockholder of any party to the actions, or who is related by blood or marriage to, or directly or indirectly associated with or employed by:

(a) Any official of the court.

(b) Any person who is interested in the outcome of the actions.

(c) Any person who is interested in the subject matter.

(d) Any person who is an officer, director or stockholder of any corporate party to the action.

(3) COMPENSATION AND EXPENSES.—The compensation and expenses of the committee shall be fixed by the court and may be taxed as costs and ordered paid by such parties in interest, and in such manner and at such time, and out of such funds or property involved in the action as the court determines. The court may remove any members of the committee and appoint a successor or successors to fill the vacancies that result from removal, resignation or death of members of the committee. The committee is subject to the supervision and control of the court at all times, and amenable to its orders until the approval of the final reports, if any, of the committee and the discharge of the committee by the court.

(4) EMPLOYMENT OF COUNSEL.—The employment of counsel by the committee shall be approved by the court and the compensation of counsel shall be fixed by the court.

(5) ONLY LEGALLY APPOINTED COMMITTEES RECOGNIZED.—Any bondholders' committee not appointed by the court in which the action is pending shall be heard in the action or permitted, directly or indirectly, to dominate or control the litigation or the action of the trustee or trustees under deed or deeds of trust under which the action is predicated, nor permitted to acquire, directly or indirectly, the property at any sale in said action.

69.031. Designated financial institutions for assets in hands of guardians, curators, administrators, trustees, receivers, or other officers.

(1) When it is expedient in the judgment of any court having jurisdiction of any estate in process of administration by any guardian, curator, executor, administrator, trustee, receiver, or other officer, because the size of the bond required of the officer is burdensome or for other cause, the court may order part or all of the personal assets of the estate placed with a bank, trust company, or savings and loan association (which savings and loan association is a member of the Federal Savings and Loan Insurance Corporation and doing business in this state) designated by the court, consideration being given to any bank, trust company or savings and loan association proposed by the officer. When the assets are placed with the designated financial institution, it shall file a receipt therefor in the name of the estate and give the officer a copy. Such receipt shall acknowledge the assets received by the financial institution. All interest, dividends, principal and other debts collected by the financial institution on account thereof shall be held by the financial institution in safekeeping, subject to the instructions of the officer authorized by order of the court directed to the financial institution.
(2) Accountings shall be made to the officer at reasonably frequent intervals. After the receipt for the original assets has been filed by the financial institution, the court shall waive the bond given or to be given or reduce it so that it shall apply only to the estate remaining in the hands of the officer, whichever the court deems proper.
(3) When the court has ordered any assets of an estate to be placed with a designated financial institution, any person or corporation having possession or control of any of the assets, or owing interest, dividends, principal or other debts on account thereof, shall pay and deliver such assets, interest, dividends, principal and other debts to the financial institution on its demand whether the officer has duly qualified or not, and the receipt of the financial institution relieves the person or corporation from further responsibility therefor.
(4) Any bank, trust company, or savings and loan association which is designated under this section, may accept or reject the designation in any instance, and shall file its acceptance or rejection with the court making the designation within 15 days after actual knowledge of the designation comes to the attention of the financial institution, and if the financial institution accepts, it shall be allowed a reasonable amount for its services and expenses which the court may allow as a charge against the assets placed with the financial institution.

69.041. State named party; lien foreclosure, suit to quiet title.

(1) Under the conditions prescribed in this section for the protection of the state, the state may be named a party to a civil action in any court of this state, or in any district court of the United States, having jurisdiction of the subject matter, either:
(a) To quiet title to real property wherein the state has or claims any adverse interest in the title to real estate; or
(b) For the foreclosure of a mortgage or other lien on real or personal property on which the state has or claims a mortgage or other lien.
(2) The complaint shall set forth with particularity the nature of the interest claimed by the state in such real property with respect to quiet title proceedings. In the case of mortgage or lien foreclosure, the complaint shall set forth with particularity the nature of the lien claimed by the state in such real property.
(3) A judicial sale in a mortgage foreclosure action shall have the same effect respecting the

discharge of the property from liens and encumbrances held by the state as is provided about such matters by the law of this state. A sale to satisfy a lien inferior to one of the state shall be made subject to and without disturbing the lien of the state, unless the state consents that the property may be sold free of its liens and the proceeds divided as the parties may be entitled.

(4)(a) The Department of Revenue has the right to participate in the disbursement of funds remaining in the registry of the court after distribution pursuant to s. 45.031(7). The department shall participate in accordance with applicable procedures in any mortgage foreclosure action in which the department has a duly filed tax warrant, or interests under a lien arising from a judgment, order, or decree for support, as defined in s. 409.2554, or interest in a reemployment assistance tax lien under contract with the Department of Economic Opportunity through an interagency agreement pursuant to s. 443.1316, against the subject property and with the same priority, regardless of whether a default against the department, the Department of Economic Opportunity, or the former Agency for Workforce Innovation has been entered for failure to file an answer or other responsive pleading.

(b) With respect to a duly filed tax warrant, paragraph (a) applies only to mortgage foreclosure actions initiated on or after July 1, 1994, and to those mortgage foreclosure actions initiated before July 1, 1994, in which no default has been entered against the Department of Revenue before July 1, 1994. With respect to mortgage foreclosure actions initiated based upon interests under a lien arising from a judgment, order, or decree for support, paragraph (a) applies only to mortgage foreclosure actions initiated on or after July 1, 1998, and to those mortgage foreclosure actions initiated before July 1, 1998, in which no default has been entered against the Department of Revenue before July 1, 1998.

69.051. General and special magistrates; compensation.

General and special magistrates appointed by the court shall be allowed such compensation for any services as the court deems reasonable, including time consumed in legal research required in preparing and summarizing their findings of fact and law.

69.061. Loss of negotiable instrument; indemnity.

The court may order that the loss of a negotiable instrument shall not be set up in any action to recover on it if satisfactory indemnity is given against the claims of any other person on the instrument.

69.071. Number of jurors.

In all civil actions when a jury is impaneled, a jury of six qualified jurors is sufficient.

69.081. Sunshine in litigation; concealment of public hazards prohibited.

(1) This section may be cited as the "Sunshine in Litigation Act."
(2) As used in this section, "public hazard" means an instrumentality, including but not limited to any device, instrument, person, procedure, product, or a condition of a device, instrument, person, procedure or product, that has caused and is likely to cause injury.

(3) Except pursuant to this section, no court shall enter an order or judgment which has the purpose or effect of concealing a public hazard or any information concerning a public hazard, nor shall the court enter an order or judgment which has the purpose or effect of concealing any information which may be useful to members of the public in protecting themselves from injury which may result from the public hazard.

(4) Any portion of an agreement or contract which has the purpose or effect of concealing a public hazard, any information concerning a public hazard, or any information which may be useful to members of the public in protecting themselves from injury which may result from the public hazard, is void, contrary to public policy, and may not be enforced.

(5) Trade secrets as defined in s. 688.002 which are not pertinent to public hazards shall be protected pursuant to chapter 688.

(6) Any substantially affected person, including but not limited to representatives of news media, has standing to contest an order, judgment, agreement, or contract that violates this section. A person may contest an order, judgment, agreement, or contract that violates this section by motion in the court that entered the order or judgment, or by bringing a declaratory judgment action pursuant to chapter 86.

(7) Upon motion and good cause shown by a party attempting to prevent disclosure of information or materials which have not previously been disclosed, including but not limited to alleged trade secrets, the court shall examine the disputed information or materials in camera. If the court finds that the information or materials or portions thereof consist of information concerning a public hazard or information which may be useful to members of the public in protecting themselves from injury which may result from a public hazard, the court shall allow disclosure of the information or materials. If allowing disclosure, the court shall allow disclosure of only that portion of the information or materials necessary or useful to the public regarding the public hazard.

(8)(a) Any portion of an agreement or contract which has the purpose or effect of concealing information relating to the settlement or resolution of any claim or action against the state, its agencies, or subdivisions or against any municipality or constitutionally created body or commission is void, contrary to public policy, and may not be enforced. Any person has standing to contest an order, judgment, agreement, or contract that violates this section. A person may contest an order, judgment, agreement, or contract that violates this subsection by motion in the court that entered such order or judgment, or by bringing a declaratory judgment action pursuant to chapter 86.

(b) Any person having custody of any document, record, contract, or agreement relating to any settlement as set forth in this section shall maintain said public records in compliance with chapter 119.

(c) Failure of any custodian to disclose and provide any document, record, contract, or agreement as set forth in this section shall be subject to the sanctions as set forth in chapter 119.

(9) A governmental entity, except a municipality or county, that settles a claim in tort which requires the expenditure of public funds in excess of $5,000, shall provide notice, in accordance with the provisions of chapter 50, of such settlement, in the county in which the claim arose, within 60 days of entering into such settlement; provided that no notice shall be required if the settlement has been approved by a court of competent jurisdiction.

CHAPTER 70. RELIEF FROM BURDENS ON REAL PROPERTY RIGHTS

70.001. Private property rights protection.

(1) This act may be cited as the "Bert J. Harris, Jr., Private Property Rights Protection Act." The Legislature recognizes that some laws, regulations, and ordinances of the state and political entities in the state, as applied, may inordinately burden, restrict, or limit private property rights without amounting to a taking under the State Constitution or the United States Constitution. The Legislature determines that there is an important state interest in protecting the interests of private property owners from such inordinate burdens. Therefore, it is the intent of the Legislature that, as a separate and distinct cause of action from the law of takings, the Legislature herein provides for relief, or payment of compensation, when a new law, rule, regulation, or ordinance of the state or a political entity in the state, as applied, unfairly affects real property.

(2) When a specific action of a governmental entity has inordinately burdened an existing use of real property or a vested right to a specific use of real property, the property owner of that real property is entitled to relief, which may include compensation for the actual loss to the fair market value of the real property caused by the action of government, as provided in this section.

(3) For purposes of this section:

(a) The existence of a "vested right" is to be determined by applying the principles of equitable estoppel or substantive due process under the common law or by applying the statutory law of this state.

(b) The term "existing use" means:

1. An actual, present use or activity on the real property, including periods of inactivity which are normally associated with, or are incidental to, the nature or type of use; or

2. Activity or such reasonably foreseeable, nonspeculative land uses which are suitable for the subject real property and compatible with adjacent land uses and which have created an existing fair market value in the property greater than the fair market value of the actual, present use or activity on the real property.

(c) The term "governmental entity" includes an agency of the state, a regional or a local government created by the State Constitution or by general or special act, any county or municipality, or any other entity that independently exercises governmental authority. The term does not include the United States or any of its agencies, or an agency of the state, a regional or a local government created by the State Constitution or by general or special act, any county or municipality, or any other entity that independently exercises governmental authority, when exercising the powers of the United States or any of its agencies through a formal delegation of federal authority.

(d) The term "action of a governmental entity" means a specific action of a governmental entity which affects real property, including action on an application or permit.

(e) The terms "inordinate burden" and "inordinately burdened":

1. Mean that an action of one or more governmental entities has directly restricted or limited the use of real property such that the property owner is permanently unable to attain the reasonable, investment-backed expectation for the existing use of the real property or a vested right to a specific use of the real property with respect to the real property as a whole, or that the property owner is left with existing or vested uses that are unreasonable such that the property owner bears permanently a disproportionate share of a burden imposed for the good of the public, which in fairness should be borne by the public at large.

2. Do not include temporary impacts to real property; impacts to real property occasioned by governmental abatement, prohibition, prevention, or remediation of a public nuisance at common law or a noxious use of private property; or impacts to real property caused by an action of a governmental entity taken to grant relief to a property owner under this section. However, a temporary impact on development, as defined in s. 380.04, that is in effect for longer than 1 year may, depending upon the circumstances, constitute an "inordinate burden" as provided in this paragraph.

(f) The term "property owner" means the person who holds legal title to the real property that is the subject of and directly impacted by the action of a governmental entity. The term does not include a governmental entity.

(g) The term "real property" means land and includes any appurtenances and improvements to the land, including any other relevant real property in which the property owner has a relevant interest. The term includes only parcels that are the subject of and directly impacted by the action of a governmental entity.

(4)(a) Not less than 150 days prior to filing an action under this section against a governmental entity, a property owner who seeks compensation under this section must present the claim in writing to the head of the governmental entity, except that if the property is classified as agricultural pursuant to s. 193.461, the notice period is 90 days. The property owner must submit, along with the claim, a bona fide, valid appraisal that supports the claim and demonstrates the loss in fair market value to the real property. If the action of government is the culmination of a process that involves more than one governmental entity, or if a complete resolution of all relevant issues, in the view of the property owner or in the view of a governmental entity to whom a claim is presented, requires the active participation of more than one governmental entity, the property owner shall present the claim as provided in this section to each of the governmental entities.

(b) The governmental entity shall provide written notice of the claim to all parties to any administrative action that gave rise to the claim, and to owners of real property contiguous to the owner's property at the addresses listed on the most recent county tax rolls. Within 15 days after the claim is presented, the governmental entity shall report the claim in writing to the Department of Legal Affairs, and shall provide the department with the name, address, and telephone number of the employee of the governmental entity from whom additional information may be obtained about the claim during the pendency of the claim and any subsequent judicial action.

(c) During the 90-day-notice period or the 150-day-notice period, unless extended by agreement of the parties, the governmental entity shall make a written settlement offer to effectuate:

1. An adjustment of land development or permit standards or other provisions controlling the development or use of land.
2. Increases or modifications in the density, intensity, or use of areas of development.
3. The transfer of developmental rights.
4. Land swaps or exchanges.
5. Mitigation, including payments in lieu of onsite mitigation.
6. Location on the least sensitive portion of the property.
7. Conditioning the amount of development or use permitted.
8. A requirement that issues be addressed on a more comprehensive basis than a single proposed use or development.
9. Issuance of the development order, a variance, special exception, or other extraordinary relief.
10. Purchase of the real property, or an interest therein, by an appropriate governmental entity or payment of compensation.
11. No changes to the action of the governmental entity.

(d)1. When a governmental entity enters into a settlement agreement under this section which would have the effect of a modification, variance, or a special exception to the application of a rule, regulation, or ordinance as it would otherwise apply to the subject real property, the relief granted shall protect the public interest served by the regulations at issue and be the appropriate relief necessary to prevent the governmental regulatory effort from inordinately burdening the real property.

2. When a governmental entity enters into a settlement agreement under this section which would have the effect of contravening the application of a statute as it would otherwise apply to the subject real property, the governmental entity and the property owner shall jointly file an action in the circuit court where the real property is located for approval of the settlement agreement by the court to ensure that the relief granted protects the public interest served by the statute at issue and is the appropriate relief necessary to prevent the governmental regulatory effort from inordinately burdening the real property.

(5)(a) During the 90-day-notice period or the 150-day-notice period, unless a settlement offer is accepted by the property owner, each of the governmental entities provided notice pursuant to paragraph (4)(a) shall issue a written statement of allowable uses identifying the allowable uses to which the subject property may be put. The failure of the governmental entity to issue a statement of allowable uses during the applicable 90-day-notice period or 150-day-notice period shall be deemed a denial for purposes of allowing a property owner to file an action in the circuit court under this section. If a written statement of allowable uses is issued, it constitutes the last prerequisite to judicial review for the purposes of the judicial proceeding created by this section, notwithstanding the availability of other administrative remedies.

(b) If the property owner rejects the settlement offer and the statement of allowable uses of the governmental entity or entities, the property owner may file a claim for compensation in the circuit court, a copy of which shall be served contemporaneously on the head of each of the governmental entities that made a settlement offer and a statement of allowable uses that was rejected by the property owner. Actions under this section shall be brought only in the county where the real property is located.

(6)(a) The circuit court shall determine whether an existing use of the real property or a vested right to a specific use of the real property existed and, if so, whether, considering the settlement offer and statement of allowable uses, the governmental entity or entities have inordinately burdened the real property. If the actions of more than one governmental entity, considering any settlement offers and statement of allowable uses, are responsible for the action that imposed the inordinate burden on the real property of the property owner, the court shall determine the percentage of responsibility each such governmental entity bears with respect to the inordinate burden. A governmental entity may take an interlocutory appeal of the court's determination that the action of the governmental entity has resulted in an inordinate burden. An interlocutory appeal does not automatically stay the proceedings; however, the court may stay the proceedings during the pendency of the interlocutory appeal. If the governmental entity does not prevail in the interlocutory appeal, the court shall award to the prevailing property owner the costs and a reasonable attorney fee incurred by the property owner in the interlocutory appeal.

(b) Following its determination of the percentage of responsibility of each governmental entity, and following the resolution of any interlocutory appeal, the court shall impanel a jury to determine the total amount of compensation to the property owner for the loss in value due to the inordinate burden to the real property. The award of compensation shall be determined by calculating the difference in the fair market value of the real property, as it existed at the time of the governmental action at issue, as though the owner had the ability to attain the reasonable investment-backed expectation or was not left with uses that are unreasonable, whichever the case may be, and the fair market value of the real property, as it existed at the time of the governmental action at issue, as inordinately burdened, considering the settlement offer together with the statement of allowable uses, of the governmental entity or entities. In determining the award of compensation, consideration may not be given to business damages relative to any development, activity, or use that the action of the governmental entity or entities, considering the settlement offer together with the statement of allowable uses has restricted, limited, or prohibited. The award of compensation shall include a reasonable award of prejudgment interest from the date the claim was presented to the governmental entity or entities as provided in subsection (4).

(c)1. In any action filed pursuant to this section, the property owner is entitled to recover reasonable costs and attorney fees incurred by the property owner, from the governmental entity or entities, according to their proportionate share as determined by the court, from the date of the filing of the circuit court action, if the property owner prevails in the action and the court determines that the settlement offer, including the statement of allowable uses, of the governmental entity or entities did not constitute a bona fide offer to the property owner which reasonably would have resolved the claim, based upon the knowledge available to the governmental entity or entities and the property owner during the 90-day-notice period or the 150-day-notice period.

2. In any action filed pursuant to this section, the governmental entity or entities are entitled to recover reasonable costs and attorney fees incurred by the governmental entity or entities from the date of the filing of the circuit court action, if the governmental entity or entities prevail in the action and the court determines that the property owner did not accept a bona fide settlement offer, including the statement of allowable uses, which reasonably would have resolved the claim fairly

to the property owner if the settlement offer had been accepted by the property owner, based upon the knowledge available to the governmental entity or entities and the property owner during the 90-day-notice period or the 150-day-notice period.

3. The determination of total reasonable costs and attorney fees pursuant to this paragraph shall be made by the court and not by the jury. Any proposed settlement offer or any proposed decision, except for the final written settlement offer or the final written statement of allowable uses, and any negotiations or rejections in regard to the formulation either of the settlement offer or the statement of allowable uses, are inadmissible in the subsequent proceeding established by this section except for the purposes of the determination pursuant to this paragraph.

(d) Within 15 days after the execution of any settlement pursuant to this section, or the issuance of any judgment pursuant to this section, the governmental entity shall provide a copy of the settlement or judgment to the Department of Legal Affairs.

(7)(a) The circuit court may enter any orders necessary to effectuate the purposes of this section and to make final determinations to effectuate relief available under this section.

(b) An award or payment of compensation pursuant to this section shall operate to grant to and vest in any governmental entity by whom compensation is paid the right, title, and interest in rights of use for which the compensation has been paid, which rights may become transferable development rights to be held, sold, or otherwise disposed of by the governmental entity. When there is an award of compensation, the court shall determine the form and the recipient of the right, title, and interest, as well as the terms of their acquisition.

(8) This section does not supplant methods agreed to by the parties and lawfully available for arbitration, mediation, or other forms of alternative dispute resolution, and governmental entities are encouraged to utilize such methods to augment or facilitate the processes and actions contemplated by this section.

(9) This section provides a cause of action for governmental actions that may not rise to the level of a taking under the State Constitution or the United States Constitution. This section may not necessarily be construed under the case law regarding takings if the governmental action does not rise to the level of a taking. The provisions of this section are cumulative, and do not abrogate any other remedy lawfully available, including any remedy lawfully available for governmental actions that rise to the level of a taking. However, a governmental entity shall not be liable for compensation for an action of a governmental entity applicable to, or for the loss in value to, a subject real property more than once.

(10)(a) This section does not apply to any actions taken by a governmental entity which relate to the operation, maintenance, or expansion of transportation facilities, and this section does not affect existing law regarding eminent domain relating to transportation.

(b) This section does not apply to any actions taken by a county with respect to the adoption of a Flood Insurance Rate Map issued by the Federal Emergency Management Agency for the purpose of participating in the National Flood Insurance Program, unless such adoption incorrectly applies an aspect of the Flood Insurance Rate Map to the property in such a way as to, but not limited to, incorrectly assess the elevation of the property.

(11) A cause of action may not be commenced under this section if the claim is presented more than 1 year after a law or regulation is first applied by the governmental entity to the property at issue.

(a) For purposes of determining when this 1-year claim period accrues:

1. A law or regulation is first applied upon enactment and notice as provided for in this subparagraph if the impact of the law or regulation on the real property is clear and unequivocal in its terms and notice is provided by mail to the affected property owner or registered agent at the address referenced in the jurisdiction's most current ad valorem tax records. The fact that the law or regulation could be modified, varied, or altered under any other process or procedure does not preclude the impact of the law or regulation on a property from being clear or unequivocal pursuant to this subparagraph. Any notice under this subparagraph shall be provided after the enactment of the law or regulation and shall inform the property owner or registered agent that the law or regulation may impact the property owner's existing property rights and that the property

owner may have only 1 year from receipt of the notice to pursue any rights established under this section.

2. Otherwise, the law or regulation is first applied to the property when there is a formal denial of a written request for development or variance.

(b) If an owner seeks relief from the governmental action through lawfully available administrative or judicial proceedings, the time for bringing an action under this section is tolled until the conclusion of such proceedings.

(12) No cause of action exists under this section as to the application of any law enacted on or before May 11, 1995, or as to the application of any rule, regulation, or ordinance adopted, or formally noticed for adoption, on or before that date. A subsequent amendment to any such law, rule, regulation, or ordinance gives rise to a cause of action under this section only to the extent that the application of the amendatory language imposes an inordinate burden apart from the law, rule, regulation, or ordinance being amended.

(13) In accordance with s. 13, Art. X of the State Constitution, the state, for itself and for its agencies or political subdivisions, waives sovereign immunity for causes of action based upon the application of any law, regulation, or ordinance subject to this section, but only to the extent specified in this section.

70.20. Balancing of interests.

It is a policy of this state to encourage municipalities, counties, and other governmental entities and sign owners to enter into relocation and reconstruction agreements that allow governmental entities to undertake public projects and accomplish public goals without the expenditure of public funds while allowing the continued maintenance of private investment in signage as a medium of commercial and noncommercial communication.

(1) Municipalities, counties, and all other governmental entities are specifically empowered to enter into relocation and reconstruction agreements on whatever terms are agreeable to the sign owner and the municipality, county, or other governmental entity involved and to provide for relocation and reconstruction of signs by agreement, ordinance, or resolution. As used in this section, a "relocation and reconstruction agreement" means a consensual, contractual agreement between a sign owner and a municipality, county, or other governmental entity for either the reconstruction of an existing sign or the removal of a sign and construction of a new sign to substitute for the sign removed.

(2) Except as otherwise provided in this section, no municipality, county, or other governmental entity may remove, or cause to be removed, any lawfully erected sign located along any portion of the interstate, federal-aid primary or other highway system, or any other road without first paying just compensation for such removal as determined by agreement between the parties or through eminent domain proceedings. Except as otherwise provided in this section, no municipality, county, or other governmental entity may cause in any way the alteration of any lawfully erected sign located along any portion of the interstate, federal-aid primary or other highway system, or any other road without first paying just compensation for such alteration as determined by agreement between the parties or through eminent domain proceedings. The provisions of this section shall not apply to any ordinance the validity, constitutionality, and enforceability of which the owner has by written agreement waived all right to challenge.

(3) In the event that a municipality, county, or other governmental entity undertakes a public project or public goal requiring alteration or removal of any lawfully erected sign, the municipality, county, or other governmental entity shall notify the owner of the affected sign in writing of the public project or goal and of the intention of the municipality, county, or other governmental entity to seek such alteration or removal. Within 30 days after receipt of the notice, the owner of the sign and the municipality, county, or other governmental entity shall attempt to meet for purposes of negotiating and executing a relocation and reconstruction agreement as

provided for in subsection (1).

(4) If the parties fail to enter into a relocation and reconstruction agreement within 120 days after the initial notification by the municipality, county, or other governmental entity, either party may request mandatory nonbinding arbitration to resolve the disagreements between the parties. Each party shall select an arbitrator, and the individuals so selected shall choose a third arbitrator. The three arbitrators shall constitute the panel that shall arbitrate the dispute between the parties and, at the conclusion of the proceedings, shall present to the parties a proposed relocation and reconstruction agreement that the panel believes equitably balances the rights, interests, obligations, and reasonable expectations of the parties. If the municipality, county, or other governmental entity and the sign owner accept the proposed relocation and reconstruction agreement, the municipality, county, or other governmental entity and the sign owner shall each pay its respective costs of arbitration and shall pay one-half of the costs of the arbitration panel, unless the parties otherwise agree.

(5) If the parties do not enter into a relocation and reconstruction agreement, the municipality, county, or other governmental entity may proceed with the public project or purpose and the alteration or removal of the sign only after first paying just compensation for such alteration or removal as determined by agreement between the parties or through eminent domain proceedings.

(6) The requirement by a municipality, county, or other governmental entity that a lawfully erected sign be removed or altered as a condition precedent to the issuance or continued effectiveness of a development order constitutes a compelled removal that is prohibited without prior payment of just compensation under subsection (2). This subsection shall not apply when the owner of the land on which the sign is located is seeking to have the property redesignated on the future land use map of the applicable comprehensive plan for exclusively single-family residential use.

(7) The requirement by a municipality, county, or other governmental entity that a lawfully erected sign be altered or removed from the premises upon which it is located incident to the voluntary acquisition of such property by a municipality, county, or other governmental entity constitutes a compelled removal that is prohibited without payment of just compensation under subsection (2).

(8) Nothing in this section shall prevent a municipality, county, or other governmental entity from acquiring a lawfully erected sign through eminent domain or from prospectively regulating the placement, size, height, or other aspects of new signs within such entity's jurisdiction, including the prohibition of new signs, unless otherwise authorized pursuant to this section. Nothing in this section shall impair any ordinance or provision of any ordinance not inconsistent with this section, including a provision that creates a ban or partial ban on new signs, nor shall this section create any new rights for any party other than the owner of a sign, the owner of the land upon which it is located, or a municipality, county, or other governmental entity as expressed in this section.

(9) This section applies only to a lawfully erected sign the subject matter of which relates to premises other than the premises on which it is located or to merchandise, services, activities, or entertainment not sold, produced, manufactured, or furnished on the premises on which the sign is located.

(10) This section shall not apply to any actions taken by the Department of Transportation that relate to the operation, maintenance, or expansion of transportation facilities, and this section shall not affect existing law regarding eminent domain relating to the Department of Transportation.

(11) Nothing in this section shall impair or affect any written agreement existing prior to the effective date of this act, including, but not limited to, any settlement agreements reliant upon the legality or enforceability of local ordinances. The provisions of this section shall not apply to any signs that are required to be removed by a date certain in areas designated by local ordinance as view corridors if the local ordinance creating the view corridors was enacted in part to effectuate a consensual agreement between the local government and two or more sign owners prior to the effective date of this act, nor shall the provisions of this section apply to any signs that are the subject of an ordinance providing an amortization period, which period has expired, and which ordinance is the subject of judicial proceedings that were commenced on or before January 1, 2001, nor shall this section apply to any municipality with an ordinance that prohibits billboards and has two or fewer billboards located within its current boundaries or its future annexed

properties.

(12) Subsection (6) shall not apply when the development order permits construction of a replacement sign that cannot be erected without the removal of the lawfully erected sign being replaced.

70.45. Governmental exactions.

(1) As used in this section, the term:

(a) "Damages" means, in addition to the right to injunctive relief, the reduction in fair market value of the real property or the amount of the fee or infrastructure cost that exceeds what would be permitted under this section.

(b) "Governmental entity" has the same meaning as provided in s. 70.001(3)(c).

(c) "Prohibited exaction" means any condition imposed by a governmental entity on a property owner's proposed use of real property that lacks an essential nexus to a legitimate public purpose and is not roughly proportionate to the impacts of the proposed use that the governmental entity seeks to avoid, minimize, or mitigate.

(d) "Property owner" has the same meaning as provided in s. 70.001(3)(f).

(e) "Real property" has the same meaning as provided in s. 70.001(3)(g).

(2) In addition to other remedies available in law or equity, a property owner may bring an action in a court of competent jurisdiction under this section to recover damages caused by a prohibited exaction. Such action may not be brought until a prohibited exaction is actually imposed or required in writing as a final condition of approval for the requested use of real property. The right to bring an action under this section may not be waived. This section does not apply to impact fees adopted under s. 163.31801 or non-ad valorem assessments as defined in s. 197.3632.

(3) At least 90 days before filing an action under this section, but no later than 180 days after imposition of the prohibited exaction, the property owner shall provide to the relevant governmental entity written notice of the proposed action. This written notice shall identify the exaction that the property owner believes is prohibited, briefly explain why the property owner believes the exaction is prohibited, and provide an estimate of the damages. Upon receipt of the written notice:

(a) The governmental entity shall review the notice of claim and respond in writing to the property owner by identifying the basis for the exaction and explaining why the governmental entity maintains that the exaction is proportionate to the harm created by the proposed use of real property, or by proposing to remove all or a portion of the exaction.

(b) The written response may not be used against the governmental entity in subsequent litigation other than for purposes of assessing attorney fees and costs under subsection (5).

(4) For each claim filed under this section, the governmental entity has the burden of proving that the exaction has an essential nexus to a legitimate public purpose and is roughly proportionate to the impacts of the proposed use that the governmental entity is seeking to avoid, minimize, or mitigate. The property owner has the burden of proving damages that result from a prohibited exaction.

(5) The court may award attorney fees and costs to the prevailing party; however, if the court determines that the exaction which is the subject of the claim lacks an essential nexus to a legitimate public purpose, the court shall award attorney fees and costs to the property owner.

(6) To ensure that courts may assess damages for claims filed under this section in accordance with s. 13, Art. X of the State Constitution, the state, for itself and its agencies or political subdivisions, waives sovereign immunity for causes of action based upon the application of this section. Such waiver is limited only to actions brought under this section.

(7) This section applies to any prohibited exaction imposed or required in writing on or after October 1, 2015, as a final condition of approval for the requested use of real property.

70.51. Land use and environmental dispute resolution.

(1) This section may be cited as the "Florida Land Use and Environmental Dispute Resolution Act."

(2) As used in this section, the term:

(a) "Development order" means any order, or notice of proposed state or regional governmental agency action, which is or will have the effect of granting, denying, or granting with conditions an application for a development permit, and includes the rezoning of a specific parcel. Actions by the state or a local government on comprehensive plan amendments are not development orders.

(b) "Development permit" means any building permit, zoning permit, subdivision approval, certification, special exception, variance, or any other similar action of local government, as well as any permit authorized to be issued under state law by state, regional, or local government which has the effect of authorizing the development of real property including, but not limited to, programs implementing chapters 125, 161, 163, 166, 187, 258, 372, 373, 378, 380, and 403.

(c) "Special magistrate" means a person selected by the parties to perform the duties prescribed in this section. The special magistrate must be a resident of the state and possess experience and expertise in mediation and at least one of the following disciplines and a working familiarity with the others: land use and environmental permitting, land planning, land economics, local and state government organization and powers, and the law governing the same.

(d) "Owner" means a person with a legal or equitable interest in real property who filed an application for a development permit for the property at the state, regional, or local level and who received a development order, or who holds legal title to real property that is subject to an enforcement action of a governmental entity.

(e) "Proposed use of the property" means the proposal filed by the owner to develop his or her real property.

(f) "Governmental entity" includes an agency of the state, a regional or a local government created by the State Constitution or by general or special act, any county or municipality, or any other entity that independently exercises governmental authority. The term does not include the United States or any of its agencies.

(g) "Land" or "real property" means land and includes any appurtenances and improvements to the land, including any other relevant real property in which the owner had a relevant interest.

(3) Any owner who believes that a development order, either separately or in conjunction with other development orders, or an enforcement action of a governmental entity, is unreasonable or unfairly burdens the use of the owner's real property, may apply within 30 days after receipt of the order or notice of the governmental action for relief under this section.

(4) To initiate a proceeding under this section, an owner must file a request for relief with the elected or appointed head of the governmental entity that issued the development order or orders, or that initiated the enforcement action. The head of the governmental entity may not charge the owner for the request for relief and must forward the request for relief to the special magistrate who is mutually agreed upon by the owner and the governmental entity within 10 days after receipt of the request.

(5) The governmental entity with whom a request has been filed shall also serve a copy of the request for relief by United States mail or by hand delivery to:

(a) Owners of real property contiguous to the owner's property at the address on the latest county tax roll.

(b) Any substantially affected party who submitted oral or written testimony, sworn or unsworn, of a substantive nature which stated with particularity objections to or support for any development order at issue or enforcement action at issue. Notice under this paragraph is required only if that party indicated a desire to receive notice of any subsequent special magistrate proceedings occurring on the development order or enforcement action. Each governmental entity must maintain in its files relating to particular development orders a mailing list of persons who have presented oral or written testimony and who have requested notice.

(6) The request for relief must contain:

(a) A brief statement of the owner's proposed use of the property.

(b) A summary of the development order or description of the enforcement action. A copy of the development order or the documentation of an enforcement action at issue must be attached to the request.

(c) A brief statement of the impact of the development order or enforcement action on the ability of the owner to achieve the proposed use of the property.

(d) A certificate of service showing the parties, including the governmental entity, served.

(7) The special magistrate may require other information in the interest of gaining a complete understanding of the request for relief.

(8) The special magistrate may conduct a hearing on whether the request for relief should be dismissed for failing to include the information required in subsection (6). If the special magistrate dismisses the case, the special magistrate shall allow the owner to amend the request and refile. Failure to file an adequate amended request within the time specified shall result in a dismissal with prejudice as to this proceeding.

(9) By requesting relief under this section, the owner consents to grant the special magistrate and the parties reasonable access to the real property with advance notice at a time and in a manner acceptable to the owner of the real property.

(10)(a) Before initiating a special magistrate proceeding to review a local development order or local enforcement action, the owner must exhaust all nonjudicial local government administrative appeals if the appeals take no longer than 4 months. Once nonjudicial local administrative appeals are exhausted and the development order or enforcement action is final, or within 4 months after issuance of the development order or notice of the enforcement action if the owner has pursued local administrative appeals even if the appeals have not been concluded, the owner may initiate a proceeding under this section. Initiation of a proceeding tolls the time for seeking judicial review of a local government development order or enforcement action until the special magistrate's recommendation is acted upon by the local government. Election by the owner to file for judicial review of a local government development order or enforcement action prior to initiating a proceeding under this section waives any right to a special magistrate proceeding.

(b) If an owner requests special magistrate relief from a development order or enforcement action issued by a state or regional agency, the time for challenging agency action under ss. 120.569 and 120.57 is tolled. If an owner chooses to bring a proceeding under ss. 120.569 and 120.57 before initiating a special magistrate proceeding, then the owner waives any right to a special magistrate proceeding unless all parties consent to proceeding to mediation.

(11) The initial party to the proceeding is the governmental entity that issues the development order to the owner or that is taking the enforcement action. In those instances when the development order or enforcement action is the culmination of a process involving more than one governmental entity or when a complete resolution of all relevant issues would require the active participation of more than one governmental entity, the special magistrate may, upon application of a party, join those governmental entities as parties to the proceeding if it will assist in effecting the purposes of this section, and those governmental entities so joined shall actively participate in the procedure.

(12) Within 21 days after receipt of the request for relief, any owner of land contiguous to the owner's property and any substantially affected person who submitted oral or written testimony, sworn or unsworn, of a substantive nature which stated with particularity objections to or support for the development order or enforcement action at issue may request to participate in the proceeding. Those persons may be permitted to participate in the hearing but shall not be granted party or intervenor status. The participation of such persons is limited to addressing issues raised regarding alternatives, variances, and other types of adjustment to the development order or enforcement action which may impact their substantial interests, including denial of the development order or application of an enforcement action.

(13) Each party must make efforts to assure that those persons qualified by training or experience

necessary to address issues raised by the request or by the special magistrate and further qualified to address alternatives, variances, and other types of modifications to the development order or enforcement action are present at the hearing.

(14) The special magistrate may subpoena any nonparty witnesses in the state whom the special magistrate believes will aid in the disposition of the matter.

(15)(a) The special magistrate shall hold a hearing within 45 days after his or her receipt of the request for relief unless a different date is agreed to by all the parties. The hearing must be held in the county in which the property is located.

(b) The special magistrate must provide notice of the place, date, and time of the hearing to all parties and any other persons who have requested such notice at least 40 days prior to the hearing.

(16)(a) Fifteen days following the filing of a request for relief, the governmental entity that issued the development order or that is taking the enforcement action shall file a response to the request for relief with the special magistrate together with a copy to the owner. The response must set forth in reasonable detail the position of the governmental entity regarding the matters alleged by the owner. The response must include a brief statement explaining the public purpose of the regulations on which the development order or enforcement action is based.

(b) Any governmental entity that is added by the special magistrate as a party must file a response to the request for relief prior to the hearing but not later than 15 days following its admission.

(c) Any party may incorporate in the response to the request for relief a request to be dropped from the proceeding. The request to be dropped must set forth facts and circumstances relevant to aid the special magistrate in ruling on the request. All requests to be dropped must be disposed of prior to conducting any hearings on the merits of the request for relief.

(17) In all respects, the hearing must be informal and open to the public and does not require the use of an attorney. The hearing must operate at the direction and under the supervision of the special magistrate. The object of the hearing is to focus attention on the impact of the governmental action giving rise to the request for relief and to explore alternatives to the development order or enforcement action and other regulatory efforts by the governmental entities in order to recommend relief, when appropriate, to the owner.

(a) The first responsibility of the special magistrate is to facilitate a resolution of the conflict between the owner and governmental entities to the end that some modification of the owner's proposed use of the property or adjustment in the development order or enforcement action or regulatory efforts by one or more of the governmental parties may be reached. Accordingly, the special magistrate shall act as a facilitator or mediator between the parties in an effort to effect a mutually acceptable solution. The parties shall be represented at the mediation by persons with authority to bind their respective parties to a solution, or by persons with authority to recommend a solution directly to the persons with authority to bind their respective parties to a solution.

(b) If an acceptable solution is not reached by the parties after the special magistrate's attempt at mediation, the special magistrate shall consider the facts and circumstances set forth in the request for relief and any responses and any other information produced at the hearing in order to determine whether the action by the governmental entity or entities is unreasonable or unfairly burdens the real property.

(c) In conducting the hearing, the special magistrate may hear from all parties and witnesses that are necessary to an understanding of the matter. The special magistrate shall weigh all information offered at the hearing.

(18) The circumstances to be examined in determining whether the development order or enforcement action, or the development order or enforcement action in conjunction with regulatory efforts of other governmental parties, is unreasonable or unfairly burdens use of the property may include, but are not limited to:

(a) The history of the real property, including when it was purchased, how much was purchased, where it is located, the nature of the title, the composition of the property, and how it was initially used.

(b) The history or development and use of the real property, including what was developed on the property and by whom, if it was subdivided and how and to whom it was sold, whether plats were filed or recorded, and whether infrastructure and other public services or improvements may have been dedicated to the public.

(c) The history of environmental protection and land use controls and other regulations, including how and when the land was classified, how use was proscribed, and what changes in classifications occurred.

(d) The present nature and extent of the real property, including its natural and altered characteristics.

(e) The reasonable expectations of the owner at the time of acquisition, or immediately prior to the implementation of the regulation at issue, whichever is later, under the regulations then in effect and under common law.

(f) The public purpose sought to be achieved by the development order or enforcement action, including the nature and magnitude of the problem addressed by the underlying regulations on which the development order or enforcement action is based; whether the development order or enforcement action is necessary to the achievement of the public purpose; and whether there are alternative development orders or enforcement action conditions that would achieve the public purpose and allow for reduced restrictions on the use of the property.

(g) Uses authorized for and restrictions placed on similar property.

(h) Any other information determined relevant by the special magistrate.

(19) Within 14 days after the conclusion of the hearing, the special magistrate shall prepare and file with all parties a written recommendation.

(a) If the special magistrate finds that the development order at issue, or the development order or enforcement action in combination with the actions or regulations of other governmental entities, is not unreasonable or does not unfairly burden the use of the owner's property, the special magistrate must recommend that the development order or enforcement action remain undisturbed and the proceeding shall end, subject to the owner's retention of all other available remedies.

(b) If the special magistrate finds that the development order or enforcement action, or the development order or enforcement action in combination with the actions or regulations of other governmental entities, is unreasonable or unfairly burdens use of the owner's property, the special magistrate, with the owner's consent to proceed, may recommend one or more alternatives that protect the public interest served by the development order or enforcement action and regulations at issue but allow for reduced restraints on the use of the owner's real property, including, but not limited to:

1. An adjustment of land development or permit standards or other provisions controlling the development or use of land.

2. Increases or modifications in the density, intensity, or use of areas of development.

3. The transfer of development rights.

4. Land swaps or exchanges.

5. Mitigation, including payments in lieu of onsite mitigation.

6. Location on the least sensitive portion of the property.

7. Conditioning the amount of development or use permitted.

8. A requirement that issues be addressed on a more comprehensive basis than a single proposed use or development.

9. Issuance of the development order, a variance, special exception, or other extraordinary relief, including withdrawal of the enforcement action.

10. Purchase of the real property, or an interest therein, by an appropriate governmental entity.

(c) This subsection does not prohibit the owner and governmental entity from entering into an agreement as to the permissible use of the property prior to the special magistrate entering a recommendation. An agreement for a permissible use must be incorporated in the special magistrate's recommendation.

(20) The special magistrate's recommendation is a public record under chapter 119. However, actions or statements of all participants to the special magistrate proceeding are evidence of an offer to compromise and inadmissible in any proceeding, judicial or administrative.

(21) Within 45 days after receipt of the special magistrate's recommendation, the governmental

entity responsible for the development order or enforcement action and other governmental entities participating in the proceeding must consult among themselves and each governmental entity must:

(a) Accept the recommendation of the special magistrate as submitted and proceed to implement it by development agreement, when appropriate, or by other method, in the ordinary course and consistent with the rules and procedures of that governmental entity. However, the decision of the governmental entity to accept the recommendation of the special magistrate with respect to granting a modification, variance, or special exception to the application of statutes, rules, regulations, or ordinances as they would otherwise apply to the subject property does not require an owner to duplicate previous processes in which the owner has participated in order to effectuate the granting of the modification, variance, or special exception;

(b) Modify the recommendation as submitted by the special magistrate and proceed to implement it by development agreement, when appropriate, or by other method, in the ordinary course and consistent with the rules and procedures of that governmental entity; or

(c) Reject the recommendation as submitted by the special magistrate. Failure to act within 45 days is a rejection unless the period is extended by agreement of the owner and issuer of the development order or enforcement action.

(22) If a governmental entity accepts the special magistrate's recommendation or modifies it and the owner rejects the acceptance or modification, or if a governmental entity rejects the special magistrate's recommendation, the governmental entity must issue a written decision within 30 days that describes as specifically as possible the use or uses available to the subject real property.

(23) The procedure established by this section may not continue longer than 165 days, unless the period is extended by agreement of the parties. A decision describing available uses constitutes the last prerequisite to judicial action and the matter is ripe or final for subsequent judicial proceedings unless the owner initiates a proceeding under ss. 120.569 and 120.57. If the owner brings a proceeding under ss. 120.569 and 120.57, the matter is ripe when the proceeding culminates in a final order whether further appeal is available or not.

(24) The procedure created by this section is not itself, nor does it create, a judicial cause of action. Once the governmental entity acts on the special magistrate's recommendation, the owner may elect to file suit in a court of competent jurisdiction. Invoking the procedures of this section is not a condition precedent to filing a civil action.

(25) Regardless of the action the governmental entity takes on the special magistrate's recommendation, a recommendation that the development order or enforcement action, or the development order or enforcement action in combination with other governmental regulatory actions, is unreasonable or unfairly burdens use of the owner's real property may serve as an indication of sufficient hardship to support modification, variances, or special exceptions to the application of statutes, rules, regulations, or ordinances to the subject property.

(26) A special magistrate's recommendation under this section constitutes data in support of, and a support document for, a comprehensive plan or comprehensive plan amendment, but is not, in and of itself, dispositive of a determination of compliance with chapter 163.

(27) The special magistrate shall send a copy of the recommendation in each case to the Department of Legal Affairs. Each governmental entity, within 15 days after its action on the special magistrate's recommendation, shall notify the Department of Legal Affairs in writing as to what action the governmental entity took on the special magistrate's recommendation.

(28) Each governmental entity may establish procedural guidelines to govern the conduct of proceedings authorized by this section, which must include, but are not limited to, payment of special magistrate fees and expenses, including the costs of providing notice and effecting service of the request for relief under this section, which shall be borne equally by the governmental entities and the owner.

(29) This section shall be liberally construed to effect fully its obvious purposes and intent, and governmental entities shall direct all available resources and authorities to effect fully the obvious purposes and intent of this section in resolving disputes. Governmental entities are encouraged to expedite notice and time-related provisions to implement resolution of disputes under this section.

The procedure established by this section may be used to resolve disputes in pending judicial proceedings, with the agreement of the parties to the judicial proceedings, and subject to the approval of the court in which the judicial proceedings are pending. The provisions of this section are cumulative, and do not supplant other methods agreed to by the parties and lawfully available for arbitration, mediation, or other forms of alternative dispute resolution.

(30) This section applies only to development orders issued, modified, or amended, or to enforcement actions issued, on or after October 1, 1995.

70.80. Construction of ss. 70.001, 70.45, and 70.51.

It is the express declaration of the Legislature that ss. 70.001, 70.45, and 70.51 have separate and distinct bases, objectives, applications, and processes. It is therefore the intent of the Legislature that ss. 70.001, 70.45, and 70.51 are not to be construed in pari materia.

CHAPTER 71. REESTABLISHMENT OF DOCUMENTS

71.011. Reestablishment of papers, records, and files.

All papers, written or printed, of any kind whatsoever, and the records and files of any official, court or public office, may be reestablished in the manner hereinafter provided.

(1) WHO MAY REESTABLISH.—Any person interested in the paper, file or record to be reestablished may reestablish it.

(2) VENUE.—If reestablishment is sought of a record or file, venue is in the county where the record or file existed before its loss or destruction. If it is a private paper, venue is in the county where any person affected thereby lives or if such persons are nonresidents of the state, then in any county in which the person seeking the reestablishment desires.

(3) REMEDY CONCURRENT.—Nothing herein shall prevent the reestablishment of lost papers, records and files at common law or in equity in the usual manner.

(4) EFFECT.—

(a) Any paper, record or file reestablished has the effect of the original. A private paper has such effect immediately on recording the judgment reestablishing it, but a reestablished record does not have that effect until recorded and a reestablished paper or file of any official, court or public officer does not have that effect until a certified copy is filed with the official or in the court or public office where the original belonged. A certified copy of any reestablished paper, the original of which is required or authorized by law to be recorded, may be recorded.

(b) When any deed forming a link in a chain of title to land in this state has been placed on the proper record without having been acknowledged or proven for record and has thereafter been lost or destroyed, certified copies of the record of the deed as so recorded may be received as evidence to reestablish the deed if the deed has been so recorded for 20 years.

(5) COMPLAINT.—A person desiring to establish any paper, record or file, except when otherwise provided, shall file a complaint in chancery setting forth that the paper, record or file has been lost or destroyed and is not in the custody or control of the petitioner, the time and manner of loss or destruction, that a copy attached is a substantial copy of that lost or destroyed, that the persons named in the complaint are the only persons known to plaintiff who are interested for or against such reestablishment.

71.021. Reestablishment of record of marks and brands.

The person desiring the reestablishment of the record of any marks or brands shall file a verified complaint in chancery describing the particular mark or brand sought to be reestablished, stating the place where it was recorded, the time of record as near as is known, that the record has been lost or destroyed, and demand reestablishment of the record of the mark or brand. On filing the complaint, the court shall order reestablishment of the mark or brand.

71.031. Reestablishment of proceedings in pending actions.

Lost or destroyed proceedings and any paper or file affecting them in any actions pending and undetermined in any court may be reestablished by the person desiring reestablishment by filing a copy of the proceedings, paper or file in chancery and giving 10 days' written notice to all parties to the action of the application for reestablishment of the proceedings, paper or file. On the hearing the judge shall ascertain the facts and determine the application.

71.041. Reestablishment of land titles destroyed by fire.

(1) JURISDICTION.—When the records in any county or any material part thereof have been destroyed by fire so that a connected chain of title cannot be deduced therefrom, the chancery court in the county has jurisdiction to inquire into the condition of any title to or interest in any land in the county and to determine and establish the title against all persons known or unknown.
(2) PLAINTIFF.—Any person claiming a freehold estate in any land in the county who, or whose grantors, were in the actual possession of the land at the time of destruction of the records and who is in possession thereof at the time of filing the complaint may file a complaint to establish and confirm his or her title to an estate in such land. Tenants in common or persons owning as aforesaid an undivided interest in the lands may join in the action.
(3) COMPLAINT.—The complaint shall state the description of the lands, the character and extent of the estate claimed by the plaintiff, from whom and when and by what mode the plaintiff derived the title, the names of all persons owning or claiming any estate or possessory interest in the lands or any part thereof, all persons who are in possession of the lands or any part thereof, all persons to whom any of the lands have been conveyed, and the date or dates that the conveyances were recorded since the time of the destruction of the records and before the filing of the complaint and if no such persons are known to plaintiff, he or she shall so state.
(4) DETERMINATION OF TITLES, ETC.—The court may determine in whom the title to any land described in the complaint is vested, whether plaintiff or any other party, but the judgment shall not affect any lien to which the land is subject, but shall leave all liens to be ascertained or established or enforced as is provided by law.

CHAPTER 72. TAX MATTERS

72.011. Jurisdiction of circuit courts in specific tax matters; administrative hearings and appeals; time for commencing action; parties; deposits.

(1)(a) A taxpayer may contest the legality of any assessment or denial of refund of tax, fee, surcharge, permit, interest, or penalty provided for under s. 125.0104, s. 125.0108, chapter 198, chapter 199, chapter 201, chapter 202, chapter 203, chapter 206, chapter 207, chapter 210, chapter 211, chapter 212, chapter 213, chapter 220, s. 379.362(3), chapter 376, s. 403.717, s. 403.718, s. 403.7185, s. 538.09, s. 538.25, chapter 550, chapter 561, chapter 562, chapter 563, chapter 564, chapter 565, chapter 624, or s. 681.117 by filing an action in circuit court; or, alternatively, the taxpayer may file a petition under the applicable provisions of chapter 120. However, once an action has been initiated under s. 120.56, s. 120.565, s. 120.569, s. 120.57, or s. 120.80(14)(b), no action relating to the same subject matter may be filed by the taxpayer in circuit court, and judicial review shall be exclusively limited to appellate review pursuant to s. 120.68; and once an action has been initiated in circuit court, no action may be brought under chapter 120.

(b) A taxpayer may not file an action under paragraph (a) to contest an assessment or a denial of refund of any tax, fee, surcharge, permit, interest, or penalty relating to the statutes listed in paragraph (a) until the taxpayer complies with the applicable registration requirements contained in those statutes which apply to the tax for which the action is filed.

(2)(a) An action may not be brought to contest an assessment of any tax, interest, or penalty assessed under a section or chapter specified in subsection (1) more than 60 days after the date the assessment becomes final. An action may not be brought to contest a denial of refund of any tax, interest, or penalty paid under a section or chapter specified in subsection (1) more than 60 days after the date the denial becomes final.

(b) The date on which an assessment or a denial of refund becomes final and procedures by which a taxpayer must be notified of the assessment or of the denial of refund must be established:

1. By rule adopted by the Department of Revenue;

2. With respect to assessments or refund denials under chapter 207, by rule adopted by the Department of Highway Safety and Motor Vehicles;

3. With respect to assessments or refund denials under chapters 210, 550, 561, 562, 563, 564, and 565, by rule adopted by the Department of Business and Professional Regulation; or

4. With respect to taxes that a county collects or enforces under s. 125.0104(10) or s. 212.0305(5), by an ordinance that may additionally provide for informal dispute resolution procedures in accordance with s. 213.21.

(c) The applicable department or county need not file or docket an assessment or a refund denial with the agency clerk or county official designated by ordinance in order for the assessment or refund denial to become final for purposes of an action initiated under this chapter or chapter 120.

(3) In any action filed in circuit court contesting the legality of any tax, interest, or penalty assessed under a section or chapter specified in subsection (1), the plaintiff must:

(a) Pay to the applicable department or county the amount of the tax, penalty, and accrued interest assessed by the department or county which is not being contested by the taxpayer; and either

(b)1. Tender into the registry of the court with the complaint the amount of the contested assessment complained of, including penalties and accrued interest, unless this requirement is waived in writing by the executive director of the applicable department or by the county official designated by ordinance; or

2. File with the complaint a cash bond or a surety bond for the amount of the contested assessment endorsed by a surety company authorized to do business in this state, or by any other security arrangement as may be approved by the court, and conditioned upon payment in full of the judgment, including the taxes, costs, penalties, and interest, unless this requirement is waived in writing by the executive director of the applicable department or by the county official designated by ordinance.

(4)(a) Except as provided in paragraph (b), an action initiated in circuit court pursuant to subsection (1) shall be filed in the Second Judicial Circuit Court in and for Leon County or in the circuit court in the county where the taxpayer resides, maintains its principal commercial domicile in this state, or, in the ordinary course of business, regularly maintains its books and records in this state.

(b) Venue in an action initiated in circuit court pursuant to subsection (1) by a taxpayer that is not a resident of this state or that does not maintain a commercial domicile in this state shall be in Leon County. Venue in an action contesting the legality of an assessment or refund denial arising under chapter 198 shall be in the circuit court having jurisdiction over the administration of the estate.

(5) The requirements of subsections (1), (2), and (3) are jurisdictional.

(6) Any action brought under this chapter is not subject to the provisions of chapter 45 as amended by chapter 87-249, Laws of Florida, relating to offers of settlement.

72.031. Actions under s. 72.011(1); parties; service of process.

(1) In any action brought in circuit court pursuant to s. 72.011(1), the person initiating the action shall be the plaintiff and the Department of Revenue shall be the defendant, except that for actions contesting an assessment or denial of refund under chapter 207 the Department of Highway Safety and Motor Vehicles shall be the defendant, for actions contesting an assessment or denial of refund under chapters 210, 550, 561, 562, 563, 564, and 565 the Department of Business and Professional Regulation shall be the defendant, and for actions contesting an assessment or denial of refund of a tax imposed under s. 125.0104 or s. 212.0305 by a county that has elected under s. 125.0104(10) or s. 212.0305(5), respectively, to administer the tax, the defendant shall be the county and the Department of Revenue. It shall not be necessary for the Governor and Cabinet, constituting the Department of Revenue, to be named as party defendants or named separately as individual parties; nor shall it be necessary for the executive director of the department to be named as an individual party.

(2) Service of process on the applicable department or county shall be perfected by service pursuant to s. 48.111, notwithstanding the provisions of s. 48.121.

72.041. Tax liabilities arising under the laws of other states.

Actions to enforce lawfully imposed sales, use, and corporate income taxes and motor and other fuel taxes of another state may be brought in a court of this state under the following conditions:

(1) The state seeking to institute an action for the collection, assessment, or enforcement of a lawfully imposed tax must have extended a like courtesy to this state;

(2) Venue for any action under this section shall be the circuit court of the county in which the defendant resides;

(3) This section does not apply to the enforcement of tax warrants of another state unless the warrant has been obtained as a result of a judgment entered by a court of competent jurisdiction in the taxing state or unless the courts of the state seeking to enforce its warrant allow the enforcement of the warrants issued by the Department of Revenue pursuant to chapters 206, 212, 213, and 220; and

(4) All tax liabilities owing to this state or any of its subdivisions shall be paid first and shall be prior in right to any tax liability arising under the laws of other states.

CHAPTER 73. EMINENT DOMAIN

73.012. Procedure.

Actions in eminent domain shall be governed by the rules of civil procedure and the appellate rules unless otherwise provided by this chapter.

73.013. Conveyance of property taken by eminent domain; preservation of government entity communications services eminent domain limitation; exception to restrictions on power of eminent domain.

(1) Notwithstanding any other provision of law, including any charter provision, ordinance, statute, or special law, if the state, any political subdivision as defined in s. 1.01(8), or any other entity to which the power of eminent domain is delegated files a petition of condemnation on or after the effective date of this section regarding a parcel of real property in this state, ownership or control of property acquired pursuant to such petition may not be conveyed by the condemning authority or any other entity to a natural person or private entity, by lease or otherwise, except that ownership or control of property acquired pursuant to such petition may be conveyed, by lease or otherwise, to a natural person or private entity:

(a) For use in providing common carrier services or systems;

(b)1. For use as a road or other right-of-way or means that is open to the public for transportation, whether at no charge or by toll;

2. For use in the provision of transportation-related services, business opportunities, and products pursuant to s. 338.234, on a toll road;

(c) That is a public or private utility for use in providing electricity services or systems, natural or manufactured gas services or systems, water and wastewater services or systems, stormwater or runoff services or systems, sewer services or systems, pipeline facilities, telephone services or systems, or similar services or systems;

(d) For use in providing public infrastructure;

(e) That occupies, pursuant to a lease, an incidental part of a public property or a public facility for the purpose of providing goods or services to the public;

(f) Without restriction, after public notice and competitive bidding unless otherwise provided by general law, if less than 10 years have elapsed since the condemning authority acquired title to the property and the following conditions are met:

1. The condemning authority or governmental entity holding title to the property documents that the property is no longer needed for the use or purpose for which it was acquired by the condemning authority or for which it was transferred to the current titleholder; and

2. The owner from whom the property was taken by eminent domain is given the opportunity to repurchase the property at the price that he or she received from the condemning authority;

(g) After public notice and competitive bidding unless otherwise provided by general law, if the property was owned and controlled by the condemning authority or a governmental entity for at least 10 years after the condemning authority acquired title to the property; or

(h) In accordance with subsection (2).

(2)(a) If ownership of property is conveyed to a natural person or private entity pursuant to

paragraph (1)(a), paragraph (1)(b), paragraph (1)(c), paragraph (1)(d), or paragraph (1)(e), and at least 10 years have elapsed since the condemning authority acquired title to the property, the property may subsequently be transferred, after public notice and competitive bidding unless otherwise provided by general law, to another natural person or private entity without restriction.
(b) If ownership of property is conveyed to a natural person or private entity pursuant to paragraph (1)(a), paragraph (1)(b), paragraph (1)(c), paragraph (1)(d), or paragraph (1)(e), and less than 10 years have elapsed since the condemning authority acquired title to the property, the property may be transferred, after public notice and competitive bidding unless otherwise provided by general law, to another natural person or private entity without restriction, if the following conditions are met:
1. The current titleholder documents that the property is no longer needed for the use or purpose for which the property was transferred to the current titleholder; and
2. The owner from whom the property was taken by eminent domain is given the opportunity to repurchase the property at the price that he or she received from the condemning authority.
(3) This section does not affect the limitation on a government entity's powers of eminent domain contained in s. 350.81(2)(j).
(4) The power of eminent domain shall be restricted as provided in this chapter and chapters 127, 163, and 166, except when the owner of a property relinquishes the property and concedes to the taking of the property in order to retain the ability to reinvest the proceeds of the sale of the property in replacement property under s. 1033 of the Internal Revenue Code.

73.014. Taking property to eliminate nuisance, slum, or blight conditions prohibited.

(1) Notwithstanding any other provision of law, including any charter provision, ordinance, statute, or special law, the state, any political subdivision as defined in s. 1.01(8), or any other entity to which the power of eminent domain is delegated may not exercise the power of eminent domain to take private property for the purpose of abating or eliminating a public nuisance. Notwithstanding any other provision of law, including any charter provision, ordinance, statute, or special law, abating or eliminating a public nuisance is not a valid public purpose or use for which private property may be taken by eminent domain and does not satisfy the public purpose requirement of s. 6(a), Art. X of the State Constitution. This subsection does not diminish the power of counties or municipalities to adopt or enforce county or municipal ordinances related to code enforcement or the elimination of public nuisances to the extent such ordinances do not authorize the taking of private property by eminent domain.
(2) Notwithstanding any other provision of law, including any charter provision, ordinance, statute, or special law, the state, any political subdivision as defined in s. 1.01(8), or any other entity to which the power of eminent domain is delegated may not exercise the power of eminent domain to take private property for the purpose of preventing or eliminating slum or blight conditions. Notwithstanding any other provision of law, including any charter provision, ordinance, statute, or special law, taking private property for the purpose of preventing or eliminating slum or blight conditions is not a valid public purpose or use for which private property may be taken by eminent domain and does not satisfy the public purpose requirement of s. 6(a), Art. X of the State Constitution.

73.015. Presuit negotiation.

(1) Effective July 1, 2000, before an eminent domain proceeding is brought under this chapter or chapter 74, the condemning authority must attempt to negotiate in good faith with the fee owner of

the parcel to be acquired, must provide the fee owner with a written offer and, if requested, a copy of the appraisal upon which the offer is based, and must attempt to reach an agreement regarding the amount of compensation to be paid for the parcel.

(a) No later than the time the initial written or oral offer of compensation for acquisition is made to the fee owner, the condemning authority must notify the fee owner of the following:

1. That all or a portion of his or her property is necessary for a project.

2. The nature of the project for which the parcel is considered necessary, and the parcel designation of the property to be acquired.

3. That, within 15 business days after receipt of a request by the fee owner, the condemning authority will provide a copy of the appraisal report upon which the offer to the fee owner is based; copies, to the extent prepared, of the right-of-way maps or other documents that depict the proposed taking; and copies, to the extent prepared, of the construction plans that depict project improvements to be constructed on the property taken and improvements to be constructed adjacent to the remaining property, including, but not limited to, plan, profile, cross-section, drainage, and pavement marking sheets, and driveway connection detail. The condemning authority shall provide any additional plan sheets within 15 days of request.

4. The fee owner's statutory rights under ss. 73.091 and 73.092, or alternatively provide copies of these provisions of law.

5. The fee owner's rights and responsibilities under paragraphs (b) and (c) and subsection (4), or alternatively provide copies of these provisions of law.

(b) The condemning authority must provide a written offer of compensation to the fee owner as to the value of the property sought to be appropriated and, where less than the entire property is sought to be appropriated, any damages to the remainder caused by the taking. The owner must be given at least 30 days after either receipt of the notice or the date the notice is returned as undeliverable by the postal authorities to respond to the offer, before the condemning authority files a condemnation proceeding for the parcel identified in the offer.

(c) The notice and written offer must be sent by certified mail, return receipt requested, to the fee owner's last known address listed on the county ad valorem tax roll. Alternatively, the notice and written offer may be personally delivered to the fee owner of the property. If there is more than one owner of a property, notice to one owner constitutes notice to all owners of the property. The return of the notice as undeliverable by the postal authorities constitutes compliance with this provision. The condemning authority is not required to give notice or a written offer to a person who acquires title to the property after the notice required by this section has been given.

(d) Notwithstanding this subsection, with respect to lands acquired under s. 253.025, the condemning authority is not required to give the fee owner the current appraisal before executing an option contract.

(2) Effective July 1, 2000, before an eminent domain proceeding is brought under this chapter or chapter 74 by the Department of Transportation or by a county, municipality, board, district, or other public body for the condemnation of right-of-way, the condemning authority must make a good faith effort to notify the business owners, including lessees, who operate a business located on the property to be acquired.

(a) The condemning authority must notify the business owner of the following:

1. That all or a portion of his or her property is necessary for a project.

2. The nature of the project for which the parcel is considered necessary, and the parcel designation of the property to be acquired.

3. That, within 15 business days after receipt of a request by the business owner, the condemning authority will provide a copy of the appraisal report upon which the offer to the fee owner is based; copies, to the extent prepared, of the right-of-way maps or other documents that depict the proposed taking; and copies, to the extent prepared, of the construction plans that depict project improvements to be constructed on the property taken and improvements to be constructed adjacent to the remaining property, including, but not limited to, plan, profile, cross-section, drainage, pavement marking sheets, and driveway connection detail. The condemning authority shall provide any additional plan sheets within 15 days of request.

4. The business owner's statutory rights under ss. 73.071, 73.091, and 73.092.

5. The business owner's rights and responsibilities under paragraphs (b) and (c) and subsection (4).

(b) The notice must be made subsequent to or concurrent with the condemning authority's making the written offer of compensation to the fee owner pursuant to subsection (1). The notice must be sent by certified mail, return receipt requested, to the address of the registered agent for the business located on the property to be acquired, or if no agent is registered, by certified mail or personal delivery to the address of the business located on the property to be acquired. Notice to one owner of a multiple ownership business constitutes notice to all business owners of that business. The return of the notice as undeliverable by the postal authorities constitutes compliance with these provisions. The condemning authority is not required to give notice to a person who acquires an interest in the business after the notice required by this section has been given. Once notice has been made to business owners under this subsection, the condemning authority may file a condemnation proceeding pursuant to chapter 73 or chapter 74 for the property identified in the notice.

(c) If the business qualifies for business damages pursuant to s. 73.071(3)(b) and the business intends to claim business damages, the business owner must, within 180 days after either receipt of the notice or the date the notice is returned as undeliverable by the postal authorities, or at a later time mutually agreed to by the condemning authority and the business owner, submit to the condemning authority a good faith written offer to settle any claims of business damage. The written offer must be sent to the condemning authority by certified mail, return receipt requested. Absent a showing of a good faith justification for the failure to submit a business damage offer within 180 days, the court must strike the business owner's claim for business damages in any condemnation proceeding. If the court finds that the business owner has made a showing of a good faith justification for the failure to timely submit a business damage offer, the court shall grant the business owner up to 180 days within which to submit a business damage offer, which the condemning authority must respond to within 120 days.

1. The business damage offer must include an explanation of the nature, extent, and monetary amount of such damage and must be prepared by the owner, a certified public accountant, or a business damage expert familiar with the nature of the operations of the owner's business. The business owner shall also provide to the condemning authority copies of the owner's business records that substantiate the good faith offer to settle the business damage claim. If additional information is needed beyond data that may be obtained from business records existing at the time of the offer, the business owner and condemning authority may agree on a schedule for the submission of such information.

2. As used in this paragraph, the term "business records" includes, but is not limited to, copies of federal income tax returns, federal income tax withholding statements, federal miscellaneous income tax statements, state sales tax returns, balance sheets, profit and loss statements, and state corporate income tax returns for the 5 years preceding notification which are attributable to the business operation on the property to be acquired, and other records relied upon by the business owner that substantiate the business damage claim.

(d) Within 120 days after receipt of the good faith business damage offer and accompanying business records, the condemning authority must, by certified mail, accept or reject the business owner's offer or make a counteroffer. Failure of the condemning authority to respond to the business damage offer, or rejection thereof pursuant to this section, must be deemed to be a counteroffer of zero dollars for purposes of subsequent application of s. 73.092(1).

(3) At any time in the presuit negotiation process, the parties may agree to submit the compensation or business damage claims to nonbinding mediation. The parties shall agree upon a mediator certified under s. 44.102. In the event that there is a settlement reached as a result of mediation or other mutually acceptable dispute resolution procedure, the agreement reached shall be in writing. The written agreement provided for in this section shall incorporate by reference the right-of-way maps, construction plans, or other documents related to the taking upon which the settlement is based. In the event of a settlement, both parties shall have the same legal rights that

would have been available under law if the matter had been resolved through eminent domain proceedings in circuit court with the maps, plans, or other documents having been made a part of the record.

(4) If a settlement is reached between the condemning authority and a property or business owner prior to a lawsuit being filed, the property or business owner who settles compensation claims in lieu of condemnation shall be entitled to recover costs in the same manner as provided in s. 73.091 and attorney's fees in the same manner as provided in s. 73.092, more specifically as follows:

(a) Attorney's fees for presuit negotiations under this section regarding the amount of compensation to be paid for the land, severance damages, and improvements must be calculated in the same manner as provided in s. 73.092(1) unless the parties otherwise agree.

(b) If business damages are recovered by the business owner based on the condemning authority accepting the business owner's initial offer or the business owner accepting the condemning authority's initial counteroffer, attorney's fees must be calculated in accordance with s. 73.092(2), (3), (4), and (5) for the attorney's time incurred in presentation of the business owner's good faith offer under paragraph (2)(c). Otherwise, attorney's fees for the award of business damages must be calculated as provided in s. 73.092(1), based on the difference between the final judgment or settlement of business damages and the counteroffer to the business owner's offer by the condemning authority.

(c) Presuit costs must be presented, calculated, and awarded in the same manner as provided in s. 73.091, after submission by the business or property owner to the condemning authority of all appraisal reports, business damage reports, or other work products for which recovery is sought, and upon transfer of title of the real property by closing, upon payment of any amounts due for business damages, or upon final judgment.

(d) If the parties cannot agree on the amount of costs and attorney's fees to be paid by the condemning authority, the business or property owner may file a complaint in the circuit court in the county in which the property is located to recover attorney's fees and costs.

(5) Evidence of negotiations or of any written or oral statements used in mediation or negotiations between the parties under this section is inadmissible in any condemnation proceeding, except in a proceeding to determine reasonable costs and attorney's fees.

73.0155. Confidentiality; business information provided to a governmental condemning authority.

(1) The following business information provided by the owner of a business to a governmental condemning authority as part of an offer of business damages under s. 73.015 is confidential and exempt from s. 119.07(1) and s. 24(a), Art. I of the State Constitution if the owner requests in writing that the business information be held confidential and exempt:

(a) Federal tax returns or tax information confidential under 26 U.S.C. s. 6103.

(b) State tax returns or tax information confidential under s. 213.053.

(c) Balance sheets, profit-and-loss statements, cash-flow statements, inventory records, or customer lists or number of customers for a business operating on the parcel to be acquired.

(d) A franchise, distributorship, or lease agreement of which the business operating on the parcel to be acquired is the subject.

(e) Materials that relate to methods of manufacture or production, potential trade secrets, patentable material, or actual trade secrets as defined in s. 688.002.

(f) Other proprietary confidential business information related to the business operating on the parcel to be acquired, if the owner attests in writing to the governmental condemning authority that:

1. The information is being relied upon to substantiate a claim for business damages under s. 73.015;

2. The information has not otherwise been publicly disclosed;

3. The information cannot be readily obtained by the public using alternative means;

4. The information is used by the business to protect or further a business advantage over those who do not know or use the information; and

5. The disclosure of the information would injure the business in the marketplace.

(2) An agency as defined in s. 119.011 may inspect and copy the confidential and exempt business information exclusively for the transaction of official business by, or on behalf of, an agency.

(3) This section does not prevent an agency from offering the confidential and exempt business information as evidence in a legal proceeding and does not prevent a court from determining whether to close a portion of a court record from subsequent public disclosure after trial in order to maintain the confidentiality of that information.

(4) Any employee or agent of an agency receiving such confidential and exempt business information who willfully and knowingly violates this section commits a misdemeanor of the first degree, punishable as provided in s. 775.082 or s. 775.083.

73.021. Petition; contents.

Those having the right to exercise the power of eminent domain may file a petition therefor in the circuit court of the county wherein the property lies, which petition shall set forth:

(1) The authority under which and the public use or purpose for which the property is to be acquired, and that the property is necessary for that public use or purpose;

(2) A description identifying the property sought to be acquired. The petitioners may join in the same action all properties involved in a planned project whether in the same or different ownership, or whether or not the property is sought for the same use;

(3) The estate or interest in the property which the petitioner intends to acquire;

(4) The names, places of residence, legal disabilities, if any, and interests in the property of all owners, lessees, mortgagees, judgment creditors, and lienholders, so far as ascertainable by diligent search, and all unknown persons having an interest in the property when the petitioner has been unable to ascertain the identity of such persons by diligent search and inquiry. If any interest in the property, or lien thereon, belongs to the unsettled estate of a decedent, the executor or administrator shall be made a defendant without joining the devisee or heir; if a trust estate, the trustee shall be made a defendant without joining the cestui que trust. The court may appoint an administrator ad litem to represent the estate of a deceased person whose estate is not being administered, and a guardian ad litem for all defendants who are infants or are under other legal disabilities; and for defendants whose names or addresses are unknown. A copy of the order of appointment shall be served on the guardian ad litem at least 10 days before trial unless he or she has entered an appearance;

(5) Whether any mobile home is located on the property sought to be acquired and, if so, whether the removal of that mobile home will be required. If such removal shall be required, the petition shall name the owners of each such mobile home as defendants. This subsection shall not apply to any governmental authority exercising its power of eminent domain when reasonable relocation or removal expenses must be paid to mobile home owners under other provisions of law or agency rule applicable to such exercise of power;

(6) A statement that the petitioner has surveyed and located its line or area of construction, and intends in good faith to construct the project on or over the described property; and

(7) A demand for relief that the property be condemned and taken for the uses and purposes set forth in the petition, and that the interest sought be vested in the petitioner.

73.031. Process; service and publication.

(1) Upon the filing of the petition, the clerk of the court shall issue a summons to show cause why the property should not be taken, directed "to all whom it may concern," containing the names of all the defendants named in the petition, commanding them and any other persons claiming any interest in the property described to serve written defenses to the petition on a day specified in the summons not less than 28 nor more than 60 days from the date of the summons. A copy of the summons and the petition shall be served upon all resident defendants in the manner provided by law and not less than 20 days before the return day.

(2) If any defendant is alleged to be a nonresident of the state, or if the name or residence of any defendant is alleged to be unknown, or if personal service cannot be had upon any defendant for any other reason, the clerk shall cause a notice to be published at least once each week for 2 consecutive weeks prior to the return day in some newspaper published in the county; provided, however, that if the petitioner be a municipality and a newspaper is published therein, the notice shall be published in such a newspaper. This notice shall contain the names of the defendants to whom it is directed, a description of the property sought to be appropriated, the nature of the action, and the name of the court in which it is pending. The clerk shall mail a copy of the summons and the petition to each out-of-state defendant at the address as set forth in the petition. The clerk shall file a certificate of mailing which, together with proof of publication, shall constitute effective service as though the defendant had been personally served with process within this state.

(3) The failure of any party to receive notice by mail shall not invalidate the proceedings of the court or any order made pursuant to this chapter.

73.032. Offer of judgment.

(1) This section shall provide the exclusive offer of judgment provisions for eminent domain actions.

(2) The petitioner may serve a defendant with an offer of judgment no sooner than 120 days after the defendant has filed an answer and no later than 20 days prior to trial.

(3) A defendant may make an offer to have judgment entered against defendant for payment of compensation by petitioner only for an amount that is under $100,000, and such offer may be served on petitioner no sooner than 120 days after the defendant has filed an answer and no later than 20 days prior to trial.

(4)(a) The offer of judgment must:

1. Be in writing;
2. Settle all pending claims with that party or parties exclusive of attorney's fees and costs;
3. State that the offer is made pursuant to this section;
4. Name the parties to whom the offer is made;
5. Briefly summarize any relevant conditions;
6. State the total amount of the offer; and
7. Include a certificate of service.

(b) The offer of judgment must be served in the same manner as other pleadings upon the parties to whom it is made, but may not be filed with the court unless it is accepted or unless filing is necessary to enforce this section.

(c) The offer of judgment shall be deemed rejected unless accepted by filing both a written acceptance and the written offer with the court within 30 days after service of the offer, or before the trial begins if less than 30 days. Upon proper filing of both the offer and acceptance, the court shall enter judgment thereon. A rejection of an offer terminates the offer.

(d) The party making the offer may withdraw the offer in a writing served on the opposing party before a written acceptance is filed with the court. Once withdrawn in this manner, an offer is void.

(e) An offer of judgment which is rejected or which is withdrawn does not preclude the making of a subsequent offer of judgment; however, any such subsequent offer of judgment shall automatically void the prior offer of judgment as if the same had never been made.

(5) If a defendant does not accept the offer of judgment made by the petitioner and the judgment obtained by the defendant, exclusive of any interest accumulated after the offer of judgment was initially made, is equal to or less than such offer, then the court shall not award any costs incurred by the defendant after the date the offer of judgment was rejected.

(6) If the petitioner rejects the offer of judgment made by defendant and the judgment obtained by defendant, exclusive of any interest accumulated after the offer of judgment was initially made, is equal to or is more than such offer, then the court shall award a reasonable attorney's fee to the defendant based on the factors set forth in s. 73.092(2) and (3).

(7) At the time an offer of judgment is made by the petitioner, the petitioner shall identify and make available to the defendant the construction plans, if any, for the project on which the offer is based.

(8) Evidence of an offer of judgment is admissible only in proceedings to enforce an accepted offer or to determine the costs to be awarded a defendant pursuant to subsection (5) or a reasonable attorney's fee pursuant to subsection (6).

73.041. Acquiring or perfecting title after appropriation.

In any instance, where the petitioner has not acquired the title to or a necessary interest in any lands which it is using, or if at any time after an attempt to acquire such title or interest, it is found to be defective, the petitioner may proceed under this chapter to acquire or perfect such title or interest; provided, however, that the compensation to be allowed the defendants shall be determined as of the date of appropriation.

73.051. Returns; defaults.

Any person interested in or having a lien upon the property, whether named as a defendant or not, may file his or her written defenses to the petition, as a matter of right, on or before the return date set in the notice or thereafter by leave of court. If a defendant does not file his or her defenses on or before the return date, defaults may be entered against the defendant, but nothing shall prevent any person who is shown by the record to be interested in the property from appearing before the jury to claim the amount of compensation that he or she conceives to be due for the property.

73.0511. Prelitigation notice.

Prior to instituting litigation, the condemning authority shall notify the fee owners of statutory rights under s. 73.091.

73.061. Pretrial hearing.

(1) Prior to the date of trial, the court may hold a hearing, in limine, to settle all disputed matters properly before it which must be determined prior to trial. Should it appear that the causes of

action joined cannot be conveniently disposed of together, the court may order separate trials; provided, however, that any such actions shall be tried in the county in which the lands are located.

(2) The court in which an action in eminent domain is pending shall have jurisdiction and authority over any and all taxes and assessments encumbering the lands involved in such actions, and may stay or defer the enforcement of such taxes and assessments, including all applications for tax deeds, foreclosures and other enforcement proceedings, until final termination of such eminent domain actions. The said court may make such orders concerning such taxes and assessments as may be equitable and proper; provided, however, that ad valorem taxes levied upon any such lands shall be prorated against the owner to the date of taking.

73.071. Jury trial; compensation; severance damages; business damages.

(1) When the action is at issue, and only upon notice and hearing to set the cause for trial, the court shall impanel a jury of 12 persons as soon as practical considering the reasonable necessities of the court and of the parties, and giving preference to the trial of eminent domain cases over other civil actions, and submit the issue of compensation to them for determination, which issue shall be tried in the same manner as other issues of fact are tried in the circuit courts.

(2) The amount of such compensation shall be determined as of the date of trial, or the date upon which title passes, whichever shall occur first.

(3) The jury shall determine solely the amount of compensation to be paid, which compensation shall include:

(a) The value of the property sought to be appropriated;

(b) Where less than the entire property is sought to be appropriated, any damages to the remainder caused by the taking, including, when the action is by the Department of Transportation, county, municipality, board, district or other public body for the condemnation of a right-of-way, and the effect of the taking of the property involved may damage or destroy an established business of more than 4 years' standing before January 1, 2005, or the effect of the taking of the property involved may damage or destroy an established business of more than 5 years' standing on or after January 1, 2005, owned by the party whose lands are being so taken, located upon adjoining lands owned or held by such party, the probable damages to such business which the denial of the use of the property so taken may reasonably cause; any person claiming the right to recover such special damages shall set forth in his or her written defenses the nature and extent of such damages; and

(c) Where the appropriation is of property upon which a mobile home, other than a travel trailer as defined in s. 320.01, is located, whether or not the owner of the mobile home is an owner or lessee of the property involved, and the effect of the taking of the property involved requires the relocation of such mobile home, the reasonable removal or relocation expenses incurred by such mobile home owner, not to exceed the replacement value of such mobile home. The compensation paid to a mobile home owner under this paragraph shall preclude an award to a mobile home park owner for such expenses of removal or relocation. Any mobile home owner claiming the right to such removal or relocation expenses shall set forth in his or her written defenses the nature and extent of such expenses. This paragraph shall not apply to any governmental authority exercising its power of eminent domain when reasonable removal or relocation expenses must be paid to mobile home owners under other provisions of law or agency rule applicable to such exercise of power.

(4) When the action is by the Department of Transportation, county, municipality, board, district, or other public body for the condemnation of a road, canal, levee, or water control facility right-of-way, the enhancement, if any, in value of the remaining adjoining property of the defendant property owner by reason of the construction or improvement made or contemplated by the

petitioner shall be offset against the damage, if any, resulting to such remaining adjoining property of the defendant property owner by reason of the construction or improvement. However, such enhancement in the value shall not be offset against the value of the property appropriated, and if such enhancement in value shall exceed the damage, if any, to the remaining adjoining property, there shall be no recovery over against such property owner for such excess.

(5) Any increase or decrease in the value of any property to be acquired which occurs after the scope of the project for which the property is being acquired is known in the market, and which is solely a result of the knowledge of the project location, shall not be considered in arriving at the value of the property acquired. For the purpose of this section, the scope of the project for which the property is being acquired shall be presumed to be known in the market on or after the condemnor executes a resolution which depicts the location of the project.

(6) The jury shall view the subject property upon demand by any party or by order of the court.

(7) If the jury cannot agree on a verdict the court shall discharge them, impanel a new jury, and proceed with the trial.

73.0715. Valuation of electric utility property.

When any person having the right to exercise the power of eminent domain seeks the appropriation of property used for the generation, transmission, or distribution of electric energy, the jury shall determine solely the amount of compensation to be paid. Such compensation shall include the reproduction cost of the property sought to be appropriated less depreciation, together with going concern value, and, when less than the entire property is sought to be appropriated, any damages to the remainder caused by the taking.

73.072. Mobile home parks; compensation for permanent improvements by mobile home owners.

(1) When all or a portion of a mobile home park as defined in s. 723.003 is appropriated under this chapter, the condemning authority shall separately determine the compensation for any permanent improvements made to each site. This compensation shall be awarded to the mobile home owner leasing the site if:

(a) The effect of the taking includes a requirement that the mobile home owner remove or relocate his or her mobile home from the site;

(b) The mobile home owner currently leasing the site has paid for the permanent improvements to the site; and

(c) The value of the permanent improvements on the site exceeds $1,000 as of the date of taking.

(2) "Permanent improvement" means any addition or improvement to the site upon which a mobile home is located, which addition or improvement cannot be detached and removed from the site without destroying its practical utility at another site. If capable of removal to another site, compensation for the expense of removal and relocation shall be as provided by law.

(3) A mobile home owner who is the lessee of the site and is required to remove his or her mobile home as the result of a taking of all or a part of a mobile home park may petition to intervene as a party defendant in proceedings under this chapter, for purposes of asserting his or her right to the separate compensation to be determined and awarded under this section. Failure to intervene shall not constitute a waiver of the right of a mobile home owner to institute a separate action to recover from a mobile home park owner the compensation awarded to such park owner for the permanent improvements made by the mobile home owner to the site on which his or her mobile home is located.

73.073. Eminent domain procedure with respect to condominium common elements.

(1) Any other provision of this chapter or any other provision of the Florida Statutes to the contrary notwithstanding, the procedure for the exercise of eminent domain with respect to the taking of a portion of the common elements of a condominium shall comply with the provisions of this section.

(2) With respect to the exercise of eminent domain or a negotiated sale for the purchase or taking of a portion of the common elements of a condominium, the condemning authority shall have the responsibility of contacting the condominium association and acquiring the most recent rolls indicating the names of the unit owners or contacting the appropriate taxing authority to obtain the names of the owners of record on the tax rolls. Notification shall be sent by certified mail, return receipt requested, to the unit owners of record of the condominium units by the condemning authority indicating the intent to purchase or take the required property and requesting a response from the unit owner. The condemning authority shall be responsible for the expense of sending notification pursuant to this section. Such notice shall, at a minimum, include:

(a) The name and address of the condemning authority.

(b) A written or visual description of the property.

(c) The public purpose for which the property is needed.

(d) The appraisal value of the property.

(e) A clear, concise statement relating to the unit owner's right to object to the taking or appraisal value and the procedures and effects of exercising that right.

(f) A clear, concise statement relating to the power of the association to convey the property on behalf of the unit owners if no objection to the taking or appraisal value is raised, and the effects of this alternative on the unit owner.

(3) In the absence of a response by the unit owner within 30 days, the unit owner shall be deemed to have acquiesced to the association acting as the unit owner's representative in any subsequent proceeding relating to the parcel at issue. Unit owners who object to the purchase or taking or the appraisal of value within 30 days after the date the notice is received shall have all of their legal rights preserved with regard to the taking, the appraisal of value, and all other rights which appertain to unit ownership. Failure to raise an objection within the 30-day period shall only constitute an acquiescence by the unit owner to the association acting as the unit owner's representative in any subsequent proceeding relating to the parcel at issue and shall not affect any other rights of the unit owner. In the event that no unit owners shall so object, the condemning authority may rely upon a power of sale vested in the condominium association. The condemning authority shall only be required to name as defendants, should eminent domain proceedings be necessitated, the association and those owners of units which shall have objected to the taking or appraisal value within the 30-day period.

(4) It is the intent of the Legislature, through the adoption of this section, to provide a mechanism to either eliminate or minimize the necessity for naming individual unit owners in eminent domain proceedings for the acquisition of a portion of the common elements of a condominium and the necessity of incidental title searches and legal actions necessitated by naming multiple unit owners as defendants.

73.081. Form of verdict.

The verdict of the jury shall state an accurate description of each parcel of the property sought to be appropriated and the amount to be paid therefor, together with any damage to the remainder caused by the taking and including business damages when allowable by statute. When severance damages, business damages, moving costs, separate compensation for permanent improvements made by a mobile home owner under s. 73.072, or other special damages are sought, the verdict shall state the amount of such damages separately from the amounts of other damages awarded.

73.091. Costs of the proceedings.

(1) The petitioner shall pay attorney's fees as provided in s. 73.092 as well as all reasonable costs incurred in the defense of the proceedings in the circuit court, including, but not limited to, reasonable appraisal fees and, when business damages are compensable, a reasonable accountant's fee, to be assessed by that court. No prejudgment interest shall be paid on costs or attorney's fees.
(2) At least 30 days prior to a hearing to assess costs under this section, the condemnee's attorney shall submit to the condemning authority for each expert witness complete time records and a detailed statement of services rendered by date, nature of services performed, time spent performing such services, and costs incurred, and a copy of any fee agreement which may exist between the expert and the condemnee or the condemnee's attorney.
(3) In assessing costs, the court shall consider all factors relevant to the reasonableness of the costs, including, but not limited to, the fees paid to similar experts retained in the case by the condemning authority or other parties and the reasonable costs of similar services by similarly qualified persons.
(4) In assessing costs to be paid by the petitioner, the court shall be guided by the amount the defendant would ordinarily have been expected to pay for the services rendered if the petitioner were not responsible for the costs.
(5) The court shall make specific findings that justify each sum awarded as an expert witness fee.

73.092. Attorney's fees.

(1) Except as otherwise provided in this section and s. 73.015, the court, in eminent domain proceedings, shall award attorney's fees based solely on the benefits achieved for the client.
(a) As used in this section, the term "benefits" means the difference, exclusive of interest, between the final judgment or settlement and the last written offer made by the condemning authority before the defendant hires an attorney. If no written offer is made by the condemning authority before the defendant hires an attorney, benefits must be measured from the first written offer after the attorney is hired.
1. In determining attorney's fees, if business records as defined in s. 73.015(2)(c)2. and kept by the owner in the ordinary course of business were provided to the condemning authority to substantiate the business damage offer in s. 73.015(2)(c), benefits for amounts awarded for business damages must be based on the difference between the final judgment or settlement and the written counteroffer made by the condemning authority provided in s. 73.015(2)(d).
2. In determining attorney's fees, if existing business records as defined in s. 73.015(2)(c)2. and kept by the owner in the ordinary course of business were not provided to the condemning authority to substantiate the business damage offer in s. 73.015(2)(c) and those records which were not provided are later deemed material to the determination of business damages, benefits for amounts awarded for business damages must be based upon the difference between the final judgment or settlement and the first written counteroffer made by the condemning authority within 90 days from the condemning authority's receipt of the business records previously not provided.
(b) The court may also consider nonmonetary benefits obtained for the client through the efforts of the attorney, to the extent such nonmonetary benefits are specifically identified by the court and can, within a reasonable degree of certainty, be quantified.
(c) Attorney's fees based on benefits achieved shall be awarded in accordance with the following

schedule:

1. Thirty-three percent of any benefit up to $250,000; plus
2. Twenty-five percent of any portion of the benefit between $250,000 and $1 million; plus
3. Twenty percent of any portion of the benefit exceeding $1 million.

(2) In assessing attorney's fees incurred in defeating an order of taking, or for apportionment, or other supplemental proceedings, when not otherwise provided for, the court shall consider:

(a) The novelty, difficulty, and importance of the questions involved.

(b) The skill employed by the attorney in conducting the cause.

(c) The amount of money involved.

(d) The responsibility incurred and fulfilled by the attorney.

(e) The attorney's time and labor reasonably required adequately to represent the client in relation to the benefits resulting to the client.

(f) The fee, or rate of fee, customarily charged for legal services of a comparable or similar nature.

(g) Any attorney's fee award made under subsection (1).

(3) In determining the amount of attorney's fees to be paid by the petitioner under subsection (2), the court shall be guided by the fees the defendant would ordinarily be expected to pay for these services if the petitioner were not responsible for the payment of those fees.

(4) At least 30 days prior to a hearing to assess attorney's fees under subsection (2), the condemnee's attorney shall submit to the condemning authority and to the court complete time records and a detailed statement of services rendered by date, nature of services performed, time spent performing such services, and costs incurred.

(5) The defendant shall provide to the court a copy of any fee agreement that may exist between the defendant and his or her attorney, and the court must reduce the amount of attorney's fees to be paid by the defendant by the amount of any attorney's fees awarded by the court.

73.101. Form of judgment.

The judgment shall recite the verdict in full and shall state that the estate or interest in the property described in the petition and sought to be appropriated by the petitioner shall vest in the petitioner upon the payment of, or securing by deposit of money, the amount found by the verdict of the jury. Where there are conflicting claims to the amount awarded for any parcel, the court, upon appropriate motion, shall determine the rights of the interested parties with respect to the amount awarded for each parcel and the method of apportionment, together with the disposition of any other matters arising from the taking.

73.111. Deposit and possession.

Within 20 days after the rendition of the judgment, the petitioner shall deposit the amount set forth therein into the registry of the court for the use of the defendants, or the proceeding shall be null and void, unless for good cause further time, not exceeding 60 days, is allowed by the court. Upon such deposit and the entry in the proper records in the clerk's office of the judgment and the clerk's certificate that the compensation has been paid into the court, the estate or interest sought shall vest in the petitioner. The court may fix the time within which, and the terms upon which, the defendants shall be required to surrender possession to the petitioner.

73.121. Writs of assistance and possession.

Whenever the judge is satisfied that any person, whether holding under the defendant or not, is preventing or obstructing the petitioner from entering upon or taking possession of the property after the petitioner is entitled to do so, the judge may grant such writs as he or she may think necessary, or the judge may proceed for contempt of court.

73.131. Appeals; costs.

(1) Appeals in eminent domain actions shall be taken in the manner prescribed by law and in accordance with the appellate rules, except that an appeal shall not prevent appropriation of the property by the petitioner where the amount awarded by the judgment has been deposited with the court as aforesaid. If, at any time after entry of the judgment, a defendant shall take out of the court the amount due him or her, any pending appeal taken by the defendant shall be dismissed by the appellate court upon the filing of a certificate by the clerk of the circuit court stating that the defendant taking the appeal has withdrawn the amount due him or her.
(2) The petitioner shall pay all reasonable costs of the proceedings in the appellate court, including a reasonable attorney's fee to be assessed by that court, except upon an appeal taken by a defendant in which the judgment of the lower court shall be affirmed.

73.141. Payment.

(1) In the event that no appeal has been taken within the time and in the manner provided by the Florida Rules of Appellate Procedure, the clerk shall pay each judgment creditor the sum necessary to satisfy the judgment from the funds on deposit, and upon order of the court shall refund to the petitioner all the funds not necessary for the satisfaction of the judgment, costs and attorney fees.
(2) In the event that a timely appeal is taken and the judgment of the trial court is affirmed, the clerk of the court shall pay each judgment creditor as hereinabove provided.

73.151. Railroads and canal companies.

(1) Whenever land sought to be condemned to the use of a railroad or canal company is in the possession, under any law of this state, of another railroad or canal company which is using the same in the construction or operation of its railroad or canal, the use of no more land than is necessary to furnish to the petitioner a right-of-way 105 feet in width across such railroad or canal shall be condemned for such use.
(2) If it shall be necessary for any railroad company organized under any law of this state to use, for the purpose of its road, any lands over which any other railroad company shall have previously acquired the right-of-way for its road, the right to use such lands may be acquired as in other cases. Such lands shall not be taken in a manner to interfere with the main track of the railroad first established except for crossing, as provided by law.

73.161. Right-of-way for telephone and telegraph over railroad right-of-way.

(1) If any telegraph or telephone company fails to secure the consent of any railroad or railway company for the construction of its lines along and upon the right-of-way of any railroad in this state, the same may be acquired by eminent domain. If the defendant railroad or railway company

has a principal office or place of business in this state, and any portion of the right-of-way sought to be condemned extends into the county wherein such principal office or place of business is located, then the eminent domain action shall be had in such county. No map need be filed with the petition, but it shall state about how many poles per mile will be erected on such right-of-way, and about how far from each other, and from the centers of the main track of the railroad, their length and size, the depth they will be planted in the ground, and the amount of land that will be occupied by them. No pole shall be set at a greater distance than 10 feet from the outer edge of the right-of-way. In such action, the petitioner shall give bond for costs in the penalty of $200, payable to the defendant, with surety to be approved by the clerk.

(2) The judgment shall authorize the petitioner to enter upon the right-of-way of the defendant and construct its lines thereon. Said judgment shall further provide that such lines shall be constructed so as not to interfere with the operation of the trains of said defendant or any telephone or telegraph line already upon such right-of-way; and, furthermore, that if, at any time, the railroad or railway company shall desire, for railway purposes, the immediate use of any land occupied by said petitioner, then the petitioner shall, upon reasonable notice in writing, at its own expense, remove its line to some other place adjacent thereto on such right-of-way so as not to interfere with the track or use of said railway or any telephone or telegraph line already on said right-of-way, and that the said line shall not be erected on any embankment or slope of any cut of such right-of-way, and if at any time the said railroad or railway company shall require for railroad purposes its entire right-of-way at any point occupied by said line, the said petitioner shall, at such point, remove said line entirely off such right-of-way.

(3) The telegraph or telephone company by such action shall acquire only an easement in and to said railroad right-of-way for the purpose of constructing, maintaining, and operating its telegraph or telephone line thereon, and only the interests of such parties as are brought before the court shall be condemned in such action. If the easement or right-of-way claimed extends in or through more counties than one, the whole right and controversy may be heard and determined in any county into or through which such right-of-way extends, except as herein otherwise provided.

CHAPTER 74. PROCEEDINGS SUPPLEMENTAL TO EMINENT DOMAIN

74.011. Scope.

In any eminent domain action, properly instituted by and in the name of the state; the Department of Transportation; any county, school board, municipality, expressway authority, regional water supply authority, transportation authority, flood control district, or drainage or subdrainage district; the ship canal authority; any lawfully constituted housing, port, or aviation authority; or any rural electric cooperative, telephone cooperative corporation, or public utility corporation, the petitioner may avail itself of the provisions of this chapter to take possession and title in advance of the entry of final judgment.

74.021. Rights under this chapter; additional.

The right to take possession and title in advance of final judgment in eminent domain actions, as provided by this law, shall be in addition to any right, power or authority conferred by laws of the state under which proceedings may be conducted and shall not be construed as abrogating, limiting or modifying any such right, power or authority.

74.031. Declaration of taking; contents.

Those having the right to take possession and title in advance of the entry of final judgment in eminent domain actions, as provided by law, may file, either with the petition or at any time prior to the entry of final judgment, a declaration of taking signed by the petitioner, or its duly authorized agent or attorney, stating that the property sought to be appropriated is thereby taken for the use set forth in the petition. The petitioner shall make a good faith estimate of value, based upon a valid appraisal of each parcel in the proceeding, which shall be made a part of the declaration of taking.

74.041. Process; service and publication.

(1) Upon the filing of the declaration of taking, the clerk of the court shall issue a summons to show cause to the defendants, containing the names of all defendants named in the petition, notifying them that the petitioner will petition for an order of taking on a specified date. A copy of the summons to show cause and the declaration of taking shall be served upon all resident defendants in the manner provided by law for service of original process in eminent domain actions, and not less than 20 days prior to the date specified.

(2) If any defendant is alleged to be a nonresident of the state, or if the name or address of any defendant is alleged to be unknown, or if personal service cannot be had upon any defendant for any other reason, the clerk of the court shall cause the summons to show cause to be published one time, not less than 20 days prior to the date specified in the petition, in some newspaper published in the county; however, if the petitioner is a municipality and a newspaper is published therein, the summons shall be published in such a newspaper. The clerk shall mail a copy of the summons to show cause and the declaration of taking to each out-of-state defendant at the address set forth in the petition. The clerk shall file a certificate of mailing, which, together with proof of publication, shall constitute effective service as to these defendants. The failure of any party to receive the summons by mail shall not invalidate the proceedings of the court or any order made pursuant to this chapter.

(3) The petition date provided in this section may be combined with the summons to show cause and the published summons provided in s. 73.031, but in no event shall the petition date provided in this section be noticed for a date earlier than 1 day following the date specified in the summons to show cause and the published summons provided in s. 73.031 for the defendants to serve written defenses to the petition in eminent domain proceedings and, if a defendant requests, a hearing on the petition for order of taking.

74.051. Hearing on order of taking.

(1) If a defendant requests a hearing pursuant to s. 74.041(3), said defendant may appear and be heard on all matters properly before the court which may be determined prior to the entry of the order of taking, including the jurisdiction of the court, the sufficiency of pleadings, whether the petitioner is properly exercising its delegated authority, and the amount to be deposited for the property sought to be appropriated. Any defendant failing to file a request for hearing shall waive any right to object to the order of taking, and title shall be vested in the petitioner, upon deposit as hereinafter provided, which date shall be the date of valuation.

(2) If a hearing is requested, the court shall make such order as it deems proper, securing to all parties the rights to which they may be entitled, not inconsistent with the provisions of this

section. The court may make such orders in respect of encumbrances, liens, rents, taxes, assessments, insurance, amount of the good faith deposit, and other charges, if any, as shall be just and equitable. If the court finds that the petitioner is entitled to possession of the property prior to final judgment, it shall enter an order requiring the petitioner to deposit in the registry of the court such sum of money as will fully secure and fully compensate the persons entitled to compensation as ultimately determined by the final judgment. Said deposit shall not be less than the amount of the petitioner's estimate of value, if the petitioner be the state or any agency thereof, any county, the city, or other public body; otherwise, double the amount of petitioner's estimate of value.

(3) If a defendant requests a hearing pursuant to s. 74.041(3) and the petitioner is an electric utility that is seeking to appropriate property necessary for an electric generation plant, an associated facility of an electric generation plant, an electric substation, or a power line, it is the intent of the Legislature that the court, when practicable, conduct the hearing no more than 120 days after the petition is filed and issue its order of taking no more than 30 days after the conclusion of the hearing.

(4) The court may fix the time within which and the terms upon which the defendants shall be required to surrender possession to the petitioner, which time of possession shall be upon deposit for those defendants failing to file a request for hearing as provided herein. The order of taking shall not become effective unless the deposit of the required sum is made in the registry of the court. If the deposit is not made within 20 days from the date of the order of taking, the order shall be void and of no further effect. The clerk is authorized to invest such deposits so as to earn the highest interest obtainable under the circumstances in state or national financial institutions in Florida insured by the Federal Government. Ninety percent of the interest earned shall be allocated in accordance with the ultimate ownership in the deposit.

74.061. Vesting of title or interest sought.

Immediately upon the making of the deposit, the title or interest specified in the petition shall vest in the petitioner, and the said lands shall be deemed to be condemned and taken for the use of the petitioner, and the right to compensation for the same shall vest in the persons entitled thereto. Compensation shall be determined in accordance with the provisions of chapter 73, except that interest shall be allowed at the same rate as provided in all circuit court judgments from the date of surrender of possession to the date of payment on the amount that the verdict exceeds the estimate of value set forth in the declaration of taking.

74.071. Paying over funds in court.

At any time, prior to the entry of final judgment, and upon motion by the proper defendants, the court may direct that the sum of money set forth in the declaration of taking be paid forthwith to such defendants from the money deposited in the registry of the court. If the compensation awarded for the property by the final judgment shall exceed the amount withdrawn by the defendant, the court shall enter judgment against the petitioner for the deficiency. If the amount withdrawn exceeds the compensation awarded for the property by the final judgment, the court shall enter a judgment against such defendant for the excess, and such judgment shall be a lien against any of the defendant's property except his or her homestead.

74.081. Proceedings as evidence.

Neither the declaration of taking, nor the amount of the deposit, shall be admissible in evidence in any action.

74.091. Effect of failure to pay final judgment.

Where an order of taking has been entered and deposit made, the failure of the petitioner to pay into the court the compensation ascertained by the jury shall not invalidate said judgment or the title of the petitioner, and such failure shall not authorize any person to molest, interfere with, enter or trespass upon said property; provided, however, persons lawfully entitled to compensation may sue out execution, in the event a timely appeal has not been filed, and such execution may be levied upon the property so condemned and any other property of the petitioner in the same manner as executions are levied in common-law actions.

74.101. Rights of housing authority after taking.

In any action in which any housing authority created under the laws of Florida has taken or may take possession of any real property in advance of final judgment therein, and the said petitioner has become irrevocably committed to pay the amount ultimately to be awarded as compensation, then it is lawful to expend moneys duly appropriated for that purpose in demolishing existing structures on said land, and in erecting buildings or public works thereon, or in improving said land or erecting and constructing buildings or works thereon, authorized by law to be constructed by any petitioner.

74.111. Drainage districts and housing authorities.

In any action instituted by a drainage or subdrainage district, or housing authority wherein the petitioner seeks to avail itself of the provisions of this chapter:
(1) Action under this chapter shall not be taken unless the chair or other legally constituted head of the petitioning authority empowered to acquire the land shall be of the opinion that the ultimate award probably will be within the limits of the authority's ability to pay.
(2) It shall be lawful for the petitioner to expend moneys duly appropriated for the purpose of availing itself of the provisions of this chapter in going forward with the project for which the land was taken; provided that, in the opinion of the attorney representing the taking authority, the title has been vested in the authority taking, or all persons having an interest therein have been made parties to such proceeding and will be bound by the final judgment therein.
(3) No money shall be paid nor contracts made for payment for any construction or maintenance proposed by the petitioner under this chapter in excess of the amount specifically appropriated therefor by the Legislature of the state, or procured by and secured to the petitioner under contracts with private persons, firms, or corporations in accordance with the laws authorizing such taking authority to negotiate contracts with private persons, firms, or corporations, or by the issuance of bonds and other debentures pursuant to tax levies duly made, all in accordance with the law in such cases made and provided.
(4) The attorney representing the petitioner is authorized to stipulate or agree in behalf of the taking authority to exclude any property, or any part thereof, or any interest therein, that may have been, or may be taken by or on behalf of the authority taking by the declaration of taking, or otherwise.

CHAPTER 75. BOND VALIDATION

75.01. Jurisdiction.

Circuit courts have jurisdiction to determine the validation of bonds and certificates of indebtedness and all matters connected therewith.

75.02. Plaintiff.

Any county, municipality, taxing district or other political district or subdivision of this state, including the governing body of any drainage, conservation or reclamation district, and including also state agencies, commissions and departments authorized by law to issue bonds, may determine its authority to incur bonded debt or issue certificates of debt and the legality of all proceedings in connection therewith, including assessment of taxes levied or to be levied, the lien thereof and proceedings or other remedies for their collection. For this purpose a complaint shall be filed in the circuit court in the county or in the county where the municipality or district, or any part thereof, is located against the state and the taxpayers, property owners, and citizens of the county, municipality or district, including nonresidents owning property or subject to taxation therein. In actions to validate bonds or certificates of debt issued by state agencies, commissions or departments, the complaint shall be filed in the circuit court of the county where the proceeds of the bond issue are to be expended, or where the seat of state government is situated, and shall be brought against the state and the taxpayers, property owners and citizens thereof, including nonresidents owning property or subject to taxation therein.

75.03. Condition precedent.

As a condition precedent to filing of a complaint for the validation of bonds or certificates of debt, the county, municipality, state agency, commission or department, or district desiring to issue them shall cause an election to be held to authorize the issuance of such bonds or certificates and show prima facie that the election was in favor of the issuance thereof, or, when permitted by law, adopt an ordinance, resolution or other proceeding providing for the issuance of such bonds or certificates in accordance with law.

75.04. Complaint.

(1) The complaint shall set out the plaintiff's authority for incurring the bonded debt or issuing certificates of debt, the holding of an election and the result when an election is required, the ordinance, resolution, or other proceeding authorizing the issue and its adoption, all other essential proceedings had or taken in connection therewith, the amount of the bonds or certificates to be issued and the interest they are to bear; and, in case of a drainage, conservation, or reclamation district, the authority for the creation of such district, for the issuance of bonds, for the levy and assessment of taxes and all other pertinent matters.

(2) In the case of an independent special district as defined in s. 218.31(7), the complaint shall allege the creation of a trust indenture established by the petitioner for a bonded trustee acceptable to the court who shall certify the proper expenditure of the proceeds of the bonds.

75.05. Order and service.

(1) The court shall issue an order directed against the state and the several property owners, taxpayers, citizens and others having or claiming any right, title or interest in property to be affected by the issuance of bonds or certificates, or to be affected thereby, requiring all persons, in general terms and without naming them and the state through its state attorney or attorneys of the circuits where the county, municipality or district lies, to appear at a designated time and place within the circuit where the complaint is filed and show why the complaint should not be granted and the proceedings and bonds or certificates validated. A copy of the complaint and order shall be served on the state attorney of the circuit in which such proceedings are pending, and when the municipality or district lies in more than one judicial circuit, on the state attorney of each of the circuits at least 20 days before the time fixed for hearing. The state attorney shall examine the complaint, and, if it appears or there is reason to believe that it is defective, insufficient, or untrue, or if in the opinion of the state attorney the issuance of the bonds or certificates in question has not been duly authorized, defense shall be made by said state attorney. The state attorney shall have access, for the purposes aforesaid, to all records and proceedings of the county, municipality, state agency, commission or department, or district, and any officer, agent or employee having charge, possession, or control of any of the books, papers, or records of the county, municipality, state agency, commission, department, or district shall exhibit them for examination on demand of the state attorney, and shall furnish, without cost, duly authenticated copies thereof which pertain to the proceedings for the issuance of the bonds or certificates or which may affect their legality.
(2) In the case of state agencies, commissions, or departments, a copy of the complaint and order shall be served on the state attorney of the circuit in which the action is pending and if pending in a county when the proceeds of the bond issue are to be expended in any other county, on the state attorney of each county in which it is proposed to expend the proceeds.
(3) Notwithstanding any other provision of law, whether a general law or special act, validation of bonds to be issued by a special district, other than a community development district established pursuant to chapter 190, as provided in s. 190.016(12), is not mandatory, but is at the option of the issuer. However, the validation of bonds issued by such community development districts shall not be required on refunding issues.

75.06. Publication of notice.

(1) Before the date set for hearing, the clerk shall publish a copy of the order in the county where the complaint is filed, and if plaintiff is a municipality or district in more than one county, then in each county, at least once each week for 2 consecutive weeks, commencing with the first publication, which shall not be less than 20 days before the date set for hearing but if there is a newspaper published in the territory to be affected by the issuance of the bonds or certificates, and in the county or counties the publication shall be therein unless otherwise ordered by the court. By this publication all property owners, taxpayers, citizens, and others having or claiming any right, title or interest in the county, municipality or district, or the taxable property therein, are made parties defendant to the action and the court has jurisdiction of them to the same extent as if named as defendants in the complaint and personally served with process.
(2) In actions to validate the bonds of state agencies, commissions or departments, the order shall be published in the same manner in a newspaper in each of the counties where the proceeds of bonds are to be expended, and in a newspaper published in the county in which the seat of state government is located if the action is brought therein.

75.07. Intervention; hearings.

Any property owner, taxpayer, citizen or person interested may become a party to the action by moving against or pleading to the complaint at or before the time set for hearing. At the hearing the court shall determine all questions of law and fact and make such orders as will enable it to properly try and determine the action and render a final judgment with the least possible delay.

75.08. Appeal and review.

Any party to the action whether plaintiff, defendant, intervenor or otherwise, dissatisfied with the final judgment, may appeal to the Supreme Court within the time and in the manner prescribed by the Florida Rules of Appellate Procedure.

75.09. Effect of final judgment.

If the judgment validates such bonds, certificates or other obligations, which may include the validation of the county, municipality, taxing district, political district, subdivision, agency, instrumentality or other public body itself and any taxes, assessments or revenues affected, and no appeal is taken within the time prescribed, or if taken and the judgment is affirmed, such judgment is forever conclusive as to all matters adjudicated against plaintiff and all parties affected thereby, including all property owners, taxpayers and citizens of the plaintiff, and all others having or claiming any right, title or interest in property to be affected by the issuance of said bonds, certificates or other obligations, or to be affected in any way thereby, and the validity of said bonds, certificates or other obligations or of any taxes, assessments or revenues pledged for the payment thereof, or of the proceedings authorizing the issuance thereof, including any remedies provided for their collection, shall never be called in question in any court by any person or party.

75.10. Recording of judgment in other counties.

If any judgment extends into more than one county it shall be recorded in each county in which the plaintiff municipality or district extends.

75.11. Stamping instruments validated.

(1) Bonds or certificates, when validated under this chapter, shall have stamped or written thereon, by the proper officers of such county, municipality or district issuing them, a statement in substantially the following form:
(2) A certified copy of the judgment or decree shall be received as evidence in any court in this state.

75.12. Payment of costs.

The costs shall be paid by the county, municipality, or district filing the complaint except when a taxpayer, citizen, or other person contests the action or intervenes, the court may tax the whole or any part of the costs against him or her as is equitable.

75.13. Certain prior proceedings validated.

Any action for validation heretofore brought by any municipality, special taxing district or political district or subdivision which extends into more than one county or judicial circuit, whereby bonds or certificates of debt have been validated in which the proceedings have been brought in one county and a decree has been entered, said decree shall be binding on all of the citizens, property owners, or taxpayers of each municipality, district or subdivision.

75.14. Landowner or taxpayer not disqualification of judge.

No judge shall be disqualified in any validation action because the judge is a landowner or taxpayer of any county, municipality, or district seeking relief hereunder.

75.16. Certain orders and decrees validated.

All orders, decrees, and judgments heretofore or hereafter made in actions for the validation of bonds or certificates of indebtedness by any judge disqualified by matters not apparent on the record are valid and binding on all parties unless attacked within 20 days of the entry thereof; and all orders, decrees, and judgments heretofore made in such validation actions by judges other than the regular judge or those mentioned or designated in the notices, or at places other than, or dates subsequent to, those mentioned in said notices, when it appears that the regular judge was disqualified, absent, or disabled from discharging the duties of his or her office, are hereby ratified.

75.17. Commencement of action after validation; affidavit of good faith.

Every person who commences an action as taxpayer or otherwise to challenge the validity of any bonds or certificates or to prevent the use of any moneys derived from the sale of the bonds or certificates after the bonds or certificates have been validated by courts of competent jurisdiction pursuant to this chapter, shall file an affidavit of good faith stating that the action is not filed for delay and setting forth with particularity why the objection was not made as part of the validation action.

CHAPTER 76. ATTACHMENT

76.01. Right to attachment.

Any creditor may have an attachment at law against the goods and chattels, lands, and tenements of his or her debtor under the circumstances and in the manner hereinafter provided.

76.02. Attachment of corporate stock.

Shares of stock in any corporation incorporated by the laws of this state are subject to attachment under the circumstances hereinafter provided and in the manner prescribed for levy of execution thereon.

76.03. Courts from which attachments shall issue.

Attachments shall be issued by a judge of the court which has jurisdiction of the amount claimed by the creditor, but if the property to be attached is being actually removed from the state and the creditor is unable to obtain process from the proper court in time to prevent such removal, any judge may issue the writ, making it returnable to the proper court and immediately sending all papers in the action to the clerk of the court to which the writ is returnable.

76.04. Grounds when debt due.

The creditor may have an attachment on a debt actually due to the creditor by his or her debtor, when the debtor:
(1) Will fraudulently part with the property before judgment can be obtained against him or her.
(2) Is actually removing the property out of the state.
(3) Is about to remove the property out of the state.
(4) Resides out of the state.
(5) Is actually moving himself or herself out of the state.
(6) Is about to move himself or herself out of the state.
(7) Is absconding.
(8) Is concealing himself or herself.
(9) Is secreting the property.
(10) Is fraudulently disposing of the property.
(11) Is actually removing himself or herself beyond the limits of the judicial circuit in which he or she resides.
(12) Is about to remove himself or herself out of the limits of such judicial circuit.

76.05. Grounds when debt not due.

Any creditor may have an attachment on a debt not due, when the debtor:
(1) Is actually removing the property out of the state.
(2) Is fraudulently disposing of the property to avoid the payment of his or her debts.
(3) Is fraudulently secreting the property to avoid payment of his or her debts.

76.06. Effect of attachment upon unmatured debt.

In attachments for debts not due, under s. 76.05, the existence of one or more of the special grounds assigned, and in case of attachment against executors or administrators for a debt not due, the existence of all the grounds assigned, shall cause the debt to become due, and plaintiff may proceed as on a debt falling due on a day before commencement of the action.

76.07. Attachment in aid of foreclosure.

Any creditor who is commencing or has commenced an action to foreclose a mortgage on personal property may have an attachment against the property, when the creditor has reason to believe and does believe that:

(1) The property or part of it will be concealed or disposed of so that it will not be forthcoming to answer a judgment on foreclosure.

(2) The property or part of it will be removed beyond the jurisdiction of the court.

(3) The property or part of it is of a perishable character and is being used and consumed by the mortgagor or other parties.

(4) The property or part of it has been disposed of without the consent of the party holding the mortgage, and stating who has the property, if known and if not known, that he or she does not know who has it.

76.08. Procurement of attachment; generally.

Upon motion by plaintiff, a writ of attachment may issue when the grounds relied on for the issuance of the writ clearly appear from specific facts shown by a verified complaint or a separate affidavit of the plaintiff, and all applicable requirements of s. 76.09, s. 76.10, or s. 76.11 are met.

76.09. Motion when debt due.

When the debt is actually due, the motion shall state the amount of the debt that is actually due, and that movant has reason to believe in the existence of one or more of the special grounds in s. 76.04, stating specifically the grounds.

76.10. Motion when debt not due.

When the debt is not actually due, the motion shall state the amount of the debt or demand; that it is actually an existing debt; and the existence of one or more of the special grounds in s. 76.05, stating specifically the grounds and plaintiff shall produce before the officer granting the attachment satisfactory proof, by affidavit (other than his or her own) or otherwise, of the existence of the special ground.

76.11. Motion for attachment in aid of foreclosure.

In attachments in aid of foreclosure of mortgages on personal property the motion shall describe the property on which the mortgage exists, and state that a complaint has been filed to foreclose the mortgage, the amount of the debt secured by the mortgage, that it is actually due, and that movant has reason to believe in the existence of one or more of the special grounds enumerated in s. 76.07, stating specifically the grounds.

76.12. Attachment bond.

No attachment shall issue until the person applying for it, the person's agent or attorney, makes a bond with surety to be approved by the clerk payable to defendant in at least double the debt demanded conditioned to pay all costs and damages which defendant sustains in consequence of plaintiff's improperly suing out the attachment. In foreclosure of a mortgage on personal property if the motion states that the property or part of it has been disposed of without the consent of the party holding the mortgage and that plaintiff does not know who has the property or part of it, the bond shall be made payable to the state for the use and benefit of all parties interested, conditioned to pay all costs and damages which are sustained in consequence of plaintiff's improperly suing out the attachment. Any party aggrieved may sue on the bond but the state is not liable for any costs, damages, or expenses that are incurred. Any bond in attachment is not void as against the obligors, nor are they discharged therefrom on account of any informality, although the attachment is dissolved because of the informality.

76.13. Writ; form.

(1) GENERALLY.—The writ of attachment shall command the sheriff to attach and take into custody so much of the lands, tenements, goods, and chattels of the party against whose property the writ is issued as is sufficient to satisfy the debt demanded with costs.
(2) IN AID OF SUITS TO FORECLOSE.—In actions to foreclose mortgages, the writ shall describe the property, and command the sheriff to take and hold such property or so much thereof as can be found sufficient to satisfy the debt to be foreclosed.

76.14. Writ; effect of levy.

The levy of a writ of attachment does not operate to dispossess the tenant of any lands or tenements, but a levy on real or personal property binds the property attached, except against preexisting liens. Levies on the same property under successive attachments have precedence as liens in the order in which they are made. A levy binds real estate as against subsequent creditors or purchasers only from the time of the record by the clerk of the circuit court of a notice of the levy and a description of the property levied on.

76.151. Writ; execution on property changing possession.

If the property to be attached is in the possession of the defendant at the time of the issuance of the writ but passes into the possession of a third person before the execution of the writ, the sheriff holding the writ shall execute it on the property in the possession of the third person and shall serve the writ on the defendant and the third person. The action, with proper amendments, shall proceed against the third person.

76.16. Writ; levy in other counties.

(1) When plaintiff states in a motion for attachment that defendant has real or personal property in some county other than the one in which the action was instituted, a writ of attachment, original or

ancillary, shall be issued and delivered to the sheriff of the county where the property is situate. The officer shall execute the writ and hold the property levied on subject to the order of the court from which the writ issued, which court has the power to order the delivery thereof to the sheriff of the county where the action was commenced or order the officer executing the writ to hold and dispose of it in his or her county.

(2) When any real property is levied on under this section, the officer levying the writ shall file a written notice of levy with the clerk of the circuit court for the county in which the property is located, which notice shall contain a description of the property levied on. The record shall be notice to all persons of the levy. If the attachment is dissolved or the action is dismissed, or for any reason the property ceases to be bound by the attachment, on due proof thereof the clerk shall note this on the record of the levy.

76.17. Writ; levy upon property removed from county pending levy.

When personal property of the defendant is located in any county at the time an action is commenced in which an attachment issues but is removed from the county pending the action, the officer to whom the writ is delivered shall make return of the fact of the removal and plaintiff may file a motion stating to what county he or she believes the property has been removed, whereupon an alias writ shall issue and be delivered to the sheriff of each county to which the property or a part thereof has been removed. On receipt of the writ, the sheriff shall take possession of the property and deliver it to the proper officer of the court from which the writ was issued, and make return of the writ. All questions about the title of the property shall be adjudicated in the county in which the action was brought, unless the court changes the venue.

76.18. Return of property upon forthcoming bond.

At any time after execution of the writ, property attached may be restored to defendant or some other person for him or her on defendant or such other person giving bond with surety to the officer levying the attachment to be approved by the officer payable to plaintiff in an amount which shall exceed by one-fourth the value of the property, as determined by the court, or which shall exceed by one-fourth the amount of the claim, whichever is less, conditioned for the forthcoming of the property restored to abide the final order of the court.

76.19. Return of property upon bond to pay debt.

Property attached may be restored to defendant (or in case of foreclosure of mortgage, to any person who makes affidavit that he or she is the owner of the equity of redemption), on his or her giving a bond with surety to be approved by the officer, conditioned for the payment to plaintiff of the debt and all costs of the action, when they are adjudicated to be payable to plaintiff.

76.20. Replevy of property taken by attachment.

If property taken under a writ of attachment is not subject to attachment, it may be replevied by defendant.

76.21. Claims of third parties to attached property.

If any attachment is levied on property claimed by any person other than defendant, such person may replevy it or interpose a claim in the manner provided in case of execution.

76.22. Custody of attached property; sale of perishables.

All personal property levied on by attachment, shall remain in custody of the officer who attached it until disposed of according to law unless it is restored to defendant or some person for him or her, or is claimed by a third person. When the property attached is perishable or liable to great deterioration in value or the costs of keeping it are greatly disproportionate to its value, the court may order the sale of the property after such notice as is expedient, and the proceeds of the sale shall be paid into court and abide the judgment.

76.24. Dissolution of attachment.

(1) The defendant by motion may obtain the dissolution of a writ of attachment unless the plaintiff proves the grounds upon which the writ was issued and a reasonable probability that the final judgment in the underlying action will be rendered in the plaintiff's favor. The court shall set down such motion for an immediate hearing. This motion shall be in lieu of the provisions of s. 76.18.
(2) On answer by defendant that any allegation in plaintiff's motion is untrue, this issue shall be tried. If the allegation in plaintiff's motion which is denied is not proved to be true, the attachment shall be dissolved.
(3) If the answer denies the debt demanded, the judge may require pleadings thereon on motion of either party to be filed in such time as he or she fixes.
(4) The issue, if any, raised by the pleadings shall be tried at the same time as the issue, if any, made by the answer on the special cause assigned in plaintiff's motion for the suit. On demand of either party a jury summoned from the body of the county shall be impaneled to try the issue.

76.25. Effect of dissolution.

(1) ON THE ACTION.—When an attachment is dissolved, the attachment only shall be dissolved, and plaintiff may prosecute the action to final judgment.
(2) ON WRITS OF GARNISHMENT.—When an attachment is dissolved and a writ of garnishment has been issued the garnishment shall not be dissolved in consequence of dissolution of the attachment, but shall remain in full force and abide the termination of the action.

76.251. When writ returnable.

A writ of attachment is returnable when fully executed or when the officer is convinced that no property can be found. If property is seized under the writ, the writ shall be returned when the property seized finally passes from the lien of the writ and control of the officer levying it. At the time of each action taken under the writ, the officer shall endorse the action thereon.

76.31. Judgments.

If a default is entered for plaintiff and defendant has retaken the property on a forthcoming bond, final judgment shall be entered at the same time against defendant and the surety on the bond for the amount of the judgment against defendant if it is less than the value of the property as fixed by the officer, or for the value of the property so fixed if the value is less than the judgment against defendant. If defendant has retaken the property on a bond to pay the debt, the judgment shall also be entered against the surety for the amount of the judgment against defendant. When judgment is entered against defendant after trial, it shall be entered against the surety as above provided except that the value of the property retaken by defendant shall be found by the court or jury, as the case may be, and stated in the finding or verdict.

76.32. Attachment of vessels.

(1) WHEN APPLICABLE.—In all actions by any person, firm, corporation or association of persons, including the state and any governmental subdivision, agency or department of the state, against any person, firm, association of persons or corporation, whether resident or nonresident, to recover damages for injury to the person or property thereof, resulting from negligence in the navigation, direction or management of any ship or boat of any kind, whether domestic or foreign and however propelled, within the territorial jurisdiction of the state, plaintiff is entitled to an attachment at law against the vessel in the manner hereinafter provided.

(2) VENUE.—Venue shall be in the county where defendants or any of them reside or the county where the damage or injury was suffered or the county where the vessel charged with the responsibility for the damage or injury is found.

(3) MOTION FOR.—Before any writ of attachment issues, plaintiff shall file in the court from which the writ is desired, a motion, which shall not be verified or negative the attachment debtor's exemptions, and which shall set forth the filing of the action, the circumstances under which the injury or damage complained of was suffered giving rise to plaintiff's cause of action and the amount of plaintiff's demand made in good faith.

(4) BOND.—No attachment shall issue until the person applying for it, the person's agent or attorney, makes a bond with surety to be approved by the clerk of the court in which the action is commenced payable to defendant in a sum at least double the amount of money in good faith demanded conditioned to pay all costs and damages which defendant may sustain in consequence of plaintiff's improperly suing out the attachment but no bond shall be required when the state, or any governmental subdivision, agency, or department is plaintiff.

(5) FORTHCOMING BOND.—Any vessel attached under this law may be restored at any time to defendant or to some other person for him or her, on defendant or the other person giving bond with surety to the officer levying the attachment to be approved by the officer payable to plaintiff in double the value of the vessel levied on, if the value does not exceed the amount of plaintiff's claim, or double the amount of plaintiff's claim, if the value exceeds the amount of plaintiff's claim, the value to be fixed by the officer, conditioned for the forthcoming of the property restored to abide the final judgment of the court but if the action is for unliquidated damages, defendant or the claimant of the offending vessel instead of furnishing a bond may apply to the court for a reduction in the amount of the bond, and the court may fix the amount and conditions of the bond at a sum sufficient to adequately secure payment of the amount of the injury or damage which may have been suffered by plaintiff with costs. The release bond shall be approved by the court. If plaintiff recovers a judgment, it shall be rendered against defendant, or the claimant of the vessel, and his or her surety on the release bond.

(6) APPLICATION OF LAW.—This law applies to those actions for injury, loss or damage which

occur without the admiralty and maritime jurisdiction of the courts of the United States.

CHAPTER 77. GARNISHMENT

77.01. Right to writ of garnishment.

Every person or entity who has sued to recover a debt or has recovered judgment in any court against any person or entity has a right to a writ of garnishment, in the manner hereinafter provided, to subject any debt due to defendant by a third person or any debt not evidenced by a negotiable instrument that will become due absolutely through the passage of time only to the defendant by a third person, and any tangible or intangible personal property of defendant in the possession or control of a third person. The officers, agents, and employees of any companies or corporations are third persons in regard to the companies or corporations, and as such are subject to garnishment after judgment against the companies or corporations.

77.02. Garnishment in tort actions.

Before judgment against a defendant no writ of garnishment shall issue in any action sounding in tort.

77.03. Issuance of writ after judgment.

After judgment has been obtained against defendant but before the writ of garnishment is issued, the plaintiff, the plaintiff's agent or attorney, shall file a motion (which shall not be verified or negative defendant's exemptions) stating the amount of the judgment. The motion may be filed and the writ issued either before or after the return of execution.

77.0305. Continuing writ of garnishment against salary or wages.

Notwithstanding any other provision of this chapter, if salary or wages are to be garnished to satisfy a judgment, the court shall issue a continuing writ of garnishment to the judgment debtor's employer which provides for the periodic payment of a portion of the salary or wages of the judgment debtor as the salary or wages become due until the judgment is satisfied or until otherwise provided by court order. A debtor's status as an employee of the state or its agencies or political subdivisions does not preclude a judgment creditor's right to garnish the debtor's wages. For the purposes of this section, the state includes the judicial branch and the legislative branch as defined in s. 216.011. The state, for itself and for its agencies and subdivisions, waives sovereign immunity for the express and limited purpose necessary to carry out this section. The court shall allow the judgment debtor's employer to collect up to $5 against the salary or wages of the judgment debtor to reimburse the employer for administrative costs for the first deduction from the judgment debtor's salary or wages and up to $2 for each deduction thereafter. The funds collected by the state under this section must be deposited in the Department of Financial Services Administrative Trust Fund for purposes of carrying out this section.

77.031. Issuance of writ before judgment.

Before judgment has been obtained by the plaintiff against the defendant:

(1) A writ of garnishment shall be issued by the court or by the clerk on order of the court.

(2) To obtain issuance of the writ, the plaintiff, or the plaintiff's agent or attorney, shall file in the court where the action is pending a verified motion or affidavit alleging by specific facts the nature of the cause of action; the amount of the debt and that the debt for which the plaintiff sues is just, due, and unpaid; that the garnishment is not sued out to injure either the defendant or the garnishee; and that the plaintiff believes that the defendant will not have in his or her possession, after execution is issued, tangible or intangible property in this state and in the county in which the action is pending on which a levy can be made sufficient to satisfy the plaintiff's claim. The writ of garnishment shall set forth a notice to the defendant of the right to an immediate hearing for dissolution of such writ pursuant to s. 77.07. Upon issuance of the writ of garnishment, the clerk of the court shall provide by mail a copy of the writ to the defendant.

(3) Except when the plaintiff has had an attachment writ issued, no writ of garnishment before judgment shall issue until the plaintiff, or the plaintiff's agent or attorney, gives a bond with surety to be approved by the clerk payable to the defendant in at least double the amount of the debt demanded, conditioned to pay all costs, damages, and attorney's fees that the defendant sustains in consequence of the plaintiff's improperly suing out the writ of garnishment. A garnishment bond is not void or voidable because of an informality in it, nor shall the obligors be discharged because of the informality, even though the garnishment is dissolved because of the informality.

(4) The motion or pleading need not negative any exemptions of the defendant.

77.04. Writ; form.

The writ shall require the garnishee to serve an answer on the plaintiff within 20 days after service of the writ stating whether the garnishee is indebted to the defendant at the time of the answer, or was indebted at the time of service of the writ, plus up to 1 business day for the garnishee to act expeditiously on the writ, or at any time between such times; in what sum and what tangible or intangible personal property of defendant the garnishee has in his or her possession or control at the time of his or her answer, or had at the time of the service of the writ, or at any time between such times; and whether the garnishee knows of any other person indebted to defendant, or who may have any of the property of defendant in his or her possession or control. The writ shall state the amount named in plaintiff's motion. If the garnishee is a business entity, an authorized employee or agent of the entity may execute, file, and serve the answer on behalf of the entity.

77.041. Notice to individual defendant for claim of exemption from garnishment; procedure for hearing.

(1) Upon application for a writ of garnishment by a plaintiff, if the defendant is an individual, the clerk of the court shall attach to the writ the following "Notice to Defendant":

1. Head of family wages. (Check either a. or b. below, if applicable.)

a. I provide more than one-half of the support for a child or other dependent and have net earnings of $750 or less per week.

b. I provide more than one-half of the support for a child or other dependent, have net earnings of more than $750 per week, but have not agreed in writing to have my wages garnished.

2. Social Security benefits.

3. Supplemental Security Income benefits.

4. Public assistance (welfare).

5. Workers' Compensation.

6. Reemployment assistance or unemployment compensation.

7. Veterans' benefits.

8. Retirement or profit-sharing benefits or pension money.

9. Life insurance benefits or cash surrender value of a life insurance policy or proceeds of annuity contract.

10. Disability income benefits.

11. Prepaid College Trust Fund or Medical Savings Account.

12. Other exemptions as provided by law.   (explain)

(2) The plaintiff must mail, by first class, a copy of the writ of garnishment, a copy of the motion for writ of garnishment, and, if the defendant is an individual, the "Notice to Defendant" to the defendant's last known address within 5 business days after the writ is issued or 3 business days after the writ is served on the garnishee, whichever is later. However, if such documents are returned as undeliverable by the post office, or if the last known address is not discoverable after diligent search, the plaintiff must mail, by first class, the documents to the defendant at the defendant's place of employment. The plaintiff shall file in the proceeding a certificate of such service.

(3) Upon the filing by a defendant of a sworn claim of exemption and request for hearing, a hearing will be held as soon as is practicable to determine the validity of the claimed exemptions. If the plaintiff or the plaintiff's attorney does not file a sworn written statement that answers the defendant's claim of exemption within 8 business days after hand delivering the claim and request or, alternatively, 14 business days if the claim and request were served by mail, no hearing is required and the clerk must automatically dissolve the writ and notify the parties of the dissolution by mail.

77.055. Service of garnishee's answer and notice of right to dissolve writ.

Within 5 days after service of the garnishee's answer on the plaintiff or after the time period for the garnishee's answer has expired, the plaintiff shall serve, by mail, the following documents: a copy of the garnishee's answer, and a notice advising the recipient that he or she must move to dissolve the writ of garnishment within 20 days after the date indicated on the certificate of service in the notice if any allegation in the plaintiff's motion for writ of garnishment is untrue. The plaintiff shall serve these documents on the defendant at the defendant's last known address and any other address disclosed by the garnishee's answer and on any other person disclosed in the garnishee's answer to have any ownership interest in the deposit, account, or property controlled by the garnishee. The plaintiff shall file in the proceeding a certificate of such service.

77.06. Writ; effect.

(1) Service of the writ shall make garnishee liable for all debts due by him or her to defendant and for any tangible or intangible personal property of defendant in the garnishee's possession or control at the time of the service of the writ or at any time between the service and the time of the garnishee's answer. Service of the writ creates a lien in or upon any such debts or property at the time of service or at the time such debts or property come into the garnishee's possession or control.

(2) The garnishee shall report in its answer and retain, subject to the provisions of s. 77.19 and subject to disposition as provided in this chapter, any deposit, account, or tangible or intangible personal property in the possession or control of such garnishee; and the answer shall state the name or names and addresses, if known to the garnishee, of the defendant and any other persons having or appearing to have an ownership interest in the involved property.

(3) In any case where a garnishee in good faith is in doubt as to whether any indebtedness or property is required by law to be included in the garnishee's answer or retained by it, the garnishee may include and retain the same, subject to the provisions of s. 77.19 and subject to disposition as provided in this chapter, and in such case the garnishee shall not be liable for so doing to the defendant or to any other person claiming the same or any interest therein or claiming to have sustained damage on account thereof.

(4) Service of a writ on a garnishee shall render him or her liable as provided in this chapter in any fiduciary or representative capacity held by him or her if the fiduciary or representative capacity is specified in the writ.

77.061. Reply.

When any garnishee answers and plaintiff is not satisfied with the answer, he or she shall serve a reply within 20 days thereafter denying the allegations of the answer as he or she desires. On failure of plaintiff to file a reply, the answer shall be taken as true and on proper disposition of the assets, if any are disclosed thereby, the garnishee is entitled to an order discharging him or her from further liability under the writ.

77.07. Dissolution of writ.

(1) The defendant, by motion, may obtain the dissolution of a writ of garnishment, unless the petitioner proves the grounds upon which the writ was issued and unless, in the case of a prejudgment writ, there is a reasonable probability that the final judgment in the underlying action will be rendered in his or her favor. The court shall set down such motion for an immediate hearing. If the writ is dissolved, the action then shall proceed as if no writ had been issued.

(2) The defendant and any other person having an ownership interest in the property, as disclosed by the garnishee's answer, shall file and serve a motion to dissolve the garnishment within 20 days after the date indicated in the certificate of service on the defendant and such other person of the plaintiff's notice required by s. 77.055, stating that any allegation in plaintiff's motion for writ is untrue. On such motion this issue shall be tried, and if the allegation in plaintiff's motion which is

denied is not proved to be true, the garnishment shall be dissolved. Failure of the defendant or other interested person to timely file and serve the motion to dissolve within such time limitation shall result in the striking of the motion as an unauthorized nullity by the court, and the proceedings shall be in a default posture as to the party involved.

(3) If the motion denies the debt demanded before judgment, the judge may require pleadings on motion of either party on the debt demanded to be filed in such time as he or she fixes.

(4) The issue, if any, raised by the pleadings shall be tried at the same time as the issue, if any, made by defendant's motion to plaintiff's motion.

(5) If the plaintiff fails to file a dismissal or motion for final judgment within 6 months after filing the writ of garnishment, the writ shall automatically be dissolved and the garnishee shall be discharged from further liability under the writ. The plaintiff has the right to extend the writ for an additional 6 months by serving the garnishee and the defendant a notice of extension and filing in the underlying proceeding a certification of such service.

77.08. Writ; jury trial.

On demand of either party a jury summoned from the body of the county shall be impaneled to try the issues.

77.081. Default; judgment.

(1) If the garnishee fails to answer as required, a default shall be entered against him or her.

(2) On the entry of judgment for plaintiff, a final judgment shall be entered against the garnishee for the amount of plaintiff's claim with interest and costs. No final judgment against a garnishee shall be entered before the entry of, or in excess of, the final judgment against the original defendant with interest and costs. If the claim of the plaintiff is dismissed or judgment is entered against the plaintiff the default against garnishee shall be vacated and judgment for the garnishee's costs entered.

77.082. No reply filed.

If no reply to garnishee's answer is served, garnishee may surrender any goods, chattels, or effects of defendant in garnishee's hands or possession to the sheriff and may pay any money or debt into registry of court. In such event or if garnishee prevails in the trial of any reply and after proper disposition of any property disclosed by garnishee's answer, the court shall discharge him or her from further liability under the writ.

77.083. Judgment.

Judgment against the garnishee on the garnishee's answer or after trial of a reply to the garnishee's answer shall be entered for the amount of his or her liability as disclosed by the answer or trial. Instead of scire facias, the court may subpoena the garnishee to inquire about his or her liability to or possession of property of the defendant. No judgment in excess of the amount remaining unpaid on the final judgment against the defendant or in excess of the amount of the liability of the garnishee to the defendant, whichever is less, shall be entered against the garnishee.

77.13. Execution on garnishee's refusal to surrender property.

If garnishee will not surrender the personal property belonging to defendant, provided he or she has the power to do so, and which garnishee has admitted is in his or her possession, the court may order execution issued against garnishee for the unpaid amount of plaintiff's judgment against defendant. The officer shall sell garnishee's property as under other executions. Garnishee may release his or her property from the levy and sale by surrendering the property of defendant to the officer levying the execution at the time appointed for the sale of garnishee's property so levied on, or at any time before the day of the sale and by paying the costs of the proceedings to sell up to the time of the surrender.

77.14. Disposition of property surrendered by garnishee.

When any garnishee has any of the personal property of defendant in his or her possession or control and surrenders it, the sheriff shall receive the property and sell it under the execution against defendant.

77.15. Proceedings against third persons named in answer.

If the answer of garnishee shows that there is any of defendant's personal property in the possession or control of any person who has not been garnished, on motion of plaintiff a writ of garnishment shall issue against the person having personal property of the defendant and the person shall answer and be liable as other garnishees.

77.16. Claims by third persons to garnisheed property.

(1) If any person other than defendant claims that the debt due by a garnishee is due to that person and not to defendant, or that the property in the hands or possession of any garnishee is that person's property and shall make an affidavit to the effect, the court shall impanel a jury to determine the right of property between the claimant and plaintiff unless a jury is waived.
(2) If the verdict is against the claimant, plaintiff shall recover costs. If the verdict is in favor of the claimant, the claimant shall recover costs against plaintiff.
(3) If the claim is interposed after a levy on property, the officer making the levy shall return the execution with the officer's levy thereon and the affidavit of the claimant to the court from which execution issued, and the proceedings shall be as in other cases of claims made to property taken on execution.

77.17. Compensation to garnishee.

The garnishee shall be allowed the pay of a witness for the garnishee's attendance out of the debt owed to defendant or the property in the garnishee's possession. If there is no debt or property in the garnishee's possession, the allowance shall be against plaintiff.

77.19. Amount retained by garnishee.

No garnishee who is indebted to or has in his or her possession the money of a person whose money or credits may be garnisheed shall retain out of the money more than double the amount which the writ of garnishment specifies as the amount plaintiff expects to recover or more than double the amount of the judgment plaintiff has recovered.

77.22. Before judgment; effect of judgment for defendant.

(1) If the judgment is for defendant in the main action, plaintiff shall pay all costs which have accrued in consequence of suing out a writ of garnishment before judgment and the money or property brought into the registry of the court or custody of the officer thereby inures to the benefit of and shall be controlled by defendant as completely as though it had been rendered in defendant's favor.
(2) If plaintiff dismisses his or her action or has a judgment against him or her on the trial, the judgment against garnishee shall become a nullity and garnishee shall have execution for garnishee's costs against plaintiff.

77.24. Before judgment; discharge.

At any time before the entry of judgment, a defendant whose property has been garnisheed may secure its release by giving a bond with surety to be approved by the clerk in at least double the amount claimed in the complaint with interest and costs, or if the value of the property garnisheed is less than this amount, then in double the value, conditioned to pay any judgment recovered against the defendant in the action with interest and costs, or so much thereof as shall equal the value. On the approval of the bond the court shall discharge the garnishment and release the property. The order shall become effective on its filing with the bond. If garnishee admits a debt to or possession of property of defendant in excess of a sum sufficient to satisfy plaintiff's claim, on motion of defendant and notice to plaintiff, the court shall release garnishee from responsibility to plaintiff for any debt to or property of defendant except in a sum deemed by the court sufficient to satisfy plaintiff's claim with interest and costs.

77.27. No appeal until fees are paid.

If the writ is dismissed or plaintiff fails to sustain his or her claim, an appeal from the judgment is not permitted until the attorney fee provided in s. 77.28 has been paid.

77.28. Garnishment; attorney fees, costs, expenses; deposit required.

Upon issuance of any writ of garnishment, the party applying for it shall pay $100 to the garnishee on the garnishee's demand at any time after the service of the writ for the payment or part payment of his or her attorney fee which the garnishee expends or agrees to expend in obtaining representation in response to the writ. On rendering final judgment, the court shall determine the garnishee's costs and expenses, including a reasonable attorney fee, and in the event of a judgment in favor of the plaintiff, the amount is subject to offset by the garnishee against the defendant whose property or debt owing is being garnished. In addition, the court shall tax the garnishee's costs and expenses as costs. The plaintiff may recover in this manner the sum advanced by him or her, and, if the amount allowed by the court is greater than the amount paid together with any offset, judgment for the garnishee shall be entered against the party against whom the costs are taxed for the deficiency.

CHAPTER 78. REPLEVIN

78.01. Right of replevin.

Any person whose personal property is wrongfully detained by any other person or officer may have a writ of replevin to recover said personal property and any damages sustained by reason of the wrongful taking or detention as herein provided. Notice of lis pendens to charge third persons with knowledge of plaintiff's claim on the property may be recorded.

78.02. What may not be taken by replevin.

No replevin shall lie:
(1) For any property taken by virtue of any warrant for the collection of any tax, assessment, or fine pursuant to any statute;
(2) For defendant in any execution or attachment to recover goods and chattels seized by virtue thereof unless such goods and chattels are exempt from the execution or attachment;
(3) By the original defendant in replevin for property taken in replevin and delivered to plaintiff while it remains in the possession of the original plaintiff or his or her agents.
(4) For any person unless that person has a right to reduce the goods taken into his or her possession.

78.03. Jurisdiction.

An action for replevin must be brought in a court of competent jurisdiction based on the value of the property sought to be replevied. When property consists of separate articles, the value of any one of which is within the jurisdiction of a lower court but taken together will exceed that jurisdiction, the plaintiff may not divide the property to give jurisdiction to the lower court to enable the plaintiff to bring separate actions therefor.

78.032. Venue.

An action for replevin may be brought in any county where the property sought to be replevied is located, where the contract was signed, where the defendant resides, or where the cause of action accrued. An action that includes a cause of action for replevin and other causes of action may be brought in any county where venue is proper under chapter 47 for any of the other causes of action or in any county where venue for the replevin is proper under this section.

78.045. Writ; court order required.

No clerk of court shall issue a writ of replevin prior to final judgment unless there has been filed with the clerk of court an order authorizing the issuance of such writ of replevin.

78.055. Complaint; requirements.

To obtain an order authorizing the issuance of a writ of replevin prior to final judgment, the plaintiff shall first file with the clerk of the court a complaint reciting and showing the following information:

(1) A description of the claimed property that is sufficient to make possible its identification and a statement, to the best knowledge, information, and belief of the plaintiff of the value of such property and its location.

(2) A statement that the plaintiff is the owner of the claimed property or is entitled to possession of it, describing the source of such title or right. If the plaintiff's interest in such property is based on a written instrument, a copy of said instrument must be attached to the complaint.

(3) A statement that the property is wrongfully detained by the defendant, the means by which the defendant came into possession thereof, and the cause of such detention according to the best knowledge, information, and belief of the plaintiff.

(4) A statement that the claimed property has not been taken for a tax, assessment, or fine pursuant to law.

(5) A statement that the property has not been taken under an execution or attachment against the property of the plaintiff or, if so taken, that it is by law exempt from such taking, setting forth a reference to the exemption law relied upon.

78.065. Order to show cause; contents.

(1) The court without delay shall examine the complaint filed; and, if on the basis of the complaint and further showing of the plaintiff in support of it the court finds that the defendant has waived in accordance with s. 78.075 his or her right to be notified and heard, the court shall promptly issue an order authorizing the clerk of the court to issue a writ of replevin.

(2) If, upon examination of the complaint filed and on further showing of the plaintiff in support of it, the court finds that the defendant has not waived in accordance with s. 78.075 his or her right to be notified and heard, the court shall promptly issue an order directed to the defendant to show cause why the claimed property should not be taken from the possession of the defendant and delivered to plaintiff. Such order shall:

(a) Fix the date and time for hearing on the order. However, the date for the hearing shall not be set sooner than 5 days after the service of the order.

(b) Direct the time within which service of the order and the complaint shall be made upon the defendant.

(c) Fix the manner in which service of the order shall be made on the defendant. The order shall direct that service as provided by law shall be made on the defendant if such service is possible or, in the event the officer serving the order is unable to serve such defendant as provided by law within the time specified in paragraph (b), that the officer shall place the order, together with the summons, on or in the claimed property or on the main entrance of the defendant's residence. The officer's return shall state that the officer was unable to locate the defendant and how the order was served.

(d) State that the nonpersonal service as provided herein shall be effective to afford notice to the defendant of the show cause order, but for no other purpose.

(e) State that the defendant has the right to file affidavits on his or her behalf with the court and may appear personally or by way of an attorney and present testimony on his or her behalf at the time of the hearing, or that the defendant may, upon a finding by the court pursuant to s. 78.067(2) that the plaintiff is entitled to the possession of the claimed property pending final adjudication of the claims of the parties, file with the court a written undertaking executed by a surety approved by the court in an amount equal to the value of the property to stay an order authorizing the delivery of the property to the plaintiff.

(f) State that if the defendant fails to appear the defendant shall be deemed to have waived his or her right to a hearing and that in such case the court may order the clerk of the court to issue a writ of replevin.

78.067. Order to show cause; hearing.

(1) If, after serving a show cause order as provided above, the court finds that the defendant has waived the right to be heard on that order in accordance with s. 78.075, it shall dispense with the hearing on the show cause order and promptly issue an order authorizing the clerk of the court to issue a writ of replevin.

(2) If the court finds that the defendant has not waived the right to be heard on the order to show cause in accordance with s. 78.075, the court shall at the hearing on the order to show cause consider the affidavits and other showings made by the parties appearing and make a determination of which party, with reasonable probability, is entitled to the possession of the claimed property pending final adjudication of the claims of the parties. This determination shall be based on a finding as to the probable validity of the underlying claim alleged against the defendant. If the court determines that the plaintiff is entitled to take possession of the claimed property, it shall issue an order directing the clerk of the court to issue a writ of replevin. However, the order shall be stayed pending final adjudication of the claims of the parties if the defendant files with the court a written undertaking executed by a surety approved by the court in an amount equal to the value of the property.

78.068. Prejudgment writ of replevin.

(1) A prejudgment writ of replevin may be issued and the property seized delivered forthwith to the petitioners when the nature of the claim and the amount thereof, if any, and the grounds relied upon for the issuance of the writ clearly appear from specific facts shown by the verified petition or by separate affidavit of the petitioner.

(2) This prejudgment writ of replevin may issue if the court finds, pursuant to subsection (1), that the defendant is engaging in, or is about to engage in, conduct that may place the claimed property in danger of destruction, concealment, waste, removal from the state, removal from the jurisdiction of the court, or transfer to an innocent purchaser during the pendency of the action or that the defendant has failed to make payment as agreed.

(3) The petitioner must post bond in the amount of twice the value of the goods subject to the writ or twice the balance remaining due and owing, whichever is lesser as determined by the court, as security for the payment of damages the defendant may sustain when the writ is obtained wrongfully.

(4) The defendant may obtain release of the property seized under a prejudgment writ of replevin by posting bond within 5 days after serving of the writ in the amount of 11/4 the amount due and

owing on the agreement for the satisfaction of any judgment which may be rendered against the defendant.

(5) A prejudgment writ of replevin shall issue only upon the signed order of a circuit court judge or a county court judge.

(6) The defendant, by contradictory motion filed with the court within 10 days after service of the writ, may obtain the dissolution of a prejudgment writ of replevin unless the petitioner proves the grounds upon which the writ was issued. The court shall set down such motion for an immediate hearing. This motion shall be in lieu of the provisions of subsection (4).

78.075. Order to show cause; waiver.

The right to be heard provided in ss. 78.065 and 78.067 is waived if the defendant, after receiving a show cause order, engages in any conduct that clearly shows that he or she wants to forego the right to be heard on that order. The defendant's failure to appear at the hearing duly scheduled on the order to show cause presumptively constitutes conduct that clearly shows that he or she wants to forego the right to be so heard. If the defendant, after service of the order to show cause, sends or delivers to the plaintiff or the court issuing the order to show cause a writing prepared by anyone but signed by the defendant after service of the order to show cause, indicating in any language that the defendant does not want to be heard on the show cause order, the defendant shall be presumed to have waived the right to be heard. For this purpose, a writing containing the following language is sufficient: "I, (name of the defendant) , am aware that I have the right and opportunity to be heard on a show cause order that has been served upon me concerning the right of plaintiff to obtain a writ of replevin authorizing the appropriate officer of the court to take (describe property) from my possession prior to final judgment against me. I hereby state that I do not want to be heard on this matter and that I expressly waive my right to be heard. I understand that the effect of my signing this paper probably will be a court order authorizing the issuance of a writ of replevin directing an officer of the court to take possession of the property described above prior to final judgment against me with respect to the claim under which the property is taken."

78.08. Writ; form.

The writ shall command the sheriff to replevy the described personal property in possession of defendant.

78.10. Writ; execution on property in buildings or enclosures.

In executing the writ of replevin, if the sheriff has reasonable grounds to believe that the property or any part thereof is secreted or concealed in any dwelling house or other building or enclosure, the sheriff shall publicly demand delivery thereof; and, if it is not delivered by the defendant or some other person, the sheriff shall cause such house, building, or enclosure to be broken open and shall make replevin according to the writ; and, if necessary, the sheriff shall take to his or her assistance the power of the county. However, if the sheriff does not have reasonable grounds to believe that the property to be replevied is secreted or concealed in any dwelling house or other building or enclosure, the plaintiff may petition the court for a "break order" directing the sheriff to enter physically any dwelling house or other building or enclosure. Upon a showing of probable cause by the plaintiff, the court shall enter such "break order."

78.11. Writ; execution on property changing possession.

If the property to be replevied is in the possession of defendant at the time of the issuance of the writ, and passes into the possession of a third person before the execution of the writ, the officer holding the writ shall execute it on the property in the possession of the third person and shall serve the writ on defendant and the third person, and the action with proper amendments, shall proceed against the third person.

78.12. Writ; execution on property removed from jurisdiction.

At the time of service of the writ if the property to be replevied is located outside the county of the court issuing the writ, the party having had the writ issued shall deliver it to the sheriff of the county where the property is located and to whom the writ is directed, and the sheriff shall execute the writ and shall, unless the writ directs otherwise, deliver the property to the plaintiff.

78.13. Writ; disposition of property levied on.

The officer executing the writ by levying on the property described shall deliver the property forthwith to plaintiff unless the writ directs otherwise. The defendant may obtain release of the property seized within 5 days after the seizure by posting with the clerk of the court who issued the writ the amount of 11/4 times the amount due and owing, conditioned to have the property forthcoming to abide the result of the action, or on the agreement for the satisfaction of any judgment which may be rendered against the defendant.

78.18. Judgment for plaintiff when goods not delivered to defendant.

If it appears that the property described in the complaint was wrongfully taken or detained by defendant and the property has been delivered to plaintiff by the officer executing the writ, plaintiff shall have judgment for his or her damages caused by the taking and detention and costs.

78.19. Judgment for plaintiff when goods retained by or redelivered to defendant.

(1) If it appears that the property was retained by, or redelivered to, defendant on his or her forthcoming bond, plaintiff shall take judgment for the property and against defendant and the surety on the forthcoming bond for the value of the property, but when plaintiff's interest in the property is based on a claim of lien or some special interest therein, the judgment shall be only for the amount of the lien or the value of such special interest and costs, and the judgment shall be satisfied by the recovery of the property or the amount adjudged against defendant and defendant's

surety.

(2) After rendition of judgment, plaintiff at his or her option may have a writ of possession for the property and execution for plaintiff's costs or have execution against defendant and defendant's surety for the amount recovered and costs. If plaintiff elects to have a writ of possession for the property and the officer returns that he or she is unable to find it or any of it, plaintiff may immediately have execution against defendant and defendant's surety for the whole amount recovered against them or for the amount recovered less the value of the property found by the officer. If he or she has execution for the whole amount, the officer shall release all property taken under the writ of possession.

(3) In any proceeding to ascertain the value of the property so that judgment for the value may be entered, the value of each article shall be found but it is not necessary to ascertain the value of each article of a lot of goods, wares, and merchandise when it has been replevied, but it is sufficient to ascertain the total value of the entire lot found.

78.20. Judgment for defendant when goods retained by, or redelivered to, defendant.

When property has been retained by, or redelivered to, defendant on his or her forthcoming bond or upon the dissolution of a prejudgment writ and defendant prevails, he or she shall have judgment against plaintiff for his or her damages for the taking, if any, of the property, attorney fees, and costs. The remedies provided in this section and s. 78.21 shall not preclude any other remedies available under the laws of this state.

78.21. Judgment for defendant when goods not retained by, or redelivered to, defendant.

When the property has not been retained by, or redelivered to, defendant and he or she prevails, judgment shall be entered against plaintiff for possession of the property and costs and against plaintiff for the value of the property and costs in the same manner as provided in s. 78.19 for judgment in favor of plaintiff. The value of each article of the goods replevied shall be found as directed in s. 78.19 with the same exception. The remedies provided in s. 78.20 and this section shall not preclude any other remedies available under the laws of this state.

CHAPTER 79. HABEAS CORPUS

79.01. Application and writ.

When any person detained in custody, whether charged with a criminal offense or not, applies to the Supreme Court or any justice thereof, or to any district court of appeal or any judge thereof or to any circuit judge for a writ of habeas corpus and shows by affidavit or evidence probable cause to believe that he or she is detained without lawful authority, the court, justice, or judge to whom such application is made shall grant the writ forthwith, against the person in whose custody the applicant is detained and returnable immediately before any of the courts, justices, or judges as the writ directs.

79.02. Bond may be required.

When it appears necessary, the court, justice, or judge granting the writ shall require bond with surety to be approved by the judge or clerk payable to the Governor executed in such manner and reasonable penalty as the court, justice, or judge prescribes; conditioned for the payment of the charges and costs awarded against the prisoner and that he or she will not escape by the way. The bond shall be filed and may be sued on in the name of the Governor for the benefit of any person interested therein. In the event of inability to give bond for the payment of charges and costs, he or she may be permitted, in the place thereof, to make deposit in such amount as the court, justice, or judge requires.

79.03. Service of writ.

When issued, the writ shall be served by the sheriff of the county in which the petitioner is alleged to be detained on the officer or other person against whom it is issued, or in his or her absence from the place where the prisoner is confined, on the person having the immediate custody of the prisoner. When the sheriff of the county is the person holding the party detained, a delivery to or receipt of the writ by the sheriff is sufficient service.

79.04. Return to writ.

(1) The person on whom the writ is served shall bring the body of the prisoner, or cause it to be brought, before the court, justice or judge before whom the writ is made returnable without delay and at the same time certify to the cause of the detention.
(2) When the writ is issued, the court shall set an early return date, at which time the formal return of the defendant shall be made. In the absence of a motion to quash or a motion for discharge notwithstanding the return, issue is joined when the return is filed and the action shall be ready for final disposition.

79.05. Compelling return and production of body.

(1) CIVIL LIABILITY.—Any person failing to return to the writ served on him or her with the cause of the prisoner's detention, or to bring the body of the prisoner before the court, justice, or judge, according to the command of the writ for 3 days after the service shall forfeit and pay to the prisoner the sum of $300.
(2) BY PROCEEDINGS BY THE COURT.—A justice or judge in vacation may enforce obedience to any writ of habeas corpus and in cases pending before the Supreme Court, or any of the justices thereof, writs for the enforcement of obedience may be directed to the sheriff or other officer.

79.06. Effect of the return.

(1) GENERALLY.—The return made to the writ may be amended, and is not conclusive as to the facts stated therein, but the court, justice or judge before whom the return is made may examine into the cause of the imprisonment or detention, receive evidence in contradiction of the return,

and determine it as the truth of the case requires.

(2) IN CASES OF CONTEMPT.—On the return of the writ when the cause of detention appears to be a contempt, plainly and specifically charged in the commitment by some court officer or body having authority to commit for the contempt so charged and for the time stated, the court, justice or judge before whom the writ is returnable shall remand the prisoner forthwith if the time for detention for contempt has not expired.

79.07. Procurement of evidence.

When it is inconvenient to procure the personal attendance of a witness, the witness's affidavit, taken upon reasonable notice to the adverse party, may be received in evidence.

79.071. Notice to prosecutor.

If the validity of any statute, criminal law proceeding or conviction is attacked by habeas corpus in the circuit court, notice of the application for the writ shall be given to the prosecuting attorney of the court in which the statute under attack is being applied, the criminal law proceeding is being maintained or the conviction has occurred.

79.08. Hearing and judgment.

The court, justice, or judge before whom the prisoner is brought shall inquire without delay into the cause of the prisoner's imprisonment, and shall either discharge the prisoner, admit him or her to bail or remand him or her to custody, as the law and the evidence require; and shall either award against the prisoner the charges of his or her transportation, not exceeding 15 cents per mile and the costs of the proceedings, or shall award the costs in the prisoner's favor, or shall award no costs or charges against either party, as is right. The clerk of the court in which such action is pending shall issue execution for the costs and charges awarded.

79.09. Filing of papers.

Before a circuit judge the petition and the papers shall be filed with the clerk of the circuit court of the county in which the prisoner is detained. Before the other courts, justices or judges, the papers shall be filed with the clerk of the court on which the justice or judge sits.

79.10. Effect of judgment.

The judgment is conclusive until reversed and no person remanded by the judgment while it continues in force shall be at liberty to obtain another habeas corpus for the same cause or by any other proceeding bring the same matter again in question except by an appeal or by action of false imprisonment; nor shall any person who is discharged from confinement by the judgment be afterward confined or imprisoned for the same cause except by order of a court of competent jurisdiction.

79.12. Trial of accused pending appeal.

When in any criminal prosecution a writ of habeas corpus is applied for by any person charged with any criminal offense and the accused has been remanded to custody by the court to which such application is made, a supersedeas of the order made on appeal being taken to an appellate court shall not prevent the state from proceeding with the prosecution of the accused pending the decision by the appellate court in the habeas corpus, but the state may prosecute the accused as if appeal had not been taken in habeas corpus. If the accused is convicted of the charge, the court shall withhold imposition of sentence and final judgment until the appellate court has determined the issues presented in the habeas corpus.

CHAPTER 80. QUO WARRANTO

80.01. Quo warranto; refusal of Attorney General to institute.

Any person claiming title to an office which is exercised by another has the right, on refusal by the Attorney General to commence an action in the name of the state upon the claimant's relation, or on the Attorney General's refusal to file a petition setting forth the claimant's name as the person rightfully entitled to the office, to file an action in the name of the state against the person exercising the office, setting up his or her own claim. The court shall determine the right of the claimant to the office, if the claimant so desires. No person shall be adjudged entitled to hold an office except upon full proof of the person's title to the office in any action of this character.

80.02. Quo warranto; control of Attorney General over certain proceedings.

When the Attorney General commences an action setting forth the name of the person rightfully entitled, or when petition is filed upon the relation of a party claiming title, the Attorney General shall not dismiss the action without the consent of the claimant, but the court shall investigate the claim and determine the right, if so desired by the person on whose relation the petition is filed, and the claimant may have counsel of his or her choice to control the action in the claimant's behalf.

80.031. Procedure.

The rules about pleading and procedure in mandamus apply to actions for quo warranto as near as may be.

80.032. Judgment of ouster.

When any petition is well-founded, a judgment of ouster may issue without further amendments to the extent that the petition is well-founded.

80.04. Quo warranto; effect of judgment.

When an individual institutes an action without the consent of the Attorney General, the judgment is conclusive as between the parties other than the state. The judgment is not a bar to any quo warranto by the state nor shall a judgment instituted by the Attorney General be a bar to actions by any claimant other than the parties thereto. The party receiving judgment shall be entitled to exercise the office until removed by quo warranto or until his or her rights thereto shall otherwise cease.

CHAPTER 81. PROHIBITION

81.011. Petition for prohibition.

The petitioner shall file a petition stating the nature of the action, the proceedings in the inferior court, tribunal or body presuming to exercise jurisdiction sought to be prohibited, and demand that writ of prohibition be granted in that behalf. When the matters appear on the face of the proceedings in the body presuming to exercise jurisdiction, the certified transcript of the record of all the proceedings shall accompany the petition. When the matters are not matters of record, they shall be verified by affidavit of petitioner or petitioner's agent, or attorney.

81.021. Prohibition; supersedeas.

If in its judgment a prima facie case is made, the court shall issue an order directed to the body presuming to exercise jurisdiction and to plaintiff to show cause why the writ of prohibition should not issue. The order is a supersedeas and shall be served on the body presuming to exercise jurisdiction and the parties at such time as the court directs and those served shall defend within the time set in the writ. In case of failure to make an answer, it may be enforced by contempt.

81.031. Prohibition; procedure.

In the circuit court the petition shall be accompanied by a supporting brief in the same manner as required for mandamus in that court.

CHAPTER 82. FORCIBLE ENTRY AND UNLAWFUL DETAINER

82.01. "Unlawful entry and forcible entry" defined.

No person shall enter into any lands or tenements except when entry is given by law, nor shall any person, when entry is given by law, enter with strong hand or with multitude of people, but only in a peaceable, easy and open manner.

82.02. "Unlawful entry and unlawful detention" defined.

(1) No person who enters without consent in a peaceable, easy and open manner into any lands or tenements shall hold them afterwards against the consent of the party entitled to possession.
(2) This section shall not apply with regard to residential tenancies.

82.03. Remedy for unlawful entry and forcible entry.

If any person enters or has entered into lands or tenements when entry is not given by law, or if any person enters or has entered into any lands or tenements with strong hand or with multitude of people, even when entry is given by law, the party turned out or deprived of possession by the unlawful or forcible entry, by whatever right or title the party held possession, or whatever estate the party held or claimed in the lands or tenements of which he or she was so dispossessed, is entitled to the summary procedure under s. 51.011 within 3 years thereafter.

82.04. Remedy for unlawful detention.

(1) If any person enters or has entered in a peaceable manner into any lands or tenements when the entry is lawful and after the expiration of the person's right continues to hold them against the consent of the party entitled to possession, the party so entitled to possession is entitled to the summary procedure under s. 51.011, at any time within 3 years after the possession has been withheld from the party against his or her consent.
(2) This section shall not apply with regard to residential tenancies.

82.045. Remedy for unlawful detention by a transient occupant of residential property.

(1) As used in this section, the term "transient occupant" means a person whose residency in a dwelling intended for residential use has occurred for a brief length of time, is not pursuant to a lease, and whose occupancy was intended as transient in nature.
(a) Factors that establish that a person is a transient occupant include, but are not limited to:
1. The person does not have an ownership interest, financial interest, or leasehold interest in the property entitling him or her to occupancy of the property.
2. The person does not have any property utility subscriptions.
3. The person does not use the property address as an address of record with any governmental agency, including, but not limited to, the Department of Highway Safety and Motor Vehicles or the supervisor of elections.
4. The person does not receive mail at the property.
5. The person pays minimal or no rent for his or her stay at the property.
6. The person does not have a designated space of his or her own, such as a room, at the property.
7. The person has minimal, if any, personal belongings at the property.
8. The person has an apparent permanent residence elsewhere.
(b) Minor contributions made for the purchase of household goods, or minor contributions towards other household expenses, do not establish residency.

(2) A transient occupant unlawfully detains a residential property if the transient occupant remains in occupancy of the residential property after the party entitled to possession of the property has directed the transient occupant to leave.

(3) Any law enforcement officer may, upon receipt of a sworn affidavit of the party entitled to possession that a person who is a transient occupant is unlawfully detaining residential property, direct a transient occupant to surrender possession of residential property. The sworn affidavit must set forth the facts, including the applicable factors listed in paragraph (1)(a), which establish that a transient occupant is unlawfully detaining residential property.

(a) A person who fails to comply with the direction of the law enforcement officer to surrender possession or occupancy violates s. 810.08. In any prosecution of a violation of s. 810.08 related to this section, whether the defendant was properly classified as a transient occupant is not an element of the offense, the state is not required to prove that the defendant was in fact a transient occupant, and the defendant's status as a permanent resident is not an affirmative defense.

(b) A person wrongfully removed pursuant to this subsection has a cause of action for wrongful removal against the person who requested the removal, and may recover injunctive relief and compensatory damages. However, a wrongfully removed person does not have a cause of action against the law enforcement officer or the agency employing the law enforcement officer absent a showing of bad faith by the law enforcement officer.

(4) A party entitled to possession of a dwelling has a cause of action for unlawful detainer against a transient occupant pursuant to s. 82.04. The party entitled to possession is not required to notify the transient occupant before filing the action. If the court finds that the defendant is not a transient occupant but is instead a tenant of residential property governed by part II of chapter 83, the court may not dismiss the action without first allowing the plaintiff to give the transient occupant the notice required by that part and to thereafter amend the complaint to pursue eviction under that part.

82.05. Questions involved in this proceeding.

No question of title, but only right of possession and damages, is involved in the action.

82.061. Process.

If no person can be found at the usual place of residence of defendant, summons may be served by posting a copy in a conspicuous place on the property, described in the complaint and summons.

82.071. Trial; evidence as to damages.

At trial evidence shall be admitted about the monthly rental value of the premises and if plaintiff recovers, the jury shall fix the plaintiff's damages at double the rental value of the premises from the time of the unlawful or wrongful holding, but the damages in no action of detainer shall be fixed at more than rental value of the premises unless the jury is satisfied that such detention is willful and knowingly wrongful.

82.081. Trial; form of verdict.

(1) IN CASES OF FORCIBLE OR UNLAWFUL ENTRY.—In forcible or unlawful entry the

form of verdict shall be substantially as follows:
(2) IN CASES OF UNLAWFUL DETAINER.—The form of verdict in unlawful detainer shall be substantially as follows:

82.091. Judgment and execution.

If the verdict is in favor of plaintiff, the court shall enter judgment that plaintiff recover possession of the property described in the complaint with his or her damages and costs, and shall award a writ of possession to be executed without delay and execution for plaintiff's damages and costs. If the verdict is for defendant, the court shall enter judgment against plaintiff dismissing the complaint and order that defendant recover costs.

82.101. Effect of judgment.

No judgment rendered either for plaintiff or defendant bars any action of trespass for injury to the property or ejectment between the same parties respecting the same property. No verdict is conclusive of the facts therein found in any action of trespass or ejectment.

CHAPTER 83. LANDLORD AND TENANT

PART I. NONRESIDENTIAL TENANCIES (SS. 83.001- 83.251)

83.001. Application.

This part applies to nonresidential tenancies and all tenancies not governed by part II of this chapter.

83.01. Unwritten lease tenancy at will; duration.

Any lease of lands and tenements, or either, made shall be deemed and held to be a tenancy at will unless it shall be in writing signed by the lessor. Such tenancy shall be from year to year, or quarter to quarter, or month to month, or week to week, to be determined by the periods at which the rent is payable. If the rent is payable weekly, then the tenancy shall be from week to week; if payable monthly, then from month to month; if payable quarterly, then from quarter to quarter; if payable yearly, then from year to year.

83.02. Certain written leases tenancies at will; duration.

Where any tenancy has been created by an instrument in writing from year to year, or quarter to quarter, or month to month, or week to week, to be determined by the periods at which the rent is payable, and the term of which tenancy is unlimited, the tenancy shall be a tenancy at will. If the rent is payable weekly, then the tenancy shall be from week to week; if payable monthly, then the tenancy shall be from month to month; if payable quarterly, then from quarter to quarter; if payable yearly, then from year to year.

83.03. Termination of tenancy at will; length of notice.

A tenancy at will may be terminated by either party giving notice as follows:
(1) Where the tenancy is from year to year, by giving not less than 3 months' notice prior to the end of any annual period;
(2) Where the tenancy is from quarter to quarter, by giving not less than 45 days' notice prior to the end of any quarter;
(3) Where the tenancy is from month to month, by giving not less than 15 days' notice prior to the end of any monthly period; and
(4) Where the tenancy is from week to week, by giving not less than 7 days' notice prior to the end of any weekly period.

83.04. Holding over after term, tenancy at sufferance, etc.

When any tenancy created by an instrument in writing, the term of which is limited, has expired and the tenant holds over in the possession of said premises without renewing the lease by some further instrument in writing then such holding over shall be construed to be a tenancy at sufferance. The mere payment or acceptance of rent shall not be construed to be a renewal of the term, but if the holding over be continued with the written consent of the lessor then the tenancy shall become a tenancy at will under the provisions of this law.

83.05. Right of possession upon default in rent; determination of right of possession in action or surrender or abandonment of premises.

(1) If any person leasing or renting any land or premises other than a dwelling unit fails to pay the rent at the time it becomes due, the lessor has the right to obtain possession of the premises as provided by law.
(2) The landlord shall recover possession of rented premises only:
(a) In an action for possession under s. 83.20, or other civil action in which the issue of right of possession is determined;
(b) When the tenant has surrendered possession of the rented premises to the landlord; or
(c) When the tenant has abandoned the rented premises.
(3) In the absence of actual knowledge of abandonment, it shall be presumed for purposes of paragraph (2)(c) that the tenant has abandoned the rented premises if:
(a) The landlord reasonably believes that the tenant has been absent from the rented premises for a period of 30 consecutive days;
(b) The rent is not current; and
(c) A notice pursuant to s. 83.20(2) has been served and 10 days have elapsed since service of such notice.

83.06. Right to demand double rent upon refusal to deliver possession.

(1) When any tenant refuses to give up possession of the premises at the end of the tenant's lease, the landlord, the landlord's agent, attorney, or legal representatives, may demand of such tenant double the monthly rent, and may recover the same at the expiration of every month, or in the same proportion for a longer or shorter time by distress, in the manner pointed out hereinafter.
(2) All contracts for rent, verbal or in writing, shall bear interest from the time the rent becomes due, any law, usage or custom to the contrary notwithstanding.

83.07. Action for use and occupation.

Any landlord, the landlord's heirs, executors, administrators or assigns may recover reasonable damages for any house, lands, tenements, or hereditaments held or occupied by any person by the landlord's permission in an action on the case for the use and occupation of the lands, tenements, or hereditaments when they are not held, occupied by or under agreement or demise by deed; and if on trial of any action, any demise or agreement (not being by deed) whereby a certain rent was reserved is given in evidence, the plaintiff shall not be dismissed but may make use thereof as an evidence of the quantum of damages to be recovered.

83.08. Landlord's lien for rent.

Every person to whom rent may be due, the person's heirs, executors, administrators or assigns, shall have a lien for such rent upon the property found upon or off the premises leased or rented, and in the possession of any person, as follows:
(1) Upon agricultural products raised on the land leased or rented for the current year. This lien shall be superior to all other liens, though of older date.
(2) Upon all other property of the lessee or his or her sublessee or assigns, usually kept on the premises. This lien shall be superior to any lien acquired subsequent to the bringing of the property on the premises leased.
(3) Upon all other property of the defendant. This lien shall date from the levy of the distress warrant hereinafter provided.

83.09. Exemptions from liens for rent.

No property of any tenant or lessee shall be exempt from distress and sale for rent, except beds, bedclothes and wearing apparel.

83.10. Landlord's lien for advances.

Landlords shall have a lien on the crop grown on rented land for advances made in money or other things of value, whether made directly by them or at their instance and requested by another person, or for which they have assumed a legal responsibility, at or before the time at which such advances were made, for the sustenance or well-being of the tenant or the tenant's family, or for preparing the ground for cultivation, or for cultivating, gathering, saving, handling, or preparing the crop for market. They shall have a lien also upon each and every article advanced, and upon all property purchased with money advanced, or obtained, by barter or exchange for any articles advanced, for the aggregate value or price of all the property or articles so advanced. The liens upon the crop shall be of equal dignity with liens for rent, and upon the articles advanced shall be paramount to all other liens.

83.11. Distress for rent; complaint.

Any person to whom any rent or money for advances is due or the person's agent or attorney may file an action in the court in the county where the land lies having jurisdiction of the amount claimed, and the court shall have jurisdiction to order the relief provided in this part. The complaint shall be verified and shall allege the name and relationship of the defendant to the plaintiff, how the obligation for rent arose, the amount or quality and value of the rent due for such land, or the advances, and whether payable in money, an agricultural product, or any other thing of value.

83.12. Distress writ.

A distress writ shall be issued by a judge of the court which has jurisdiction of the amount claimed. The writ shall enjoin the defendant from damaging, disposing of, secreting, or removing any property liable to distress from the rented real property after the time of service of the writ until the sheriff levies on the property, the writ is vacated, or the court otherwise orders. A violation of the command of the writ may be punished as a contempt of court. If the defendant does not move for dissolution of the writ as provided in s. 83.135, the sheriff shall, pursuant to a further order of the court, levy on the property liable to distress forthwith after the time for answering the complaint has expired. Before the writ issues, the plaintiff or the plaintiff's agent or attorney shall file a bond with surety to be approved by the clerk payable to defendant in at least double the sum demanded or, if property, in double the value of the property sought to be levied on, conditioned to pay all costs and damages which defendant sustains in consequence of plaintiff's improperly suing out the distress.

83.13. Levy of writ.

The sheriff shall execute the writ by service on defendant and, upon the order of the court, by levy on property distrainable for rent or advances, if found in the sheriff's jurisdiction. If the property is in another jurisdiction, the party who had the writ issued shall deliver the writ to the sheriff in the other jurisdiction; and that sheriff shall execute the writ, upon order of the court, by levying on the property and delivering it to the sheriff of the county in which the action is pending, to be disposed of according to law, unless he or she is ordered by the court from which the writ emanated to hold the property and dispose of it in his or her jurisdiction according to law. If the plaintiff shows by a sworn statement that the defendant cannot be found within the state, the levy on the property suffices as service on the defendant.

83.135. Dissolution of writ.

The defendant may move for dissolution of a distress writ at any time. The court shall hear the motion not later than the day on which the sheriff is authorized under the writ to levy on property liable under distress. If the plaintiff proves a prima facie case, or if the defendant defaults, the court shall order the sheriff to proceed with the levy.

83.14. Replevy of distrained property.

The property distrained may be restored to the defendant at any time on the defendant's giving bond with surety to the sheriff levying the writ. The bond shall be approved by such sheriff; made payable to plaintiff in double the value of the property levied on, with the value to be fixed by the sheriff; and conditioned for the forthcoming of the property restored to abide the final order of the court. It may be also restored to defendant on defendant's giving bond with surety to be approved by the sheriff making the levy conditioned to pay the plaintiff the amount or value of the rental or advances which may be adjudicated to be payable to plaintiff. Judgment may be entered against the surety on such bonds in the manner and with like effect as provided in s. 76.31.

83.15. Claims by third persons.

Any third person claiming any property so distrained may interpose and prosecute his or her claim for it in the same manner as is provided in similar cases of claim to property levied on under execution.

83.18. Distress for rent; trial; verdict; judgment.

If the verdict or the finding of the court is for plaintiff, judgment shall be rendered against defendant for the amount or value of the rental or advances, including interest and costs, and against the surety on defendant's bond as provided for in s. 83.14, if the property has been restored to defendant, and execution shall issue. If the verdict or the finding of the court is for defendant, the action shall be dismissed and defendant shall have judgment and execution against plaintiff for costs.

83.19. Sale of property distrained.

(1) If the judgment is for plaintiff and the property in whole or in part has not been replevied, it, or the part not restored to the defendant, shall be sold and the proceeds applied on the payment of the execution. If the rental or any part of it is due in agricultural products and the property distrained, or any part of it, is of a similar kind to that claimed in the complaint, the property up to a quantity to be adjudged of by the officer holding the execution (not exceeding that claimed), may be delivered to the plaintiff as a payment on the plaintiff's execution at his or her request.
(2) When any property levied on is sold, it shall be advertised two times, the first advertisement being at least 10 days before the sale. All property so levied on shall be sold at the location advertised in the notice of sheriff's sale.
(3) Before the sale if defendant appeals and obtains supersedeas and pays all costs accrued up to the time that the supersedeas becomes operative, the property shall be restored to defendant and there shall be no sale.
(4) In case any property is sold to satisfy any rent payable in cotton or other agricultural product or thing, the officer shall settle with the plaintiff at the value of the rental at the time it became due.

83.20. Causes for removal of tenants.

Any tenant or lessee at will or sufferance, or for part of the year, or for one or more years, of any houses, lands or tenements, and the assigns, under tenants or legal representatives of such tenant or lessee, may be removed from the premises in the manner hereinafter provided in the following cases:

(1) Where such person holds over and continues in the possession of the demised premises, or any part thereof, after the expiration of the person's time, without the permission of the person's landlord.

(2) Where such person holds over without permission as aforesaid, after any default in the payment of rent pursuant to the agreement under which the premises are held, and 3 days' notice in writing requiring the payment of the rent or the possession of the premises has been served by the person entitled to the rent on the person owing the same. The service of the notice shall be by delivery of a true copy thereof, or, if the tenant is absent from the rented premises, by leaving a copy thereof at such place.

(3) Where such person holds over without permission after failing to cure a material breach of the lease or oral agreement, other than nonpayment of rent, and when 15 days' written notice requiring the cure of such breach or the possession of the premises has been served on the tenant. This subsection applies only when the lease is silent on the matter or when the tenancy is an oral one at will. The notice may give a longer time period for cure of the breach or surrender of the premises. In the absence of a lease provision prescribing the method for serving notices, service must be by mail, hand delivery, or, if the tenant is absent from the rental premises or the address designated by the lease, by posting.

83.201. Notice to landlord of failure to maintain or repair, rendering premises wholly untenantable; right to withhold rent.

When the lease is silent on the procedure to be followed to effect repair or maintenance and the payment of rent relating thereto, yet affirmatively and expressly places the obligation for same upon the landlord, and the landlord has failed or refused to do so, rendering the leased premises wholly untenantable, the tenant may withhold rent after notice to the landlord. The tenant shall serve the landlord, in the manner prescribed by s. 83.20(3), with a written notice declaring the premises to be wholly untenantable, giving the landlord at least 20 days to make the specifically described repair or maintenance, and stating that the tenant will withhold the rent for the next rental period and thereafter until the repair or maintenance has been performed. The lease may provide for a longer period of time for repair or maintenance. Once the landlord has completed the repair or maintenance, the tenant shall pay the landlord the amounts of rent withheld. If the landlord does not complete the repair or maintenance in the allotted time, the parties may extend the time by written agreement or the tenant may abandon the premises, retain the amounts of rent withheld, terminate the lease, and avoid any liability for future rent or charges under the lease. This section is cumulative to other existing remedies, and this section does not prevent any tenant from exercising his or her other remedies.

83.202. Waiver of right to proceed with eviction claim.

The landlord's acceptance of the full amount of rent past due, with knowledge of the tenant's breach of the lease by nonpayment, shall be considered a waiver of the landlord's right to proceed with an eviction claim for nonpayment of that rent. Acceptance of the rent includes conduct by the landlord concerning any tender of the rent by the tenant which is inconsistent with reasonably prompt return of the payment to the tenant.

83.21. Removal of tenant.

The landlord, the landlord's attorney or agent, applying for the removal of any tenant, shall file a complaint stating the facts which authorize the removal of the tenant, and describing the premises in the proper court of the county where the premises are situated and is entitled to the summary procedure provided in s. 51.011.

83.22. Removal of tenant; service.

(1) After at least two attempts to obtain service as provided by law, if the defendant cannot be found in the county in which the action is pending and either the defendant has no usual place of abode in the county or there is no person 15 years of age or older residing at the defendant's usual place of abode in the county, the sheriff shall serve the summons by attaching it to some part of the premises involved in the proceeding. The minimum time delay between the two attempts to obtain service shall be 6 hours.
(2) If a landlord causes, or anticipates causing, a defendant to be served with a summons and complaint solely by attaching them to some conspicuous part of the premises involved in the proceeding, the landlord shall provide the clerk of the court with two additional copies of the complaint and two prestamped envelopes addressed to the defendant. One envelope shall be addressed to such address or location as has been designated by the tenant for receipt of notice in a written lease or other agreement or, if none has been designated, to the residence of the tenant, if known. The second envelope shall be addressed to the last known business address of the tenant. The clerk of the court shall immediately mail the copies of the summons and complaint by first-class mail, note the fact of mailing in the docket, and file a certificate in the court file of the fact and date of mailing. Service shall be effective on the date of posting or mailing, whichever occurs later; and at least 5 days from the date of service must have elapsed before a judgment for final removal of the defendant may be entered.

83.231. Removal of tenant; judgment.

If the issues are found for plaintiff, judgment shall be entered that plaintiff recover possession of the premises. If the plaintiff expressly and specifically sought money damages in the complaint, in addition to awarding possession of the premises to the plaintiff, the court shall also direct, in an amount which is within its jurisdictional limitations, the entry of a money judgment in favor of the plaintiff and against the defendant for the amount of money found due, owing, and unpaid by the defendant, with costs. However, no money judgment shall be entered unless service of process has been effected by personal service or, where authorized by law, by certified or registered mail, return receipt, or in any other manner prescribed by law or the rules of the court, and no money judgment may be entered except in compliance with the Florida Rules of Civil Procedure. Where otherwise authorized by law, the plaintiff in the judgment for possession and money damages may also be awarded attorney's fees and costs. If the issues are found for defendant, judgment shall be entered dismissing the action.

83.232. Rent paid into registry of court.

(1) In an action by the landlord which includes a claim for possession of real property, the tenant shall pay into the court registry the amount alleged in the complaint as unpaid, or if such amount is contested, such amount as is determined by the court, and any rent accruing during the pendency of the action, when due, unless the tenant has interposed the defense of payment or satisfaction of the rent in the amount the complaint alleges as unpaid. Unless the tenant disputes the amount of accrued rent, the tenant must pay the amount alleged in the complaint into the court registry on or before the date on which his or her answer to the claim for possession is due. If the tenant contests the amount of accrued rent, the tenant must pay the amount determined by the court into the court registry on the day that the court makes its determination. The court may, however, extend these time periods to allow for later payment, upon good cause shown. Even though the defense of payment or satisfaction has been asserted, the court, in its discretion, may order the tenant to pay into the court registry the rent that accrues during the pendency of the action, the time of accrual being as set forth in the lease. If the landlord is in actual danger of loss of the premises or other hardship resulting from the loss of rental income from the premises, the landlord may apply to the court for disbursement of all or part of the funds so held in the court registry.

(2) If the tenant contests the amount of money to be placed into the court registry, any hearing regarding such dispute shall be limited to only the factual or legal issues concerning:

(a) Whether the tenant has been properly credited by the landlord with any and all rental payments made; and

(b) What properly constitutes rent under the provisions of the lease.

(3) The court, on its own motion, shall notify the tenant of the requirement that rent be paid into the court registry by order, which shall be issued immediately upon filing of the tenant's initial pleading, motion, or other paper.

(4) The filing of a counterclaim for money damages does not relieve the tenant from depositing rent due into the registry of the court.

(5) Failure of the tenant to pay the rent into the court registry pursuant to court order shall be deemed an absolute waiver of the tenant's defenses. In such case, the landlord is entitled to an immediate default for possession without further notice or hearing thereon.

83.241. Removal of tenant; process.

After entry of judgment in favor of plaintiff the clerk shall issue a writ to the sheriff describing the premises and commanding the sheriff to put plaintiff in possession.

83.251. Removal of tenant; costs.

The prevailing party shall have judgment for costs and execution shall issue therefor.

PART II. RESIDENTIAL TENANCIES (SS. 83.40-83.683)

83.40. Short title.

This part shall be known as the "Florida Residential Landlord and Tenant Act."

83.41. Application.

This part applies to the rental of a dwelling unit.

83.42. Exclusions from application of part.

This part does not apply to:
(1) Residency or detention in a facility, whether public or private, when residence or detention is incidental to the provision of medical, geriatric, educational, counseling, religious, or similar services. For residents of a facility licensed under part II of chapter 400, the provisions of s. 400.0255 are the exclusive procedures for all transfers and discharges.
(2) Occupancy under a contract of sale of a dwelling unit or the property of which it is a part in which the buyer has paid at least 12 months' rent or in which the buyer has paid at least 1 month's rent and a deposit of at least 5 percent of the purchase price of the property.
(3) Transient occupancy in a hotel, condominium, motel, roominghouse, or similar public lodging, or transient occupancy in a mobile home park.
(4) Occupancy by a holder of a proprietary lease in a cooperative apartment.
(5) Occupancy by an owner of a condominium unit.

83.43. Definitions.

As used in this part, the following words and terms shall have the following meanings unless some other meaning is plainly indicated:
(1) "Building, housing, and health codes" means any law, ordinance, or governmental regulation concerning health, safety, sanitation or fitness for habitation, or the construction, maintenance, operation, occupancy, use, or appearance, of any dwelling unit.
(2) "Dwelling unit" means:
(a) A structure or part of a structure that is rented for use as a home, residence, or sleeping place by one person or by two or more persons who maintain a common household.
(b) A mobile home rented by a tenant.
(c) A structure or part of a structure that is furnished, with or without rent, as an incident of employment for use as a home, residence, or sleeping place by one or more persons.
(3) "Landlord" means the owner or lessor of a dwelling unit.
(4) "Tenant" means any person entitled to occupy a dwelling unit under a rental agreement.
(5) "Premises" means a dwelling unit and the structure of which it is a part and a mobile home lot and the appurtenant facilities and grounds, areas, facilities, and property held out for the use of tenants generally.
(6) "Rent" means the periodic payments due the landlord from the tenant for occupancy under a rental agreement and any other payments due the landlord from the tenant as may be designated as rent in a written rental agreement.
(7) "Rental agreement" means any written agreement, including amendments or addenda, or oral agreement for a duration of less than 1 year, providing for use and occupancy of premises.
(8) "Good faith" means honesty in fact in the conduct or transaction concerned.

(9) "Advance rent" means moneys paid to the landlord to be applied to future rent payment periods, but does not include rent paid in advance for a current rent payment period.

(10) "Transient occupancy" means occupancy when it is the intention of the parties that the occupancy will be temporary.

(11) "Deposit money" means any money held by the landlord on behalf of the tenant, including, but not limited to, damage deposits, security deposits, advance rent deposit, pet deposit, or any contractual deposit agreed to between landlord and tenant either in writing or orally.

(12) "Security deposits" means any moneys held by the landlord as security for the performance of the rental agreement, including, but not limited to, monetary damage to the landlord caused by the tenant's breach of lease prior to the expiration thereof.

(13) "Legal holiday" means holidays observed by the clerk of the court.

(14) "Servicemember" shall have the same meaning as provided in s. 250.01.

(15) "Active duty" shall have the same meaning as provided in s. 250.01.

(16) "State active duty" shall have the same meaning as provided in s. 250.01.

(17) "Early termination fee" means any charge, fee, or forfeiture that is provided for in a written rental agreement and is assessed to a tenant when a tenant elects to terminate the rental agreement, as provided in the agreement, and vacates a dwelling unit before the end of the rental agreement. An early termination fee does not include:

(a) Unpaid rent and other accrued charges through the end of the month in which the landlord retakes possession of the dwelling unit.

(b) Charges for damages to the dwelling unit.

(c) Charges associated with a rental agreement settlement, release, buyout, or accord and satisfaction agreement.

83.44. Obligation of good faith.

Every rental agreement or duty within this part imposes an obligation of good faith in its performance or enforcement.

83.45. Unconscionable rental agreement or provision.

(1) If the court as a matter of law finds a rental agreement or any provision of a rental agreement to have been unconscionable at the time it was made, the court may refuse to enforce the rental agreement, enforce the remainder of the rental agreement without the unconscionable provision, or so limit the application of any unconscionable provision as to avoid any unconscionable result.

(2) When it is claimed or appears to the court that the rental agreement or any provision thereof may be unconscionable, the parties shall be afforded a reasonable opportunity to present evidence as to meaning, relationship of the parties, purpose, and effect to aid the court in making the determination.

83.46. Rent; duration of tenancies.

(1) Unless otherwise agreed, rent is payable without demand or notice; periodic rent is payable at the beginning of each rent payment period; and rent is uniformly apportionable from day to day.

(2) If the rental agreement contains no provision as to duration of the tenancy, the duration is determined by the periods for which the rent is payable. If the rent is payable weekly, then the tenancy is from week to week; if payable monthly, tenancy is from month to month; if payable quarterly, tenancy is from quarter to quarter; if payable yearly, tenancy is from year to year.

(3) If the dwelling unit is furnished without rent as an incident of employment and there is no agreement as to the duration of the tenancy, the duration is determined by the periods for which wages are payable. If wages are payable weekly or more frequently, then the tenancy is from week to week; and if wages are payable monthly or no wages are payable, then the tenancy is from month to month. In the event that the employee ceases employment, the employer shall be entitled to rent for the period from the day after the employee ceases employment until the day that the dwelling unit is vacated at a rate equivalent to the rate charged for similarly situated residences in the area. This subsection shall not apply to an employee or a resident manager of an apartment house or an apartment complex when there is a written agreement to the contrary.

83.47. Prohibited provisions in rental agreements.

(1) A provision in a rental agreement is void and unenforceable to the extent that it:
(a) Purports to waive or preclude the rights, remedies, or requirements set forth in this part.
(b) Purports to limit or preclude any liability of the landlord to the tenant or of the tenant to the landlord, arising under law.
(2) If such a void and unenforceable provision is included in a rental agreement entered into, extended, or renewed after the effective date of this part and either party suffers actual damages as a result of the inclusion, the aggrieved party may recover those damages sustained after the effective date of this part.

83.48. Attorney fees.

In any civil action brought to enforce the provisions of the rental agreement or this part, the party in whose favor a judgment or decree has been rendered may recover reasonable attorney fees and court costs from the nonprevailing party. The right to attorney fees in this section may not be waived in a lease agreement. However, attorney fees may not be awarded under this section in a claim for personal injury damages based on a breach of duty under s. 83.51.

83.49. Deposit money or advance rent; duty of landlord and tenant.

(1) Whenever money is deposited or advanced by a tenant on a rental agreement as security for performance of the rental agreement or as advance rent for other than the next immediate rental period, the landlord or the landlord's agent shall either:
(a) Hold the total amount of such money in a separate non-interest-bearing account in a Florida banking institution for the benefit of the tenant or tenants. The landlord shall not commingle such moneys with any other funds of the landlord or hypothecate, pledge, or in any other way make use of such moneys until such moneys are actually due the landlord;
(b) Hold the total amount of such money in a separate interest-bearing account in a Florida banking institution for the benefit of the tenant or tenants, in which case the tenant shall receive and collect interest in an amount of at least 75 percent of the annualized average interest rate payable on such account or interest at the rate of 5 percent per year, simple interest, whichever the landlord elects. The landlord shall not commingle such moneys with any other funds of the landlord or hypothecate, pledge, or in any other way make use of such moneys until such moneys are actually due the landlord; or
(c) Post a surety bond, executed by the landlord as principal and a surety company authorized and

licensed to do business in the state as surety, with the clerk of the circuit court in the county in which the dwelling unit is located in the total amount of the security deposits and advance rent he or she holds on behalf of the tenants or $50,000, whichever is less. The bond shall be conditioned upon the faithful compliance of the landlord with the provisions of this section and shall run to the Governor for the benefit of any tenant injured by the landlord's violation of the provisions of this section. In addition to posting the surety bond, the landlord shall pay to the tenant interest at the rate of 5 percent per year, simple interest. A landlord, or the landlord's agent, engaged in the renting of dwelling units in five or more counties, who holds deposit moneys or advance rent and who is otherwise subject to the provisions of this section, may, in lieu of posting a surety bond in each county, elect to post a surety bond in the form and manner provided in this paragraph with the office of the Secretary of State. The bond shall be in the total amount of the security deposit or advance rent held on behalf of tenants or in the amount of $250,000, whichever is less. The bond shall be conditioned upon the faithful compliance of the landlord with the provisions of this section and shall run to the Governor for the benefit of any tenant injured by the landlord's violation of this section. In addition to posting a surety bond, the landlord shall pay to the tenant interest on the security deposit or advance rent held on behalf of that tenant at the rate of 5 percent per year simple interest.

(2) The landlord shall, in the lease agreement or within 30 days after receipt of advance rent or a security deposit, give written notice to the tenant which includes disclosure of the advance rent or security deposit. Subsequent to providing such written notice, if the landlord changes the manner or location in which he or she is holding the advance rent or security deposit, he or she must notify the tenant within 30 days after the change as provided in paragraphs (a)-(d). The landlord is not required to give new or additional notice solely because the depository has merged with another financial institution, changed its name, or transferred ownership to a different financial institution. This subsection does not apply to any landlord who rents fewer than five individual dwelling units. Failure to give this notice is not a defense to the payment of rent when due. The written notice must:

(a) Be given in person or by mail to the tenant.

(b) State the name and address of the depository where the advance rent or security deposit is being held or state that the landlord has posted a surety bond as provided by law.

(c) State whether the tenant is entitled to interest on the deposit.

(d) Contain the following disclosure:

(3) The landlord or the landlord's agent may disburse advance rents from the deposit account to the landlord's benefit when the advance rental period commences and without notice to the tenant. For all other deposits:

(a) Upon the vacating of the premises for termination of the lease, if the landlord does not intend to impose a claim on the security deposit, the landlord shall have 15 days to return the security deposit together with interest if otherwise required, or the landlord shall have 30 days to give the tenant written notice by certified mail to the tenant's last known mailing address of his or her intention to impose a claim on the deposit and the reason for imposing the claim. The notice shall contain a statement in substantially the following form:

(b) Unless the tenant objects to the imposition of the landlord's claim or the amount thereof within 15 days after receipt of the landlord's notice of intention to impose a claim, the landlord may then deduct the amount of his or her claim and shall remit the balance of the deposit to the tenant within 30 days after the date of the notice of intention to impose a claim for damages. The failure of the tenant to make a timely objection does not waive any rights of the tenant to seek damages in a separate action.

(c) If either party institutes an action in a court of competent jurisdiction to adjudicate the party's right to the security deposit, the prevailing party is entitled to receive his or her court costs plus a reasonable fee for his or her attorney. The court shall advance the cause on the calendar.

(d) Compliance with this section by an individual or business entity authorized to conduct business in this state, including Florida-licensed real estate brokers and sales associates, constitutes compliance with all other relevant Florida Statutes pertaining to security deposits held pursuant to a rental agreement or other landlord-tenant relationship. Enforcement personnel shall look solely to this section to determine compliance. This section prevails over any conflicting provisions in chapter 475 and in other sections of the Florida Statutes, and shall operate to permit licensed real estate brokers to disburse security deposits and deposit money without having to comply with the notice and settlement procedures contained in s. 475.25(1)(d).

(4) The provisions of this section do not apply to transient rentals by hotels or motels as defined in chapter 509; nor do they apply in those instances in which the amount of rent or deposit, or both, is regulated by law or by rules or regulations of a public body, including public housing authorities and federally administered or regulated housing programs including s. 202, s. 221(d)(3) and (4), s. 236, or s. 8 of the National Housing Act, as amended, other than for rent stabilization. With the exception of subsections (3), (5), and (6), this section is not applicable to housing authorities or public housing agencies created pursuant to chapter 421 or other statutes.

(5) Except when otherwise provided by the terms of a written lease, any tenant who vacates or abandons the premises prior to the expiration of the term specified in the written lease, or any tenant who vacates or abandons premises which are the subject of a tenancy from week to week, month to month, quarter to quarter, or year to year, shall give at least 7 days' written notice by certified mail or personal delivery to the landlord prior to vacating or abandoning the premises which notice shall include the address where the tenant may be reached. Failure to give such notice shall relieve the landlord of the notice requirement of paragraph (3)(a) but shall not waive any right the tenant may have to the security deposit or any part of it.

(6) For the purposes of this part, a renewal of an existing rental agreement shall be considered a new rental agreement, and any security deposit carried forward shall be considered a new security deposit.

(7) Upon the sale or transfer of title of the rental property from one owner to another, or upon a change in the designated rental agent, any and all security deposits or advance rents being held for the benefit of the tenants shall be transferred to the new owner or agent, together with any earned interest and with an accurate accounting showing the amounts to be credited to each tenant account. Upon the transfer of such funds and records to the new owner or agent, and upon transmittal of a written receipt therefor, the transferor is free from the obligation imposed in subsection (1) to hold such moneys on behalf of the tenant. There is a rebuttable presumption that any new owner or agent received the security deposit from the previous owner or agent; however, this presumption is limited to 1 month's rent. This subsection does not excuse the landlord or agent for a violation of other provisions of this section while in possession of such deposits.

(8) Any person licensed under the provisions of s. 509.241, unless excluded by the provisions of this part, who fails to comply with the provisions of this part shall be subject to a fine or to the suspension or revocation of his or her license by the Division of Hotels and Restaurants of the Department of Business and Professional Regulation in the manner provided in s. 509.261.

(9) In those cases in which interest is required to be paid to the tenant, the landlord shall pay directly to the tenant, or credit against the current month's rent, the interest due to the tenant at least once annually. However, no interest shall be due a tenant who wrongfully terminates his or her tenancy prior to the end of the rental term.

83.50. Disclosure of landlord's address.

In addition to any other disclosure required by law, the landlord, or a person authorized to enter into a rental agreement on the landlord's behalf, shall disclose in writing to the tenant, at or before the commencement of the tenancy, the name and address of the landlord or a person authorized to receive notices and demands in the landlord's behalf. The person so authorized to receive notices and demands retains authority until the tenant is notified otherwise. All notices of such names and addresses or changes thereto shall be delivered to the tenant's residence or, if specified in writing by the tenant, to any other address.

83.51. Landlord's obligation to maintain premises.

(1) The landlord at all times during the tenancy shall:

(a) Comply with the requirements of applicable building, housing, and health codes; or

(b) Where there are no applicable building, housing, or health codes, maintain the roofs, windows, doors, floors, steps, porches, exterior walls, foundations, and all other structural components in good repair and capable of resisting normal forces and loads and the plumbing in reasonable working condition. The landlord, at commencement of the tenancy, must ensure that screens are installed in a reasonable condition. Thereafter, the landlord must repair damage to screens once annually, when necessary, until termination of the rental agreement.

(2)(a) Unless otherwise agreed in writing, in addition to the requirements of subsection (1), the landlord of a dwelling unit other than a single-family home or duplex shall, at all times during the tenancy, make reasonable provisions for:

1. The extermination of rats, mice, roaches, ants, wood-destroying organisms, and bedbugs. When vacation of the premises is required for such extermination, the landlord is not liable for damages but shall abate the rent. The tenant must temporarily vacate the premises for a period of time not to exceed 4 days, on 7 days' written notice, if necessary, for extermination pursuant to this subparagraph.

2. Locks and keys.

3. The clean and safe condition of common areas.

4. Garbage removal and outside receptacles therefor.

5. Functioning facilities for heat during winter, running water, and hot water.

(b) Unless otherwise agreed in writing, at the commencement of the tenancy of a single-family home or duplex, the landlord shall install working smoke detection devices. As used in this paragraph, the term "smoke detection device" means an electrical or battery-operated device which detects visible or invisible particles of combustion and which is listed by Underwriters Laboratories, Inc., Factory Mutual Laboratories, Inc., or any other nationally recognized testing laboratory using nationally accepted testing standards.

(c) Nothing in this part authorizes the tenant to raise a noncompliance by the landlord with this subsection as a defense to an action for possession under s. 83.59.

(d) This subsection shall not apply to a mobile home owned by a tenant.

(e) Nothing contained in this subsection prohibits the landlord from providing in the rental agreement that the tenant is obligated to pay costs or charges for garbage removal, water, fuel, or utilities.

(3) If the duty imposed by subsection (1) is the same or greater than any duty imposed by subsection (2), the landlord's duty is determined by subsection (1).

(4) The landlord is not responsible to the tenant under this section for conditions created or caused by the negligent or wrongful act or omission of the tenant, a member of the tenant's family, or other person on the premises with the tenant's consent.

83.52. Tenant's obligation to maintain dwelling unit.

The tenant at all times during the tenancy shall:

(1) Comply with all obligations imposed upon tenants by applicable provisions of building, housing, and health codes.

(2) Keep that part of the premises which he or she occupies and uses clean and sanitary.

(3) Remove from the tenant's dwelling unit all garbage in a clean and sanitary manner.

(4) Keep all plumbing fixtures in the dwelling unit or used by the tenant clean and sanitary and in

repair.

(5) Use and operate in a reasonable manner all electrical, plumbing, sanitary, heating, ventilating, air-conditioning and other facilities and appliances, including elevators.

(6) Not destroy, deface, damage, impair, or remove any part of the premises or property therein belonging to the landlord nor permit any person to do so.

(7) Conduct himself or herself, and require other persons on the premises with his or her consent to conduct themselves, in a manner that does not unreasonably disturb the tenant's neighbors or constitute a breach of the peace.

83.53. Landlord's access to dwelling unit.

(1) The tenant shall not unreasonably withhold consent to the landlord to enter the dwelling unit from time to time in order to inspect the premises; make necessary or agreed repairs, decorations, alterations, or improvements; supply agreed services; or exhibit the dwelling unit to prospective or actual purchasers, mortgagees, tenants, workers, or contractors.

(2) The landlord may enter the dwelling unit at any time for the protection or preservation of the premises. The landlord may enter the dwelling unit upon reasonable notice to the tenant and at a reasonable time for the purpose of repair of the premises. "Reasonable notice" for the purpose of repair is notice given at least 12 hours prior to the entry, and reasonable time for the purpose of repair shall be between the hours of 7:30 a.m. and 8:00 p.m. The landlord may enter the dwelling unit when necessary for the further purposes set forth in subsection (1) under any of the following circumstances:

(a) With the consent of the tenant;

(b) In case of emergency;

(c) When the tenant unreasonably withholds consent; or

(d) If the tenant is absent from the premises for a period of time equal to one-half the time for periodic rental payments. If the rent is current and the tenant notifies the landlord of an intended absence, then the landlord may enter only with the consent of the tenant or for the protection or preservation of the premises.

(3) The landlord shall not abuse the right of access nor use it to harass the tenant.

83.535. Flotation bedding system; restrictions on use.

No landlord may prohibit a tenant from using a flotation bedding system in a dwelling unit, provided the flotation bedding system does not violate applicable building codes. The tenant shall be required to carry in the tenant's name flotation insurance as is standard in the industry in an amount deemed reasonable to protect the tenant and owner against personal injury and property damage to the dwelling units. In any case, the policy shall carry a loss payable clause to the owner of the building.

83.54. Enforcement of rights and duties; civil action; criminal offenses.

Any right or duty declared in this part is enforceable by civil action. A right or duty enforced by civil action under this section does not preclude prosecution for a criminal offense related to the lease or leased property.

83.55. Right of action for damages.

If either the landlord or the tenant fails to comply with the requirements of the rental agreement or this part, the aggrieved party may recover the damages caused by the noncompliance.

83.56. Termination of rental agreement.

(1) If the landlord materially fails to comply with s. 83.51(1) or material provisions of the rental agreement within 7 days after delivery of written notice by the tenant specifying the noncompliance and indicating the intention of the tenant to terminate the rental agreement by reason thereof, the tenant may terminate the rental agreement. If the failure to comply with s. 83.51(1) or material provisions of the rental agreement is due to causes beyond the control of the landlord and the landlord has made and continues to make every reasonable effort to correct the failure to comply, the rental agreement may be terminated or altered by the parties, as follows:
(a) If the landlord's failure to comply renders the dwelling unit untenantable and the tenant vacates, the tenant shall not be liable for rent during the period the dwelling unit remains uninhabitable.
(b) If the landlord's failure to comply does not render the dwelling unit untenantable and the tenant remains in occupancy, the rent for the period of noncompliance shall be reduced by an amount in proportion to the loss of rental value caused by the noncompliance.
(2) If the tenant materially fails to comply with s. 83.52 or material provisions of the rental agreement, other than a failure to pay rent, or reasonable rules or regulations, the landlord may:
(a) If such noncompliance is of a nature that the tenant should not be given an opportunity to cure it or if the noncompliance constitutes a subsequent or continuing noncompliance within 12 months of a written warning by the landlord of a similar violation, deliver a written notice to the tenant specifying the noncompliance and the landlord's intent to terminate the rental agreement by reason thereof. Examples of noncompliance which are of a nature that the tenant should not be given an opportunity to cure include, but are not limited to, destruction, damage, or misuse of the landlord's or other tenants' property by intentional act or a subsequent or continued unreasonable disturbance. In such event, the landlord may terminate the rental agreement, and the tenant shall have 7 days from the date that the notice is delivered to vacate the premises. The notice shall be in substantially the following form:
(b) If such noncompliance is of a nature that the tenant should be given an opportunity to cure it, deliver a written notice to the tenant specifying the noncompliance, including a notice that, if the noncompliance is not corrected within 7 days from the date that the written notice is delivered, the landlord shall terminate the rental agreement by reason thereof. Examples of such noncompliance include, but are not limited to, activities in contravention of the lease or this part such as having or permitting unauthorized pets, guests, or vehicles; parking in an unauthorized manner or permitting such parking; or failing to keep the premises clean and sanitary. If such noncompliance recurs within 12 months after notice, an eviction action may commence without delivering a subsequent notice pursuant to paragraph (a) or this paragraph. The notice shall be in substantially the following form:
(3) If the tenant fails to pay rent when due and the default continues for 3 days, excluding Saturday, Sunday, and legal holidays, after delivery of written demand by the landlord for payment of the rent or possession of the premises, the landlord may terminate the rental agreement. Legal holidays for the purpose of this section shall be court-observed holidays only. The 3-day notice shall contain a statement in substantially the following form:
(4) The delivery of the written notices required by subsections (1), (2), and (3) shall be by mailing or delivery of a true copy thereof or, if the tenant is absent from the premises, by leaving a copy

thereof at the residence. The notice requirements of subsections (1), (2), and (3) may not be waived in the lease.

(5)(a) If the landlord accepts rent with actual knowledge of a noncompliance by the tenant or accepts performance by the tenant of any other provision of the rental agreement that is at variance with its provisions, or if the tenant pays rent with actual knowledge of a noncompliance by the landlord or accepts performance by the landlord of any other provision of the rental agreement that is at variance with its provisions, the landlord or tenant waives his or her right to terminate the rental agreement or to bring a civil action for that noncompliance, but not for any subsequent or continuing noncompliance. However, a landlord does not waive the right to terminate the rental agreement or to bring a civil action for that noncompliance by accepting partial rent for the period. If partial rent is accepted after posting the notice for nonpayment, the landlord must:

1. Provide the tenant with a receipt stating the date and amount received and the agreed upon date and balance of rent due before filing an action for possession;

2. Place the amount of partial rent accepted from the tenant in the registry of the court upon filing the action for possession; or

3. Post a new 3-day notice reflecting the new amount due.

(b) Any tenant who wishes to defend against an action by the landlord for possession of the unit for noncompliance of the rental agreement or of relevant statutes must comply with s. 83.60(2). The court may not set a date for mediation or trial unless the provisions of s. 83.60(2) have been met, but must enter a default judgment for removal of the tenant with a writ of possession to issue immediately if the tenant fails to comply with s. 83.60(2).

(c) This subsection does not apply to that portion of rent subsidies received from a local, state, or national government or an agency of local, state, or national government; however, waiver will occur if an action has not been instituted within 45 days after the landlord obtains actual knowledge of the noncompliance.

(6) If the rental agreement is terminated, the landlord shall comply with s. 83.49(3).

83.561. Termination of rental agreement upon foreclosure.

(1) If a tenant is occupying residential premises that are the subject of a foreclosure sale, upon issuance of a certificate of title following the sale, the purchaser named in the certificate of title takes title to the residential premises subject to the rights of the tenant under this section.

(a) The tenant may remain in possession of the premises for 30 days following the date of the purchaser's delivery of a written 30-day notice of termination.

(b) The tenant is entitled to the protections of s. 83.67.

(c) The 30-day notice of termination must be in substantially the following form:

(d) The 30-day notice of termination shall be delivered in the same manner as provided in s. 83.56(4).

(2) The purchaser at the foreclosure sale may apply to the court for a writ of possession based upon a sworn affidavit that the 30-day notice of termination was delivered to the tenant and the tenant has failed to vacate the premises at the conclusion of the 30-day period. If the court awards a writ of possession, the writ must be served on the tenant. The writ of possession shall be governed by s. 83.62.

(3) This section does not apply if:

(a) The tenant is the mortgagor in the subject foreclosure or is the child, spouse, or parent of the mortgagor in the subject foreclosure.

(b) The tenant's rental agreement is not the result of an arm's length transaction.

(c) The tenant's rental agreement allows the tenant to pay rent that is substantially less than the fair market rent for the premises, unless the rent is reduced or subsidized due to a federal, state, or local subsidy.

(4) A purchaser at a foreclosure sale of a residential premises occupied by a tenant does not assume the obligations of a landlord, except as provided in paragraph (1)(b), unless or until the purchaser assumes an existing rental agreement with the tenant that has not ended or enters into a new rental agreement with the tenant.

83.57. Termination of tenancy without specific term.

A tenancy without a specific duration, as defined in s. 83.46(2) or (3), may be terminated by either party giving written notice in the manner provided in s. 83.56(4), as follows:

(1) When the tenancy is from year to year, by giving not less than 60 days' notice prior to the end of any annual period;

(2) When the tenancy is from quarter to quarter, by giving not less than 30 days' notice prior to the end of any quarterly period;

(3) When the tenancy is from month to month, by giving not less than 15 days' notice prior to the end of any monthly period; and

(4) When the tenancy is from week to week, by giving not less than 7 days' notice prior to the end of any weekly period.

83.575. Termination of tenancy with specific duration.

(1) A rental agreement with a specific duration may contain a provision requiring the tenant to notify the landlord within a specified period before vacating the premises at the end of the rental agreement, if such provision requires the landlord to notify the tenant within such notice period if the rental agreement will not be renewed; however, a rental agreement may not require more than 60 days' notice from either the tenant or the landlord.

(2) A rental agreement with a specific duration may provide that if a tenant fails to give the required notice before vacating the premises at the end of the rental agreement, the tenant may be liable for liquidated damages as specified in the rental agreement if the landlord provides written notice to the tenant specifying the tenant's obligations under the notification provision contained in the lease and the date the rental agreement is terminated. The landlord must provide such written notice to the tenant within 15 days before the start of the notification period contained in the lease. The written notice shall list all fees, penalties, and other charges applicable to the tenant under this subsection.

(3) If the tenant remains on the premises with the permission of the landlord after the rental agreement has terminated and fails to give notice required under s. 83.57(3), the tenant is liable to the landlord for an additional 1 month's rent.

83.58. Remedies; tenant holding over.

If the tenant holds over and continues in possession of the dwelling unit or any part thereof after the expiration of the rental agreement without the permission of the landlord, the landlord may recover possession of the dwelling unit in the manner provided for in s. 83.59. The landlord may also recover double the amount of rent due on the dwelling unit, or any part thereof, for the period during which the tenant refuses to surrender possession.

83.59. Right of action for possession.

(1) If the rental agreement is terminated and the tenant does not vacate the premises, the landlord may recover possession of the dwelling unit as provided in this section.

(2) A landlord, the landlord's attorney, or the landlord's agent, applying for the removal of a tenant, shall file in the county court of the county where the premises are situated a complaint describing the dwelling unit and stating the facts that authorize its recovery. A landlord's agent is not permitted to take any action other than the initial filing of the complaint, unless the landlord's agent is an attorney. The landlord is entitled to the summary procedure provided in s. 51.011, and the court shall advance the cause on the calendar.

(3) The landlord shall not recover possession of a dwelling unit except:

(a) In an action for possession under subsection (2) or other civil action in which the issue of right of possession is determined;

(b) When the tenant has surrendered possession of the dwelling unit to the landlord;

(c) When the tenant has abandoned the dwelling unit. In the absence of actual knowledge of abandonment, it shall be presumed that the tenant has abandoned the dwelling unit if he or she is absent from the premises for a period of time equal to one-half the time for periodic rental payments. However, this presumption does not apply if the rent is current or the tenant has notified the landlord, in writing, of an intended absence; or

(d) When the last remaining tenant of a dwelling unit is deceased, personal property remains on the premises, rent is unpaid, at least 60 days have elapsed following the date of death, and the landlord has not been notified in writing of the existence of a probate estate or of the name and address of a personal representative. This paragraph does not apply to a dwelling unit used in connection with a federally administered or regulated housing program, including programs under s. 202, s. 221(d)(3) and (4), s. 236, or s. 8 of the National Housing Act, as amended.

(4) The prevailing party is entitled to have judgment for costs and execution therefor.

83.595. Choice of remedies upon breach or early termination by tenant.

If the tenant breaches the rental agreement for the dwelling unit and the landlord has obtained a writ of possession, or the tenant has surrendered possession of the dwelling unit to the landlord, or the tenant has abandoned the dwelling unit, the landlord may:

(1) Treat the rental agreement as terminated and retake possession for his or her own account, thereby terminating any further liability of the tenant;

(2) Retake possession of the dwelling unit for the account of the tenant, holding the tenant liable for the difference between the rent stipulated to be paid under the rental agreement and what the landlord is able to recover from a reletting. If the landlord retakes possession, the landlord has a duty to exercise good faith in attempting to relet the premises, and any rent received by the landlord as a result of the reletting must be deducted from the balance of rent due from the tenant. For purposes of this subsection, the term "good faith in attempting to relet the premises" means that the landlord uses at least the same efforts to relet the premises as were used in the initial rental or at least the same efforts as the landlord uses in attempting to rent other similar rental units but does not require the landlord to give a preference in renting the premises over other vacant dwelling units that the landlord owns or has the responsibility to rent;

(3) Stand by and do nothing, holding the lessee liable for the rent as it comes due; or

(4) Charge liquidated damages, as provided in the rental agreement, or an early termination fee to the tenant if the landlord and tenant have agreed to liquidated damages or an early termination fee, if the amount does not exceed 2 months' rent, and if, in the case of an early termination fee, the tenant is required to give no more than 60 days' notice, as provided in the rental agreement, prior

to the proposed date of early termination. This remedy is available only if the tenant and the landlord, at the time the rental agreement was made, indicated acceptance of liquidated damages or an early termination fee. The tenant must indicate acceptance of liquidated damages or an early termination fee by signing a separate addendum to the rental agreement containing a provision in substantially the following form:

(a) In addition to liquidated damages or an early termination fee, the landlord is entitled to the rent and other charges accrued through the end of the month in which the landlord retakes possession of the dwelling unit and charges for damages to the dwelling unit.

(b) This subsection does not apply if the breach is failure to give notice as provided in s. 83.575.

83.60. Defenses to action for rent or possession; procedure.

(1)(a) In an action by the landlord for possession of a dwelling unit based upon nonpayment of rent or in an action by the landlord under s. 83.55 seeking to recover unpaid rent, the tenant may defend upon the ground of a material noncompliance with s. 83.51(1), or may raise any other defense, whether legal or equitable, that he or she may have, including the defense of retaliatory conduct in accordance with s. 83.64. The landlord must be given an opportunity to cure a deficiency in a notice or in the pleadings before dismissal of the action.

(b) The defense of a material noncompliance with s. 83.51(1) may be raised by the tenant if 7 days have elapsed after the delivery of written notice by the tenant to the landlord, specifying the noncompliance and indicating the intention of the tenant not to pay rent by reason thereof. Such notice by the tenant may be given to the landlord, the landlord's representative as designated pursuant to s. 83.50, a resident manager, or the person or entity who collects the rent on behalf of the landlord. A material noncompliance with s. 83.51(1) by the landlord is a complete defense to an action for possession based upon nonpayment of rent, and, upon hearing, the court or the jury, as the case may be, shall determine the amount, if any, by which the rent is to be reduced to reflect the diminution in value of the dwelling unit during the period of noncompliance with s. 83.51(1). After consideration of all other relevant issues, the court shall enter appropriate judgment.

(2) In an action by the landlord for possession of a dwelling unit, if the tenant interposes any defense other than payment, including, but not limited to, the defense of a defective 3-day notice, the tenant shall pay into the registry of the court the accrued rent as alleged in the complaint or as determined by the court and the rent that accrues during the pendency of the proceeding, when due. The clerk shall notify the tenant of such requirement in the summons. Failure of the tenant to pay the rent into the registry of the court or to file a motion to determine the amount of rent to be paid into the registry within 5 days, excluding Saturdays, Sundays, and legal holidays, after the date of service of process constitutes an absolute waiver of the tenant's defenses other than payment, and the landlord is entitled to an immediate default judgment for removal of the tenant with a writ of possession to issue without further notice or hearing thereon. If a motion to determine rent is filed, documentation in support of the allegation that the rent as alleged in the complaint is in error is required. Public housing tenants or tenants receiving rent subsidies are required to deposit only that portion of the full rent for which they are responsible pursuant to the federal, state, or local program in which they are participating.

83.61. Disbursement of funds in registry of court; prompt final hearing.

When the tenant has deposited funds into the registry of the court in accordance with the provisions of s. 83.60(2) and the landlord is in actual danger of loss of the premises or other personal hardship resulting from the loss of rental income from the premises, the landlord may apply to the court for disbursement of all or part of the funds or for prompt final hearing. The court shall advance the cause on the calendar. The court, after preliminary hearing, may award all or any portion of the funds on deposit to the landlord or may proceed immediately to a final resolution of the cause.

83.62. Restoration of possession to landlord.

(1) In an action for possession, after entry of judgment in favor of the landlord, the clerk shall issue a writ to the sheriff describing the premises and commanding the sheriff to put the landlord in possession after 24 hours' notice conspicuously posted on the premises. Saturdays, Sundays, and legal holidays do not stay the 24-hour notice period.
(2) At the time the sheriff executes the writ of possession or at any time thereafter, the landlord or the landlord's agent may remove any personal property found on the premises to or near the property line. Subsequent to executing the writ of possession, the landlord may request the sheriff to stand by to keep the peace while the landlord changes the locks and removes the personal property from the premises. When such a request is made, the sheriff may charge a reasonable hourly rate, and the person requesting the sheriff to stand by to keep the peace shall be responsible for paying the reasonable hourly rate set by the sheriff. Neither the sheriff nor the landlord or the landlord's agent shall be liable to the tenant or any other party for the loss, destruction, or damage to the property after it has been removed.

83.625. Power to award possession and enter money judgment.

In an action by the landlord for possession of a dwelling unit based upon nonpayment of rent, if the court finds the rent is due, owing, and unpaid and by reason thereof the landlord is entitled to possession of the premises, the court, in addition to awarding possession of the premises to the landlord, shall direct, in an amount which is within its jurisdictional limitations, the entry of a money judgment with costs in favor of the landlord and against the tenant for the amount of money found due, owing, and unpaid by the tenant to the landlord. However, no money judgment shall be entered unless service of process has been effected by personal service or, where authorized by law, by certified or registered mail, return receipt, or in any other manner prescribed by law or the rules of the court; and no money judgment may be entered except in compliance with the Florida Rules of Civil Procedure. The prevailing party in the action may also be awarded attorney's fees and costs.

83.63. Casualty damage.

If the premises are damaged or destroyed other than by the wrongful or negligent acts of the tenant so that the enjoyment of the premises is substantially impaired, the tenant may terminate the rental agreement and immediately vacate the premises. The tenant may vacate the part of the premises rendered unusable by the casualty, in which case the tenant's liability for rent shall be reduced by the fair rental value of that part of the premises damaged or destroyed. If the rental agreement is terminated, the landlord shall comply with s. 83.49(3).

83.64. Retaliatory conduct.

(1) It is unlawful for a landlord to discriminatorily increase a tenant's rent or decrease services to a tenant, or to bring or threaten to bring an action for possession or other civil action, primarily because the landlord is retaliating against the tenant. In order for the tenant to raise the defense of retaliatory conduct, the tenant must have acted in good faith. Examples of conduct for which the landlord may not retaliate include, but are not limited to, situations where:
(a) The tenant has complained to a governmental agency charged with responsibility for enforcement of a building, housing, or health code of a suspected violation applicable to the premises;
(b) The tenant has organized, encouraged, or participated in a tenant organization;
(c) The tenant has complained to the landlord pursuant to s. 83.56(1);
(d) The tenant is a servicemember who has terminated a rental agreement pursuant to s. 83.682;
(e) The tenant has paid rent to a condominium, cooperative, or homeowners' association after demand from the association in order to pay the landlord's obligation to the association; or
(f) The tenant has exercised his or her rights under local, state, or federal fair housing laws.
(2) Evidence of retaliatory conduct may be raised by the tenant as a defense in any action brought against him or her for possession.
(3) In any event, this section does not apply if the landlord proves that the eviction is for good cause. Examples of good cause include, but are not limited to, good faith actions for nonpayment of rent, violation of the rental agreement or of reasonable rules, or violation of the terms of this chapter.
(4) "Discrimination" under this section means that a tenant is being treated differently as to the rent charged, the services rendered, or the action being taken by the landlord, which shall be a prerequisite to a finding of retaliatory conduct.

83.67. Prohibited practices.

(1) A landlord of any dwelling unit governed by this part shall not cause, directly or indirectly, the termination or interruption of any utility service furnished the tenant, including, but not limited to, water, heat, light, electricity, gas, elevator, garbage collection, or refrigeration, whether or not the utility service is under the control of, or payment is made by, the landlord.
(2) A landlord of any dwelling unit governed by this part shall not prevent the tenant from gaining reasonable access to the dwelling unit by any means, including, but not limited to, changing the locks or using any bootlock or similar device.
(3) A landlord of any dwelling unit governed by this part shall not discriminate against a servicemember in offering a dwelling unit for rent or in any of the terms of the rental agreement.
(4) A landlord shall not prohibit a tenant from displaying one portable, removable, cloth or plastic United States flag, not larger than 4 and 1/2 feet by 6 feet, in a respectful manner in or on the dwelling unit regardless of any provision in the rental agreement dealing with flags or decorations. The United States flag shall be displayed in accordance with s. 83.52(6). The landlord is not liable for damages caused by a United States flag displayed by a tenant. Any United States flag may not infringe upon the space rented by any other tenant.
(5) A landlord of any dwelling unit governed by this part shall not remove the outside doors, locks, roof, walls, or windows of the unit except for purposes of maintenance, repair, or replacement; and the landlord shall not remove the tenant's personal property from the dwelling unit unless such action is taken after surrender, abandonment, recovery of possession of the dwelling unit due to the death of the last remaining tenant in accordance with s. 83.59(3)(d), or a lawful eviction. If provided in the rental agreement or a written agreement separate from the rental

agreement, upon surrender or abandonment by the tenant, the landlord is not required to comply with s. 715.104 and is not liable or responsible for storage or disposition of the tenant's personal property; if provided in the rental agreement, there must be printed or clearly stamped on such rental agreement a legend in substantially the following form:

(6) A landlord who violates any provision of this section shall be liable to the tenant for actual and consequential damages or 3 months' rent, whichever is greater, and costs, including attorney's fees. Subsequent or repeated violations that are not contemporaneous with the initial violation shall be subject to separate awards of damages.

(7) A violation of this section constitutes irreparable harm for the purposes of injunctive relief.

(8) The remedies provided by this section are not exclusive and do not preclude the tenant from pursuing any other remedy at law or equity that the tenant may have. The remedies provided by this section shall also apply to a servicemember who is a prospective tenant who has been discriminated against under subsection (3).

83.681. Orders to enjoin violations of this part.

(1) A landlord who gives notice to a tenant of the landlord's intent to terminate the tenant's lease pursuant to s. 83.56(2)(a), due to the tenant's intentional destruction, damage, or misuse of the landlord's property may petition the county or circuit court for an injunction prohibiting the tenant from continuing to violate any of the provisions of that part.

(2) The court shall grant the relief requested pursuant to subsection (1) in conformity with the principles that govern the granting of injunctive relief from threatened loss or damage in other civil cases.

(3) Evidence of a tenant's intentional destruction, damage, or misuse of the landlord's property in an amount greater than twice the value of money deposited with the landlord pursuant to s. 83.49 or $300, whichever is greater, shall constitute irreparable harm for the purposes of injunctive relief.

83.682. Termination of rental agreement by a servicemember.

(1) Any servicemember may terminate his or her rental agreement by providing the landlord with a written notice of termination to be effective on the date stated in the notice that is at least 30 days after the landlord's receipt of the notice if any of the following criteria are met:

(a) The servicemember is required, pursuant to a permanent change of station orders, to move 35 miles or more from the location of the rental premises;

(b) The servicemember is prematurely or involuntarily discharged or released from active duty or state active duty;

(c) The servicemember is released from active duty or state active duty after having leased the rental premises while on active duty or state active duty status and the rental premises is 35 miles or more from the servicemember's home of record prior to entering active duty or state active duty;

(d) After entering into a rental agreement, the servicemember receives military orders requiring him or her to move into government quarters or the servicemember becomes eligible to live in and opts to move into government quarters;

(e) The servicemember receives temporary duty orders, temporary change of station orders, or state active duty orders to an area 35 miles or more from the location of the rental premises, provided such orders are for a period exceeding 60 days; or

(f) The servicemember has leased the property, but prior to taking possession of the rental premises, receives a change of orders to an area that is 35 miles or more from the location of the rental premises.

(2) The notice to the landlord must be accompanied by either a copy of the official military orders or a written verification signed by the servicemember's commanding officer.

(3) In the event a servicemember dies during active duty, an adult member of his or her immediate family may terminate the servicemember's rental agreement by providing the landlord with a written notice of termination to be effective on the date stated in the notice that is at least 30 days after the landlord's receipt of the notice. The notice to the landlord must be accompanied by either a copy of the official military orders showing the servicemember was on active duty or a written verification signed by the servicemember's commanding officer and a copy of the servicemember's death certificate.

(4) Upon termination of a rental agreement under this section, the tenant is liable for the rent due under the rental agreement prorated to the effective date of the termination payable at such time as would have otherwise been required by the terms of the rental agreement. The tenant is not liable for any other rent or damages due to the early termination of the tenancy as provided for in this section. Notwithstanding any provision of this section to the contrary, if a tenant terminates the rental agreement pursuant to this section 14 or more days prior to occupancy, no damages or penalties of any kind will be assessable.

(5) The provisions of this section may not be waived or modified by the agreement of the parties under any circumstances.

83.683. Rental application by a servicemember.

(1) If a landlord requires a prospective tenant to complete a rental application before residing in a rental unit, the landlord must complete processing of a rental application submitted by a prospective tenant who is a servicemember, as defined in s. 250.01, within 7 days after submission and must, within that 7-day period, notify the servicemember in writing of an application approval or denial and, if denied, the reason for denial. Absent a timely denial of the rental application, the landlord must lease the rental unit to the servicemember if all other terms of the application and lease are complied with.

(2) If a condominium association, as defined in chapter 718, a cooperative association, as defined in chapter 719, or a homeowners' association, as defined in chapter 720, requires a prospective tenant of a condominium unit, cooperative unit, or parcel within the association's control to complete a rental application before residing in a rental unit or parcel, the association must complete processing of a rental application submitted by a prospective tenant who is a servicemember, as defined in s. 250.01, within 7 days after submission and must, within that 7-day period, notify the servicemember in writing of an application approval or denial and, if denied, the reason for denial. Absent a timely denial of the rental application, the association must allow the unit or parcel owner to lease the rental unit or parcel to the servicemember and the landlord must lease the rental unit or parcel to the servicemember if all other terms of the application and lease are complied with.

(3) The provisions of this section may not be waived or modified by the agreement of the parties under any circumstances.

PART III. SELF-SERVICE STORAGE SPACE (SS. 83.801-83.809)

83.801. Short title.

Sections 83.801-83.809 shall be known and may be cited as the "Self-storage Facility Act."

83.803. Definitions.

As used in ss. 83.801-83.809:

(1) "Self-service storage facility" means any real property designed and used for the purpose of renting or leasing individual storage space to tenants who are to have access to such space for the purpose of storing and removing personal property. No individual storage space may be used for residential purposes. A self-service storage facility is not a "warehouse" as that term is used in chapter 677. If an owner issues any warehouse receipt, bill of lading, or other document of title for the personal property stored, the owner and the tenant shall be subject to the provisions of chapter 677, and the provisions of this act shall not apply.

(2) "Self-contained storage unit" means any unit not less than 200 cubic feet in size, including, but not limited to, a trailer, box, or other shipping container, which is leased by a tenant primarily for use as storage space whether the unit is located at a facility owned or operated by the owner or at another location designated by the tenant.

(3) "Owner" means the owner, operator, lessor, or sublessor of a self-service storage facility or self-contained storage unit or his or her agent or any other person authorized by him or her to manage the facility or to receive rent from a tenant under a rental agreement.

(4) "Tenant" means a person or the person's sublessee, successor, or assign entitled to the use of storage space at a self-service storage facility or in a self-contained unit, under a rental agreement, to the exclusion of others.

(5) "Rental agreement" means any agreement or lease which establishes or modifies terms, conditions, rules, or any other provisions concerning the use and occupancy of a self-service storage facility or use of a self-contained storage unit.

(6) "Last known address" means the street address or post office box address provided by the tenant in the latest rental agreement or in a subsequent written change-of-address notice provided by hand delivery, first-class mail, or e-mail.

83.805. Lien.

The owner of a self-service storage facility or self-contained storage unit and the owner's heirs, executors, administrators, successors, and assigns have a lien upon all personal property, whether or not owned by the tenant, located at a self-service storage facility or in a self-contained storage unit for rent, labor charges, or other charges, present or future, in relation to the personal property and for expenses necessary for its preservation or expenses reasonably incurred in its sale or other disposition pursuant to ss. 83.801-83.809. The lien provided for in this section attaches as of the date that the personal property is brought to the self-service storage facility or as of the date the tenant takes possession of the self-contained storage unit, and the priority of this lien shall be the same as provided in s. 83.08; however, in the event of default, the owner must give notice to persons who hold perfected security interests under the Uniform Commercial Code in which the tenant is named as the debtor.

83.8055. Withholding access to personal property upon nonpayment of rent.

Upon the failure of a tenant to pay the rent when it becomes due, the owner may, without notice, after 5 days from the date the rent is due, deny the tenant access to the personal property located in the self-service storage facility or self-contained storage unit. In denying the tenant access to personal property contained in the self-contained storage unit, the owner may proceed without judicial process, if this can be done without breach of the peace, or may proceed by action.

83.806. Enforcement of lien.

An owner's lien as provided in s. 83.805 may be satisfied as follows:
(1) The tenant shall be notified by written notice delivered in person, by e-mail, or by first-class mail with a certificate of mailing to the tenant's last known address and conspicuously posted at the self-service storage facility or on the self-contained storage unit. If the owner sends notice of a pending sale of property to the tenant's last known e-mail address and does not receive a response, return receipt, or delivery confirmation from the same e-mail address, the owner must send notice of the sale to the tenant by first-class mail with a certificate of mailing to the tenant's last known address before proceeding with the sale.
(2) The notice shall include:
(a) An itemized statement of the owner's claim, showing the sum due at the time of the notice and the date when the sum became due.
(b) The same description, or a reasonably similar description, of the personal property as provided in the rental agreement.
(c) A demand for payment within a specified time not less than 14 days after delivery of the notice.
(d) A conspicuous statement that, unless the claim is paid within the time stated in the notice, the personal property will be advertised for sale or other disposition and will be sold or otherwise disposed of at a specified time and place.
(e) The name, street address, and telephone number of the owner whom the tenant may contact to respond to the notice.
(3) Any notice given pursuant to this section shall be presumed delivered when it is deposited with the United States Postal Service and properly addressed with postage prepaid.
(4) After the expiration of the time given in the notice, an advertisement of the sale or other disposition shall be published once a week for 2 consecutive weeks in a newspaper of general circulation in the area where the self-service storage facility or self-contained storage unit is located.
(a) A lien sale may be conducted on a public website that customarily conducts personal property auctions. The facility or unit owner is not required to hold a license to post property for online sale. Inasmuch as any sale may involve property of more than one tenant, a single advertisement may be used to dispose of property at any one sale.
(b) The advertisement shall include:
1. A brief and general description of what is believed to constitute the personal property contained in the storage unit, as provided in paragraph (2)(b).
2. The address of the self-service storage facility or the address where the self-contained storage unit is located and the name of the tenant.
3. The time, place, and manner of the sale or other disposition. The sale or other disposition shall take place at least 15 days after the first publication.
(c) If there is no newspaper of general circulation in the area where the self-service storage facility or self-contained storage unit is located, the advertisement shall be posted at least 10 days before

the date of the sale or other disposition in at least three conspicuous places in the neighborhood where the self-service storage facility or self-contained storage unit is located.

(5) Any sale or other disposition of the personal property shall conform to the terms of the notification as provided for in this section and shall be conducted in a commercially reasonable manner, as that term is used in s. 679.610.

(6) Before any sale or other disposition of personal property pursuant to this section, the tenant may pay the amount necessary to satisfy the lien and the reasonable expenses incurred under this section and thereby redeem the personal property. Upon receipt of such payment, the owner shall return the property to the tenant and thereafter shall have no liability to any person with respect to such personal property. If the tenant fails to redeem the personal property or satisfy the lien, including reasonable expenses, he or she will be deemed to have unjustifiably abandoned the self-service storage facility or self-contained storage unit, and the owner may resume possession of the premises for himself or herself.

(7) A purchaser in good faith of the personal property sold to satisfy a lien provided for in s. 83.805 takes the property free of any claims, except those interests provided for in s. 83.808, despite noncompliance by the owner with the requirements of this section.

(8) In the event of a sale under this section, the owner may satisfy his or her lien from the proceeds of the sale, provided the owner's lien has priority over all other liens in the personal property. The lien rights of secured lienholders are automatically transferred to the remaining proceeds of the sale. The balance, if any, shall be held by the owner for delivery on demand to the tenant. A notice of any balance shall be delivered by the owner to the tenant in person or by first-class mail with a certificate of mailing to the last known address of the tenant. If the tenant does not claim the balance of the proceeds within 2 years after the date of sale, the proceeds shall be deemed abandoned, and the owner shall have no further obligation with regard to the payment of the balance. In the event that the owner's lien does not have priority over all other liens, the sale proceeds shall be held for the benefit of the holders of those liens having priority. A notice of the amount of the sale proceeds shall be delivered by the owner to the tenant or secured lienholders in person or by first-class mail with a certificate of mailing to their last known addresses. If the tenant or the secured lienholders do not claim the sale proceeds within 2 years after the date of sale, the proceeds shall be deemed abandoned, and the owner shall have no further obligation with regard to the payment of the proceeds.

(9) If the rental agreement contains a limit on the value of property stored in the tenant's storage space, the limit is deemed to be the maximum value of the property stored in such space.

(10) If a lien is claimed on property that is a motor vehicle or a watercraft and rent and other charges related to the property remain unpaid or unsatisfied for 60 days after the maturity of the obligation to pay the rent and other charges, the facility or unit owner may sell the property pursuant to this section or have the property towed. If a motor vehicle or watercraft is towed, the facility or unit owner is not liable for the motor vehicle or watercraft or any damages to the motor vehicle or watercraft once a wrecker takes possession of the property. The wrecker taking possession of the property must comply with all notification and sale requirements provided in s. 713.78.

83.808. Contracts.

(1) Nothing in ss. 83.801-83.809 shall be construed as in any manner impairing or affecting the right of parties to create liens by special contract or agreement nor shall it in any manner impair or affect any other lien arising at common law, in equity, or by any statute of this state or any other lien not provided for in s. 83.805.

(2) A rental agreement or an application for a rental agreement must contain a provision disclosing whether the applicant is a member of the uniformed services as that term is defined in 10 U.S.C. s. 101(a)(5).

(3) A facility or unit owner may charge a tenant a reasonable late fee for each period that he or she does not pay rent due under the rental agreement. The amount of the late fee and the conditions for imposing such fee must be stated in the rental agreement or in an addendum to such agreement. For purposes of this subsection, a late fee of $20, or 20 percent of the monthly rent, whichever is greater, is reasonable and does not constitute a penalty. In addition to late fees, a facility or unit owner may also charge a tenant a reasonable fee for any expenses incurred as a result of rent collection or lien enforcement.

83.809. Application of act.

(1) Nothing in this act shall be construed as in any manner impairing or affecting the right of parties to create additional rights, duties, and obligations in and by virtue of a rental agreement. The provisions of ss. 83.801-83.809 shall be in addition to all other rights allowed by law in a creditor-debtor or landlord-tenant relationship.
(2) Chapter 82-151, Laws of Florida, shall apply to all rental agreements entered into, extended, or renewed after July 1, 1982.

CHAPTER 85. ENFORCEMENT OF STATUTORY LIENS

85.011. Enforcement by persons in privity with the owner.

All liens on real or personal property provided for by part I or part II of chapter 713 are enforceable by persons in privity with the owners, except when otherwise provided, as follows:
(1) RETENTION OF POSSESSION.—By retention of possession of the property on which the lien has attached for a period of not exceeding 3 months by the person entitled to the lien, if the person was in possession at the time the lien attached.
(2) BY ACTION IN CHANCERY.—By an action in chancery, however this is the exclusive remedy for enforcement of liens on the separate statutory property of married women and against estates by the entireties.
(3) ORDINARY ACTION AT LAW.—By an ordinary action at law and levy of the execution obtained therein on the property on which the lien is held.
(4) SPECIAL ACTION AT LAW.—By an action at law in which the complaint shall state the manner in which the lien arose, the amount for which the lien is held, the description of the property and demand that the property be sold to satisfy the lien. The judgment for plaintiff is a personal judgment against defendant as well as a lien on the property, which it shall describe, and shall direct execution against the property, as well as against the property generally of defendant.
(5) SUMMARY ACTION.—
(a) By a person claiming a lien for labor performed, or claiming a landlord's lien under s. 713.691, filing in the court having jurisdiction of the amount of the lien claimed, a complaint describing the property on which a lien is claimed and stating the facts which authorize or create the lien. Such person is entitled to the summary procedure under s. 51.011.
(b) If the issues are found for plaintiff, judgment shall be entered for the amount found to be due him or her with 15 percent attorney's fee and costs. The judgment is a prior lien on the property described in the petition over all other liens accruing or that may be filed subsequent to the day the lien for such labor performed or unpaid rent accrued, but if such issues are found for defendant, judgment shall be entered dismissing the action.

85.021. Enforcement by persons not in privity with the owner.

A person not in privity with the owner may resort to any of the remedies prescribed by s. 85.011. The judgment may provide for the recovery from the contractor or other person for whom the labor or material was furnished, if the contractor or other person is joined in the action, of the amount due by him or her, and from the owner of the amount due by the owner to the contractor or other person as aforesaid, at the time of the service of the notice provided for by s. 713.75 of part II of chapter 713, as well as enforce the lien against the property of such owner for such amount, but only one satisfaction of the judgment shall be had. Although no lien is found to exist and no judgment rendered against the owner, judgment may be rendered against the contractor or other person for whom the labor or materials were furnished for the amount due by him or her.

85.031. Remedies against personal property only; all lienors.

(1) BY INJUNCTION AND ATTACHMENT.—If any person entitled to a lien under part II of chapter 713 on personal property has reason to believe that it is about to be removed from the county in which it is, the person may enjoin its removal in the manner provided for enjoining the removal of property subject to a mortgage or, if the lien has been perfected, may attach it in the manner provided for attachment in aid of foreclosure of mortgages.
(2) BY SALE WITHOUT JUDICIAL PROCEEDINGS.—When any person entrusts to any mechanic or laborer, materials with which to construct, alter, or repair any article of value, or any article of value to be altered or repaired, and if the article is completed and not taken away, and the reasonable charges not paid, such mechanic or laborer may sell it after 3 months from the time such charges become due at public auction for cash but before the sale the mechanic or laborer shall give public notice of the time and place thereof, by notices posted for 10 days in 3 public places in the county, one of which shall be at the courthouse, and another in some conspicuous part of his or her shop or place of business. The proceeds of the sale, after payment of charges for construction or repair with the costs of the sale, shall be deposited with the clerk of the circuit court for the county, if the owner is absent, where they shall remain subject to the order of the person legally entitled thereto. The clerk shall be entitled to receive 5 percent on the proceeds for the care and disbursement thereof. Any person claiming a lien under s. 713.65, of part II of chapter 713, may enforce it by sale without judicial proceedings in the manner set forth herein after 1 month after the time the charges for which a lien is claimed become due.

85.041. Joinder.

All persons who have liens under part I or part II of chapter 713, may join to enforce their respective liens.

85.051. Time of bringing action.

When there has been no record of a notice of lien, action to enforce a lien (if it exists without such record) must be brought within 12 months from the accrual of the unpaid rent, the performance of the work, or the furnishing of the materials, and if there has been such record, the action must be brought within 12 months from the time of such record.

CHAPTER 86. DECLARATORY JUDGMENTS

86.011. Jurisdiction of trial court.

The circuit and county courts have jurisdiction within their respective jurisdictional amounts to declare rights, status, and other equitable or legal relations whether or not further relief is or could be claimed. No action or procedure is open to objection on the ground that a declaratory judgment is demanded. The court's declaration may be either affirmative or negative in form and effect and such declaration has the force and effect of a final judgment. The court may render declaratory judgments on the existence, or nonexistence:
(1) Of any immunity, power, privilege, or right; or
(2) Of any fact upon which the existence or nonexistence of such immunity, power, privilege, or right does or may depend, whether such immunity, power, privilege, or right now exists or will arise in the future. Any person seeking a declaratory judgment may also demand additional, alternative, coercive, subsequent, or supplemental relief in the same action.

86.021. Power to construe.

Any person claiming to be interested or who may be in doubt about his or her rights under a deed, will, contract, or other article, memorandum, or instrument in writing or whose rights, status, or other equitable or legal relations are affected by a statute, or any regulation made under statutory authority, or by municipal ordinance, contract, deed, will, franchise, or other article, memorandum, or instrument in writing may have determined any question of construction or validity arising under such statute, regulation, municipal ordinance, contract, deed, will, franchise, or other article, memorandum, or instrument in writing, or any part thereof, and obtain a declaration of rights, status, or other equitable or legal relations thereunder.

86.031. Before breach.

A contract may be construed either before or after there has been a breach of it.

86.041. Actions by executors, administrators, trustees, etc.

Any person interested as or through an executor, administrator, trustee, guardian, or other fiduciary, creditor, devisee, legatee, heir, next of kin, or cestui que trust, in the administration of a trust, a guardianship, or the estate of a decedent, an infant, a mental incompetent, or insolvent may have a declaration of rights or equitable or legal relations to:
(1) Ascertain any class of creditors, devisees, legatees, heirs, next of kin, or others;
(2) Direct the executor, administrator, or trustee to refrain from doing any particular act in his or her fiduciary capacity; or
(3) Determine any question relating to the administration of the guardianship, estate, or trust,

including questions of construction of wills and other writings.

86.051. Enumeration not exclusive.

The enumeration in ss. 86.021, 86.031 and 86.041 does not limit or restrict the exercise of the general powers conferred in s. 86.011 in any action where declaratory relief is sought. Any declaratory judgment rendered pursuant to this chapter may be rendered by way of anticipation with respect to any act not yet done or any event which has not yet happened, and in such case the judgment shall have the same binding effect with respect to that future act or event, and the rights or liability to arise therefrom, as if that act or event had already been done or had already happened before the judgment was rendered.

86.061. Supplemental relief.

Further relief based on a declaratory judgment may be granted when necessary or proper. The application therefor shall be by motion to the court having jurisdiction to grant relief. If the application is sufficient, the court shall require any adverse party whose rights have been adjudicated by the declaratory judgment to show cause on reasonable notice, why further relief should not be granted forthwith.

86.071. Jury trials.

When an action under this chapter concerns the determination of an issue of fact, the issue may be tried as issues of fact are tried in other civil actions in the court in which the proceeding is pending. To settle questions of fact necessary to be determined before judgment can be rendered, the court may direct their submission to a jury. When a declaration of right or the granting of further relief based thereon concerns the determination of issues of fact triable by a jury, the issues may be submitted to a jury in the form of interrogatories, with proper instructions by the court, whether a general verdict is required or not. Neither this section nor any other section of this chapter shall be construed as requiring a jury to determine issues of fact in chancery actions.

86.081. Costs.

The court may award costs as are equitable.

86.091. Parties.

When declaratory relief is sought, all persons may be made parties who have or claim any interest which would be affected by the declaration. No declaration shall prejudice the rights of persons not parties to the proceedings. In any proceeding concerning the validity of a county or municipal charter, ordinance, or franchise, such county or municipality shall be made a party and shall be entitled to be heard. If the statute, charter, ordinance, or franchise is alleged to be unconstitutional, the Attorney General or the state attorney of the judicial circuit in which the action is pending shall be served with a copy of the complaint and be entitled to be heard.

86.101. Construction of law.

This chapter is declared to be substantive and remedial. Its purpose is to settle and to afford relief from insecurity and uncertainty with respect to rights, status, and other equitable or legal relations and is to be liberally administered and construed.

86.111. Existence of another adequate remedy; effect.

The existence of another adequate remedy does not preclude a judgment for declaratory relief. The court may order a speedy hearing of an action for a declaratory judgment and may advance it on the calendar. The court has power to give as full and complete equitable relief as it would have had if such proceeding had been instituted as an action in chancery.

CHAPTER 88. UNIFORM INTERSTATE FAMILY SUPPORT ACT

PART I. GENERAL PROVISIONS (SS. 88.0011-88.1041)

88.0011. Short title.

This act shall be known and may be cited as the "Uniform Interstate Family Support Act."

88.1011. Definitions.

As used in this act:
(1) "Child" means an individual, whether over or under the age of majority, who is or is alleged to be owed a duty of support by the individual's parent or who is or is alleged to be the beneficiary of a support order directed to the parent.
(2) "Child support order" means a support order for a child, including a child who has attained the age of majority under the law of the issuing state or foreign country.
(3) "Convention" means the Convention on the International Recovery of Child Support and Other Forms of Family Maintenance, concluded at The Hague on November 23, 2007.
(4) "Duty of support" means an obligation imposed or imposable by law to provide support for a child, spouse, or former spouse, including an unsatisfied obligation to provide support.
(5) "Foreign country" means a country, including a political subdivision thereof, other than the United States, that authorizes the issuance of support orders and:
(a) Which has been declared under the law of the United States to be a foreign reciprocating country;
(b) Which has established a reciprocal arrangement for child support with this state as provided in s. 88.3081;
(c) Which has enacted a law or established procedures for the issuance and enforcement of support orders which are substantially similar to the procedures under this act; or

(d) In which the convention is in force with respect to the United States.

(6) "Foreign support order" means a support order of a foreign tribunal.

(7) "Foreign tribunal" means a court, administrative agency, or quasi-judicial entity of a foreign country which is authorized to establish, enforce, or modify support orders or to determine parentage of a child. The term includes a competent authority under the convention.

(8) "Home state" means the state or foreign country in which a child lived with a parent or a person acting as parent for at least 6 consecutive months immediately preceding the time of filing of a petition or comparable pleading for support and, if a child is less than 6 months old, the state or foreign country in which the child lived from birth with any of them. A period of temporary absence of any of them is counted as part of the 6-month or other period.

(9) "Income" includes earnings or other periodic entitlements to money from any source and any other property subject to withholding for support under the law of this state.

(10) "Income-withholding order" means an order or other legal process directed to an obligor's employer or other debtor, as defined by the income deduction law of this state, or payor as defined by s. 61.046, to withhold support from the income of the obligor.

(11) "Initiating tribunal" means the tribunal of a state or foreign country from which a petition or comparable pleading is forwarded or in which a petition or comparable pleading is filed for forwarding to another state or foreign country.

(12) "Issuing foreign country" means the foreign country in which a tribunal issues a support order or a judgment determining parentage of a child.

(13) "Issuing state" means the state in which a tribunal issues a support order or renders a judgment determining parentage of a child.

(14) "Issuing tribunal" means the tribunal of a state or foreign country that issues a support order or a judgment determining parentage of a child.

(15) "Law" includes decisional and statutory law and rules and regulations having the force of law.

(16) "Obligee" means:

(a) An individual to whom a duty of support is or is alleged to be owed or in whose favor a support order or a judgment determining parentage of a child has been issued;

(b) A foreign country, state, or political subdivision of a state to which the rights under a duty of support or support order have been assigned or which has independent claims based on financial assistance provided to an individual obligee in place of child support;

(c) An individual seeking a judgment determining parentage of the individual's child; or

(d) A person that is a creditor in a proceeding under part VII of this chapter.

(17) "Obligor" means an individual, or the estate of a decedent that:

(a) Owes or is alleged to owe a duty of support;

(b) Is alleged but has not been adjudicated to be a parent of a child;

(c) Is liable under a support order; or

(d) Is a debtor in a proceeding under part VII.

(18) "Outside this state" means a location in another state or a country other than the United States, whether or not the country is a foreign country.

(19) "Person" means an individual, corporation, business trust, estate, trust, partnership, limited liability company, association, joint venture, public corporation, government, or governmental subdivision, agency, or instrumentality or any other legal or commercial entity.

(20) "Record" means information that is inscribed on a tangible medium or that is stored in an electronic or other medium that is retrievable in perceivable form.

(21) "Register" means to record or file in a tribunal of this state a support order or judgment determining parentage of a child issued in another state or a foreign country.

(22) "Registering tribunal" means a tribunal in which a support order or judgment determining parentage of a child is registered.

(23) "Responding state" means a state in which a petition or comparable pleading for support or to determine parentage of a child is filed or to which a petition or comparable pleading is forwarded for filing from another state or a foreign country.

(24) "Responding tribunal" means the authorized tribunal in a responding state or a foreign country.

(25) "Spousal-support order" means a support order for a spouse or former spouse of the obligor.

(26) "State" means a state of the United States, the District of Columbia, Puerto Rico, the United States Virgin Islands, or any territory or insular possession under the jurisdiction of the United States. The term includes an Indian nation or tribe.

(27) "Support enforcement agency" means a public official, governmental entity, or private agency authorized to:

(a) Seek enforcement of support orders or laws relating to the duty of support;

(b) Seek establishment or modification of child support;

(c) Request determination of parentage of a child;

(d) Attempt to locate obligors or their assets; or

(e) Request determination of the controlling child support order.

(28) "Support order" means a judgment, decree, order, decision, or directive, whether temporary, final, or subject to modification, issued in a state or foreign country for the benefit of a child, a spouse, or a former spouse, which provides for monetary support, health care, arrearages, retroactive support, or reimbursement for financial assistance provided to an individual obligee in place of child support. The term may include related costs and fees, interest, income withholding, automatic adjustment, reasonable attorney's fees, and other relief.

(29) "Tribunal" means a court, administrative agency, or quasi-judicial entity authorized to establish, enforce, or modify support orders or to determine parentage of a child.

88.1021. State tribunal and support enforcement agency.

(1) The circuit court or other appropriate court, administrative agency, quasi-judicial entity, or combination is the tribunal of this state.

(2) The Department of Revenue is the support enforcement agency of this state.

88.1031. Remedies cumulative.

(1) Remedies provided by this act are cumulative and do not affect the availability of remedies under other law, or the recognition of a foreign support order on the basis of comity.

(2) This act does not:

(a) Provide the exclusive method of establishing or enforcing a support order under the law of this state; or

(b) Grant a tribunal of this state jurisdiction to render judgment or issue an order relating to child custody or visitation in a proceeding under this act.

88.1041. Application of act to resident of foreign country and foreign support proceeding.

(1) A tribunal of this state shall apply parts I through VI of this chapter, and, as applicable, part VII of this chapter, to a support proceeding involving:

(a) A foreign support order;

(b) A foreign tribunal; or

(c) An obligee, obligor, or child residing in a foreign country.

(2) A tribunal of this state that is requested to recognize and enforce a support order on the basis of

comity may apply the procedural and substantive provisions of parts I through VI of this chapter. (3) Part VII of this chapter applies only to a support proceeding under the convention. In such a proceeding, if a provision of part VII of this chapter is inconsistent with parts I through VI of this chapter, part VII of this chapter controls.

PART II. JURISDICTION (SS. 88.2011-88.2111)

88.2011. Bases for jurisdiction over nonresident.

(1) In a proceeding to establish or enforce a support order or to determine parentage of a child, a tribunal of this state may exercise personal jurisdiction over a nonresident individual or the individual's guardian or conservator if:
(a) The individual is personally served with citation, summons, or notice within this state;
(b) The individual submits to the jurisdiction of this state by consent in a record, by entering a general appearance, or by filing a responsive document having the effect of waiving any contest to personal jurisdiction;
(c) The individual resided with the child in this state;
(d) The individual resided in this state and provided prenatal expenses or support for the child;
(e) The child resides in this state as a result of the acts or directives of the individual;
(f) The individual engaged in sexual intercourse in this state and the child may have been conceived by that act of intercourse;
(g) The individual asserted parentage of a child in a tribunal or in a putative father registry maintained in this state by the appropriate agency; or
(h) There is any other basis consistent with the constitutions of this state and the United States for the exercise of personal jurisdiction.
(2) The bases of personal jurisdiction set forth in subsection (1) or in any other law of this state may not be used to acquire personal jurisdiction for a tribunal of this state to modify a child support order of another state unless the requirements of s. 88.6111 are met, or, in the case of a foreign support order, unless the requirements of s. 88.6151 are met.

88.2021. Duration of personal jurisdiction.

Personal jurisdiction acquired by a tribunal of this state in a proceeding under this act or other law of this state relating to a support order continues as long as a tribunal of this state has continuing, exclusive jurisdiction to modify its order or continuing jurisdiction to enforce its order as provided by ss. 88.2051, 88.2061, and 88.2111.

88.2031. Initiating and responding tribunal of state.

Under this act, a tribunal of this state may serve as an initiating tribunal to forward proceedings to a tribunal of another state and as a responding tribunal for proceedings initiated in another state or a foreign country.

88.2041. Simultaneous proceedings in another state.

(1) A tribunal of this state may exercise jurisdiction to establish a support order if the petition or comparable pleading is filed after a petition or comparable pleading is filed in another state or a foreign country only if:

(a) The petition or comparable pleading in this state is filed before the expiration of the time allowed in the other state or the foreign country for filing a responsive pleading challenging the exercise of jurisdiction by the other state or the foreign country;

(b) The contesting party timely challenges the exercise of jurisdiction in the other state or the foreign country; and

(c) If relevant, this state is the home state of the child.

(2) A tribunal of this state may not exercise jurisdiction to establish a support order if the petition or comparable pleading is filed before a petition or comparable pleading is filed in another state or a foreign country if:

(a) The petition or comparable pleading in the other state or the foreign country is filed before the expiration of the time allowed in this state for filing a responsive pleading challenging the exercise of jurisdiction by this state;

(b) The contesting party timely challenges the exercise of jurisdiction in this state; and

(c) If relevant, the other state or the foreign country is the home state of the child.

88.2051. Continuing exclusive jurisdiction.

(1) A tribunal of this state that has issued a child support order consistent with the law of this state has and shall exercise continuing, exclusive jurisdiction to modify its child support order if the order is the controlling order and:

(a) At the time of the filing of a request for modification, this state is the residence of the obligor, the individual obligee, or the child for whose benefit the support order is issued; or

(b) Even if this state is not the residence of the obligor, the individual obligee, or the child for whose benefit the support order is issued, the parties consent in a record or in open court that the tribunal of this state may continue to exercise jurisdiction to modify its order.

(2) A tribunal of this state that has issued a child support order consistent with the law of this state may not exercise continuing, exclusive jurisdiction to modify the order if:

(a) All of the parties who are individuals file consent in a record with the tribunal of this state that a tribunal of another state that has jurisdiction over at least one of the parties who is an individual or that is located in the state of residence of the child may modify the order and assume continuing, exclusive jurisdiction; or

(b) Its order is not the controlling order.

(3) If a tribunal of another state has issued a child support order pursuant to this act or a law substantially similar to this act which modifies a child support order of a tribunal of this state, tribunals of this state shall recognize the continuing, exclusive jurisdiction of the tribunal of the other state.

(4) A tribunal of this state that lacks continuing, exclusive jurisdiction to modify a child support order may serve as an initiating tribunal to request a tribunal of another state to modify a support order issued in that state.

(5) A temporary support order issued ex parte or pending resolution of a jurisdictional conflict does not create continuing exclusive jurisdiction in the issuing tribunal.

88.2061. Continuing jurisdiction to enforce child support order.

(1) A tribunal of this state that has issued a child support order consistent with the law of this state

may serve as an initiating tribunal to request a tribunal of another state to enforce:

(a) The order if the order is the controlling order and has not been modified by a tribunal of another state that assumed jurisdiction pursuant to the Uniform Interstate Family Support Act; or

(b) A money judgment for arrears of support and interest on the order accrued before a determination that an order of a tribunal of another state is the controlling order.

(2) A tribunal of this state having continuing jurisdiction over a support order may act as a responding tribunal to enforce the order.

88.2071. Determination of controlling child support order.

(1) If a proceeding is brought under this act and only one tribunal has issued a child support order, the order of that tribunal controls and must be recognized.

(2) If a proceeding is brought under this act, and two or more child support orders have been issued by tribunals of this state, another state, or a foreign country with regard to the same obligor and the same child, a tribunal of this state having personal jurisdiction over both the obligor and individual obligee shall apply the following rules and by order shall determine which order controls and must be recognized:

(a) If only one of the tribunals would have continuing, exclusive jurisdiction under this act, the order of that tribunal controls.

(b) If more than one of the tribunals would have continuing, exclusive jurisdiction under this act:

1. An order issued by a tribunal in the current home state of the child controls; or

2. If an order has not been issued in the current home state of the child, the order most recently issued controls.

(c) If none of the tribunals would have continuing, exclusive jurisdiction under this act, the tribunal of this state shall issue a child support order, which controls.

(3) If two or more child support orders have been issued for the same obligor and the same child, upon request of a party who is an individual or that is a support enforcement agency, a tribunal of this state having personal jurisdiction over both the obligor and the obligee who is an individual shall determine which order controls under subsection (2). The request may be filed with a registration for enforcement or registration for modification pursuant to part VI of this chapter, or may be filed as a separate proceeding.

(4) A request to determine which is the controlling order must be accompanied by a copy of every child support order in effect and the applicable record of payments. The requesting party shall give notice of the request to each party whose rights may be affected by the determination.

(5) The tribunal that issued the controlling order under subsection (1), subsection (2), or subsection (3) has continuing jurisdiction to the extent provided in s. 88.2051 or s. 88.2061.

(6) A tribunal of this state that determines by order which is the controlling order under paragraph (2)(a), paragraph (2)(b), or subsection (3) or that issues a new controlling order under paragraph (2)(c) shall state in that order:

(a) The basis upon which the tribunal made its determination;

(b) The amount of prospective support, if any; and

(c) The total amount of consolidated arrears and accrued interest, if any, under all of the orders after all payments made are credited as provided by s. 88.2091.

(7) Within 30 days after issuance of an order determining which is the controlling order, the party obtaining the order shall file a certified copy of it in each tribunal that issued or registered an earlier order of child support. A party or support enforcement agency obtaining the order that fails to file a certified copy is subject to appropriate sanctions by a tribunal in which the issue of failure to file arises. The failure to file does not affect the validity or enforceability of the controlling order.

(8) An order that has been determined to be the controlling order, or a judgment for consolidated arrears of support and interest, if any, made pursuant to this section must be recognized in proceedings under this act.

88.2081. Child support orders for two or more obligees.

In responding to registrations, petitions, or comparable pleadings for enforcement of two or more child support orders in effect at the same time with regard to the same obligor and different individual obligees, at least one of which was issued by a tribunal of another state or a foreign country, a tribunal of this state shall enforce those orders in the same manner as if the orders had been issued by a tribunal of this state.

88.2091. Credit for payments.

A tribunal of this state shall credit amounts collected for a particular period pursuant to any child support order against the amounts owed for the same period under any other child support order for support of the same child issued by the tribunal of this state, another state, or a foreign country.

88.2101. Application of act to nonresident subject to personal jurisdiction.

A tribunal of this state exercising personal jurisdiction over a nonresident in a proceeding under this act, under another law of this state relating to a support order, or recognizing a foreign support order may receive evidence from outside this state pursuant to s. 88.3161, communicate with a tribunal outside this state pursuant to s. 88.3171, and obtain discovery through a tribunal outside this state pursuant to s. 88.3181. In all other respects, parts III through VI of this chapter do not apply, and the tribunal shall apply the procedural and substantive law of this state.

88.2111. Continuing, exclusive jurisdiction to modify spousal support order.

(1) A tribunal of this state issuing a spousal support order consistent with the law of this state has continuing, exclusive jurisdiction to modify the spousal support order throughout the existence of the support obligation.
(2) A tribunal of this state may not modify a spousal support order issued by a tribunal of another state or foreign country having continuing, exclusive jurisdiction over that order under the law of that state or foreign country.
(3) A tribunal of this state that has continuing, exclusive jurisdiction over a spousal support order may serve as:
(a) An initiating tribunal to request a tribunal of another state to enforce the spousal support order issued in this state; or
(b) A responding tribunal to enforce or modify its own spousal support order.

PART III. CIVIL PROVISIONS OF GENERAL APPLICATION (SS. 88.3011-88.3191)

88.3011. Proceedings under this act.

(1) Except as otherwise provided in this act, this part applies to all proceedings under this act.
(2) An individual petitioner or a support enforcement agency may initiate a proceeding authorized under this act by filing a petition or a comparable pleading in an initiating tribunal for forwarding to a responding tribunal or by filing a petition or a comparable pleading directly in a tribunal of another state or a foreign country which has or can obtain personal jurisdiction over the respondent.

88.3021. Proceeding by minor parent.

A minor parent, or a guardian or other legal representative of a minor parent, may maintain a proceeding on behalf of or for the benefit of the minor's child.

88.3031. Application of law of state.

Except as otherwise provided in this act, a responding tribunal of this state shall:
(1) Apply the procedural and substantive law generally applicable to similar proceedings originating in this state and may exercise all powers and provide all remedies available in those proceedings; and
(2) Determine the duty of support and the amount payable in accordance with the law and support guidelines of this state.

88.3041. Duties of initiating tribunal.

(1) Upon the filing of a petition or comparable pleading authorized by this act, an initiating tribunal of this state shall forward the petition and its accompanying documents or a comparable pleading and its accompanying documents:
(a) To the responding tribunal or appropriate support enforcement agency in the responding state; or
(b) If the identity of the responding tribunal is unknown, to the state information agency of the responding state with a request that they be forwarded to the appropriate tribunal and that receipt be acknowledged.
(2) If requested by the responding tribunal, a tribunal of this state shall issue a certificate or other document and make findings required by the law of the responding state. If the responding tribunal is in a foreign country, upon request the tribunal of this state shall specify the amount of support sought, convert that amount into the equivalent amount in the foreign currency under applicable official or market exchange rate as publicly reported, and provide any other documents necessary to satisfy the requirements of the responding foreign tribunal.

88.3051. Duties and powers of responding tribunal.

(1) When a responding tribunal of this state receives a petition or comparable pleading from an initiating tribunal or directly pursuant to s. 88.3011(2), it shall cause the petition or comparable pleading to be filed and notify the petitioner where and when it was filed.

(2) A responding tribunal of this state, to the extent not prohibited by other law, may do one or more of the following:

(a) Establish or enforce a support order, modify a child support order, determine the controlling child support order, or determine parentage of a child.

(b) Order an obligor to comply with a support order, specifying the amount and the manner of compliance.

(c) Order income withholding.

(d) Determine the amount of any arrearages, and specify a method of payment.

(e) Enforce orders by civil or criminal contempt, or both.

(f) Set aside property for satisfaction of the support order.

(g) Place liens and order execution on the obligor's property.

(h) Order an obligor to keep the tribunal informed of the obligor's current residential address, electronic mail address, telephone number, employer, address of employment, and telephone number at the place of employment.

(i) Issue a bench warrant, capias, or writ of bodily attachment for an obligor who has failed after proper notice to appear at a hearing ordered by the tribunal and enter the bench warrant, capias, or writ of bodily attachment in any local and state computer systems for criminal warrants.

(j) Order the obligor to seek appropriate employment by specified methods.

(k) Award reasonable attorney's fees and other fees and costs.

(l) Grant any other available remedy.

(3) A responding tribunal of this state shall include in a support order issued under this act, or in the documents accompanying the order, the calculations on which the support order is based.

(4) A responding tribunal of this state may not condition the payment of a support order issued under this act upon compliance by a party with provisions for visitation.

(5) If a responding tribunal of this state issues an order under this act, the tribunal shall send a copy of the order to the petitioner and the respondent and to the initiating tribunal, if any.

(6) If requested to enforce a support order, arrears, or judgment, or modify a support order stated in a foreign currency, a responding tribunal of this state shall convert the amount stated in the foreign currency to the equivalent amount in dollars under the applicable official or market exchange rate as publicly reported.

88.3061. Inappropriate tribunal.

If a petition or comparable pleading is received by an inappropriate tribunal of this state, the tribunal shall forward the pleading and accompanying documents to an appropriate tribunal of this state or another state and notify the petitioner where and when the pleading was sent.

88.3071. Duties of support enforcement agency.

(1) In a proceeding under this act, a support enforcement agency of this state, upon request:

(a) Shall provide services to a petitioner residing in a state;

(b) Shall provide services to a petitioner requesting services through a central authority of a foreign country as described in s. 88.1011(5)(a) or (d); and

(c) May provide services to a petitioner who is an individual not residing in a state.

(2) A support enforcement agency that is providing services to the petitioner as appropriate shall:

(a) Take all steps necessary to enable an appropriate tribunal in this state, another state, or a foreign country to obtain jurisdiction over the respondent.

(b) Request an appropriate tribunal to set a date, time, and place for a hearing.

(c) Make a reasonable effort to obtain all relevant information, including information as to income and property of the parties.

(d) Within 10 days, exclusive of Saturdays, Sundays, and legal holidays, after receipt of a written notice from an initiating, responding, or registering tribunal, send a copy of the notice to the petitioner.

(e) Within 10 days, exclusive of Saturdays, Sundays, and legal holidays, after receipt of a written communication from the respondent or the respondent's attorney, send a copy of the communication to the petitioner.

(f) Notify the petitioner if jurisdiction over the respondent cannot be obtained.

(3) A support enforcement agency of this state that requests registration of a child support order in this state for enforcement or for modification shall make reasonable efforts:

(a) To ensure that the order to be registered is the controlling order; or

(b) If two or more child support orders exist and the identity of the controlling order has not been determined, to ensure that a request for such a determination is made in a tribunal having jurisdiction to do so.

(4) A support enforcement agency of this state that requests registration and enforcement of a support order, arrears, or judgment stated in a foreign currency shall convert the amounts stated in the foreign currency into the equivalent amounts in dollars under the applicable official or market exchange rate as publicly reported.

(5) A support enforcement agency of this state shall issue or request a tribunal of this state to issue a child support order and an income-withholding order that redirect payment of current support, arrears, and interest if requested to do so by a support enforcement agency of another state pursuant to s. 88.3191.

(6) This act does not create or negate a relationship of attorney and client or other fiduciary relationship between a support enforcement agency or the attorney for the agency and the individual being assisted by the agency.

88.3081. Duty of Governor and Cabinet.

(1) If the Governor and Cabinet determine that the support enforcement agency is neglecting or refusing to provide services to an individual, the Governor and Cabinet may order the agency to perform its duties under this act or may provide those services directly to the individual.

(2) The Governor and Cabinet may determine that a foreign country has established a reciprocal arrangement for child support with this state and take appropriate action for notification of the determination.

88.3091. Private counsel.

An individual may employ private counsel to represent the individual in proceedings authorized by this act.

88.3101. Duties of state information agency.

(1) The Department of Revenue is the state information agency under this act.

(2) The state information agency shall:

(a) Compile and maintain a current list, including addresses, of the tribunals in this state which have jurisdiction under this act and any support enforcement agencies in this state and transmit a copy to the state information agency of every other state.

(b) Maintain a register of tribunals and support enforcement agencies received from other states.

(c) Forward to the appropriate tribunal in the place in this state in which the obligee who is an individual or the obligor resides, or in which the obligor's property is believed to be located, all documents concerning a proceeding under this act received from another state or a foreign country.

(3) Obtain information concerning the location of the obligor and the obligor's property within this state not exempt from execution, by such means as postal verification and federal or state locator services, examination of telephone directories, requests for the obligor's address from employers, and examination of governmental records, including, to the extent not prohibited by other law, those relating to real property, vital statistics, law enforcement, taxation, motor vehicles, driver licenses, and social security.

88.3111. Pleadings and accompanying documents.

(1) In a proceeding under this act, a petitioner seeking to establish a support order, to determine parentage of a child, or to register and modify a support order of a tribunal of another state or a foreign country must file a petition or comparable pleading. Unless otherwise ordered under s. 88.3121, the petition or comparable pleading or the documents accompanying either the petition or comparable pleading must provide, so far as known, the name, residential address, and social security numbers of the obligor and the obligee or the parent and alleged parent, and the name, sex, residential address, social security number, and date of birth of each child for whose benefit support is sought or whose parentage of a child is to be determined. Unless filed at the time of registration, the petition must be accompanied by a copy of any support order known to have been issued by another tribunal. The petition may include any other information that may assist in locating or identifying the respondent.

(2) The petition must specify the relief sought. The petition and accompanying documents must conform substantially with the requirements imposed by the forms mandated by federal law for use in cases filed by a support enforcement agency.

88.3121. Nondisclosure of information in exceptional circumstances.

If a party alleges in an affidavit or a pleading under oath that the health, safety, or liberty of a party or child would be jeopardized by disclosure of specific identifying information, that information must be sealed and may not be disclosed to the other party or the public. After a hearing in which a tribunal takes into consideration the health, safety, or liberty of the party or child, the tribunal may order disclosure of information that the tribunal determines to be in the interest of justice.

88.3131. Costs and fees.

(1) The petitioner may not be required to pay a filing fee or other costs.

(2) If an obligee prevails, a responding tribunal of this state may assess against an obligor filing fees, reasonable attorney's fees, other costs, and necessary travel and other reasonable expenses

incurred by the obligee and the obligee's witnesses. The tribunal may not assess fees, costs, or expenses against the obligee or the support enforcement agency of either the initiating or the responding state or foreign country, except as provided by other law. Attorney's fees may be taxed as costs, and may be ordered paid directly to the attorney, who may enforce the order in the attorney's own name. Payment of support owed to the obligee has priority over fees, costs, and expenses.

(3) The tribunal shall order the payment of costs and reasonable attorney's fees if it determines that a hearing was requested primarily for delay. In a proceeding under part VI, a hearing is presumed to have been requested primarily for delay if a registered support order is confirmed or enforced without change.

88.3141. Limited immunity of petitioner.

(1) Participation by a petitioner in a proceeding under this act before a responding tribunal, whether in person, by private attorney, or through services provided by the support enforcement agency, does not confer personal jurisdiction over the petitioner in another proceeding.

(2) A petitioner is not amenable to service of civil process while physically present in this state to participate in a proceeding under this act.

(3) The immunity granted by this section does not extend to civil litigation based on acts unrelated to a proceeding under this act committed by a party while physically present in this state to participate in the proceeding.

88.3151. Nonparentage as defense.

A party whose parentage of a child has been previously determined by or pursuant to law may not plead nonparentage as a defense to a proceeding under this act.

88.3161. Special rules of evidence and procedure.

(1) The physical presence of a nonresident party who is an individual in a tribunal of this state is not required for the establishment, enforcement, or modification of a support order or the rendition of a judgment determining parentage of a child.

(2) An affidavit, a document substantially complying with federally mandated forms, or a document incorporated by reference in any of them, which would not be excluded under the hearsay rule if given in person, is admissible in evidence if given under penalty of perjury by a party or witness residing outside this state.

(3) A copy of the record of child support payments certified as a true copy of the original by the custodian of the record may be forwarded to a responding tribunal. The copy is evidence of facts asserted in it, and is admissible to show whether payments were made.

(4) Copies of bills for testing for parentage of a child, and for prenatal and postnatal health care of the mother and child, furnished to the adverse party at least 10 days before trial, are admissible in evidence to prove the amount of the charges billed and that the charges were reasonable, necessary, and customary.

(5) Documentary evidence transmitted from outside this state to a tribunal of this state by telephone, telecopier, or other electronic means that do not provide an original record may not be excluded from evidence on an objection based on the means of transmission.

(6) In a proceeding under this act, a tribunal of this state shall permit a party or witness residing outside this state to be deposed or to testify by telephone, audiovisual means, or other electronic

means at a designated tribunal or other location. A tribunal of this state shall cooperate with other tribunals in designating an appropriate location for the deposition or testimony.

(7) If a party called to testify at a civil hearing refuses to answer on the ground that the testimony may be self-incriminating, the trier of fact may draw an adverse inference from the refusal.

(8) A privilege against disclosure of communications between spouses does not apply in a proceeding under this act.

(9) The defense of immunity based on the relationship of husband and wife or parent and child does not apply in a proceeding under this act.

(10) A voluntary acknowledgment of paternity, certified as a true copy, is admissible to establish parentage of a child.

88.3171. Communications between tribunals.

A tribunal of this state may communicate with a tribunal outside this state in a record, or by telephone, electronic mail, or other means, to obtain information concerning the laws of that state, the legal effect of a judgment, decree, or order of that tribunal, and the status of a proceeding. A tribunal of this state may furnish similar information by similar means to a tribunal outside this state.

88.3181. Assistance with discovery.

A tribunal of this state may:
(1) Request a tribunal outside this state to assist in obtaining discovery.
(2) Upon request, compel a person over which it has jurisdiction to respond to a discovery order issued by a tribunal outside this state.

88.3191. Receipt and disbursement of payments.

(1) A support enforcement agency or tribunal of this state shall disburse promptly any amounts received pursuant to a support order, as directed by the order. The agency or tribunal shall furnish to a requesting party or tribunal of another state or a foreign country a certified statement by the custodian of the record of the amounts and dates of all payments received.

(2) If neither the obligor, nor the obligee who is an individual, nor the child resides in this state, upon request from the support enforcement agency of this state or another state, the support enforcement agency of this state or a tribunal of this state shall:

(a) Direct that the support payment be made to the support enforcement agency in the state in which the obligee is receiving services; and

(b) Issue and send to the obligor's employer a conforming income-withholding order or an administrative notice of change of payee, reflecting the redirected payments.

(3) The support enforcement agency of this state receiving redirected payments from another state pursuant to a law similar to subsection (2) shall furnish to a requesting party or tribunal of the other state a certified statement by the custodian of the record of the amount and dates of all payments received.

PART IV. ESTABLISHMENT OF SUPPORT ORDER (SS. 88.4011, 88.4021)

88.4011. Establishment of support order.

(1) If a support order entitled to recognition under this act has not been issued, a responding tribunal of this state with personal jurisdiction over the parties may issue a support order if:
(a) The individual seeking the order resides outside this state; or
(b) The support enforcement agency seeking the order is located outside this state.
(2) The tribunal may issue a temporary child support order if the tribunal determines that such an order is appropriate and the individual ordered to pay is:
(a) A presumed father of the child;
(b) Petitioning to have his paternity adjudicated;
(c) Identified as the father of the child through genetic testing;
(d) An alleged father who has declined to submit to genetic testing;
(e) Shown by clear and convincing evidence to be the father of the child;
(f) An acknowledged father as provided in s. 382.013, s. 382.016, or s. 742.10;
(g) The mother of the child; or
(h) An individual who has been ordered to pay child support in a previous proceeding and the order has not been reversed or vacated.
(3) Upon finding, after notice and opportunity to be heard, that an obligor owes a duty of support, the tribunal shall issue a support order directed to the obligor and may issue other orders pursuant to s. 88.3051.

88.4021. Proceeding to determine parentage.

A tribunal of this state authorized to determine parentage of a child may serve as a responding tribunal in a proceeding to determine parentage of a child brought under this act or a law or procedure substantially similar to this act.

PART V. ENFORCEMENT OF SUPPORT ORDER OF ANOTHER STATE WITHOUT REGISTRATION (SS. 88.5011-88.5071)

88.5011. Employer's receipt of income-withholding order of another state.

An income-withholding order issued in another state may be sent by or on behalf of the obligee, or by the support enforcement agency, to the person defined as the obligor's employer under the income deduction law of this state or payor as defined by s. 61.046, without first filing a petition or comparable pleading or registering the order with a tribunal of this state.

88.50211. Employer's compliance with income-withholding order of another state.

(1) Upon receipt of an income-withholding order, the obligor's employer shall immediately provide a copy of the order to the obligor.

(2) The employer shall treat an income-withholding order issued in another state which appears regular on its face as if it had been issued by a tribunal of this state.

(3) Except as otherwise provided by subsection (4) and s. 88.5031, the employer shall withhold and distribute the funds as directed in the withholding order by complying with the terms of the order which specify:

(a) The duration and amount of periodic payments of current child support, stated as a sum certain;

(b) The person designated to receive payments and the address to which the payments are to be forwarded;

(c) Medical support, whether in the form of periodic cash payment, stated as a sum certain, or ordering the obligor to provide health insurance coverage for the child under a policy available through the obligor's employment;

(d) The amount of periodic payments of fees and costs for a support enforcement agency, the issuing tribunal, and the obligee's attorney, stated as sums certain; and

(e) The amount of periodic payments of arrearages and interest on arrearages, stated as sums certain.

(4) An employer shall comply with the law of the state of the obligor's principal place of employment for withholding from income with respect to:

(a) The employer's fee for processing an income-withholding order;

(b) The maximum amount permitted to be withheld from the obligor's income; and

(c) The times within which the employer must implement the withholding order and forward the child support payment.

88.5031. Employer's compliance with two or more income-withholding orders.

If the obligor's employer receives two or more income-withholding orders with respect to the earnings of the same obligor, the employer satisfies the terms of the orders if the employer complies with the law of the state of the obligor's principal place of employment to establish the priorities for withholding and allocating income withheld for two or more child support obligees.

88.5041. Immunity from civil liability.

An employer that complies with an income-withholding order issued in another state in accordance with this article is not subject to civil liability to an individual or agency with regard to the employer's withholding of child support from the obligor's income.

88.5051. Penalties for noncompliance.

An employer that willfully fails to comply with an income-withholding order issued by another state and received for enforcement is subject to the same penalties that may be imposed for noncompliance with an order issued by a tribunal of this state.

88.5061. Contest by obligor.

(1) An obligor may contest the validity or enforcement of an income-withholding order issued in another state and received directly by an employer in this state by registering the order in a tribunal of this state and filing a contest to that order as provided in part VI of this chapter, or otherwise contesting the order in the same manner as if the order had been issued by a tribunal of this state.

(2) The obligor shall give notice of the contest to:

(a) A support enforcement agency providing services to the obligee;

(b) Each employer that has directly received an income-withholding order relating to the obligor; and

(c) The person designated to receive payments in the income-withholding order, or if no person is designated, to the obligee.

88.5071. Administrative enforcement of orders.

(1) A party or support enforcement agency seeking to enforce a support order or an income-withholding order, or both, issued in another state or a foreign support order may send the documents required for registering the order to a support enforcement agency of this state.

(2) Upon receipt of the documents, the support enforcement agency, without initially seeking to register the order, shall consider and, if appropriate, use any administrative procedure authorized by the law of this state to enforce a support order or an income-withholding order, or both. If the obligor does not contest administrative enforcement, the order need not be registered. If the obligor contests the validity or administrative enforcement of the order, the support enforcement agency shall register the order pursuant to this act.

PART VI. REGISTRATION, ENFORCEMENT, AND MODIFICATION OF SUPPORT ORDER (SS. 88.6011-88.6161)

PART VII. SUPPORT PROCEEDING UNDER CONVENTION (SS. 88.70111-88.7131)

88.70111. Definitions.

As used in this part, the term:

(1) "Application" means a request under the convention by an obligee or obligor, or on behalf of a child, made through a central authority for assistance from another central authority.

(2) "Central authority" means the entity designated by the United States or a foreign country described in s. 88.1011(5)(d) to perform the functions specified in the convention.

(3) "Convention support order" means a support order of a tribunal of a foreign country described in s. 88.1011(5)(d).

(4) "Direct request" means a petition filed by an individual in a tribunal of this state in a proceeding involving an obligee, obligor, or child residing outside the United States.

(5) "Foreign central authority" means the entity designated by a foreign country described in s. 88.1011(5)(d) to perform the functions specified in the convention.

(6) "Foreign support agreement":

(a) Means an agreement for support in a record that:

1. Is enforceable as a support order in the country of origin;

2. Has been:

a. Formally drawn up or registered as an authentic instrument by a foreign tribunal; or

b. Authenticated by or concluded, registered, or filed with a foreign tribunal; and

3. May be reviewed and modified by a foreign tribunal; and

(b) Includes a maintenance arrangement or authentic instrument under the convention.

(7) "United States central authority" means the Secretary of the United States Department of Health and Human Services.

88.7021. Applicability.

This part applies only to a support proceeding under the convention. In such a proceeding, if a provision of this part is inconsistent with parts I through VI, this part controls.

88.7031. Relationship of Department of Revenue to United States central authority.

The Department of Revenue is recognized as the agency designated by the United States central authority to perform specific functions under the convention.

88.7041. Initiation by Department of Revenue of support proceeding under convention.

(1) In a support proceeding under this part, the Department of Revenue shall:

(a) Transmit and receive applications; and

(b) Initiate or facilitate the institution of a proceeding regarding an application in a tribunal of this state.

(2) The following support proceedings are available to an obligee under the convention:

(a) Recognition or recognition and enforcement of a foreign support order.

(b) Enforcement of a support order issued or recognized in this state.

(c) Establishment of a support order if there is no existing order, including, where necessary, determination of parentage of a child.

(d) Establishment of a support order if recognition of a foreign support order is refused under s. 88.7081(2)(b), (d), or (i).

(e) Modification of a support order of a tribunal of this state.

(f) Modification of a support order of a tribunal of another state or a foreign country.

(3) The following support proceedings are available under the convention to an obligor against whom there is an existing support order:

(a) Recognition of an order suspending or limiting enforcement of an existing support order of a tribunal of this state.

(b) Modification of a support order of a tribunal of this state.

(c) Modification of a support order of a tribunal of another state or foreign country.

(4) A tribunal of this state may not require security, bond, or deposit, however described, to guarantee the payment of costs and expenses in proceedings under the convention.

88.7051. Direct request.

(1) A petitioner may file a direct request seeking establishment or modification of a support order or determination of parentage of a child. In the proceeding, the law of this state applies.

(2) A petitioner may file a direct request in a tribunal of this state seeking recognition and enforcement of a support order or support agreement. In such a proceeding, the provisions of ss. 88.7061-88.7131 apply.

(3) In a direct request for recognition and enforcement of a convention support order or foreign support agreement:

(a) A security, bond, or deposit is not required to guarantee the payment of costs and expenses; and

(b) An obligee or obligor that in the issuing country has benefited from free legal assistance is entitled to benefit, at least to the same extent, from any free legal assistance provided for by the law of this state under the same circumstances.

(4) An individual filing a direct request is not entitled to assistance from the Department of Revenue.

(5) This part does not prevent the application of laws of this state that provide simplified, more expeditious rules regarding a direct request for recognition and enforcement of a foreign support order or foreign support agreement.

88.7061. Registration of convention support order.

(1) Except as otherwise provided in this part, a party who is an individual or a support enforcement agency seeking recognition of a convention support order shall register the order in this state as provided in part VI of this chapter.

(2) Notwithstanding ss. 88.3111 and 88.6021(1), a request for registration of a convention support order must be accompanied by the following:

(a) A complete text of the support order, or an abstract or extract of the support order drawn up by the issuing foreign tribunal, which may be in the form recommended by the Hague Conference on Private International Law.

(b) A record stating that the support order is enforceable in the issuing country.

(c) If the respondent did not appear and was not represented in the proceedings in the issuing country, a record attesting, as appropriate, either that the respondent had proper notice of the proceedings and an opportunity to be heard, or that the respondent had proper notice of the support order and the opportunity to be heard in a challenge or appeal on fact or law before a tribunal.

(d) A record showing the amount of any arrears, and the date the amount was calculated.

(e) A record showing a requirement for automatic adjustment of the amount of support, if any, and the information necessary to make the appropriate calculations, if necessary.

(f) A record showing the extent to which the applicant received free legal assistance in the issuing country.

(3) A request for registration of a convention support order may seek recognition and partial enforcement of the order.

(4) A tribunal of this state may vacate the registration of a convention support order without the filing of a contest under s. 88.7071 only if, acting on its own motion, the tribunal finds that recognition and enforcement of the order would be manifestly incompatible with public policy.

(5) The tribunal shall promptly notify the parties of the registration or the order vacating the registration of a convention support order.

88.7071. Contest of registered convention support order.

(1) Except as otherwise provided in this part, ss. 88.6051-88.6081 apply to a contest of a registered convention support order.
(2) A party contesting a registered convention support order shall file a contest not later than 30 days after notice of the registration, but if the contesting party does not reside in the United States, the contest must be filed not later than 60 days after notice of the registration.
(3) If the nonregistering party fails to contest the registered convention support order by the time specified in subsection (2), the order is enforceable.
(4) A contest of a registered convention support order may be based only on grounds set forth in s. 88.7081. The contesting party bears the burden of proof.
(5) In a contest of a registered convention support order, a tribunal of this state:
(a) Is bound by the findings of fact on which the foreign tribunal based its jurisdiction; and
(b) May not review the merits of the order.
(6) A tribunal of this state deciding a contest of a registered convention support order shall promptly notify the parties of its decision.
(7) A challenge or appeal, if any, does not stay the enforcement of a convention support order unless there are exceptional circumstances.

88.7081. Recognition and enforcement of convention support order.

(1) Except as otherwise provided in subsection (2), a tribunal of this state shall recognize and enforce a registered convention support order.
(2) The following grounds are the only grounds on which a tribunal of this state may refuse recognition and enforcement of a registered convention support order:
(a) Recognition and enforcement of the order is manifestly incompatible with public policy, including the failure of the issuing tribunal to observe minimum standards of due process, which include notice and an opportunity to be heard;
(b) The issuing tribunal lacked personal jurisdiction consistent with s. 88.2011;
(c) The order is not enforceable in the issuing country;
(d) The order was obtained by fraud in connection with a matter of procedure;
(e) A record transmitted in accordance with s. 88.7061 lacks authenticity or integrity;
(f) A proceeding between the same parties and having the same purpose is pending before a tribunal of this state and that proceeding was the first to be filed;
(g) The order is incompatible with a more recent support order involving the same parties and having the same purpose if the more recent support order is entitled to recognition and enforcement under this act in this state;
(h) Payment, to the extent alleged arrears have been paid in whole or in part;
(i) In a case in which the respondent neither appeared nor was represented in the proceeding in the issuing foreign country:
1. If the law of that country provides for prior notice of proceedings, the respondent did not have proper notice of the proceedings and an opportunity to be heard; or
2. If the law of that country does not provide for prior notice of the proceedings, the respondent did not have proper notice of the order and an opportunity to be heard in a challenge or appeal on fact or law before a tribunal; or

(j) The order was made in violation of s. 88.7111.

(3) If a tribunal of this state does not recognize a convention support order under paragraph (2)(b), paragraph (2)(d), paragraph (2)(f), or paragraph (2)(i):

(a) The tribunal may not dismiss the proceeding without allowing a reasonable time for a party to request the establishment of a new convention support order; and

(b) The Department of Revenue shall take all appropriate measures to request a child support order for the obligee if the application for recognition and enforcement was received under s. 88.7041.

88.7091. Partial enforcement.

If a tribunal of this state does not recognize and enforce a convention support order in its entirety, it shall enforce any severable part of the order. An application or direct request may seek recognition and partial enforcement of a convention support order.

88.7101. Foreign support agreement.

(1) Except as provided in subsections (3) and (4), a tribunal of this state shall recognize and enforce a foreign support agreement registered in this state.

(2) An application or direct request for recognition and enforcement of a foreign support agreement must be accompanied by:

(a) A complete text of the foreign support agreement; and

(b) A record stating that the foreign support agreement is enforceable as an order of support in the issuing country.

(3) A tribunal of this state may vacate the registration of a foreign support agreement only if, acting on its own motion, the tribunal finds that recognition and enforcement would be manifestly incompatible with public policy.

(4) In a contest of a foreign support agreement, a tribunal of this state may refuse recognition and enforcement of the agreement if it finds:

(a) Recognition and enforcement of the agreement is manifestly incompatible with public policy;

(b) The agreement was obtained by fraud or falsification;

(c) The agreement is incompatible with a support order issued between the same parties and having the same purpose in this state, another state, or a foreign country if the support order is entitled to recognition in this state; or

(d) The record submitted under subsection (2) lacks authenticity or integrity.

(5) A proceeding for recognition and enforcement of a foreign support agreement must be suspended during the pendency of a challenge to or appeal of the agreement before a tribunal of another state or a foreign country.

88.7111. Modification of convention child support order.

(1) A tribunal of this state may not modify a convention child support order if the obligee remains a resident of the foreign country where the support order was issued unless:

(a) The obligee submits to the jurisdiction of a tribunal of this state, either expressly or by defending on the merits of the case without objecting to the jurisdiction at the first available opportunity; or

(b) The foreign tribunal lacks or refuses to exercise jurisdiction to modify its support order or issue a new support order.

(2) If a tribunal of this state does not modify a convention child support order because the order is

not recognized in this state, the provisions of s. 88.7081(3) apply.

88.7121. Personal information; limit on use.

Personal information gathered or transmitted under this part may be used only for the purposes for which it was gathered or transmitted.

88.7131. Record in original language; English translation.

A record filed with a tribunal of this state under this part must be in the original language and, if not in English, must be accompanied by an English translation.

PART VIII. INTERSTATE RENDITION (SS. 88.8011, 88.8021)

88.8011. Grounds for rendition.

(1) For purposes of this article, "Governor" includes an individual performing the functions of Governor or the executive authority of a state covered by this act.
(2) The Governor of this state may:
(a) Demand that the Governor of another state surrender an individual found in the other state who is charged criminally in this state with having failed to provide for the support of an obligee; or
(b) On the demand of the Governor of another state, surrender an individual found in this state who is charged criminally in the other state with having failed to provide for the support of an obligee.
(3) A provision for extradition of individuals not inconsistent with this act applies to the demand even if the individual whose surrender is demanded was not in the demanding state when the crime was allegedly committed and has not fled therefrom.

88.8021. Conditions of rendition.

(1) Before making demand that the Governor of another state surrender an individual charged criminally in this state with having failed to provide for the support of an obligee, the Governor of this state may require a prosecutor of this state to demonstrate that at least 60 days previously the obligee had initiated proceedings for support pursuant to this act or that the proceeding would be of no avail.
(2) If, under this act or a law substantially similar to this act, the Uniform Reciprocal Enforcement of Support Act, or the Revised Uniform Reciprocal Enforcement of Support Act, the Governor of another state makes a demand that the Governor of this state surrender an individual charged criminally in that state with having failed to provide for the support of a child or other individual to whom a duty of support is owed, the Governor may require a prosecutor to investigate the demand and report whether a proceeding for support has been initiated or would be effective. If it appears that a proceeding would be effective but has not been initiated, the Governor may delay honoring the demand for a reasonable time to permit the initiation of a proceeding.

(3) If a proceeding for support has been initiated and the individual whose rendition is demanded prevails, the Governor may decline to honor the demand. If the petitioner prevails and the individual whose rendition is demanded is subject to a support order, the Governor may decline to honor the demand if the individual is complying with the support order.

PART IX. MISCELLANEOUS PROVISIONS (SS. 88.9011-88.9031)

88.9011. Uniformity of application and construction.

In applying and construing this uniform act, consideration must be given to the need to promote uniformity of the law with respect to its subject matter among states that enact it.

88.9021. Transitional provision.

This act applies to proceedings begun on or after the effective date of this act to establish a support order or determine parentage of a child or to register, recognize, enforce, or modify a prior support order, determination, or agreement, whenever issued or entered.

88.9031. Severability.

If any provision of this act or its application to any person or circumstance is held invalid, the invalidity does not affect other provisions or applications of this act which can be given effect without the invalid provision or application, and to this end the provisions of this act are severable.

CPSIA information can be obtained
at www.ICGtesting.com
Printed in the USA
LVHW022355220323
742367LV00010B/518

9 781719 116466